# Personnel Policy Handbook

# Personnel Policy Handbook

## How to Develop a Manual That Works

## William S. Hubbartt

**McGraw-Hill, Inc.**

New York  San Francisco  Washington, D.C.  Auckland  Bogotá
Caracas  Lisbon  London  Madrid  Mexico City  Milan
Montreal  New Delhi  San Juan  Singapore
Sydney  Tokyo  Toronto

Library of Congress Cataloging-in-Publication Data

Hubbartt, William S.
    Personnel policy handbook : how to develop a manual that works /
William S. Hubbartt.
        p.    cm.
    Includes index.
    ISBN 0-07-030833-0
    1. Personnel procedure manuals.   I.  Title.
HF5549.5.C62H82   1993
    658.3—dc20                                                          93-9807
                                                                          CIP

2 3 4 5 6 7 8 9 10 11 12 13 14 BKMBKM 9 9 8 7 6 5 4

ISBN 0-07-030833-0

*The sponsoring editor for this book was Betsy Brown, the editing supervisor was Fred
Dahl, and the production supervisor was Donald Schmidt. It was set in Baskerville
by Inkwell Publishing Services.*

# Contents

## 6. Writing Your Policy Manual

**85**

## Part 2.  Policy Development Guidelines

### 7.  Hiring, Promoting, and Other Employment Policies

**111**

## 12.  Holidays, Vacations, and Other Employee Benefits                319

## 16. Current Issues: Addressing Workplace Drug Abuse, Smoking, Disability Accommodation, Etc.

## Part 3.  Auditing Your Policy Manual

## Part 4.  Implementing Your Policy Manual

## APPENDIXES

# Preface

The human resource management field is continually changing. Changing labor laws and government regulations impose new restrictions affecting the way employers hire, retain, and terminate employees. Recent regulations define requirements relating to immigrant work authorization, polygraph testing limits, drug use testing, hazard communication, minimum wage adjustment, layoff notification, and handicap hiring, in addition to the many other laws affecting employment practices.

Many new and emerging issues are causing changes in employee relations practices. Health concerns prompt the need to define protective guidelines on matters such as AIDS, smoking, drug abuse, and chemical safety on the job. Changing workforce demographics require new policies relating to family and medical leave, employment of older workers, acces- sibility for handicapped, and increasing minority labor force participation.

A simple hiring or firing employment decision of years past is now a complex matter. Managers must be educated in the proper techniques for dealing with personnel issues in order to avoid costly legal liabilities.

*Personnel Policy Handbook: How to Develop a Manual That Works* is intended to provide guidance and direction to business managers and executives who will be coping with these vital human resource issues in the coming decade. This book will be of particular interest to:

Human resource managers

Personnel administrators and practitioners

Small business owners

Administrative and office managers

Government personnel administrators

Operations and plant managers

Labor relations specialists

Instructors, trainers, and teachers

Others involved in defining personnel policies

The reader of *Personnel Policy Handbook* will receive the following valuable benefits:

- Useful ideas on how to plan and organize a policy manual
- Practical tips on preparing a supervisor's policy manual and an employee handbook
- Objective recommendations on what subjects to include in a policy manual, and what topics to avoid
- Invaluable suggestions on how to carefully write personnel policies to achieve clear understanding and interpretation
- Time-saving checklists, worksheets, and reference charts
- Proven policies and samples that have been tested and used successfully at other firms
- A handy desk reference that will be used repeatedly by the reader

*William S. Hubbartt*

# How to Use
# This Handbook

*Personnel Policy Handbook* is organized into five main sections:

Part 1: Planning and Preparation

Part 2: Policy Development Guidelines

Part 3: Auditing Your Policy Manual

Part 4: Implementing Your Policy Manual

Appendix A: Sample Employee Handbook

Appendix B, "Topic List for Personnel Policy Manual," serves as a quick reference.

If you are starting work on a new policy manual, begin with Part 1, "Planning and Preparation," and continue through the book. Its organization is designed to bring you from concept, to policy development, to implementation.

If you are updating or revising an existing policy manual, begin with Part 3, "Auditing Your Policy Manual." The audit section will help you to identify issues and the need for revisions to your policy manual. Then proceed to Part 1 and succeeding parts to develop policies and to write and publish your manual.

If you are developing a specific policy, begin with Part 2, "Policy Development Guidelines," where tips and suggestions are provided on over 100 policy issues. Then check Appendix A for samples of how other firms have dealt with similar issues.

A summary of each chapter and its key topics are highlighted here to aid in finding information based on the reader's specific needs.

## PART 1: PLANNING AND PREPARATION

Chapter 1, "Why Prepare Personnel Policies?," identifies the need for policies and the benefits of having written personnel policies. Various case examples have been used to demonstrate the problems of managing an organization without policies and the problem-solving benefits of policies. Government requirements for written policies are noted. Chapter 1 provides the background and foundation for you to sell management on a policy manual project and justify the commitment of resources to a policy manual project.

Chapter 2, "The Contract Controversy," addresses the issue of employment at will and the relationship of this legal concept to personnel policies. A clear understanding of this issue is vital to proper preparation of personnel policies while avoiding potential liabilities in wrongful discharge cases. From a personnel practitioner's point of view, Chapter 2 highlights key employment-at-will concepts and lists specific preventative actions.

Chapter 3, "Getting Started: Organizing Your Policy Project to Achieve Results," provides nuts-and-bolts, how-to information to guide you in organizing your efforts and getting results. Sources of policy information in the organization are identified (i.e., policy memos, letters of understanding, bulletin board messages, payroll desk procedures, and unwritten practices). Specific examples are given to help you analyze your organization's current personnel practices. Tips are provided to help you recognize management style and organizational culture in order to develop suitable policy guidelines. Specific suggestions aid the reader to plan and organize the policy manual project. Pros and cons of a policy committee are listed, together with tips on leading a policy committee to obtain results.

Chapter 4, "Competitive Practices: What Is Everybody Else Doing?," helps you to draw upon information resources which identify competitive practices. Selected personnel practices and benefit surveys are identified. Suggestions on reading and using survey data are provided. Highlights of selected survey data are provided with policy examples to aid you in developing personnel policies which reflect competitive practice.

Chapter 5, "Avoiding Legal Pitfalls," alerts you to various labor law issues which must be considered in order to avoid legal pitfalls. You are alerted to check federal law, state law, administrative regulations, and leading court decisions to ensure that personnel policies are properly defined. Then, labor law issues are correlated to typical personnel policies to focus your research and to aid policy preparation which recognizes labor law restraints. Selected sources of information on labor laws are provided. Professional review of the policy manual is addressed to minimize the likelihood of legal liability.

Chapter 6, "Writing Your Policy Manual," offers encouragement to the novice policy writer and numerous valuable time-saving tips. Covered issues include selecting writing style and format, writing for the reading audience, and organizing information with selected samples to illustrate key points. Basic reminders on grammar and punctuation have been included. You are cautioned against 10 common writing pitfalls and errors.

Chapter 6 also addresses the unique issues of writing an employee handbook as distinguished from a personnel policy manual for supervisors. Suggested topics, writing style, organization, and writing tips are provided. Special precautions are noted to protect against the "contract" issues being raised in the courts.

# PART 2: POLICY DEVELOPMENT GUIDELINES

Each chapter in Part 2 identifies selected policy topics in a format which provides the following information:

- Policy objective and important issues to consider
- Checklist of points to cover when writing the policy
- Comments on competitive practices
- Pitfalls to avoid
- Sample policy and procedures
- Sample employee handbook paragraph
- Typical forms to be used with the policy

Chapter 7, "Hiring, Promoting, and Other Employment Policies," defines guidelines related to common employment practices such as recruiting and testing, staffing and hiring, preemployment physical examination, employee definitions, defining exempt/nonexempt status, orientation of new employees, equal employment opportunity, sexual harassment, transfers, promotions and job postings, personnel records, and job descriptions.

Chapter 8, "Define Work Hours, Set Employee Schedules, and Control Attendance," defines guidelines related to attendance control issues including working hours/work week, lunch and break periods, overtime work, flex-time schedules, attendance control, time records, and voting time.

Chapter 9, "Planning and Administering Leaves of Absence," defines policies for jury service, medical leave, maternity leave, military leave, personal or family leave, funeral leave, and reemployment from leave.

Chapter 10, "Pay, Performance, and Other Compensation Policies," defines guidelines related to pay periods, pay day, overtime pay, pay reviews, performance reviews, wage garnishments, and bonuses.

Chapter 11, "Discipline, Discharges, Retirements, and Other Separations," defines guidelines related to disciplinary procedures, disciplinary rules, dismissals, layoffs, voluntary quits, retirement, and severance pay.

Chapter 12, "Holidays, Vacations, and Other Employee Benefits," defines guidelines related to holidays, vacations, education, sick pay, salary continuation, savings plans, insurances, retirement plans, and legislated benefits.

Chapter 13, "Employee and Union Relations: Policies to Motivate the Workforce," defines guidelines related to important employee relations issues such as open door/employee communications, employee committees, preventing/countering union-organizing activity, union agreements, and grievance/complaint procedure.

Chapter 14, "Controlling Use of Telephones, Protecting Confidentiality, Setting Dress Codes, and Handling Related Administrative Issues," defines guidelines related to common administrative issues such as telephone use, dress codes, confidentiality, relocation, vehicles, secondary employment, and ethical business practices.

Chapter 15, "Miscellaneous Policy Issues: Safety, Hazard Communication, Security, Sanitation, and Others," defines guidelines related to a variety of important policy issues.

Chapter 16, "Current Issues: Addressing Workplace Drug Abuse, Smoking, Disability Accommodation, Etc.," defines guidelines related to new issues affecting the workplace in the 1990s.

# PART 3: AUDITING YOUR POLICY MANUAL

Chapter 17, "Personnel Policy Audit: A Comprehensive 50-Item Checklist," provides a comprehensive 50-item personnel policy checklist designed to serve as a self-audit. Readers who have an existing policy manual will find the audit to be an excellent starting point to evaluate and improve policies. Readers who have used this book to write their policy manual will find the audit to be a useful quality-control tool to check and evaluate their writing effort.

Chapter 18, "Employee Handbook Audit: A Comprehensive 50-Item Checklist," provides a 50-item employee handbook self-audit checklist. Readers who have an employee handbook will find the audit to be a useful tool for identifying needed revisions. Readers who have used this book in the preparation of their employee handbook will find the audit to be useful in evaluating their work.

# PART 4: IMPLEMENTING YOUR POLICY MANUAL

Chapter 19, "Publishing Ideas and Suggestions," provides ideas and tips relating to a variety of alternatives for publishing. Included is an analysis with pros and cons of typesetting, printing, photocopying, word processing, desktop publishing, and other similar publishing alternatives for the personnel policy manual. Issues such as image, audience, cost, and related concerns are analyzed. Tips on dealing with printers are provided.

Chapter 20, "Distributing and Updating Your Policy Manual," provides instructions for manual distribution, tips on orienting supervisory personnel to the new policy manual, and suggested ways to announce the manual to employees. Sample employee letters and training exercises are included. Policy manual maintenance instructions, suggestions for keeping the manual up-to-date, and related control procedures are identified.

## APPENDIXES: SAMPLE EMPLOYEE HANDBOOK AND LIST OF TOPICS

Appendix A contains a sample employee handbook which shows policy issues and a writing style typical of an employee handbook. Appendix B is a comprehensive list of personnel policy manual topics.

## PRECAUTIONS FOR THE READER

This publication is not designed to render legal advice or legal opinions. Highlights of various laws and court decisions are provided to aid the reader in careful development of personnel policies. The human resource management field is subject to a wide variety of laws, regulations, and court decisions from the federal and state government levels. Because these regulations and court decisions vary widely from one jurisdiction to another, the reader should conduct appropriate research of applicable laws for his or her respective jurisdiction. When specific legal advice is sought, the reader is encouraged to contact legal counsel or the appropriate government agency.

## ACKNOWLEDGEMENTS

I want to acknowledge the following persons for their support and suggestions in the preparation of this book: Dr. Arthur Malinowski of Loyola University of Chicago, Senior Editor Betsy Brown of McGraw-Hill, Production Supervisor Fred Dahl of Inkwell Publishing Services, and the Associates of Hubbartt & Associates.

# PART 1

# Planning and Preparation

# 1
# Why Prepare
# Personnel Policies?

**Read Chapter 1 for:**

The benefits of personnel policies

The consequences of operating without personnel policies

Guidelines to determine when your organization should start a policy manual

Tips on getting management support for personnel policies

Suggestions for selling your policy manual to management

## What Is our Policy on...?

One important responsibility of the human resource specialist is to answer a multitude of personnel policy questions. Most likely, every human resource specialist has had to answer personnel policy questions such as, "When is the newly hired employee entitled to paid vacation?" "What is excessive absenteeism and how should the employee be warned?" "If I work over the upcoming holiday weekend, will I get overtime pay?"

These questions and others are raised daily by employees, supervisors, and managers. Some issues may seem trivial to you, while others may seem of great significance. For individuals who turn to the Human Resource Department seeking answers, these questions are important.

In responding to these inquiries, you will typically consider a number of issues, such as the following:

How was this issue handled before?

Does this issue require management approval?

Is this a competitive practice that is typical for this area or industry?

Shall I consult with other managers to see how they have handled the issue before?

What is the law (federal, state, local) on this issue?

What will be the cost to the organization?

You need answers to these questions to answer the employee's original policy question. You can get these answers through a series of phone calls, informal discussions with different managers, or even an emergency staff meeting to survey prevailing organizational opinion on the matter. Clearly, this fact-finding process of surveying other managers each time a policy question arises is a costly and inefficient use of management time. An organization could easily waste $5000 of management time to resolve a $50 question.

Or, the matter can be defined quickly and economically by checking the firm's written policy guidelines.

## Definition of Policy

A policy is a statement of how an organization intends to deal with an issue. A policy statement can be brief, such as, "We are an equal opportunity employer." Or, a policy can be a multipage detailed document with definitions, procedures, sample forms, and interpretive guidelines.

A key element of policy is that it is a predetermined guideline providing a specified course of action for dealing with prescribed circumstances.

## Operating without Policies

Many newly formed organizations, small businesses, or family-run enterprises operate without written policies. One reason why some managers operate without written policies is that they want the flexibility to decide issues on a case-by-case basis. Unfortunately, employees may see a manager's prerogative for flexibility as favoritism or discrimination. They may perceive entrepreneurs who use a free-wheeling management style for employment decisions as unfair and capricious.

In many organizations, there is a tendency for the business owner or manager to follow certain past practices. "We always take Thursday and Friday off to provide a four-day weekend at Thanksgiving." Customary practices are soon established for working hours, holidays, vacation entitlement, and other employment or attendance issues. Such practices become unwritten policy.

As a management consultant who assists firms in defining personnel policies, I have observed many situations in which a lack of policy guidelines created problems for an organization. For example, a growing financial services firm permitted department managers to develop policies in their respective departments, which led to conflicting policies on sick leave, vacation, and employee discipline. As a result of these conflicting practices, the firm experienced productivity and morale problems.

In another instance, an unwritten commitment made by company owners about accumulation of sick pay resulted in a significant cost liability for a metal-working firm when several employees began to "cash in" on the plan.

Finally, a high-tech company experienced considerable employee dissatisfaction and wasted management time each year trying to explain and administer its poorly defined vacation plan for employees.

## How Policies Evolve

Organizations are formed to manufacture a product or to render a service. It is highly unlikely that most new organizations start with detailed policy guidelines. Rather, personnel issues are typically handled on a case-by-case basis as situations occur. Decisions usually are made based on past practice and expediency. Unwritten practices tend to become informal policy.

As an organization grows, adding employees and then supervisors, more and more personnel policy questions arise. These questions typically relate to pay, time off, pay for time off, and various misconduct issues. Ad hoc policy is sometimes summarized by a payroll clerk who is seeking some guidance for consistently handling pay issues. Misconduct issues such as absenteeism, tardiness, or other serious forms of misconduct often prompt a supervisor or manager to list rules of conduct on the job.

As more problems occur, more memos or rules are written in an attempt to resolve each matter. The rules guide management's decision for the next time, and let employees know how the matter will be handled.

Soon the organization has a collection of notes, memos, and rules relating to personnel policies or benefits. These documents represent a personnel policy manual or employee handbook in an evolutionary stage.

## Policies Prevent Problems

As organizations grow and more supervisors become involved in making personnel decisions, the need for a personnel policy manual becomes self-evident. Different supervisors tend to handle employment or attendance issues based on their perspective and need, which sometimes results in different solutions for the same issue. If the organization limits supervisory authority by centralizing decision making, then much of top management time is spent resolving the details of petty policy questions. Neither alternative represents the best use of management time.

Unfortunately, some managers recognize the benefits of a personnel policy manual only after receiving a discrimination charge. The absence of policies permits flexibility. Excessive flexibility, however, can lead to favoritism, discriminatory practices, or individual negotiations between an employee and the company. Employees who do not receive the best deal view such actions as unfair. At the very least, these employees are likely to become dissatisfied.

The common needs that prompt organizations to define personnel policies are as follows:

- The need to establish uniform personnel practices among managers at various locations
- The need to achieve better consistency between managers and supervisors making personnel decisions
- The need to define practices and improve communication of policy issues to employees
- The need to control personnel costs resulting from absences, tardiness, accidents, and similar issues
- The need to prevent or respond to administrative claims or litigation
- The need to comply with government laws and regulations
- The need to delegate routine personnel decisions to supervisors and managers
- The need to define personnel practices to prevent union-organizing activity

## Government Requirements

Government regulations touch nearly every aspect of personnel and benefits administration. Many of the laws or regulations require covered employers to define written policies or procedures for compliance with the law. Some of these requirements are as follows:

- Federal government contractors are required to maintain written affirmative action plans.
- Federal government contractors are required to develop a policy statement and a drug awareness program to comply with the Drugfree Workplace Act of 1988.
- Many state wage hour laws require employers to provide to employees notice of pay rate and pay day. For example, Section 195.5 of the New York State Labor Law provides as follows: "Every employer shall notify his employees in writing or by publicly posting the employer's policy on sick leave, vacation, personal leave, holidays, and hours."[1]

- Various state laws regulating workplace drug testing require employers to have a written policy.

- The Occupational Safety and Health Administration's (OSHA) Hazard Communication Standard requires covered employers to develop a written hazard communication program defining responsibilities and procedures to notify employees about chemical hazards in the workplace.

- The U.S. Equal Employment Opportunity Commission recommends that employers define and communicate to employees a policy statement prohibiting sexual harassment.

Various federal and state laws require employers to post notices or notify employees regarding provisions of the law. A policy manual or employee handbook can help the firm to comply with these requirements.

Laws and government regulations affecting the employment process define a minimum standard for employment practices. It makes good sense to define personnel policies in a way which reflects the law or regulation. This helps assure that the firm's personnel practices are in compliance with the law.

## When Is a Policy Manual Needed?

Why is it that some firms with 15 employees make an effort to define personnel policies while others wait until the employment level reaches 150? One answer lies in the management style of the chief executive. Some entrepreneurs who left the big corporations frustrated by bureaucracy or red tape are likely to resist efforts of subordinates to define policies. Other entrepreneurs who tend toward a more systematic approach are more likely to prefer the structure and consistency which defined policies provide.

Organizational size, number of locations, government requirements, legal claims, and other similar factors influence an executive's recognition of the benefits of personnel policies.

Based on 10 years of consulting, I offer the following recommendations:

1. At 15 employees or more, your organization can benefit from an employee handbook or a basic personnel policy guide for managers. By this stage of development, your organization is subject to most state and federal labor laws. Further, your 15 or more employees will have a variety of policy questions and expect some consistency in your reply.

2. At five or more supervisors or two or more locations, your organization can benefit from a basic policy and procedure guide for supervisors and managers. Your five or more supervisors probably direct 25 to 50 employees or more and are likely to have varying interpretation of company policies and benefits. Likewise, with two or more locations, your off-site managers are under the gun to make policy decisions in

response to personnel issues. A policy and procedure manual will guide them toward sound personnel decisions.

## Benefits of a Personnel Policy Manual

The Controller of a growing electronics equipment distributor summed up the benefits of defining a personnel policy manual. He said, "We were busy before and did not have much time to devote to policy issues until a problem occurred. Now that our policies are defined, it is an impulse reaction to reach for the policy manual and provide an answer when questions arise."

A personnel policy manual has many uses in helping growing firms to prevent personnel problems. It

- Minimizes the need for management staff meetings to resolve routine policy questions
- Promotes fair and uniform administration of company policies
- Permits routine matters to be handled by supervisors
- Provides a ready reference for orientating new employees
- Serves as an aid in recruiting new employees
- Helps to control costly absenteeism, tardiness, accidents, or sick leave abuse
- Promotes compliance with government employment and wage hour laws
- Defines authority and responsibility for supervisory personnel
- Provides a basis for defense against legal claims made by employees or former employees

## Nine Tips for Getting Management Support

Support from top management is essential in accomplishing anything significant in an organization. Whether you are developing a new policy on family leave or smoking cessation, or defining a complete personnel policy manual, your task will be made easier when you have active interest and support from superiors.

Since human resources is a staff support function, your proper role is to advise line managers. From this context, if top management wants a new policy defined, it is typically your assignment to sort out issues and define the policy.

Often, however, top management's time is committed to sales, profits, manufacturing, service, finances, or other issues. As a result, unresolved personnel problems are likely to come to your attention. As problems recur, the need for a policy guideline emerges. In seeking to resolve the issue, you may become the advocate for a new policy (or a policy manual). If so, you must "sell" management on the idea.

As a human resource consultant, I find that the nature of my business is selling: first to sell the manager on the merits and value of the policy or project, and second to convince the manager that I am the best one to do the job. Based on this experience, I have gained some valuable ideas on how to sell a policy to management.

1. *Show need.* According to basic motivational concepts, we are not motivated to act unless we perceive a need. Similarly, you must identify the need for a policy in order to prompt management interest and support of the issue. Identify examples, situations, or problems which would be resolved by the policy.

2. *Detail costs.* Line managers who are held accountable to profit goals, budgets, and expense limits will pay close attention to data showing unnecessary costs incurred. Costs of absences, lost time, overtime, accidents, litigation, or other similar issues can be used to justify a policy which will help control or prevent the costs.

3. *Compute return on investment (ROI).* Line managers whose responsibilities include the making of large purchases are accustomed to computing a return on investment, or ROI, of the capital expense. Calculate the time and cost to develop your personnel policy or manual together with the costs savings attained when it is in place, compared to expenses incurred without the policy guidelines. Most human resource projects should recoup the investment within one or two years.

4. *Show benefits.* Sales personnel learn the importance of selling benefits of their product or service rather than dwelling on its features. Benefits focus on why the policy or policy manual will be useful and make the supervisor's or manager's job easier. Identifying costs, savings, and ROI issues is an important aspect of showing benefits.

5. *Offer solutions.* Seasoned human resource specialists know the importance of presenting solutions to problems, not just identifying problems. It is good to identify the problems (show need), but it is equally important to recommend solutions. With this extra step and effort you become part of the solution, not the problem.

6. *Present alternatives.* A personnel manager for a growing printing company encountered management ambivalence to his draft of an equal employment opportunity policy, even after the firm had received a formal discrimination charge. The problem was that the entrepreneurial president was uncomfortable with the detailed eight-page policy statement including detailed definitions of various kinds of discrimina-

tion and employee complaint procedures. That policy was never implemented because it did not reflect the executive's management style. The firm ultimately adopted a brief, more basic policy statement in an employee handbook prepared by a consultant. The lesson here: Consider alternative solutions. Costs, time, procedural details, organizational culture, and management style are all factors that influence management's acceptance or rejection of a policy or policy manual.

7. *Elicit support.* Many executives accord substantial consideration to the recommendations of trusted advisors, and they address issues in which there is a consensus among the management staff. If this is the case in your organization, you should enlist the support of other managers or supervisors.

8. *Timing is everything.* Everyone knows better than to ask for a raise when the boss is having an off day. Likewise, a proper sense of timing is important when selling management on a personnel policy or policy manual. Since personnel policies are intended to guide decisions on a particular matter, a proposal for a policy to solve a current or pending dilemma is likely to be viewed as an effective solution to the matter.

9. *Consider outside support.* Many management functions routinely draw on outside specialists for advice and direction. Common examples include auditors who critique accounting practices; actuaries who compute probabilities and design insurance plans; and pension specialists who update retirement plans to comply with changing tax or regulatory laws. Likewise, human resource advisors who specialize in personnel policy development can provide valuable assistance. Outside specialists can effectively sell the project, audit current practices, provide objective recommendations, and review policy issues or provide actual writing assistance.

## Summary

A policy is a predetermined guideline providing a specified course of action for dealing with prescribed circumstances. New and smaller organizations tend to follow unwritten practices rather than written policies. But as firms grow, questions and problems arise which prompt the need to define policy guidelines. Some government regulations also require written policies. By the time an organization reaches 15 or more employees, or two or more locations, or five or more supervisors, it can benefit from written policy guidelines. It is important, however, to stimulate management support when defining policies. The next concern is to recognize the impact of the legal concepts of employment at will and wrongful discharge. These concepts play a significant role in how policies are defined. Chapter 2 sheds some light on these important issues.

## Notes

1. Notice Requirements for Fringe Benefits and Hours, New York State Department of Labor Interpretive Guideline LS 606 (7-86).

# 2

# The Contract Controversy

**Read Chapter 2 for:**

Employment at will

Limitations to employment at will

Highlights of selected leading employment-at-will cases

23 tips on avoiding the contract controversy

## Understanding Employment at Will

Years ago, employment decisions seemed simpler. Workers were hired to meet business needs and dismissed when the work slacked off. This was the free-market exercise of employment at will.

Unfortunately, there were some abuses of management prerogative. As a result, the employment process is now much more complex. Labor laws, government regulations, and court decisions influence nearly every aspect of the employment process. Your job as a human resource specialist is much like that of an infantry soldier walking "point," leading the platoon across a minefield. Each step of the employment process must be carefully considered to avoid potentially explosive liabilities.

One of the leading issues facing human resource specialists is the interpretation by some courts that personnel policy handbooks are contractually binding. In a growing number of states, fired employees have won court decisions and sizeable awards after showing that their separation was a wrongful discharge. A basic understanding of employment at will and wrongful discharge issues is essential to preparing personnel policies.

The employment-at-will concept evolved from the master–servant relationship as the United States evolved from an agrarian and craft society to a more industrialized society. The basic definition of employment at will is that the employee is hired for an indefinite period without an employment contract and that separation of employment may occur at any time for any reason. Likewise, the employee may seek employment or quit employment at any time.

Approximately 18 percent of the U.S. workforce is unionized. Many executives and other high-level technical or sales personnel have individual employment contracts. When an individual or collectively bargained employment contract exists, the contract controls the employment relationship. The remainder of the workforce (approximately 75 percent of workers) has no formal contract and may be considered employed at will unless otherwise protected by an applicable law.

## Legislated Limitations

During the past 25 years, the employment-at-will doctrine has been eroded. Limitations to the employer's unfettered right to hire and fire have occurred through legislation and court decisions.

State and federal labor laws which prohibit employment discharge for specified reasons limit employment at will. The National Labor Relations Act of 1935 protects employees from discharge for participation in union activities. Similarly, Title VII of the Civil Rights Act of 1964 and the Occupational Safety and Health Act of 1970 prohibit an employer from discharging an individual from employment for exercising rights under those laws.

Various other local, state, and federal labor laws impose prohibitions on discharges. Among these laws are the following:

Equal Employment Opportunity Laws

Equal Pay Laws

Workers' Compensation Laws

Wage Hour Laws

Wage Deduction for Creditors Laws

Labor Relations Law

Whistle Blower Protection Laws

These legislated limitations reduce the employer's prerogative to fire at will. For a further discussion of the effects of various labor laws on the personnel policy development process, see Chap. 5, "Avoiding Legal Pitfalls."

## Litigated Limitations

The center of the contract controversy focuses on litigated limitations to employment at will. Many of the limitations to the employment-at-will doctrine are based on case law rather than a specific state or federal law. As a result, the interpretations and limitations to employment at will occur through state courts applying or creating legal precedents when rendering decisions to individual lawsuits. Further, this allows separated employee plaintiffs, through their lawsuits, to advance a variety of legal theories to support their wrongful discharge claims.

One of the leading cases occurred in Michigan in 1978. When he was hired by Blue Cross/Blue Shield of Michigan, Charles Toussaint was given verbal assurances that he would not be terminated without cause. Further, he received an employee handbook which stipulated that progressive discipline procedures would be used for all terminations. Upon discharge, Toussaint filed a wrongful discharge lawsuit against his former employer alleging breach of implied contract because the discharge did not follow company procedures. Since Toussaint prevailed in a lawsuit which was filed in state court anppd heard by a jury, the law allowed a jury award of more than $70,000.00.[1]

Following the Toussaint case, the floodgates opened. Jurisdictions in the various states heard a variety of wrongful discharge cases. The number of wrongful discharge lawsuits multiplied rapidly, as did the jury awards to the plaintiff former employees. A study by the Rand Corp.'s Institute for Civil Justice shows that 1000 wrongful discharge lawsuits were filed in California in 1986. In Los Angeles, the number of such suits grew from 90 in 1980 to 600 in 1986. A recent television news feature on wrongful discharge reported that wrongful discharge lawsuits rose from 200 in 1970 to more than 25,000 in 1990.[2]

Courts in various jurisdictions are drawing different conclusions. Courts in some states have concluded that employee handbooks or personnel policy information does rise to the level of a contract. Some of these states define certain requirements which must be met before a policy manual may be construed as a contract. Other states have reached different findings, concluding that employee handbooks or policy manuals are not contractual in nature.

There are, however, some common trends in case decisions which limit the employment-at-will prerogative. Legal challenges to the employment-at-will doctrine can be grouped into four broad categories: implied contract, good faith and fair dealing, public policy, and various tort law theories. Selected leading cases are summarized here to give you a basic understanding of some litigated limitations to employment at will.

## Implied Contract

In many states the courts have concluded that written or oral statements made to an employee about job security or discharge procedures have created an implied contract binding upon the employer. Interview statements about job security, promises that discharge would only be for cause, or detailed predischarge procedures contained in an employee handbook are common examples in which the employer's actions disregarding such statements constituted wrongful discharge. These wrongful discharge lawsuits created case law precedent in their respective jurisdictions and influenced other jurisdictions as well.

In a Michigan case, Mr. Ebling, an employee of Masco Corp., was told by management that he would be with the company as long as he did his job. Subsequently discharged, Ebling sued, asserting that management's promise of employment constituted an oral contract of employment. A jury ruled in favor of Ebling, and the case was upheld by the Court of Appeals and the State Supreme Court.[3]

The implied contract issue is frequently focused on a firm's employee handbook. In one leading case, the Minnesota Supreme Court held that Mettille's discharge from a Pine River, Minnesota bank was without cause and inconsistent with progressive discipline procedures listed in the bank's employee handbook. The Court concluded that the employee handbook was contractually binding on the employer.[4]

Following the line of thinking in the Pine River case, a growing number of jurisdictions have held that, under certain conditions, an employee handbook does create contractually binding obligations on the employer.

In Illinois, for example, the state supreme court agreed with the Pine River court in deciding a wrongful discharge claim of a hospital employee. In the case of *Dudulao* v. *St. Mary of Nazareth Hospital* the Court stated, "We hold that an employee handbook or other policy statement creates enforceable contractual rights if the traditional requirements for contracts formation are present. First, the language of the policy statement must contain a promise clear enough that an employee would reasonably believe that an offer has been made. Second, the statement must be disseminated to the employee in such a manner that the employee is aware of its contents and reasonably believes it to be an offer. Third, the employee must accept the offer by commencing or continuing to work after learning of the policy statement. When these conditions are present, then the employee's continued work constitutes a consideration for the promises contained in the statement, and under traditional principles, a valid contract is formed."[5]

Courts in some states have recognized that employment-at-will status can be preserved by specific language. Contract disclaimers in personnel policy documents, policy manuals, and employee handbooks have helped several firms to prevail in wrongful discharge lawsuits. For example, the language in the employment application affirming an employee's at-will status was upheld in *Batchelor* v. *Sears Roebuck & Co.*[6]

As another example, the Illinois Appellate Court recognized that a disclaimer in the Evanston Hospital employee handbook was sufficient to prevent the handbook from being interpreted as a contract.[7]

In another case, an Illinois court held that an employer's discipline policy guidelines for management were not distributed to employees and did not constitute clear promise which employees could believe to be an offer of employment, and therefore did not reach the level of a contract.[8]

Considerable caution is necessary to ensure that all personnel policy documents given to employees consistently reflect language designed to protect employment-at-will status. For example, a New York court noted that, in spite of the at-will language appearing on a Sears Roebuck application, policy manual requirements for certain pre-discharge conditions created an employment contract that was distinguishable from employment at will.[9]

## Good Faith and Fair Dealing

The doctrine of good faith and fair dealing asserts that every contract contains an unwritten provision or covenant that the parties will deal with each other fairly. The courts, in applying this doctrine to employment discharge cases, have concluded that a discharge in bad faith or for a bad cause is a wrongful discharge limitation to the employment-at-will concept.

A leading case which reflects the good faith and fair dealing doctrine is *Cleary* v. *American Airlines*.[10] Cleary, an 18-year employee with satisfactory employment ratings, was fired without an objective investigation and a fair review hearing as defined by Company policies. Cleary prevailed in his lawsuit. The court held that discharge of a satisfactorily performing employee of 18 years, without legal cause, violated the implied covenant of good faith and fair dealing contained in all contracts.

Another California case with significant implications is *Foley* v. *Interactive Data Corp.*[11] Foley, a seven-year employee who had received salary increases, bonuses, and oral assurances of job security, was transferred and then fired. Foley's wrongful discharge lawsuit was based on three issues: public policy, breach of implied contract, and breach of the good faith and fair dealing covenant. The trial court dismissed his claims. But on appeal to the State Supreme Court, Foley prevailed with the breach of implied contract claim and the breach of good faith and fair dealing. In a notable departure from past practice, the Court held that remedies would be limited only to actual losses such as back pay and not the punitive damages customarily allowed in tort cases. (The legal concept of torts is explained briefly in the next section.)

The good faith and fair dealing doctrine is not recognized as an exception to employment at will in all states. According to the Bureau of National Affairs, only 13 states currently recognize the good faith and fair dealing covenant in the employment relationship.

## Tort Theories

In some wrongful discharge cases, various tort theories have been advanced. *Tort* is the legal term for a civil wrong in which an individual is negligently or willfully harmed in some way. Tort cases are distinguished from breach of contract cases, which rise from a violation of an express or implied contract.

One example is the tort of intentional infliction of emotional distress. In cases where this theory has been used successfully, the terminated employee plaintiff was able to show that the employer's conduct was intentional and outrageous in nature and had a severe effect on the employee's emotional tranquility. An illustrative case was *Rulon-Miller* v. *IBM*.[12]

Various other tort theories which have been used successfully by terminated employee plaintiffs are fraudulent misrepresentation, defamation, negligence, and invasion of privacy.

## Public Policy

Courts in many jurisdictions have held that discharge of an employee for exercising rights under labor law or discharge for refusing to perform illegal acts directed by the employer is employer conduct which violates public policy. There is substantial case law which demonstrates that the courts will view such actions by employers as wrongful discharge. In one of the leading cases, Petermann was discharged for refusing to commit perjury during a legislative hearing. The court held that the discharge was a wrongful discharge which violated the state's public policy.[13]

Through a number of cases, the public policy exception to employment at will has grown to include "whistle blowing" (an employee reporting an employer's wrongdoing,) filing worker's compensation claims, participating in jury service, responding to a witness subpoena, cooperating with law enforcement authorities, or other similar cases in which an employee has exercised a right allowed by law.

## Emerging Law

The employment at will and wrongful discharge issues represent an area of rapidly emerging law. Since this area of employment law is based largely on case law at the state court level, there are many different cases and decisions. A detailed examination of all these cases is beyond the scope of this book. However, human resource specialists who are preparing personnel policies must stay continually alert to the impact of these court decisions. Careful and current research is necessary to make sure that your firm's policies and procedures reflect the current labor law requirements.

Currently, one state, Montana, has passed a wrongful discharge law (see Table 2.1). The law requires employers to follow any written policies

**Table 2.1.** Employment at Will: State Comparison Chart

| State | Implied contracts (employer policies, handbooks) | Public policy | Good faith covenant |
|---|---|---|---|
| Alabama | Yes | Yes | Yes |
| Alaska | Yes | Yes | Yes |
| Arizona | Yes | Yes | Yes |
| Arkansas | Yes | Yes | No* |
| California | Yes | Yes | Yes |
| Colorado | Yes | No | Yes |
| Connecticut | Yes | Yes | Yes |
| Delaware | No | No | Yes |
| District of Columbia | Yes | NR | NC |
| Florida | No | No | NC |
| Georgia | Yes* | No | No |
| Hawaii | Yes | Yes | NC |
| Idaho | Yes* | Yes | Yes |
| Illinois | Yes | Yes | No |
| Indiana | No | Yes* | No |
| Iowa | NR | Yes | Yes |
| Kansas | Yes | Yes* | No |
| Kentucky | NC | Yes* | NC |
| Louisiana | NC | No | NC |
| Maine | Yes* | NC | No |
| Maryland | Yes | Yes | No |
| Massachusetts | NC | Yes | Yes |
| Michigan | Yes | Yes* | NC |
| Minnesota | Yes | Yes | No |
| Mississippi | NC | NR | NC |
| Missouri | No | Yes | NC |
| Montana | Yes | Yes | Yes |
| Nebraska | NC | Yes | NC |
| Nevada | NC | Yes | Yes |
| New Hampshire | Yes | Yes | Yes |
| New Jersey | Yes | Yes | No |
| New Mexico | Yes | Yes | NC |
| New York | Yes* | No | No |

**Table 2.1.** Employment at Will: State Comparison Chart (*Continued*)

| State | Implied contracts (employer policies, handbooks) | Public policy | Good faith covenant |
|---|---|---|---|
| North Carolina | No | Yes | NC |
| North Dakota | NC | Yes | No |
| Ohio | Yes | Yes | NC |
| Oklahoma | Yes | Yes | No |
| Oregon | Yes | Yes | NC |
| Pennsylvania | NR | Yes | No |
| Rhode Island | NC | NC | NC |
| South Carolina | Yes | Yes | NC |
| South Dakota | Yes | Yes | No |
| Tennessee | No | Yes | NC |
| Texas | Yes | Yes | NC |
| Utah | Yes | NC | NC |
| Vermont | Yes | NC | NC |
| Virginia | NR | Yes | NR |
| Washington | Yes | Yes | No |
| West Virginia | Yes | Yes | NC |
| Wisconsin | Yes | Yes | No |
| Wyoming | Yes | Yes | No |

*–Qualifiedly.
NC—No cases or no clear expression.
NR—No definite state ruling; there may be federal rulings in the subject area.
Reprinted with permission from *Employment Guide*, pp 10:87–88A. Copyright 1991 by the Bureau of National Affairs, 1231 25th Street, Washington D.C. 20037.
*Caution to reader*: The Employment at Will State Comparison Chart is intended as a general information guide to acquaint the reader with employment at will issues in the various states. New laws are passed by state legislatures, and court decisions can create new legal trends in a particular state or jurisdiction. The reader is urged to check local labor laws and/or professional counsel to define policy information that complies with the law.

and limits discharges to certain broadly defined good cause reasons. Additionally, a committee of the National Conference of Commissioners in Uniform State Laws in 1990 drafted a proposed employee termination law referred to as the Uniform Employment Termination Act. This proposed law is still under development. In light of the continued growth of wrongful discharge lawsuits and substantial jury awards being rendered, it is likely that more states will adopt some form of employee termination legislation.

## The Policy Debate

The growing number of wrongful discharge cases and sizeable damage awards are causing some organizations to reconsider the use of written policy manuals. The absence of a written employee handbook removes one possible source of liability. A careful assessment of the issues shows, however, that an organization which elects not to publish a policy manual still opens itself up to the same or possibly greater potential liabilities.

Some courts have held that verbal statements made by supervisors to employees are binding. As a result, the lack of written policies does not protect the firm from breach of an implied contract created by a supervisor's statement. Rather, without policy guidelines for supervisors, there could be a greater likelihood of promises or statements by a supervisor which negate the employment-at-will relationship.

After more than 20 years in the human resource field, I have observed that a key process for preventing employee relations problems, and for defending against any employee allegations, is to

1. Define a policy guideline (which is in compliance with the law).

2. Communicate the policy to employees.

3. Demonstrate uniform, fair administration of the policy.

## What the Experts Say

Many lawyers and human resource experts have advocated the benefits of written policy manuals, even in the current litigation climate. Several examples are highlighted in this section.

Attorney John D. Coombe, writing in *Employee Relations Law Journal* stated that employee handbooks have a positive and beneficial employee relations aspect that easily outweighs the legal hazards of the handbook. Coombe writes, "Simply eliminating the use of employee handbooks for fear of a breach of contract claim is tantamount to throwing the baby out with the bath water."[14]

Another example, appears in "Avoiding Liability in Employee Handbooks," an article from the summer, 1988 issue of *Employee Relations Law Journal.* In this article, attorneys Maureen Reidy Witt and Sandra R. Goldman summarize by stating, "Employers that have rejected publishing employee handbooks because of fear of contractual liability should re-evaluate their options."[15]

The "Managers' Newsfront" column in the April, 1987 *Personnel Journal,* written by attorneys, cites recent trends in cases involving personnel policy manuals and offers the following assessment: "Employer personnel policy and procedure manuals can go far toward establishing an orderly workplace by informing employees of what is expected of them and setting forth the consequences of a failure to perform."[16]

Attorney Gerald D. Skoning, writing in the "Your Turn" opinion column of *Crain's Chicago Business* urges companies not to discontinue use of employee handbooks entirely. Skoning acknowledges that eliminating an employee handbook would make it more difficult for a court to find an implied contract. However, Skoning adds that the absence of a handbook would violate important rules of human resource management such as providing notice, uniformity, predictability, and fairness.[17]

Washington, D.C. attorney Lawrence Lorber was quoted in an *Inc. Magazine* article on legal challenges to personnel policies as saying, "Having policies in place creates the perception—and the reality—that you have made an attempt at fair play. It protects you from frivolous charges."[18]

## Summary

One of the leading labor law issues is the interpretation by some courts that personnel policy handbook can be contractually binding upon the employer. The traditional common law principle of employment at will—that an employer can separate the employment relationship at any time for any reason—has become significantly limited by recent laws and court decisions.

The leading theories being advocated are as follows:

1. Personnel policy information may become an implied contract;

2. A discharge should not be in violation of public policy; and

3. An agreement contains an implied covenant of good faith and fair dealing.

Proper wording of policy information, use of disclaimers, and training of supervisors are several key practices which an employer can institute to minimize legal liability of claims.

The task of writing a personnel policy manual typically falls upon the human resource practitioner in the organization. Chapter 3 provides nuts and bolts how-to information to help you get started on this project.

## Notes

1. *Toussaint* v. *Blue Cross and Blue Shield of Michigan* (292 NW 2nd 880. Mich. 1980).
2. C. Kleiman, "Wrongful Discharge Lawsuits Multiplying," *Chicago Tribune,* January 29, 1989.
3. *Ebling* v. *Masco Corp.* (2902 NW 2nd 32 880. Mich. 1980) (4).
4. *Pine River State Bank* v. *Mettille* (333 NW 2nd 622 Minn. 1983).

5. *Dudulao* v. *St. Mary of Nazareth Hospital* (1 IER cases 1431), copyright 1987 by The Bureau of National Affairs. Reprinted with permission

6. *Batchelor* v. *Sears Roebuck & Co.* (575 F Supp. 1480 E.D. Mich. 1983).

7. *Bennett* v. *Evanston Hospital* (540 NE 2nd 979 1989).

8. *Koch* v. *Illinois Power Co.* (529 NE 2nd 281. 1988).

9. *Tiorranno* v. *Sears Roebuck & Co.* (472 N.Y.S. 2nd 49 1984).

10. *Cleary* v. *American Airlines* (168 Cal. Rptr. 722. Cal., 1980).

11. *Foley* v. *Interactive Data Corp.* (110 LC. 55, 978 Cal. Sup. Ct., 1984).

12. *Rulon-Miller* v. *IBM* (162 Cal. Ap. 3rd. 241 1984).

13. *Petermann* v. *Teamsters Local 396* (344 P. 2nd 25 1959).

14. J. D. Coombe, "Employee Handbooks: Asset or Liability," *Employee Relations Law Journal*, Vol. 12, 1986, p. 10.

15. M. Reidywitt, S. Goldman, "Avoiding Liability in Employee Handbooks," *Employee Relations Law Journal*, Vol. 14, Summer, 1988, p. 17. Reprinted with permission. Copyright © 1988 by Executive Enterprises, Inc., 22 West 21st Street, New York, NY 10010-6900. All rights reserved.

16. B. S. Murphy, W. Barlow, D. D. Hutch, "Employee Handbooks and Wrongful Termination," Managers' Newsfront column, *Personnel Journal*, April, 1987, p. 24.

17. G. Skoning, "Beware New Court Rulings Limiting Firms' Right to Fire," Your Turn column, *Crain's Chicago Business*, April 9, 1984, p. 9.

18. E. Kolton, "An Ounce of Prevention," *Inc. Magazine*, October, 1984, p. 156.

**CHECKLIST**
**23 Tips to Avoid the Contract Controversy:**
**Actions You Can Take to Prevent Lawsuits**

There are a number of actions which organizations can take to avoid the contract controversy. Your goal should be protecting management prerogatives of employment at will and minimizing the likelihood of a wrongful discharge lawsuit.

A checklist of preventive actions follows

1. Place a prominent disclaimer in the employee handbook which asserts that the handbook is not a contract, that policies or benefits may be changed or withdrawn, and that the employment is at will, meaning that either the company or employee may separate employment at any time for any reason.

2. Utilize the disclaimer in an acknowledgment/sign-off sheet in which the employee signs for receipt of the handbook and acknowledges employment at will.

3. Avoid references to "permanent" employment when defining employment status. Rather, identify that full-time employees are hired for an indefinite period of employment.

4. Include a disclaimer on your employment application in which the applicant certifies an understanding that employment and compensation can be terminated with or without cause and with or without notice at any time by either the company or the applicant.

5. Avoid references to "probationary" status for new employees. Passing probation may imply permanent or tenured status and create potential barriers to employment at will. The terms *introductory period* or *orientation period* may be used to describe the training and evaluation phase during the first few weeks of employment.

6. Avoid making promises about job security or discharge protection during the recruiting and interviewing process.

7. Avoid statements committing to a "just cause" basis for involuntary terminations. The just cause requirement will limit management prerogative to separate an employee at will.

8. Avoid defining detailed predischarge procedures in your employee handbook. Typical predischarge procedures may include detailed predischarge disciplinary steps, or requirements for counselling, probation, or performance reviews. These are excellent human resource procedures to follow, but the publishing of the procedures as discharge prerequisites in an employee manual limits management prerogative to separate an employee at will.

9. If disciplinary rules are listed in your employee manual, be sure to specify that the list is not all inclusive, that separation may occur as a result of other misconduct.

10. If disciplinary guidelines are defined in your employee manual, list such guidelines broadly, stating that corrective action for any offense may include

warnings, suspension, or immediate discharge, as deemed appropriate by management.

11. Define policies which reflect the culture and management style of the organization. For example, if management of an organization prefers flexibility, broadly written policies which allow some flexibility will be more effective than rigid, detailed procedures. The key issue here: Avoid publishing a policy or rule which is likely to be disregarded by management.

12. Require that all dismissals be subject to the review and approval of a second-level manager and/or human resource specialist. This review process helps to assure that the dismissal complies with policy, is consistent with other similar instances, and that all relevant labor law or nondiscriminatory issues have been considered.

13. Avoid making promises about job security, career tenure, or discharge protection when discussing performance evaluations or career plans.

14. Take care to utilize a due process approach when considering discharges. Make sure that the employee was adequately trained on job tasks, counseled on improper behavior, warned about misconduct, appraised of poor performance, given an opportunity to correct behavior, and that corrective actions are adequately documented. *Note:* These predischarge procedures are important to follow. However, to minimize the likelihood of creating an implied contract from a detailed predischarge procedure in an employee handbook, avoid publishing detailed discharge procedures in a manual given to employees. Rather, include any detailed discharge procedures in a supervisor's policy manual.

15. Train supervisors and managers on proper techniques for interviewing, appraising performance, disciplining, and handling discharges. Training should include effective techniques, awareness of how employment decisions influence employment at will, and precautions to help prevent wrongful discharge lawsuits.

16. Research labor laws and case decisions relating to wrongful discharge and employment at will in your state. Seek professional counsel when unsure of the proper way to define policy issues.

17. Review old employee handbooks and policy manuals to ensure that policies, procedures, and employment documents are revised to maximize employment-at-will prerogatives and minimize liability of a wrongful discharge lawsuit.

18. Avoid the tendency to disregard published policies or to make exceptions to predischarge procedures.

19. Carefully evaluate and justify the discharge of long-term employees. A significant job performance problem or serious economic limitations resulting in layoff are a firm's best justification for discharge of a long-term employee with a history of pay raises.

20. Carefully document misconduct or poor performance ratings uniformly for all employees. An employee's personnel file with records reflecting management's efforts to correct performance or misconduct problems provides a clear justifi-

cation of a discharge and can be your first line of defense in a wrongful discharge lawsuit.

21. Respond promptly and truthfully to unemployment claims. It may be beneficial in subsequent legal proceedings to get an administrative determination that the termination was justified by the employee's misconduct.

22. Consider outplacement services to direct the terminated employee's energies toward constructive job search efforts. A disgruntled individual who feels cheated or angry at the former employer is more likely to seek legal redress than one who finds reemployment quickly.

23. Avoid the tendency to delay a discharge following an incident or performance problem. If the incident is serious enough to warrant discharge, make the separation on a timely basis following investigation of the circumstances. Unreasonable delay clouds the real reason for discharge.

# 3

# Getting Started: Organizing Your Policy Project to Achieve Results

**Read Chapter 3 for:**

A definition of policy project action steps from start to finish

Analysis of organizational needs, priorities, and culture

Evaluating benefits of an employee handbook versus management policy manual

Selecting appropriate policy topics for your policy manual

Time management tips and organization checklists

Implementation tips on organizing and working with a personnel policy committee.

## A Starting Point

An ancient oriental proverb states that the longest journey begins with one step. Likewise, your personnel policy manual must be written word by word. To be completed properly, a personnel policy manual will require planning, organizing, some research, considerable writing, and careful editing. This process may seem like a formidable task. Chapter 3 will assist you in breaking this project into manageable segments or steps.

Often, the development of a personnel policy manual is delayed because other pressing issues and emergencies require your immediate attention, or because you procrastinate. The responsible manager rationalizes the delay by saying, "We'll get around to it one of these days." In fact, "we'll get around to it" is such a universal excuse for procrastination that sales representatives frequently carry a novelty wooden coin imprinted with the words "round tuitt," which they present to sales prospects in a humorous yet persistent effort to close a sale.

In the human resource arena a "round tuitt" is often in the form of a serious incident that affects customer relations or a legal claim, such as a discrimination charge or a wrongful discharge lawsuit. The seriousness of the situation prompts management to define policy issues to prevent recurrence of similar incidents.

## Organize Project Steps

The key to success with any large project is to break it into manageable chunks. (See Table 3.1.) You can then plan and organize your efforts to complete the project. Here is a recommended approach:

**Set a Goal.**   When you set a personal goal and write it down, you have taken the first big step toward accomplishing that goal. The goal should be specific and attainable, with a defined deadline. For example, "I plan to prepare a personnel policy and procedure manual with 20 management policies, to be completed within six months." By writing the goal, you are beginning the process which commits you to action. For a real commitment, give a copy of the goal to your superior (if he or she hasn't already assigned the project to you.) Now that you have made a public commitment in your organization, you will be motivated to finish the job.

**Define Project Objectives.**   All too often, an inexperienced manual writer begins an employee handbook, but midway through the project inserts

**Table 3.1.** Flowchart for a Policy Manual Project

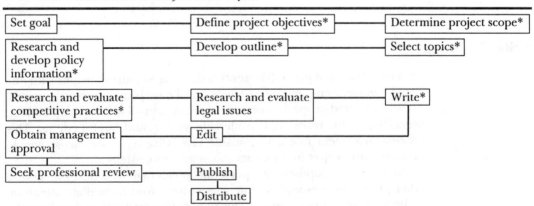

*Activities appropriate for a policy manual committee.

procedural instructions for supervisors. You can prevent this problem when you define project objectives to focus your efforts. Will your policy manual be a procedural guide for supervisors or a concise handbook with a positive message for employees? Will your manual provide broad guidelines or specific procedures? The answers to these questions will help you stay on course.

**Determine Project Scope.**   A personnel policy manual can contain as few as five topics or as many as 100 or more. Determine the size and scope of your project. This will prevent you from tackling more than what you can handle. In one small company of less than 50 employees, for example, an overzealous personnel specialist developed over 55 policies, procedures, and forms, creating a bureaucratic nightmare for the entrepreneur owner.

**Select Topics.**   After you have determined the scope of your policy manual, you can begin to focus on which policy topics will be addressed. As a general rule, employees want to know about issues relating to pay, time off, or a combination of these issues. Management, on the other hand, typically wants the policy manual to deal with issues relating to working hours, attendance, discipline, and similar work conduct issues. One tip: Focus on those topics about which frequent questions or issues arise.

**Develop an Outline.**   Once you identify the policy manual topics, develop an outline which organizes topics into a logical sequence. Subpoints on your outline can focus on scheduled key policy and procedure issues. Lack of an outline is one reason many inexperienced manual writers produce poorly organized material.

**Research and Develop Policy Information.**   Development of policy information can be one of the more challenging aspects of preparing a personnel policy manual. In this phase you ask, "What is our policy on...?" The answers are drawn from management interviews, policy memos or letters, or policy committee discussions.

**Research and Evaluate Competitive Practices.**   Most organizations operate in a competitive environment. All organizations compete for workers from the local labor market. This means that firms must control personnel costs yet provide policies and benefits which will help attract and retain qualified workers. Failure to maintain competitive personnel practices or benefits may contribute to costly turnover and hiring difficulties. For these reasons, it is essential to research and evaluate competitive practices in the industry and the local community when preparing a policy manual. Personnel practices and benefits surveys are a leading source of information on competitive practices.

**Research and Evaluate Legal Issues.**  All personnel policies are subject to various state and federal labor laws, administrative regulations, and court decisions. A properly defined personnel policy is a firm's first step in guiding supervisors or managers to make employment decisions which are consistent with the law. Experienced human resource specialists are likely to be familiar with various labor laws or sources of information on the law. Take care to define policy issues which reflect current labor law trends. Inadequate research may result in defining a personnel practice which violates the law. If you are weak in this area, be sure to arrange for professional review of your manual prior to its distribution.

**Write the Manual.**  Writing the manual is the heart of the project. Without preparation, this can be an arduous task. But with some planning, organization, and collection of relevant information, the writing process is much easier. Policy samples are one resource which can give you ideas on writing personnel policies. Take care, however, to adapt policies to reflect the management style and practices of your organization.

**Edit the Manual.**  Careful reading and editing of your manual is an important quality check. Ideally, the editor should be someone, other than yourself, who has excellent grammar skills and a thorough understanding of personnel policy issues. The editing process is a second look at the written material to ensure consistently error-free writing, correction of grammatical errors, and fine-tuning of the material to improve organization or content.

**Obtain Management Approval.**  A major hurdle for many policy manual writers is obtaining management approval of their effort. Many policy manual attempts have ended up as unused draft manuscripts collecting dust in a desk or file drawer. Management read the manuscript but was unmoved or even reluctant to release the manual. Careful organization, preparation, and writing are keys for gaining management approval.

**Seek Professional Review.**  In the current employment arena, professional review of your personnel policy manual is strongly recommended. Changing labor laws, administrative regulations, and court decisions affect the legality of personnel policies. Your best protection is to have your manual reviewed by a consultant, attorney, or other human resource specialist who is familiar with current labor law issues.

**Publish and Distribute Your Manual.**  Publishing your policy manual and distributing it to supervisors or employees is the culmination of your efforts. But don't rest on your laurels. This is just a milestone. You must periodically update and revise the manual to reflect changing policies, benefits, and labor laws, or to correct misinterpretations.

The foregoing paragraphs provide an overview of the policy manual development process. Now we will focus on some project management tips.

## Who Is Your Writing Audience?

At the beginning of the policy manual project, you need to identify your writing audience. Will your manual be prepared for employees or for managers and supervisors? This decision is critical. It will affect what you write, the tone of your message, and the degree to which you cover procedural details.

There are three basic approaches or formats for preparing policy information:

1. Policy statement
2. Policy and procedure guide
3. Employee handbook.

Use the following guidelines and samples to select the format for your policy manual.

| Policy format | Characteristic | Suggested audience |
| --- | --- | --- |
| Policy statement | Narrative paragraph describing broad policy objective | Employees or management |
| Policy and procedure guide | Contains policy statement and a series of procedural instructions for administering the policy | Supervisors and managers exclusively |
| Employee handbook | Contains brief summaries of policy information concisely written with a positive flair | All employees, including supervisors and managers |

**Policy Statement.** The policy statement broadly describes the organization's policy on a particular subject. It is defined to communicate top management's commitment to a particular issue. While policy statements may be assembled in a policy manual, they are frequently used as the lead-in to a major corporate program. Common examples include a commitment to quality statement which emphasizes the importance of quality in the firm's quality control manual, or an equal employment opportunity statement which serves as the introduction to a written affirmative action plan.

The policy statement is often signed by the chief executive to emphasize executive commitment to the issue, and it can often be seen on a fancy plaque or framed for display in the company's lobby or on the company bulletin board. The following is a sample policy statement:

> XYZ Corporation is dedicated to a policy of maintaining equal employment opportunities for all individuals in every phase of the employment relationship. Our policy of equal employment opportunity is intended to assure that all employment decisions are made without regard to race, color, age, sex, religion, national origin, physical or mental disability, status as a military veteran, or other protected status defined by law. Our policy of equal employment opportunity covers but is not limited to recruitment, selection, promotion, transfer, training, compensation, benefits, social or business activities, and other terms or conditions of employment. Each employee and manager is accountable for treating others with individual respect and for complying with the spirit and intent of this policy. Any individual who has a complaint or has experienced any form of discrimination is entitled to seek redress through his or her respective manager or the human resource department.

**Policy or Procedure Guideline.**    The policy and procedure statement typically consists of a brief one- or two-sentence policy statement and procedural guidelines for carrying out the policy. This format is intended for distribution solely to managers and supervisors.

Procedural guidelines serve as a series of instructions that aid the supervisor in taking action and making appropriate decisions under the policy. A sample procedure statement follows.

**XYZ CORPORATION**
**PERSONNEL POLICY MANUAL**

| | |
|---|---|
| Equal Employment Opportunity | No. 1.06 |
| | Page 1 of 3 |
| Applies to: All Employees | Effective: 1-1-89 |

*Policy*: It is the policy of XYZ Corporation to provide employment opportunities without regard to race, sex, age, national origin, religion, marital status, physical or mental disability, or status as a military veteran.

*Procedure:*
1. All employment decisions are to be made without regard to race, sex, age, national origin, religion, marital status, physical or mental disability, status as a military veteran, or union affiliation. Employment decisions covered by this policy include recruiting, hiring, promotion, transfer, training, compensation, benefits, discipline, termination, and other decisions, terms, or conditions of employment.

2. Each Supervisor or Manager is responsible for administering employment practices in a manner which is consistent with this policy. The

Supervisor or Manager is encouraged to confer with his or her superior and the Personnel Manager in making employment decisions which may be in conflict with the intent of this policy.

3. The Corporate Personnel Manager is responsible for keeping abreast of current issues, labor laws, etc. and for recommending changes to personnel policies or practices as appropriate. The Corporate Personnel Manager is responsible for investigating allegations or complaints of discrimination and for advising and assisting management in resolving such issues in the best interests of the Company.

4. If an employee has a question or complaint about equal opportunity employment matters, the employee should speak with his or her superior. If the employee is uncomfortable discussing the matter with his or her superior, the employee may speak with a Personnel Department representative. Employee complaints shall be handled as defined in Policy No. 1.05, Open Door Policy.

5. The Corporate Personnel Manager is responsible for maintaining necessary records and completing any required government reports.

**Employee Handbook.** Personnel policy information in an employee handbook should be a brief summary of the company's policy. It is usually written with more flair or style than the procedure statements. A sample employee handbook paragraph follows.

*Equal Employment Opportunity*
It is the policy of XYZ Corporation to afford equal opportunity for employment. All employment decisions are made without regard to race, color, age, sex, religion, national origin, ancestry, marital status, handicap, or unfavorable discharge from military service.

XYZ Corporation will not tolerate any form of harassment or discrimination, and any complaint relating to such matters may be brought directly to the attention of top management.

## Analyze the Corporate Culture

Each organization has a corporate culture, which represents the beliefs and attitudes of the organization's owners or managers. These beliefs and attitudes filter through the different levels of management and supervision to employees. The corporate culture is reflected in leadership or management styles, in acceptable norms of dress or appearance, and in many other factors affecting employment decisions and communication in an organization.

The management style of the chief executive is a significant factor which influences the corporate culture. To a lesser degree, a facility manager or branch manager influences the culture of his or her facility in a multilocation organization.

What does this mean to you as a policy manual writer? You must be aware of the corporate culture to effectively write policies for that organization.

The differences can be significant: strict policy detail versus a loose-goose approach, or a pleasant and flowery policy versus no-nonsense, military-like rigidity.

Inability to recognize the corporate culture factor and failure to write policies which reflect management style are two leading causes of management's failure to approve policy manuals.

In over eight years of policy writing, I have begun to categorize management styles and their influence on personnel policy preparation. Evaluate your organization in light of the following management styles and tailor your policy development efforts accordingly.

**The King.**   The king wields total control through a centralized and autocratic decision-making management style. All decisions, however minute, require his or her approval. The king is likely to resist defining detailed policies because doing so may dilute his or her power. The king may authorize subordinates to publish policy information which does not limit executive discretion. Decision-making procedures most likely will require that the king exercise final approval in all employment matters.

**The Gunslinger.**   The gunslinger typically is an entrepreneur with a shoot-from-the-hip decision-making style. He or she probably comes from a sales, marketing, design, or creative background, and is a whiz kid who takes pride in creating and launching a new product or service idea. The gunslinger feels that rules were made to be broken. He or she probably left a corporate bureaucracy because of frustration over rules and red tape. The gunslinger will resist the red tape of the bureaucracy, but may allow broad policy statements permitting flexibility in policy matters.

**The Technocrat.**   The technocrat is typically in or from a large corporation, government, or other bureaucratic organization in which policies, rules, and procedures are a way of life. The technocrat is comfortable in a management style which is structured by detailed policy guidelines. Technocrats prefer detailed policies, procedures, or instructions in codified policy manual form.

**Mother Goose.**   The mother goose manager tends to be protective and paternalistic toward his or her employees. Often, mother goose is the founder of a family-run firm or a long-term manager with many long-term loyal employees. Mother goose achieves results by providing little favors and often cannot say no to an employee. Sooner or later, mother goose recognizes the need for policy guidelines to limit favoritism or to control attendance or some other problem which has gotten out of hand. Detailed policy and procedure guidelines are often needed to control personnel problems and help mother goose say no to some employee requests.

**Committee Coordinator.**   The committee coordinator achieves results by consensus, negotiation, and coordinating of committees. The committee coordinator may come from a union environment in which most issues were subject to conferences with the union, or a highly employee-oriented organization which seeks maximum employee input on operational issues before making decisions. The committee coordinator is likely to prefer policy statements which set broad directions and procedural guidelines which can facilitate activities of participants in the committee process.

## Select Policy Manual Topics

Clients often ask, "What topics should we put in our policy manual?" My reply is simple: Select those topics that answer important questions raised by employees or issues of management concern such as controlling employee behavior on the job.

The selection of topics for your policy manual is part of the project organization process. How many policy issues should be defined? What policy topics should be covered? The answers to these questions set some limits for the policy manual project.

One reason many personnel policy manual projects fail to be implemented is that the policy writer tried to cover too many issues. When you have identified a manageable number of topics to be addressed, you can then focus your efforts to complete the task.

## Identify Critical Policy Issues

The critical policy issues are those about which questions occur frequently and for which there is an important need for management control. While critical policy issues may vary from organization to organization, there are some common, recurring issues. For example, employees often ask about

Pay day

Pay raises/promotions

Overtime pay

Vacation

Holidays

Sick pay

Eligibility for benefits

Leave of absence

Equal employment opportunity.

Supervisors or management often want to clarify policies on

Attendance

Punctuality

Performance

Discipline

Notice for vacation

Leave of absence controls

Specified misconduct issues

Pay administration

Terminations.

In some organizations a problem situation or government requirement prompts the need to define policies. Common policies needed to solve personnel problems or comply with government regulations include

Safety/accident reporting

Sexual harassment

Drug testing

Smoking

Grievance or complaint system

Hazard communication

Drug-free workplace

Affirmative action.

Part II of this book provides detailed information that will help you in selecting and defining relevant policy issues.

## How Many Topics Should My Manual Have?

The number of topics for your policy manual should be secondary to identifying critical policy issues. However, if every issue is critical, you need to set priorities or select immediate "hot" issues to address so you can keep the policy manual project at a manageable scale. Here are some guidelines:

| Company Size (Number of employees) | Policy Statement (Number of policies) | Policy and Procedure Guide (Number of policies) | Employee handbook (Number of topics) |
|---|---|---|---|
| 1–14 | 5–15 | 0–15 | 5–20 |
| 15–49 | 10–25 | 10–25 | 10–30 |
| 50–199 | 10–25 | 15–30 | 20–40 |
| 200–499 | 10–25 | 15–50 | 30–50 |
| 500+ | 15+ | 20–75 | 30–100 |

Explanatory Notes:

1. Many state and federal laws key coverage to the number of employees and may be a factor in the number of policies defined by your organization.

2. You may elect to do any or all of the policy formats.

3. Suggested number of policies is a guideline to aid you in developing your policy manual. Add or delete topics based on your organization's needs.

## Time Management Tips

One critical element in preparing your policy manual is committing the time necessary to complete the project. Your policy manual will not write itself. You need to set a reasonable deadline and then establish a schedule to meet your goal. Here are some time management tips to help you reach your goal:

- Break the project into phases or segments. Set interim deadlines for each phase or segment. For example: Complete 12 policies in three months; commit to doing one policy each week or four policies each month.

- Get organized. Do your necessary research first. Collect policy information and outline key points. It is easier to write when your thoughts and material are organized.

- Set aside a specific time period to do your writing. Get to work early, or stay late, so that you can write during quiet periods with no interruptions.

- Delegate certain tasks to others if you are working with a policy manual committee. Again, set deadlines to keep the policy project on schedule.

Table 3.2 shows a sample project timeline.

## Where to Find Policy Information

Personnel policy information may come in a variety of forms. In an organization without written policy information, personnel policies come from management decisions. As decisions are repeated, a personnel prac-

**Table 3.2.** Sample Timeline Chart

| Activity | Month: | 1 | 2 | 3 | 4 | 5 | 6 |
|---|---|---|---|---|---|---|---|
| Define objectives | | ——— | | | | | |
| Determine scope/topics | | | ——— | | | | |
| Research | | | ——— | | | | |
| Write | | | | ———————————— | | | |
| Edit/approval | | | | | ——— | | |
| Publish | | | | | | ——————— | |

tice or unwritten policy is born. Many new and smaller organizations operate on the basis of management decisions and past practice. Sooner or later, many of these practices find their way into some form of written document. Unwritten or informal personnel practices can serve as the foundation for your personnel policy manual.

The following are some sources for policy information in the organization.

**Policy Memos.**    Policy information is usually developed or defined to clarify an employee benefit or in response to some form of employee misconduct. Often, the manager will write a memo to supervisors or employees which is intended to define or clarify the issue in question. Over the years, these memos may accumulate as new policy memos are written or old memos are revised. These memos can serve as an important resource for policy information. However, you should verify whether the policy memo reflects current practice.

**Letters.**    Letters can be another source of policy information. A letter may be directed to an individual employee and may deal with a unique issue or personnel question as distinguished from a policy memo written to supervisors or employees. Examples include a job offer letter that also describes eligibility for benefits, or a letter of understanding describing reemployment conditions upon return from a leave of absence. When developing policy information from letters, determine whether the letter writer intended the letter to serve as a precedent for future policy and whether the letter reflects current practice.

**Bulletin Board.**    In many organizations, it is customary to post certain benefits or policy announcements on the company bulletin board. Holidays, vacation schedules, safety rules, disciplinary rules, and equal opportunity statements are common examples of policy information which may be posted on the bulletin board. Be sure to check this resource when researching policy information in your organization.

**Payroll Procedures.**   The payroll clerk is often a storehouse of information about company pay practices. This person typically does not create policy, but plays an instrumental role in carrying out pay practices based on instructions from managers. Payroll clerks sometimes will prepare written procedures for their own guidance in carrying out prior instructions. "Do we pay for jury service?" "Is Saturday work considered overtime, or does the employee have to work 40 hours first?" The payroll clerk deals with these issues each week. The payroll clerk or payroll records are a useful resource when researching policy information in your organization.

**Old Manuals or Handbooks.**   If your organization issued a policy manual or employee handbook in the past, this can be useful in identifying current policies. Any manual that is over five years old, however, should be scrutinized to verify current practices and to identify personnel practices which may be illegal under current labor laws.

**Union Agreements.**   A union agreement is, in a sense, a policy manual defining certain policies and benefits for union employees. If your firm is unionized, then the labor agreement is an important source of policy information. Many firms implement similar policies or benefits for non-union workers based on issues defined by the labor agreement for union workers. Another approach is to define policy guidelines covering management rights issues which are not defined in the labor agreement. For firms that are nonunion, but in a heavily unionized area or industry, it is wise to keep track of union-negotiated pay and benefits so that you can set pay, benefits, and policies at a competitive level.

**Current Practices.**   There are likely to be numerous current personnel practices in your organization which are based on past practice. Such practices are not written, but have customarily been observed over the years. For example, "We always take Friday after Thanksgiving as a holiday," or "The company has always shut down for a week between Christmas and New Year's." These practices can easily be defined as you prepare a policy manual. Interviews with key managers or long-term supervisors are a key source of information about current practices.

**External Source of Policy Information.**   There are various sources of policy information outside the company as well. Policy manuals from other firms and personnel practice or benefits surveys are two important sources. Further details on these issues are provided in Chap. 4.

## Form a Policy Committee

The use of employee committees to achieve operations improvement is a growing trend in the 1990s. Quality improvement teams, safety committees, or computer systems implementation task forces are common examples of an employee committee process. Likewise, some firms have formed a personnel policy committee to develop their personnel policy manual.

The purpose of a policy committee is to promote greater input and assistance from the various members of the organization. The committee process allows you to delegate research and writing tasks. As a result, your role becomes that of a project coordinator and editor. There are advantages and disadvantages to the committee process.

**Advantages of a Policy Committee.** The formation of a policy committee has a variety of advantages:

- Broad, cross-section input is attained when your policy committee consists of supervisors and/or employees from various sectors of the organization.

- Thorough treatment of policy issues is promoted through input of a policy committee. Important policies or issues are less likely to be omitted because of cross-section input in the development of policy information.

- Employee or supervisor interest and commitment to the policy manual is enhanced because these individuals played a role in its development.

- Greater employee and supervisor understanding of the complexity of policy issues is achieved, promoting more cooperation in working through policy interpretation difficulties.

- Shared research and writing activities reduce the demands on your time. In most organizations, the human resource specialist or administrative manager is responsible for preparing the manual in addition to keeping up with all other daily tasks.

**Disadvantages of a Policy Committee.** The formation of a policy committee also has some disadvantages:

- Committee indecision or inaction is a common complaint of people who have worked with committees. Because the committee process encourages participation of all members, the process also can lead to disagreements or indecision.

- The committee process is slow. Because it encourages various viewpoints, the committee process will take longer in reaching consensus or agreement on policy issues.

- There are too many meetings. Many managers complain that the amount of meetings leaves no time for their regular job.

- A policy committee may produce a wish list of desired policies or benefits. Committee members may use the policy committee as a form to push for a desired benefit.

■ An employee committee may be judged as an unfair labor practice by the National Labor Relations Board. See cautionary comments on page 93.

## Tips for Working with a Policy Committee

A policy committee can be an effective medium for developing your personnel policy manual. Here are some tips for working with a committee to achieve results.

**Develop an Agenda.**   One of the keys to leading a committee meeting is developing an agenda. Decide what topics will be discussed at the committee meeting. Avoid trying to cover too much at one meeting. Write up your agenda, and then stick with it as you lead the meeting.

**Define the Committee's Mission.**   To increase the effectiveness of your personnel policy committee, you need to define its mission. Define a specific purpose or objective for the group. Do you want your committee to define new benefits or develop guidelines to eliminate confusion about current benefits? Is your group a sounding board to test reaction to new policies, or will the group members be given specific research and writing assignments? Take care to define and communicate your committee's mission. Otherwise, your committee meeting is likely to turn into a grievance session with wish lists and complaints.

**Establish a Meeting Schedule.**   A policy committee most likely will meet a number of times over the course of the policy project. Establish a meeting schedule so that your group meets at a regular time (e.g., on alternate Wednesdays at 4:00 p.m.). A regular schedule allows participants to plan other activities around the schedule. You will have better attendance and fewer conflicts if you establish a regular schedule.

**Provide Advance Notice of Meetings.**   Advance notice of the policy committee meeting will improve attendance. Include your agenda so that participants can come to the meeting prepared to discuss the planned topics. These actions will significantly improve the effectiveness of your committee.

**Start and End on Time.**   Set a time limit for your meetings. One hour is a suggested length. Be sure to start on time and end on time. This will take some self-discipline, but committee members will appreciate that you stick with the established schedule. Starting promptly will help assure that you end on time. It also alerts committee members to arrive on time. Delaying the start of your meeting for tardy members is disconcerting to those who arrived on time. Be sure to end the meeting on schedule, because your participants have other commitments and responsibilities.

**Stay on Track.**   Committee meetings or group discussions can easily stray off the planned topic of discussion. As the meeting leader, be sure that the group focuses discussion on planned topics. Occasionally one or two committee members become concerned about a personal issue which is not relevant to the whole committee. To keep the meeting on track, tell these individuals that their topic can be covered individually after the group meeting is concluded.

**Demonstrate Leadership.**   Committees need a leader to set a direction and achieve results. The committee process promotes discussion and consensus. But a leader is needed to draw conclusions and identify the decisions reached. As a leader, after a reasonable period of discussion, assert control over the meeting, summarize conclusions, and move on to the next issue.

**Assign Responsibility.**   The purpose of a policy committee is to obtain assistance in researching and writing policy information. You need to be assertive in eliciting volunteers or assigning individuals to accomplish specified tasks. When assigning responsibility, define the task, provide any necessary instructions on work procedures, and set a deadline for the task.

**Record Results.**   It is important to keep a record of policy decisions, assignments, and results achieved in the policy committee meetings. Designate one individual as a recorder to keep track of the various issues covered in a committee meeting. Accurate notes will aid you in achieving results through the committee.

Tables 3.3 and 3.4 show sample forms. A policy worksheet can be used to collect and organize policy information. A policy committee worksheet can be used to delegate and monitor committee assignments.

## Select Personnel for Your Policy Committee

In my work as a consultant helping firms to prepare personnel policy manuals, I have developed policy materials that I have used with individuals and with groups of 10 or more. From an outside advisor's perspective, it is easier to define policy details by meeting with a single individual. In small to mid-size companies, this can be the president, owner, controller, human resource manager, or another individual who has a thorough knowledge of company policies and personnel practices.

In most organizations, however, a personnel policy committee needs a cross section of input from various sectors of the organization. Broad input

**Table 3.3.** Personnel Policy Committee Policy Worksheet

Policy/topic: _____

Applies to:       \_\_\_\_ Exempt       \_\_\_\_ Management      \_\_\_\_ Union

                  \_\_\_\_ Nonexempt    \_\_\_\_ Office           \_\_\_\_ Nonunion

                                   \_\_\_\_ Plant

                                   \_\_\_\_ Other _____

Eligibility: _____

_____

Policy summary: _____

_____

Procedures: _____

_____

_____

_____

_____

_____

_____

_____

_____

_____

Forms: _____

_____

is advisable so that the policy adequately recognizes the needs of the various sectors of the organization. The size and complexity of the organization will influence the makeup of your personnel policy committee.

Your personnel policy committee can be as small as three individuals, such as an office manager, plant or operations manager, and human resource or payroll administrator. A larger organization, on the other hand, would benefit from broader input from a committee consisting of 6 to 10 departmental managers. If the organization operates various branch facilities, then one or more branch managers should be on the policy committee.

Some organizations may elect to include office or operations employees in the policy committee. If you plan to involve employees, try to select individuals from various departments in the organization. A committee of half employees and half supervisors or managers can provide a balanced perspective on worker and management concerns. Table 3.5 shows suggested sizes of policy committees.

**Table 3.4.** Personnel Policy Committee Assignments Worksheet

| Topic/Activity | Assigned To | Date Due | Date Completed | Comment |
|---|---|---|---|---|
|  |  |  |  |  |
|  |  |  |  |  |
|  |  |  |  |  |
|  |  |  |  |  |
|  |  |  |  |  |
|  |  |  |  |  |
|  |  |  |  |  |
|  |  |  |  |  |
|  |  |  |  |  |
|  |  |  |  |  |
|  |  |  |  |  |
|  |  |  |  |  |
|  |  |  |  |  |
|  |  |  |  |  |
|  |  |  |  |  |
|  |  |  |  |  |
|  |  |  |  |  |
|  |  |  |  |  |

## A Word of Caution

Considerable care must be exercised when organizing a personnel policy committee with a membership of rank and file employees. Despite an employer's best intentions, the National Labor Relations Board (NLRB) determined that some employee committees constituted a labor organization.

The NLRB is the federal government agency that oversees union and management relations. The National Labor Relations Act, one of the laws enforced by the NLRB, defines certain prohibited unfair labor practices. Section 8(a)(2) of the law in part makes it an unfair labor practice for an employer "to dominate or interfere with the formulation or administration of any labor organization or contribute financial or other support;..."[1]

**Table 3.5.** Suggested Size of Policy Committee

| Organization size (number of employees) | Committee size |
|---|---|
| 1–15 | Committee of the whole |
| 16–50 | 3–5 |
| 51–500 | 5–12* |
| 500+ | 10–15* |

*Larger organizations may consider a two-tiered committee approach: (1) an employee group to offer ideas and suggestions, and (2) a management group to evaluate employee suggestions and define policy issues.

A leading court case on employee committees at Cabot Carbon Company was decided by the U.S. Supreme Court in 1959. In this case, an employee committee was established to handle employee grievances and discuss other issues such as seniority, job classifications, job bidding, overtime records, vacation, and sick leave. The Supreme Court concluded that the employee committee fit the definition of a labor organization because the committee existed at least in part for the purpose of dealing with the employer concerning grievances.[2]

Many subsequent cases before the NLRB have followed the Cabot Carbon holding. In some cases, employee committees were found to be a labor organization. Whether or not an employee committee may be unlawful depends on the facts of each case, employee committee activities, and methods used to select employees.

One example is the employee advisory committee established at Memphis Truck and Trailer, Inc. The employee committee met monthly with management and discussed retirement, parking, uniforms, tool storage, and other various issues. Finding that the committee represented the company's employees in discussions with management that involved employee benefits and working conditions, the NLRB concluded that the committee possessed all the elements of a labor organization.[3]

In other cases, however, the NLRB has determined that employee committees were not a labor organization within the meaning of the National Labor Relations Act. In a 1977 case, for example, General Foods Corp. divided its workforce into four teams which met periodically to discuss matters of concern. At these meetings, employees spoke on their own behalf. The NLRB affirmed the Administrative Law Judge's decision that the employee teams were not labor organizations. The facts showed that the teams did not act as agents for the employees. Further, the judge stated that any conclusion that the teams were a labor organization would mean

## CHECKLIST
## Issues to Consider When Forming a Personnel Policy Committee

The following precautions are provided to help you create an effective employee committee while avoiding an unfair labor practice charge:

1. If there is a union, involve union representatives in the committee early to avoid the appearance of bypassing the union.

2. Maintain a separation of union agreement issues and issues discussed by your committee.

3. Rotate members on and off the committee on a periodic basis to maximize participation.

4. Voluntary memberships are recommended. Management appointment of employees may also be considered. Avoid any form of election of committee members by other employees.

5. Make sure that employee participation in committee activities is as an individual and not as a representative or spokesperson for the work group.

6. Limit the committee to an informational or advisory role. Any committee recommendations are subject to approval or rejection at management's discretion.

7. Do not let the committee initiate any complaints or grievances.

8. Do not negotiate with the committee.

9. Avoid creating permanent committees. Rather, create an ad hoc committee to deal with a specific issue and disband the committee once the objective is accomplished.

that the employer could never hold a staff conference without creating a labor organization.[4]

In another case involving Scott & Fetzer Co., a federal court reversed an NLRB decision, holding that a company-established employee committee was not a labor organization under the Act. The court noted that employee membership on the committee rotated, that there was no continuous interaction between the company and the committee, and that meetings were informative in nature, and not a method for pursuing a course of dealings.[5]

As this book goes to press, a definition guideline on the legal status of employee committees has yet to be determined. A long awaited decision by the NLRB on the Electromation case failed to provide broad direction sought by observers of the labor-management scene. In this case, an Indiana employer formed employee action committees to resolve employee complaints. A union-organizing drive occurred, and the union filed an unfair labor practice charge alleging that the committees were company-dominated labor organizations. The NLRB agreed, finding the company in violation of the National Labor Relations Act. The case is being appealed to a federal appeals court. In the meantime, employers should exercise caution when forming employee committees.[6] A checklist of precautions appears on page 46.

## Summary

Your personnel policy project should now be planned, organized, and off to a running start. As you begin to define personnel policy and benefits issues, one question invariably arises: "What are other companies doing?"

This question has a twofold purpose. First, by finding out how other companies are handling a particular matter, you learn competitive practices. Second, you learn how other organizations have solved the personnel problems which you face in attempting to define personnel policies. For further guidance, read Chap. 4, "Competitive Practices: What Is Everybody Else Doing?"

## Notes

1. 29 U.S.C. S. 151.

2. *NLRB* v. *Cabot Carbon Co.*, 360 U.S. 203 (1959).

3. *Memphis Truck and Trailer, Inc.*, 284 NLRB 900 (1987).

4. *General Foods Corp.*, 231 NLRB 1232 (1977).

5. *NLRB* v. *Streamway Divl. of Scott & Fetzer Co.*, 691 F.2nd 288 (6th Cir. 1982).

6. 309 NLRB No. 163 (Dec. 16, 1992).

# 4

# Competitive Practices: What Is Everybody Else Doing?

**Read Chapter 4 for:**

The benefits of evaluating competitive practices

Various sources of personnel policy and benefits information

How to read and interpret personnel policy and benefits surveys

Organizations that provide surveys on personnel policies and benefits

Tips on how to develop and conduct your own personnel practices survey

## Why Consider Competitive Practices?

Most organizations in the free world operate in a market economy resulting in competition for goods, services, and a qualified labor force. This means that, in order to succeed, the organization must attract and retain capable workers who can produce goods or provide efficient services at a fair price. To the human resource specialist, these economic factors affect recruiting, staffing, compensating, and retaining employees. Normally, workers are recruited from the community surrounding the organization. Other employers in the area also are recruiting workers. What this all means, of course, is that employers must compete in the labor market for employees. Competitive personnel policies, practices, benefits, and pay are necessary to attract capable workers.

Job applicants seek employment, and your employees continue to work for a variety of reasons. Among these reasons are pay, benefits, work hours, job location, working conditions, and the work itself. If any one factor is less than satisfactory, the employee most likely will stay on the job. However, if the employee perceives that several of the aforementioned factors are inadequate, he or she is likely to be dissatisfied with the job. This dissatisfaction typically takes the form of excessive absences, marginal work quality, lower productivity, or a search for other employment.

The competitive market to hire qualified workers and the need to retain a motivated workforce are the primary reasons why it is important for an organization to maintain competitive personnel policies, pay levels, and benefits.

# Benefits of Competitive Personnel Policies

One of the more valuable tasks that a human resource specialist can do for his or her employer is to keep management informed of competitive personnel practices. By keeping abreast of competitive practices and trends, the organization achieves the following benefits:

**Maintain a Competitive Position.** The organization can better maintain a competitive position in the marketplace when its personnel policies and benefits are comparable to those provided by other firms. Personnel policies and benefits have a direct bottom-line impact. The cost of benefits—including insurances, vacations, holidays, etc.—represents approximately 30 percent of total compensation. Likewise, policies defining whether overtime pay is computed after eight hours daily or 40 hours weekly directly affect labor costs and profitability. Clearly, based on these examples, an organization needs to monitor industry or area trends in order to establish competitive personnel policies and benefits. Disregard for the competitive picture can seriously affect a firm's competitive position in the marketplace.

**Attract a Qualified Workforce.** Competitive personnel policies are an essential ingredient in recruiting and attracting qualified workers. Capable workers—with good qualifications—have a sense of self-worth in the job market and seek jobs with the better firms. It can be embarrassing to a hiring manager to be told by an applicant, "I'd like working for you, but frankly, your company is way behind the times in the policies and benefits that you've described to me." This comment in a job interview was representative of applicant replies to job offers extended by a growing high-tech firm. After failing to hire several badly needed engineers, company management retained a consultant to analyze competitive practices, develop a personnel policy manual, and assist in recruiting.

When you're recruiting job candidates, remember that they too are actively interviewing at other firms and comparing the jobs, evaluating benefits, and forming job preferences. One company involved in the distribution of industrial products experienced difficulty in finding qualified office workers. Their first choice of applicants, it seemed, often declined the job offer and accepted other employment. One step taken by management in response to this difficulty was to implement personnel policies and benefits which were equal to or better than many other area firms. As a result, job seekers were impressed with the firm's policy and benefits package, and company managers were better able to hire their "first choice" applicants.

**Retain Valued Employees.**   An organization with competitive personnel policies and benefits has eliminated a major cause of unwanted turnover. While an employee is not likely to change jobs solely to get an extra week of vacation, he or she is less likely to seek other work when the employer operates with competitive personnel policies.

One midwest manufacturing company, for example, had a major competitor in the same community. The competitor was larger, unionized, and paid higher wages. To prevent loss of employees to the competitor, the company adopted a positive employee relations philosophy, competitive personnel policies, and proactive communications. The firm effectively minimized unwanted turnover because employees felt they were treated fairly by supervisors.

**Control Personnel Costs.**   Controlling costs is important to every organization. By monitoring competitive personnel practices, company management can make considered decisions to control costs of company policies and benefits. For example, company managers may be considering a paid sick leave benefit. One manager suggests 10 days yearly, while another conservatively recommends five days a year. In their 100-employee company with an average salary of $25,000, the benefit cost estimate ranges from $48,000 for the five-day plan to $96,000 for the 10-day plan. Very clearly, a look at competitive personnel practices in the community will help these managers reach a decision which can benefit employees as well as the bottom line.

**Learn How Other Firms Handle Policies.**   Smaller family businesses and newly formed entrepreneurial firms often make up policy only after being confronted with an issue or a personnel problem. This approach sometimes results in uncertainty when management is unfamiliar with human resource matters. A look at competitive personnel practices can help management learn how other firms have handled a particular policy issue. For example, managers of a publishing company in a large city were uncertain about how to deal with the Martin Luther King birthday holiday. Minority employees were asking for time off, but the company had not observed this holiday in the past. Management checked a local personnel practices survey. The survey showed that, while many banks and government offices closed for Dr. King's birthday, only 12 percent of area firms participating in the survey were closed in observation of the holiday.

## Finding and Using Competitive Practice Information

There are a variety of information sources for competitive personnel practices. The real trick is recognizing the information when you see it. An executive recruiter once explained that he compared his recruiting assignments to the military intelligence work he performed while in the army. This work, he said, involves collecting bits and pieces of information from various sources and then putting these pieces together to get an overall picture. Likewise, information on competitive personnel practices is everywhere. The human resource specialist merely needs to recognize it, retain it, and then assemble it with other data to form some general conclusions.

This intelligence-gathering process is not without its pitfalls. One common problem is viewing an isolated fact and construing it to be a general truth. One or two bits of personnel policy information obtained from employees about former employers should not be viewed as representative of personnel practices in the area. Every human resource manager can relate a story about an employee complaining that pay or benefits are better at the company down the street. Except for those small communities with one or two major employers, we need to compare personnel practices to the broader business community or industry.

A second and related pitfall in the intelligence-gathering process is failing to recognize the significance of competitive practice data. Some of the isolated facts that we uncover should be discarded as irrelevant while other facts warrant serious consideration. Data from our competitors, other firms in our industry, prominent employers in the community, or from firms which represent the leading industry in the area will be of value. Likewise, data from unrelated sectors will not be as significant in its value.

A third pitfall is assimilating so much data that it becomes overwhelming. I have seen human resource specialists buy four, five, or six expensive surveys only to become confused with the abundance and apparent conflict of information.

If your firm has the staff capability and time to adequately assess available data, you can define your personnel policies competitively and confidently. However, having experienced the aforementioned difficulties, some firms have opted for professional assistance in obtaining and evaluating information on competitive personnel practices.

# Competitive Practice
# Information Sources

Information on competitive personnel practices is all around us. The most common and useful sources are discussed in this section.

**Personnel Practice and Benefits Surveys.** Personnel surveys are the leading source of information about competitive practices. Surveys identify what other firms are doing in the area of personnel policies, benefits, and pay. Surveys are conducted by the federal government, national trade associations, local employer associations, chambers of commerce, and consulting organizations. Costs may vary from $25 to $500 or more to purchase a survey. Some associations only distribute survey data to members, so it may be necessary to join the association to receive their survey.

Some policies and benefits surveys are national and cover practices at firms across the United States, while other surveys may focus on practices in a particular industry, region, or city. Carefully evaluate your needs before purchasing a survey. If your firm has facilities in various states, then a national survey would be appropriate. If your organization has only one location, check for a survey of practices in your immediate area.

A list of organizations that provide survey information appears on page 55.

**Business Periodicals.** Business magazines and trade publications often run feature articles or conduct readership surveys on personnel issues. Articles often deal with current trends or new requirements imposed by government regulations. Trade publications provide an editorial focus for an occupational specialty (e.g., *Personnel, Personnel Journal,* and *HR Magazine* address human resource issues) or for an industry (e.g., *Modern Machine Shop* and *American Machinist* address interests of machine shops). General business magazines address a broader range of issues of interest to management (e.g., *Industry Week, Inc. Magazine,* or *Nation's Business*).

Monitor the publications that are relevant to your industry and occupational specialty. Clip and save those articles or surveys that relate to competitive practices and personnel policy issues.

**Newspaper Articles.** Your local newspaper as well as national business news periodicals such as the *Wall Street Journal* occasionally run news stories which provide insights on trends and competitive personnel practices. Newspaper articles tend to cover current events, while the magazines tend to be more feature oriented. News stories may cover new trends, release of government regulations, or highlights of surveys released by the government or private organizations. Clip and save the articles. If appropriate, contact the organization in the news story for further information.

**Union Agreements.**   Information from union agreements can be beneficial even if your firm is nonunion. If your firm is in an area or industry that is highly unionized, it is wise to keep abreast of union settlements as well as policies or benefits covered in union agreements. Managers in unionized firms will sometimes share copies of a contract. Also, some local employer associations keep a library of union agreements submitted by member firms.

**Government Publications.**   The U.S. Department of Labor Bureau of Labor Statistics (BLS) is an agency whose full-time job is surveying, analyzing, and publishing statistics about labor, wages, benefits, union settlements, and related data. In addition to wage and benefits surveys, the BLS publishes a professional journal entitled *Monthly Labor Review*. This journal contains articles and statistics about personnel policies, benefits, and wages. Another BLS publication, *Compensation and Working Conditions,* reports on wage and benefit changes resulting from collective bargaining settlements and unilateral management decisions.

**Shared Policy Information.**   Some business owners, managers, or human resource specialists are willing to share personnel policy or benefits information. The practice of sharing policy or benefits information typically occurs when there is no danger of disclosure of proprietary information to a direct competitor. Information can be shared by exchange of employee handbooks or policy manuals.

There is one major pitfall with this practice. Do not copy the other firm's policy information verbatim! Two serious liabilities can occur. First, if you copy another firm's policy because it sounds good, but fail to follow that policy in a discharge situation, you have disregarded a published rule and could be on the losing end of a wrongful discharge lawsuit. Second, by copying another firm's policy manual you have violated copyright laws.

Another way of sharing policy information is through networking at local employer association meetings. You can get a sense of competitive practices by asking an individual or the group at large, "What is your policy on...?"

**Consulting Firms.**   Consulting firms that specialize in personnel policies, benefits, or compensation have competitive practice information on file. Some consulting firms conduct their own surveys of policies, benefits, or compensation and then publish survey results. If you do not have the time or expertise to sort through all the issues, it makes sense to engage a professional. Consultants can analyze your firm's practices, provide competitive comparisons, recommend solutions, and then develop the policies or benefits based on your firm's needs.

## Sources of Personnel Policy and Benefits Surveys

Personnel policy and benefits surveys and information are available through a variety of organizations. Costs will vary. This list is provided for information purposes only and does not represent any form of endorsement of a particular organization or survey.

*Business Publishers*

Commerce Clearing House
4025 W. Peterson Ave.
Chicago, IL 60646

Business & Legal Reports Inc.
39 Academy St.
Madison, CT 06443

The Bureau of National Affairs, Inc.
1231 25th St. N.W.
Washington, DC 20037

*United States Government*

Bureau of Labor Statistics—Regional Offices

Region I
1 Congress Street, 10th Fl.
Boston, MA 02114
617-565-2327

Region II
Room 808, 201 Varick St.
New York, NY 10014
212-337-2400

Region III
3535 Market St., Box 13309
Philadelphia, PA 19101
215-596-1154

Region IV
1371 Peachtree St. N.E.
Atlanta, GA 30367
404-347-4416

Region V
9th Fl., Federal Office Bldg.
230 S. Dearborn St.
Chicago, IL 60604
312-353-1880

Region VI
Federal Building
525 Griffin St., Rm. 221
Dallas, TX 75202
214-767-6970

Regions VII & VIII
911 Walnet St.
Kansas City, MO 64106
816-426-2481

Regions IX & X
71 Stevenson St., Box 193766
San Francisco, CA 94119
415-744-6600

*Trade Associations*

American Compensation Association
14040 Northsight Blvd.
Scottsdale, AZ 85260
602-951-9191

Human Resource Planning Society
41 E. 42nd St., Ste. 1500

Administrative Management Society
1101 14th St. N.W., Ste. 1100
Washington, DC 20005
202-371-8299

Merchants & Manufacturers
  Association*

*Members only

New York, NY 10017
212-490-6387

National Restaurant Association
1200 17th St. N.W.
Washington, DC 20036
202-331-5900

Bank Adm Institute
One North Franklin
Chicago, IL 60606
312-553-4600

National Air Transportation Association
4226 King St.
Alexandria, VA 22302
703-845-9000

National Association of Convenience
   Stores
1605 King St.
Alexandria, VA 22314
703-684-3600

National Retail Merchants Association*
100 W. 31st St.
New York, NY 10001
212-244-8780

International Business Forms Ind.
2111 Wilson Blvd., #350
Arlington, VA 22201
703-841-9191

Society of Plastics Industry
1275 K St. N.W., #400
Washington, DC 20005
202-371-5200

1150 S. Olive St., Box 15013
Los Angeles, CA 90005
       213-748-0421

Chamber of Commerce U.S.*
1615 H St. N.W.
Washington, DC 20062
202-659-6000

Employee Benefit Research Institute
2121 K St. N.W., #600
Washington, DC 20037
202-659-0670

American Bankers Association
1120 Connecticut Ave. N.W.
Washington, DC 20036
202-663-5000

Society of Human Resource
   Management
606 N. Washington St.
Alexandria, VA 22314
703-548-3440

Employment Management Association
4101 Lake Boone Trail, Ste. 201
Raleigh, NC 27607
919-787-6010

National Automatic Merchants
   Association*
20 N. Wacker Dr.
Chicago, IL 60606
312-346-0370

*Members only

## Reading and Understanding
## Benefits Surveys

Benefits and personnel practice surveys appear in a wide variety of formats. Some surveys come with detailed charts and statistical analysis. Others are simple, consisting of series of questions with a percentage tabulation of yes and no responses.

One difficulty in surveying policy and benefits practices is the wide range of variables that may be difficult to categorize. A survey may report, for example, that 66 percent of employers in a major city provide a paid sick leave plan. This information is helpful, but your next question is likely to be, "How many days of paid sick leave are allowed?" Then you will want to know if there is a length of service requirement. Some surveys will address these issues, while others will avoid a detailed breakout of data.

Here are some suggestions for reading and understanding survey data:

1. Surveys with larger numbers of participants are generally more representative pictures of competitive practices.

2. Read introductory information in the survey to understand its scope, number of firms, and industries represented. Make sure that the data is relevant to your organization.

3. Note the date of the survey and the base period in which the survey was conducted. Personnel policies and benefits surveys may be fairly representative for up to two or three years. After that period, there are sufficient changes and new developments that it is best to get a new, up-to-date survey.

4. Surveys generally report data in a percentage form. The fact that 477 firms conduct performance appraisals is not meaningful by itself. But when the data is identified as "87 percent of large firms provide a formal performance appraisal for managers," the data is relevant and useful.

5. Carefully read the headings, captions, and explanatory notes when working with charted data. Does the data reflect that 67 percent of employees receive a benefit or 67 percent of companies provide the benefit? Some surveys break out data to reflect a total of 100 percent. Other surveys report multiple responses to various questions so that totals will exceed 100 percent.

6. Avoid trying to correlate or compare data between two different surveys. While you may compare your firm's practices to each survey, you must recognize that different surveys seek different information from a different base of participants. Accordingly, there will be differences in survey findings.

### Samples of Survey Data

Three different samples of survey data are shown in Figs. 4.1, 4.2, and 4.3.

## Conducting a Policy and Benefits Survey

There may be occasions when current policy and benefits survey data is unavailable or inappropriate for your specific needs. One company, for example, was located in an industrial park near a large city. Company

| Employer, union, and number of workers covered | Current general wage increase and effective date | Related information |
|---|---|---|

## MANUFACTURING

### Food and kindred products

| | | |
|---|---|---|
| E.J. Brach & Son, Inc. Chicago, IL Teamsters—2,200 | 2.2 percent 7/14/91 | Deferred increase negotiated 11/90 (CWD, January 1991). |
| Iowa Beef Processors, Inc. Waterloo, IA Food and Commercial Workers —1,550 | 20 cents 7/22/91 | Deferred increase negotiated 10/90 (CWD, February 1991); see CWD, April 1991. |
| Wholesale bread and cake bakeries Los Angeles, CA Bakery, Confectionery and Tobacco Workers—1,400 | 45 cents 6/30/91 | Deferred increase negotiated 7/1/89 (CWD, August 1989); see CWD, July 1990. |

### Apparel and other textile products

| | | |
|---|---|---|
| Apparel Manufacturers Association; Affiliated Apparel Manufacturers; United Better Dress Association; and Rain Apparel Contractors Interstate Ladies' Garment Workers—20,000 | 4 percent 6/1/91 | A 3-year agreement negotiated 5/91 also provided: 4-percent hourly wage increases on 6/1/92 and 6/1/93; cost-of-living clause provides for 1/93 adjustments of 10 cents (2 percent outside of New York and New Jersey) if the rise in the CPI-W exceeds 8.5 percent during 5/91–11/92, 15 cents (or 3 percent) if it exceeds a full 9 percent, 20 cents (or 4 percent) for a full 9.5 percent, and 25 cents (or 4.5 percent) maximum increase if it rises 10 percent or more; 13.4 percent (was 12.9 percent) company payment to health and welfare fund, increasing to 13.9 percent on 6/1/92, and 14.4 percent on 6/1/93; 3.375 percent (was 2.375 percent) employer payment to Health Services Plan for prescription drugs; 6 months' unpaid leave established for serious illness in the family; and reimbursement established for difference between jury duty pay and daily earned pay (CWD, July 1988); see CWD, June 1990. |
| Association of Garment Contractors Boston, MA, area Ladies' Garment Workers—3,800 | 4 percent 6/1/91 | A 3-year agreement negotiated 6/91 also provided: wage increases of 4 percent on both on 6/1/92 and 6/1/93; cost-of-living clause provides for 1/93 adjustment of 2 percent if a rise in the CPI-W during 5/91–11/92 exceeds 8.5 percent, 3 percent if it exceeds 9 percent, 4 percent for a full 9.5 percent, and 4.5 percent maximum increase if it rises 10 percent or more; 13.5 percent (was 13 percent) company payment to health and welfare fund, increasing to 14 percent on 6/1/92, and 14.5 percent on 6/1/93; 3.375 percent (was 2.375 percent) employer payment to Health Services Plan for prescription drugs; 6 months' unpaid leave established for serious illness in the family; and reimbursement established for difference between jury duty pay and daily earned pay (CWD, July 1988); see CWD, June 1990. |
| Atlantic Apparel Contractors Association Northeastern and western PA Ladies' Garment Workers—18,000 | 4 percent 6/1/91 | A 3-year agreement negotiated 6/91 also provided: wage increases of 4 percent on both on 6/1/92 and 6/1/93; cost-of-living clause provides for 1/93 adjustment of 2 percent if a rise in the CPI-W during 5/91–11/92 exceeds 8.5 pecent, 3 percent if it exceeds a full 9 percent, 4 percent for a full 9.5 percent, and 4.5 percent maximum increase if it exceeds 10 percent or more; 13.5 percent (of payroll) company payment to health and welfare fund (was 13 percent), increasing to 14 percent on 6/1/92, and 14.5 percent on 6/1/93; 3.38 percent (was 2.38 percent) employer payment to Health Services Plan for prescription drugs; 6 months' unpaid leave established for serious illness in the family; and reimbursement established for difference between jury duty pay and daily earned pay (CWD, July 1988); see CWD, June 1990. |

**Figure 4.1.** Sample survey information: selected wage and benefit changes. (*From *Compensation and Working Conditions, U.S. Dept. of Labor, Bureau of Labor Statistics, July, 1991, p. 12.*)

| Employee benefit program | All employees[3] | Professional and administrative employees[3] | Technical and clerical employees[3] | Production and service employees[3] | Employee benefit program | All employees[3] | Professional and administrative employees[3] | Technical and clerical employees[3] | Production and service employees[3] |
|---|---|---|---|---|---|---|---|---|---|
| **Paid:** | | | | | **Dental care—Continued** | | | | |
| Holidays | 97 | 97 | 96 | 97 | Family coverage: | | | | |
| Vacations | 97 | 98 | 99 | 95 | Wholly employer financed | 25 | 23 | 21 | 28 |
| Personal leave | 22 | 28 | 30 | 14 | Partly employer financed | 42 | 46 | 46 | 37 |
| Lunch period | 10 | 4 | 4 | 16 | | | | | |
| Rest time | 71 | 57 | 69 | 80 | Life insurance | 94 | 95 | 94 | 93 |
| Funeral leave | 84 | 87 | 86 | 80 | Wholly employer financed | 82 | 82 | 81 | 83 |
| Jury duty leave | 90 | 95 | 92 | 87 | Partly employer financed | 12 | 13 | 14 | 11 |
| Military leave | 53 | 61 | 57 | 45 | | | | | |
| Sick leave | 68 | 93 | 87 | 44 | All retirement[4] | 81 | 85 | 81 | 80 |
| Maternity leave | 3 | 4 | 2 | 3 | | | | | |
| Paternity leave | 1 | 2 | 1 | 1 | Defined benefit pension | 63 | 64 | 63 | 63 |
| | | | | | Wholly employer financed | 60 | 61 | 61 | 60 |
| **Unpaid:** | | | | | Partly employer financed | 3 | 3 | 2 | 3 |
| Maternity leave | 37 | 39 | 37 | 35 | | | | | |
| Paternity leave | 18 | 20 | 17 | 17 | Defined contribution[5] | 48 | 59 | 52 | 40 |
| | | | | | Uses of funds: | | | | |
| Sickness and accident insurance | 43 | 29 | 29 | 58 | Retirement[6] | 36 | 43 | 39 | 31 |
| Wholly employer financed | 36 | 22 | 22 | 51 | Wholly employer financed[7] | 14 | 15 | 14 | 12 |
| Partly employer financed | 7 | 7 | 7 | 7 | Partly employer financed | 22 | 28 | 24 | 18 |
| | | | | | Capital accumulation[8] | 14 | 18 | 14 | 11 |
| Long-term disability insurance | 45 | 65 | 57 | 27 | Wholly employer financed[7] | 2 | 1 | 1 | 3 |
| Wholly employer financed | 35 | 50 | 43 | 23 | Partly employer financed | 12 | 17 | 13 | 8 |
| Partly employer financed | 9 | 15 | 14 | 4 | Types of plans: | | | | |
| | | | | | Savings and thrift | 30 | 41 | 35 | 21 |
| Medical care | 92 | 93 | 91 | 93 | Deferred profit sharing | 15 | 13 | 13 | 16 |
| Employee coverage: | | | | | Employee stock ownership | 3 | 4 | 3 | 3 |
| Wholly employer financed | 48 | 45 | 41 | 54 | Money purchase pension | 5 | 8 | 6 | 3 |
| Partly employer financed | 44 | 48 | 50 | 39 | Stock bonus | (*) | (*) | (*) | (*) |
| Family coverage: | | | | | | | | | |
| Wholly employer financed | 31 | 28 | 25 | 37 | Stock option | (*) | (*) | (*) | (*) |
| Partly employer financed | 60 | 64 | 66 | 54 | | | | | |
| | | | | | Stock purchase | 2 | 3 | 2 | 1 |
| Dental care | 66 | 69 | 66 | 65 | | | | | |
| Employee coverage: | | | | | Cash only profit-sharing | 1 | 1 | 1 | 1 |
| Wholly employer financed | 34 | 32 | 31 | 38 | | | | | |
| Partly employer financed | 32 | 37 | 36 | 27 | Flexible benefits plans | 9 | 14 | 15 | 3 |
| | | | | | Reimbursement accounts | 23 | 36 | 31 | 11 |

[1] Participants are workers covered by a paid time off, insurance, retirement, or capital accumulation plan. Workers eligible for paid or unpaid maternity and paternity leave are also covered. Employees subject to a minimum service requirement before they are eligible for benefit coverage are counted as participants even if they have not met the requirement at the time of the survey. If employees are required to pay part of the cost of a benefit, only those who elect the coverage and pay their share are counted as participants. Benefits for which the employee must pay the full premium are outside the scope of the survey. Only current employees are counted as participants; retirees are excluded.

[2] See appendix A for scope of study.

[3] See appendix A for definitions of the occupational groups.

[4] Includes defined benefit pension plans and defined contribution retirement plans. The total is less than the sum of the individual items because many employees participated in both types of plans.

[5] The total is less than the sum of the individual items because some employees participated in both retirement and capital accumulation plans, and in more than one type of plan.

[6] Plans were counted as retirement plans if employer contributions had to remain in the participant's account until retirement age, death, disability, separation from service, age 59 1/2, or hardship.

[7] Employees participating in two or more plans were counted as participants in wholly employer-financed plans only if all plans were noncontributory.

[8] Includes plans in which employer contributions may be withdrawn from participant's account prior to retirement age, death, disability, separation from service, age 59 1/2, or hardship.

[9] Less than 0.5 percent.

NOTE: Because of rounding, sums of individual items may not equal totals. Where applicable, dash indicates no employees in this category.

**Figure 4.2.** Sample survey information: percent of full-time employees. (*Employee Benefits in Medium and Large Firms, 1989, U.S. Dept. of Labor, Bureau of Labor Statistics, 1990 Bulletin 2363, p. 4.)

| Occupational Group/ Union Status | Percentage of Employees On: | |
|---|---|---|
| | Flexible Work Schedules | Part-Time Work Schedules |
| Managers | 17.7% (440) | 0.7% (420) |
| Union Professional and Technical Employees | 1.8 (47) | 2.7 (46) |
| Nonunion Professional and Technical Employees | 14.7 (421) | 2.5 (404) |
| Union Clerical Employees | 4.3 (72) | 2.4 (74) |
| Nonunion Clerical Employees | 10.8 (432) | 4.9 (449) |
| Union Manufacturing and Production Employees | 1.7 (145) | 1.5 (142) |
| Nonunion Manufacturing and Production Employees | 8.4 (300) | 4.7 (302) |

Sample size is in parentheses.

| | Percentage of "yes" responses to the job analysis question | | | | | |
|---|---|---|---|---|---|---|
| | Professional Employees | | Clerical Employees | | Manufacturing Employees | |
| Managers | Union | Nonunion | Union | Nonunion | Union | Nonunion |
| 58% (478) | 38% (52) | 60% (453) | 48% (85) | 61% (465) | 47% (160) | 55% (328) |

**Figure 4.3.** Sample survey information on work scedules and on management, union, or nonunion status of employees. (*From *Human Resource Policies and Practices in American Firms*, U.S. Dept. of Labor, Bureau of Labor—Management Relations and Cooperative Programs, BLMR 137, p. 50.)

management periodically checked the personnel practices survey published by an employer association in the city. However, as the number of firms in the industrial park grew, company managements wanted to keep abreast of personnel practices in the immediate area. In circumstances such as these, you may decide to conduct your own policy and benefits survey.

When you conduct your own survey, you can focus the survey toward the information, geographical area, or industry of concern. Conducting a survey, however, does take considerable time as you develop a questionnaire, collect information, and analyze data. Another area of concern is getting adequate survey participation. I recommend that you promise to provide survey results to cooperating firms in order to encourage their participation.

## Steps in Designing and Conducting a Survey

The following are recommended steps for designing and conducting a personnel policy and benefits survey.

**Define Your Objective.**    Identify and define the objective of your survey. This first step helps to focus your efforts and the survey to obtain the desired information. For example, the objectives of the XYZ Company personnel practices survey are

- To obtain information on employee benefits and policies provided by firms in the Central City industrial corridor
- To evaluate the competitiveness of current policies and benefits
- To identify which policies or benefits need improvement in order to be competitive with firms in the area

**Select Topics to Be Surveyed.**    Carefully evaluate which topics, policies, or benefits will be covered by your survey. Limit your survey to those issues of significance. This will help keep your survey to a manageable length. Also, it will avoid the appearance of a fishing expedition. Your survey objectives will help to focus your selection of survey topics.

Examples of survey topics may include

- Length of work week
- Length of lunch and break periods
- Number of paid sick days allowed
- Number or identification of paid holidays
- Vacation benefits eligibility
- What benefits are provided to part-time workers
- Number of days of paid funeral leave
- Frequency of performance or pay reviews

**Design a Structured Questionnaire.**    A structured questionnaire is needed in order to elicit responses that can be easily tabulated. This is done by structuring responses to survey questions into multiple choice answers or multiple choice categories. Also, some questions can be phrased to allow for a yes, no, or not applicable response.

When drafting survey questions, keep the statements short and simple. Cover only one issue or topic in each question. Use commonly understood terms. It may be helpful to attach a brief definition to terms used to insure a common understanding. Take care to avoid bias. Prepare questions in an objective manner. Several sample questions are as follows:

Does your firm provide paid funeral leave for full-time
employees?   ____Yes   ____No

How many days of paid funeral leave are allowed:
____0   ____1   ____2   ____3   ____4 or more

How many days of paid sick leave are allowed?
____0   ____1 to 4   ____5 to 9   ____10 or more

**Select Employers to Be Surveyed.**   The selection of employers to be included in your survey can significantly influence survey findings. Select employers to be surveyed based upon your survey objectives. Are you seeking data from firms in your immediate vicinity, your industry, or some other criteria? For best results, your survey should include a representative sample of organizations.

When more organizations participate in your survey, your data will better reflect prevailing practice. For example, if your firm is in an industrial park with 20 other firms, data from 10, 12, 15, or more would be preferable. If your organization is a bank in a medium-sized city with 12 other financial institutions in the area, you may wish to survey all 12 financial institutions. Or you may elect to survey other commercial or industrial establishments as well as the banks. If you elect to survey the broader employer community, take care to include a random cross-section sampling of firms so that your data is not biased by a particular industry with more generous (or stingy) policies or benefits.

**Determine the Survey Method.**   There are several alternatives for conducting the survey: face-to-face interview, telephone interview, or mail. Pros and cons of each are as follows:

| Survey method | Pro | Con |
|---|---|---|
| Face-to-face interview | Minimizes misunderstanding<br>Maximizes responses | Time consuming<br><br>Requires appointments |
| Telephone interview | Maximizes responses<br>Minimizes misunderstanding<br>Effective for short surveys | Time consuming<br>Hard to reach respondents<br>May require appointments |
| Mail | Minimal time commitment | Lower response rate<br>Requires telephone follow-up |

**Tabulate Data.**    After the survey responses have been collected, tabulate the data. Personnel policy and benefits data is typically presented in the form of averages (responding firms observe an average of 8.5 holidays) or percentages (70 percent of surveyed firms provide paid funeral leave to full-time employees). You will want to total the data and compare it to your firm's practices.

If you have promised survey results to participants, you will need to organize and display data in a way which identifies each question and the percentage of replies in each response. There are many database and filer software packages for personal computers that can be adapted to total and display survey data. Take care to avoid displaying data that is clearly identifiable to one firm.

## Summary

An understanding of competitive personnel practices is essential in properly defining a personnel policy manual. There are a wide variety of informative sources for competitive practice data. The most commonly used sources are personnel policy and benefits surveys. These surveys are available from the government, employer associations, and certain business publishers. In some instances, however, an organization may elect to conduct its own survey to identify competitive personnel practices.

In addition to competitive issues, the personnel policy writer needs to prepare policy information in a way which reflects applicable state and federal labor laws. This issue is covered next in Chap. 5, "Avoiding Legal Pitfalls."

# 5

# Avoiding Legal Pitfalls

**Read Chapter 5 for:**

Tips on using the law as a source of personnel policy information

Common state laws which affect employment policies

Handy sources of information on federal and state labor laws, regulations and court decisions

The variety of laws and regulations which affect personnel policies

Common-sense suggestions for a professional review of your policy manual

## The Need to Be Legal

Every personnel policy or human resource decision is subject to some type of employment or labor law. As a result, willful or even inadvertent disregard for employment laws or employee rights can create significant and costly liability for the organization. Too many organizations have learned about employment law the hard way—a government ruling against their firm because of personnel policies and practices which violated a state or federal law.

One of the responsibilities of the human resource specialist is to advise his or her employer on making employment decisions which are within the law. To meet this responsibility, you must keep abreast of a wide variety of laws, court decisions, and administrative regulations. The employment law arena is one of the more rapidly changing segments of the law. The job of the human resource specialist has become more complex because of these legal requirements. However, the human resource function has also risen substantially in the hierarchy of many organizations. This is because human resource specialists advise management on practical solutions to personnel problems while avoiding costly liabilities.

The objective of this chapter is to aid you in identifying and avoiding typical legal pitfalls occurring because of a poorly prepared manual. It is not likely that an organization will deliberately set out to prepare a personnel policy which violates the law. However, a personnel policy which is inconsistent with the law will be clear evidence of the organization's liability in a government hearing. Accordingly, some basic understanding of employment and labor laws is needed to prepare a personnel policy manual that works.

## If Your Policy Violates the Law

There are many problems that an organization can incur when it disregards any of the various employment and labor laws. Some common examples are as follows:

- An employee who quit his job received his final paycheck, but according to the employer's policy did not receive any pay for unused vacation. The employee filed a claim with the State Labor Department. The State Claims Examiner determined that the employer's policy was inconsistent with the law and that the employee was entitled to vacation pay at separation. The employer was ordered by the state to pay for earned vacation prorated through the date of separation.

- A medium-sized manufacturing firm created a policy which declared that plant employees were paid on an hourly basis and that office employees were salaried and therefore ineligible for overtime pay. Over a period of frequent overtime work, a secretary filed a complaint with the Wage-Hour Division of the U.S. Department of Labor about the lack of overtime pay. As a result of the employee's complaint, the government conducted an audit of the firm's pay and overtime practices. The firm was found in violation of the Fair Labor Standards Act for failing to properly classify office clerical workers as nonexempt and for failing to provide overtime pay as specified by the law. The back pay to employees cost the firm tens of thousands of dollars.

- A national communications company had defined a pregnancy leave policy requiring pregnant workers to leave their jobs during the sixth or seventh month of pregnancy. This widespread policy affected thousands of women and failed to provide the same benefits guaranteed to other workers on disability leave. The Equal Employment Opportunity Commission (EEOC) filed a class action suit which was eventually settled for $66 million, at that time the largest cash recovery in EEOC history.

- A manufacturing firm had defined a performance appraisal policy and required supervisors to conduct evaluations of employees each year. The policy was vague and did not provide detailed guidelines to supervisors. One employee who was fired as a result of poor ratings filed a discrimination suit. The employer's performance appraisal system was ruled unfair, because supervisors were allowed to choose performance variables and there were no guidelines to aid in obtaining objective appraisals.

As the foregoing examples show, poorly prepared personnel policies can be very costly. Further examples of the costs of disregard for labor laws are the following data:

- During the fiscal year 1991, the U.S. Department of Labor Wage-Hour Division conducted 60,685 compliance actions. As a result, more than $142.7 million in unpaid back wages was found due to over 382,000 workers.[1]

- In fiscal year 1991, the Occupational Safety and Health Administration conducted 82,484 state and 42,113 federal inspections. The dollar amount of proposed penalties by the state exceeded $32 million. Proposed federal penalties were in excess of $91 million.[2]

- For fiscal year 1992, the U.S. Equal Employment Opportunity Commission (EEOC) received 70,339 discrimination complaints against employers. The agency secured settlements from employers totalling $65.6 million during the year.[3]

In addition to these enforcement activities, many more employers were subject to compliance requirements of the various state government agencies.

## Finding Labor Law Information

One of the biggest challenges facing the human resource specialist is keeping informed about labor and employment law issues. Keeping informed is also a necessity in order to do your job properly. When you have access to information on employment law issues, you can improve your ability to define policy issues or resolve human resource matters in a way which is consistent with the law.

Here are some common sources of information about labor and employment laws.

**Government Agencies.** Government agencies that are responsible for enforcing the law are a good source of information and regulations about the law. Most government agencies provide literature, booklets, copies of the law, or information on administrative regulations which affect employers. Often this information is available at no charge (you pay for it when you pay your taxes) or is sold at a nominal cost.

The Wage-Hour Division of the U.S. Labor Department, for example, provides publications on minimum wage, overtime pay, and definitions to aid in determining whether a job is exempt or nonexempt. The Equal Employment Opportunity Commission offers publications on avoiding discrimination, dealing with sexual harassment, and developing affirmative action plans. The Occupational Safety and Health Administration offers a variety of booklets on safety guidelines and copies of its innumerable lists of safety regulations. Many State Labor Departments also provide literature or booklets on the state labor laws under their jurisdiction.

Generally the information is there for the asking. But you must make the effort to contact each agency for information on their respective laws or regulations. Further, you need to update your file periodically to keep abreast of changes or new laws.

Some managers are reluctant to contact the government to request information for fear that a government representative will show up at the firm's front door requesting an inspection. However, such fears are unfounded. I have worked in the public sector side (State Labor Department employee) and the private section side (Plant and Corporate Level Personnel Manager), and it has been my experience that government employees are eager to provide information and to respond to an employer's sincere effort to comply with the law.

**Federal Register.** The *Federal Register* is the U.S. government's official publisher of laws, regulations, and proposed regulations. This voluminous publication is issued daily, detailing the regulatory requirements of the many federal agencies. The *Federal Register* is available on a subscription basis. However, an annual subscription will provide a ton of information ranging from agriculture to zoology.

For the human resource specialist, the trick is to learn the dates that major laws or regulations appear in the *Federal Register*, and then request or purchase copies of the specific regulations from the Government Printing Office, government book store, or appropriate agency.

**Topical Law Reporters.** Various business and legal publishers offer subscription services which keep subscribers up to date on laws, regulations, and court decisions. These services generally focus on national laws, but some of the services also cover state labor law developments. A key benefit of these services is that you can subscribe to the specific topical law reporting services which relate to your area of interest. Also, these services provide a large binder of background information, interpretive comments, copies of regulations, periodic updates, and often a newsletter subscription. The costs of these services can run from $300 to $1000 yearly or more.

**Books.** There are a wide variety of books available on labor and employment laws for the human resource specialist. These are not law books for lawyers, but rather books on employment and labor laws written to help human resource specialists understand the many laws, regulations, and major court decisions that impact on human resource management. The labor law books for human resource specialists generally address national labor law issues, current trends, and general employment information such as developments in employment at will. The cost of these books can range from $10 for brief paperbacks to $100 or more for a hardbound text. If you are serious about a career in human resources, I recommend that you purchase one of these publications for your professional library.

**Magazines and Trade Journals.**   Professional magazines and trade journals generally keep up to date with current trends and issues affecting human resource management. A subscription to *Personnel Journal, HR Magazine,* or *Personnel,* for example, will provide the subscriber with monthly articles on a variety of human resource topics including significant labor law and personnel policy issues. The magazine articles are also a source of information about how other companies are dealing with employee concerns or responding to government regulations. The magazines often feature how-to or analysis articles written by fellow professionals or experts in the field.

**Newsletters.**   In the last 20 years, the publication of newsletters has grown into a full-fledged communications industry. The Human Resource field has its share of various newsletters. Some of these newsletters even focus on labor law issues affecting the human resource field. A subscription to a newsletter will provide periodic news and information about current events in human resources. If your newsletter editor is worth his or her salt, your subscription will keep you apprised of new laws, government regulations, and significant court decisions.

Newsletters, however, are intended to provide brief highlights only of newsworthy items. You will find it necessary to do further research on the details of the legal issues featured in the newsletter.

**Professional/Trade Associations.**   Many professional or trade associations and chambers of commerce are a source of information about employment and labor laws. Many firms join an employer association in order to gain an information source about human resources and employment law issues. Some associations have various subgroups which meet to discuss issues of importance such as sales, government relations, financial management, human resources, etc. By attending these meetings, you have an opportunity to hear speakers on current topics and network with people in other firms who share similar problems and concerns. Some associations also offer a variety of services such as research, library reference materials, referral to experts, newsletters, or publications on human resources employment or labor law issues.

**Seminars and Courses.**   Various organizations offer workshops and seminars on employment and labor law issues. A wide variety of programs are offered, providing one-, two-, or three-day programs. You can select from seminars on basic employment laws to advance presentations dealing with employment at will, or drug-free workplace implementation, or other specialized issues. Many seminar attenders receive literature or publications relating to the topics covered. Many colleges and universities offer business, human resources, or labor relations curriculums. These courses can provide a foundation to understanding the many labor law issues affecting human resources management.

**Libraries.**   Your local library may be a good source of information about employment and labor laws. Check the business section, reference section, or pamphlet file for books or publications on employment and labor laws. Also, ask the librarian if you cannot find the book or publication you need. Some libraries participate in cooperative lending programs with other libraries in the area, thus widening the array of reference materials that may be available to you.

## Understanding the Priority of Laws

In order to have an adequate grasp of the various labor laws that affect the employment process, it helps to have a basic understanding of the U.S. legal system. The legal system in the United States is based upon a hierarchy of laws. The U.S. Constitution is the foundation of the legal system. The Constitution defines the federal/state relationships and the separation of powers between the executive, judicial, and legislative branches of government. The Constitution and its amendments, referred to as the Bill of Rights, guarantees certain rights to individuals. Subordinate to the Constitution are the following forms of law:

**Federal Statutes.**   Statutes are the laws passed by Congress. The various federal laws affect all covered organizations based upon criteria defined in the law such as number of employees or volume of business affecting interstate commerce. Examples of federal laws include the Age Discrimination in Employment Act of 1967 or the Americans with Disabilities Act of 1990.

**State Statutes.**   Statutes passed by the various state legislatures affect covered organizations in the respective state. The state may define a number of employees or dollar volume of business as a criterion for coverage of the law. Depending upon coverage of the law, an organization may be subject to both federal and state laws. In the event of a conflict of laws, the federal law preempts or takes precedence over the state law. However, if a state law requires greater protection for the employee and it does not conflict with a federal law, the employer must also comply with the state law.[4]

**Local Laws.**   Various cities, counties, and other local governmental jurisdictions have passed laws which may affect the employment process. The local laws will cover organizations located within their jurisdiction. An example of a local law is the Human Rights Ordinance passed in 1989 by the city of Chicago. As a result of this law's passage, a Chicago employer is subject to the

Chicago Human Rights Ordinance, the Illinois Human Rights Law, Title VII of the Civil Rights Act of 1964, and other federal non-discrimination laws.

**Court Decisions.**    Court decisions serve to interpret the various laws. State circuit courts hear matters brought by state agencies or individuals seeking enforcement or interpretation of a state law. Likewise, federal government agencies or individuals can initiate suits in Federal District Court for enforcement or interpretation of a federal law. The decisions of the courts are generally precedent setting within their respective jurisdiction.

Within the federal and state court systems there is a hierarchy of courts, permitting cases to be appealed to a higher court. Cases appealed from a State Circuit Court or Federal District Court are heard by the State or Federal Appeals Court, respectively. From there, a case may go to the State or U.S. Supreme Court, respectively, for a final determination. A matter of constitutional significance may be appealed from a State Supreme Court to the U.S. Supreme Court. An example of a Supreme Court decision is *Meritor Savings Bank* v. *Vinson.* In this 1986 case, the court held that a claim of a sexually hostile environment was a form of sex discrimination which was protected under the Title VII employment discrimination statute.[5]

**Administrative Regulations.**    Many of the state and federal government agencies issue administrative regulations as a means to enforce the laws under their jurisdiction. On the federal side, these rules and regulations appear in the *Federal Register.* In the *Federal Register,* they are assigned locations in the Code of Federal Regulations. These regulations generally carry the force of law. An employer's disregard for the regulations can result in administrative hearings and penalties by the agency, which can be enforced by a suit in federal court if necessary. An example of an administrative regulation is the OSHA Hazard Communication Standard, which is listed as 29 CFR 1910.1200 in the Code of Federal Regulations.

**Private Labor Law.**    Private labor law takes the form of collective bargaining agreements and agreements to arbitrate which are negotiated between union and management in the collective bargaining process. These labor agreements are binding upon the parties. Further, any disputes or questions of interpretation may be resolved by the arbitration process or enforced by the federal court. Any labor agreement negotiated between an employer and a union is an example of private labor law.

## Preparing Policies Based on the Law

The best way to make sure that your firm's personnel policies are consistent with the law is to prepare your policies based on the law. To do this, you must first obtain information on laws or regulations that relate to the policy in question. Then, write your policy statement drawing from the language of the law or regulations. The net result of this approach is that the law becomes your policy; and, therefore, your policy is consistent with the law.

Unfortunately, most laws and administrative regulations are written in a stilted legalese style. The stilted language of the law is sometimes difficult to understand or simply not phrased appropriately for an easy-to-read personnel policy manual. You may need to make changes to the language, explain procedures, add details, or define responsibilities. However, when making such changes, take care not to change the meaning of the policy statement so that it is inconsistent with the law. A sample of a policy statement follows, and is then compared to the applicable labor law.

### Policy Statement–Jury Service
It is the policy of the company to grant time off from work without pay for jury service, as described by the procedures below:

1. Any employee who receives a jury summons is responsible for giving reasonable notice to the company by submitting a copy of the juror summons to management. Reasonable notice is one full work day or more prior notice.
2. The employee will receive time off from work without pay for jury service.
3. Night shift employees are not required to work during jury service. However, if a night shift employee requests to work and jury service does not conflict with work, the employee may be permitted to work.
4. The supervisor shall record the absence as jury service without pay on the employee's time record.

### Illinois State Law on Jury Duty
33.1 Jury duty—Notice to employer—Right to time off
10.1. Jury duty, notice to employer, right to time off. Any person who is not legally disqualified to serve on juries, has been duly summoned for jury duty for either petit or grand jury service, and notifies his employer of such jury service summons, shall be given time off from employment to serve upon the jury for which such employee is summoned, regardless of the employment shift such employee is assigned to at the time of service of such summons. An employer may not deny an employee time off for jury duty because such employee is then assigned to work a night shift of employment, that is, an employer cannot require a night shift worker to work while such employee is doing jury duty in the daytime.

No employer shall discharge an employee for taking time off for jury duty as provided in this Section, if such employee, prior to taking such time off, gives reasonable notice to his employer that he is required to serve.

However, no employer shall be obligated to compensate such employee for such time taken off for jury duty.[6]

## State Labor Law Checklist

Employment and labor laws vary from state to state. The significance of labor law variations from state to state is seen in the following example: I was advising an Illinois employer on various issues including preparation of an employee handbook. The handbook was written to reflect the Illinois Labor Law requirements for a minimum 20-minute lunch period for full-time employees. There was no mention of a break period. In a subsequent consulting assignment with this firm, I was called upon to advise the firm's Kentucky facility. In the preparation of personnel policies, my research revealed that Kentucky labor laws require the employer to grant a 10-minute rest break during each half of the workday, without specific time requirements for the lunch period. While these labor law differences may seem minor, the lunch and break periods allowed by law are of significant concern to employees at each location.

To assist the policy manual preparer in identifying relevant state laws that may affect a personnel policy manual, we have prepared a chart of 13 common labor law issues identifying whether an applicable state law exists on that issue. This checklist will be particularly useful for firms with facilities or branch locations in various states. Further research of the labor laws in your state will be necessary to define your policies in a manner that is consistent with state law.

## Should You Have a Lawyer
## Review Your Policy Manual?

For every manager who has sought legal review of his or her policy manual, there is likely to be an equal number who have said, "Let's not get the lawyers involved, they'll just complicate things."

A legal review of your policy manual does not guarantee that your firm will not get sued by a current, former, or prospective employee. And if sued, prior legal review does not guarantee that your firm will prevail in litigation. In fact, one law firm places a prominent disclaimer to this effect at the end of its legal review of the client's personnel policies. The Human Resources Manager of that company was nonplussed after spending over $2000 for legal advice.

Another firm prepared a policy manual and then sent the manuscript to the two law firms it kept on retainer. The company president received back two legal reports in which several recommendations were conflicting. This president then asked me to update his policy manual and reconcile the various recommendations he had received.

Stephenie Overman's article on "How to Work with Your Lawyer" in *HR Magazine* identifies a lawyer's perspective on advising human resource specialists. In the article, Boston attorney Susan L. Lennox is quoted as saying, "Don't wait until the deal is done. Call us before it is cast in concrete. An ounce of prevention is worth a pound of cure." According to Overman, "Lennox compares a lawyer's advice to a 'doctor's diagnosis. It's an educated guess.' "[7]

Without a doubt, there are many legal issues to consider in preparing a personnel policy manual. It is essential that your personnel policy manual be consistent with applicable employment laws. Here are some common-sense suggestions.

- Professional review of your personnel policy manual is recommended if you are unfamiliar with current labor law issues or lack in-house staff expertise.

- If your firm is a high-profile or large organization, you are a more likely target for litigation, and for this reason, professional review of your personnel policy manual is recommended.

- Select a qualified professional who is up to date on human resource policy issues as well as employment law. Your lawyer who serves as a corporation counsel or specializes in product liability may not be "up to speed" on employment issues. Human resource consultants or labor attorneys must stay abreast of the ever-changing labor law arena to do their job properly.

- Specify exactly what you want from a professional review. I know of more than one organization that received a detailed legal treatise explaining numerous applicable laws and court decisions when all the firm really wanted was a protective employment-at-will disclaimer.

## Summary

The writer of a personnel policy manual needs to be aware of the various laws and regulations which affect the employment process. Employment and labor law is defined in federal statutes, state laws, local ordinances, administrative regulations, and court decisions. The personnel policy writer can use the law as a source of information to define a policy.

Now you're ready to begin the heart of the job: writing your policy manual.

## Notes

1. U.S. Department of Labor Annual Report, Fiscal Year 1991, p. 76.
2. U.S. Department of Labor Annual Report, Fiscal Year 1991, p. 68.
3. *Chicago Tribune*, Dec. 12, 1992, p. 10.
4. *Labor Law Course*, 26th edition, Commerce Clearing House, Chicago, 1987, pp. 512–23.
5. *Meritor Savings Bank* v. *Vinson* (477 U.S. 57).
6. Illinois Revised Statutes, 33.1, Sec. 10.1.
7. S. Overman, "How to Work with Your Lawyer," *HR Magazine*, July, 1992, p. 43.

**CHECKLIST**
**Labor Law for 15 Common Personnel Policies**

This checklist for 15 common personnel policies is designed to identify significant labor laws which affect policy preparation. State law issues are identified as a category of laws. Use this chart as a guide to aid in complying with the various laws that affect personnel policies.

*Policy Issue and Major Labor Laws to Consider*

1. Recruiting/Staffing

| *Federal* | *State\** |
|---|---|
| Fair Labor Standard Act | Fair Employment Practices |
| Title VII, Civil Rights Act | |
| Pregnancy Discrimination | Employment of Minors |
| Equal Pay | Minimum Wage |
| Executive Order 11241 | Workplace Testing |
| Age Discrimination in Employment | Drug Testing |
| Rehabilitation Act | AIDS Testing |
| Americans with Disability Act | Arrest/Conviction Records |
| Veterans' Re-employment Rights | |
| Guidelines on Selection Procedures | Use of Consumer Credit Reports |
| Employee Polygraph Protection | Blacklisting—References |
| National Labor Relations Act | |
| Immigration Reform and Control Act | |

2. Setting/Administering Pay

| *Federal* | *State* |
|---|---|
| Fair Labor Standards Act | Fair Employment Practices |
| Title VII, Civil Rights Act | |
| Equal Pay Act | Minimum Wage |
| Age Discrimination | Recordkeeping Requirements |
| Rehabilitation Act | |
| Americans with Disabilities Act | Wage Payment Laws |
| Fair Credit Reporting Act | Use of Consumer Credit Reports |
| | Meal Periods and Rest Periods |
| | Wage Garnishment |

3. Working Hours/Lunches, Breaks

| *Federal* | *State* |
|---|---|
| Fair Labor Standards Act | Fair Employment Practices |
| Title VII, Civil Rights Act | |
| Pregnancy Discrimination | Employment of Minors |

\*Generic titles or examples of state laws are shown here. Specific laws vary from state to state.

Age Discrimination in
  Employment
Rehabilitation Act
Americans with Disabilities Act
National Labor Relations Act
Railway Labor Act
Jury System Improvement Act

Recordkeeping Requirements

Wage Payment Laws
Meal Periods and Rest Periods

Sunday Labor Laws
Time Off for Voting
Jury Service Laws

4. Overtime Work/Pay
*Federal*
Fair Labor Standards Act
National Labor Relations Act
Title VII, Civil Rights Act
Railway Labor Act

*State*
Fair Employment Practices

Employment of Minors
Minimum Wage
Recordkeeping Requirements
Wage Payment Laws
Meal Periods and Rest Periods
Sunday Labor Laws

5. Medical Leave/Maternity Leave
*Federal*
Title VII, Civil Rights Act
Pregnancy Discrimination Act
Family and Medical Leave Act
Age Discrimination in
  Employment
The Rehabilitation Act
Americans with Disabilities Act
Drugfree Workplace Act
National Labor Relations Act

*State*
Fair Employment Practices
Parental Leave Laws

Workers' Compensation Laws

Drug Testing
AIDS Testing

6. Time Records
*Federal*
Fair Labor Standards Act

*State*
Employment of Minors
Minimum Wage
Recordkeeping Requirements
Wage Payment Laws
Sunday Labor Laws

7. Military Leave
*Federal*
Fair Labor Standards Act
Vietnam Era Veterans
  Readjustment Assistance Act
Veterans' Re-employment
  Rights Law

*State*
Recordkeeping Requirements
Wage Payment Laws

8. Funeral Leave

| *Federal* | *State* |
|---|---|
| Fair Labor Standards Act | Fair Employment Practices |
| Title VII, Civil Rights Act | Recordkeeping Requirements |
| National Labor Relations Act | Wage Payment Laws |

9. Personal/Family Leave

| *Federal* | *State* |
|---|---|
| Fair Labor Standards Act | Fair Employment Practices |
| Title VII, Civil Rights Act | Recordkeeping Requirements |
| Pregnancy Discrimination Act | Wage Payment Laws |
| Age Discrimination in Employment | Parental Leave Laws |
| The Rehabilitation Act | Family and Medical Leave Laws |
| Americans with Disabilities Act | |
| National Labor Relations Act | |
| Family and Medical Leave Laws | |

10. Personnel Records

| *Federal* | *State* |
|---|---|
| Fair Labor Standards Act | Fair Employment Practices |
| Title VII, Civil Rights Act | Employment of Minors |
| Americans with Disabilities Act | Recordkeeping Requirements |
| Consolidated Omnibus Budget Reconciliation Act | Blacklisting—References |
| | Access to Personnel Records |
| National Labor Relations Act | Wage Garnishments |
| Immigration Reform and Control Act | |

11. Union Relations/Avoidance

| *Federal* | *State* |
|---|---|
| National Labor Relations Act | Wage Garnishments |
| Railway Labor Act | |

12. Disciplinary Procedures

| *Federal* | *State* |
|---|---|
| Fair Labor Standards Act | Fair Employment Practices |
| Title VII, Civil Rights Act | |
| Employee Polygraph Protection | |
| Drugfree Workplace Act | |
| National Labor Relations Act | |

13. Separation of Employment

| *Federal* | *State* |
|---|---|
| Employee Retirement Income Security Act | Fair Employment Practices |
| Title VII, Civil Rights Act | Wage Payment Laws |
| Pregnancy Discrimination Act | Unemployment Compensation |
| Age Discrimination in | Use of Consumer Credit Reports |

Employment
The Rehabilitation Act
Americans with Disabilities Act        Wage Garnishments
Vietnam Era Veterans                   Jury Service Laws
   Readjustment Assistance Act
Veterans Re-employment Rights
   Law
Jury System Improvement Act            Whistle Blower Laws
Consolidated Omnibus Budget
   Reconciliation Act
Employee Polygraph Protection
Drugfree Workplace Act
Fair Credit Reporting Act
National Labor Relations Act
Worker Adjustment and Retraining
   Notification Act

14. Jury Service
    *Federal*                          *State*
    Fair Labor Standards Act           Wage Payment Laws
    Jury System Improvement Act        Jury Service Laws
    National Labor Relations Act

15. Workplace Safety
    *Federal*                          *State*
    Occupational Safety Health Act     Workers' Compensation Laws
    Americans with Disabilities Act    State/Municipal Smoking Laws
    National Labor Relations Act       Safety Laws

## CHECKLIST
### State and Federal Labor Laws Affecting Personnel Policies

| Federal Laws | State Laws* |
|---|---|
| Fair Labor Standards Act | Fair Employment Practices |
| Employee Retirement Income Security Act | Employment of Minors |
| Occupational Safety Health Act | Recordkeeping Requirements |
| Title VII, Civil Rights Act | Wage Payment Laws |
| Pregnancy Discrimination Act | Parental Leave Laws |
| Equal Pay Act | Workers' Compensation Laws |
| Executive Order 11246 | Unemployment Compensation |
| Civil Rights Act 1866 | Workplace Testing |
| Age Discrimination in Employment | Drug Testing |
| The Rehabilitation Act | AIDS Testing |
| Americans with Disabilities Act | Arrest/Conviction Records |
| Vietnam Era Veterans Readjustment Assistance Act | Use of Consumer Credit Reports |
| The Veterans' Re-employment Rights Law | Blacklisting—References |
| | Access to Personnel Records |
| Uniform Guidelines on Employee Selection Procedures | State/Municipal Smoking Laws |
| | Meal Periods and Rest Periods |
| Jury System Improvement Act | Wage Garnishment |
| Consumer Credit Protection Act | Sunday Labor Law |
| Consolidated Omnibus Budget Reconciliation Act | Time for Voting |
| | Jury Service Laws |
| Employee Polygraph Protection Act | Safety Laws |
| Drugfree Workplace Act | |
| Fair Credit Reporting Act | |
| National Labor Relations Act | |
| Railway Labor Act | |
| Immigration Reform and Control Act | |
| Worker Adjustment and Retraining Notification Act | |
| Whistleblower Laws | |
| Civil Rights Act of 1991 | |

*Generic titles or examples of state laws are shown here. Specific laws vary from state to state.

**CHECKLIST**
**State Labor Law: 13 Common Labor Laws Affecting Personnel Policies**

| State | 1<br>Wage<br>payment | 2<br>Vacation<br>pay due<br>at term-<br>ination | 3<br>Fair<br>employ-<br>ment prac-<br>tice laws<br>discrimination | 4<br>Workplace<br>smoking<br>limits | 5<br>Whistle-<br>blower<br>protection<br>law | 6<br>Child<br>labor<br>limits<br>under<br>16 years |
|-------|---------|---------|---------|---------|---------|---------|
| AL | NO | NO | NO | NO | NO | YES |
| AK | YES | NO | YES | YES | YES | YES |
| AZ | YES | YES | YES | YES | YES | YES |
| AR | YES | NO | NO | YES | NO | YES |
| CA | YES | YES | YES | YES | YES | YES |
| CO | YES | YES** | YES | NO | YES | YES |
| CT | YES | YES** | YES | YES | YES | YES |
| DE | YES | YES | YES | NO | YES | YES |
| DC | YES | YES** | YES | YES | NO | YES |
| FL | NO | NO | YES | YES | YES | YES |
| GA | YES | NO | YES* | NO | NO | YES |
| HI | YES | NO | YES | YES | YES | YES |
| ID | YES | NO | YES | NO | NO | YES |
| IL | YES | NO | YES | YES | YES | YES |
| IN | YES | YES** | YES | YES | YES | YES |
| IA | YES | YES | YES | YES | YES | YES |
| KS | YES | YES** | YES | YES | YES | YES |
| KY | YES | YES | YES | NO | YES | YES |
| LA | YES | YES** | YES | NO | YES | YES |
| ME | YES | YES | YES | YES | YES | YES |
| MD | YES | YES | YES | NO | NO | YES |
| MA | YES | YES | YES | NO | NO | YES |
| MI | YES | YES | YES | NO | YES | YES |
| MN | YES | YES | YES | YES | YES | YES |
| MS | YES | NO | YES* | NO | NO | YES |
| MO | YES | YES** | YES | NO | YES | YES |
| MT | YES | NO | YES | YES | YES | YES |
| NE | YES | YES** | YES | YES | YES | YES |
| NV | YES | NO | YES | YES | NO | YES |
| NH | YES | YES | YES | YES | YES | YES |
| NJ | YES | NO | YES | YES | YES | YES |

| 7 | 8 | 9 | 10 | 11 | 12 | 13 |
|---|---|---|---|---|---|---|
| Off-duty smokers rights protected | Jury service | Employee access to personnel records | Drug tests limits/ require-ments | Overtime pay required | Parental/ family leave | Accident reporting |
| NO | YES | NO | NO | NO | YES | YES |
| NO | YES | NO | NO | YES | NO | YES |
| YES | YES | NO | YES | NO | NO | YES |
| NO | YES | YES* | NO | YES | NO | YES |
| NO | YES | YES | NO | YES | NO | YES |
| NO | YES | NO | NO | YES | YES | YES |
| YES | YES | YES | YES | YES | YES | YES |
| NO | YES | YES | NO | NO | NO | YES |
| NO | NO | YES* | NO | YES | YES | YES |
| NO | YES | YES* | YES | NO | NO | YES |
| NO | YES | NO | NO | NO | NO | YES |
| NO | YES | NO | YES | YES | NO | YES |
| NO | YES | YES* | NO | YES | NO | YES |
| YES | YES | YES | NO | YES | NO | YES |
| YES | YES | NO | NO | NO | NO | YES |
| NO | YES | NO | YES | NO | NO | YES |
| NO | NO | NO | NO | YES | YES | YES |
| YES | YES | NO | NO | YES | YES | YES |
| YES | YES | YES* | YES | NO | YES | YES |
| YES | YES | YES | YES | YES | YES | YES |
| NO | NO | NO | YES | YES | NO | YES |
| NO | YES | YES | NO | YES | YES | YES |
| NO | YES | YES | NO | YES | NO | YES |
| NO | YES | YES | YES | YES | YES | YES |
| YES | YES | NO | NO | NO | NO | YES |
| NO | NO | NO | NO | YES | NO | YES |
| NO | NO | NO | YES | YES | YES | YES |
| NO | YES | NO | YES | NO | NO | YES |
| NO | YES | YES | NO | YES | NO | YES |
| YES | YES | YES | NO | YES | NO | YES |
| NO | YES | NO | NO | YES | YES | YES |

## CHECKLIST
### State Labor Law: 13 Common Labor Laws Affecting Personnel Policies

| State | 1<br><br>Wage<br>payment | 2<br>Vacation<br>pay due<br>at term-<br>ination | 3<br>Fair<br>employ-<br>ment prac-<br>tice laws<br>discrimination | 4<br><br>Workplace<br>smoking<br>limits | 5<br>Whistle-<br>blower<br>protection<br>law | 6<br>Child<br>labor<br>limits<br>under<br>16 years |
|-------|------|------|------|------|------|------|
| NM | YES | NO | YES | YES | NO | YES |
| NY | YES | YES | YES | YES | YES | YES |
| NC | YES | YES | YES | NO | NO | YES |
| ND | YES | YES** | YES | NO | NO | YES |
| OH | YES | YES | YES | NO | YES | YES |
| OK | YES | YES | YES | NO | NO | YES |
| OR | YES | YES** | YES | NO | YES | YES |
| PA | YES | YES | YES | YES | YES | YES |
| RI | YES | YES | YES | YES | YES | YES |
| SC | YES | YES | YES | NO | YES | NO |
| SD | YES | NO | YES | NO | NO | YES |
| TN | YES | YES** | YES | NO | YES | YES |
| TX | YES | YES | YES | NO | NO | YES |
| UT | YES | NO | YES | YES | YES | YES |
| VT | YES | YES | YES | YES | YES | YES |
| VA | YES | NO | YES | YES | YES | YES |
| WA | YES | NO | YES | YES | YES | YES |
| WV | YES | YES | YES | NO | YES | YES |
| WI | YES | YES | YES | YES | NO | YES |
| WY | YES | NO | YES | NO | YES | YES |

*Applies to public or educational employment only.
**Case law appears to define this issue.
*Key*: YES = A state law or regulation deals with this issue.
NO = There is not statute or regulation on this issue.
*Caution to the reader*: The state-by-state labor law checklist is intended as a general informational guide to acquaint the reader with the various state laws that affect the 13 policy issues shown in the chart. The information summarized here is believed to be current at the time the data was assembled for publication. New laws are passed by state legislatures, and state laws change from time to time through amendments or interpretations of the courts. The reader is urged to check local labor laws and/or professional counsel to define policy information that complies with the law.

| 7 | 8 | 9 | 10 | 11 | 12 | 13 |
|---|---|---|---|---|---|---|
| Off-duty smokers rights protected | Jury service | Employee access to personnel records | Drug tests limits/ require- ments | Overtime pay required | Parental/ family leave | Accident reporting |
| YES | YES | NO | NO | YES | NO | YES |
| NO | YES | YES*, ** | NO | NO | YES | YES |
| NO | YES | YES* | NO | YES | NO | YES |
| NO | YES | NO | NO | YES | NO | NO |
| NO | YES | NO | NO | YES | NO | YES |
| YES | YES | NO | NO | NO | NO | YES |
| YES | YES | YES | NO | YES | YES | YES |
| NO | YES | YES | NO | YES | NO | YES |
| YES | YES | YES | YES | YES | YES | YES |
| YES | YES | NO | NO | NO | NO | YES |
| YES | YES | YES* | NO | NO | NO | YES |
| YES | YES | YES* | NO | NO | YES | YES |
| NO | YES | NO | NO | NO | NO | YES |
| NO | YES | YES* | YES | NO | NO | YES |
| NO | YES | YES* | YES | YES | YES | YES |
| YES | YES | NO | NO | NO | NO | YES |
| NO | YES | YES | NO | YES | YES | YES |
| YES | YES | NO | NO | YES | NO | YES |
| NO | YES | YES | NO | YES | YES | YES |
| YES | YES | NO | NO | NO | NO | YES |

SOURCES: Personnel Practices/Communications Volume of *Human Resources Management Reporter*, para. 1589, 1598, 3250. Copyright 1992. Reproduced with permission of Commerce Clearing House, Inc., 4025 W. Peterson Ave., Chicago, IL 60646.

Ronald M. Green, William A. Carmell, and Peter S. Gray, 1992 *State-by-State Guide to Human Resources Law*. Excerpts from tables 1.1-2, 2.3-1, 2.5-1, 7.2-2, 4.5-1, 7.2-3, 7.5-2. Reproduced with permission. Copyright 1992. Panel Publishers, Inc., 36 W. 44th St., New York, NY 10036.

# 6

# Writing Your Policy Manual

**Read Chapter 6 for:**

Tips on defining an appropriate writing style

Basic grammar tips

Selecting a policy format

Organizing policy information in your manual

Twelve tips for better readability

Seven sample policy formats

Four employee handbook writing styles.

## The Art and Skill of Writing

Written communication comes easy for some people. However, for many individuals, written communication requires major effort. Many find that writing a letter to a friend or relative is an awkward process. These are the people who struggled through the required book reports in high school literature class, or "pulled an all-nighter" in college, agonizing over each word in a term paper that was due the next day.

Now, in an administrative, human resource, or other management role, your daily job tasks probably encompass various meetings, telephone calls, one-on-one interviews, various computations, some computer terminal operation, and writing an occasional letter or policy memo. Even in an employment setting, the writing skills of many individuals are often underdeveloped. For this reason, the task of writing a detailed personnel policy manual may seem like a formidable challenge.

Effective writing is both an art and a skill. There is an element of artistic creativity in the preparation of a letter, memo, or policy statement. More importantly, writing is a communication skill which, like other skills, can be learned. The objective of this chapter is to share some useful writing tips to help you prepare a personnel policy manual that works.

## Define the Purpose of Your Policy Manual

An important first step in writing your policy manual is to define its purpose. Is your policy manual intended to provide policy information for employees or procedures and guidelines for supervisors? The answer to this question will clarify a variety of issues as you prepare your policy manual.

As described in Chap. 3, there are three types of policy manuals: (1) a policy manual, (2) a personnel policy and procedure guide, and (3) an employee handbook for distribution to the workforce. Here are some guidelines to aid in defining the purpose of your policy manual:

| If your manual's purpose is: | And your intended audience is: | Then your manual selection should be: |
| --- | --- | --- |
| A broad definition of personnel policies | Employees and/or management | The personnel policy manual |
| A specific definition of policies, procedures, and forms | Supervisors and management | Personnel policy and procedure guide |
| A broad or specific definition of policies and benefits | Employees | The employee handbook |

Once you have made your decision regarding purpose, intended audience, and type of manual, it is then easier to write an employee handbook without supervisor's procedures creeping into your manuscript.

## Contrasting Writing Styles

Writing styles for a policy manual typically differ from the writing style for an employee handbook. The following guidelines are offered to assist you in contrasting these writing styles.

| Personnel policy manual | Personnel policy and procedure guide | Employee handbook |
|---|---|---|
| *Policy length*:<br>1 page | 1–5 pages | 1–2 paragraphs or 1/2 page |
| *Writing style*:<br>impersonal, semiformal, or formal | impersonal, semiformal | friendly, personalized, or informal |
| *Written voice*:<br>2nd person (you) or 3rd person (employee) | 3rd person (employee) | 1st person (we), 2nd person (you), or 3rd person (employee) |
| *Procedural details*:<br>minimal | extensive | minimal to moderately extensive |
| *Use of forms*:<br>may be attached to policy | forms with instructions included with procedures | selected forms may be displayed in handbook |
| *Use of illustrations*:<br>none used | none used | optional—may be used |

## Getting Yourself Organized for Writing

The task of writing is much easier when the writer is organized. In the preparation of a personnel policy manual, this includes defining policy issues, evaluating competitive issues, and completing any relevant research on policy issues or applicable labor and employment laws.

One suggestion is to develop a file on each policy topic. Your file may include an old policy memo, notes on current practices, a sample policy from this book or a sample policy from another firm, a copy of the personnel practice survey on the subject, and a copy of any applicable labor law. Now you have all the information needed to write your policy.

Next, develop an outline. The first outline can identify each policy topic to be covered in your manual. This outline, in a sense, may become the table of contents for your policy manual. Then, for each policy issue, prepare a brief outline. This outline identifies essential elements of the policy such as who is covered, when the policy applies, what decisions are made by supervisors or management, and what forms are used to document the personnel action or decision. Of course, draw from the reference materials in your policy file as you draft the outline.

**Sample Outline for a Policy**

I.   Summary
     A. Company recognizes civic responsibility of jury service.
     B. Employee is permitted time off.
II.  Employees Covered by Policy
     A. Full-time employees
     B. Part-time employees
     C. Temporary employees
     D. Night shift employees
III. Notification
     A. Employee responsibility
     B. Timing
     C. Copy of summons
IV.  Supervisor Authorization
V.   Pay
     A. Differential between jury and regular pay
     B. Based on 40 hours
     C. Turn in jury pay warrant
     D. Pay for part-time employees
VI.  Benefits Continuation
     A. Holidays
     B. Vacation accrual
     C. Insurances or premiums
VII. Time Records

## Writing the Employee Handbook

The policy manual writer must exercise special care when preparing an employee handbook. Clear writing is essential for employee understanding. In addition, the handbook's written message must be consistent with applicable labor laws and protect employment-at-will prerogatives. Guidelines on the legal issues were covered in Chap. 2, "The Contract Controversy," and Chap. 5, "Avoiding Legal Pitfalls."

The employee handbook is designed to inform employees about company policies and benefits. The handbook must be written at a level that is understandable for the reading audience. To do this, write for the lowest common denominator. For example, if your organization consists of a mixture of professionals, technicians, clericals, and semi-skilled production workers, then your handbook should be written so that the clericals and production workers can easily understand policy information.

## Employee Handbook Writing Styles

Generally, the employee handbook reflects the management style of the organization. The handbook tends to be written in a personalized style which conveys a sense of the corporate culture. Personnel policy manuals or personnel policy and procedure guides, on the other hand, tend to be written in a more impersonal style.

Four different employee handbook writing styles are discussed.

**Friendly.**   A friendly writing style is characterized by use of the first person plural "we" referring to the company and "you" the employee. It tends to be a more personalized message which reflects the corporate attitudes and culture. Policy issues are typically stated in a more positive manner, often with explanation as to why a policy is necessary. Topic headlines may be more informal, such as "Working Together" for the handbook sections dealing with employment policies. A sample of the friendly writing style follows.

> At XYZ Company, our Employee Relations Department protects the confidentiality of personnel records. These records help us to keep track of your insurances, retirement plan, pay raises, and related records. If you ever have a question about information in your personnel file, you are encouraged to speak with your team leader. Also, don't forget to keep us informed if there are changes in your personal life which might affect your personnel file. Let us know if you move, get married (or divorced), add dependents, or want to change tax exemptions. Please help us keep your records up to date.

**Firm.**   A firm writing style is likely to be a more formal, no-nonsense approach to defining policy issues. Policy information in a firm writing style is typically in the third person voice. With this style, it is customary to identify the employer as the "company," "bank," or "hospital," etc. The term *employees* is usually used when referring to the organization's workforce. Negative issues such as disciplinary procedures, rules, or grounds for discharge are likely to be defined in greater detail. Topic headlines will be practical and to the point, such as "Employment Policies" or "Attendance Policies." A sample of the firm writing style follows.

> XYZ Company maintains certain records in order to administer employee benefits, insurances, payroll, and other employment policies. Each employee is required to inform the company of any change in status affecting personnel records. Be sure to report change of name, address, telephone, marital status, dependents, tax exemptions, or beneficiary for insurance. All personnel records are confidential. An employee must submit a signed statement to authorize release of credit or employment reference information. Speak to the Human Resource Administrator if there are questions about personnel records.

**Brief.**   The management of many smaller organizations prefers a brief writing style. The brief style highlights only basic policy information. Often, many details of policy issues are subject to management discretion. The brief policy writing approach works best for smaller organizations where policy issues are not as complex or where management prefers greater flexibility in handling personnel matters. Brief writing is characterized by concise policy statements, written in the second person (you) or third person (employee, company) voice. The policy statement is summarized in two or three sentences omitting many discretionary details. A sample of the brief writing style follows.

> In order to keep company personnel records current, please notify the Office Manager if there is a change of address, telephone number, name, tax exemption, or insurance beneficiary. Please cooperate with this request in order to keep payroll and benefits information up to date.

**Detailed.**  In some organizations, management prefers detailed policy information in the employee handbook. A detailed writing style is likely to be written in the second person (you) or the third person (employee, company) voice. The first person plural voice ("we" referring to the company, or the friendly writing style) may be used to soften the message. The detailed employee handbook typically includes a statement with explanation about every policy or benefit and other administrative issues. The detailed employee handbook is likely to include certain procedures for employees, such as step-by-step instructions on filing an insurance claim, getting authorization to work overtime, or applying for tuition aid. A sample of a detailed writing style follows.

> XYZ Company maintains personnel records to comply with employment laws and to administer payroll and benefits for employees. The master personnel file for each employee is kept in the Human Resource Department.
>
> In order to protect individual privacy and the confidentiality of personnel records, XYZ Company has defined the following policy guidelines:
>
> 1. Access to an individual's personnel file is strictly limited by the Personnel Records Clerk. Only management or Human Resource Department representatives with an official "need to know" may view an employee's personnel file.
>
> 2. An employee may view his or her personnel file during nonworking time. To view information in your file, contact the Personnel Records Clerk at extension 1234. You will be permitted to view information under the supervision of the Personnel Records Clerk. No information or records may be removed from your file. An employee may photocopy information from his or her file, at a cost of $.10 per copy.
>
> 3. If you feel that there is an error in your personnel records, you are encouraged to discuss the matter with your supervisor or the Human Resource Manager. We will do our best to correct any errors.
>
> 4. It is your responsibility to keep the company informed of changes in status which affect your employment, pay, or benefits at XYZ. Be sure to notify your supervisor in the event of change of any of the following:
> Name
> Address
> Telephone number

Marital status
Dependents
Beneficiary
Tax exemptions
Emergency notification
Educational achievements

5. In the event you have applied for a loan or mortgage, you must provide a written release to the company authorizing release of employment information to your creditors. For further details speak with your supervisor.

## Twelve Tips for Better Readability

Careful writing of your personnel policy manual is essential to ensure that it can be easily read, interpreted, and understood. Poor grammar or awkward writing will only confuse the reader and contribute to misunderstandings. Here are 12 writing tips that will help achieve better readability:

1. Use a straightforward writing style. The purpose of a policy manual is to clearly define a policy, benefit, or procedural issue. This is not the time for cutesy writing, slang, editorial license, or exaggeration that is often associated with advertising copy.

2. Keep the message clear and concise. Avoid long or complex descriptions or definitions. Try to break a complex issue down into a clear sequence of smaller, less complex topics.

3. Write in sentences that are short and simple. As much as possible, limit each sentence to one thought or point. A sentence with three or four points that becomes a paragraph is probably too complex. Break up compound sentences into two or more simple sentences.

4. Observe basic grammar guidelines. Write in full sentences which contain a subject and predicate. Take care to use correct spelling. Observe guidelines for proper punctuation.

5. Consider your audience and write at a level that will be understood by your reader. When writing policy information, it is better to err on the side of simplicity and understanding. If your message is too complex or awkward, your readers will have difficulty interpreting policy.

6. Use common terms which are in customary use in daily communications. Also, use terms with common definitions or meanings to aid in uniform understanding of your policy message.

7. Avoid use of technical jargon that may not be understood by your reading audience. Technical jargon may be suitable if your policy issue

deals with a technical, scientific, or legal issue and your readers are familiar with the concepts and terms.

8. Write policy or procedural information in a manner which follows the policy sequence. In other words, start at the beginning and then lead your reader through to the end. An outline or a flowchart is useful in guiding the writer to define policy information in sequence.

9. Stay within the scope of your policy. For example, when writing about working hours, avoid straying into details about overtime pay if this issue is being defined in a separate policy.

10. Anticipate possible questions that may be asked by the reader or by employees. Try to provide answers to these questions as you write the policy.

11. Proofread and edit your policy statement or manual carefully. After you have written the material, set it aside for a day or two. Then look at it again with a fresh perspective. This is an effective way to catch errors that may be overlooked in an initial proofreading.

12. Ask another individual to read your policy draft to ensure understanding of meaning and procedures. Be open to suggestions for improvement or clarifications that may be needed.

## Say What You Mean—Mean What You Say

Careless writing of a personnel policy manual is a leading cause of employee misunderstanding of company policies. Careless writing is also a significant factor contributing to a firm's liability in wrongful discharge lawsuits. When writing your policy manual, say what you mean and mean what you say! The following are some precautions to help you avoid common policy writing problems.

- *Consistency*—Take care to use the same word for the same meaning throughout your manuscript. Also, recognize that a different word will denote a different meaning. For example, if you're writing about your firm's performance appraisal policy and then use the term *review*, confusion and misunderstanding are likely to occur. Careful proofreading is the best cure for this error.

- *Time traps*—Be alert for time traps. Many personnel policies and benefits define a policy time period or length of service eligibility criteria. Carefully select words which convey the proper meaning about time in your policy. A typical vacation policy, for example, deals with two measurements of time. Several sample statements are shown.

*To define a continuous time period*: Vacation may be granted for a period of one week.

*To define a cumulative time period*: An employee must have a total of five years service to be eligible for three weeks vacation.

*To define time limits*: An employee may schedule up to two consecutive weeks of vacation, OR, Vacation requests must be submitted not later than one month prior to the requested vacation date.

- *Criteria cut-offs*—Many policies use length of service or other criteria to start or end the policy or benefits. Take care to define the cut-off to avoid confusion. A discipline policy may, for example, state that a warning is required "after three instances" of tardiness. This statement, however, can be confusing. It means that the fourth tardiness occurrence is actionable. A better way to state this criterion is, "A disciplinary warning shall be issued as a result of four or more instances of tardiness."

- *Can–may–shall–will*—These four auxiliary verbs are often misused and misunderstood. Improper use of these words has resulted in firms losing some wrongful discharge lawsuits. If you want to commit to a specific action in a policy, indicate that an action *shall* occur. If you want to retain discretion and flexibility, indicate that at management's discretion, an action *may* occur. Consider the following meanings when writing your policy information.

  *Can*: to know how to; to be able to

  *May*: a possibility, opportunity, or permission

  *Shall*: imperative; implies a command

  *Will*: am about to or going to; future action[1]

- *The calendar quandary*—Many policies define eligibility, notice, or pay requirements based on a specified number of days. To avoid misunderstanding, you must clearly specify a definition of a day. Do you intend day to be a calendar day, a 24-hour period, or an 8-hour period commonly referred to as a workday? Likewise, how do you define a week's vacation, or the number of absences allowed in a month without penalty? Several examples are shown.

  An employee must provide at least two calendar days' notice when requesting a personal day.

  Funeral leave pay is computed based on the employee's regular straight time pay rate for an eight-hour workday.

  Three or more instances of tardiness in a calendar month are grounds for corrective disciplinary action.

- *Covered employees*—Many policies or benefits apply to specific groups or categories of employees. When writing policy information, it is important to clarify which employees are covered by the policy. This can be done in two ways: specified employee groups can be included or excluded. To include employees, you might state, " All full-time employees are eligible for..." or "Employees assigned to work in the plant must wear..." It is advisable to define these terms in the policy or elsewhere in the policy manual. Again, be consistent in use of the same term throughout the policy manual to define a particular category of employees.

An example of defining a category of employees by exclusion is: "All nonmanagement employees, or all employees excluding part-time workers."

- *Lists*—When a policy lists a series of items, such as a listing of disciplinary rules, there is an implication that the list is all inclusive unless otherwise stated. In other words, if you define a policy that lists five reasons for discharge, a court may interpret that your policy does not permit discharge except for any of the five stated reasons. For this reason, be very careful with lists. If the list is intended to be an example of misconduct that is grounds for discharge, be sure to include an introductory statement that the list "includes but is not limited to..." or other similar language.

## Interpretation Guidelines

The realm of collective bargaining provides a perspective on how labor agreements are interpreted by arbitrators. An arbitrator's award does not create binding law which affects personnel policy manuals. However, arbitrators do tend to follow broad legal guidelines when construing the intent of the parties to a labor agreement. These broad legal guidelines can serve as a benchmark to the personnel policy writer. Attorney Thomas Williams, writing in *Personnel Journal*, offers the following suggestions.

Employee handbooks and personnel manuals are a potential source of significant problems. The handbooks should be drafted as if they were collective bargaining agreements. In doing so, it is best to remember the basic rules of collective bargaining agreement interpretation.
  These rules include:
  1) The intent of the parties will be to govern.
  2) Clear and unambiguous language will control.
  3) Specific terms will always control over general provisions.
  4) The agreement should be construed as a whole and affect should be given to all clauses and words.
  5) The agreement will be interpreted so as to be a legal agreement.
  6) The agreement will be interpreted so as to avoid harsh, absurd, or nonsensical results.
  7) The agreement will be construed in light of the particular factual context.

8) The agreement will be construed so as to avoid a forfeiture. [an unintended penalty]

9) The agreement will be construed in accordance with industry practice.

10) The agreement will be construed against the drafter.

11) The agreement will be construed in accordance with reason and equity.

12) The agreement will be construed in accordance with pre-contract negotiations. [Consider verbal promises made to applicants or employees in this light.]

13) The agreement will be construed in accordance with custom and practice.[2]

## Grappling with Grammar

One of the keys to clear writing is good grammar. By the time you are half-way through your policy manual's first draft, the importance of good grammar will become evident. We will not attempt to re-create an eighth-grade grammar class here; however, several basic grammar guidelines are offered.

1. A sentence is a basic unit of writing which expresses an idea. A sentence contains a subject (noun) and a predicate (verb).

2. The subject and the predicate must be in agreement. Both noun and verb must be singular or plural. For example: *he is* (singular) or *they are* (plural).

3. Avoid fragments or incomplete sentences. Many writers get involved in a long thought and omit the subject or predicate.

4. Eliminate run-on sentences. These are actually several sentences joined by a series of and's or other conjunction. Divide the long run-on sentence into several smaller sentences.

5. A paragraph is a group of sentences dealing with the same thought or idea. Be sure to start a new paragraph when you introduce a new idea.

6. Beware of dangling participles. These are modifying phrases which become separated from the noun which they are modifying.

7. Use the active voice. In the active voice, the noun acts upon the verb. For example, "The supervisor may authorize overtime work." Try not to use the passive voice.

8. Proofread your policy manuscript for grammar as well as accurate definition of policy issues. If a sentence is awkward or unclear, check your grammar. Edit and simplify the sentence until it is clear and makes sense. Ask another person to read your policy to insure a clear understanding.

9. Try to use words that have one or two syllables. An occasional word with three syllables is permissible, but avoid overuse of long words.

10. Limit sentence length to approximately 10 to 20 words. Periodically check your writing. If sentences become too long, editing is necessary.

## Policy Numbering Systems

A system of numbering policies in your personnel policy manual is recommended. Numbered policies aid in the organization of policy information. When each policy is numbered, it aids the reader in finding information. Further, a numbering system for each policy, rather than sequential page numbers, aids in maintenance of your manual. Numbered policies permit the addition or deletion of a policy without affecting a page number sequence.

Two examples of policy numbering systems are shown.

| | |
|---|---|
| A. Employment Policies | 1.00 Employment Policies |
|    1. Employment Status | 1.01 Employment Status |
|    2. Selection/Hiring | 1.02 Selection/Hiring |
|    3. Orientation and Training | 1.03 Orientation & Training |
|    4. Personnel Records | 1.04 Personnel Records |
| B. Attendance Policies | 2.00 Attendance Policies |
|    1. Working Hours | 2.01 Working Hours |
|    2. Leaves of Absence | 2.02 Leaves of Absence |
|    3. Time Records | 2.03 Time Records |
| C. Pay Policies | 3.00 Pay Policies |
|    1. Pay Period/Check Disbursement | 3.01 Pay Period/Check Disbursement |
|    2. Setting Pay Levels | 3.02 Setting Pay Levels |
|    3. Pay Reviews | 3.03 Pay Reviews |
|    4. Performance Appraisals | 3.04 Performance Appraisals |

## Personnel Forms Numbering Systems

Many large organizations assign a form number to each printed form. The form number aids in form identification, inventory control, and reordering. Form numbers can also be designed to correlate to specified personnel policies. Several examples of form numbering systems are shown.

| Numerical Sequence | Alphanumeric Sequence |
|---|---|
| 1 | Actg 101 Accounting Forms |
| 2 | Actg 102 |
| 3 | Pers 201 Personnel Forms |
| 4 | Pers 202 |
| ... | Sls 301 Sales Forms |
| 155 | Sls 302 |
| 156 | |
| 157, etc. | |

*Policy Sequence*

| *Policy No.* | *Form Number* |
|---|---|
| Employment Status 1.01 | Payroll Change Form 1.01A |
| Selection/Hiring 1.02 | Employee Requisition 1.02A |
| Orientation/Hiring 1.03 | Orientation Checklist 1.03A |
| | Tuition Aid Request 1.03B |

## Organize Your Manual

Organized information is readable information. A carefully organized policy manual will help your reader to locate, read, and understand the policy guidelines that you worked so hard to prepare. Your readers will notice the absence of organization. And you will, too. If your firm's supervisors have difficulty reading or finding information in your manual, you will notice that

- The manual will not be used.
- Supervisors will make their own decisions.
- Supervisors will be coming to you or other managers for answers to policy questions.

Here are some suggestions for organizing your policy manual for maximum readability.

**Chapters/Sections.**  Divide policy issues or topics into sections or chapters. This will help the reader to quickly locate a specific policy within a broad policy section. In this book, for example, I have devoted Part II to personnel policy issues. Within Part II, Chap. 8 deals with attendance policies such as working hours, time records, overtime, etc.

**Policy/Page Numbers.**  A numbering system will organize your policy information to help your reader find policy answers quickly.

An absence of policy or page numbers leads to a lot of unnecessary page turning as the reader looks for a topic or issue.

**Contents.**  Do your reader a real favor by putting a contents page in your policy manual. When clients ask me to review or revise their manuals, I am simply amazed at the number of policy manuals that lack the basic organizational tool of a contents page.

**Index.**  An index page is recommended to aid the reader in quickly locating a specific subject or issue. The index differs from the contents page in that it is an alphabetical listing of subjects, including specific subjects that may be defined under a major topic heading. Index preparation can be time consuming, but it is another organizational tool that your reader will appreciate.

**Revisions List.** Include a summary sheet that shows each policy, policy number, issuance date, and latest revision date. This list will serve as an excellent tool to aid supervisors in maintaining their manuals with the last policy revision.

## Sample Policy Manual Contents

A sample policy manual contents page follows to illustrate a policy organization and numbering system.

**XYZ COMPANY
PERSONNEL POLICY MANUAL
CONTENTS**

---

## Sample Employee Handbook Contents

Organize your employee handbook for ease in reading. A sample employee handbook contents page is shown.

**XYZ COMPANY**

**EMPLOYEE HANDBOOK**

**CONTENTS**

---

Welcome Message
The XYZ Tradition
   Our Products and Market
   Our Commitment to Quality
   Equal Employment Opportunity
   Open Door Policy
Benefits at XYZ
   Holidays
   Vacations
   Insurances
   Tuition Aid
   Retirement Plan
   Cafeteria Benefit Plan
XYZ Employee Practices
   New Employee Orientation
   Pay Periods
   Performance Reviews
   Advancement Opportunities
   Transfers
   Working Hours
   Lunch and Break Periods
   Overtime
   Jury Service

Leave of Absence
Separation of Employment
Employee Responsibilities
Reporting Absence
Attendance and Punctuality
Time Records
Drugs and Alcohol
Confidential Information
Address Changes
Telephone Use
Smoking
Accident Reporting

## Sample Policy Formats

There are many different ways to prepare the format or design of a personnel policy statement. A variety of sample policy formats are reproduced here to show the various approaches.

### POLICY STATEMENT

To: All Employees
Subject: Statement of Policy on Equal Employment Opportunity and Affirmative Action

The success of XYZ Company is founded on the skill, efforts, and dedication of our employees. In order to achieve our goals, management is committed to a philosophy of employee relations in which each employee is treated fairly, with respect, and is recognized as an individual. It is, therefore, the policy of XYZ Company to afford Equal Employment Opportunity for all employees and candidates for employment.

To effect this policy, we are committed to making all employment decisions without regard to an individual's race, color, religion, sex, national origin, ancestry, age, marital status, physical or mental handicap, or status as a military veteran. This policy includes employment practices such as recruitment, hiring, promotions, training, compensation, benefits, discipline, appraisal, termination, and other terms or conditions of employment.

Our belief in fair employment practices includes a commitment to establishing and implementing affirmative employment practices which will provide opportunities for minorities, females, handicapped persons, and Vietnam era veterans.

To accomplish this objective, XYZ Company has developed an Affirmative Action Plan. Our Affirmative Action Plan details management responsibilities, goals, and positive action plans. I urge each employee to give their full support and cooperation toward this program.

John J. Jones
President
XYZ Company

## PERSONNEL RECORDS POLICY

SUBJECT: PERSONNEL RECORDS          POLICY NO.: PERS 1.03
                                    PAGE: 1

All Personnel and payroll records are confidential, and access is limited to a need to know basis. Employee records are stored in a confidential central file maintained by an individual designated by the President. Personnel records for Corporate Officers may be stored separately as directed by the President.

The employee is responsible for keeping the Company informed of any changes affecting personnel records such as

a)  Name, address, telephone number
b)  Marital status or number of dependents
c)  Number of income tax exemptions
d)  Beneficiary of group insurances
e)  Persons to notify in case of emergency

_____     _____
Approved                          Date


## ABSENCES AND TARDINESS POLICY

SECTION 9                                    Rev. May 1, 1993
                                             Replaces 6-15-88

ABSENCES/TARDINESS

*Policy Statement*: It is the policy of MMM, Inc. to establish reasonable and necessary controls to ensure adequate attendance and to meet business and production needs.

1.  *Working Schedules*: Working schedules and starting times are established by the department Supervisor or Manager based on business and production needs. (See Section 8, Hours of Employment.) The department supervisor or manager is responsible for communicating work schedules to subordinates. Employees are expected to be at their work station in a fit condition and ready to work at start time. Work activity should commence at starting time and continue until the normal designated stopping times for breaks, lunch, or end of work.

2.  *Reporting Absence*: In the event of absence or tardiness from an assigned work schedule, the employee is required to report absence to the Company. When reporting absence, the employee must telephone his or her supervisor, or other designated individual. The employee must call not later than the scheduled start time.

3.  *Authorized Absences*: The Company recognizes that an occasional absence may occur, as defined by Company policies for holidays, vacations, jury service, funerals, medical leave, personal leave, military leave, voting, etc. Time off from work is unpaid unless the Company has established a specific policy providing pay for time off. (See appropriate policy for details.)

4. *Physician's Certification*: The employee is required to submit a physician's certification in the event of medical absences exceeding three days or in the event of repeated absences for medical reasons.

5. *Excused Absences*: An employee's absence will be considered excused if covered by policy and the employee provides proper and timely notification deemed satisfactory to the supervisor or manager. Timely notification means calling in not later than the employee's scheduled start time on the day of absence or providing advance notice for absences which can be anticipated.

6. *Unexcused Absences*: An employee's absence will be deemed unexcused when an employee fails to call in, gives late notice, fails to give advance notice for absence which could be anticipated, or exceeds the number or length of absences as defined by policy or authorized in advance by the supervisor or manager. Unexcused absences are subject to corrective discipline, which may include termination.

7. *Excessive Absenteeism*: Excessive absenteeism is defined as two or more instances of unexcused absence in a calendar month. Such excessive absenteeism is subject to corrective discipline. Any eight instances of unexcused absenteeism in a calendar year are considered grounds for discharge.

8. *Unreported Absence*: In the event an employee is absent for three days or more without prior notice or approval, such absence is considered to be grounds for dismissal.

9. *Tardiness*: In the event a nonexempt employee reports to work late, he or she will be docked for time missed. Any lateness of six minutes or a portion thereof shall result in loss of pay equivalent to six minutes.

10. *Excessive Tardiness*: Tardiness includes reporting to work late or returning late from lunches or breaks. Excessive tardiness shall be subject to corrective discipline or termination. Excessive tardiness is defined as three or more instances of lateness in a calendar month and is subject to corrective discipline. After any eight instances of tardiness in a calendar year, each subsequent instance of tardiness shall be subject to disciplinary warnings or other corrective action deemed appropriate by management. Any 12 instances of tardiness in a calendar year are considered grounds for discharge.

11. *Leaving Early*: An employee's request to leave work early may be considered by the supervisor or manager. Approval of such absences should be based upon the urgency of the reason for absence and department staffing needs. As a general guide, early leaving should not exceed one instance per month or four instances in a calendar year.

12. *Records*: The Personnel Department or other designated individual is responsible for maintaining attendance records and for advising respective supervisors if an employee's absence or lateness exceeds the guidelines of this policy.

PERSONNEL POLICY MANUAL
___

ATTENDANCE POLICIES
Working Hours                                    No. 3.01
Applies to: All Employees                        Page 1 of 4
Effective: 8-1-85                                Revised: 4-1-92

*Policy*: It is the policy of the Company to establish working schedules based on business conditions and customer requirements.
*Purpose*: To define working schedules, overtime, and related practices.

*Procedure*:

1. The regular work week is based upon working hours from 8:30 a.m. to 5:00 p.m. Monday through Friday.

2. The pay period begins on Sunday and runs through Saturday. Employees are paid on Fridays as shown below:

   Weekly on Friday—Hourly paid employees
   Biweekly on alternating Fridays—Salaried employees

3. Changes to work schedules may be made at any time, as deemed necessary by management, based upon business needs and production requirements. Employees are expected to work all available hours. Some employees may be placed on different schedules based on department needs.

4. Rest periods may be permitted as defined by the department supervisor. Employee lunch periods are scheduled based upon departmental needs as shown below:

   Office employees—1-hour lunch
   Production employees—1/2-hour lunch

5. A time slip is used to record hours worked by nonexempt employees for the purpose of computing payroll and tracking attendance.

   a. The employee receives a time slip at the beginning of each week. Time must be recorded at the start of work, end of work, or when leaving/returning to the premises for nonbusiness reasons during the work day.

   b. The time slip shall be turned in to the supervisor at the end of each week.

   c. The supervisor shall review time slips of subordinates each week and initial approval of overtime as appropriate.

6. Nonexempt employees are entitled to receive one and one-half times their regular hourly pay rate for time worked over 40 hours in a week. (*Note*: Nonexempt office employees receive regular straight time pay for working from 37.5 to 40 hours in a week.) All overtime work must be authorized in advance by the supervisor.

7. An employee who will be absent or late for work must call in not later than his or her scheduled starting time to report the absence. Absences must be reported to the employee's supervisor or the Personnel Manager.

8. Absences which can be anticipated or planned must be requested in advance. To be considered an authorized absence, the absence must be requested by the employee and approved by management (one) 1 week

| SECTION: | EMPLOYMENT POLICIES | POLICY NO. | 1.03 |
|---|---|---|---|
| SUBJECT: | Performance Review | EFFECTIVE: | 12-1-84 |
| | | REVISED: | |
| APPLICABLE TO: | | PAGE: | 1 of 2 |
| | All XYZ Employees | ISSUED BY: | R. Zacc |
| APPROVALS: | | | |

POLICY: It is the policy of the Company to provide employees with a fair and periodic appraisal of their performance on the job.

PURPOSE: To ensure periodic Supervisor-Employee discussions designed to improve job performance.

PROCEDURE:

1) The appraisal of an employee's performance may be conducted for the following reasons:

  a) Evaluation Review - A periodic review and appraisal of results achieved by the employee.

  b) Corrective Review - A critical review of employee performance short-comings, specifying corrective actions needed.

2) Performance appraisals are conducted at the end of the two week orientation period, at six months of employment, and then annually thereafter during the month of the individual's anniversary of employment. The corrective review may be conducted at any time deemed necessary by the Supervisor. All performance appraisal discussions are to be recorded on the MIMA Performance Appraisal form.

3) Approximately two weeks prior to the scheduled review date, the Supervisor is responsible for collecting Company records or data which may be helpful in preparing the performance appraisal of an employee. (Examples include production, installation or other activity reports, quality or error records, attendance records, accident reports, etc.) The Supervisor then prepares the performance appraisal form making ratings and comments as appropriate based upon the performance data.

4) The Supervisor and management may confer and discuss employee ratings or appraisals at the time that the Supervisor prepares the appraisal form. At its discretion, management may require a second level approval of performance appraisals.

**Figure 6.1.** Policy and procedure guide. Some organizations use preprinted form for a uniform policy format, as shown here.

PROCEDURE:     (cont'd)

5) After the performance appraisal form is prepared (and approved by management if required) the Supervisor schedules and conducts a private meeting with the employee to discuss performance issues.  Performance factors such as job knowledge, skills, abilities, productivity, attitude, and attendance are covered in the discussion. The Supervisor shall offer suggestions for improvement where necessary.  The employee shall be afforded the apportunity to sign the appraisal. (Note: it is important that the employee understand that the appraisal is a discussion of performance issues, NOT pay issues which are discussed at a separate meeting between employee and Supervisor.)

6) The completed and signed performance appraisal shall be returned to the Office Manager for inclusion in the employee's personnel file.

**Figure 6.1.** Policy and procedure guide (*Continued*)

in advance. Failure to provide advance notice and receive approval will result in denial of any applicable paid absence benefits.

9. Absences from work may be authorized as defined by Company policies. See Policy No. 3.02 Leave of Absence, Policy No. 1.01 Vacation, or the employee handbook. An absence is unpaid unless expressly provided as a paid absence as defined by Company policy or management decision.

10. The employee is responsible for preparing and submitting an absence report to his or her supervisor when absent. This form shall be forwarded to Personnel. The Personnel Manager shall maintain attendance records for all employees.

11. In the event that absenteeism or tardiness becomes excessive, or there is other disregard of attendance policies, the supervisor shall take corrective disciplinary action or address attendance problems through the Company's Performance Appraisal Policy No. 2.01.

**XYZ COMPANY**
**PERSONNEL POLICY MANUAL**
**JURY SERVICE**

I. Policy Summary
   A. XYZ Company recognizes an employee's civic responsibility for serving as a juror when summoned.
   B. Employees shall receive time off from work for jury service without loss of regular pay, as defined by this policy.
II. Employees Covered by the Jury Service Policy
   A. All employees are covered by this policy effective immediately at the start of employment. This includes employees in full-time, part-time, and temporary work classifications.
   B. Employees performing night shift work shall be granted time off from work for the period of jury service even if there is no conflict between the employee's work schedule and jury service.
III. Procedures for Notification of Absence
   A. The employee is responsible for notifying his/her supervisor by the next workday after receipt of a jury summons.
   B. The employee must submit a copy of the jury summons to support the absence request.
IV. Authorization for Absence
   A. Upon receipt of a copy of the jury summons, the supervisor shall authorize the employee's absence.
   B. The copy of the summons shall be routed to the individual's personnel file.
V. Jury Service Pay
   A. Employees in an authorized jury service absence shall receive jury service pay. Jury service pay is computed based on the difference between the employee's regular weekly or daily pay rate and the weekly or daily jury service pay, so that there is no loss of pay by the employee.
   B. The jury pay differential is computed based upon a regular 40-hour workweek or an eight-hour workday as applicable.
   C. To receive jury pay, the employee must turn in to payroll a copy of the juror pay warrant each week or at the end of the period of jury

service, whichever occurs first. The jury pay will be issued on the next normal pay day which follows receipt of the jury pay warrant.

   D. Jury pay shall continue for the duration of the jury service.

   E. In the event that a part-time employee normally receives less pay than jury pay, the employee shall not receive any compensation from the company for the jury service absence.

VI. Benefits Continuation during Jury Service

   A. The employee retains original length-of-service credit for any company-administered benefits which are based on length of service (i.e., vacation).

   B. An employee on jury service is not eligible for holiday pay for any holidays occurring during the period of absence.

   C. An employee continues to accrue vacation benefits as if there were no absence from work.

   D. The employee is responsible to continue to pay any contributory insurance premiums, such as dependent's insurance coverage.

   E. The company-paid portion of insurance premiums is continued during the period of jury service.

VII. Attendance Records

   A. The supervisor shall record the employee's absence on the time records as "JS" to designate jury service.

**PERSONNEL POLICY MANUAL**

---

3.00 ATTENDANCE POLICIES
3.02 Leave of Absence                 Applies to: All Employees
Effective: 8-1-85                         Revised: 4-1-93

---

3.02.01 *Policy*: It is the policy of the Company to grant a leave of absence when warranted by significant medical, personal, or civic reasons and subject to management discretion after considering the needs of the business.

3.02.02 *Purpose*: To define policy and benefits requirements when an employee is granted a leave of absence.

3.02.03 *Procedure*:

3.02.0301. A leave of absence is defined as an approved absence from work normally lasting five days or more during which time the employee's regular salary is suspended. The absence may be for medical reasons including pregnancy, urgent personal reasons, or civic reasons such as jury duty or military reserve training.

3.02.0302. The employee must request a leave of absence in advance and submit supporting documentation such as physician's statement, juror summons, military orders, etc. In cases of absence for medical reasons including pregnancy, the employee must submit a physician's statement at the start of leave, at succeeding 30-day intervals, and upon return to work.

3.02.0303. Approval of a leave of absence is at management discretion after considering the needs of the business and the circumstances of the case. The length of approved leave is decided by management on a case-by-case basis. In cases of family health emergencies, care of a new child in the home, or employee disability, up to 12 weeks of leave per year may be granted.

3.02.0304. In the event of a question regarding a medical leave, or an employee's ability to perform available work, the Company may elect to obtain a second medical opinion prior to considering or extending a medical leave of absence. In the event of a conflict of medical opinions, the company may elect at its expense to obtain a third medical opinion.

3.02.0305. In the event an employee incurs a medical condition which may affect the employee's ability to work safely or which may adversely affect other employees, the employee has a responsibility to report the condition to management and to seek appropriate medical care. In such cases, the Company may elect to schedule the individual for medical exams, tests, or arrange a medical leave of absence as appropriate.

3.02.0306. An employee's regular wage or salary is suspended during the leave. The employee retains length of service credit; however, profit sharing benefits may be affected by the absence. The employee is ineligible for holiday pay while on leave. Accrual of vacation benefits is suspended in the event of a leave of absence for 30 days or more. The Company-paid portion of insurance premiums is continued for up to 12 weeks. Thereafter, the employee may elect to pay the full insurance premium cost if uninterrupted insurance is desired. The employee is responsible for maintaining payments for dependent insurances during the period of leave.

3.02.0307. The Company shall make every reasonable effort to hold open the employee's job during leave periods of 12 weeks or less. However, during any period of leave, the Company reserves the right to fill, change, or eliminate a vacant position if required by the needs of the business. In such cases an employee returning from leave may be placed into another comparable position if any such position is available or may be placed in a layoff status. Return from military leave shall be handled in accordance with applicable government laws on reemployment.

3.02.0308. All leaves of absence shall be recorded on the employee's attendance record.

*Note*: See Chap. 9 for information on leaves and the new Family and Medical Leave Act.

## Summary

Writing is an art and a skill which can be learned. It is important to define the purpose of your policy manual in order to write the manual properly. Prepare an outline to organize your thoughts and information. Write in a clear, concise style that the reader will understand. Organize your manual into sections with contents, index, and page or topic number systems. Take care to say what you mean and mean what you say.

In Part II, numerous personnel policies issues are defined, with sample policies and employee handbook paragraphs provided.

## Notes

1. L. Marceau, *Drafting A Union Contract*, Little, Brown & Co., Boston, 1965, p. 16.
2. Thomas H. Williams, "Fire At Will" article, *Personnel Journal*, June, 1985, p. 76. Reprinted with permission of *Personnel Journal*, Costa Mesa, Cal. All rights reserved.

# PART 2

# Policy Development Guidelines

# 7

# Hiring, Promoting, and Other Employment Policies

**Read Chapter 7 for:**

Staffing selection

Recruitment and testing

Physical exams

Employment definitions

Orientation

Equal employment opportunity

Sexual harassment

Transfers

Promotions

Personnel records

Job descriptions

## Recruiting Qualified Employees

Attracting and retaining qualified employees is vital to the success of any organization. Despite the continued growth of technology, the human element is still the central ingredient in every organization.

A personnel policy on recruiting will guide managers to hire the right person for the job. The primary purpose of the recruiting policy is to attract qualified candidates at a minimum cost and time. A recruiting policy also will enable the organization to contact a diverse variety of recruiting resources, which helps to avoid charges of bias in recruiting practices.

In the absence of a defined recruiting policy, hiring managers will do whatever method works best for attracting candidates. Some will ask employees for referrals, and others will talk to employment agencies or place an ad in the local paper. These efforts will produce varying results. Some recruiting methods will be more costly than others. A recruiting policy will help managers to achieve the best result.

## Recruiting Resources

Common recruiting resources include one or more of the following:

Promotion/transfer of current employees

Help wanted ads in local newspaper

Help wanted ads in major/regional newspaper

Help wanted ads in trade journals

Employment agencies

Executive search firms

Public employment service (Job Service)

Job training services and programs

Temporary help services

College placement offices

Trade and technical schools

Employee referrals

Help wanted sign in door, window, or on plant gate

Referrals from business contacts

Walk-in applicants

Unsolicited resumes

Community service organizations

Situation wanted ads

Job fairs

Career days at local schools

Professional associations

Union hiring halls

### Competitive Practices

Figure 7.1 shows employer recruitment practices.

**CHECKLIST**
**Recruiting Policy**

The following checklist identifies important issues to consider when preparing a recruiting policy:

- Who has the authority to authorize hiring of a replacement employee or an addition to staff?

- What categories of jobs are covered by the recruiting policy? (full time, part time, temporary, union, nonunion, etc.)

- Who is responsible for recruiting activities—the hiring supervisor, department manager, or human resource specialist?

- What recruiting resources are recommended? What recruiting resources should be avoided?

- Is there a cost limit on recruiting? How large (and costly) a help wanted ad is permissible? How much can be spent on employment agency fees?

- Does the organization consider current employees for promotion before recruiting candidates from outside the firm?

- What procedures are necessary to assure equal employment opportunities for all and will aid in reaching affirmative action plan goals?

**Pitfalls to Avoid**

There are several common pitfalls that can occur when recruiting employees. These pitfalls are identified with some suggestions on how to avoid the problem.

1. The hiring of applicants referred by current employees is a low-cost and effective means for recruiting employees. Generally, when an employee refers a friend or relative for employment, it is an indicator that the employee likes his or her job well enough to recommend it to others. Second, an employee is more likely to recommend someone who will be a good worker.

However, excessive reliance on employee referrals can be counterproductive and even result in legal problems for the employer. Some firms have found that frequent hiring of employee referrals results in employee cliques. A packaging company, for example, had in one department a tight-knit clique of employees all from a nearby community. This clique contributed to excessive turnover because newly hired workers felt like outsiders. In another case, a metalworking firm frequently hired relatives of employees, resulting in large family units working in the plant. One day, a supervisor's disciplinary dispute with one worker resulted in 15 employees walking off the job.

| Occupational Group/ Union Status | Recruitment Source | | | | | | | |
|---|---|---|---|---|---|---|---|---|
| | Newspapers | Colleges | Graduate Schools | Search Firms | Gov't Agencies | Private Agencies | Employee Referrals | Walk Ins |
| Managers | 82% | 31% | 36% | 75% | 18% | 62% | 83% | 44% |
| | (455) | (409) | (412) | (461) | (396) | (424) | (434) | (406) |
| Union Professional and Technical Employees | 68 | 43 | 33 | 14 | 36 | 41 | 83 | 63 |
| | (53) | (51) | (51) | (49) | (50) | (51) | (48) | (48) |
| Nonunion Professional and Technical Employees | 93 | 63 | 52 | 46 | 32 | 64 | 91 | 65 |
| | (454) | (436) | (422) | (416) | (395) | (422) | (433) | (414) |
| Union Clerical Employees | 56 | 10 | 1 | 0 | 54 | 23 | 84 | 85 |
| | (75) | (72) | (73) | (75) | (76) | (73) | (76) | (78) |
| Nonunion Clerical Employees | 83 | 11 | 15 | 6 | 59 | 44 | 94 | 88 |
| | (459) | (385) | (391) | (397) | (415) | (418) | (451) | (445) |
| Union Manufacturing and Production Employees | 56 | 4 | 3 | 1 | 59 | 7 | 84 | 84 |
| | (147) | (137) | (140) | (139) | (149) | (139) | (151) | (151) |
| Nonunion Manufacturing and Production Employees | 76 | 10 | 5 | 5 | 63 | 16 | 95 | 90 |
| | (312) | (271) | (273) | (275) | (280) | (281) | (312) | (312) |

Sample size is in parentheses.

**Figure 7.1.** Sources of recruitment by occupation group and union status (percent reporting use)[1]

2. Another recruiting pitfall is failure to attract a diverse applicant pool, resulting in charges of employment discrimination. Firms have been found guilty of discriminatory hiring practices by limiting recruiting contacts to newspapers read by non-minorities, only hiring from the immediate neighborhood, avoiding contacts in the broader community which includes minorities, or relying on employee referrals. Such actions tend to perpetuate the current racial makeup of the workforce to the exclusion of others. Such practices are viewed as discriminatory by the Equal Employment Opportunity Commission (EEOC). For example, in a recent highly publicized case, a small firm employing about 20 workers in a Hispanic neighborhood of Chicago was charged with discrimination for failing to hire a black applicant who had left an unsolicited application with the receptionist. A subsequent job opening, filled by another Hispanic from the neighborhood, was evidence of discrimination according to the EEOC.

3. Except in cases of a confidential search, it is best to communicate job opening information to employees This practice provides an opportunity for an interested employee to come forth and apply for the job. It also helps to reduce the likelihood of an employee sending a resume thinking that the job is with another company.

4. Carefully consider how a promotion-from-within policy fits into the recruiting process. While promotion from within is a positive benefit for employees, some line managers say that promotion policies complicate the hiring process by delaying the filling of the job or require the promotion of a marginally qualified worker when a fully qualified applicant from outside the company is available.

## Sample Policy

A sample recruiting policy follows:

**XYZ COMPANY**
**PERSONNEL POLICY & PROCEDURE**

---

SUBJECT: EMPLOYEE RECRUITMENT          DATE: May 1, 1993

---

*Policy*: It is the policy of XYZ Company to use a variety of cost-effective employee recruitment resources to attract a qualified applicant pool for consideration for employment.

*Applies to*: All positions, except for temporary reassignment.

*Procedure*:

1. Each department manager is responsible for recommending department staffing levels when preparing the annual budget. Upon receipt of their approved department budget, the Department Manager can authorize the filling of new or replacement positions. Exceptions to budgeted staffing must be authorized by the General Manager.

2. When a job opening occurs, the Department Manager and supervisor shall confer to identify job duties, skills, and requirements for the job. The Human Resource Administrator can provide assistance in defining job specifications if requested. The Department Supervisor shall then prepare a job description or revise the existing job description.

3. The supervisor shall prepare a recruiting requisition. The requisition, together with the job description, shall be approved by the Department Manager and then routed to the Human Resource Department.

4. Consideration shall be given to qualified employees available through transfer or promotion. The Human Resource Manager shall confer with line managers and check employee files to identify possible candidates. See "Policies on Promotions and Transfers." In the event there is no current employee selected for the open position, the Human Resources Administrator shall begin employee recruitment.

5. The Human Resource Administrator is responsible for developing and maintaining effective recruiting contacts. Recruiting resources may include:
   Newspaper advertisements
   Referrals from employees
   Help wanted sign on building or premises
   Applications on file
   Walk-in applicants

Local schools or colleges
Public employment referral/training services or other similar resources

6. In the event that recruiting costs will exceed $1000 (such as for a large ad or employment agency fee), the cost must be approved by the General Manager.

7. The Human Resource Administrator is responsible for contacting recruiting resources and providing information on the job opening. Refer to the job description for qualifications and job information. Advise the recruiting source of the firm's equal employment opportunity policy.

8. Except in cases of a confidential search, the Human Resource Administrator is responsible for notifying current employees of the job opening by a bulletin board posting and for notifying the switchboard/receptionist so that inquiries may be properly routed.

9. In the event of unsolicited inquires from job seekers or employment agencies to supervisors or managers, such inquiries shall be referred to the Human Resource Department.

## Sample Employee Handbook Paragraph

*Employee Recruitment*

XYZ Company contacts a variety of sources in the community when the company has a job opening. This helps to assure our goals for promoting equal employment opportunities and selecting qualified candidates. Information on job openings is normally posted on the bulletin board. If you know of a friend or relative who may qualify for the position, you are encouraged to refer the individual to the Human Resource Department.

## Sample Form

**EMPLOYEE REQUISITION**

Job Title _____ Desired date
                                 to fill position _____

___New position          ___Replacement position

Job Duties (attach job description) _____

_____

_____

Qualifications _____

_____

_____

*Sample Form (Continued)*

Check applicable boxes:

____Full Time      ____Part Time      ____Temporary

____Exempt      ____Nonexempt      ____Please determine exempt/non-

exempt status

Is this job in approved budget?   ____yes   ____no

If no, attach justification.

Comments: _____

_____

_____

Requested Supervisor  _____   Date  _____

Approved Manager  _____   Date  _____

Approved General Mgr.  _____   Date  _____

## Employee Selection and Testing

After the recruiting process has attracted job candidates, the next issue involves screening, testing, and selecting the best applicant. Careful employee selection is an important human resource responsibility because capable, hard-working employees affect the productivity and profitability of the organization.

The objective of a policy on employee selection and testing is to provide guidelines on selection procedures which will aid supervisors or managers in selecting a qualified worker while avoiding legal liabilities. Policy guidelines promote a uniform and thorough approach to employee selection. With selection guidelines, there is a great likelihood that supervisors will make better selection decisions.

In the absence of guidelines, supervisors or managers will try different employee selection techniques. Some managers conduct detailed interviews. Others may ask only a few questions about job skills or personal interests and then make a hiring decision based on applicant personality. Some supervisors devise tests for applicants or ask applicants to demonstrate their skill at running a machine used on the job. At best, these techniques will have varying degrees of success and, at worse, such practices have been shown to be improper and discriminatory selection devices.

All employee selection techniques are subject to the uniform selection guidelines issued by the EEOC in 1978. The EEOC guidelines are designed to serve as a workable set of standards to determine whether selection procedures comply with Title VII of the Civil Rights Act of 1964. In its regulations, EEOC defines tests as any paper and pencil or performance measure used as a basis for an employment decision. The regulations offer as examples any formal, scored, quantified, or standardized technique of assessing job suitability including any skill or ability tests, interviewer rating scales, or other educational or work history requirements. The regulations further require that the test be a valid measure of required performance on the job. Requirements for validation studies are also defined in the regulations. The personnel policy writer should check to ensure that selection procedures comply with these regulations.[2]

The checklist on page 119 is designed to identify important issues to consider when preparing an Employee Selection Policy.

Typical employee selection procedures include one or more of the following:

Screening of resumes

Review of employment applications

Telephone screening of applicants

Broad screening interviews

Detailed selection interviews

Skill testing (i.e., keyboard, typing, math aptitude)

Psychological evaluations

Verification of employment references

Verification of educational or professional credentials

Drug abuse screening

Physical exam (subject to limitations under the Americans with Disabilities Act)

Polygraph testing for preemployment screening of applicants by nongovernmental employers is now a prohibited employment practice under the Polygraph Protection Act of 1990.[3]

The Americans with Disabilities Act (ADA) has added a new dimension to the employee selection process. For example, in the event that an applicant with a disability is unable to complete a test due to his or her disability, the employer is responsible for making a reasonable accommodation by identifying an alternative means to permit the applicant to demonstrate the skill or knowledge which the test purports to measure.

**CHECKLIST**
**An Employee Selection Policy**

---

Who participates in the employee selection process—the Supervisor, Manager, Human Resource Administrator, or others?

Will preliminary applicant screening be done by a Human Resource Administrator?

Are any currently used selection procedures limited or prohibited by law?

Will the supervisor have full hiring discretion?

Will the supervisor recommend hire, subject to approval of a higher-level manager?

What applicant screening techniques will be used in the selection process?

Will tests (ability, skill, or aptitude) be used to help evaluate the candidate's qualifications?

Will drug tests, honesty tests, handwriting analysis, or other testing techniques be used?

Who will be responsible for administering tests, checking references, etc.?

Who will have responsibility for the hiring decision?

Who will have responsibility for determining starting pay and communicating the job offer?

What checks or procedures will be taken to ensure that selection procedures are nondiscriminatory?

---

### Competitive Practices

The chart in Fig. 7.2 shows employee selection practices.

### Pitfalls to Avoid

The major pitfalls in the employee selection process typically fall into two categories: use of inadequate selection techniques, and improper use of employee selection procedures causing discriminatory and legal liabilities. Here are some suggestions for avoiding these problems:

1. Make sure that employee selection devices or procedures are in compliance with the law. Potential troublesome areas include

   Polygraph testing—prohibited by the Polygraph Protection Act
   Physical exams—limited by the Americans with Disabilities Act (ADA)
   Drug testing—may be subject to limits under state/local laws
   HIV/AIDS testing—prohibited by ADA and certain state laws
   Tests or rating scales—are subject to EEOC guidelines on employee selection procedures

2. Check to ensure that the employment application complies with recent labor law changes by avoiding inquiries about physical or mental handicaps, age, sex, national origin, or other protected categories.

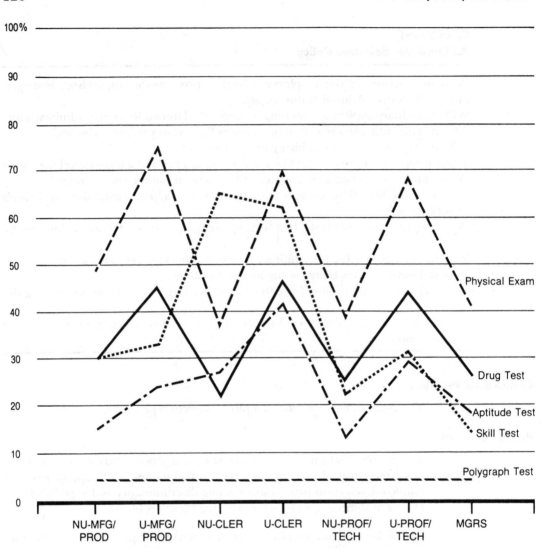

**Figure 7.2.** Employee selection practices, by occupation and union status[4]

3. Check to ensure that your firm's employment application has an applicant certification which authorizes prior employers to release information for reference checks, asserts that employment is at will, and states that falsification or omission of information on the application is grounds for refusing employment or for dismissal from employment.

4. Avoid misunderstandings by confirming job offers in a letter which specifies job, start date, and pay rate—specifying pay in an hourly, weekly, or monthly rate.

5. Use objective, job-related criteria throughout the selection process. Job

descriptions are a useful aid in the selection process. The ADA recognizes written job descriptions, prepared before advertising or interviewing for the job, as evidence of the essential functions of the job.

6. Be consistent in the use of selection techniques. If a selection procedure, such as reference checking, physical exam, or drug screen, is used on one candidate, it should be used on all candidates for the same job or similar class of jobs. Sporadic use of a selection procedure could be viewed as a discriminatory hiring practice.

**Sample Policy**

A sample Employee Selection Policy follows:

**XYZ COMPANY**
**PERSONNEL POLICY & PROCEDURE**

SUBJECT: EMPLOYEE TESTING
          AND SELECTION                      DATE: May 1, 1993

*Policy*: It is the policy of XYZ Company to use a uniform and thorough selection process to promote equal employment opportunities in the hiring of qualified employees.

*Procedure*:

1. The employee selection procedures apply to the filling of all positions except for temporary reassignment of job duties or consolidation of job duties or functions.

2. The Supervisor or Department Manager has authority to define staffing needs and job skill requirements needed to efficiently complete department work tasks. The authorized number of employees in a department is subject to approval of the second-level Manager (and the Company President or third-level Manager, if required).

3. When a job opening occurs, the Supervisor or Department Manager shall confer with the second-level Manager and the Personnel Department. Consideration shall be given to qualified employees available through transfer or promotion. (See Policy on Promotions and Transfers.)

4. Job applicants must complete an Employment Application. The selection process should include interviews by one or more of the following individuals: a Personnel Department representative and/or hiring Supervisor or Manager. The individual responsible for recruiting may elect to conduct reference checks, skill tests, or other similar procedures designed to aid selection of qualified employees. Use of any tests must be approved by the Corporate Personnel Department. All selection criteria shall be based upon job-related factors, and selection decisions shall be made in a nondiscriminatory manner as defined by the Equal Employment Opportunity Policy.

5. Hiring decisions and starting pay rates may be formulated by the Department Manager. Supervisors or Managers authorized to make hiring decisions are encouraged to confer with the Personnel Department for

advice on employee selection, setting pay levels, etc. Hiring decisions and starting pay rates may be subject to approval of a Company Officer.

6. All new employees are subject to the following standards of employment:

   a) They must be legally qualified to work in the U.S. as evidenced by submitting appropriate identity and employment authorization documents. (I-9 and related sample forms appear as attachments to this policy.)

   b) They must be physically and mentally fit to perform assigned job duties as evidenced by results of a preemployment physical exam including appropriate tests to determine the presence of drugs or alcohol in the body. The physical exam shall be scheduled *after* the employee has accepted the job offer and prior to the start of work. (A positive test result indicating presence of drugs or alcohol shall be sufficient grounds to refuse or withdraw an offer of employment.)

   c) They must possess a valid driver's license appropriate for any vehicle which may be operated in the course of performing job duties, if the job requires regular or frequent travel.

7. The communication of the job offer is normally done by the Personnel Manager. A job offer should specify start date, starting pay (in hourly, weekly, or monthly terms), and position.

8. The employment classification of the position shall be determined by the Manager responsible for the position after conferring with the Personnel Manager.

9. See the Orientation Policy for new employee orientation guidelines.

## Sample Employee Handbook Paragraph

*New Employee Selection*

New employees are selected by management based upon an assessment of the individual's experiences, skills, abilities, education, and related factors. All new employees are subject to the following standards of employment:

a. They must be legally qualified to work in the U.S. as evidenced by submitting appropriate identity and employment authorization documents.

b. They must be physically and mentally fit to perform assigned job duties as evidenced by results of a preemployment physical exam including appropriate tests to determine the presence of drugs or alcohol in the body. To assure the safety of all employees on the job, it is our policy that a positive test result indicating presence of drugs or alcohol shall be sufficient grounds to refuse or withdraw an offer of employment. We will, of course, make a reasonable accommodation for qualified disabled workers.

c. They must possess a valid driver's license appropriate for any vehicle which may be operated in the course of performing job duties, if the job requires regular or frequent travel.

**Sample Form**

## EMPLOYMENT APPLICATION

Name _____ Type of Work Sought _____

Address _____ Telephone Number _____

City, State, Zip _____

Social Security Number _____

| Education | School Name | Degree | Course of Study |
|---|---|---|---|
| Grammar School | | | |
| High School | | | |
| Bus/Trade School | | | |
| College/University | | | |
| Advanced Studies | | | |

Military:

Branch of Service _____ Dates Served _____

List military training or skills _____

_____

*Statement of Equal Employment Opportunity*: All applicants are considered for employment without regard to race, sex, age, national origin, religion, military status, physical or mental disability, or other status as protected by law.

Job Skills:

List machines that you operate _____

List computers that you operate _____

List computer software/languages _____

List any occupational license/certification _____

List any other information which would be helpful in evaluating you for this position: _____

_____

_____

Employment History: (List most recent job first.)

Employer _____ Dates of Employment _____

*Sample Form (Continued)*

Address _____          Start/End Pay _____

Phone _____            Job Duties _____

Supervisor _____       May we contact?  __yes  __no

Reason for Leaving _____

_____

_____


Employer _____         Dates of Employment _____

Address _____          Start/End Pay _____

Phone _____            Job Duties _____

Supervisor _____       May we contact?  __yes  __no

Reason for Leaving _____

_____

_____


Employer _____         Dates of Employment _____

Address _____          Start/End Pay _____

Phone _____            Job Duties _____

Supervisor _____       May we contact?  __yes  __no

Reason for Leaving _____

_____

_____


*Applicant Certification*:
1. I certify that the information provided in this application is true and accurate to the best of my knowledge. I understand that submission of false information on this application or in an employment interview is grounds for withdrawal of a job offer or for dismissal of employment.

2. I authorize release of employment, salary, education, and other related records to the Company for the purpose of checking my references and verifying my employment and educational history.

3. In consideration of my employment, I agree to conform to the rules and regulations of the company, and my employment and compensa-

*Sample Form (Continued)*

> tion can be terminated with or without cause and with or without notice at any time at the option of either the Company or myself.

_____    _____

(Signature of Applicant)                          (Date)

# Employment Classifications

Every organization has various employment classifications. The employment classification is a method of grouping or categorizing jobs or employees to define a policy, procedure, or benefit for that group. Employment classifications help to sort out issues such as eligibility for benefits, payment of salaries, and entitlement to overtime pay.

Typical employment classifications or categories are as follows:

| | |
|---|---|
| Full-time employee | Exempt employee* |
| Part-time employee | Nonexempt employee* |
| Temporary employee | Salaried employee |
| Union employee | Hourly employee |
| Nonunion employee | Commission employee |
| Office employee | Management employee |
| Plant employee | Nonmanagement employee |
| At-will employee | Tenured employee |
| | Nontenured employee |
| | Probationary employee |
| | Appointed employee |
| | Civil service employee |

## Pitfalls to Avoid

Employment classifications help to bring administrative order and consistency to employment practices. Here are some pitfalls to avoid when defining employment classifications.

1. Avoid excessive or unnecessary employment classifications. Develop only those employment classifications that are needed to efficiently administer benefits or employment policies.

2. Check employment classifications to ensure that they do not create a category which groups employees by race, age, sex, or other protected class defined by antibias laws. Even if the classifications are not inten-

*Exempt from the Fair Labor Standards Act (FLSA). A nonexempt employee is one who is covered by the FLSA.

### CHECKLIST
### An Employment Classification Policy

The following checklist identifies important issues to consider when preparing an Employment Classification Policy.

- Who is responsible for defining employment classifications?

- Who is responsible for evaluating jobs and determining their employment classification (i.e., supervisor, manager, human resource administrator)?

- What legal or contractual requirements create or affect employment classifications (i.e., benefit plans, insurance contracts, FLSA requirements, union agreement, etc.)?

- How will changes in an employee's classification affect entitlement to benefits or application of policy?

- When and how will employment classifications be recorded?

- Do employment classifications avoid classifying employees on the basis of race, age, sex, religion, national origin, disability, military status, or other protected class?

tionally biased, if their effect tends to group employees in categories that are predominantly or exclusively female or minority, such a practice could be viewed as discrimination by the government.

3. Take care to protect employment-at-will prerogatives when defining employment classifications. Two problem areas are these:

    a. Avoid defining full-time employees as permanent employees.

    b. Avoid defining new nonunion employees as probationary because passing probation may imply some form of employment security.

4. Avoid overlooking legal requirements that affect employment classifications. The Fair Labor Standards Act defines certain executive, professional, administrative, and outside sales jobs as exempt from the law requirements for minimum wage, recording hours worked, and overtime pay. Likewise, the law specifies that full-time and part-time employees who enter military service are entitled to reemployment rights under certain conditions. For further guidance on defining exempt and nonexempt job categories, see WH Publication 1281, Regulations, Part 541: Defining Terms "Executive," "Administrative," "Professional," and "Outside Salesman," published by the U.S. Department of Labor.

5. Avoid the tendency to classify plant workers as hourly paid employees and all office workers as salaried and therefore ineligible for overtime pay. Under the FLSA, certain office employees who do not meet the exemption tests should be classified as nonexempt salaried employees who are eligible for overtime pay.

**Sample Policy**

A sample Employee Classification Policy follows:

**XYZ COMPANY**
**PERSONNEL POLICY & PROCEDURE**

SUBJECT: EMPLOYMENT CLASSIFICATIONS          DATE: May 1, 1993

*Policy*: It is the policy of XYZ Company to define employment classifications in order to uniformly administer policies and benefits, and to comply with relevant wage-hour or labor laws.

*Procedure*:

1. Employment classifications are determined by the Manager responsible for the position after conferring with the Corporate Personnel Manager. The employment classification must be specified prior to hiring an employee so that pay and employment benefits may be properly communicated when making a job offer.

2. In determining employment classifications, the Manager and Human Resource Administrator shall evaluate the following factors:

   a) Job duties, responsibilities, and job description, if any

   b) Planned work schedule and duration of job

   c) Relevant state or federal labor laws and employment or collective bargaining agreements, if any

3. In order to achieve compliance with the Fair Labor Standards Act, all employees are classified into one of the following categories:

   a) Exempt Employees—Employees performing jobs determined to be Executive, Professional, Administrative, or Sales positions. Exempt employees are not eligible for overtime pay. However, when an exempt supervisor is scheduled by management to work on Saturday, Sunday, or a Company observed holiday, overtime pay will be paid at the employee's regular straight time pay rate. A guideline sheet defining exempt positions is maintained in the Human Resource Department.

   b) Nonexempt Employees—Employees performing all other jobs not determined to be exempt. Examples include clerical, factory, and warehouse jobs. Employees assigned to nonexempt positions are required to maintain a record of hours worked and may receive overtime pay when performing overtime work.

4. An employee's work schedule affects employment classifications as defined below:

   a) Full-Time Employee—One who is hired for an indefinite period for a full-time work schedule which normally averages 40 hours or more weekly.

   b) Part-Time Employee—One who is hired for an indefinite period for a less than full-time work schedule that normally averages less than 40 hours weekly.

   c) Temporary Employee—One who is hired for a short term, seasonal, or specific period of time or for a specified work project. Temporary employees may work full-time or part-time work schedules as determined by management. A temporary employee is hired with the understanding that employment will cease at the expiration of a specific period of time or when services are no longer needed.

5. The Company has recognized a union, and certain specified jobs are covered by a collective bargaining agreement. Employees hired for union jobs are considered to be probationary employees until successful completion of the probationary period. (See Probationary Period Policy.)

6. In the event of promotion, transfer, or change of work schedules or responsibilities, the responsible Manager shall confer with the Human Resource Administrator to evaluate employment classification of the job.

7. Assignment of or changes to employment classifications shall be recorded on the Payroll Change Notice Form.

8. The designation of employment classifications in no way alters the employment-at-will nature of the employment relationship. The Company reserves the right to change an employee's work hours and employment category if warranted by business needs in the judgment of the Department Manager or a Company Officer.

9. When necessary, a Department Manager or Company Officer may authorize the use of services contracted through a temporary help firm or a self-employed independent contractor. Individuals performing tasks on a contract basis are not deemed to be employees.

## Employee Handbook Paragraph

### Employment Classifications

At time of hire, each new employee is assigned an employment classification based upon job responsibilities and work schedule. The employment classification determines one's eligibility for benefits and requirements for time recording for overtime pay computations. An employee will be classified as defined below:

Full-Time Employee—One who is hired to work for an indefinite period with a work schedule averaging 40 hours per week. Full-time employees meeting appropriate length of service requirements are eligible to participate in all Company benefits programs.

Part-Time Employee—One who is hired to work for an indefinite period with a work schedule of less than 40 hours per week. Part-time employees meeting appropriate length of service requirements are entitled to receive holiday and vacation pay prorated to the equivalent number of hours normally worked weekly.

Temporary Employee—One who is hired for special projects or short-term periods such as summer employment. Temporary employees are not eligible for Company benefits.

Temporary changes in the number of hours do not affect your status, and the above definitions are not to be construed as a guarantee of work hours.

**Sample Form**

**PAYROLL CHANGE NOTICE FORM**

Effective Date _____

Employee _____ Social Security No. _____

____ New Hire ____ Status Change ____ Separation

|  | Old | New |
|---|---|---|
| Job | _____ | _____ |
| Pay Rate | _____ | _____ |
| Department | _____ | _____ |
| Shift | _____ | _____ |
| Other | _____ | _____ |
| Other | _____ | _____ |

| Leave of Absence: | From | To |
|---|---|---|
| Family or Medical | _____ | _____ |
| Personal | _____ | _____ |
| Jury | _____ | _____ |
| Military | _____ | _____ |
| Other | _____ | _____ |

Separation

____ Voluntary   Reason: _____

____ Involuntary   Reason: _____

Comments: _____

_____

_____

_____

| Supervisor | Manager | Human Resource | Date |
|---|---|---|---|

# Physical Exams

A preemployment physical exam has been used by many organizations as part of the employee selection process. The physical exam was seen as an effective way to evaluate the employee's physical ability to perform job duties. From an insurance loss control perspective, the preemployment physical served to identify job applicants with preexisting medical conditions which limited or prevented the individual from safely performing job duties. This provided a basis to screen out of the hiring process those applicants with medical conditions that made them prone to injury, which would cause lost productivity, costly medical claims, and higher worker's compensation costs.

In certain occupational areas, preemployment physical exams are required by government regulations. For example, employees working in noisy environments are required to have a preemployment hearing test and periodic retesting. These requirements are part of a hearing conservation program which is required by the Occupational Safety and Health Administration (OSHA).

The U.S. Department of Transportation (DOT) requires preemployment and biannual physical exams for truck drivers operating large vehicles in interstate commerce.

The Americans with Disabilities Act (ADA) of 1990 prohibits inquiries about an applicant's medical condition and imposes major limitations on preemployment physical exams. The ADA requires that a physical exam be conducted after making the job offer and that its use as a screening tool be applied to all applicants for the position. If the physical exam identifies a medical condition, the employer is required to make reasonable accommodation for the condition.

### Pitfalls to Avoid

The passage of the Americans with Disabilities Act (ADA) places specific limitations on the use of physical exams in the employment relationship. Here are some pitfalls to avoid when developing a policy on physical exams:

1. Be sure to check ADA requirements regarding physical exams. The preemployment physical exam is now prohibited by ADA. A postoffer physical is allowed so long as it is not used to screen out qualified disabled applicants.

2. Avoid using physical exams on a sporadic or inconsistent basis. Identify a specific job or class of jobs and use the physical consistently for all applicants who have accepted an offer of a job in the covered category.

3. Do not overlook OSHA requirements regarding physical exams and maintenance of health records.

4. Various states have laws defining limits to physical exams and requiring that the preemployment physical exams be paid for by the employer.

5. Avoid using the physical exam to check for medical conditions which are not job related or are inconsistent with business necessity.

6. Avoid careless use or unauthorized release of confidential medical records.

**CHECKLIST**
**A Physical Exam Policy**

The following checklist identifies important issues to consider when preparing a Physical Exam Policy.

- Which jobs are covered by the physical exam policy: production, warehouse, truck drivers, or other categories?

- What doctor, clinic, or occupational health facility will be used for the physical exam?

- What medical checks or lab tests will be included in the exam?

- Will physical exams be conducted for preemployment, or periodically during employment, or upon return from medical leave or other circumstance?

- What actions will be taken if the physical shows a medical condition that may affect the individual's ability to safely perform job tasks?

- What steps will be taken to comply with the Americans with Disabilities Act?

- What reasonable accommodations will be made for qualified disabled applicants or employees?

- Who will pay for the cost of the physical exam?

- Where and for how long will medical records be stored?

---

**XYZ COMPANY**
**PERSONNEL POLICY & PROCEDURE**

SUBJECT: PHYSICAL EXAMS                    DATE: May 1, 1993

*Policy*: It is the policy of XYZ Company to use a pre-employment physical examination as part of the screening and selection process for sales employees.

*Procedure*:
1. The successful completion of a preemployment physical exam is a condition of employment for all sales employees hired after the effective date of this policy. All new sales employees are subject to the preemployment physical exam regardless of disability.

2. Due to the fact that sales employees are working with confidential business information and operating a motor vehicle on the job, a physical exam shall include a drug screen. The physical exam with drug screen is deemed to be necessary to assure the safety and health of employees, customers, and the general public.

3. The physical exam and drug screen shall be performed by a Company designated physician. The exam shall include procedures and tests as specified by the Company. The physical exam shall be paid for by the Company. The Human Resource Administrator is responsible for identifying the servicing organization and/or local physician for this policy.

4. The interviewing manager is responsible for advising the candidate about the physical exam and drug screen during the employment interview. The candidate should be advised that:

   a) Completion of the physical exam is a condition of employment for sales positions.

   b) The physical exam includes lab tests for detection of drug abuse.

   c) Refusal to submit to the physical exam and/or evidence of drug use is considered grounds to deny employment.

   d) The company affords equal employment opportunity for all individuals, and reasonable accommodations will be made for qualified disabled individuals.

5. Recommended referral form, consent form, and sales representative job outline are attached to this policy. All information obtained regarding the medical condition or history of the applicant is collected and maintained on separate forms and in separate medical files.

6. A job offer shall be extended to the candidate conditioned on successful completion of the physical exam. Once the candidate has accepted the job offer, the hiring manager shall refer the candidate to the designated physician for the exam. The physical exam should be completed prior to the individual's start date.

7. The results of the physical exam are confidential and may be viewed only by the manager authorizing the exam, a hiring manager, or other executive managers involved in the employee selection or placement decision. Where necessary for the safety and health of the employee or other employees, a supervisor may be advised of an employee's medical condition with precautions or instructions for emergency treatment or accommodations to be made.

8. Employment decisions based upon the physical exam must be made on a nondiscriminatory basis. The hiring manager shall consider the following issues when reviewing the results of the physical exam:

   a) Consider the individual's abilities in relation to the physical demands of the job.

   b) Consider what "reasonable accommodations" may be made to the work environment or job duties in order to accommodate qualified disabled individuals.

   c) When reasonable accommodations are not feasible and where a physical or mental condition impairs an individual's ability to meet normal job performance standards, such factor(s) may disqualify the individual from employment.

   d) Candidates receiving a positive test result on the drug screening test shall be deemed disqualified due to the potential danger of their presence in the work environment or their operation of a motor vehicle, unless the candidate submits documented evidence showing use of prescription drugs under the care of a physician which do not adversely affect performance of job duties.

9. The Company reserves the right to schedule physical exams and/or drug/alcohol screening tests at any time during employment if deemed necessary by management. The cost of such exams or tests will be paid

by the Company, and medical records shall remain confidential company property.

10. Confidential medical records may be viewed by properly identified government officials investigating compliance with employment, health, and safety laws.

## Sample Employee Handbook Paragraph

*Physical Exams*

Good health is important for your personal well-being as well as your effectiveness on the job. Upon acceptance of a job offer, all new employees are expected to pass a physical exam as a condition of employment. The cost of the physical exam is paid by XYZ Company. Its purpose is to ensure that you are physically able to perform your job duties.

Employees in certain jobs may be required to participate in periodic physical exams or lab tests as part of an on-going program to ensure good safety and health.

## Sample Form

To: (applicant or employee)
From: XYZ Company

Successful completion of a preemployment physical exam is a condition of employment at XYZ Company. The purpose of the physical exam is to promote a safe and healthful working environment by ensuring that each employee is physically able to perform job duties.

You have been scheduled for a physical exam as shown:

Exam appointment: _____

Facility name: _____

Address: _____

Please sign and return indicating your consent for the exam. Upon completion, return this form to the hiring manager. Note: It is the policy of XYZ Company to make employment decisions without regard to physical or mental disability and to make reasonable accommodations for qualified disabled employees.

---

### CERTIFICATION

_____ I consent to the preemployment physical exam with drug screen for the purpose of evaluating my physical or mental condition to perform work at XYZ Company. I understand that omission or falsification of information from my medical history/records to the physician performing the Company physical exam is grounds for the company to withdraw or refuse to make an offer of employment.

*Sample Form (Continued)*

_____ I do not consent to the preemployment physical exam with drug screen. I understand that refusal to participate in the exam is grounds for the Company to withdraw or refuse to make an offer of employment.

_____          _____
Employee/applicant                                     Date

# New Employee Orientation

A new employee must adjust to many factors during the first few days and weeks on the job. Learning about the work area and lunchroom, meeting fellow employees and managers, and learning job responsibilities can seem bewildering when starting a new job. Even seasoned workers with many years experience must get acquainted with new work procedures and different coworkers during the initial period of employment.

A Company policy and program on new employee orientation is an effective way to aid the adjustment to the new job. A newly hired employee who has received a thorough introduction to the workplace will be more productive sooner than the employee who learns employer policies on a trial-and-error basis. Lack of an effective orientation program for new employees is often a contributing factor to unwanted employee turnover.

An orientation policy can help to assign responsibility to specific individuals in the organization. This defined responsibility helps to ensure that new employees become acquainted with the organization, its products or services, the facility, other workers, and assigned job duties.

The Personnel Manager at a midwest pump company developed a new orientation procedure after learning that several recently hired employees were not properly enrolled in insurance plans. The Personnel Manager created an orientation checklist which assigned responsibility for the various procedures needed to enroll new employees into payroll and benefits plans. The checklist designated the supervisor responsible for telling the new employee about job responsibilities, attendance procedures, and safety. The payroll specialist was accountable to obtain tax forms and to start time records. Explanation of benefits information, enrollment into benefits plans, and discussion of policies were handled by the Personnel Department. With this procedure, new employees received a thorough orientation with timely benefits enrollment.

## Pitfalls to Avoid

There are several common errors which reduce the effectiveness of new employee orientation procedures. Take care to avoid the following pitfalls:

1. A common orientation practice is to turn the new employee over to a senior worker for informal on-the-job instruction. The problem with

this practice is that the new employee most likely will not receive a thorough orientation. Further, employees in other departments under other supervisors will probably be told different things during orientation. As a result, orientation of new employees is likely to be sketchy and inconsistent.

2. Don't rely solely on a new employee orientation outline to assure a thorough introduction. Better results will be attained when supervisors are trained in what to say and how to conduct the orientation.

3. Avoid placing sole responsibility for new employee orientation on one person. Consider dividing responsibilities among several individuals who can provide information with which they are more familiar. For example, the supervisor can cover job duties, a manager can cover policy issues, and the human resource specialist can cover benefits issues.

4. Decline the requests of a supervisor who wants to place the employee directly on the job before orientation because of a pressing workload. Except in emergencies, it is best to complete orientation and training before placing an unfamiliar employee on a strange job.

5. Try to limit the number of forms, booklets, and information that the employee will be confronted with at orientation. Too much information presented quickly in too complex a fashion will only confuse the employee.

6. Avoid the tendency to refer to the initial period of employment as a probationary period. While the probation period implies a trial period with discharge possible once the employee passes probation, there is a greater implication of job security or tenure which may limit the firm's discretion to discharge an employee at will.

7. Avoid the tendency to specify a time period for orientation. As noted, once the probation or orientation period has passed, the implication of greater job security may affect a court judgment in a wrongful discharge lawsuit.

8. Take care not to tell an employee that he or she will receive a review after 30 or 60 days. This creates an expectation of a pay increase. Use the term *performance appraisal* as distinguished from a salary adjustment.

**Sample Policy**

**XYZ COMPANY**
**PERSONNEL POLICY & PROCEDURE**

---

SUBJECT: NEW EMPLOYEE ORIENTATION            DATE: May 1, 1993

---

*Policy*: It is the policy of XYZ Company to orientate employees to Company policies and benefits and to consider the employment relationship as

## CHECKLIST
## A New Employee Orientation Policy

The following checklist identifies important issues to consider when preparing a new employee orientation policy.

- Who will be responsible for conducting the new employee orientation—supervisor, department manager, human resource specialist?

- Will orientation responsibilities be centered on one individual or divided among several persons?

- Will fellow employees participate in the orientation process?

- What information will be included in the orientation (i.e., job duties, benefits, company policies, and/or other information)?

- Will employees be enrolled into benefits or insurance plans as part of the orientation?

- Will employees receive insurance booklets, plan descriptions, employee handbooks, or similar information?

- What forms are necessary to start the employee on payroll or to enroll into benefits plans?

- Will videocassettes, filmstrips, or other audiovisual materials be used in the orientation process?

---

"employment at will," in which the employee and the Company may elect to terminate employment at any time.

*Procedure*:

1. All employees are hired with the understanding that the employment relationship is at the will of either party, and that their continued employment is subject to the needs of the business and an acceptable level of performance, and that employment may be altered at any time at the discretion of management, or be terminated at any time with or without notice by either the employee or the Company.

2. New employees shall be instructed to report to the Personnel Department on the first day of employment. The Personnel Department representative shall instruct/assist the employee in preparing tax forms, benefits enrollment forms, and related records which are needed to place the employee on the payroll. At this time, the employee shall be advised of benefits information, employment policies, attendance policies, and related information. The Personnel Department representative shall check and sign the Orientation Checklist.

3. The Department Supervisor is responsible for orientating the employee to job duties, department procedures, safety guidelines, and related

information. Orientation details may be delegated to a designated employee so long as the Supervisor insures that employee orientation is adequate. The Supervisor and the employee are responsible for signing the Orientation Checklist and returning the form to the Personnel Department for inclusion in the individual's personnel file.

4. The orientation period provides an opportunity for the employee to evaluate the job, and it provides the Company an opportunity to carefully evaluate the employee's suitability for the job. During this time, the Supervisor is responsible for orientating the employee to work procedures and job responsibilities. The Supervisor or other designated individual shall provide job instructions, coaching, or on-the-job training as appropriate.

5. During the orientation, the Supervisor shall give careful attention to the employee's ability to learn or perform job tasks, willingness to perform assignments, attendance, punctuality, and related performance factors.

6. Corrective job instructions or disciplinary warnings shall be provided to the employee by the Supervisor as appropriate. If the employee fails to perform adequately, or does not respond to corrective job instructions or disciplinary measures, or any other reason deemed sufficient by management, the employee may be dismissed at any time during orientation or at any other time during employment. For guidelines on discipline and dismissal, see Disciplinary Procedures and Separation of Employment Policies.

7. After 60 days' employment, the Supervisor or Manager is responsible for preparing a performance evaluation form, conferring with a second-level Manager if directed, and then discussing performance issues with the employee. A pay adjustment may be recommended at this time if warranted by appropriate performance ratings. See Performance Reviews and Pay Adjustment Policies.

8. The completed performance evaluation shall be signed by the employee and then placed in the individual's personnel file. Any pay adjustment is recorded on the Payroll Change Notice and processed through payroll.

## Sample Employee Handbook Paragraph

*New Employee Orientation*

The first few weeks on a new job are a period of learning and adjustment. We recognize the importance of a new employee's orientation. During this time the employee learns Company procedures and job responsibilities with careful evaluation by the supervisor to ensure the employee's suitability for the job. An employee's failure to perform adequately, or any other reason deemed sufficient by management, could result in dismissal during the orientation period or at any other time during employment. Be sure to speak with your supervisor if you have any questions about job responsibilities.

**Sample Form**

_____<br>Employee

**NEW HIRE ORIENTATION CHECKLIST**

*Instructions*: The hiring supervisor or Manager is responsible for preparing this orientation checklist on an employee's first day of employment. This checklist, together with the specified forms, must be routed to the Personnel/Payroll Office in order to begin payroll and benefits for the new employee.

*Discuss these topics with the new employee*:

_____ Company products, services

_____ Pay information, pay day, pay reviews

_____ Job responsibilities

_____ Work schedules, lunch period

_____ Time card or time slip procedures

_____ Procedure and phone number to report absences

_____ Importance of advance notice on absences, leaves, vacation, etc.

_____ Employee handbook (provide), personnel policies, disciplinary

rules, etc.

_____ Highlights of Company benefits:

| | |
|---|---|
| Holidays | Salary continuation |
| Birthday holiday | Short-term disability |
| Vacations | Savings and investment plan |
| Health & dental insurance | Educational benefits |
| Life insurance | Service awards |
| Worker's compensation | Credit union |
| Personal/sick days | Jury pay |

_____ Proper use of telephones

_____ Conduct, appearance, and customer relations

_____ Other _____

*The following Personnel/Payroll forms must be completed*:

_____ Employment Application

_____ Reference check results (if any)

_____ State W-4 Tax Form

_____ Federal W-4 Tax Form

_____ I-9 Employment Eligibility Form

*Sample Form (Continued)*

\_\_\_\_\_ Health, Dental, Life Insurance Enrollment or Waiver

\_\_\_\_\_ Employee Handbook Orientation Receipt

\_\_\_\_\_ Receipt for Tools, Equipment, Beeper, etc.

\_\_\_\_\_ Copy of Certificate Insurance (if personal auto is used for business travel)

\_\_\_\_\_ Time record or time card for employee (start)

\_\_\_\_\_ Other _____

_____

_____          _____

Supervisor/Manager                                          Date

## Equal Employment Opportunity

More than just a legal requirement, providing equal employment opportunity is a sound business practice. The growing diversity of the labor force means that there are greater numbers of minorities and females in the job market. The aging of the U.S. population will contribute to growing numbers of older workers. Individuals with physical or mental disabilities are seeking greater workforce participation, encouraged by the provisions of the Americans with Disabilities Act of 1990.

These factors are representative of a changing labor market. The employer who limits employment opportunities by avoiding employment of protected class individuals is limiting the pool of qualified applicants. If an employer focuses employment on Caucasian males, the employer is in fact considering a class of individuals that is now a minority in terms of numbers in the labor force.

Nearly every employing organization is subject to equal employment opportunity laws. Firms employing 15 or more employees are subject to Title VII of the Civil Rights Act of 1964 enforced by the Equal Employment Opportunity Commission (EEOC). Every state except Arizona has an equal employment opportunity statute, with many state laws covering organizations as small as one or two employees. Further, in some areas there are municipal laws addressing non-discrimination in employment.

A policy statement asserting equal employment opportunity, by itself, is not enough to prevent discriminatory practices. Since equal employment laws cover all employment decisions, specific guidelines are needed to aid managers in effectively implementing this policy.

**CHECKLIST**
**Equal Employment Opportunity Policy**

The following checklist identifies important issues to consider when preparing an Equal Employment Opportunity Policy.

- Check which federal equal employment opportunity laws affect your organization (i.e., Title VII, Age Discrimination, Equal Pay, Disability Act, etc.).

- Check your state antibias laws to identify whether your organization is covered.

- Identify all protected classes covered by the various laws that apply to your organization (i.e., age, race, sex, marital status, sexual orientation, etc.).

- Specify which employment practices are covered by your policy.

- Specify who is responsible for implementing the EEO policy. What are responsibilities of employees, supervisors, managers, and human resource personnel?

- How will complaints be handled? Will there be a complaint and investigation procedure?

- Are there any municipal antibias laws which affect your organization?

- How will personnel decisions be documented to prove nondiscrimination in the event of a charge or allegation?

- What action should a supervisor take when he or she becomes aware of a discriminatory practice or complaint?

- What internal controls or audits will be defined to ensure that the organization is complying with the spirit and the letter of the law?

A policy on equal employment opportunity must accomplish a variety of purposes. First, it must identify protected class employees, specify covered employment decisions, outline guidelines for managers, provide a mechanism for individuals to present claims, and define procedures for resolution of those claims.

**Pitfalls to Avoid**

The greatest pitfall with an Equal Employment Opportunity Policy is getting past the high-sounding rhetoric and creating a policy which guides supervisors to make fair employment decisions. Here are some suggestions:

1. Don't just write a boilerplate equal employment policy and expect to be in full compliance with the law. For employees, management actions will speak much louder than words.

2. Weave equal employment opportunity guidelines into all personnel policies. Nondiscrimination issues must be addressed when writing personnel policies for recruiting, selection, training, promotions, pay administration, discipline, appraisals, discharges, and other policy areas.

3. Avoid creating a policy that is unworkable due to excessive detail or procedural limitations that hamper effective management action.

4. Take care not to confuse the concepts of affirmative action and equal employment opportunity. Firms which have a specified dollar volume of contracts with the federal government or some other government jurisdictions are subject to affirmative action requirements. Under certain circumstances, affirmative action requirements also carry through to subcontractor firms who supply goods or services to the organization with the prime contract. Affirmative action requirements generally specify that the organization develop a written plan which includes the following: a race-sex breakout of the workforce, compared to a race-sex breakout of the area labor force, with policies and procedures to achieve affirmative action hiring and employment goals. Equal employment opportunity policies, on the other hand, specify nondiscriminatory and nonpreferential treatment for all candidates and employees.

5. Take care to administer the Equal Employment Opportunity Policy and all other policies in a consistent manner for all employees. For example, excessive attention to or documentation of the discharge of a minority when other cases are not similarly documented could be viewed as a discriminatory practice. Likewise, a firm's failure to document the performance problems of a minority female because of fear of a discrimination claim and then subsequent termination of the individual was judged to be a discriminatory employment practice.

6. Avoid the tendency to oversimplify equal employment opportunity issues. Because there are so many laws, covered employment practices, and protected class individuals, it may be wise to address these topics in several different policies. Many firms, for example, define separate policies for sexual harassment or reasonable accommodation procedures for compliance with disabilities act provisions.

## Sample Policy

A sample Equal Employment Opportunity Policy follows:

**XYZ COMPANY**
**PERSONNEL POLICY & PROCEDURE**

SUBJECT: EQUAL EMPLOYMENT OPPORTUNITY    DATE: May 1, 1993

*Policy:* It is the policy of XYZ Company to provide employment opportunities without regard to race, sex, age, national origin, religion, marital status, physical or mental disability which can be reasonably accommodated, status as a military veteran, or union affiliation.

*Procedure*:

1. All employment decisions are to be made without regard to race, sex, age, national origin, religion, marital status, physical or mental disability which can be reasonably accommodated, status as a military veteran, or union affiliation. Employment decisions covered by this policy include recruiting, hiring, promotion, transfer, training, compensation, benefits, discipline, termination, and other decisions, terms, or conditions of employment.

2. Each Supervisor and Manager is responsible for administering employment practices in a manner which is consistent with this policy. The Supervisor or Manager is encouraged to confer with his or her superior and the Human Resource Administrator in making employment decisions which may be in conflict with the intent of this policy.

3. The Human Resource Administrator is responsible for keeping abreast of current issues, labor laws, etc. and for recommending changes to personnel policies or practices as appropriate. The Human Resource Administrator is responsible for investigating allegations or complaints of discrimination and for advising and assisting management in resolving such issues in the best interests of the Company.

4. In the event an employee has a question or complaint about equal opportunity employment matters, the employee should speak with his or her superior. In the event the employee is uncomfortable discussing the matter with his or her superior, the employee may speak with a Human Resource Department representative. Employee complaints shall be handled as defined in the Open Door Policy.

5. The Human Resource Administrator is responsible for maintaining necessary records and completing any required government reports.

## Sample Employee Handbook Paragraph

*Equal Employment Opportunity*

It is the policy of XYZ Company to afford equal opportunity for employment. All employment decisions are made without regard to race, color, age, sex, religion, national origin, ancestry, marital status, handicap, or unfavorable discharge from military service. Our policy applies to all employment decisions including recruitment, selection, hiring, training, promotions, transfers, appraisals, pay, benefits, discipline, separation, company activities, and other terms and conditions of employment. In the event you believe that you have been treated unfairly in any way, you may speak to the Human Resource Administrator.

# Sexual Harassment

During televised proceedings for the confirmation of Supreme Court Justice Clarence Thomas in the fall of 1991, the public witnessed firsthand the complexities of the sexual harassment controversy. Although the EEOC had issued regulations prohibiting sexual harassment 11 years earlier in 1980, the televised hearings served to reintroduce this important issue to the public. Viewers observed as Anita Hill, a law professor and former EEOC legal assistant, and Clarence Thomas, Supreme Court nominee and former head of the EEOC, related their interpretations of various incidents. The fact that sexual harassment allegations had been raised between two people whose job responsibilities were to enforce antibias laws shows just how difficult it can be to determine what is sexual harassment, to prevent harassment incidents, and to resolve claims of sexual harassment.

In early court decisions on matters related to what is now described as sexual harassment, courts held that matters of sexual relationships between employees were personal issues beyond the realm of the employment relationship or labor laws.

However, women's groups advocated a stronger government role. Pressure for governmental action continued to grow. According to a survey by a leading women's magazine in the mid-1970s, over 90 percent of women surveyed reported unwanted sexual attention on the job.[5] By 1980, the EEOC had issued regulations defining sexual harassment as a form of sex discrimination violating Title VII of the Civil Rights Act of 1964. The heart of the EEOC's regulations are as follows:

> Part 1604 Guidelines on Discrimination because of sex
> 1064.11 Sexual Harassment
> (a) Harassment on the basis of sex is a violation of Sec. 703 of Title VII. Unwelcome sexual advances, requests for sexual favors, and other verbal or physical conduct of a sexual nature constitute sexual harassment when (1) submission to such conduct is made either explicitly or implicitly a term or condition of an individual's employment, (2) submission to or rejection of such conduct by an individual is used as the basis for employment decisions affecting such individual, or (3) such conduct has the purpose or effect of unreasonably interfering with an individual's work performance or creating an intimidating, hostile, or offensive working environment.[6]

These regulations are quite vague and subject to interpretation. In issuing the regulations, the EEOC stated that each case will be evaluated on the totality of the circumstances. In one leading case which reached the U.S. Supreme Court, the Court held that a hostile or offensive working environment constitutes unlawful sexual harassment even if the employee bringing the suit suffers no economic or job benefit losses as a result of such harassment. Further, the employer, Meritor Savings Bank, was still held

**CHECKLIST**
**A Sexual Harassment Policy**

The following checklist identifies important issues to consider when preparing a Sexual Harassment Policy.

■ Who is covered by the Sexual Harassment Policy—employees, supervisors and management, customers, vendors, the public?

■ Will specific actions be identified as examples of sexual harassment? If so, what actions are viewed as harassment?

■ What responsibilities are assigned to employees, supervisors, or managers to prevent or control harassment?

■ How will complaints be handled? Will there be a complaint investigation procedure?

■ What actions should a supervisor take when he or she becomes aware of a discriminatory practice?

■ Will the Human Resource Administrator or other specialist be identified as an independent resource to handle and resolve claims of sexual harassment?

■ What steps will be taken to protect the confidentiality of the harassment victim and alleged offender?

■ What investigatory procedures will be used to ascertain the facts of the case?

■ What corrective measures will be used on the offender to address confirmed instances of sexual harassment (i.e., transfer, warning notice, demotion, discharge, etc.)?

■ What steps will be taken to prevent any retaliation against an individual for raising a harassment complaint or assisting in a harassment investigation?

liable even though employee Vinson failed to raise the issue under the organization's complaint procedure.[7]

For human resource specialists, the sexual harassment issue presents a whole host of issues and problems to address. What about romantic relations between employees? What are the liabilities of a consenting relationship between a supervisor and an employee? What if someone complains because our best sales rep is a womanizer? The EEOC holds the employer accountable for controlling unwanted sexual attention occurring between employees, supervisors, and subordinates, or customers if the employer knows or should have known of the conduct.

Further, the EEOC recommends that firms take proactive measures to prevent sexual harassment by developing a policy and communicating information to employees.

## Pitfalls to Avoid

One of the greatest difficulties in developing a Sexual Harassment Policy is defining what actions constitute sexual harassment. Here are some pitfalls to avoid when preparing your policy on sexual harassment.

1. Avoid trying to list every conceivable incident that might be viewed as sexual harassment. Rather, in a manner similar to the EEOC regulations, identify broad categories and examples of conduct which may be considered sexual harassment.

2. Take care to avoid making light of the sexual harassment issue when defining policy and in responding to any sexual harassment claims. When an individual presents a claim of sexual harassment, it is often with a great deal of trepidation, fear for job security, and concern for reputation of self and the offending party.

3. Do not limit sexual harassment complaints to normal grievance or complaint channels. Often, the sexual harasser is an individual's supervisor or other manager with authority to exercise adverse control over the victim's employment relationship. Be sure to define a complaint procedure in the harassment policy which allows the aggrieved employee to present his or her complaint to a human resource specialist, counselor, employee advocate, chief executive, or other independent third party.

4. In administration of the sexual harassment policy, take care to ensure that it does not result in an adverse employment decision affecting only the female complainant. Such outcome will limit the effectiveness of your policy in resolving harassment allegations and may even be judged to be a discriminatory practice in any claims which come before the EEOC or state antibias agency.

## Sample Policy

**XYZ COMPANY**
**PERSONNEL POLICY & PROCEDURE**

---

SUBJECT: SEXUAL HARASSMENT                     DATE: May 1, 1993

---

*Policy*: It is the policy of XYZ Company to maintain a work environment which is free from intimidation, coercion, or harassment, including sexual harassment.

*Procedure*:
1. All employees are responsible for conducting themselves in a business-like manner which provides respect to others. Any behavior or action which is unduly coercive, intimidating, harassing, or sexual in nature is inappropriate and prohibited. This guideline applies to all business or related interactions between employees, supervisors or managers, customers, vendors, visitors, etc.

2. Each supervisor or manager is responsible for administering employment practices in a manner which is consistent with this policy. The supervisor or manager is encouraged to confer with his or her superior or the Human Resource Administrator in making employment decisions which may be in conflict with the intent of this policy.

3. All individuals are urged to exercise common sense and respect for individuals in the exercise of this policy. Incidents of harassment may be subjective in nature. As a guide for supervisors and managers, sexual harassment is defined below based on government definitions:

    Unwelcome sexual advances, requests for sexual favors, and other verbal or physical conduct of a sexual nature constitute sexual harassment when a) submission to such conduct is made either explicitly or implicitly a term or condition of an individual's employment, b) submission to or rejection of such conduct by an individual is used as the basis for employment decisions affecting such individual, or c) such conduct has the purpose or effect of unreasonably interfering with an individual's work performance or creating an intimidating, hostile, or offensive working environment.

4. In the event of a question, complaint, or allegation regarding fair employment practices, any employee may speak with his or her supervisor or manager. In the event the employee is not comfortable discussing the matter with the supervisor or manager, the employee may contact the designated individual responsible for personnel.

5. When or if a supervisor or manager becomes aware of an incident of harassment, the matter should be discussed with his or her superior or the individual responsible for personnel. The matter shall be investigated in a discreet and confidential manner. Investigation may include private discussions with the complainant, the alleged harasser, and any witnesses.

6. Company management shall consider the facts of the case and take corrective action as deemed appropriate in the best interests of the Company and the individual(s). Such action may include counseling, disciplinary warning, transfer, demotion, discharge, or other action as deemed appropriate.

7. Employees, supervisors, and managers are cautioned to consider allegations of harassment as a serious matter which should be resolved discreetly and confidentially in order to minimize work disruption and potential liability.

8. In the event the complaining employee is not satisfied with the results of action taken as defined above, the employee may request that the matter be reviewed by a Company officer or the Company President, if necessary, for a final decision.

## Transfers

Every organization deals with employee transfers. Transfers can occur between jobs, work locations, shifts, or departments. Transfers may be initiated by the organization to move an employee to another assignment

## CHECKLIST
## A Transfer Policy

- What kinds of transfers will be defined in the transfer policy—temporary transfer, indefinite transfer, or employee-requested transfer?

- Will transfers be permitted between jobs, departments, work shifts, locations?

- Is the likelihood of job transfers sufficiently significant to make acceptance of transfers a requirement or condition of employment?

- Will an employee's family or personal needs be considered a reasonable basis for an employee to turn down a job transfer offered by the company?

- Are there any different benefits, pay rates, or pay differentials associated with different job categories?

- How will pay or benefits differentials be applied to employees transferring in? transferring out? to temporary transfers? to indefinite transfers?

- What criteria will be used to evaluate candidates for transfer if two or more persons are considered for a job opening?

- What factors will be considered when evaluating an employee's request for transfer?

- Are there union agreement limitations to transfers?

- What reasonable accommodations may be made for disabled workers or for the religious beliefs of the employee?

in response to staffing requirements. Employees may also request transfers. Transfers may be temporary, lasting a day, a week, or a month. Or transfers may be indefinite in duration. A personnel policy on transfers helps to sort out these various issues and guide the reassignment of employees to other jobs.

The process of transferring employees raises questions about pay rates, shift differential pay, reporting relationships, and duration of assignments. Transfers can also result in relocations for employees and their families. If these issues are not resolved, the employee will not be fully effective on the new job assignment.

As a general guide for most organizations, transfers can be addressed in three categories: temporary, indefinite, and employee requested.

Temporary transfer of an employee to a special short-term assignment is a common practice in many organizations. Typical examples of temporary transfers are assignment to perform physical inventory, reassignment to another job or department to help complete a rush order for a major customer, or transfer from a branch store to the main store during a special clearance sale.

Management wants the flexibility to move or reassign individuals to perform special tasks in response to unique situations or for prompt handling of rush orders. In temporary transfers, the employee typically performs the same job or another routine task that can be easily learned. At the conclusion of the temporary assignment, the employee is returned to his or her regular job assignment. Temporary transfer assignments are normally initiated by management. If the organization has a practice of periodically reassigning employees for temporary transfers, it is important to let new employees know that transfers are a normal part of job responsibilities.

An indefinite transfer of an employee is made when management needs to move an employee from one job to another for an extended time period. For example, if a manufacturing firm is adding a night shift, some employees from the day shift may be transferred to nights, assuring a core of experienced workers qualified to train other newly hired night shift workers. Likewise, an organization opening a new branch office or store is likely to transfer some experienced workers from existing locations to the new location.

An indefinite transfer is distinguished from a promotion. A transfer is a lateral move that involves performing the same or similar job, often without increase in compensation because of the similarity of job responsibilities. The transferred employee may, however, receive a pay differential because of a shift change or other similar factor. This is different from a promotion, in which the employee assumes a new job with greater responsibilities and increased compensation.

In an employee-requested transfer, management considers the employee's request for transfer and then makes the job change if the change is beneficial to the organization. As in the other transfer categories, the transfer may be to another job, department, shift, or work location.

In evaluating an employee's transfer request, several factors are considered: job opening, employee qualifications, and availability of a trained replacement. Another factor considered by some organizations is a requirement for a specified time period on the present job, which minimizes frequent transfers and excessive job changes.

The checklist on page 147 identifies important issues to consider when preparing a Transfer Policy.

## Pitfalls to Avoid

A major concern with a transfer policy is protecting the organization's flexibility in reassigning employees to meet business needs while minimizing the disruption of unnecessary or excessive job changes. Here are some potential troublespots to avoid:

1. Don't give up the flexibility to make temporary transfers when needed to respond to unique business conditions. Protect the prerogative to assign employees to special tasks. There are several ways to address this issue. First, explain special projects or temporary transfer possibilities during the employee selection process and during orientation when discussing job responsibilities. Second, include a reference to special projects or assignments in job descriptions as well as a statement that the incumbent is expected to perform other duties as assigned. Third, assert management's right to transfer employees in policy manuals and employee handbooks.

2. If frequent transfers are an important aspect of meeting staffing needs, protect this prerogative by making availability for transfer a condition of employment. A regional retail organization, for example, operated 20 small stores in a metropolitan area. To assure adequate supervision of its many stores, the firm required new store managers to be available for transfer or reassignment to any store in the area.

3. On the other hand, you can avoid hardships to employees (which cause unnecessary turnover) by allowing employes to accept or decline transfers. In the present U.S. workforce, with large numbers of dual career families and single-parent workers, job transfers may cause serious interference with personal schedules. From this perspective, transfer policies can be tailored to be responsive to employee needs as well as business requirements.

**Sample Policy**

**XYZ COMPANY**
**PERSONNEL POLICY & PROCEDURE**

---

SUBJECT: TRANSFERS                                        DATE: May 1, 1993

---

*Policy*: It is the policy of XYZ Company to transfer employees as needed to respond to business requirements and to consider employee requests for transfers.

*Procedure*:
1. The company reserves the right to transfer employees on a temporary basis to other jobs or special assignments as needed to meet staffing needs. For the purpose of this policy, a temporary transfer is defined as a job assignment of 30 calendar days or less.

2. When a job opening occurs, the supervisor is responsible for preparing an employee requisition defining the job, responsibilities, and qualifi-

cations. The requisition, with attached job description if available, shall be routed to the Department Manager for approval and then to the Human Resource Department.

3. The Human Resource Specialist is responsible for scanning employee files to identify current employees who may be suitable candidates for transfer or promotion to the open position.

4. In the event an employee requests transfer to another job, the transfer request shall be handled in the following manner:

   a) The employee shall submit a transfer request form to his or her supervisor, listing new position sought and reason for transfer. The employee must have a minimum of six months in his or her present position to request a transfer.

   b) Transfer requests shall be held in the Human Resource Department for review when job openings occur.

   c) At the time that a suitable opening occurs, the transfer request shall be forwarded to the hiring supervisor.

   d) The transfer may be approved at the discretion of the hiring supervisor and Department Manager if the employee is qualified to perform the job and a suitable replacement is identified for the transferred employee.

5. Any candidates for transfer shall be evaluated based upon their experience, skills, abilities, and education compared to the job requirements.

6. Compensation for transferred employees shall be handled as follows:

   a) There is no change in regular pay for an employee who is transferred on a temporary basis.

   b) Employees transferred to nights receive the night shift differential. Employees transferring indefinitely from nights to days lose the night shift differential; the night shift differential is continued during temporary transfers from nights to days.

   c) A transfer to a job at the same pay grade results in no pay adjustment. An indefinite transfer to a job at a lower pay grade will result in the employee's pay being adjusted to the new pay range.

7. The scheduling of the transfer shall be coordinated and agreed upon by the respective supervisors.

8. All transfers shall be recorded on the employee change notice. The hiring supervisor is responsible for preparing the change notice and routing it through the Department Manager to the Human Resource Department.

## Sample Employee Handbook Paragraph

*Transfers*

XYZ Company is a growing company where all employees must work together to make our operation a success. There are occasions when it is necessary to transfer employees from one job to another on a temporary basis in order to meet the needs of our customers. Please cooperate when your supervisor asks you to handle a special assignment.

If there is an available opening and an employee wants to change shifts, the Company will try to accommodate an employee's request. However, the Company does not make a habit of frequently changing shifts for employees.

**Sample Form**

**TRANSFER REQUEST FORM**

Employee _____ Date _____

I request a transfer as shown below:

| Present | Requested |
|---------|-----------|
| Job _____ | Job _____ |
| Shift _____ | Shift _____ |
| Department _____ | Department _____ |
| Location _____ | Location _____ |

Reason for Transfer: _____

_____

_____

Authorized:

_____     _____
Supervisor                                                    Date

_____     _____
Human Resource Department                         Date

# Promotions

Promotion to a higher-paying job with greater responsibilities is an excellent way to reward a deserving employee. For many employees, career advancement and the opportunity for greater earnings are significant motivators which can contribute to organizational loyalty.

Promotion policies are generally seen as good for morale. Often, employees seek employment at a particular firm because of career advancement potential. For these reasons, many organizations have a philosophy of trying to promote from within whenever possible.

Some managers, however, report concerns about promotion policies. The Plant Manager at a graphic arts facility complained that promotion policies complicate the hiring process. He stated that when he promotes a helper to a press operator, this results in succeeding openings for press helper, press trainee, and jogger—creating a total of four openings, three promotions, one new hire, and all four employees on the press learning the job so productivity and quality are down.

Likewise, an office manager expressed dismay over a promotion dilemma in which two equally qualified subordinates were under consideration for the job. Although both deserved the job, only one could be promoted and the other would be disappointed.

In spite of the difficulties discussed in these examples, there is a greater likelihood of low employee morale and productivity problems if the firm disregards qualified employees on staff to hire an outsider.

A common practice at many organizations is the use of a job bidding promotion procedure. With a job bidding procedure, job openings are posted on the bulletin board for several days. Employees who are interested in the opening are encouraged to bid on the job by following specified application procedures. Advantages of a job bid procedure are that employees are aware of job openings, interested individuals may seek consideration, and management is in a position to respond to individuals who seek career advancement.

Organizations that have a union generally must comply with a job bid procedure. In some union contracts, a more rigid promotion process requires the job to go to the most senior worker in the next lower job category.

The checklist on the next page identifies important issues to consider when preparing a job bid Promotion Policy.

### Pitfalls to Avoid

While a promotion-from-within policy is a good employee relations tool, supervisors may see it as a hindrance to quickly filling a job opening. Here are some pitfalls to avoid:

1. Don't make this policy too cumbersome or complex. Generally, when a job opening occurs, line management wants to move quickly to fill the vacancy. If the job bid procedure seems to cause excessive delays in filling the job, managers are likely to subvert the process.

2. Take care to assure that all jobs covered by the policy are posted, even if a Department Manager has a "shoe-in" candidate who is in line for the job. Failure to post all covered jobs will lead to charges of favoritism. Posting the job and interviewing all candidates allows management to evaluate candidates and counsel those who are not selected.

3. Avoid the tendency to disregard hiring criteria or qualifications. Employees will be quick to note if an unqualified employee is selected.

### Competitive Practice

The chart in Fig. 7.3 shows promotion-from-within practices.

## CHECKLIST
## A Promotion Policy

Which jobs are covered by the job bid promotion policy—plant, office, union, nonmanagerial, etc.?

- Must the job bid promotion policy be concluded by consideration and rejection of all internal candidates before recruiting from outside sources, or may job bid and external recruitment occur simultaneously?

- How long are jobs posted?

- What application process will be specified?

- Will a supervisor be permitted to pass over all job bid candidates if none is judged qualified for the job?

- If two candidates are judged to be equally qualified, what criteria will be used to select the one for promotion?

- Who will be responsible for counseling those job bid candidates who are not selected for promotion?

- Are there any labor agreement requirements for a job bid procedure?

- What candidate evaluation and selection techniques will be used?

- How will promotions and transfer of individuals be coordinated?

- What steps will be taken to insure that promotions are made on a nondiscriminatory basis?


**Sample Policy**

### XYZ COMPANY
### PERSONNEL POLICY & PROCEDURE

SUBJECT: JOB BID PROMOTION POLICY        DATE: May 1, 1993

*Policy*: It is the policy of XYZ Company to encourage promotion from within by posting nonmanagement jobs and considering current employees before considering new hires.

*Procedure*:

1. When a full-time job opening occurs, the supervisor is responsible for preparing a personnel requisition specifying job title, qualifications, and a summary of responsibilities. The requisition shall be referred through the Department Manager to the Human Resource Administrator.

2. The Human Resource Administrator is responsible for preparing the job bid form and posting copies on Company bulletin boards. The job bid form shall remain posted for four workdays.

3. The job bid form shall instruct interested candidates to notify their

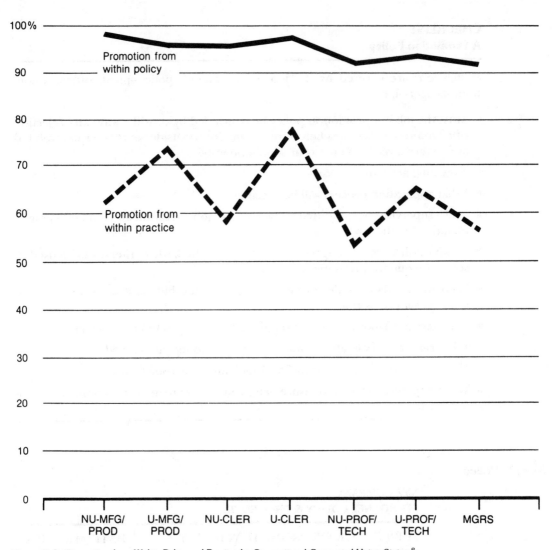

**Figure 7.3.** Promotion from Within Policy and Practice by Occupational Group and Union Status.[8]

    supervisor of their interest in the posted position and then complete a job interest form in the Human Resource Department.

4. At the completion of the four-day job posting period, the Human Resource Administrator shall remove all job postings from bulletin boards. Employment and education information on the individuals completing the job interest forms shall be referred to the hiring supervisor.

5. The Human Resource Administrator shall

    a) Conduct a preliminary screening interview with interested candidates to ascertain basic qualifications and explain job functions of the posted position. At this time, clearly unqualified or disinterested candidates should be screened out of the selection process.

b) Coordinate and schedule interviews of interested candidates with the hiring supervisor.

6. Once the hiring supervisor has conducted interviews and conferred with the Department Manager, a job offer and pay rate may be formulated. The hiring supervisor must then confer with the individual's present supervisor to coordinate the transfer. The hiring supervisor may then contact the employee to communicate the job offer.

7. The Human Resource Administrator is responsible for counseling any employees who bid for the job but were not selected.

8. In the event that no internal candidates are deemed suitable for the position in the judgment of the hiring supervisor and Department Manager, the supervisor may request that the Human Resource Administrator begin recruitment of candidates from outside the organization. At the request of a Department Manager, outside recruitment contacts may be made concurrently with the job bid procedure.

9. Any promotion or transfer resulting from the job bid procedure shall be recorded on the employee change notice. The employee change notice shall be prepared by the hiring supervisor. The employee change notice is routed for signature/approval through the Department Manager, Human Resource Administrator, Payroll Clerk, and then returned to the individual's personnel file.

## Sample Employee Handbook Paragraph

*Job Bid Promotion Policy*

Promotion from within is an important part of our practice of recognizing and rewarding capable employees. Employees meeting the qualifications for job vacancies will receive consideration for promotion. Plant job openings are posted on the Company bulletin board. If you feel that you are qualified to perform a posted job, you are encouraged to speak with your supervisor and arrangements will be made for an interview with the hiring supervisor. There are occasions, however, when it becomes necessary to select job candidates from outside the Company because there are no employees possessing the qualifications and skills required for an open position.

## Sample Forms

### JOB BID ANNOUNCEMENT

| | | |
|---|---|---|
| Job Opening: | Accounting Clerk | Posting Period: |
| Department: | Accounting | June 1–4, 1993 |

*Summary*: Performs accounts payable entries on computerized record system. Verifies invoices, computes, discounts, and posts data to ledgers.

*Sample Form (Continued)*

*Qualifications*: High school education; knowledge of accounting, accounts payable procedures, and double entry bookkeeping, computer literate; accurate math skills.

To be considered, contact: Human Resource Department

**JOB INTEREST FORM**

Employee Name: _____

Job Sought: _____

Present Job: _____

List any skills, abilities, or experience which you believe qualifies you for the

job sought: _____

_____

_____

_____

_____

_____

_____        _____
Employee Signature                                      Date

## Personnel Records

Most organizations keep some type of personnel records for the administration of payroll and benefits. Federal government labor laws, wage hour laws, and many similar state laws specify certain records that must be maintained by employers. These laws define certain minimum records retention requirements. In some instances, the law specifies a certain form upon which personnel information must be recorded. The I-9 employment eligibility form required by the Immigration and Naturalization Service or the EEO-1 reporting form required by the Equal Employment Opportunity Commission are examples. In many instances, however, the employer is free to select the form in which the records will be maintained. Some states have laws which deal with the issues of personnel records privacy and employee access to personnel files.

A policy on personnel records is important because it helps to clarify two important issues: (1) retention of records required by law, and (2) protection of records confidentiality.

Many firms use Human Resources Information Systems (HRIS) to maintain computerized personnel records. Larger organizations are likely to tailor HRIS systems to their specific needs. Smaller and mid-sized firms, on the other hand, are more likely to purchase one of the many packaged HRIS programs available on the market for personal computer applications.

Accurate personnel records serve a variety of useful purposes, including the following:

- They ensure compliance with federal and state laws. A firm that has records as required by law will avoid penalties for failure to maintain the specified records.

- A firm that has accurate personnel records has a better framework for consistency and fairness in personnel decisions. A lack of records contributes to inconsistency and discriminatory practices, which can result in staff dissension, lower morale, or discrimination charges.

- Maintenance of personnel records helps an organization to better utilize its human resources. As organizations grow, it becomes harder for top managers to know each employee's capabilities personally. With personnel records that reflect the individual's education, experience, job history, and performance levels, management can make more informed personnel decisions.

- Accurate records of personnel actions can help a company to prevail in unemployment compensation hearings.

- Adequate records documenting personnel decisions are an important basis for defending against discrimination charges or wrongful discharge lawsuits.

Among the factors that a Personnel Records Policy should define are which records to maintain. An organization may elect, for example, to keep records on wage, hours, employee name/address, benefits enrollment, performance ratings, physical exams, preemployment drug screen, and workplace accidents. While all of this information could be kept in the firm's personnel files, I recommend that separate files be maintained for certain information. The following chart shows one approach for separating personnel files.

| File | Items Included |
|------|----------------|
| Payroll File | Wages, hours |
|  | Tax exemptions |
|  | Wage deduction orders |
| Personnel File | Application/resume |

| File | Items Included |
|------|----------------|
| | Pay rates |
| | Performance ratings* |
| | Disciplinary warnings |
| | I-9 |
| | Orientation checklist |
| | Policy receipts |
| | Absence requests; attendance |
| Health Records | Physical exam |
| | Drug screen |
| | Health records |
| Safety File | Accident records |
| | Safety training |
| | Hazard communication orientation |

The checklist on page 159 identifies important issues to consider when preparing a Personnel Records Policy.

## Pitfalls to Avoid

There are several pitfalls to avoid when defining a Personnel Records Policy.

1. One major concern is to protect the confidentiality of personnel records. The best way to do this is to assign responsibility for file maintenance to a designated individual. Also, be sure that records are kept in locked drawers or file cabinets. Make sure that computerized records are protected by access codes which are periodically revised.

2. Don't allow personnel records to become an accumulation of miscellaneous documents about employees. Limit personnel files for storage of job-related information about the employee. Avoid accumulation of records that are not job related.

3. Avoid the tendency to allow supervisors unrestricted latitude in responding to reference check inquiries by other area employers. Some firms have found themselves on the losing end of a lawsuit by a former employee because of poor handling of employment references. An untrained supervisor carelessly giving a bad reference about a former employee could create a liability for libel or defa-

*I-9 records may be kept in a file that is separate from personnel files. This has the advantage of easy accessability of I-9 records in the event of inspection by representatives of the Labor Department or Immigration and Naturalization Service.

**CHECKLIST**
**A Personnel Records Policy**

- What records requirements are specified by federal or state labor laws?

- What information and records should go into personnel files?

- Will separate files be maintained for medical, payroll, safety, or other related issues?

- Will employees receive copies of personnel documents such as approvals or disciplinary warnings?

- Will computerized personnel records systems be used?

- What steps will be taken to protect confidentiality of computerized records?

- Who is responsible for maintaining personnel records?

- Will supervisors be permitted to keep duplicate or separate personnel records on their subordinates?

- Where will files be stored, and what actions will be taken to protect records confidentiality?

- Who will have access to employee records—managers, supervisors, payroll specialists, etc.?

- How will reference or credit check inquiries be handled?

- Will employees be permitted access to their own personnel files?

mation lawsuit. The best preventative action is to refer reference inquiries to the personnel records specialist. Release references only in response to written inquiries. Limit the reference check to verifying dates of employment and job title(s) and confirming salary if the other employer provides data given by the employee. Avoid detailed subjective evaluations of unverifiable performance information.

4. Avoid unnecessary restrictions on employees viewing their own files. While some states have laws requiring the employer to grant the employee access to his or her file, most states are silent on the matter. In my 20-plus years' experience in human resources, I have found that it is best to grant an employee's request to see his or her personnel file. When permitting the employee to view the file, the viewing should take place in the presence of a supervisor, manager, or human resource specialist. This prevents unauthorized removal of documents and permits an exploratory discussion to ascertain the employee's concern. By learning about the employee's concern, management can take action to remedy the situation.

**Sample Policy**

XYZ COMPANY
PERSONNEL POLICY & PROCEDURE

SUBJECT: PERSONNEL RECORDS                         DATE: May 1, 1993

*Policy*: It is the policy of XYZ Company to maintain confidential employee records as necessary for administration of benefits and management of personnel.

*Procedure*:

1. All employee records are to be stored in a central file maintained by the Vice President or a designated office employee. Records for salary and insurance information are stored separately and maintained by the individual responsible for payroll administration. Medical records, medical claims, physical exams, or drug/alcohol screening tests shall be stored separately in a file maintained by the Vice President.

2. All personnel and payroll records are confidential and shall be stored in locked filing cabinets when not in use. Access to personnel records is limited to a need-to-know basis. Top management, the Plant Manager, or supervisors may be permitted access to personnel records of those employees under their supervision. Access to review a personnel file shall be approved by the Plant Manager or top management.

3. The employee is responsible for keeping the Company notified of any changes of information such as change of address, name, telephone number, marital status, number of dependents and tax exemptions, insurance beneficiary, and related information.

4. An employee may be granted limited and supervised access to his or her personnel file to verify accuracy of information contained in the file. Under no circumstances will an employee be permitted access to personnel records of other employees.

5. All credit or reference check inquiries are to be referred to the Bookkeeper or management. Information released for reference checks shall be pursuant to written inquiries and limited to verifying an employee's date of employment, job title(s), and salary or salary history.

6. An employee's personnel file shall normally consist of the following records:

   Employment application or resume
   Employee information or records update notice
   Income tax withholding forms
   Job assignment/history record
   Attendance record
   Schooling or training records
   Documents supporting leave of absence requests
   Letters of commendation, warning, or discipline
   Any other similar records necessary for effective management of personnel
   Separate records are maintained for benefits enrollment, salary, and salary history.

7. Records of information which is not reasonably job related shall not be maintained. Disciplinary warnings which are more than 12 months old shall be removed from the file and shall not be considered under the Company's policy of corrective discipline.

8. Personnel files of separated employees shall be removed from the regular personnel file and stored in another file section or drawer.

## Sample Employee Handbook Paragraph

*Personnel Records*

At the start of employment, the Company establishes a personnel file for you in order to administer the benefits and insurances. Your cooperation is requested to keep these records up to date. Please notify the Human Resource Department if there is a change in any of the following records:

a. name, address, and telephone number
b. marital status or number of dependents
c. number of income tax exemptions
d. beneficiary of group insurance
e. persons to notify in case of emergency

If there is a question regarding information in your personnel file, you may speak to the Human Resource Manager.

# Job Descriptions

The job description's usefulness in recruiting, screening, training, compensating, and evaluating employees makes it an important part of an organization's personnel practices. Job descriptions are assuming even greater importance under the Americans with Disabilities Act (ADA). The ADA states that employers must give equal treatment to qualified disabled workers who are able to perform essential functions of the job. Further, the law recognizes a job description, prepared before advertising and interviewing, as evidence of essential job functions.

For these reasons, every organization should have a policy to guide management in the preparation and maintenance of job descriptions. A personnel policy can guide supervisors and managers in preparation, use, and maintenance of job descriptions. The preparation and updating of a job description should be a management responsibility. The Human Resource Specialist can provide advice to assure that the description is accurate, thorough, and in a proper format. These details can be defined in the personnel policy on job descriptions.

The checklist on page 162 identifies important issues to consider when preparing a Job Description Policy.

**CHECKLIST**
**A Job Description Policy**

- Who is responsible for preparing the job descriptions (i.e., supervisor, manager, or other specialist)?

- Who is responsible for reviewing and editing job descriptions (i.e., manager or Human Resource Specialist)?

- Who is responsible for updating or revising job descriptions?

- What information, style, and format will be used for job descriptions?

- Who will be permitted to see and/or receive job description copies (i.e., supervisor, employee, manager)?

- What procedures will be used to reevaluate the job following any changes in duties or responsibilities?

**Pitfalls to Avoid**

The following are several suggestions for avoiding problems with job descriptions:

1. One challenge to the Human Resource Specialist is to make sure that job descriptions are prepared in a uniform format by supervisors or managers. Training and instruction in proper job description preparation techniques, provision of format samples, and review of job descriptions are keys to consistency in job description preparation. Firms that have old job descriptions should review and revise the descriptions to reflect actual job tasks now performed by employees.

2. Timely revision of job descriptions is another major concern. Since jobs, responsibilities, and incumbents change from time to time, the job description must be reviewed for accuracy periodically and revised when necessary.

3. Avoid the tendency to use gender-based terms or arbitrary requirements in job descriptions. Gender-based terms such as *foreman* or arbitrary requirements such as high school or college degree could be viewed as discriminatory and in violation of antibias laws.

4. As with all employment documents, job descriptions should include a disclaimer which asserts management's right to change job duties. Likewise, policy guidelines for supervisors should include precautions against promises or commitments which could limit employment-at-will prerogatives.

**Sample Policy**

**XYZ COMPANY**
**PERSONNEL POLICY & PROCEDURE**

SUBJECT: JOB DESCRIPTIONS                    DATE: May 1, 1993

*Policy*: It is the policy of XYZ Company to define job descriptions to promote effective communication of job duties and qualifications and to aid in making reasonable accommodations for qualified disabled workers.

*Procedure*:

1. The supervisor is responsible for preparing a job description for each full-time and part-time position in the work unit. A job description shall be prepared when a new job is created or when job duties are significantly changed. The job description is subject to review and approval of the Department Manager.

2. Job descriptions shall be prepared in a standardized format with a job title, job summary, qualifications, and typical duties. The following guidelines are provided:

   a) Avoid use of gender-based job titles, such as *foreman*.

   b) List major job functions and provide examples of tasks performed.

   c) Begin each job function with an action verb, such as *plans, analyzes, sorts, checks, assembles, operates*, etc.

   d) Identify tasks performed, examples of decisions made, equipment operated, and nature of contacts with others.

3. A sample job description is attached to this policy. Upon completion of the job description and its approval by the Department Manager, the description shall be referred to the Human Resource Specialist, who is responsible for the following:

   a) Review and edit the job description to fit the designated format.

   b) Check the description to ensure it complies with non-discrimination requirements.

   c) Analyze job to determine exempt, nonexempt status.

   d) Evaluate the job and assign pay level.

   e) Maintain a central file of all job descriptions.

4. The supervisor is responsible for providing a copy of the job description to new employees at time of hire.

5. The supervisor is encouraged to refer to the job description for the following personnel activities:

   a) when interviewing job candidates

   b) when orienting and training new employees

   c) when preparing an employee performance appraisal

**Sample Employee Handbook
Paragraph**

*Job Descriptions*

At time of hire, each employee receives a job description as part of the new employee orientation materials. Your job description is a brief summary of typical duties. Be sure to speak with your supervisor if you have questions about job responsibilities. Please recognize that job responsibilities may change from time to time. Also, all employees are expected to fill in to assist others and perform other duties as directed by their supervisor.

**Sample Job Description**

**JOB DESCRIPTION**

Order Entry Clerk                                                    Page 1
                                                                    June 1, 1991

*Summary*: Under general supervision, the Order Entry Clerk is responsible for entering and processing orders for established accounts, monitoring inventory levels, and related tasks. REPORTS TO: Director of Administration.

*Qualifications*:
- High school education, preferably supplemented by advanced training in office procedures and business skills.
- 2 years' experience in customer service and order entry.
- Possess understanding of customer service and order entry procedures, excellent telephone skills, ability to handle pressure, and typing skill of approximately 40–45 wpm. Knowledge of computerized record systems helpful.
- Any other equivalent combination of training and experience.

*Typical Duties and Responsibilities*:
1. Receives customer orders by mail or telephone for products to be drop-shipped from inventory or directly from supplier. Verifies accuracy of data and contacts customer or superior in the event of discrepancy. Checks account book for order processing instructions. Operates computer terminal to enter order onto computerized record system by key entering data for price codes, part numbers, etc. Enters data to change orders when necessary. Writes notes or special instructions on order processing documents as necessary to assure proper handling of order by others.
2. Confers with superior to review new customer orders to identify need for special procedures or inventory control program. Creates files, procedures, and reports as needed to properly administer orders.
3. Receives customer telephone inquiries regarding status of orders or deliveries. Checks order status and reports information to customer. Communicates order information or changes between departments.

May solve routine problems related to order information, changes, status, or delivery. May provide information about product availability or established prices. Uses tact and diplomacy when dealing with customers on the telephone.

4. Operates computer printer to create open order report. Compares report to original orders and resolves discrepancies. Prints packing lists and routes to appropriate department.

5. Monitors inventory records on computerized record system. Operates computer terminal to query stock status when handling customer orders or checking inventory levels. Notifies Sales Coordinator when inventories become low. Operates computer printer to periodically print and distribute order status report, inventory report, and related data. Tracks and resolves inventory discrepancies.

6. Sets up customer file and inventory records for new accounts in computerized record system. Based on instructions from sales, sets up customer records, product information, part numbers, and related data. Records any special order handling procedures.

7. Operates computer terminal to access data, enter data, and change or delete data as necessary according to prescribed procedures for order entry. Selects prescribed screen format, follows menu cues, and reads or enters data as necessary. May refer to computer reference manual or superior in the event of computer entry difficulty. May operate computer system to prepare back-up diskettes.

8. May perform related duties or fill in for others in the department or other departments when requested. May train or instruct fellow workers regarding own duties. Fills in at switchboard in the absence of Receptionist/Switchboard Attendant.

9. Operates necessary office equipment such as telephone, calculator, copier, computer terminal, etc. Requisitions office supplies needed in the department.

10. Collects, sorts, and organizes data for routine or special business reports. May copy, collate, assemble, and distribute reports as requested. Performs special projects or tasks when requested by superior.

11. Maintains records and files related to own work. Organizes records and work efforts to assure timely accomplishment of tasks.

12. Periodically checks work area and maintains a neat and orderly work area. Observes Company policies related to dress, appearance, attendance, employment, etc.

13. Performs other duties as assigned.

Job duties are subject to change as directed by management.[9]

## Notes

1. *Human Resource Policies and Practices in American Firms,* U.S. Dept. of Labor, BLMR 137, 1989, p. 53.

2. 29 CFR, Part 1607, Uniform Guidelines on Employee Selection Procedures, © 1978.

3. Title 29, USCA Chapter 22, Employee Polygraph Protection.

4. *Human Resource Policies and Practices in American Firms,* U.S. Dept. of Labor, BLMR 137, 1989, p. 41.

5. W. Hubbartt, "How to Limit Liability in Sexual Harassment Cases," *Office Systems '87,* July, 1987, p. 25.

6. 29 CFR, Part 1604. Discrimination Because of Sex Under Title VII of the Civil Rights Act of 1964 as Amended, Adoption of Final Interpretive Guidelines. Section 1604.11(a).

7. *Meritor Savings Bank FSB* v. *Vinson* (477 U.S. 57).

8. *Human Resource Policies and Practices in American Firms,* U.S. Department of Labor, BLMR 137, 1989, p. 42.

9. W. Hubbartt, *Performance Appraisal Manual for Managers and Supervisors,* Commerce Clearing House, Chicago, IL, 1992, p. 70.

# 8

# Work Hours, Employee Schedules, and Control Attendance

**Read Chapter 8 for:**

Work hours and the work week
Lunch and break periods
Overtime work
Flex-time schedules
Attendance control
Time records
Voting time

## Work Hours and the Work Week

The establishment of working hours, starting times, and work schedules is a necessity in every organization. While many firms schedule employees on a traditional 9:00 a.m. to 5:00 p.m. day shift schedule, numerous other organizations have work schedules that include evenings, weekends, and overnight work.

There are many factors that influence working hours. Business hours must be defined to identify when the organization will be open to serve customers. For example, most retail firms have evening and weekend work schedules as well as daytime hours.

The public service nature of some organizations dictates around-the-clock service. Health care, public transportation, police, fire, and utilities are common examples of sectors which provide 24-hour service to the community. Business volume affects manufacturing hours. As a result, many factories schedule overtime work or 24-hour production operations when customer orders increase.

Scheduling of workflow within an organization also influences employee work schedules. In restaurant or catering operations, for example, food handlers begin preparations hours before meals are served to the eating clientele. Likewise, in many office and manufacturing facilities, employees responsible for start-up of computers or machines often begin activities before the regular workday.

Competitive issues also influence the setting of work schedules. In the manufacturing arena, for example, a firm is likely to have overtime hours or extra shifts in order to beat the competition in the introduction of a new product to the marketplace. As another example, retail or service organizations often expand business hours in order to obtain an advantage over other competitors.

Definition of the work week is important for two reasons: first, to comply with wage hour laws, and second, to establish a uniform pay period. Firms subject to the Fair Labor Standards Act are required to define a seven-day pay period for the purpose of determining overtime pay eligibility. Further, wage payment laws in many states require the employer to post information on pay periods and pay days. These laws allow the employer to specify on which day the pay period will start and end, so long as the pay period does not fluctuate from week to week.

When defining a working hours policy, one must also understand what work activities are compensable. There are a variety of work-related activities for which the employee should receive pay. Likewise, some activities are deemed by the Labor Department to be noncompensable. A chart showing common examples of compensable activities follows:

**Compensable Work Activities
Time Spent during Regular
Work Hours**

*Compensable*

Coffee and snack breaks

Fire drills

Grievance adjustment during time employee is required to be on premises

Meal periods if employees are not relieved of duties, if not free to leave posts, or if too short to be useful (less than 1/2 hour)

Meal periods of 24-hour on-call employees

Sleeping time if tour of duty is less than 24 hours

Stand by time—remaining at post during lunch period or temporary shutdown

Time spent participating in suggestion systems

Travel:
1. from job site to job site
2. from work site to outlying job
3. to customers
4. from preliminary instructional meeting to work site

### CHECKLIST
### A Working Hours Policy

What factors must be considered when establishing business hours and work schedules (i.e., customer needs/preferences, production requirements, industry/area trends, competitive issues, workflow issues, etc.)?

- Will work schedules be set for an 8-hour day/40-hour week, 7.5-hour day/37.5-hour week, or other schedule?

- Will work be scheduled for a day shift, or will evening or night work shifts be needed also?

- Will different work schedules be needed to address the requirements of different work units or departments?

- Will employee work schedules vary from business hours?

- If there is a union, is the firm required to negotiate work schedules with the union?

- Will overtime work be mandatory if scheduled in advance by the company?

- Will the pay period be weekly, biweekly, semimonthly, or monthly?

Medical attention on plant premises or if employer directs outside treatment

Meetings to discuss daily operations problems

Principal duties

Rest periods of 20 minutes or less

Retail sales product meetings sponsored by employer

Show-up time if employees required to remain on premises before being sent home

Waiting:
1. by homeworker to deliver or obtain work
2. by truck driver standing guard while loading
3. for work after reporting at a required time
4. while on duty

*Noncompensable*

Absence for illness, holiday, or vacation

Meal periods of 1/2 hour or longer if relieved of all duties and free to leave post (but can be confined to plant premises)

Medical attention by employee choice of outside doctor

Shutdown for regular maintenance

Sleeping time up to eight hours if tour of duty is 24 hours or longer

Union meetings concerning solely internal union affairs

Voting time (unless required by state law)

## Time Spent Before, After, or Between Regular Work Hours

*Compensable**

Arranging or putting merchandise away

Bank employees waiting for audit to finish

Changing clothes, showering, or washing if required by nature of the work (such as job with chemicals requires bathing for worker health)

Civic or charitable work if requested by employer or controlled by employer or if required to be performed on employer's premises

Clearing cash register or totaling receipts

Discussing work problems at shift change

Distributing work to work benches

Equipment maintenance before or after shift

Homework under contract with employer

Make-ready work, preparatory work necessary for principal activity

On-call time if employee must stay on or near premises so as to have liberty restricted or not use time as pleases

Photography and finger-printing for identification purposes

Physical exam required for continued service

Travel time to customer on after-hour emergency

*Noncompensable*

Changing clothes, washing, or showering for employees' convenience

Homework of which the employer has no knowledge

Meal periods while on out-of-town business

Medical attention by company doctor even if injury was at work

On-call time when only telephone number to be reached or other similar contact device is required so that employee can come and go as pleases

Opening plant and turning on lights and heat

Preemployment tests

Retail sales meeting sponsored

Travel time:
1. from home to work site or vice versa (even if employer provided transportation)
2. from plant entrance to work site
3. from time clock to work site
4. to and from dressing room
5. from outlying job to home

Unauthorized overtime if prohibited and without employer's knowledge

Voluntary attendance at industry meetings to keep abreast of technological change

Waiting:
1. for paycheck
2. at time clock
3. to start work at designated time after arriving

* Note: Custom or contract may also influence compensable activities.[1]

SOURCE: Exerpted and reproduced with permission from *Labor Law Course*, 26th Edition, by CCH Editors, pp. 6091, 6092. © 1987. Published by Commerce Clearing House, Inc., 4025 W. Peterson Ave. Chicago, IL 60646.

by manufacturer if attendance
is voluntary
Reporting early to promptly relieve
prior shift
Training programs sponsored by
employer if outside regular work
hours, attendance is voluntary,
employee does no productive
work while attending, and
program is not directly related
to employee's present job

## Competitive Practices

The charts in Figs. 8.1a and 8.1b show work schedules for full-time employees in medium and large firms and in small, private establishments.

## Pitfalls to Avoid

One of the main problems that organizations experience with working hours practices is failure to comply with the Federal Fair Labor Standards Act (FLSA) and similar state wage hour laws. Here are some tips:

1. Avoid state wage payment law violations by determining wage payment requirements in your state. If your firm has multistate locations, you will need to check requirements for each state. Be alert for maximum allowable pay periods requirements and timeliness of pay day following the pay period.

2. Take care to comply with FLSA requirements. Two troublesome areas are noted: First, for all nonexempt job categories covered by FLSA, specify a seven-day pay period for overtime pay computation. Second, take care to properly classify jobs as exempt and nonexempt. A common mistake made by many firms is to consider plant employees as hourly and all office employees as salaried and therefore exempt. To be in compliance, office clerical, technical, and administrative jobs should be properly evaluated to determine their exempt or nonexempt status. (See Chap. 10 for more information.)

3. Do not violate child labor laws. Check FLSA and state labor laws for limitations on working hours for children. Work hour limits for children vary from state to state. Also, the age of the child and whether or not school is in session may affect child work schedules.

4. Recognize that old state protective laws on working hours for women have been superseded by Title VII of the Civil Rights Act of 1964. This means that there is no longer a legal requirement or justification for work hour limitations exclusively for women.

| Work schedule | All employees | Professional, technical, and related employees | Clerical and sales employees | Production and service employees |
|---|---|---|---|---|
| Total ................................ | 100 | 100 | 100 | 100 |
| **Hours per week:** | | | | |
| Under 35 ............................. | 4 | 2 | 3 | 6 |
| 35 ......................................... | 5 | 6 | 7 | 4 |
| Over 35 and under 37.5 ............. | 2 | 4 | 2 | 2 |
| 37.5 ..................................... | 5 | 8 | 8 | 1 |
| Over 37.5 and under 40 ............. | 1 | 1 | 2 | 1 |
| 40 ........................................ | 77 | 69 | 74 | 82 |
| Over 40 and under 50 ................. | 3 | 4 | 3 | 3 |
| 50 and over ............................ | 2 | 8 | 1 | 1 |
| Hours per week not available ..... | (¹) | (¹) | (¹) | (¹) |
| Non-fixed work hours ................. | (¹) | (¹) | (¹) | (¹) |
| **Hours per day:** | | | | |
| Under 6 ................................. | 1 | (¹) | 1 | 2 |
| 6 .......................................... | 2 | 1 | 1 | 2 |
| Over 6 and under 7 .................... | 1 | 1 | (¹) | 2 |
| 7 .......................................... | 6 | 6 | 7 | 5 |
| Over 7 and under 8 .................... | 7 | 13 | 10 | 3 |
| 8 .......................................... | 78 | 70 | 76 | 82 |
| Over 8 and under 9 .................... | 1 | 2 | 1 | 1 |
| 9 .......................................... | 1 | 2 | 1 | 1 |
| Over 9 and under 10 ................... | (¹) | (¹) | (¹) | (¹) |
| 10 ........................................ | 2 | 5 | 1 | 2 |
| Over 10 ................................. | (¹) | (¹) | (¹) | 1 |
| Hours per day not available ........ | (¹) | (¹) | (¹) | (¹) |
| Non-fixed work days .................. | (¹) | (¹) | (¹) | (¹) |

¹ Work schedule data include regularly scheduled overtime, paid lunch, and paid rest periods.
² Less than 0.5 percent.

NOTE: Because of rounding, sums of individual items may not equal totals. Where applicable, dash indicates no employees in this category.

**Figure 8.1a.** Work schedules: percent of full-time employees by number of hours scheduled per week,[1] small establishments, 1990.[2]

5. There are no federal government requirements on the maximum number of hours worked daily or weekly for adult employees. Some state laws, however, limit the number of hours per week or require one day of rest in a seven-day period for covered employees. Check these state law requirements when establishing overtime or seven-day work schedules. This issue is important to recognize because some employees believe that they cannot be required to work over 40 hours. The fact is, the employer can set work schedules (such as 40 or 48 hours weekly) and require adult employees to work scheduled hours so long as all non-exempt employees receive overtime pay for time worked over 40 hours in a week. The FLSA does have some time limits for youths aged 15 and under.

| Work schedule | All employees | Professional and administrative employees | Technical and clerical employees | Production and service employees |
|---|---|---|---|---|
| Total ..................................... | 100 | 100 | 100 | 100 |
| **Hours per week:** | | | | |
| Under 30 ........................... | (²) | (²) | – | (²) |
| 30 ....................................... | (²) | (²) | (²) | 1 |
| Over 30 and under 35 ................. | (²) | (²) | (²) | (²) |
| 35 ....................................... | 3 | 6 | 4 | 1 |
| Over 35 and under 37.5 .............. | 1 | 2 | 3 | (²) |
| 37.5 .................................... | 7 | 9 | 13 | 3 |
| Over 37.5 and under 40 ............. | 1 | 2 | 2 | (²) |
| 40 ....................................... | 82 | 78 | 77 | 88 |
| Over 40 and under 50 ................. | 2 | 1 | 1 | 4 |
| 50 and over ................................ | (²) | 1 | (²) | 1 |
| Hours per week not available ..... | 1 | (²) | (²) | 1 |
| Non-fixed work hours ................... | 1 | 1 | 1 | 1 |

[1] Work schedule data include regularly scheduled overtime, paid lunch, and paid rest periods.
[2] Less than 0.5 percent.

NOTE: Because of rounding, sums of individual items may not equal totals. Where applicable, dash indicates no employees in this category.

**Figure 8.1b.** Work schedules: Percent of full-time employees by number of hours scheduled per week,[1] medium and large firms, 1990.[3]

## Sample Policy

**XYZ COMPANY**
**PERSONNEL POLICY & PROCEDURE**

SUBJECT: WORKING HOURS                    DATE: May 1, 1993

*Policy*: It is the policy of XYZ Company to establish working schedules based on business conditions and customer requirements.

*Procedure*:
1. A regular work week shall consist of five 8-hour work days, Monday through Friday, providing a 40-hour work week. The normal schedule is:

Plant Working Hours

| Shift/Hours | Lunch | Break |
|---|---|---|
| **1st Shift** | | |
| Office 8:00 a.m.–4:30 p.m. | 12:30–1:00 | 10:10–10:20 |
| Prod. 7:00 a.m.–3:30 p.m. | 11:30–12:00 | 9:45–9:55 |
| | 12:00–12:30 | 10:00–10:10 |

2nd Shift

3:00 p.m.–11:00 p.m.                5:55–6:20              9:00–9:10

3rd Shift

11:00 p.m.–7:00 a.m.                2:00–2:25              5:00–5:10

---

Working hours, lunch, and break schedules may change from time to time. On occasion, the Company may schedule a 10-minute "change-over" period at the end of the shift to coordinate work activities and conditions between shifts.

2. The weekly pay period shall begin at the start of the first shift on Monday (7:00 a.m.) and run through Sunday for hourly paid employees (Tuesday–Saturday for third shift employees).

3. Changes to work schedules may be made at any time, as deemed necessary by management, based upon business needs and production requirements. Employees are expected to work all available hours. Some employees may be placed on different schedules based on department needs.

4. All employees receive a 10-minute break period at a time designated by management.

5. All employees receive a lunch period at a time designated by management as summarized below:

| | |
|---|---|
| Office employees | 1/2 hour unpaid lunch |
| 1st shift prod. | 1/2 hour unpaid lunch |
| 2nd shift | 20-minute paid lunch |
| 3rd shift | 20-minute paid lunch |

6. All plant employees are entitled to a five-minute washup period prior to lunch and at the end of the work shift.

7. Employees who are assigned to work on the second and third shifts are entitled to receive shift premium differential. In the event that the Company requires any second or third shift employees to work days for a short-term period (30 days or less), the employee will continue to receive the shift premium. The amount of the shift premium is set by management. However, a shift change to day shift at the request or convenience of an employee may result in loss of the shift premium differential.

8. A time card shall be used to record hours worked by hourly paid employees for the purpose of computing payroll, tracking attendance, and recording time spent on each work activity.

   a) Each employee receives an assigned time card in the card rack at the beginning of each week, and additional cards may be obtained as needed through the supervisor.

   b) The employee is responsible for recording time with a time clock at the start of work, end of work, and when leaving the premises. Time must not be recorded earlier than 15 minutes before the start of work nor later than 15 minutes after the end of work.

    c) The employee is responsible for manually recording work times on the time card throughout the day when starting or stopping each work activity or job function.

    d) The supervisor shall review time cards of subordinates each week, and initial approval of overtime as appropriate.

9. Overtime work may be scheduled at management discretion when needed to meet production schedules. Hourly paid employees and hourly paid first line plant supervisors shall receive overtime pay at a rate of one and one-half times their regular pay rate for all time worked over 40 hours in a week. Actual hours worked, Company-observed holidays, and prior approved vacation count toward the 40-hour requirement for overtime eligibility. Other absences, paid or unpaid, do *not* count toward overtime eligibility.

10. All overtime work must be approved by the supervisor before an employee is permitted to work extra hours. Distribution or frequency of overtime is based on customer or production requirements affecting certain machines or jobs in the various departments. Employees are expected to work overtime as scheduled by the Company.

## Sample Employee Handbook Paragraph

*Working Hours*

Employees are normally scheduled to work an 8-hour workday, Monday through Friday, providing a 40-hour work week. The normal work schedule is:

| Plant | 1st shift | 7:00 a.m.–3:30 p.m. |
|-------|-----------|---------------------|
|       | 2nd shift | 3:00 p.m.–11:00 p.m. |
|       | 3rd shift | 11:00 p.m.–7:00 a.m. |
| Office |          | 8:00 a.m.–4:30 p.m. |

Note: A 10-minute shift changeover scheduled at the end of the shift may be in effect from time to time. This allows the operators finishing their shifts to pass on to the incoming operators the conditions of the jobs and machines.

Changes to work schedules may be made at any time, based upon business needs and production requirements. Employees are expected to work all available hours.

Employees assigned to second or third shift work receive a shift premium. In the event that the Company requires any second or third shift employee to work days for a short-term period, the employee will continue to receive the shift premium. However, a shift change to day shift at the request or convenience of an employee may result in loss of the shift premium.

There is a five-minute washup period prior to lunch and at the end of the workday for plant employees. Please do not leave your work area or stop working prior to washup time.

## Lunch and Break Periods

Lunch and break periods are an important element of the daily work schedule. Employees are refreshed and more productive following a rest period during the workday. Further, in many areas, state law requires the employer to grant employees either a lunch or break period.

The practice for rest and break periods varies by area and industry. In many organizations, it is customary to permit a break period during each half of the work shift and a lunch period at midday. Another common practice in many offices is to permit a lunch period but no defined break periods because employees are permitted to consume drinks and snacks at their work area during the day. In the graphic arts and printing industry, it is common practice to grant a brief break period while requiring that press employees "eat on the fly." This practice began because it was too costly to shut down and start up a press each day because of lunch period interruptions.

State laws regarding lunch and break periods also vary. New York and Illinois, for example, require a lunch period. Kentucky, on the other hand, mandates two 10-minute break periods in addition to a lunch period, but the law does not specify a time period for lunches. Kentucky Labor Department staffers recommend a 20- or 30-minute lunch period.

Lunch periods typically run 20 minutes or 30 minutes, or up to an hour. Break periods are commonly 10 to 15 minutes in length.

Interpretive guidelines on the FLSA and various state laws require that the 10- to 15-minute break periods be paid time. Lunch periods of 20 minutes or more, however, may be deemed noncompensable time.

### Competitive Practices

Figures 8.2a and 8.2b show paid lunch time granted to employees.

### Pitfalls to Avoid

One of the biggest problems with lunch and break periods is getting employees to return to work on a timely basis. Here are some suggestions:

1. Avoid the tendency to permit lunches and breaks to expand beyond the allotted time period. Specify clearly in your policy what the time limits are for lunches or breaks. Also, specify that supervisors are accountable for enforcing the time limits. Consider late return from lunch or breaks as a tardiness. Use discussions, disciplinary warnings, or performance ratings to deal with abusers.

2. Reduce worker's compensation liabilities by requiring hourly paid employees to punch out when leaving the premises for lunch. This clarifies that they have left the premises for non-job-related reasons,

### CHECKLIST
### A Lunch and Break Policy

- What are state and federal labor law requirements affecting lunch and break periods in your area?

- What are competitive practices for lunch and breaks in your area and industry?

- How many minutes will be granted for lunches and breaks?

- Will all employees be on the same lunch/break schedule, or will different schedules be established for certain work units, shifts, or employment categories?

- Do health or safety requirements prohibit employees from consuming food or drink in work areas?

- Will the lunch period be paid or unpaid?

- Will employees be permitted to leave the premises during lunch or breaks?

- Will employees be required to punch out or sign out for lunch or when leaving the premises?

- Will an employee be permitted to work through lunch based upon business needs or the employee's request?

| Minutes per day | All employees | Professional and administrative employees | Technical and clerical employees | Production and service employees |
|---|---|---|---|---|
| Total | 100 | 100 | 100 | 100 |
| Provided paid lunch time | 10 | 4 | 4 | 16 |
| Under 20 minutes | 1 | (¹) | (¹) | 2 |
| 20 minutes | 4 | (¹) | (¹) | 8 |
| Over 20 and under 30 minutes | (¹) | – | (¹) | (¹) |
| 30 minutes | 4 | 2 | 3 | 5 |
| Over 30 minutes | 1 | 1 | 1 | 1 |
| Number of minutes not available | (¹) | (¹) | (¹) | (¹) |
| Not provided paid lunch time | 90 | 96 | 96 | 84 |

¹ Less than 0.5 percent.

NOTE: Because of rounding, sums of individual items may not equal totals. Where applicable, dash indicates no employees in this category.

**Figure 8.2a.** Paid lunch time: Percent of full-time employees by minutes of paid lunch time per day, medium and large firms, 1989.[4]

| Minutes per day | All employees | Professional, technical, and related employees | Clerical and sales employees | Production and service employees |
|---|:---:|:---:|:---:|:---:|
| Total ..................................................... | 100 | 100 | 100 | 100 |
| Provided paid lunch time .................... | 8 | 7 | 7 | 8 |
| Under 30 minutes ......................... | 1 | (¹) | (¹) | 1 |
| 30 minutes .................................... | 5 | 3 | 3 | 6 |
| Over 30 minutes ............................ | 2 | 3 | 4 | 1 |
| Number of minutes not available ..................................... | (¹) | (¹) | – | 1 |
| Not provided paid lunch time ............. | 92 | 93 | 93 | 92 |

¹ **Less than 0.5 percent.**

NOTE: **Because of rounding, sums of individual items may not equal totals. Where applicable, dash indicates no employees in this category.**

**Figure 8.2b.** Paid lunch time: Percent of full-time employees by minutes of paid lunch time per day, small establishments, 1990.[5]

and minimizes the likelihood of a worker's compensation claim in the event of an off-premises accident while the employee is on his or her own time.

3. Schedule lunches and breaks so that there is adequate coverage of telephones, reception areas, or sales counters to serve customers visiting your facility during the lunch period.

4. Check state labor law requirements before allowing employees to work through lunch in order to leave work early at the end of the day. Some states require that employees receive the designated lunch period.

**Sample Policy**

**XYZ COMPANY**
**PERSONNEL POLICY & PROCEDURE**

SUBJECT: LUNCH & BREAK PERIODS            DATE: May 1, 1993

*Policy*: It is the policy of XYZ Company to permit lunch and break periods which minimize disruption to customer service while promoting employee productivity.

*Procedure*:
1. Supervisors and Department Managers are responsible for establishing department schedules for lunch and break periods within the guidelines of this policy. When setting lunch and break periods, consideration shall be given to business needs so that business operations continue during the day with minimum disruption.

2. Lunch periods shall be a half hour in duration, normally occurring between the third and the fifth hours of the work shift. In instances of a business lunch with customers or vendors, up to one-hour lunch is permissible, with approval of one's superior.

3. Break periods shall be 10 minutes in duration. One break period is permitted during each half of the workday. In the event employees are working an overtime work schedule of 10 or more hours daily, one additional break period shall be permitted after the normal eight-hour work shift.

4. Lunch periods are unpaid time. Hourly paid employees must punch out when leaving the premises and punch in upon return to work. Break periods are paid time. Employees are not permitted to leave the premises during paid time.

5. The following guidelines are provided for scheduling of lunches and breaks:

   a) Not more than half of the department may take lunch or breaks at one time.

   b) Lunch and break schedules may be changed as needed in response to work requirements.

   c) An employee may not work through lunch in order to leave early; such a practice is in violation of state law.

   d) In the event employees are in the middle of a major task or involved in direct service to the customer, the employee is expected to finish the task and then take lunch.

6. All food and drinks must be consumed in the break room. Consumption of food and drinks is not permitted in work areas due to health and sanitation reasons.

7. In the event of excessive tardiness or late return to work from lunch or breaks, the supervisor is responsible for using corrective discipline. See the Disciplinary Warning Policy.

**Sample Employee Handbook Paragraph**

*Breaks and Lunches*

Employees are permitted a 15-minute break period during each half of the work day, and a 30-minute lunch period. The schedule for lunch and break periods is set by the department supervisor in a manner which allows business operations to continue uninterrupted during the day. Your supervisor will advise you of the schedule for lunch and breaks in your department. In fairness to your fellow workers, please observe the time limits set for rest and lunch periods.

# Overtime

Overtime refers to the time worked by an employee that is beyond the employee's normal work schedule. Since overtime is a complex and trouble-

**CHECKLIST**
**An Overtime Policy**

What federal or state labor laws affect the overtime policy?

What is the normal work schedule and what constitutes overtime work?

What jobs or categories of jobs are covered by the overtime policy?

Will overtime be mandatory or may an employee turn down an overtime work request?

Will overtime work require supervisory authorization?

What procedures will be taken to prevent employee abuse or unauthorized working of overtime?

How will overtime be distributed fairly among employees?

Will overtime assignments be based on business need, employee seniority, skills and abilities, requirements for machine or job function, etc.?

What records will be maintained to track overtime work?

How much prior notice of overtime work will be given to employees?

Will availability for overtime work be considered a condition of employment for the job?

some issue, it is dealt with in two sections in this book. This section deals with overtime work schedules. For information on overtime pay, see Chap. 10.

The establishment of work schedules, including overtime, is a prerogative of the employer. There are, however, some limitations on overtime work schedules:

1. Most states and the FLSA have child labor law provisions which limit the number of daily and weekly hours that may be worked by a youth under a specified age limit.

2. Some states have a six-day week law which prohibits covered employees from working seven consecutive workdays.

3. Firms with unions may have overtime limits or controls defined in the labor agreement.

4. Certain safety regulations define rest time limits for truck drivers, pilots, and others involved in transportation occupations.

Therefore, unless otherwise limited as defined above, the employer can set work schedules including overtime work and require employees to work hours as scheduled. This means that the adult employee who refuses overtime work saying, "You can't make me work over 40 hours in a week," is wrong.

Employers are cautioned, however, to give reasonable advance notice to employees when scheduling overtime work. Generally, 24 hours' notice is considered reasonable advance notice of short periods of overtime. For extended periods of overtime, a week's notice or more is recommended.

Most employees will cooperate with an employer's occasional request for overtime. However, with the predominance of two working spouses and growing number of single working parents, lack of prior notice of overtime work can become a significant employee relations issue.

## Pitfalls to Avoid

Overtime work is generally a change from the normal work schedule requiring additional work hours. A major concern for the employer is adequate staffing to meet the increased workload requirement. Here are some pitfalls to avoid when scheduling overtime.

1. Do not permit employee abuse of overtime work. Some hourly paid employees will stay a few extra minutes each day to accumulate extra overtime pay at the end of the week. In some production operations, managers complain that employees work slowly during the week, causing the firm to schedule overtime work on Saturday, thus providing added income for employees and unnecessary higher costs to the company. Be sure that your overtime policy specifies that overtime work is at management direction and not at employee election.

2. Another way to avoid overtime abuse is by supervisory review and approval of time records each week. If employees are working unauthorized extra hours, the supervisor can immediately deal with the matter through corrective discussions or disciplinary warnings.

3. If overtime work is a frequent occurrence at the organization, the employer should communicate this practice to new employees during the interview and hiring process. Unless specifically limited by law or contract, the employer is free to require mandatory overtime, make availability for overtime a condition of employment, and enforce overtime attendance through disciplinary procedures which may include discharge.

4. In some firms, employees view overtime work as a special prerequisite or benefit because of the premium pay. As a result, the employer must be concerned with fair distribution of overtime work. Various schemes have been devised to deal with this issue. Collective bargaining agreements, for the most part, specify that overtime work shall be to qualified employees on a seniority basis. Other firms have tried an overtime duty roster procedure to assure that qualified workers are offered overtime in proper turn.

5. Avoid excessive overtime work requirements. Employees generally will be cooperative with overtime work schedules of a week or two or even several months. But when heavy work demands produce continual 10-

to 12-hour days and six-or seven-day work schedules, this schedule becomes a strain to employees and their families. Excessive overtime can cause family conflicts, lower morale and productivity, and contribute to workplace accidents.

**Sample Policy**

**XYZ COMPANY**
**PERSONNEL POLICY & PROCEDURE**

SUBJECT: OVERTIME                                    DATE: May 1, 1993

*Policy*: It is the policy of XYZ Company to schedule overtime work when needed to meet business workload requirements.

*Procedure*:

1. Department work schedules are set by the Department Manager within the guidelines of management direction and the Working Hours Policy. A normal workday is an eight-hour period; a normal work week is a 40-hour period, Monday through Friday. Work beyond the eight-hour day or 40-hour week is considered overtime.

2. Department Managers are responsible for estimating overtime work schedules based upon business plans and incorporating these estimates into the annual budget. The Department Manager may approve overtime work within budgetary estimates.

3. All XYZ employees are hired with the understanding that there will be occasions of overtime work. When reasonable notice is provided, employees must perform work as scheduled. The following guidelines are provided:

   a) In cases of scheduled periods of overtime, one-week notice to employees is recommended. Scheduled overtime is viewed as a mandatory work schedule; an unauthorized absence will result in corrective discipline.

   b) In cases of emergency overtime, one-day notice to employees is recommended. Employees are expected to perform emergency overtime work when requested. However, the supervisor may consider an employee's personal emergency or other circumstances as a reasonable basis to decline overtime work.

4. The supervisor shall recommend the need for overtime work, subject to the approval of the Department Manager. The supervisor is responsible for communicating overtime work requirements to subordinates.

5. Overtime work shall be assigned according to the supervisor's judgment, considering the following criteria:

   a) The machines, equipment, or operations necessary to complete the required work.

   b) Skill/ability of the employee(s) to perform the required work.

      c) If all other factors are equal, length of company service shall be considered.

6. The supervisor or another designated supervisor must be working on the premises when employees are performing overtime work.

7. The supervisor is responsible for reviewing weekly time records and initial approval of overtime work. In the event a review of time records shows unauthorized work, the supervisor shall instruct the employees not to work overtime unless authorized by management. In the event of subsequent offenses, see the Disciplinary Rules Policy.

**Sample Employee Handbook
Paragraph**

*Overtime*

There are occasions when extra work hours must be scheduled to meet the needs of our customers; in some instances when critical work deadlines must be met, overtime work may be required. We make every effort to provide reasonable notice of overtime work and expect your cooperation in working scheduled hours.

Hourly paid employees will receive one and one-half times their regular hourly pay rate for all time worked over 40 hours per week. All overtime work must be approved by your supervisor. Company-paid holidays count as time worked when computing overtime.

# Attendance Control

Getting employees to come to work—every day, on time—is a major concern to many managers and supervisors. Every supervisor can lament about one or two employees in his or her work group who miss too many days or regularly have difficulty in arriving to work on time.

Unscheduled absences have a disruptive effect on business operations. Absences cause delayed or unfinished work, changes in work assignments, poor customer service, and extra work demands upon other employees. Scheduled absences, though less disruptive, also contribute to adjustments in work assignments and extra workloads for other employees.

A major concern for the employer is to control absences and promote good attendance. Carefully defined attendance policies can help to achieve these objectives. An attendance control policy helps to clarify allowable absences, identify absence reporting guidelines, limit number of absences, and outline corrective action for excessive or unauthorized absences.

A carefully defined attendance control policy assumes even greater importance with the currently higher labor force participation of single

**CHECKLIST**
**An Attendance Control Policy**

- What employee groups or categories are covered by the Attendance Control Policy?
- Will there be different policy or procedure guidelines based on the unique needs of exempt, nonexempt, union, non-union employees, etc.?
- To whom and by when should absences be reported?
- Will time and attendance records be maintained? By whom?
- What kinds of absences are considered authorized? Unauthorized?
- Will authorized absences be paid or unpaid?
- How many absences are allowable? At what point will absences be considered excessive?
- Will a no-fault absence policy be used?
- What corrective action will be taken for violations of attendance policies?
- Will there be any incentives or rewards for good attendance?
- How will the attendance policy be communicated to employees?

parents and dual working spouses. The result is that a majority of workers now have greater demands upon personal time. These time demands are likely to cause some conflict with work schedules. So while attendance policies of the last several decades were oriented toward reducing absences, we are now seeing new and innovative approaches to balance the employer's need for attendance control and the employee's need to handle personal or family matters which conflict with the job.

The recently passed federal Family and Medical Leave Act of 1993 reflects the changing needs of the American workforce. This new law requires covered firms to grant unpaid leave benefits to employees in the event of disability, family health emergency, or care of a new child in the home. The law permits employees and employers to agree to a part-time work schedule if scheduled absences are medically necessary.

An effective attendance control policy really should be a series of policies which define allowable absences and specify requirements to control abuse of absences.

Here are some other policy areas to consider as a cross reference when defining attendance control issues:

- *Employee selection*—Include guidelines on screening recruits for attendance when defining employee selection and reference checking policies. (See Chap. 7.)

- *Employee orientation*—Make sure that new employee orientation procedures include instructions on reporting absences and the importance of regular attendance. (See Chap. 7.)

- *Employee benefits*—Recognize that proper definition of employee benefits is an important part of attendance control. This can include benefits such as vacations, sick leave, funeral absences, and other paid absences. (See Chap. 12.)

- *Leaves of absence*—Policies which define leaves of absence are an integral part of the attendance control process. (See Chap. 9.)

- *Disciplinary procedures*—The use of corrective disciplinary procedures is generally regarded as one tool to control abuse of attendance policies. (See Chap. 11.)

- *Performance ratings*—When an employee's absences are identified in performance ratings and performance appraisals, this can influence pay adjustments. There can be a financial incentive for the employee to maintain good attendance. (See Chap. 10.)

A growing number of firms are trying to control absences with a "no-fault" attendance policy. The objective of the no-fault policy is to avoid judging the reason for absence. Rather, this plan focuses on defining a limited number of allowable instances for absence, regardless of reason. Once the employee exceeds the allowable instances of absence, then disciplinary measures are imposed. No-fault attendance plans also typically include a provision granting the employee credit for good attendance.

The principal advantage of a no-fault attendance plan is that it specifies objective absence limits, which eliminates the need for the supervisor to make judgments on employee absence requests. The absence, regardless of reason, will be granted upon timely notice by the employee, but once absences exceed defined limits, then discipline is imposed.

## Pitfalls to Avoid

Attendance control is a nagging problem that affects many organizations. Accurate attendance records are an important part of attendance control. A sample attendance record is shown in Figure 8.3. Here are some pitfalls to avoid when defining an Attendance Control Policy.

1. Many smaller and mid-size organizations fall into a trap of allowing unlimited sick leave for salaried or exempt workers. This practice creates a twofold problem. First, there will be some absence abusers who take advantage of this lax practice, causing absences which disrupt operations or affect productivity. Second, employee relations problems

# ATTENDANCE RECORD

Employee _____    Department _____

| Month \ Day | 1 | 2 | 3 | 4 | 5 | 6 | 7 | 8 | 9 | 10 | 11 | 12 | 13 | 14 | 15 | 16 | 17 | 18 | 19 | 20 | 21 | 22 | 23 | 24 | 25 | 26 | 27 | 28 | 29 | 30 | 31 | Total Absences |
|---|---|---|---|---|---|---|---|---|---|---|---|---|---|---|---|---|---|---|---|---|---|---|---|---|---|---|---|---|---|---|---|---|
| January | | | | | | | | | | | | | | | | | | | | | | | | | | | | | | | | |
| February | | | | | | | | | | | | | | | | | | | | | | | | | | | | | | | | |
| March | | | | | | | | | | | | | | | | | | | | | | | | | | | | | | | | |
| April | | | | | | | | | | | | | | | | | | | | | | | | | | | | | | | | |
| May | | | | | | | | | | | | | | | | | | | | | | | | | | | | | | | | |
| June | | | | | | | | | | | | | | | | | | | | | | | | | | | | | | | | |
| July | | | | | | | | | | | | | | | | | | | | | | | | | | | | | | | | |
| August | | | | | | | | | | | | | | | | | | | | | | | | | | | | | | | | |
| September | | | | | | | | | | | | | | | | | | | | | | | | | | | | | | | | |
| October | | | | | | | | | | | | | | | | | | | | | | | | | | | | | | | | |
| November | | | | | | | | | | | | | | | | | | | | | | | | | | | | | | | | |
| December | | | | | | | | | | | | | | | | | | | | | | | | | | | | | | | | |

Absence Codes:

V = Vacation
S = Sickness/Illness
L = Leave of Absence
J = Jury Service
H = Holiday

F = Funeral
O = Other
T = Tardy
— = Present

Additional comments to explain absence may be made on reverse side.

Reorder Form 9103
(708) 406-1590

© 1991 Hubbartt & Associates

**Figure 8.3.** Sample attendance record. ©1991 Hubbartt & Associates, reprinted with permission.

occur if the nonexempt or hourly paid employees are held to a more restrictive attendance policy or lose pay for absences. A consistently applied attendance control guideline is recommended for all employee categories.

2. Avoid the tendency to grant excused absences based solely on the supervisor's evaluation of the employee's reason for absence. Some supervisors can't say no. And some employees seem to become very creative with reasons causing absence. When absences increase and become troublesome, the key to absence control is to quantify allowable instances of absence. A quantified limit to absences gives the supervisor a basis to turn down an absence request or provides a guideline to start corrective action.

3. Recognize employee needs as well as business needs when defining attendance control guidelines. Today's workforce has large numbers of working spouses and single parents. These individuals are likely to incur child, family, and health care problems which conflict with work. Responsive employers are creating "family friendly" policies—policies that allow greater flexibility for absence and promote better employee relations.

4. Avoid the tendency to define attendance control policies that are too rigid or strict. A graphic arts company had defined a procedure requiring discipline for any absence or tardiness over two occurrences in a month. The firm's policy required two written warnings and then discharge. The firm's supervisors, however, were reluctant to strictly enforce the policy because they sympathized with the child care problems experienced by the large number of working parents. As a result, attendance control was a continual problem. The occasional enforcement of attendance rules for cases of extreme absenteeism was ruled inappropriate in unemployment insurance hearings because many other employees had poor attendance records.

5. Exercise caution when dealing with absences caused by employee disability or by an employee or a family health condition. Two recently passed laws have added new constraints on employers' attendance control policies. First, the Americans with Disabilities Act requires covered employers to make reasonable accommodations for individuals with a chronic or permanent physical or mental condition that meets the criteria of a disability. Second, an employee's absences due to disability, health condition of self or family member, or a new child in the home must now be handled in a manner that is consistent with the Family and Medical Leave Act. Carefully defined administrative controls will need to distinguish between unscheduled casual absences and a scheduled absence for a chronic condition that interferes with work.

**Sample Attendance Control
Policy**

**XYZ COMPANY
PERSONNEL POLICY MANUAL**

---

SUBJECT: ATTENDANCE AND PUNCTUALITY     No. 2.02
                                                                        Page 1 of 3
APPLIES TO: ALL EMPLOYEES                            Effective: 5-1-93

---

*Policy*: It is the policy of XYZ Company to establish reasonable and necessary controls to ensure adequate attendance and to meet business and production needs.

*Procedure*:

1. Working schedules and starting times are established by the department Supervisor or Manager based on business and production needs. (See Working Hours Policy.) The department Supervisor is responsible for communicating work schedules to subordinates.

2. Employees are expected to be at their work station in a fit condition and ready to work at start time. Work activity should commence at starting time and continue until the normal designated stopping times for breaks, lunch, or end of work.

3. In the event of absence or tardiness from an assigned work schedule, the employee is required to report absence to the Company. When reporting absence, the employee must telephone his or her supervisor, or other designated individual as specified by management. In the event the employee cannot reach a Supervisor or Manager, the absence should be reported to the Human Resource Department. The employee must call within one hour of scheduled start time.

4. The Company reserves the right to require an employee to submit a physician's certification in the event of repeated absences for medical reasons or in the event of medical absences exceeding three days.

5. The Company recognizes that an occasional absence may occur, as defined by Company policies for holidays, vacations, jury service, funerals, family and medical leave, personal leave, military leave, voting, etc. Time off from work is unpaid unless the Company has established a specific policy providing pay for time off.

6. An employee's absence will be considered excused if covered by policy and the employee provides proper and timely notification deemed satisfactory to the Supervisor or Manager. Timely notification means calling in on the day of absence or providing advance notice for absences which can be anticipated.

7. An employee's absence will be deemed unexcused when an employee fails to call in, gives late notice, fails to give advance notice for an absence which could be anticipated, exceeds the number or length of absences as defined by policy or authorized in advance by the Supervisor or Manager. Unexcused absences are subject to corrective discipline or

termination as defined in policies on Disciplinary Procedures and Separation of Employment.

8. Excessive absenteeism is defined as two or more instances of unexcused absence in a calendar month. Such excessive absenteeism is subject to corrective discipline. Any eight instances of unexcused absenteeism in a calendar year are considered grounds for discharge.

9. In the event an employee is absent for three days or more without prior notice or approval, such absence is viewed as job abandonment. The employee is then separated from employment as a voluntary quit.

10. In the event a nonexempt employee reports to work late, he or she will be docked for time missed. Any lateness of up to six minutes shall result in loss of pay equivalent to $1/10$ of an hour for each six minutes of lateness or portion thereof.

11. Excessive tardiness shall be subject to corrective discipline or termination. Excessive tardiness is defined as three or more instances of lateness in a calendar month and is subject to corrective discipline. Any 12 instances of lateness in a calendar year are considered grounds for discharge.

12. An employee's request to leave work early may be considered by the Supervisor or Manager. Approval of such absences should be based upon the urgency of the reason for absence and department staffing needs. As a general guide, early leaving should not exceed one instance per month or five instances in a calendar year.

13. The Personnel Records Clerk is responsible for maintaining attendance records and for advising respective supervisors if an employee's absence or lateness exceeds the guidelines of this policy.

## Sample Employee Handbook Paragraph

*No-Fault Attendance Plan*

The Company has established a no-fault attendance plan in order to encourage good attendance. Under this plan, an employee is permitted a certain number of absences without penalty and an opportunity to earn attendance credits which are a reward for good attendance.

Authorized absences are permitted as defined by Company policies for vacation, holidays, personal/sick days, jury service, bereavement, voting, medical leave, personal leave, or military service. Of course, the employee must provide timely notice of absence or receive prior approval for the absence as defined by the respective policy. The Company reserves the right to require documentation in support of the absence.

Any other absences which are not covered by policy or exceed the limits of policy will be handled under the no-fault attendance plan. Under this plan, such instance of absence or tardiness accumulates absence points as shown:

a. Each instance of absence is recorded as one absence point. (Note that a two-day absence—i.e., Tuesday/Wednesday or Friday/Monday—

counts as one absence point. But two separate absences—i.e., Tuesday and Friday—count as two absence points.)

b. Each instance of tardiness counts as a half absence point. Tardiness includes reporting to work late or returning to work late from lunch.

c. An absence of less than four hours, including leaving work for nonbusiness reasons during the day, leaving early, or failing to work assigned overtime, counts as a half absence point.

An employee may accumulate up to four absence points without penalty. Four or more absence points will result in corrective action as summarized below:

4 Absence Points = Verbal Warning
5 Absence Points = Written Warning
6 Absence Points = 2nd Written Warning and/or Suspension without Pay for up to 2 Days
7 Absence Points = Subject to Dismissal

The absence points may be "erased" by maintaining perfect attendance for a calendar month to receive an absence credit. Each absence credit erases an absence point. Continuous perfect attendance can result in accumulation of up to five absence credits. Then, absences or tardies are charged against the individual's absence credits without penalty before additional absence points are accumulated. The absence credit rewards an employee for good attendance; and our no-fault attendance plan helps assure that all attendance matters are handled on an objective basis. Attendance records are maintained in the Personnel Department.

## Sample Attendance Control Forms

*Absence Request Form*

Employee _____  Date _____

Job _____  Department _____

I request absence from work on the day (dates) shown below:

Absent from _____  to _____

Reason for Absence _____

_____

_____

Employee Signature:

_____

### SUPERVISOR'S ABSENCE REPORT

*Instructions*: Complete and route to Payroll Department by 9:00 a.m. daily. Reasons for absence: V—Vacation, S—Sick, D—Disability/Medical/Maternity Leave, J—Jury Service, M—Military Leave, P—Personal/Family Leave, O—Other.

*Sample Attendance Control Forms (Continued)*

Department _____ Date _____

| Employees Absent | Reason Code | Paid Yes/No | Excused Yes/No |
|---|---|---|---|
| _____ | _____ | _____ | _____ |
| _____ | _____ | _____ | _____ |
| _____ | _____ | _____ | _____ |
| _____ | _____ | _____ | _____ |
| _____ | _____ | _____ | _____ |
| _____ | _____ | _____ | _____ |
| _____ | _____ | _____ | _____ |
| _____ | _____ | _____ | _____ |
| _____ | _____ | _____ | _____ |
| _____ | _____ | _____ | _____ |
| _____ | _____ | _____ | _____ |
| _____ | _____ | _____ | _____ |

Signature of Supervisor:

_____

# Time Records

Employee time records are among the most important documents maintained in any organization. Employee time records are important because they affect pay and because they are a source for compliance with various state and federal laws.

Employee time records can be used for four different purposes:

**Compute Payroll.** A record of hours worked is necessary to compute payroll for hourly paid employees. It is customary in many organizations to have employees record time at the start of work, end of work, and whenever leaving the premises for non-job-related reasons.

The available methods of time recording vary widely. Many organizations have employees complete a time slip which is turned in at the end of the pay period. Other organizations, particularly factories, often use a time clock to record hours worked. Employees are required to insert a time card into an electromechanical clock, which stamps on the card. Newer time systems are now more likely to be electronic. With an electronic system, the employee receives a plastic or laminated identification card, which is inserted into an electronic card reader that displays current time and records the employee's time entry. These systems generally are fully automated, with preprogrammed work schedules tracking employee work hours, recording overtime hours, totaling hours for the pay period, and computing paycheck amounts.

**Wage Hour Compliance.**   The Fair Labor Standards Act (FLSA) requires employers to keep a record of hours worked for covered employees. The law does not specify in what form the records must be maintained. Likewise, many similar state wage payment laws require the employee to keep certain records on employees, pay rates, work schedules, and hours worked. Generally, these laws exempt certain employees such as executives, professionals, outside sales representatives, and certain administrative employees. An employer's failure to maintain the requisite records can result in fines.

The FLSA requires that employers provide overtime pay for covered employees who work over 40 hours in a week. Further, some organizations have elected to provide overtime pay for certain exempt employees such as plant supervisors, engineers, data processing employees, or others who tend to have large amounts of overtime work. Time records are necessary to keep track of hours worked and compute overtime pay as required by law or specified by company policy.

**Attendance Control.**   Employee time records are the foundation of any attendance control effort. The time record shows the days and times that the employee arrived to work. This data is essential in tracking attendance and dealing with attendance problems. Some firms, however, fail to track attendance in a systematic way or to use time records to control attendance. A midwest pump manufacturer, for example, was experiencing attendance and tardiness problems. Management announced that time clocks would be installed to deal with the problem. After two months of using the time clocks, managers recognized that they had not corrected the attendance problem; the time clocks merely documented the problem more accurately. Ultimately, company managers defined an attendance policy, tracked absences, and issued disciplinary warnings when needed. These follow-up actions brought about improved attendance.

**Labor and Cost Reporting.**   A growing number of firms, particularly those in the manufacturing environment, use employee time records for labor

### CHECKLIST
### A Time Records Policy

- What jobs or job categories are covered by the FLSA and therefore require the keeping of time records?

- Who is responsible for maintaining the actual time records—employees or supervisors?

- Will time be recorded on a time sheet, or with a time clock or other automated system?

- What is the pay period? When must time records be turned in?

- Will supervisors be required to review and/or approve time records?

- Is there a time limit within which employees should punch in?

- How will mistakes or errors on time records be handled?

- Will there be disciplinary action for falsifying time records or recording time on another employee's card?

and cost reporting. Labor and cost reporting can be done with time slips, a time clock, or an automated time reporting system. With labor cost reporting, the employee makes time entries at the start and end of each task, job, or work activity. Some organizations use one set of time records for both payroll and for labor/cost reporting.

## Pitfalls to Avoid

There are several common problems that occur with time reporting policies. Here are some pitfalls to avoid.

1. One of the biggest areas of misunderstanding is in determining which employees are covered by the FLSA (for which time records must be maintained) and which employees are exempt from the law. A common practice is to treat office workers as salaried and exempt from the FLSA. Such a practice can lead to fines and back pay penalties in the event of a wage hour audit by the U.S. Department of Labor. It is important to properly classify jobs as covered by the FLSA to avoid these liabilities. See Chap. 10 for more information.

2. Take care to properly define the firm's policy or practice for "docking" of pay when an employee is late. Generally, it is the employer's obligation to pay the employee for time actually worked. Therefore, it is permissible to dock or withhold pay for time not worked by hourly paid employees. It is not permissible to penalize the employee by withholding more pay than the work time actually missed for lateness. Several examples are provided.

a. With a time clock that records minute to minute, a pay deduction for lateness should be equivalent to the number of minutes actually lost.

b. With a time clock that records time in tenths of an hour, a six-minute pay deduction may be made for each six-minute period of lateness or portion thereof.

c. Likewise, if a firm's time clock records time in 15-minute segments, a deduction for lateness may occur for each 15-minute period or portion thereof.

In my discussions with wage hour department representatives, they recommend that the docking practice begin midway through the time clock segment, such as at seven minutes or three minutes. The wage hour people feel that, since the firm doesn't pay the employee overtime for punching out for one or two minutes past quitting time, it evens out if you don't dock the employee for being one or two minutes late.

3. When a time recording device is used, take care to require employees to record time within 15 minutes of their scheduled start and quit times. Since all employees cannot possibly punch in exactly at start time, the 15-minute limit allows a brief time period for employees to record time without creating an overtime pay liability. In many organizations there are one or two employees who come to work early, punch in, read the paper or have their morning coffee, and then begin work at the designated start time. In the event of a wage hour audit, the time records of these individuals become suspect, because the time card appears to show daily overtime work which was not paid. For this reason, I recommend that employees on a time clock be required to record times close to their scheduled work time.

4. Many firms fail to carefully monitor time records. As a result, they incur excessive absences, tardies, and abuse of overtime. Overtime work should be allowed only with management's direction and approval. Supervisors should review time records to check for absences, lateness, or overtime work abuses. A sample time slip appears in Fig. 8.4.

**Sample Policy**

**XYZ COMPANY**
**PERSONNEL POLICY & PROCEDURE**

---

SUBJECT: TIME RECORDS                                    DATE: May 1, 1993

---

*Policy*: It is the policy of XYZ Company to maintain time records to record hours worked, compute payroll, and track attendance.

*Procedure*:
1. All nonexempt employees are responsible for recording hours worked on their respective time cards using the time clock. The definition of

# BIWEEKLY TIME SLIP

Employee _____  ID # _____  Pay Period Ending _____

| | Mon. | Tues. | Weds. | Thurs. | Fri. | Sat. | Sun. | Mon. | Tues. | Weds. | Thurs. | Fri. | Sat. | Sun. |
|---|---|---|---|---|---|---|---|---|---|---|---|---|---|---|
| | / | / | / | / | / | / | / | / | / | / | / | / | / | / |
| Start | | | | | | | | | | | | | | |
| Lunch - out | | | | | | | | | | | | | | |
| Lunch - return | | | | | | | | | | | | | | |
| End | | | | | | | | | | | | | | |
| Absence | | | | | | | | | | | | | | |
| Daily Total Regular Hours Overtime | | | | | | | | | | | | | | |

Total for period _____

Authorization
of Overtime: _____  Supervisor's signature _____  Date _____

Reorder Form 9109
(708) 406-1590

© 1991 Hubbartt & Associates

**Figure 8.4.** Biweekly time slip. ©1991 Hubbartt & Associates, reprinted with permission

195

   nonexempt employees is covered in the Company policy on Employment Categories.

2. Due to the frequency of overtime work in production operations, production supervisors are responsible for recording time on the time slip.

3. The employee is responsible to record times as follows:

   a) at the start of work

   b) when leaving and upon return to the premises for non-business reasons including lunch

   c) at the end of work

4. Time must be recorded not sooner than 15 minutes before the start of work and not later than 15 minutes after the end of work unless the supervisor has authorized overtime work.

5. At the end of each pay period, the supervisor is responsible for collecting time cards of subordinates and for reviewing cards to monitor absences, lateness, and overtime work. The supervisor shall initial approval on the time cards. See Disciplinary Procedures if time cards show excessive absences or other disregard for attendance policies.

6. In the event of lateness, the following guidelines are provided for docking of employees:

   a) The time clock records time in tenths of an hour. For any lateness of three minutes or more, pay shall be deducted.

   b) The pay deduction shall be in six-minute increments for any subsequent six minutes of lateness or portion thereof.

7. The supervisor is responsible for turning time cards in to the Payroll Department by 9:00 a.m. on the workday following the end of the pay period.

## Employee Handbook Paragraph

### Time Records

A time card is used to record hours worked by hourly paid employees in order to compute payroll. Time must be recorded at the start of work, at the end of work, and when leaving the premises for nonbusiness reasons. It is the employee's responsibility to accurately record time worked and to turn the card in to the supervisor at the end of the week. Be sure to punch only your own card. As a reminder, do not punch in earlier than 10 minutes before the start of work or later than 10 minutes after the end of work unless your supervisor has authorized overtime work. Speak to your supervisor if there is an error or question about your time card.

## Sample Form

A biweekly timeslip is shown in Fig. 8.4 on page 195.

# Voting Time

The public's participation in government by voting in elections is the cornerstone of democracy in the United States. Periodic elections are conducted by various levels of government including city, county, state, and the federal government. General elections are scheduled on the first Tuesday in November on even-numbered years. However, primary elections and other elections occur at other times of the year.

In most areas, the polls are open for 12 hours, usually 6:00 a.m. to 6:00 p.m. This polling schedule allows many employees to vote before or after work. Further, absentee voting procedures provide for voting by individuals who will be out of town on election day.

When the scheduling of elections interferes with working schedules of employees, the employer has a civic responsibility to grant reasonable time off for voting.

While there is no federal law requiring time off for voting in governmental elections, some states have defined requirements in this area.

One area of elections is covered by federal labor law: elections to vote for or against a union to represent employees in a private-sector business enterprise. In the event the National Labor Relations Board sanctions a union election or a decertification election, the voting is conducted at the employer's premises during work time. This issue, however, is sufficiently unique that it should not be covered by a policy dealing with voting in governmental elections.

There are two key reasons for defining a policy on voting. The recurrence of elections means that the issue of time off for voting will come up every two years or so. Further, the practice of granting time off for voting causes absences which can disrupt business operations.

If a state law defines voting requirements, then the law should serve as a guide to formulate the company policy. In the absence of specific legal requirements, I recommend that a voting policy cover issues listed in the checklist which follows.

## Pitfalls to Avoid

The main concern with defining a policy on voting is balancing the employee's desire for absence to perform a civic responsibility with the firm's need to minimize the likelihood of disruption to operations. Here are some pitfalls to avoid.

1. Maintain adequate work schedules on election day by requiring the employee to request in advance for time off from work. Advance notice of absence permits the supervisor to make adequate adjustments to work assignments. One day or one week of advance notice should be satisfactory.

**CHECKLIST**
**A Voting Time Policy**

---

- What employees are covered by the voting policy (i.e., full time, part time, eligible voters, etc.)?

- What laws or regulations define requirements for voting?

- What elections will be included under the policy (federal, state, local, etc.)?

- When and how should employees request time off for voting?

- What time period of absence will be allowed?

- Will voting time off be paid or unpaid?

- Will voting time off be granted to all eligible employees or only if there is a conflict with work schedules?

- Will the company establish a schedule to plan and control voting absences?

- Will time off for voting count toward overtime pay eligibility?

- Will documentation of voter registration and/or voter participation be required?

---

2. Exercise initiative to schedule times off for voting to minimize work disruptions. For example, time off for voting may be granted at the start of the work shift or end of the work shift.

3. Recognize that a policy which defines voting time as a paid absence is more likely to be used by employers than a policy which permits unpaid time off.

4. If allowable by applicable state law, limit voting time off to circumstances in which there is a conflict between work schedules and voting time. It hardly makes sense, for example, to grant voting time off from work to a night shift employee who has all day to go to the polls before starting work.

**Sample Policy**

**XYZ COMPANY**
**PERSONNEL POLICY & PROCEDURE**

---

SUBJECT: VOTING TIME                                    DATE: May 1, 1993

---

*Policy*: It is the policy of XYZ Company to permit time off for voting if work schedules conflict with voting in a state or federal general election.

*Procedure*:
1. In the event an employee is eligible to vote in a state or federal general election, and the employee's work schedule conflicts with voting times, the employee may request time off in advance for voting.

2. The Supervisor shall grant to the employee time off without pay up to the limits defined by state law when the above conditions are met. The Supervisor may schedule employee voting absences in a manner which minimizes disruption to work schedules (under current work schedules and extended voting hours it is expected that most employees can fulfill voting obligations with no conflict to work).

3. The employee is responsible for recording the voting absence on his or her time record.

**Sample Employee Handbook Paragraph**

*Voting in Elections*

XYZ Company recognizes an employee's civic responsibility for voting in state or federal general elections. Employees who are eligible to vote may request up to two hours off work without pay when their work schedule interferes with voting. Your request for time off must be submitted in advance, and the Company reserves the right to schedule employee absences in a manner which will minimize work disruptions.

# Flexible Work Schedules

The growing numbers of dual income families, working spouses, and single working parents means that employees must juggle personal and family activities around work schedules. These employees often must get children off to school or day care, or hurry home after work to pick up children and prepare dinner.

Increasingly, companies are adopting personnel policies to accommodate the changing needs of the labor force. One of these changes has been the use of flexible work schedules.

With flexible work schedules, certain employees are assigned earlier starting and quitting times while others are allowed to schedule later starting and quitting times. All employees work during a core time period in the middle of the workday. The earlier or later work schedule is intended to allow the employee to maintain a work schedule which does not interfere with personal or family activities.

In addition to accommodating the employee's needs, flexible work schedules are intended to promote productivity for the organization. Flexible work schedules provide the following benefits for employers:

- Improved employee morale and productivity because employees are less likely to be distracted by personal or family issues which conflict with work schedules.

- Early and late staggered work shifts provide a longer workday. Longer workdays can help improve customer service or promote increased departmental work activities.

- The staggered work shifts created by flexible scheduling also can help alleviate congestion in Company facilities such as lunch rooms, parking lots, elevators, or other similar facilities.

Flexible work schedules may be more effective in certain kinds of working environments. Many retail and food service organizations, for example, place workers on early and late schedules with the overlapping portion of the schedule to cover peak customer service periods. Likewise, many office environments are able to function effectively when a portion of employees are on earlier or later work schedules. On the other hand, managers in production environments, where one work station supplies the next work station throughout the day, report that all employees are needed on the job at the same time.

When considering flexible schedules, the manager must carefully evaluate work demands, workflows, customer needs, and the degree of interaction needed between employees. Other factors such as building access, security, computer system support, and availability of supervision must also be evaluated. However, careful evaluation of these factors with creative scheduling of employees can result in productivity improvements.

### Competitive Practices

The chart in Fig. 8.5 shows the prevalence of flexible work schedules at large companies.

### Pitfalls to Avoid

Flexible scheduling is not without its pitfalls. Here are some potential problems to avoid.

1. Make sure that employees on flexible schedules are adequately supervised. Occasionally, employees on flexible schedules tend to take advantage of the unsupervised "flexible" portion of the workday. Some firms have caught employees abusing flexible schedules by unproductive socializing, excessive use of telephones, conducting of personal business, or even participation in secondary employment on company time.

2. Avoid the tendency to freely grant flexible schedules unless there is adequate work available to be performed during the flex time periods. For example, a sales clerk reporting to work two hours before the store opens is clearly unproductive. However, a stock clerk or merchandise display worker could make excellent use of a two-hour period before the store opens.

3. Avoid miscommunications regarding flex time. Plan meetings, training, or other activities during the core work period when all employees are present. Develop systems or procedures to ensure timely, accurate

## CHECKLIST
## Key Points to Consider when Developing a Flexible Schedule Policy

- What departments, work groups, or jobs will be included in flexible schedules?

- Will there be work available for the employees on flexible schedules?

- Is there a need for interaction between employees, or can flexible schedule employees perform tasks independently of other employees?

- Will flexible schedules help to improve customer service or will they limit the firm's ability to effectively serve the customer?

- Will business support systems such as telephones, switchboards, computers, etc. be operational during flexible schedule periods?

- Will there be adequate supervision for employees on flexible schedules?

- Is there an adequate basis to monitor work results of employees on flexible schedules?

- Is there adequate back-up staffing to fill in for absences of employees on flexible schedules?

- Do special arrangements need to be made with customers, suppliers, vendors, or other work units when implementing flexible schedules?

- What portion of employees will be placed on or allowed to go on flexible schedules?

- Will flexible schedules be permitted at the convenience of the employee or the direction of the Company, or both?

communication about job issues between employees on different schedules or work shifts. New electronic systems such as telephone system voice mail or computer system electronic or E mail can help improve communication of job matters.

**Sample Policy**

**XYZ COMPANY**
**PERSONNEL POLICY & PROCEDURE**

SUBJECT: FLEXIBLE HOURS                     DATE: May 1, 1993

*Policy*: It is the policy of XYZ Company to establish flexible work hours schedules as necessary to promote efficient operations and to respond to reasonable requests from employees.

*Procedure*:
1. Working hours and starting times are set by the Department Manager, subject to the limitations of Company policies and direction from

|                                          | Percentage of Employees On: | |
| Occupational Group/ Union Status         | Flexible Work Schedules | Part-Time Work Schedules |
| --- | --- | --- |
| Managers | 17.7% (440) | 0.7% (420) |
| Union Professional and Technical Employees | 1.8 (47) | 2.7 (46) |
| Nonunion Professional and Technical Employees | 14.7 (421) | 2.5 (404) |
| Union Clerical Employees | 4.3 (72) | 2.4 (74) |
| Nonunion Clerical Employees | 10.8 (432) | 4.9 (449) |
| Union Manufacturing and Production Employees | 1.7 (145) | 1.5 (142) |
| Nonunion Manufacturing and Production Employees | 8.4 (300) | 4.7 (302) |

Sample size is in parentheses.

**Figure 8.5.** Employees on flexible work schedules[6]

management. Working hours and starting times may be changed at any time at the discretion of Company management.

2. The department Manager is responsible for evaluating work unit activities and for scheduling employees in a manner which promotes maximum efficiency for the department and the Company. Employees may be placed on earlier or later work schedules as needed to efficiently accomplish work unit objectives.

3. Company management recognizes that flexible work schedules can be helpful for employees handling personal matters before or after work. A Department Manager may authorize an employee to work a flexible work schedule as shown:

|                  | Start      | Quit       |
| --- | --- | --- |
| Early Schedule #1 | 6:00 a.m. | 3:00 p.m. |
| Early Schedule #2 | 7:00 a.m. | 4:00 p.m. |
| Normal Schedule   | 8:00 a.m. | 5:00 p.m. |
| Late Schedule #1  | 9:00 a.m. | 6:00 p.m. |

4. When considering a flexible work schedule, the manager is responsible for ensuring that the following conditions are met:

a) There is adequate work available during the flexible time period.

b) Computer, telephone, and other support systems are operational for completion of job tasks.

    c) There must be adequate supervision and back-up staffing arrangements.

    d) The assignment does not adversely affect customer relations or other work units.

5. The manager is responsible for evaluating workflow, coordinating work activities, and discussing the planned schedule changes with other Department Managers affected by the change before authorizing a new work schedule.

6. Once an employee is placed on a new work schedule, the employee is accountable to maintain proper attendance and punctuality.

## Sample Employee Handbook Paragraph

*Flexible Work Hours*

XYZ Company has established a flexible work hours program. Under our flexible hours program, an employee may be placed on an earlier or later starting time. An employee may be placed on a flexible work schedule based upon departmental needs. Also, the Company will consider employee requests for flexible work schedules. Please recognize that when you are on a flexible schedule, you are responsible for maintaining regular attendance and on-time punctuality. Speak with your supervisor if there are questions about work schedules.

# Notes

1. *Labor Law Course,* 26th ed., Commerce Clearing House, Chicago, 1987, pp. 6091, 6092.
2. *Employee Benefits in Small Private Establishments, 1990,* U.S. Dept. of Labor Bulletin 2388, September, 1991, p. 9.
3. *Employee Benefits in Medium and Large Firms, 1989,* U.S. Dept. of Labor Bulletin 2363, June, 1989, p. 10.
4. *Employee Benefits in Medium and Large Firms, 1989,* U.S. Dept. of Labor Bulletin 2363, June, 1990, p. 10.
5. *Employee Benefits in Small Firms, 1989,* U.S. Dept. of Labor Bulletin 2363, June, 1990, p. 9.
6. *Human Resource Policies and Practices in American Firms,* U.S. Dept. of Labor, BLMR 137, 1989, p. 50.

# 9

# Planning and Administering Leaves of Absence

**Read Chapter 9 for:**

Jury service

Family and medical leave

Medical leave

Maternity leave

Military leave

Personal/family leave

Funeral leave

Sick leave

Conditions of leave

## Jury Service

The constitutional guarantee of a trial by a jury of one's peers is a cornerstone of individual rights in the United States. To assure defendants of this right, the various levels of government draw jurors from the lists of eligible voters. This means, of course, that various employees will be called upon from time to time to serve as jurors.

Jurors typically receive a summons in the mail providing instructions on when and where to report for jury duty. The summons provides a week or two of advance notice to the individual. The governmental unit requiring jury service generally provides some sort of stipend or jury pay. Depending on the needs of the court, the juror may be dismissed after a day or juror's service may be required for a week, a month, or more.

The uncertainty of the timing and duration of jury service can create hardships for employees and employers alike. Most employees report they are unable to get by on jury pay alone. Employers must juggle work tasks or reassign responsibilities to cover for individuals who are absent for jury service. Major policy concerns, therefore, relate to absence notification, work, scheduling, and pay for jurors.

Various laws define certain requirements for employers to grant jury leave for employees. The Jury System Improvement Act makes it unlawful for an employer to discharge or otherwise discriminate against an employee because of federal jury duty. The law also requires firms to consider employees on a leave of absence for jury service, reinstate the employee without loss of service or seniority credit, and provide benefits in the same manner as for other leaves of absence. There are no federal requirements to pay an employee while on leave, except that exempt employees should not receive a pay deduction for an absence of less than a week. Likewise, most states have laws prohibiting employers from discharging or otherwise discriminating against an employee who participates in the jury process. The issue of pay for jury service varies from state to state.

## Competitive Practices

The charts shown in Figs. 9.1a and 9.1b reveal jury service practices in small firms and in medium and large firms.

## Pitfalls to Avoid

1. Be sure to check applicable jury service laws and define your policy to comply. This is one area where the employer's actions or inaction comes directly to the attention of the court. A firm's refusal to grant jury leave or other disciplinary action against an employee for jury service participation could result in fines or even a citation for being in contempt of court.

2. Avoid the tendency to discharge an absentee-prone employee if the final absence incident is related to jury service. The Office Manager of a communications company became fed up with the repeated absences of a receptionist. When the receptionist brought a juror summons to work one day, the irate manager told the employee, "If you are absent again, you're fired!" The employee reported to jury service as summoned and told the judge of her dilemma. By the end of the jury service, the court had directed the employee's reinstatement with back pay and severely admonished the employer for its personnel practices.

3. Take care to maintain reasonable attendance controls for jury service

## CHECKLIST
## A Jury Service Policy

- What are the state and federal requirements for jury service?
- What classes or categories of employees are covered by the jury service policy?
- When and how must the employee notify the company of jury service?
- Will time off for jury service be paid or unpaid?
- If paid time is provided for jury service, what amount and for how long will pay be continued?
- How will the jury absence affect the employee's entitlement to benefits and insurance?
- What documents will be needed to substantiate jury duty or jury pay?
- Will the company request postponement of jury duty if juror service creates a hardship?
- Will the jury service policy include a summons to serve as a witness?
- What attendance records will be maintained?
- Will a jury service absence count as time worked toward overtime pay eligibility for nonexempt employees?

| Number of days | All employees | Professional, technical, and related employees | Clerical and sales employees | Production and service employees |
|---|---|---|---|---|
| Total ............................................ | 100 | 100 | 100 | 100 |
| Provided paid jury-duty leave .............. | 54 | 72 | 62 | 43 |
| Under 10 days ............................... | 2 | 1 | 2 | 1 |
| 10 days ........................................ | 3 | 3 | 4 | 2 |
| 11-19 days .................................... | (¹) | (¹) | (¹) | (¹) |
| 20 days ........................................ | 1 | 2 | 1 | (¹) |
| Over 20 days ................................. | 1 | 1 | (¹) | 1 |
| No maximum specified² ................. | 48 | 64 | 55 | 38 |
| Number of days not available ....... | (¹) | (¹) | (¹) | - |
| Not provided paid jury-duty leave ....... | 46 | 28 | 38 | 57 |

¹ Less than 0.5 percent.
² Jury-duty leave is provided as needed.

NOTE: Because of rounding, sums of individual items may not equal totals. Dash indicates no employees in this category.

**Figure 9.1a.** Paid jury-duty leave: percent of full-time employees by number of paid jury-duty leave days available per occurrence, small establishments, 1990.[1]

| Number of days | All employees | Professional and administrative employees | Technical and clerical employees | Production and service employees |
|---|---|---|---|---|
| Total .............................................. | 100 | 100 | 100 | 100 |
| Provided paid jury-duty leave .............. | 90 | 95 | 92 | 87 |
| Under 10 days ............................... | 1 | 1 | 2 | 1 |
| 10 days ......................................... | 5 | 5 | 5 | 5 |
| 11-19 days .................................... | 1 | 1 | 1 | 1 |
| 20 days ......................................... | 2 | 2 | 1 | 2 |
| 21-29 days .................................... | 1 | 1 | 1 | (¹) |
| 30 days ......................................... | 1 | 2 | 1 | 1 |
| More than 30 days ........................ | (¹) | (¹) | (¹) | 1 |
| No maximum specified² ................ | 79 | 83 | 82 | 75 |
| Number of days not available ....... | (¹) | (¹) | (¹) | (¹) |
| Not provided paid jury-duty leave ....... | 10 | 5 | 8 | 13 |

¹ Less than 0.5 percent.
² Jury-duty leave is provided as needed.

NOTE: Because of rounding, sums of individual items may not equal totals. Where applicable, dash indicates no employees in this category.

**Figure 9.1b.** Paid jury-duty leave: percent of full-time employees by number of paid jury-duty leave days available per occurrence, medium and large firms, 1989.[2]

absences as well as other absences. Attendance controls can include a requirement for advance notice of absence, providing a copy of the jury summons to substantiate the absence, and requiring the employee to return to work if a half day or more of work can be performed at the conclusion of jury service.

**Sample Policy**

**XYZ COMPANY**
**PERSONNEL POLICY & PROCEDURE**

SUBJECT: JURY SERVICE                                    DATE: May 1, 1993

*Policy*: It is the policy of XYZ Company to recognize the civic responsibility of jury service by permitting time off work as necessary for jury duty and to provide limited financial protection when an employee is summoned to jury service.

*Procedure*:
1. The employee is responsible for notifying the company as soon as a juror summons is received. A minimum of two days' prior notice is needed for the company to plan for the absence. The employee must

provide a copy of the jury summons to the supervisor. The summons is routed to the office for inclusion in the employee's personnel file.

2. An employee who participates in jury service shall receive pay for the difference between his or her regular pay rate per day up to eight hours and daily jury pay, for a period up to two weeks (10 working days).

3. Upon return to work, the employee is responsible for turning in a copy of the juror pay stub to his or her supervisor. The supervisor shall route the pay stub copy to the Payroll Department. The employee will receive a paycheck with the jury pay differential on the next regular pay day.

4. Jury service which exceeds the 10 days is considered an unpaid leave of absence.

5. The period of jury service shall be recorded on the employee's attendance record. Time off for jury service counts as time worked for overtime pay eligibility for nonexempt employees.

6. In the event the employee is released from jury duty early in the day (permitting a half day of work or more), the employee is expected to return to work.

7. All benefits continue uninterrupted during the period of jury service. In the event of an extended jury service obligation, the company will make arrangements to delay payroll deductions for group insurance premiums if requested by the employee.

8. In the event an employee fails to provide timely notice of jury service, a warning may be issued to the employee for late or lack of notice.

**Sample Employee Handbook Paragraph**

*Jury Duty*

Employees who are summoned to and participate in jury duty will receive pay for the difference between their regular pay rate for up to eight hours and daily jury pay, for a period of up to two weeks. Please notify your supervisor when you receive a juror summons and provide a juror's pay warrant upon your return to work.

In cases where jury service would cause a hardship, the Company may request that the employee be excused from jury service.

Time off without pay may be granted for circumstances which exceed the limits of this policy.

# Medical Leave

A Medical Leave Policy is intended to cover absences for medical reasons such as accidents, hospitalization, extended illness, in-patient substance abuse treatment, work injury, pregnancy, or other health-related conditions. A medical leave is distinguished from a policy allowing absence or providing pay for occasional instances of illness, commonly referred to as a sick leave benefit. While a Sick Leave Policy (see page 211) covers an occasional sick day, the Medical Leave Policy focuses on major or long-term periods of absence for medical reasons.

A broadly written Medical Leave Policy can cover various medical conditions that may include accidents or disability arising from employment, non-job-related medical conditions, or pregnancy. Some organizations, on the other hand, may develop separate policies to cover each of these issues independently.

A Medical Leave Policy should define circumstances covered by the leave such as

- Absences for a medical reason as certified by a physician and when the employee is under the care of a physician
- Absences involving hospitalization
- Absences for a medial reason occurring for an extended period, such as five days or more

By using these broad criteria to define the leave, you have a basis to deal with a wide variety of circumstances which cause an employee to be absent for medical-related reasons.

When defining a medical leave, consider the absence separately from pay. First define the circumstances under which an employee may be placed on a medical leave of absence. Include a statement that the employee's regular salary will be suspended during the period of leave. Then, if desired by company management, define what type of salary continuation or disability income benefit may be provided.

Other important issues to consider when developing a Medical Leave Policy include requirements for notification of absence, allowable duration of absence, reinstatement following absence, and eligibility for benefits during the period of leave. In addition, when the company is providing compensation to the employee during a medical leave, it may be wise insurance to reserve the right to require a second medical opinion from a company-paid doctor before granting a leave, extending a leave, or paying disability income benefits.

Many of the foregoing issues are now defined by the Family and Medical Leave Act of 1993. Employers with an existing medical leave policy should review and update their medical leave policy for consistency with the new law. Firms that are defining a new policy are referred to the Family and Medical Leave section of this chapter.

Many companies have asked what is the best way to deal with an employee who has an infectious or contagious condition which could infect other employees, customers, or contaminate products or food items. These far-ranging issues really require a variety of policy guidelines which promote safety, health, and well-being on the job. In part, this issue can be covered in the Medical Leave Policy by requiring an employee who incurs a medical condition which may adversely affect the safety or health of other employ-

## CHECKLIST
### A Medical Leave Policy

- What are state and federal requirements relating to medical leave of absence?

- What classes or categories of employees are covered by the medical leave of absence policy?

- When and how must the employee notify the company about a medical leave of absence?

- Will the firm define one broad policy for medical leaves, or will separate policies be defined for job-related absence, non-job-related absence, etc.?

- Will the policy cover family and medical leaves in one policy, or will separate policies be defined for medical issues and for family issues?

- Will regular salary be suspended during medical leave, or will the company provide some form of disability pay benefit?

- If a disability pay benefit is provided, what amount and for how long will pay be continued? (See "Salary Continuation Benefit," Chap. 12.)

- Will the employee be required to submit a doctor's statement identifying the nature of illness/disability and duration of absence?

- Will a doctor's statement be required periodically during leave or upon return to work?

- How will the medical leave of absence affect the employee's entitlement to benefits or insurances?

- What responsibility will the employee have to seek medical care for conditions which may infect other employees, customers, or products?

- How will a medical leave of absence affect overtime pay eligibility?

- What reemployment rights does the employee have?

- What attendance records will be maintained?

ees, customers, products, or food items to report the condition to the company and to seek appropriate medical care. When the employee's medical condition interferes with the performance of job duties, placing the employee on a medical leave may be one alternative.

The American's with Disabilities Act (ADA) creates an obligation to make reasonable accommodations for employees with a disability. For example, an employee with a chronic medical condition or a permanent partial disability may seek reemployment from a medical leave. While the ADA excludes temporary medical conditions, an employee with a permanent or chronic condition would be subject to ADA reasonable accommodation requirements.

This means that the employer must evaluate the employee's ability to perform essential functions of the job and, if necessary, make a reasonable accommodation for the individual. Be sure that your Medical Leave Policy covers such contingencies.

## Pitfalls to Avoid

The medical leave issue presents some sensitive concerns which can result in serious liabilities for the employer if matters aren't properly handled. Here are some pitfalls to avoid.

1. Define your Medical Leave Policy to include pregnancy as a temporary disability. The major legal guidelines from the EEOC stipulate that policies and benefits for pregnancy and related medical conditions be the same as policies and benefits for other temporary disabilities. Some states, such as California, have a maternity leave law. Check the requirements in your state to make sure that your policy complies with local requirements.

2. Avoid confusing disability pay benefits with medical leave. While a disability pay benefit is normally provided to an employee on a medical leave, it is best to define these two issues as separate policies. Not all firms provide a disability pay benefit. Yet every organization, at one time or another, will have to deal with an employee's extended absence for medical reasons. The solution is to define the procedures which control the absence. If desired, the company can also define its practice of compensating an employee while on a medical leave.

3. Take care to clarify benefits entitlements and re-employment rights, if any. Summarize the Medical Leave Policy on an employee information sheet and require sign-off to document that the employee understands the policy. A leave of absence, by its definition, does imply a degree of job attachment and reemployment. Now, under the Family and Medical Leave Act, a covered employer is required to place the returning employee into the same or similiar job at the end of the leave period.

   A typical problem occurs when the temporary replacement worker is a better performer than the prior employee who is currently on leave of absence. The employer then wants to retain the replacement worker and not rehire the employee on leave. Such action will be illegal under the new leave law. However, in order to maintain the maximum degree of staffing flexibility, I recommend a policy statement that asserts the company's right to fill, alter, or eliminate a vacant position during any period of leave. The policy may state that the returning employee may be placed into the same or similar position if available, or offered another suitable job, or placed on a layoff status if no suitable work is available.

**Sample Policy**

**XYZ COMPANY
PERSONNEL POLICY & PROCEDURE**

SUBJECT: MEDICAL LEAVE OF ABSENCE            DATE: May 1, 1993

*Policy*: It is the policy of XYZ Company to grant a medical leave of absence subject to business needs when an employee becomes seriously ill or disabled.

*Procedure*:

1. A medical leave of absence is defined as an absence due to serious illness or disability of the employee normally lasting five (5) workdays or more, during which time the employee is under the care of a physician. Absences for maternity are included under this policy.

2. The employee is responsible for submitting a Leave Request Form together with a physician's certification to his or her Supervisor in advance or as soon as possible after the start of leave. The physician's statement should identify the nature of the disability and anticipated duration of absence.

3. The Supervisor shall evaluate the leave request with consideration given to staffing needs and the facts of the case. Normally, the length of a medical leave is determined by the physician's evaluation of the employee's condition and ability to work. During the period of leave, the Company may direct the employee to submit updated physician's certifications.

4. In the event of a question regarding a medical leave, the Supervisor may elect at company expense to obtain a second medical opinion prior to considering or extending a medical leave of absence. In the event of a difference in medical opinions, the company may elect at its expense to obtain a third medical opinion in the evaluation of the leave of absence.

5. An employee's regular wage or salary is suspended during the medical leave. During medical leave, the employee may be eligible for compensation from one or more of the following benefits as applicable: sick pay, disability pay, union health and welfare, vacation, worker's compensation, or other similar plans as defined by the Company, except that no two forms of compensation shall be paid simultaneously.

6. In the event an employee incurs a medical condition which may infect other employees or the ability to work safely, the employee has a responsibility to seek appropriate medical care and take appropriate steps to minimize the spread of the condition to others. If a Supervisor becomes aware of an employee's contagious condition, it is recommended that the situation be discussed with one's superior and the Human Resource Manager. In such cases, the Company may elect to refer the employee for medical tests or treatment, make a reasonable accommodation for the condition, or place the employee on a medical leave of absence.

7. During a period of medical leave, the employee retains length-of-service credit, but is not entitled to receive holiday pay. Accrual of vacation benefits is suspended during leave. The company paid portion of insurance will be continued for up to 12 weeks. The employee is

responsible for continuing to pay normal insurance contributions if uninterrupted insurance is desired.

8. At the conclusion of the leave period, the employee must submit a physician's certification that he or she can resume normal job duties. In the event an employee fails to return to work on an agreed date at the end of leave or fails to receive approval for a leave extension, the continued absence will be viewed as a voluntary quit.

9. The Supervisor shall place the returning employee in the same or similar job for any medical absence of 12 weeks or less. However, during any period of leave, the Company reserves the right to fill, change, or eliminate a vacant position if required by the needs of the business. In those cases when no suitable work is available, customary layoff procedures shall apply.

10. The individual responsible for maintaining time records shall record the absence as medical leave on the employee's time card.

## Sample Employee Handbook Paragraph

*Medical Leave of Absence*

An employee who becomes seriously ill or disabled may be placed on medical leave. Medical leaves are normally approved for periods of up to 30 days, and may be extended at 30-day intervals up to a total of 12 weeks. A medical statement is required to place the employee on leave, when requesting extensions, and upon return to work. Absence for maternity is treated in a manner similar to temporary disability.

An employee on medical leave may be paid in accordance with the Company's disability insurance if eligible, or worker's compensation, if applicable. During a medical leave, the employee is responsible for paying normal insurance premium contributions in order to maintain insurance coverages.

In the event an employee incurs a medical condition which may affect the employee's ability to work safely or which may adversely affect other employees, the employee has a responsibility to report the condition to management and to seek appropriate medical care. In such cases, the Company may elect to schedule the individual for medical exams and tests, arrange a medical leave of absence as appropriate, or make a reasonable accommodation for the condition. Further details on leaves of absence are defined in the company policy on Conditions of Leave.

# Maternity Leave

The growing number of women of childbearing age in the workforce means that most firms sooner or later will have to deal with a maternity leave issue. A firm that has a clear policy which properly defines procedures for childbearing absence will eliminate many questions, concerns, and potential legal liabilities.

The Family and Medical Leave Act of 1993 defines important issues relating to pregnancy, maternity, and care of a new child. A woman who is disabled and unable to work due to pregnancy must be granted leave under the new law. Further, once there is a new child in the household, the employee can request time off work to care for the child. Further details on family and medical leaves are defined elsewhere in this chapter.

The Pregnancy Disability Act of 1978, which amends Title VII of the Civil Rights Act of 1964, prohibits discrimination on the basis of pregnancy or related conditions. This law requires the employer to treat pregnancy as any other temporary medical disability with regard to leave of absence policies, compensation, benefits, and other terms or conditions of employment.

As a result of the pregnancy disability law, I recommend that firms define a medical leave policy which includes absence for pregnancy and related conditions. This approach promotes uniformity in the handling of maternity absences like any other temporary medical disability. The only exception to this guideline would be in those areas where state or local laws define greater requirements which do not violate Title VII.

One example of such a law is the California Maternity Leave Law. In 1987, the U.S. Supreme Court upheld the state law, requiring California Savings and Loan Association to grant reemployment to receptionist Lillian Garland following her maternity leave. In deciding this case, the court acknowledged that a state law which provides greater protections for women was not in violation of Title VII.[3]

Whether a firm defines one medical leave policy including maternity absences in compliance with Title VII, or separate maternity and medical leave policies to comply with state law, the leave of absence policies should contain similar procedures. The policy should include provisions to define the nature of covered absences, require the employee to report the absence to the company, rely on a physician's statement certifying period of disability, define any pay or benefits entitlements, and clarify reemployment procedures. Further details are highlighted in the following checklist.

## Pitfalls to Avoid

Effective handling of maternity leaves has been an area of continued concern for many employers. Some firms which failed to define a clear policy or developed inappropriate policies ultimately were on the losing end of a lawsuit. Here are some pitfalls to avoid.

1. Unless specifically required by state or local law, avoid the tendency to define separate policies for maternity and medical leaves of absence. Where your state defines specific requirements for maternity leave, be sure to develop a policy which is in compliance. In addition to complying with any state requirements, medical and maternity leaves should provide the same terms, conditions, and benefits in order to comply with the Pregnancy Discrimination Act.

**CHECKLIST**
**A Maternity Leave of Absence Policy**

- Are there any state or local laws requiring specific policies, pay, or benefits for women on a maternity leave?

- What classes or categories of employees are covered by the medical leave of absence policy?

- When and how must the employee notify the company about a maternity leave of absence?

- Will regular salary be suspended during maternity leave, or will the company provide some form of disability pay benefit?

- If a disability pay benefit is provided, what amount and for how long will pay be continued? (See "Salary Continuation Benefit," Chap. 12.)

- Will the employee be required to submit a doctor's statement identifying the nature of illness/disability and duration of absence?

- Will a doctor's statement be required periodically during leave or upon return to work?

- How will the maternity leave of absence affect the employee's entitlement to benefits or insurances?

- How will a maternity leave of absence affect overtime pay eligibility?

- What reemployment rights does the employee have?

- What attendance records will be maintained?

- How will an employee's request for extended absence for child care be handled?

2. Take care not to define a specified period or time limit for maternity leaves which differs from medical leaves. The Maternity Leave Policy of a generation ago often defined a maternity leave as an absence of up to three months. Such a practice is now prohibited if it differs from the firm's practice for other medical disabilities. The period of disability will vary from woman to woman. Some women may only miss a week or two from work. Others, due to medical complications, may require an absence of several months or more.

   The key to the period of absence should be the time period in which the female employee's doctor certifies that she is unable to work due to the temporary disability of pregnancy or related conditions. The woman's general health, medical conditions related to pregnancy, physical demands of the job, or complications arising from delivery are factors which may influence a physician's certification of disability during periods before and after delivery.

3. Often following a delivery, a new mother will request additional time

off from work to care for the newborn child. Unless there are medical complications affecting the female employee, this type of request should be considered under a personal, family, parental, or family and medical leave of absence policy. When there is no longer a medical condition affecting the employee, as certified by a physician, the period of medical leave should come to an end. Any further requests for absence may be considered under other applicable policies.

**Sample Policy**

See policy for Medical Leave of Absence (page 213).

**Sample Employee Handbook Paragraph**

See policy for Medical Leave of Absence.

## Personal/Family Leave

The growing number of single working parents and employees with working spouses has led to greater employer interest in providing family-friendly policies. Family-friendly policies are personnel practices or benefits which aid the employee in meeting family obligations. One example of a family-friendly policy is the granting of a personal/family leave of absence. Another term for this type of leave is parental leave.

A Personal/Family Leave Policy defines a basis to grant employee absences for a variety or reasons such as a child care absence following pregnancy or adoption, an absence to care for a sick or disabled family member, an extended vacation period, or other circumstance requiring the employee to be absent from work.

In recent years, some states have passed laws requiring employers to grant personal or family leave up to specified limits when requested by an employee. Currently, 13 states have statutory requirements for family or parental leave. States with parental leave laws are CO, CT, OK, KS, KY, ME, MA, MN, MT, NJ, NY, OR, RI, TN, VT, WA, and WI.

Typically, these laws relate to absence for childbirth, adoption, or care for a sick child. The U.S. Congress passed similar legislation at a national level. The Family and Medical Leave Act received presidential approval in February, 1993.

Your firm may elect to define a Personal/Family Leave policy in order to provide leave benefits which exceed requirements of the state or federal law. Leave typically would be unpaid. Your policy should define covered absences, eligibility requirements and level of authority for approving leave.

**CHECKLIST**
**A Personal/Family Leave Policy**

- Are there any state law requirements for personal, family, or parental leave?

- What classes or categories of employees are covered by the family/personal leave policy?

- When and how must the employee request leave or notify the company regarding absence?

- Will time off for personal/family leave be paid or unpaid?

- If paid time is provided, what amount and for how long will pay be continued?

- How will the personal/family leave affect the employee's entitlement to benefits and insurance?

- How long of a time period will be permitted for absence?

- What documents, if any, will be needed to substantiate the employee's request for absence?

- Will the absence count as time worked toward overtime pay eligibility for nonexempt employees?

- What attendance records will be maintained?

- What circumstances, if any, may be used as a basis to grant or deny leave?

As with other forms of a leave of absence, a Personal/Family Leave Policy should include a requirement for reasonable notice to the employer, limits or conditions of leave, and clarification of benefits entitlements while the employee is on leave.

## Competitive Practices

The charts shown in Figs. 9.2a and 9.2b reveal personal leave and parental leave practices in small firms and in medium and large firms.

## Pitfalls to Avoid

A major concern with any leave of absence policy is balancing the employer's need for adequate staffing versus the employee's need for time away from work for handling personal matters. Here are some pitfalls to avoid when developing your personal/family leave policy.

1. Avoid a "head in the sand" attitude about personal and family leaves. Various lobbying groups speaking for business have advocated against proposed laws required for parental or personal/family leaves of absence. Owners of many small and mid-sized businesses complain that

| Employer leave policy | All employees | Profes- sional and admini- strative employees | Technical and clerical employees | Production and service employees |
|---|---|---|---|---|
| Total ................................. | 100 | 100 | 100 | 100 |
| Eligible for parental leave[1] ................. | 41 | 45 | 41 | 39 |
| Eligible for maternity leave ........... | 41 | 44 | 41 | 39 |
| Paid days only ......................... | 2 | 2 | 1 | 2 |
| Unpaid days only ..................... | 35 | 37 | 36 | 34 |
| Both unpaid and paid days ..... | 1 | 2 | 1 | 1 |
| Information not available on type of days .......................... | 2 | 3 | 2 | 2 |
| Not eligible for maternity leave ......................................... | ([2]) | 1 | ([2]) | ([2]) |
| Eligible for paternity leave ........... | 20 | 23 | 20 | 19 |
| Paid days only ......................... | 1 | 2 | 1 | 1 |
| Unpaid days only ..................... | 18 | 20 | 17 | 17 |
| Both unpaid and paid days ..... | ([2]) | ([2]) | ([2]) | ([2]) |
| Information not available on type of days .......................... | 1 | 1 | 1 | 1 |
| Not eligible for paternity leave ......................................... | 21 | 21 | 21 | 20 |
| Not eligible for parental leave ........... | 59 | 55 | 59 | 61 |

[1] Parental leave includes plans providing maternity leave only, paternity leave only, and both maternity and paternity leave.
[2] Less than 0.5 percent.

NOTE: Because of rounding, sums of individual items may not equal totals. Where applicable, dash indicates no employees in this category.

**Figure 9.2a.** Parental leave: Percent of full-time employees by leave policy, medium and large firms, 1989.[3]

mandated leaves will affect staffing and create absences which affect the cost of doing business. Many of these very same employers, however, are likely to grant an absence for a valued employee in time of need and hold the vacant job open until the employee returns. The simple fact is, with large numbers of dual working spouses and single parents in the workforce, there will be personal emergencies causing employees to request a leave of absence. The employer who arbitrarily refuses such requests or fails to define a policy for dealing with these issues is likely to experience personnel problems. When an employee's personal matters interfere with work, there are likely to be increased instances of absence, lower productivity, and greater likelihood of errors. Some experienced workers may even be forced to quit work to solve personal matters. For the employer, these circumstances also

| Employer leave policy | All employees | Professional, technical, and related employees | Clerical and sales employees | Production and service employees |
|---|---|---|---|---|
| Total ........................................ | 100 | 100 | 100 | 100 |
| Eligible for parental leave[1] ................... | 19 | 30 | 23 | 13 |
| Eligible for maternity leave ........... | 19 | 29 | 23 | 13 |
| Paid days only ......................... | 2 | 3 | 2 | 1 |
| Unpaid days only .................... | 16 | 26 | 19 | 11 |
| Both unpaid and paid days ..... | ([2]) | ([2]) | 1 | ([2]) |
| Information not available on type of days ......................... | ([2]) | ([2]) | 1 | ([2]) |
| Not eligible for maternity leave ......................................... | ([2]) | ([2]) | ([2]) | ([2]) |
| Eligible for paternity leave ........... | 8 | 13 | 9 | 6 |
| Paid days only ........................ | ([2]) | ([2]) | ([2]) | ([2]) |
| Unpaid days only .................... | 7 | 13 | 8 | 5 |
| Both unpaid and paid days ..... | ([2]) | ([2]) | ([2]) | ([2]) |
| Information not available on type of days ......................... | ([2]) | ([2]) | ([2]) | ([2]) |
| Not eligible for paternity leave ......................................... | 11 | 16 | 14 | 7 |
| Not eligible for parental leave ........... | 81 | 70 | 77 | 87 |

[1] Parental leave includes plans providing maternity leave only, paternity leave only, and both maternity and paternity leave.
[2] Less than 0.5 percent.

NOTE: Because of rounding, sums of individual items may not equal totals. Where applicable, dash indicates no employees in this category.

**Figure 9.2b.** Parental leave: Percent of full-time employees by leave policy, small establishments, 1990.[4]

increase personnel costs. I recommend a Personal Leave Policy which balances employer and employee needs.

2.  Maintain control of leave of absence situations by defining eligibility criteria and conditions of leave. Managers at some firms complain that a Leave of Absence Policy gives employees the right to come and go as they please. One manager, for example, lamented that 10 percent of the workforce would "return to the old country" each year to visit family members for three to six months at a time and then suddenly return and expect their jobs back. In this case, the firm solved its dilemma by writing a policy that required a one year service eligibility, limited leaves to 30 days, and defined requirements for benefits and insurance eligibility.

3. Avoid confusion about reemployment rights by defining conditions of leave. If a particular law requires reinstatement following leave, then the policy should comply accordingly. However, in the absence of a legal requirement or union agreement, the employer is free to define a policy regarding reinstatement procedures. In order to maximize flexibility, some firms reserve the right to fill, alter, or eliminate a vacant position if required by the needs of the business. In such cases, it is best to have the employee sign a statement which clarifies the leave policy, reinstatement procedures, and benefits eligibility during leave.

4. Take care to consistently administer a leave of absence policy. For example, if management holds a high-level job open for a male while on leave, but hires a replacement for a female on leave and then fails to reinstate her, this may be sufficient cause for a sex discrimination claim by the woman.

## Sample Policy

### XYZ COMPANY
### PERSONNEL POLICY & PROCEDURE

| SUBJECT: LEAVE OF ABSENCE | DATE: May 1, 1993 |
|---|---|

*Policy*: It is the policy of XYZ Company to recognize that an employee may need time off from work for medical or personal reasons. An absence for maternity is included under this policy.

*Procedure*:
1. An employee with one year or more Company service working a minimum of 1000 hours may schedule a leave of absence by providing reasonable advance notice. Our policy for leaves of absence is designed to be consistent with state law.

2. Family leave of up to six weeks in a 12-month period for the birth, adoption, or preadoption placement of a child, provided the leave begins within 16 weeks of the child's birth or placement.

3. Time off up to two weeks in a 12-month period to care for the employee's child, spouse, or parent, if there is a serious health condition involving inpatient care in a hospital or nursing home or outpatient care requiring continuing treatment by a health care provider.

4. The leaves described in paragraphs 1 and 2 may not exceed eight weeks in a 12-month period and may be scheduled by the employee as a partial absence.

5. The employee may have two weeks of medical leave during a 12-month period for a serious health condition which makes the employee unable to perform his or her duties.

6. In cases involving illness or disability of the employee, the employee must submit a physician's certification when requesting leave. The employee's regular salary is suspended during leave. The employee may

be eligible for compensation through one or more of the Company's disability or sick pay plans.

7. In the event an employee incurs a medical condition which may affect the employee's ability to work safely or which may adversely affect other employees, the employee has a responsibility to report the condition to management and to seek appropriate medical care. In such cases, the Company may elect to schedule the individual for medical exams and tests, arrange a medical leave of absence as appropriate, or make a reasonable accommodation for the condition.

8. In the event of a question regarding a medical leave or an employee's ability to perform available work, the Company may elect to obtain a second medical opinion prior to considering or extending a medical leave of absence.

9. The Company may consider unpaid leaves of absence exceeding the guidelines defined above or requests from individuals who are ineligible as defined above. In such cases, approval of any leave is at management discretion after considering the circumstances of the case and staffing needs.

10. The leave of absence shall be recorded on the employee's attendance record.

### Sample Employee Handbook Paragraph

*Leave of Absence*

We expect that employees will plan normal personal business obligations to avoid conflict with work schedules. However, the Company recognizes that certain circumstances may compel absence from work for medical or urgent personal reasons. In such cases, an employee may request a leave of absence.

Each request for leave will be handled on an individual basis, in writing, and approval is at management discretion, subject to the needs of the business. In cases involving illness, injury, or maternity, a medical statement is required to place an employee on leave and upon return to work. An employee on a medical leave is paid in accordance with the Company's disability plan if eligible.

An employee on leave loses all benefits during the period of absence except seniority. A leave of absence, when granted, is with the understanding that the employee will return to work on a specified return date.

## Family and Medical Leave

The Family and Medical Leave Act of 1993 defines requirements for employers to grant leave of absence when requested by eligible employees. The passage of this law was the result of an eight-year effort in Congress to achieve a consensus that balanced employer staffing concerns with employee needs. Several prior leave bills were vetoed by Presidents Reagan and Bush before the current Act cleared Congress and was signed into law on February 5, 1993 by President Clinton.

The Family and Medical Leave law reflects the changing needs of the workforce. A significant number of married employees now are likely to have a working spouse. As our population ages, many individuals have undertaken responsibility for the care of an aged or infirm parent. In addition, our society has a growing number of households with an employed single parent.

All of these factors place added family care pressures upon employees. As a result, care of dependents is an emerging concern that distracts employees from job duties. The Family and Medical Leave law helps to balance the sometimes conflicting needs of employees and their employers.[5]

To date, 35 states have passed varying laws dealing with family leave issues. Some of the state laws are limited only to public sector employees. Employers in these states will be subject to their respective state law if it provides greater benefit or protection for the employee. According to the February 10, 1993 issue of *Labor Relations Week*, a publication of the Bureau of National Affairs, the following states have family leave laws or regulations:[6]

| States allowing leave for public employees only | States allowing leave for public and private sector employees |
|---|---|
| Alaska | California |
| Arizona | Connecticut |
| Delaware | District of Columbia |
| Florida | Hawaii |
| Georgia | Kentucky |
| Idaho | Maine |
| Illinois | Minnesota |
| Iowa | New Jersey |
| Louisiana | Oregon |
| Maryland | Rhode Island |
| Missouri | Vermont |
| North Dakota | Washington |
| Oklahoma | Wisconsin |
| South Carolina | |
| West Virginia | |

An understanding of the new Family and Medical Leave Act is essential to define a leave policy that complies with the law. Highlights of the new law drawn from the February 11, 1993 issue of *Labor Law Reports* (Issue Number 541, Report 463, published by Commerce Clearing House) are summarized below.

The Family and Medical Leave Act covers private employers and public agencies with 50 or more employees. Excluded are individuals who work for an employer who has fewer than 50 employees within 75 miles of the employee's worksite. Eligible employees are those individuals who have worked for 12 months and accumulate 1250 hours of service.

Under the law, an eligible employee is entitled to 12 unpaid work weeks of leave during any 12-month period for any of the following reasons:

1. Birth of a child

2. Adoption or placement of a new child in the home including a foster child

3. Serious health condition of a spouse, parent, or child

4. Disability due to the employee's own serious health condition

Leave should be requested 30 days in advance or the employee should provide other such notice as practicable. Leave may be taken on an intermittent or reduced basis. The employer may require the employee to submit a medical certification of the serious health condition of the employee or family member when requesting leave and at reasonable intervals during leave. The employer may require the employee to use available paid vacation or sick leave benefits during the mandated 12-week leave period.

The law specifies certain benefit protections for employees. Most notable, the law requires that the employee returning from leave be placed in the same or equivalent position with like pay, benefits, and conditions of employment. The highest paid 10 percent of the employer's workforce are exempted from reemployment requirements.

Health insurance benefits must be continued under the conditions coverage would have been provided to the employee during the employment.

The employer is prohibited from discharging or otherwise discriminating against an employee for exercise of rights under the law. A notice of the Act's provisions must be displayed in the workplace.

Special rules for teachers are defined affecting leave scheduling and intermittent leaves. The law also covers federal civil service workers and employees of the U.S. Congress.

The law takes effect six months after the February 5, 1993 enactment. In the case of a collective bargaining agreement, the Act takes effect upon the termination of the agreement but not later than 12 months after enactment.

The law allows civil suits by employees and the U.S. Department of Labor may take certain enforcement actions. In writing the Family and Medical Leave Act, Congress also directed the Labor Department to issue regulations for administration of the law.[7]

During congressional hearings on the law, business groups had argued that the law was another example of government's intrusion into the employment process. Opponents charged that the law would increase employment costs, disrupt work scheduling, and adversely affect smaller businesses.

Many firms, however, were already providing leaves of absence to employees. (See Figure 9.2) This new law serves as a guideline to aid employers in defining leave of absence policies. State and federal laws are fairly clear in defining employer obligations to grant leave for jury duty and military service. Prior to now, guidelines for absences due to family or employee medical disabilities were not clearly defined except in those states with a leave law.

The Pregnancy Discrimination Act of 1978 merely mandated that pregnancy be treated as a temporary disability and required employers to provide like benefits or policies for pregnancy and other medical conditions. Under the 1978 law, an employer could operate without a medical leave policy. There was no federal requirement to grant leave of absence for medical or pregnancy reasons. Now this gap has been filled. A female employee's application for leave due to pregnancy and care of a newborn child is likely to be a leading cause of employee leave requests under the new law. Employers now have definitive guidelines for handling employee leave requests.

The checklist on the following page provides ideas to help define a Family and Medical Leave Policy.

## Pitfalls to Avoid

Enforcement provisions of the new Family and Medical Leave Act include employer liability to the affected employee for monetary damages for lost salary or benefits, interest owed on monetary damages, additional liquidated damages, court costs, attorney's fees, court-ordered reinstatement, or other equitable relief. The employee may sue the employer in state or federal court to seek relief. In addition, the U.S. Department of Labor may investigate complaints and take certain enforcement actions. To minimize these liabilities, here are some pitfalls to avoid:

1. As noted earlier in this book, most employee policy questions relate to pay, time off from work, or a combination of these issues. Many employers currently deal with family and medical leave issues on a case-by-case basis. Such informal practices are ripe for discrimination claims. To avoid costly claims and disruption to work schedules, employers should define leave of absence policies, using the applicable laws as a guideline.

   The employer is permitted under the law to define certain control procedures to minimize abuse of leave policies. Among the control procedures are leave eligibility, unpaid absence, doctor certification,

## CHECKLIST
## A Family and Medical Leave Policy

- What are the provisions of the new federal law and regulations relating to family and medical leaves?

- Does your state define requirements for a family or medical leave of absence?

- How should existing leave policies or collective bargaining agreements be modified to comply with the new law?

- Prior to scheduling a family and medical leave, will employees be required to use other paid leave benefits such as vacation, paid personal days, or paid sick days?

- What classes or categories of employees are covered by the Family and Medical Leave Policy?

- What eligibility requirements will be defined for leave benefits?

- Will the leave be paid or unpaid?

- Will the employee be required to submit a doctor's statement identifying the nature of the illness/disability and duration of absence?

- Will a doctor's statement be required periodically during leave or upon return to work?

- What limits will be defined for leave duration or frequency of allowed leave?

- Will leave be permitted on an intermittent or reduced work schedule basis?

- What leave request procedures will be defined?

- How will the leave affect the employee's entitlement to benefits and insurances?

- How will the family and medical leave absence affect overtime pay eligibility?

- What reemployment rights does the employee have?

- What attendance records will be maintained?

use of vacation or other paid absences as part of the leave period, advance request requirements, and authority to recoup insurance premium costs if the employee fails to return from leave. Be sure to include these controls in your leave policy.

2. Recognize that employees are likely to have a high level of interest in leave benefits and an awareness of reinstatement rights following leave. Define your policy and guide supervisors to make employment decisions fairly. If a firm's leave practices adversely affect women, minorities, or disabled individuals, the firm may be subject to discrimination claims as well as enforcement action under the new law.

3. Avoid an arbitrary or inflexible response to employee leave requests. Disruption to work schedules can be minimized with prior notice of

leave request and use of intermittent or reduced schedule absences. When possible, transfer assignments and cross train employees to ensure that back-up workers are available.

4. Take care to comply with the law's reinstatement provisions. Congressional intent is that the employee be reinstated to a position equivalent in pay, benefits, and other employment terms. This provides a greater degree of job protection than a return to a "comparable" or "similar" position.

**Sample Policy**

**XYZ COMPANY**
**PERSONNEL POLICY & PROCEDURE**

---

SUBJECT: FAMILY AND MEDICAL LEAVE                    Date: May 1, 1993
APPLIES TO: All Employees

---

*Policy*: It is the policy of the XYZ Company to grant a family and medical leave of absence when an employee or immediate family member becomes seriously ill or disabled, or when a new child is in the home.

*Procedure*:

1. To be eligible for a family and medical leave, an employee must have 12 months of continuous Company service during which 1250 or more hours were worked. Employees failing to meet eligibility requirements are not entitled to leave under this policy.

2. An eligible employee may request and receive up to 12 work weeks of unpaid leave during any 12-month period, for any or all of the following reasons:

   a) Serious illness or disability of the employee during which time the employee is under the care of a physician, including pregnancy and related conditions;

   b) Serious illness or disability of the employee's spouse, parent, or child, requiring the employee's assistance to care for the individual; and

   c) Birth of a new child or placement of a new child in the home through adoption or other similar procedure.

3. The employee is responsible to submit a leave request form to the supervisor 30 days prior to any leave that can be anticipated, or as soon as possible prior to start of leave if the absence cannot be anticipated. Together with the leave request, the employee must submit a physician's certification describing the nature of the medical condition and anticipated duration of absence. Copies of adoption papers should be provided if the leave is due to child adoption.

4. The employee is responsible for scheduling absences in a manner which minimizes disruption to work activities. Upon receipt of the leave request, the supervisor shall confer with the employee to evaluate suitability for intermittent leave, reduced work schedules, transfer or

reassignment of tasks, or other arrangements which meet work scheduling needs and employee needs.

5. In the event of a question regarding the medical justification for leave, the Company, at its own expense, may obtain a second medical opinion. In the event of a difference between medical opinions, the Company, at its own expense, may obtain a third medical opinion.

6. An employee's regular wage and salary is suspended during the family and medical leave. During medical leave, the employee may be eligible for compensation from one or more of the following benefits as applicable: sick pay, disability pay, union health and welfare, vacation, workers compensation, or other similar plans as defined by the Company, except that no two forms of compensation shall be paid simultaneously.

7. During a period of family and medical leave, the employee retains length of service credit, but is not entitled to receive holiday pay. Accrual of vacation benefits is suspended during leave. The employee is responsible to continue paying normal insurance contributions, and the Company-paid portion continues for up to 12 weeks.

8. At the conclusion of leave period, an employee, who has been absent due to illness or disability, must submit a physician's certification that he or she can resume normal job duties.

9. In the event an employee fails to return to work on an agreed date at the end of leave or fails to receive approval for a leave extension, the continued absence will be viewed as a voluntary quit. In the event the employee quits employment during leave, or fails to return to work at the end of the leave period, the Company is entitled to recoup from the employee any health insurance premiums paid for the employee's insurance coverage during their leave of absence.

10. Following any leave of 12 weeks or less, the Supervisor shall place the returning employee into the same or equivalent job. However, during any period of leave exceeding 12 weeks, the Company reserves the right to fill, change, or eliminate a vacant position if required by the needs of the business.

11. The individual responsible for maintaining time records shall record the absence as medical leave on the employee's time card.

**Sample Employee Handbook
Paragraph**

*Family and Medical Leave of Absence*

XYZ Company recognizes that family obligations and medical conditions may occasionally cause absence from work. In such cases, an eligible employee may request a leave of absence under our Family and Medical Leave of Absence Policy. Employees with 12 months' service and 1250 hours worked are eligible for leave under this policy.

Under this policy, an employee may request leave in the event of: the employee's illness or disability; pregnancy or related conditions affecting a female employee; serious health condition of one's spouse, parent, or child; or in the event of a new child in the home through birth, adoption, or foster care.

Please notify your supervisor 30 days in advance, or as soon as possible if the leave cannot be anticipated. A certificate from your physician will be needed. Try to arrange your absences to minimize disruption to work. Speak with your supervisor if an intermittent or reduced work schedule can be arranged.

A family and medical leave is unpaid and is limited to a maximum of 12 weeks in a 12-month period. You may request to receive sick pay or vacation pay during the absence. Your benefits and length of service continue uninterrupted during leave. Upon return to work, you will be placed into the same or equivalent job. The above provisions regarding benefits, length of service, and reinstatement of employment are limited to a period not to exceed 12 weeks. After 12 weeks, approval of leave, provision of continued benefits, and reemployment are at the discretion of management, considering staffing needs and the circumstances of the case.

## Military Leave

In the decade that followed the Vietnam War the military draft was eliminated, a volunteer army was instituted, and there were no major military actions affecting reserve units. As a result, many firms did not see a need to define a military leave policy. However, the activation of the military reserves in 1990 for the Gulf War called attention to the need for a Military Leave Policy. Many firms which had operated without a clearly defined policy were suddenly scrambling to clarify reemployment rights of military reservists.

A leave of absence for military service is subject to specific governmental requirements. It has long been governmental policy to require employers to release employees when needed for national defense. Further, to support the military veteran's readjustment back to civilian life at the end of the service, the government has provided various veteran's benefits and specified certain employment reinstatement rights.

The controlling law is the Veteran's Re-employment Rights Law of 1958. It requires reinstatement of full-time or part-time employees who volunteer or are inducted into military service, for a four-year period (or five years, if service is extended by the government). To be reinstated, the individual must apply for reemployment within 90 days of military separation or within one year of release from service-connected hospitalization.

A key feature of the law is the requirement that, if the veteran is still qualified to perform job duties, he or she shall be restored to the former job or to a position of like seniority, status, and pay. If the veteran is not qualified to perform the former job by reason of service-connected disability, he or she shall be offered another suitable position. Further, the law prohibits discrimination in employment because of an individual's obligation as a member of a reserve unit.

The major policy concerns for the employer are to grant leave, reinstate the veteran upon timely application, and to provide benefits and pay in a manner as if the employee had not left. Two examples are provided:

1. For employees in military reserves, the law directs employers to grant a leave of absence exclusive of earned vacation and provide employees with equal consideration for job benefits and promotions as all other employees. Military reserve training can be paid, unpaid, or the employer may provide the difference between military pay and the employee's regular pay. The employee can be required to notify the company of his or her absence upon receipt of military orders.

2. For employees enlisting or being activated for an extended military tour of duty, the law requires a leave of absence and reinstatement upon timely application. The returning veteran must be accorded length-of-service or seniority credit as though employment were uninterrupted. However, the employer is not required to pay actual salary for time not worked, nor to pay actual vacation pay benefits for the period of absence. The employee is not required to give advance notice of enlistment or call-up to active duty. At time of employment separation, the employer can require a copy of military orders to document the nature of leave.

## Competitive Practices

The charts shown in Figs. 9.3a and 9.3b give an indication of how firms handle military leave issues.

## Pitfalls to Avoid

1. Avoid the tendency to penalize military reservists because of their military absences. Federal law requires that a reservist be granted earned vacation in addition to absences for military services. The employer may allow the employee's request for vacation pay during the military training absence.

2. Take care to prevent misunderstandings about leave and reinstatement by defining a written policy and having the employee sign an acknowledgment at time of leave. The acknowledgment should specify nature of leave, period of absence, and reemployment procedures.

3. Recognize that, for private employers, there is no federal requirement to pay the employee salary for time actually missed. Actual salary may be suspended during leave.

**CHECKLIST**
**A Military Leave of Absence Policy**

- What are the federal law requirements for a military leave of absence?
- What classes or categories of employees are covered by the military leave policy?
- When and how must the employee notify the company about military reserve training? Military enlistment or induction?
- Will time off for military reserve training or active service be paid or unpaid?
- If paid time is provided, what amount and for how long will pay be continued?
- What documents will be needed to substantiate military reserve training, enlistment, or induction?
- How will military service absence affect the employee's entitlement to benefits and insurance?
- Will a military reserve training absence count toward overtime pay eligibility for nonexempt employees?
- What attendance records will be maintained during periods of military reserve training?
- By what time limits should an employee apply for re-instatement following military service?

**Sample Policy**

**XYZ COMPANY**
**PERSONNEL POLICY & PROCEDURE**

SUBJECT: MILITARY LEAVE OF ABSENCE          DATE: May 1, 1993

*Policy*: It is the policy of XYZ Company to recognize the civic responsibility of military service by permitting time off work as necessary for an employee to fulfill military obligations.

*Procedure*:
1. The employee is responsible for notifying the Company as soon as military orders are received. The employee must submit to the Supervisor a Leave Request Form together with a copy of military orders. The leave request shall be routed to the Personnel Department for inclusion in the individual's personnel file.
2. Management is responsible for permitting the employee to take time off from work for military service. Military leave may be granted for military obligations such as reserve summer training camp, guard activation in a declared emergency, or for an extended tour of duty up to four years (or five years if at the convenience of the military).

| Number of days | All employees | Professional, technical, and related employees | Clerical and sales employees | Production and service employees |
|---|---|---|---|---|
| Total ........................................ | 100 | 100 | 100 | 100 |
| Provided paid military leave ................ | 21 | 29 | 26 | 15 |
| Under 5 days ............................... | (¹) | (¹) | – | (¹) |
| 5-9 days ..................................... | 1 | (¹) | 1 | 1 |
| 10 days ...................................... | 12 | 16 | 14 | 9 |
| 11-14 days .................................. | 1 | 1 | 1 | (¹) |
| 15 days ...................................... | (¹) | 1 | (¹) | (¹) |
| Over 15 days ............................... | 1 | 1 | 1 | 1 |
| No maximum specified² ................ | 6 | 9 | 8 | 5 |
| Number of days not available ....... | 1 | 1 | 1 | – |
| Not provided paid military leave ......... | 79 | 71 | 74 | 85 |

¹ Less than 0.5 percent.
² Military leave is provided as needed.

NOTE: Because of rounding, sums of individual items may not equal totals. Where applicable, dash indicates no employees in this category.

**Figure 9.3a.** Paid military leave: Percent of full-time employees by number of paid military leave days available per year, small establishments, 1990.[9]

3. A military leave of absence is unpaid. An employee may request to receive earned vacation pay during an absence for military reserve training.

4. During a military leave of absence, benefits are administered as defined below:

a) Military reserve summer training camp—All benefits and length of service continue on an uninterrupted basis. The employee is responsible for continuing to pay any normal insurance premium contributions. The employee is entitled to holiday pay for any Company observed holiday occurring during absence.

b) Extended military obligation, enlistment, or conscription—The employee is separated from the payroll and entitled to receive final pay, vacation pay, etc. The employee does not receive any benefits during leave. Upon reinstatement as defined herein, the employee is rehired without loss of length-of-service credits. Benefits and pay are computed based upon uninterrupted length of service.

5. A former employee who is discharged from military service under honorable conditions and applies for reinstatement within 90 days shall be reinstated for the same or similar position and status.

6. The individual responsible for maintaining time records shall record the absence as military leave on the employee's time card.

| Number of days | All employees | Professional and administrative employees | Technical and clerical employees | Production and service employees |
|---|---|---|---|---|
| Total ........................................... | 100 | 100 | 100 | 100 |
| Provided paid military leave ............... | 53 | 61 | 57 | 45 |
| 5 days ...................................... | 2 | 1 | 4 | 1 |
| 6-9 days ................................... | (¹) | (¹) | (¹) | 1 |
| 10 days ..................................... | 31 | 37 | 34 | 26 |
| 11-14 days ................................. | 1 | 1 | 1 | 1 |
| 15 days ..................................... | 2 | 3 | 3 | 2 |
| 16-19 days ................................. | 1 | 1 | 1 | 1 |
| 20 days ..................................... | 2 | 3 | 1 | 1 |
| 21-29 days ................................. | (¹) | (¹) | (¹) | (¹) |
| 30 days ..................................... | 2 | 2 | 1 | 2 |
| More than 30 days ...................... | (¹) | (¹) | (¹) | (¹) |
| No maximum specified² ................ | 12 | 13 | 12 | 11 |
| Number of days not available ....... | (¹) | (¹) | (¹) | (¹) |
| Not provided paid military leave ......... | 47 | 39 | 43 | 55 |

¹ Less than 0.5 percent.
² Military leave is provided as needed.

NOTE: Because of rounding, sums of individual items may not equal totals. Where applicable, dash indicates no employees in this category.

**Figure 9.3b.** Paid military leave: Percent of full-time employees by number of paid military leave days available per year, medium and large firms, 1989.[10]

## Sample Employee Handbook Paragraph

*Military Leave*

Employees who participate in military reserve training exercises may receive time off without pay for the two-week training period. At an employee's request, the Company will provide any earned vacation pay during this time. Please advise your supervisor as soon as you are scheduled for military training.

Employees may be released, without pay, for extended military obligations. A military veteran is eligible for re-employment rights to the same or similar job if the individual a) reapplies within 90 days of military separation, and b) he or she is qualified to perform the job. Monetary benefits such as vacation pay are not paid during a leave of absence. However, a returning military veteran retains length-of-service credit based upon the latest date of hire immediately preceding military service for reinstatement of pay and benefits.

# Funeral Leave

A death in one's immediate family is a traumatic time requiring a period of bereavement. Needless to say, an individual who has lost a spouse or parent, or other member of the immediate family, has many personal concerns on his or her mind. To be responsive to the employee's need at this time, employers customarily grant a period of funeral leave.

A funeral leave is typically granted as a period of authorized absence when the employee notifies management about a death in the family. The absence may be paid or unpaid depending on the employer's practice. The period of absence is usually one to five days in length. In many firms, the period between date of death and date of funeral is considered the funeral leave period. Firms commonly state that funeral leave is provided in the event of death in the immediate family. What constitutes immediate family is an important issue to clarify. Based on my experience writing policies for firms, I have observed the following practices:

1. Most frequently defined as immediate family:
   Current spouse—husband and/or wife
   Child
   Parent—mother and/or father
   Sibling—brother and/or sister (stepparent and stepchild relationships are often included in this category)

2. Other commonly defined family relationships covered in funeral leave policies:
   Spouse's parent
   Brother-in-law
   Sister-in-law
   Grandparent

3. Other family relationships that may be covered by funeral leave:
   Uncles
   Aunts
   Cousins

My advice to clients is to focus their definition of immediate family on the category 1 relationships. Category 2 relationships may also be considered, or perhaps covered by a policy which grants time off on the day of the funeral. If you allow the funeral leave policy to get into category 3 relationships, it is my opinion that you are giving away the store. A policy which covers that many varied relationships will tend to promote unnecessary absences.

Funeral leave absences are not typically covered by state labor law. However, check the laws in your jurisdiction to make sure that your policy does not violate a specific statute. There are, however, several federal laws which influence a funeral leave policy.

Federal and most state fair employment practice laws prohibit discrimination on the basis of religious beliefs. Further, federal law requires the employer to make a reasonable accommodation for an employee's religious beliefs. Since many funeral services and burials are keyed to religious

## CHECKLIST
### A Funeral Leave Policy

- Are there any state or federal laws which affect funeral leave?

- What classes or categories of employees are covered by the funeral leave policy?

- When and how should the employee notify the company about absence due to death in the family?

- Will time off for funeral leave be paid or unpaid?

- If paid time is provided, what amount and for how long will pay be continued?

- What immediate family relationships are covered by the funeral leave policy?

- How will the funeral leave absence affect the employee's entitlement to benefits and insurance?

- What documents will be needed to substantiate death in the family or attendance at a funeral?

- How will absences be handled for other relatives not defined as immediate family?

- Will a funeral leave absence count as time worked toward overtime pay eligibility for nonexempt employees?

- What attendance records will be maintained?

practices, the employer should make a reasonable effort to accommodate the employee's request for funeral leave. As an example, if the employer's policy provides for three days paid funeral leave, the employer may accommodate the employee's request for additional time off without pay.

## Competitive Practices

Bureau of Labor Statistics surveys are shown in Figs. 9.4a and 9.4b to provide an indication of how other firms are handling funeral leaves.

## Pitfalls to Avoid

Accommodating the employee's personal bereavement needs and religious beliefs is an important aspect of a funeral leave policy. Here are some pitfalls to avoid:

1. One of the greatest difficulties with developing and administering a funeral leave policy is clarifying which relationships are included as immediate family. One reason for this difficulty is the many varied family relationships in people's lives. As a result of divorce, death, remarriage, and live-in relationships, the customary terms used to define immediate family may have different meanings to different people. For example,

| Number of days | All em-ployees | Profes-sional, techni-cal, and re-lated employ-ees | Clerical and sales employ-ees | Produc-tion and service employ-ees |
|---|---|---|---|---|
| Total ........................................... | 100 | 100 | 100 | 100 |
| Provided paid funeral leave ................. | 47 | 57 | 54 | 38 |
| 1 day ................................................ | 3 | 4 | 3 | 3 |
| 2 days .............................................. | 4 | 3 | 3 | 5 |
| 3 days .............................................. | 30 | 35 | 36 | 25 |
| 4 days .............................................. | 1 | 2 | 1 | (¹) |
| 5 days .............................................. | 4 | 7 | 5 | 1 |
| More than 5 days ......................... | (¹) | – | (¹) | (¹) |
| No maximum specified ................. | 4 | 6 | 5 | 3 |
| Varies by length of service ........... | (¹) | (¹) | (¹) | – |
| Not provided paid funeral leave ......... | 53 | 43 | 46 | 62 |
| Number of days varies by relation-ship to deceased² ............................ | 10 | 14 | 13 | 7 |

¹ Less than 0.5 percent.
² The maximum number of days provided for any occurrence was in-cluded in the distribution of funeral leave days.

NOTE: Because of rounding, sums of individual items may not equal totals. Where applicable, dash indicates no employees in this category.

**Figure 9.4a.** Paid funeral leave: Percent of full-time employees by number of paid funeral leave days available per occurrence, small establishments, 1990.[11]

some individuals raised by an aunt, uncle, or grandparent tend to view that person as a parent. Divorce and remarriage complicate immediate family definitions. An employee whose parents divorced and then re-married other spouses could claim two sets of parents for funeral leave purposes. When defining your policy, recognize these variations either in the definitions or in policy administration.

2. Avoid abuse of the funeral leave policy by defining a requirement for (or reserving the right to require) the employee to provide proof of relationship or attendance at the funeral. Many managers can cite situations in which an employee seemed to report an unusually large number of deaths in the family, requesting funeral leave for each. If abuse or questionable use of the funeral leave policy is a problem, it is best to require the employee to submit documented proof of relation-ship to the deceased and attendance at the funeral. A funeral card or obituary clipping are common examples of requested documents.

3. Sometimes a family death occurs while an employee is on vacation or other absence. Some firms will allow the employee to charge the time to a funeral leave benefit. Take care not to provide two forms of compen-sation for the same period. Also, what if a family death occurs while an

| Number of days | All employees | Professional and administrative employees | Technical and clerical employees | Production and service employees |
|---|---|---|---|---|
| Total ............................................. | 100 | 100 | 100 | 100 |
| Provided paid funeral leave ................ | 84 | 87 | 86 | 80 |
|   1 day ............................................ | 1 | 1 | 1 | 1 |
|   2 days .......................................... | 3 | 3 | 4 | 2 |
|   3 days .......................................... | 62 | 59 | 58 | 66 |
|   4 days .......................................... | 3 | 4 | 3 | 2 |
|   5 days .......................................... | 9 | 13 | 13 | 5 |
|   More than 5 days ......................... | (') | (') | (') | 1 |
|   Varies by length of service .......... | 5 | 9 | 6 | 3 |
|   Number of days not available ....... | (') | (') | (') | (') |
| Not provided paid funeral leave ......... | 16 | 13 | 14 | 20 |
| Number of days varies by relationship to deceased[2] ............................ | 19 | 19 | 20 | 18 |

[1] Less than 0.5 percent.
[2] The maximum number of days provided for any occurrence was included in the distribution of funeral leave days.

NOTE: Because of rounding, sums of individual items may not equal totals. Where applicable, dash indicates no employees in this category.

**Figure 9.4b.**  Paid funeral leave: Percent of full-time employees by number of paid funeral leave days available per occurrence, medium and large firms, 1989.[12]

employee is on an extended leave of absence? There is no legal obligation to pay for time not worked; therefore, the policy may be defined to provide a paid funeral leave benefit only for time missed from work.

4. Avoid confusion about handling funeral leave on weekends. Following the foregoing reasoning, most firms do not provide paid funeral leave benefits for Saturday or Sunday if the employee's regular work schedule is Monday through Friday. This is done by defining the benefit in the following manner: In the event of death in the immediate family, an employee may receive up to three consecutive days of paid funeral leave for time missed from work during the Monday through Friday work week.

**Sample Policy**

**XYZ COMPANY**
**PERSONNEL POLICY & PROCEDURE**

SUBJECT: FUNERAL LEAVE                                DATE: May 1, 1993

*Policy*: It is the policy of XYZ Company to grant funeral leave in the event of death in an employee's immediate family.

*Procedure*:

1. The employee is responsible for notifying his or her Manager as soon as possible when a death occurs in the family.

2. Employees may receive up to three consecutive days of funeral leave for the immediate family, which should include the day of the funeral. Full-time employees are eligible for funeral leave pay computed based upon the employee's regular pay rate for an eight-hour workday. Funeral leave pay is not paid with any other compensation received from the Company.

3. Immediate family is defined as mother, father, sister, brother, child, stepchild, spouse, mother-in-law, father-in-law.

4. In the event an employee requests additional time off, or attends the funeral of other relatives or is not eligible as defined above, the Manager may permit time off without pay. In all cases the employee is responsible for keeping the Manager informed of the anticipated duration of absence.

5. Time off without pay may be granted to part-time or temporary employees based on the guidelines of this policy.

6. The Company may request proof of relationship and/or proof of attendance at the funeral, such as an obituary clipping, funeral card, or other similar document.

7. The Manager is responsible for recording the individual's absence on the payroll sheet. Time off for funeral leave does not count as time worked toward overtime computations for hourly paid personnel.

## Sample Employee Handbook Paragraph

*Funeral Leave*

In the event of death in the immediate family, employees may be granted up to three days off with pay to attend to funeral matters. Immediate family is defined as spouse, children, parents, brother, or sister.

One day off with pay will be permitted to attend the funeral of mother-in-law, father-in-law, grandparent, or grandchild.

Funeral leave is based on the employee's regular hourly rate for up to eight hours, and an employee may be requested to provide evidence of relationship such as a copy of obituary clipping or funeral card. Please notify your supervisor when you will be absent. Any additional time off may be permitted under the Company policy for a personal leave.

In the event of death of a family member or relative, employees will be permitted an authorized absence without pay to attend to funeral matters. Please notify your supervisor when you will be absent.

## Sick Leave

Just about every employee gets sick once in a while. In recognition of this, many firms provide a paid sick leave benefit for employees. A paid sick leave benefit is intended to provide limited income protection for an employee in cases of non-job-related illness normally lasting only a few days. For extended medical absences lasting beyond a few days, see "Medical Leave."

Not all firms provide a paid sick leave benefit. Some managers or business owners do not believe in paying employees for absence due to occasional illness. Others feel that, once a sick leave benefit is defined, employees will use all available sick days. Says one manager, "It's like giving them (employees) another five days of vacation. They're gonna use it!"

Firms that provide a paid sick leave benefit generally find that most employees do not use all of their sick leave benefit. Admittedly, there typically are a few absentee abusers who use all sick leave or other paid absence benefits and continually test the limits of company policy and supervisory will. Close supervision and consistent administration of attendance and discipline policies are needed for these individuals.

A paid sick leave plan is a valued benefit for many employees. An inquiry about sick leave benefits is a commonly asked question by job seekers. For some individuals, a paid sick leave benefit can influence acceptance of one job offer over another. While managers may deride such an attitude among employees, the paid sick leave benefit helps a firm to provide a competitive pay and benefit package.

Once management decides to provide a paid sick leave benefit, the primary concerns are providing a competitive benefit and controlling abuse of sick leave. To control abuse of sick leave, this policy must be carefully defined and coordinated with other attendance policies. Certain attendance controls are needed in the sick leave policy. Among these controls are call-in or notification requirements, eligibility requirements, benefit limits, and guidelines for handling situations of benefits abuse.

Since a paid sick leave benefit provides pay for time not worked, it is not a legally mandated benefit. However, several federal labor laws can impact on a firm's sick leave policy. Employees exempt from the Fair Labor Standards Act normally are not subject to a pay deduction for an individual absence due to illness. However, interpretive information from the Labor Department indicates that exempt employees may be subject to a pay deduction of a full day or more where a defined sick leave benefit has been exhausted.

Needless to say, all sick leave benefits must be defined and administered in a way which avoids discrimination against protected class individuals. Further, under the new ADA law, an employer may consider greater flexibility and adjustments to enforcement of sick leave or attendance controls as an example of reasonable accommodation for a disabled worker.

The Employee Retirement Income Security Act (ERISA), which defines reporting and plan description requirements for health, welfare, and retirement plans, may create requirements for a firm's sick leave plan. Advice of legal counsel or other specialist is recommended to insure ERISA compliance. State wage payment laws may define requirements for sick leave pay if such a benefit is provided. Further, state laws may specify whether or not

**CHECKLIST**
**A Sick Leave Policy**

- Are there any state or federal laws which affect the Sick Leave Policy?

- What classes or categories of employees are covered by the Sick Leave Policy?

- When and how should the employee notify the company of a sick leave absence?

- Is it permissible to schedule a sick leave absence in advance for a doctor appointment?

- Will time off for sick leave be paid or unpaid?

- If paid time is provided, what amount and for how long will pay be continued?

- How will the sick leave absence affect the employee's entitlement to benefits and insurance?

- Will a doctor's statement be required to substantiate a sick leave absence? If so, will this practice be required with the first absence or a subsequent absence?

- Will employees be permitted to use sick leave pay for personal absences, extended vacation, etc.?

- How will unused sick leave pay benefits be handled (forfeiture, bank for future use, or a cash payout at year end)?

- Will a sick leave absence count as time worked toward overtime pay eligibility for nonexempt employees?

- What corrective action will be taken for abuse of sick leave or falsification of reason for absence?

- What attendance records will be maintained?

---

unused sick leave pay benefits are to be paid to an employee upon separation of employment.

**Competitive Practices**

The charts in Figs. 9.5a and 9.5b show competitive practices for paid sick leave.

**Pitfalls to Avoid**

An effective Sick Leave Policy should help achieve a balance between a benefit providing pay for occasional absence and controlling abuse of absences. Here are some pitfalls to avoid:

1. Avoid confusing attendance control policies with a sick leave policy. On various occasions when assisting a firm to define attendance policies,

| Provision | All employees | Professional, technical, and related employees | Clerical and sales employees | Production and service employees |
|---|---|---|---|---|
| Total ............................................. | 100 | 100 | 100 | 100 |
| Provided paid sick leave .................... | 47 | 70 | 61 | 29 |
| Sick leave provided on: | | | | |
| An annual basis only[1] ............... | 41 | 62 | 53 | 26 |
| A per disability basis only[2] ........ | 2 | 3 | 3 | 2 |
| Both an annual and per | | | | |
| disability basis .......................... | 2 | 3 | 3 | 1 |
| As needed basis[3] ...................... | 1 | 2 | 2 | ([4]) |
| Other basis[5] ............................... | ([4]) | ([4]) | ([4]) | ([4]) |
| Not provided paid sick leave ............. | 53 | 30 | 39 | 71 |

[1] Employees earn a specified number of sick leave days per year. This number may vary by length of service.
[2] Employees earn a specified number of sick leave days for each illness or disability. This number may vary by length of service.
[3] Plan does not specify maximum number of days.
[4] Less than 0.5 percent.
[5] Includes formal plans with provisions that change from a specified number of days per year to a specified number of days per absence after a certain service period.

NOTE: Because of rounding, sums of individual items may not equal totals. Where applicable, dash indicates no employees in this category.

**Figure 9.5a.** Paid sick leave: Percent of full-time employees by type of provision, small establishments, 1990.[13]

the client seems to focus on paid sick leave benefits. While these policies need to be closely related, I recommend one policy on attendance control. If a paid sick leave benefit is provided, prepare a separate policy on sick leave which defines certain conditions under which sick leave benefits will be paid. The sick leave benefit can be one of various allowable reasons for absence, provided the employee provides timely notice and absences are within policy limits.

2. Be wary of undefined sick leave practices. Many smaller and mid-sized firms operate without defining specific sick leave benefits. "We treat employees as professionals," or "If I give five days of sick leave, they (employees) will take them all," are common refrains. The problem is, this practice is viewed by some employees as unlimited sick leave. And, in fact, because some employers fail to keep attendance records, a few employees tend to be absentee or sick leave abusers. Further, a lack of a clearly defined policy makes it difficult to fairly enforce attendance or impose discipline. As a result, some firms find themselves facing discrimination charges or other allegations from discharged employees.

| Provision | All employees | Professional and administrative employees | Technical and clerical employees | Production and service employees |
|---|---|---|---|---|
| Total ............................................. | 100 | 100 | 100 | 100 |
| Provided paid sick leave ................... | 68 | 93 | 87 | 44 |
| Sick leave provided on: | | | | |
| An annual basis only[1] ................ | 51 | 62 | 64 | 37 |
| A per disability basis only[2] ........ | 9 | 16 | 10 | 5 |
| Both an annual and per disability basis ......................... | 6 | 8 | 10 | 2 |
| As needed basis[3] ...................... | 3 | 7 | 2 | (4) |
| Other basis[5] .............................. | (4) | (4) | 1 | (4) |
| Not provided paid sick leave ............ | 32 | 7 | 13 | 56 |

[1] Employees earn a specified number of sick leave days per year. This number may vary by length of service.
[2] Employees earn a specified number of sick leave days for each illness or disability. This number may vary by length of service.
[3] Plan does not specify maximum number of days.
[4] Less than 0.5 percent.
[5] Includes formal plans with provisions that change from a specified number of days per year to a specified number of days per absence after a certain service period.

NOTE: Because of rounding, sums of individual items may not equal totals. Where applicable, dash indicates no employees in this category.

**Figure 9.5b.** Paid sick leave: Percent of full-time employees by type of provision, medium and large firms, 1989.[14]

3. If starting a new paid Sick Leave Policy, avoid being too generous with benefits. It is always easier to add a new benefit or improve upon a benefit rather than take away benefits. Here are some tips for gradually introducing a sick leave benefit:

   ■ If competitive practice is six paid sick days annually, introduce your new policy by granting three or four days per year. You can add another day or two later to reach a competitive level so long as the benefit is not abused.

   ■ Define eligibility requirements which begin after 3, 6, or 12 months of service. This practice minimizes sick leave abuse by new employees or high turnover individuals who may leave during the first few months of service.

   ■ Reduce paid sick leave abuse by new employees by providing a pro rata benefit or requiring the employee to complete a specified period of service before earning each sick day. For example, begin benefits after 60 days' service; then grant one sick day upon completion of each succeeding 60-day period.

4. Clarify how the paid sick leave benefit may be used. Is it for sickness of the employee only or for caring for an ill family member as well? Some firms permit sick days to be used for personal absence such as court date, house closing, etc. Many firms permit use of sick leave benefits for a doctor's appointment. These kinds of questions will come up, so consider these issues when defining your policy.

5. Decide what will happen to unused paid sick leave benefits. Recognize that a forfeiture of unused sick leave benefits—often referred to as a "use or lose" policy—will prompt some employees to call in sick rather than lose the benefit. Also, check for state wage payment laws that may define a "vesting" requirement for sick leave benefits. If the firm elects to pay employees for unused benefits, there is an added cost associated with the payout. If benefits are banked for future use, there will be a need for controls to prevent abuse of this practice.

## Sample Policy

**XYZ COMPANY**
**PERSONNEL POLICY & PROCEDURE**

---

SUBJECT: SICK LEAVE                                          DATE: May 1, 1993

---

*Policy*: It is the policy of XYZ Company to provide a basic sick pay plan which provides limited income maintenance in the event of illness.

*Eligibility*: Full-time nonsupervisory employees with one year service or more.

*Procedure*:

1. Eligible employees are permitted paid sick day absences during each calendar year as summarized below:

   All nonsupervisory employees with one year service or more may receive paid sick days following each January 1 as shown below:

   | Length of service as of January 1 | Paid sick days |
   | --- | --- |
   | 1 year | 1 day |
   | 2 years | 2 days |
   | 8 years | 3 days |
   | 15 years | 4 days |

2. The sick pay benefit may be used when an employee calls in sick, or may be scheduled in advance for medically related absences such as a doctor's appointment. In order to receive pay for a sick day, the employee must call in on the day of the absence, or provide advance notice for absences which can be anticipated.

3. The sick pay benefit is paid based on the employee's regular pay rate for up to eight hours.

4. Any sick pay days which are unused at the end of the calendar year will be paid to the employee, in order to encourage good attendance.

5. Time off on sick pay shall be recorded on the employee's attendance record.

6. Time off for illness (whether paid or unpaid) is *not* counted as time worked when computing overtime.

7. Upon separation of employment, covered employees shall receive pay for any unused sick days based on a proration of one (1) sick day for each two full months of service, up to the limits defined in paragraph 1 of this policy.

8. Abuse of sick pay benefits or falsification of reason for absence is grounds for corrective disciplinary action, which may include immediate discharge.

## Sample Employee Handbook Paragraph

*Sick Days*

XYZ Company provides a sick pay benefit for full-time employees. This benefit may be used for a non-job-related illness, injury, or doctor's appointment for the employee only.

New employees with one year service or more may receive paid sick days following January 1 as shown below:

| Length of service as of January 1 | Paid sick days |
| --- | --- |
| 1 year | 1 day |
| 2 years | 2 days |
| 8 years | 3 days |
| 15 years | 4 days |

The paid sick day is computed based on the employee's regular straight time pay rate for an eight-hour day plus any applicable shift differential. A sick day absence (paid or unpaid) *does not* count toward overtime pay eligibility.

The Company reserves the right to require a physician's statement for sick pay. Any falsification of reason for absence or other abuse of this benefit is grounds for corrective action.

To encourage good attendance, the Company will pay eligible employees for any unused sick days at the end of the calendar year.

## Conditions of Leave

When an employee has been granted a leave of absence, it is assumed that he or she intends to return to work at the end of the leave period. For the employee, the leave of absence provides a degree of job attachment and an expectation of reemployment. However, sometimes circumstances can change causing the employee or the company to separate the employment relationship. Other questions can arise concerning eligibility for benefits, continuation of insurance, or eligibility for income maintenance plans. A carefully prepared policy helps to clarify these circumstances.

A New York company, for example, had defined a leave of absence policy and required employees to sign a letter of understanding when going on leave. One employee went on leave and then failed to contact the company or to return on the designated date at the end of the leave. In accordance with its policy, the company separated the employee and hired a replacement. When the employee finally returned, he sought to reclaim his job by filing an unfair labor practice charge. Upon hearing the facts of the case, the Labor Department Referee sided for the company, citing the "conditions of leave" memo signed by the employee.

## Pitfalls to Avoid

Careful definition of conditions of leave will help to minimize employee complaints, reduce misunderstandings, and prevent legal liabilities. Here are some pitfalls to avoid:

1. Check state and federal laws to make sure that your leave policy is in compliance. Absences for military service, jury service, and to a growing degree parental leave are covered by specific laws in many jurisdictions. Avoid unnecessary legal liabilities by using the laws as a guide for policy provisions.

2. Minimize confusion about leaves of absence, benefits entitlements, and reemployment procedures by defining conditions of leave. A leave of absence involves a form of separation of employment. Such separations can sometimes become permanent. If the separation involves misunderstandings, discriminatory practices, or disregard for procedures, there is a likelihood for costly legal claims by the former employee.

## Sample Policy

**XYZ COMPANY**
**PERSONNEL POLICY & PROCEDURE**

---

SUBJECT: CONDITIONS OF LEAVE          DATE: May 1, 1993

---

*Policy*: It is the policy of XYZ Company to grant a leave of absence when warranted by significant medical, personal, or civic reasons and subject to management discretion after considering the needs of the business.

*Procedure*:
1. A leave of absence is defined as an approved absence from work normally lasting five days or more, during which time the employee's

**CHECKLIST**
**A Conditions of Leave Policy**

---

- Are there any state or federal laws that define requirements for leaves of absence?

- Are there any eligibility or length-of-service requirements which apply to granting a leave or providing benefits?

- Will regular salary be suspended, or will the employee receive some form of income continuation?

- Will the employee be permitted to claim two or more forms of income continuation while on leave (i.e., receiving funeral leave pay while on a medical leave receiving disability)?

- How long will income maintenance be provided?

- During a leave, will the employee be eligible for any of the following benefits?
    Vacation pay
    Holiday pay
    Funeral pay
    Accrual of vacation benefits
    Medical insurance
    Life insurance
    Tuition aid benefits
    or other similar benefits

- During leave, will the employee be required to continue to pay normal contributory insurance premium costs?

- During leave, how long will the company continue to pay insurance coverage for the employee by paying its portion of insurance premium costs?

- Will the employee be permitted to seek or accept other employment while on leave?

- What reemployment rights, if any, does the employee have?

- Will the company reserve the right to fill, alter, or eliminate a vacant position if required by business needs?

- If the employee's former position is no longer available, will the employee be offered another suitable job?

- If there is no suitable work available, will the employee be placed on a layoff status?

---

regular salary is suspended. The absence may be for medical reasons including pregnancy, urgent personal reasons, or civic reasons such as jury duty or military reserve training.

2. The employee must request a leave of absence in advance and submit supporting documentation such as physician's statement, juror summons, military orders, etc. In cases of absence for medical reasons including pregnancy, the employee must submit a physician's statement

at the start of leave, at succeeding 30-day intervals, and upon return to work.

3. Approval of a leave of absence is at management discretion after considering the needs of the business and the circumstances of the case. The length of approved leave is decided by management on a case-by-case basis.

4. In the event of a question regarding a medical leave, or an employee's ability to perform available work, the Company may elect to obtain a second medical opinion prior to considering or extending a medical leave of absence.

5. In the event an employee incurs a medical condition which may affect the employee's ability to work safely or which may adversely affect other employees, the employee has a responsibility to report the condition to management and to seek appropriate medical care. In such cases, the Company may elect to schedule the individual for medical exams and tests, arrange a medical leave of absence as appropriate, or make a reasonable accommodation for the condition.

6. An employee's regular wage or salary is suspended during the leave. The employee retains length-of-service credit; however, profit sharing benefits may be affected by the absence. The employee is ineligible for holiday pay while on leave. Accrual of vacation benefits is suspended in the event of a leave of absence for 30 days or more. The Company-paid portion of insurance premiums is continued for up to three months. Thereafter, the employee may elect to pay the full insurance premium cost if uninterrupted insurance is desired. The employee is responsible for maintaining payments for dependent insurances during the period of leave.

7. The Company shall make every reasonable effort to hold open the employee's job during shorter periods of absence. However, during any period of leave, the Company reserves the right to fill, change, or eliminate a vacant position if required by the needs of the business. In such cases an employee returning from leave may be placed into another comparable position if any such position is available or otherwise placed in a layoff status. Return from leave shall be handled in accordance with government laws on reemployment.

8. All leaves of absence shall be recorded on the employee's attendance record.

## Sample Employee Handbook Paragraph

*Conditions of Leave*

All requests for leave of absence are subject to management approval after considering Company needs and the nature of the employee's request. A leave of absence is approved with the understanding that the employee intends to return to work on an agreed date at the conclusion of the leave. Failure to return or request a leave extension by the agreed return date will be considered a voluntary resignation.

An employee's regular wage or salary is suspended during a leave of absence. The employee retains length-of-service credit; however, profit sharing benefits may be affected by the absence. The employee is ineligible for holiday pay while on leave. Accrual of vacation benefits is suspended in the event of a leave of absence for 30 days or more. The Company-paid portion of insurance premiums is continued for three months. The employee is responsible for maintaining payments for dependent insurances.

Every effort is made to place the returning employee into the same or similar position if possible. However, during any period of leave, the Company retains the right to fill, alter, or eliminate a vacant position if required by business needs.

## Notes

1. *Employee Benefits in Small Private Establishments, 1990,* Bulletin 2388, U.S. Dept. of Labor, September, 1991, p. 15.

2. *Employee Benefits in Medium and Large Firms, 1989,* Bulletin 2363, U.S. Dept. of Labor, June, 1990, p. 15.

3. Daily Labor Report, DLR No. 9, Bureau of National Affairs, Washington, D.C., January 14, 1987.

4. *Employee Benefits in Small Private Establishments, 1990,* Bulletin 2388, U.S. Dept. of Labor, September, 1991, p. 15.

5. William S. Hubbartt, "Family Leave Law Reflects Changing Workforce Needs," Management and Memo Column, *Kane County Chronicle*, Geneva, Illinois (February 19, 1993), p. 12.

6. The Family and Medical Leave Act of 1993, Summary and Full Test, *Labor Relations Week* (Washington, D.C.: Bureau of National Affairs, February 10, 1993), pp. 5–9.

7. Family and Medical Leave Act of 1993, P.L. 103-3. *Labor Law Reports*, Issue Number 541, Report 463 (Chicago: Commerce Clearing House, February 11, 1993).

8. *Employee Benefits in Medium and Large Firms, 1989,* Bulletin 2363, U.S. Dept. of Labor, June, 1990, p. 15.

9. *Employee Benefits in Small Private Establishments, 1990,* Bulletin 2388, U.S. Dept. of Labor, September, 1991, p. 15.

10. *Employee Benefits in Medium and Large Firms, 1989,* Bulletin 2363, U.S. Dept. of Labor, June, 1990, p. 16.

11. *Employee Benefits in Small Private Establishments, 1990,* Bulletin 2388, U.S. Dept. of Labor, September, 1991, p. 14.

12. *Employee Benefits in Medium and Large Firms, 1989,* Bulletin 2363, U.S. Dept. of Labor, June, 1990, p. 15.

13. *Employee Benefits in Small Private Establishments, 1990,* Bulletin 2388, U.S. Dept. of Labor, September, 1991, p. 20.

14. *Employee Benefits in Medium and Large Firms, 1989,* Bulletin 2363, U.S. Dept. of Labor, June, 1990, p. 23.

# 10

# Pay, Performance, and Other Compensation Policies

**Read Chapter 10 for:**

Pay periods

Defining exempt and nonexempt employees

Overtime pay

Performance appraisals

Pay administration

Bonus incentives

Wage garnishments

## Pay Periods

Every employee looks forward to pay day. Receiving the paycheck on pay day is one of the key reasons for the employment relationship. Many employees plan their lives around receipt of the paycheck. With the cost of living and demands of today's society, many employees live virtually from paycheck to paycheck. For some people, even one day's delay in receiving a paycheck can create financial personal problems. For these reasons, effective administration of payroll is an important element of good employee relations.

A clearly defined personnel policy providing a guide to processing employee time records and dispensing paychecks helps promote effective payroll administration.

An important issue to consider when defining a payroll procedure is the State Wage Payment Law, which defines time limit requirements for pay periods and for the payment of wages following the end of the pay period. Check the state law in those areas where your firm is conducting business.

Many firms define separate pay periods and run separate payrolls for various categories of employees. So long as your pay periods comply with relevant laws, it is permissible to have different pay periods for different employment categories. For example, a midwest manufacturing company pays its production employees weekly while administrative employees are paid biweekly. A service firm pays hourly nonexempt employees each week but schedules a semimonthly pay period for all salaried exempt personnel. Another sales/distribution firm pays weekly but puts all sales personnel on a monthly pay cycle.

The Fair Labor Standards Act defines certain recordkeeping requirements. Also, many states specify certain employment or payroll recordkeeping requirements for employers. While these requirements vary from state to state (10 states have no records requirements), the law typically requires the employer to keep a record of employee name, address, occupation, pay rate, pay period, and hours worked.

Another important issue to consider in establishing a pay period is the portion of employees subject to overtime pay laws. If a large number of employees are subject to overtime pay, then a weekly pay period makes sense to facilitate computation and payment of overtime pay.

Payroll administration is subject to numerous Internal Revenue Service (IRS) regulations. The IRS requires the employer to deduct income taxes, deduct social security taxes, compute matching social security contributions, send payroll taxes to government depositories according to specified schedules, and follow various reporting requirements on earnings and taxes paid. Most of the information needed for complying with payroll tax issues is included in IRS Circular E.

## Pitfalls to Avoid

A primary objective of a Pay Period Policy is to define procedures for timely disbursement of employee paychecks. Here are some pitfalls to avoid:

1. One common situation when issuing paychecks is proper handling of the check when an employee is absent on pay day. Customary practice at many firms is to hold the check until the employee's return or to mail the check to the employee's home. On occasion, an employee may ask a spouse, relative, or friend to pick up the paycheck. This can present a dilemma to the employer. On the one hand, you want to accommodate the employee with timely release of a paycheck. On the other hand, however, the employer needs to protect privacy of pay information and release the paycheck only to the employee or to someone designated by the employee. The solution then is to release the paycheck only to

**CHECKLIST**
**A Pay Period Policy**

- What state law requirements relate to length of pay period and timeliness of paycheck disbursement?

- What wage hour law requirements affect your policy?

- Will all employees be paid on the same pay period and pay day or will different pay periods be established?

- Will the pay period be weekly, biweekly, semimonthly, monthly, or other interval?

- How many days after the end of the pay period will paychecks be disbursed?

- Will paychecks be released early prior to normal pay day if requested by the employee because of an emergency?

- When and to whom must employee time records be turned in at the end of the pay period?

- If an employee has a question about pay, to whom should the employee speak (Supervisor, Manager, Payroll Clerk, or Human Resource Specialist)?

- How will paychecks be handled when an employee is absent on pay day?

- Will a third party be permitted to pick up an employee's paycheck? If so, what form of authorization from the employee will be required?

- When and how will pay be disbursed when an employee separates employment?

the employee or to a specified individual as designated by the employee. A written instruction (signed by the employee) to the employer provides the best assurance of protecting pay while responding to an employee's request.

2. Avoid advance release of paychecks. Supervisors in many organizations report that there is at least one employee who encounters a personal financial crisis and simply must have the paycheck a few days early. "After all, it is money the Company owes me for working last week. And it is an emergency. I won't ask for it again." Unfortunately, these hapless individuals can never seem to manage their finances. Every month or so, they are back in the Payroll Department asking for another pay advance. This situation can be a particularly troublesome problem in smaller or mid-sized privately held firms with a paternalistic management style. The simple solution is a firm policy against pay advances. If this practice is strictly followed, employees won't take advantage of the employer's kindness.

3. An organization can prevent unnecessary wage claims by being familiar with the state's wage pay law. One particular troublesome area for some firms is the issuance of final pay for separating employees. Some

state laws specify that the final paycheck must be given to the employee within a specified number of hours or days following separation. Some states require a termination letter detailing reason for separation, final pay, and benefits owed. (See Chap. 11 for more on this.) Make sure that your pay policy details proper guidelines for release of pay at separation.

**Sample Policy**

**XYZ COMPANY**
**PERSONNEL POLICY & PROCEDURE**

SUBJECT: PAY PERIOD/PAY DAYS                      DATE: May 1, 1993

*Policy*: It is the policy of XYZ Company to administer employee pay on a weekly pay period basis.

*Procedure*:
1. The pay period shall be a weekly pay period beginning at 12:00 a.m. on Monday morning. The pay period shall run through a seven consecutive day period ending at 11:59 p.m. following Sunday night.
2. The Payroll Clerk is responsible for inserting time cards into the time card racks at the end of the preceding work week. Note: This means that time cards are placed in the rack on Friday for use the following work week.
3. At the end of the pay period the supervisor is responsible for removing the time cards, giving initial approval of employee work hours, and turning time cards in to the Payroll Clerk not later than noon each Monday.
4. The Payroll Clerk is responsible for computing payroll for release each week by Friday at noon. Paychecks normally shall be given to department supervisors for distribution to their respective employees. To protect confidentiality, each paycheck shall be placed in a window envelope and sealed.
5. In compliance with state law, the Payroll Clerk is responsible for maintaining a payroll register showing employee, employee address, pay rate, jobs, and hours worked for the week.
6. Pay advances are not permitted. In the event an employee going on vacation desires to receive pay prior to the start of vacation, the employee must notify the Payroll Clerk one week (seven days) prior to the start of vacation.
7. In the event an employee is absent on pay day, the supervisor is responsible for holding the check and providing it to the employee upon his or her return. If the absence will be for a week or more, the check shall be mailed to the employee's home address.
8. In the event the employee wishes to have a third party pick up his or her paycheck, the employee must submit a written note through the supervisor to the Payroll Clerk.

9. At separation of employment, paychecks shall normally be disbursed on the normal pay day for the pay period in which the separation occurs.

## Sample Employee Handbook Paragraph

### Pay Periods

Paychecks are distributed weekly on Friday by your supervisor. The paycheck will cover all hours worked from Monday to Sunday of the previous week.

In the event you are absent on pay day, your check will be held until your return. Your written authorization is needed if you request another person to pick up your check. If you have a question regarding your paycheck, you may speak to your supervisor.

# Defining Exempt and Nonexempt Employees

The terms *exempt* and *nonexempt* refer to the Fair Labor Standards Act (FLSA). Under the law, certain jobs are defined as exempt from the law's provisions. Other jobs, defined as nonexempt, are covered by the requirements of the FLSA. Basically, the FLSA specifies a minimum wage, requires overtime wages for covered jobs, directs employers to maintain time records on covered employees, and limits employment of minors.

Many firms fail to properly classify jobs as exempt from this law. A fairly common practice among smaller firms is to consider all office employees as salaried (and therefore exempt) while production or service employees are paid on an hourly basis and considered nonexempt. This practice, however, does not comply with the FLSA. As a result, some firms are faced with employee complaints about overtime pay resulting in wage hour audits by the Department of Labor.

The Labor Department has issued regulations to aid employers in properly classifying jobs as exempt and nonexempt. These regulations are defined in a booklet entitled *Regulations, Part 541 Defining the Terms "Executive," "Administrative," "Professional," and "Outside Salesman,"* WH Publication 1281. The regulations provide explanations, definitions, examples, and interpretations to assist employers in defining which jobs are exempt.

A written job description is needed to effectively analyze the job to determine its exempt or nonexempt status. The job description, with its written list of duties and responsibilities, provides an objective basis for comparison of job duties to the FLSA guidelines.

The following questionnaires may be used in the analysis of jobs to determine their exempt or nonexempt status.

Conclusion: *Exempt _____     Nonexempt _____

**SALES QUESTIONNAIRE**
**For Determining Exempt Status**

_____    _____    _____
Job                                  Department                            Grade

1. Is the individual customarily and regularly engaged
   away from the employer's place or places of business and employed for the purpose of:

   a. Making sales within the meaning of Section 3(k)      Yes ___  No ___
      of the Act? (The Act states that "Sale" or "Sell"
      includes any sale, exchange, contract to sell,
      consignment for sale, shipment for sale, or
      other disposition.)

   b. Obtaining orders or contracts for services** or      Yes ___  No ___
      for the use of facilities for which a consideration
      will be paid by the client or customer?

2. Does the individual devote at least 80 percent of       Yes ___  No ___
   the work week to activities which are directly re-
   lated to questions #1a or #1b above?

Reference: *Regulations, Part 541 Defining the Terms "Executive," "Ad-*
*ministrative," "Professional," and "Outside Salesman,"* WH Publication
1281

   *Conclusion: If the answer to one of the two subparagraphs under #1 *and* the answer
to #2 are YES, the employee is exempt. See above.

   **The inclusion of the word *services* is not intended to exempt persons who are
sometimes described as selling "services." For example, it does not include persons such
as service employees even though they may sell the service which they themselves perform.
Selling the service in such cases would be incidental to the servicing rather than the reverse.
Nor does it include outside buyers, who are sometimes described as selling their employer's
"service" to the person from whom they obtain their goods. It is obvious that the
relationship here is the reverse of that of salesperson–customer.

Conclusion: *Exempt _____     Nonexempt _____

**EXECUTIVE QUESTIONNAIRE**
**For Determining Exempt Status**

_____    _____    _____
Job                                  Department                            Grade

1. Does the primary duty of this position consist of       Yes ___  No ___
   the management of the enterprise in which this
   individual is employed or of a customarily recognized department or subdivision thereof?

2. Does this individual customarily and regularly di-      Yes ___  No ___
   rect the work of two or more employees?

3. Does this individual have the authority to hire or fire other employees or make suggestions and recommendations as to the hiring or the advancement and promotion or any other change of status of the employees?                                 Yes ___ No ___

4. Does this individual customarily and regularly exercise discretionary powers?                                 Yes ___ No ___

5. Does this individual devote at least 80 percent of the work week to activities which are directly and clearly related to the performance of the job described in questions #1–4 of this section?                                 Yes ___ No ___

6. Is this individual compensated (except as provided in Section 541.5b) for services on a basis of not less than $155.00 per week, exclusive of board, lodging, or other facilities?                                 Yes ___ No ___

7. OR, if an employee is compensated (except as provided in Section 541.5b) on a basis of not less than $250.00 per week (exclusive of board, lodging, or other facilities) AND his or her primary duty consists of the management of the enterprise in which he or she works, or of a recognized department or subdivision thereof, and includes the regular direction of work of two or more employees, the individual is exempt.

Reference: *Regulations, Part 541 Defining the Terms "Executive," "Administrative," "Professional," and "Outside Salesman,"* WH Publication 1281

*Conclusion: If the answers from #1–6 are *all* YES *or* meet the standards of #7, the employee is exempt. See above.

Conclusion: *Exempt _____     Nonexempt _____

## PROFESSIONAL QUESTIONNAIRE
### For Determining Exempt Status

| Job | Department | Grade |
| --- | --- | --- |

1. Does the individual's primary duty consist of the performance of work which requires:

   a) Knowledge of an advanced type in a field of science or learning customarily acquired by a prolonged course of specialized intellectual instruction and study, as distinguished from a general academic education, apprenticeship, or training received in the performance of routine mental, manual, or physical processes?                                 Yes ___ No ___

   b) Original and creative skills in a recognized field of artistic endeavor, the result of which depends primarily on the invention, imagination, or creative talent of the employee?                                 Yes ___ No ___

2. Does the individual's work require the consistent       Yes ___   No ___
   exercise of discretion and judgment in its perfor-
   mance?

3. Is the individual's work predominantly intellectual     Yes ___   No ___
   and varied in character (as opposed to routine
   mental, manual, mechanical, or physical work) in
   which the result accomplished cannot be standardized in relation to a given period of time?

4. Does the individual devote at least 80 percent of       Yes ___   No ___
   the work week to activities which are an essential
   part of the job described in questions #1 through
   3 of this section?

5. Is the individual (except as provided in Section        Yes ___   No ___
   541.5b) compensated for services on a basis of not
   less than $170.00 per week, exclusive of board,
   lodging, or other facilities? NOTE: This does not
   apply to those who hold a valid license or certificate
   to practice law or medicine and are currently engaged in the practice thereof.

6. OR, if the individual (except in Section 541.5b) is
   compensated on a basis of not less than $250.00
   per week (exclusive of board, lodging, or other
   facilities) and his or her primary duty consists of
   the performance of work either requiring knowledge of an advanced type in a field of science or
   learning, which includes work requiring the consistent exercise of discretion and judgment, or requiring invention, imagination, or talent in a recognized field of artistic endeavor, the employee is
   exempt.

Reference: *Regulations, Part 541 Defining the Terms "Executive," "Administrative," "Professional," and "Outside Salesman,"* WH Publication 1281

*Conclusion: If the answers to #2,3,4, & 5 are all YES, and the answer to "a" or "b" of
the subparagraphs under #1 is YES or MEETS THE STANDARDS OF #6, the employee
is exempt. See above.

Conclusion: *Exempt _____      Nonexempt _____

**ADMINISTRATIVE QUESTIONNAIRE**
**For Determining Exempt Status**

_____  _____  _____
Job                            Department                         Grade

1. Does the individual's primary duty consist of the      Yes ___   No ___
   performance of office or nonmanual work directly
   related to management policies of general business
   operations of his or her employer or their customers?

2. Does the individual customarily and regularly exercise discretion and independent judgment?     Yes ___   No ___

3. Does the individual regularly and directly assist a proprietor, or an employee employed in a bona fide executive or administrative capacity (as defined in this regulation)?     Yes ___   No___

4. Does the individual perform work along specialized or technical lines requiring special training, experience, or knowledge and only under general supervision?     Yes ___   No ___

5. Does the individual execute special assignments and tasks only under general supervision?     Yes ___   No ___

6. Does the individual devote at least 80 percent of the work week to activities which are directly related to the job described in questions #1 through 3 of this section?     Yes ___   No ___

7. Is the individual (except as provided in Section 541.5b) compensated for services on a salary or fee basis of not less than $155.00 per week, exclusive of board, lodging, or other facilities?     Yes ___   No ___

8. OR, if the individual (except in Section 541.5b) is compensated on a salary basis of not less than $250.00 per week (exclusive of board, lodging, or other facilities) and his or her primary duty consists of the performance of office or nonmanual work directly related to management policies or general business operations of an employer or its customers (work requiring the exercise of discretion and independent judgment), the employee is exempt.

Reference: *Regulations, Part 541 Defining the Terms "Executive," "Administrative," "Professional," and "Outside Salesman,"* WH Publication 1281

*Conclusion: If the answers to #1, 2, 6, & 7 are *all* YES, and the answer to #3, 4, or 5 is YES *or* MEETS THE STANDARDS OF #8, the employee is exempt. See above.

### Pitfalls to Avoid

Failure to properly classify jobs and administer their pay according to the law results in the many wage hour violations identified each year by the Labor Department. Here are some pitfalls to avoid:

1. Avoid the tendency to oversimplify the exempt/nonexempt designation. Firms which consider all office workers as salaried and therefore exempt are likely to be in violation of the law. The wage hour criterion for exempt status does not consider an employer's criteria for paying on a salary. The focus is, instead, on job duties. An organization can pay both exempt and nonexempt employees on a salaried basis, so long as the nonexempt employees maintain a record of hours

**CHECKLIST**
**Exempt/Nonexempt Status Policy**

- Does the firm have or will the firm prepare job descriptions for use in analyzing jobs?

- Does the firm have a copy of WH Publication 1281 or other similar reference materials to aid in analyzing jobs?

- Who will be responsible for performing exempt/nonexempt analysis of jobs (Supervisor, Manager, Human Resource Specialist, etc.)?

- When will exempt/nonexempt analysis be conducted (i.e., when a new job is defined or when job duties change)?

- How will the exempt/nonexempt status affect payroll processing, time records, application of policies, or eligibility for benefits?

- Who will be responsible for communicating exempt or non-exempt status to the employee?

- When and how should information on exempt/nonexempt status be communicated to the employee?

- What documents will be maintained to document the analysis of jobs?

worked and receive overtime pay for time worked over 40 hours in a week.

2. Make sure that all nonexempt employees maintain time records showing starting and ending times each day. Even salaried office workers who are nonexempt should maintain time records. The government does not require employers to use time clocks, but instead allows the employer to select the time reporting method.

3. Correct classification errors as soon as they are identified. If a job has been incorrectly viewed as salaried exempt, but analysis of the job and regulations shows that the job should be a nonexempt position, institute the change as soon as possible and inform the employee.

4. Avoid the tendency to permit employees to select exempt or nonexempt status for their job. In some firms, employees view exempt jobs as having a special status because exempt employees can come and go at various times or call in sick without a pay deduction. In other organizations, where there are large amounts of overtime work, exempt employees sometimes request that their jobs be reclassified to non-exempt in order to receive overtime pay. While it is good employee relations to be responsible to employees, this is one area where the firm's personnel practices should comply with the law.

## Sample Policy

**XYZ COMPANY**
**PERSONNEL POLICY & PROCEDURE**

SUBJECT: FLSA EXEMPTIONS                    DATE: May 1, 1993

*Policy*: It is the policy of XYZ Company to evaluate jobs and define their exempt or nonexempt status as required by the Fair Labor Standards Act (FLSA).

*Procedure:*

1. The Human Resource Administrator is responsible for conducting analysis and determining the exempt or nonexempt status of the job.

2. When conducting analysis for exempt or nonexempt status, the Human Resource Administrator should include the following activities in the analysis:
   - Confer with the responsible supervisor or manager who has supervisory authority over the position.
   - Review the job description.
   - Review wage hour definitions for executive, administrative, professional, and outside salesperson.
   - Compare the job with other similar jobs in the organization.

3. Jobs shall be evaluated when a new job is created and whenever an existing job or job duties are changed.

4. The Human Resource Administrator is responsible for maintaining a record of analysis of jobs in the event of a wage hour audit.

5. The Human Resource Administrator is responsible for helping supervisors and managers to understand the FLSA exemptions and for explaining requirements to employees.

## Sample Employee Handbook Paragraph

*Employment Classification*

At time of hire, each new employee is assigned an employment classification based upon job responsibilities and work schedule. The employment classification determines one's eligibility for benefits and requirements for time recording for overtime pay computations.

In addition, government wage hour laws define certain jobs as nonexempt positions which are paid on an hourly basis. Nonexempt employees are entitled to receive overtime pay, for which a record of actual hours worked must be maintained. Other positions such as executive, professional, supervisory, or sales jobs are defined as exempt and are paid on a salary basis. You will be advised of your employment classification at time of hire.

## Overtime Pay

Overtime pay is extra compensation paid for working additional hours beyond a 40 hour work week or other specified schedule.

The Fair Labor Standards Act (FLSA) requires covered employers to provide overtime pay to certain employees. FLSA defines a minimum requirement for overtime pay. Employers are free to provide greater overtime pay compensation.

The primary purpose of a personnel policy on overtime pay is to clarify when premium pay is provided in accordance with the law.

When defining an overtime pay policy, several issues need to be identified. First, the employer must specify the work week. A work week is a period of 168 hours during seven consecutive 24-hour periods. The employer may designate the date and time that is the start of the work week. Each work week should stand alone as a basis for computing overtime pay. Generally, two weeks cannot be combined and there can be no averaging of hours between two weeks. (An exception in the regulations has been defined for certain health care employees.)

A second requirement is that covered employees must be paid for all hours worked in a work week. Hours worked include the time that the employee is on duty, including time which the employee is suffered or permitted to work. Certain activities are deemed to be compensable time. Other activities are noncompensible. A chart of compensible time appears at Chap. 8.

Under the FLSA, overtime pay should be one and one-half times the employee's regular straight time pay rate for nonexempt employees for all time worked over 40 hours in a week. For example, an hourly paid employee who earns $5.00 per hour and works 44 hours in a work week should receive pay as follows:

| | | |
|---|---|---|
| First 40 hours worked at $5.00 | = | $200.00 |
| plus next 4 hours worked (1 1/2 | = | 30.00 |
| or $7.50/hr) | | |
| for a total weekly pay of | = | $230.00 |

If an employee works on a piece rate basis, there is another method for computing overtime pay. The piece rate employee is entitled to one-half of his or her average hourly earnings for the time worked over 40 hours. For example, if the employee paid in piece work works 45 hours per week and is paid $250.00 for the week, the employee's average hourly rate would be $5.56. The employee would be entitled to an additional $2.78 for each hour over 40 as shown:

| | | |
|---|---|---|
| Piece work pay for 45 hours worked | = | $250.00 |
| (equivalent to $5.56 per hour) | | |

| | | |
|---|---|---|
| plus half-time rate of $2.78 for each hour over 40 | = | 13.90 |
| for a total weekly pay of | = | $263.90 |

As an alternative, if agreed to before the work is performed, the employee may be given a piece rate which is one and one-half times the normal piece rate, for each piece produced during the overtime period.

For nonexempt employees paid on a salaried basis, the employer is responsible for computing an hourly rate and providing overtime pay for time worked over 40 hours in the work week. The employee's regular rate is determined by dividing the salary by the number of hours in the employee's specified work week. The employee must then be paid a half-time rate for the overtime hours. For example, if a salaried employee is paid $300.00 weekly for whatever number of hours work is required, overtime pay may be computed as shown:

| | | |
|---|---|---|
| Salary for 48-hour work week (equivalent to $6.25 per hour) plus half-time rate of $3.13 | = | $300.00 |
| for each hour over 40 | = | 25.04 |
| for a total weekly pay of | | $325.04 |

Under the overtime pay arrangement shown, if the employee works more or fewer hours during the week, the hourly rate will fluctuate based upon the number of hours worked.

In the event an employee is paid on a different pay period than weekly, the employee's pay must be converted to a weekly basis in order to compute regular rate and overtime. For example,

- For a biweekly pay period, compute each work week separately.
- For a semimonthly pay period, multiply pay by 24 and then divide by 52 to obtain a weekly equivalent.
- For a monthly salary, multiply pay by 12 and then divide by 52 to obtain a weekly equivalent.[1]

In addition to the FLSA, various states have legislation which defines overtime pay requirements. (Nineteen states have no statutory requirements for overtime pay.) Depending upon the state, overtime pay may be required after eight hours daily, or on a weekly basis of 40, 45, 46, or 48 hours. Also, occupational categories covered by the state law may vary from FLSA requirements. Students, learners, apprentices, outside salespersons, domestic service workers, and agricultural employees may be covered under state law. Several states require overtime pay coverage for executives and professionals—a significant departure from federal requirements.[2]

In addition, numerous states stipulate that certain handicapped workers are covered by overtime pay requirements. These unique state requirements are noteworthy because the Americans with Disabilities Act will prompt greater numbers of disabled workers to seek employment. Employers in those states must take care to assure proper compensation for disabled workers. Be sure to check state requirements when preparing your overtime pay policy.

Overtime pay is a mandatory subject for bargaining for those firms which have a union. Often, unions will negotiate an overtime pay provision for their members which is better than the minimum requirements of the law. Common overtime provisions negotiated by unions may include overtime pay for work over eight hours per day, work on Saturday or Sunday, work on a holiday, and premium overtime pay such as double time or triple time.

**Pitfalls to Avoid**

Employee complaints and employer misunderstandings about overtime pay are key reasons leading to wage hour investigations by the Department of Labor. Many of these employers are liable for millions of dollars of back wages owed to thousands of employees. Here are some pitfalls to avoid:

1. One of the leading difficulties causing back pay liability for unpaid overtime is improperly classifying employees as salaried exempt workers ineligible for overtime pay. See the prior section on defining exempt and nonexempt employees.

2. Some organizations improperly try to limit overtime pay by offering employees time off work equivalent to the overtime worked. This practice is sometimes referred to as granting compensatory time off or "comp" time. I am aware of one firm (no doubt there are many others) which allowed employees to work overtime and then save unpaid overtime for future use as paid vacation time. Such a practice for nonexempt employees, however, is contrary to the FLSA. Overtime pay must be computed and paid based upon each work week. According to my contacts at the Wage-Hour Division, compensatory time off may be granted within the same work week. However, at the end of the work week, the employee must receive any owed overtime pay on the next regular paycheck.

3. During a recent personnel practices audit of a graphic arts firm, I uncovered a practice of delaying payment for a portion of overtime work until the next following pay period. This was done, management stated, at the request of employees. The employees wanted a more uniform paycheck week to week and sought to minimize the larger tax bite which occurred with larger paychecks reflecting greater overtime pay. Even though this practice was done to accommodate employees,

**CHECKLIST**
**An Overtime Pay Policy**

- What are the minimum FLSA requirements for overtime pay?
- What are state requirements for overtime pay?
- What categories of employees are covered by the overtime pay policy?
- What categories of employees are excluded or exempted from overtime pay?
- How will overtime pay be computed?
- Who will authorize overtime work and overtime pay?
- Will overtime pay be computed only after 40 hours actually worked by the employee, or will paid time off such as holidays or vacation count as time worked for overtime pay eligibility?
- What is the start and end of the work week for overtime pay purposes?
- What time records are maintained to track hours worked for overtime pay computations?

the practice violated FLSA. Overtime pay must be computed each week and paid at the following pay period.

4. Control of unauthorized overtime work is a concern for some organizations. This issue becomes troublesome when employees are permitted to clock out late or to work extra time in order to pad their paychecks. The employer is responsible for paying the employee for time worked. There are several things an employer can do to control overtime:

   - Permit overtime work only at the direction and approval of supervisor.
   - Require supervisors to review time records and authorize overtime pay.
   - Put employees on notice that overtime work may be performed only at supervisory direction.
   - Take corrective disciplinary action if deemed necessary to deal with repeat offenders who disregard work schedules and time reporting procedures.

5. Should salaried exempt employees receive overtime pay? To exempt employees who work a lot of hours, overtime pay would be welcomed. Contrary to some misconceptions, the FLSA does not prohibit an employer from providing overtime pay to exempt workers; it merely exempts these jobs from the requirement. Since there is no legislated requirement under FLSA (check your state law requirements, however), the employer may elect to provide overtime pay to exempt workers. I have seen firms pay overtime to

- plant supervisors who direct groups of production employees who work frequent overtime

- field service engineers or other exempt workers whose jobs require extensive travel, emergency work at unusual hours, or jobs which perform tasks on a billable hours basis for customers

- selected occupational groups, jobs, or departments when there is a pattern of frequent and extensive overtime work

Similarly, unless otherwise defined by a specific law, an employer may define what overtime pay will be provided to exempt workers. Among various overtime pay plans for exempt workers, I have seen plans that

- pay straight time rate for over 40 hours

- pay straight time rate for hours over a specified limit such as 45 hours or 48 hours

- pay time and a half for hours worked over 40, or other similar variations

**Sample Policy**

**XYZ COMPANY**
**PERSONNEL POLICY & PROCEDURE**

SUBJECT: OVERTIME PAY                    DATE: May 1, 1993

*Policy*: It is the policy of XYZ Company to provide overtime pay for certain employees for authorized overtime work.

*Procedure*:
1. Nonexempt employees who perform authorized overtime work are entitled to receive overtime pay as outlined below:

   a) Nonunion employees are entitled to receive overtime pay computed at 1 1/2 times the employee's straight time pay rate for all time worked over 40 hours in a week.

   b) Union employees are entitled to receive overtime pay computed at 1 1/2 times the employee's straight time pay rate for all time worked:
      - over 8 hours per day or
      - over 40 hours per week or
      - beyond their regular work schedule or
      - on Saturday

   c) Union employees are entitled to receive two times their regular straight time pay rate for time worked on Sundays, holidays, or in excess of 10 hours per day.

2. Salaried exempt plant supervisors who exercise direct supervision over a department or work unit are entitled to receive overtime pay, computed at a straight time hourly rate, for time worked over 48 hours in a week. Time worked for the period under 48 hours is included in the employee's regular weekly salary.

3. All overtime work must be directed and authorized by the Department Supervisor.

4. All employees eligible for overtime pay are required to maintain a record of hours worked. This may be a manually completed time slip by office employees and by time clock for plant employees. Time must be recorded at the start of work, end of work, or when leaving the premises for nonbusiness reasons. In facilities where a time clock is used, employees should punch in not earlier than 15 minutes before the start of work and not later than 15 minutes after the end of work.

5. Each supervisor is responsible for reviewing time records of subordinate employees at the end of each pay period to authorize overtime pay. The supervisor is responsible for clarifying discrepancies to assure accurate time records.

## Sample Employee Handbook Paragraph

### Overtime Pay

There are occasions when additional work hours are scheduled by the Company in order to meet the needs of our customers. Hourly paid employees will receive one and one-half times their regular hourly pay rate for all time worked over 40 hours per week. All overtime work must be approved by your supervisor. Company-paid holidays count as time worked when computing overtime.

Salaried nonexempt employees are entitled to receive overtime pay computed by dividing the number of weekly hours worked into the weekly salary to determine hourly rate for the week. One-half of the employee's hourly rate is then multiplied by the number of hours worked beyond the normal full-time work schedule of 40 hours worked in the week.

# Performance Appraisals

Performance appraisals have long been recognized by human resource specialists as an important management tool. A performance appraisal is a structured discussion between employee and supervisor. It provides an opportunity for the supervisor to recognize an employee's achievements, offer suggestions for improvement when needed, discuss job responsibilities, define objectives, counsel for career advancement, and justify a pay adjustment.

A policy on performance appraisals provides guidelines for supervisors to conduct effective performance appraisals. The policy can identify when performance appraisals should be scheduled, who is responsible for preparation of the appraisal, and how the appraisal influences pay adjustments. In addition, the policy can provide ideas for supervisors on how to prepare for and conduct performance appraisals.

There are several important issues to stress in a policy on performance appraisals:

- Performance appraisals should be based on objective data of performance results rather than subjective opinion. Use the policy to guide supervisors on identifying and using work records or data to improve the objectivity of appraisals.

- Emphasize the importance of accurately documenting the employee's performance—good or bad. Recognition of good performance can be a motivation for employees. Likewise, when the employee performs poorly, the supervisor should rate the employee accordingly. If the supervisor fails to identify poor performance, the employee is likely to assume that performance is satisfactory unless told otherwise.

- Use the performance appraisal mid-year, or at any time during the rating period to address poor performance. Often, a supervisor will have a brief discussion with an employee about a performance problem, but fail to make any record of the discussion. If the employee's performance deteriorates, there is no record of the problem or prior discussions to justify a dismissal. However, when the supervisor prepares a performance appraisal and discusses that problem with the employee, there is a greater likelihood that the problem will be resolved. If the employee is unable to improve performance, then the supervisor has documented evidence of prior performance discussions which help to justify discharge.

## Competitive Practices

Figure 10.1 contains performance appraisal practices.

## Pitfalls to Avoid

1. "It's time for your review." This simple statement causes misunderstandings in so many organizations. The employee enters the discussion expecting a pay raise. The supervisor, on the other hand, is prepared to discuss performance issues with the employee. Clearly, employee and supervisor are not communicating. There are several ways to minimize this common misunderstanding. First of all, avoid the term *review*. Rather, use the term *performance appraisal* to identify the performance discussion. Second, during new employee orientation, explain the performance appraisal policy and give the employee a copy

## CHECKLIST
### A Performance Appraisal Policy

- How often will performance appraisals be conducted (annually, semiannually, or some other interval)?

- Will an appraisal be conducted for periodic discussions of performance, completion of orientation or probation, justification of pay increase, or correcting poor performance?

- Who is responsible for preparing and conducting performance appraisals?

- Will all employees be rated on a specific day, or will performance appraisals coincide with the employee's anniversary date?

- Will appraisals be reviewed by a second-level manager, a general manager, or a human resource specialist?

- What guidelines will be given to supervisors to prepare appraisals and document performance issues?

- Will the employee be required to sign the appraisal form?

- Will employees be permitted to prepare a self-evaluation for discussion with their supervisor?

- Will the human resource administrator notify supervisors of performance review due dates?

- Will the performance appraisal be correlated to the pay adjustment process? If so, how?

of the appraisal form. Third, you may consider separating performance and pay discussions by several days or a week.

2. Low ratings from "hard" supervisors compared to high ratings from "easy" supervisors are a matter of great concern to employees. This inconsistency in ratings is a common problem with performance appraisals at many firms. One important way to reduce this kind of inconsistency is to include performance-level definitions in the performance appraisal policy guidelines. Performance-level definitions will aid supervisors in distinguishing between excellent and superior or superior and good or whatever other performance levels may be identified. A second approach to achieve better consistency in performance ratings is to have appraisals routed through the Human Resource Administrator for review. If a pattern of high or low ratings is observed from a particular manager, then the Human Resource Administrator can counsel and advise the supervisor to get better consistency in ratings.

| Issue | Managers | Professional/ Technical Employees | | Clerical Employees | | Manufacturing/ Production Employees | |
| --- | --- | --- | --- | --- | --- | --- | --- |
| | | Union | Nonunion | Union | Nonunion | Union | Nonuni |
| Percent Covered by Formal Perform- ance Appraisal Program | 87% (477) | 71% (51) | 90% (461) | 47% (76) | 87% (471) | 40% (151) | 81% (317) |
| Average Age of Program in Years | 14 (374) | 18 (27) | 14 (368) | 19 (26) | 13 (368) | 17 (47) | 13 (238) |
| Average Number of Appraisals Per Year | 1.1 (421) | 1.2 (34) | 1.2 (406) | 1.1 (39) | 1.2 (402) | 1.3 (66) | 1.4 (255) |
| Who Conducts the Appraisal? | | | | | | | |
|   Supervisor | 99% (427) | 95% (39) | 99% (423) | 89% (44) | 100% (421) | 89% (79) | 99% (268) |
|   HR Staff | 11% (182) | 9% (23) | 9% (170) | 17% (24) | 11% (166) | 15% (39) | 12% (113) |
|   Job Holder | 37% (196) | 37% (24) | 38% (187) | 9% (23) | 32% (180) | 16% (38) | 29% (120) |
|   Consultant | 2% (174) | 0% (23) | 0% (165) | 0% (24) | 0% (160) | 0% (39) | 0% (109) |
|   Subordinate | 2% (173) | 0% (23) | 2% (165) | 0% (24) | 2% (159) | 8% (39) | 4% (108) |
|   Multiple | 14% (412) | 25% (36) | 12% (411) | 10% (39) | 10% (411) | 13% (61) | 10% (252) |
| Percent Training Appraisers | 58% (455) | 58% (43) | 53% (428) | 54% (46) | 50% (426) | 55% (80) | 46% (267) |
| Percent Holding Formal Performance Review Sessions | 74% (452) | 56% (45) | 75% (437) | 62% (50) | 75% (434) | 55% (95) | 70% (275) |
| Percent Using MBO | 72% (418) | 40% (40) | 67% (406) | 37% (41) | 51% (397) | 32% (80) | 38% (252) |
| Percent Using Assessment Centers | 8% (464) | 10% (49) | 6% (450) | 9% (66) | 2% (450) | 6% (126) | 4% (295) |

Sample size is in parentheses.

**Figure 10.1.** *Human Resources Policies and Practices in American Firms.*[3]

3. Late ratings are another common problem. Supervisors claim that they are too busy to get the rating done on time. Employees feel cheated because their review date has been missed. The supervisor should be responsible for conducting performance appraisals on time for his or her subordinates, and this issue can be spelled out in the policy.

However, many firms have found it useful to have the Human Resource Administrator maintain a list of performance appraisal due dates, notify supervisors prior to the due date, and monitor appraisals for on-time submission.

## Sample Policy[4]

I. *Purpose*: To define the policy of the company to assure that employees receive periodic performance feedback, recognition, and corrective instructions to promote effective job performance.

II. *Coverage*: All employees.

III. *Management responsibilities*: Each supervisor and manager is responsible for conducting performance appraisals on a timely basis according to the guidelines of this policy. To promote consistency and objectivity, each performance appraisal shall be reviewed by the next higher level manager and the manager of Human Resources.

IV. *Policy implementation*:
 A. The new performance appraisal policy becomes effective January 1, 1992. All performance appraisals conducted after this date should be in accordance with the new policy guidelines.
 B. All managers and supervisors are responsible for implementing this policy in their respective work unit, department, facility, or division.
 C. All performance appraisals should be conducted in an objective manner which avoids discrimination on the basis of race, color, religion, sex, national origin, age, physical or mental disability, status as a military reservist or veteran, or any other protected class defined by state or local law.

V. *Policy guidelines*:
 A. Procedure
 1. Each supervisor or manager is responsible for conducting a performance appraisal for each subordinate according to the following schedule:
 a) At six months employment for new hires;
 b) On or about the individual's employment anniversary; and
 c) At any time deemed necessary to address and correct performance problems.
 2. The human resource manager maintains a performance appraisal tickler file with appraisal due dates. Approximately 30 days prior to scheduled performance appraisal dates, the human resource manager is responsible for notifying supervisors or managers of performance appraisals due.
 3. The supervisor or manager should refer to policy guidelines, performance rating definitions, employee objectives, department and individual productivity records, and related data when preparing the performance appraisal form.
 4. Complete all sections of the form. Mark appropriate performance ratings. Make written comments in the space provided to clarify or explain ratings.

     5. In the event that the individual's performance warrants a pay adjustment recommendation, see company policy on pay administration.

     6. The completed performance appraisal should be routed to the next higher manager and the human resource manager for review.

     7. Upon receiving appropriate approvals as initiated on the performance appraisal form, the supervisor or manager then schedules and conducts the performance discussion with the employee.

     8. The performance appraisal discussion should be conducted in a private room or office. Approximately a 30–45 minute discussion is recommended.

     9. At the conclusion of the performance appraisal discussion, the supervisor or manager should request the employee to sign the appraisal form to document participation in the discussion.

  B. Appraisal Form

     1. All performance appraisals shall be documented on the company performance appraisal form. Copies of the form are available from the Human Resource Department.

     2. At the conclusion of the performance appraisal discussion, a copy of the appraisal form should be provided to the employee and a copy is returned to the individual's personnel file in the Human Resource Dept.

## Sample Employee Handbook Paragraph

*Performance and Salary Reviews*

At XYZ Company, we are committed to a philosophy of recognizing each employee's contribution to the Company, and administering salaries in proportion to an employee's efforts. Your performance and work quality are under continual review by your supervisor. Periodically during your employment, your supervisor will conduct a performance appraisal discussion covering performance factors such as work skills, job knowledge, attendance, quality and quantity of work. Performance appraisals are normally scheduled to coincide with your employment anniversary. Please recognize that a performance appraisal discussion is different from a salary review.

Consideration for pay changes may occur at time of appraisal. However, actual pay adjustments will be made only if warranted by appropriate business conditions and satisfactory performance ratings.

## Sample Form

For best results, a performance appraisal form should be developed based upon jobs to be appraised, relevant performance factors, management style, and organizational culture. To copy and use an inappropriate performance appraisal form could create greater performance problems and liabilities. For this reason, a sample performance appraisal form has not been included here.

## Pay Administration

A discussion about salary with an employee can be a difficult task for the supervisor. There are two key reasons why supervisors have a difficult time discussing pay: one is lack of understanding about the firm's pay practices, and the second is the supervisor's limited authority for pay decisions which must be approved by top management.

A Pay Administration Policy helps to resolve these issues. The Pay Administration Policy provides instructions to aid supervisors in understanding the organization's compensation philosophy, formulating pay offers, and handling salary adjustments. Further, it can define guidelines which allow supervisors to make pay decisions within prescribed limits. Exceptions to pay policy can be referred to human resources or top management for decisions.

An organization's compensation philosophy sets the direction for its pay policy. The pay philosophy determines whether the firm is going to be a pay leader or follower, or match competitive norms. Management at most firms generally states that they want to set pay rates which match a competitive norm.

Many large firms tend to have defined compensation programs with formalized job evaluation systems and salary ranges. Many smaller and mid-sized organizations, on the other hand, operate without a formal pay structure. Employee pay rates at these firms tend to be individually negotiated between the employee and top manager. Competitive or prevailing salaries for similar jobs may be considered, but outside data tends to take a back seat. More often than not, the best pay goes to the best negotiators and long-term loyal employees. As a result, these firms have inequities in pay levels. Pay fails to correspond to responsibility or performance.

A carefully defined Pay Administration Policy also helps an organization comply with the Equal Pay Act of 1963. This Act prohibits unequal wages for women and men who work in the same establishment performing substantially equal work with respect to skill, effort, and responsibility under similar working conditions.

### Competitive Practices

Figure 10.2 contains a chart showing competitive pay practices.

## CHECKLIST
### A Pay Administration Policy

- Does the firm have a pay structure with designated pay ranges for each job?

- Who is responsible for performing job evaluation to determine pay levels or for assigning pay ranges to each job?

- During the hiring process, who is responsible for formulating pay offers for newly hired employees?

- Who is responsible for communicating pay information to employees?

- Who will be responsible for evaluating jobs for compliance with the Equal Pay Act?

- What factors will influence salary changes, such as merit increase, cost of living increase, skill level increase, promotion, demotion, shift change, location change, etc.?

- At what intervals will pay adjustments be considered (i.e., six months, annually, or other interval)?

- Who is responsible for recommending pay adjustments, and who approves pay adjustments?

- Are pay levels and pay increases budgeted each year?

- Who participates in the salary budget planning process?

- Will performance appraisals influence pay adjustments, and if so, how?

- What forms or records will be used to document pay changes?

- Where and how will pay records be maintained to protect confidentiality?

### Pitfalls to Avoid

Employee salaries can represent from 40 percent to 80 percent of a business's expenses depending upon industry. For this reason, a firm's Pay Administration Policy can have a significant impact on the bottom line. Here are some pitfalls to avoid:

1. Avoid Equal Pay Act liabilities which can occur when separate but similar jobs are defined for men and women. A common example of this problem would be defining two production machine operator job categories where one category is predominantly women and the other category is high-paid men due to occasional lifting. Specify in your policy that a human resource or compensation specialist is responsible for determining pay levels of jobs and check for equal pay violations.

2. Minimize the likelihood of inequity in pay rates by having a human resource or compensation specialist review all pay offers and pay

| Issue | Managers | Professional/Technical Employees | | Clerical Employees | | Manufacturing/Production Employees | |
|---|---|---|---|---|---|---|---|
| | | Union | Nonunion | Union | Nonunion | Union | Nonunion |
| Percent Conducting Market Wage Survey | 88% (488) | 75% (55) | 91% (466) | 72% (82) | 88% (479) | 69% (159) | 88% (329) |
| Percent Using Point System | 40% (483) | 20% (53) | 41% (462) | 24% (78) | 38% (472) | 19% (154) | 32% (320) |
| Percent with Two-Tier Pay System | 9% (474) | 34% (53) | 11% (454) | 39% (80) | 15% (465) | 39% (160) | 18% (319) |
| Percent Where Second Tier Merges with First Tier | 91% (44) | 69% (16) | 96% (48) | 74% (31) | 88% (67) | 67% (63) | 91% (58) |
| Percent Using Lump Sums... | | | | | | | |
| In lieu of wage increases | 14% (432) | 8% (49) | 11% (413) | 22% (76) | 11% (420) | 33% (152) | 19% (298) |
| In addition to wage increases | 33% (427) | 20% (51) | 25% (401) | 15% (74) | 15% (404) | 22% (148) | 19% (280) |

**Figure 10.2.** *Human Resources Policies and Practices in American Firms.*[5]

adjustments. Advise supervisors if pay rates or pay ranges are unusually high or low. Whether you give the human resource specialist authority to veto pay rates, change pay adjustments, or merely make recommendations to the line manager is a management policy decision. On the one hand, a strong human resource role in reviewing pay adjustments promotes consistency and equity. On the other hand, most line managers prefer to make pay decisions based upon their assessment of the individual and the individual's performance, without limitation or interference from human resources. An alternative solution is to allow supervisory discretion within defined guidelines for pay levels and pay adjustments. All exceptions to the guidelines must be approved by the human resource specialist and top management.

3. Improve control and consistency by defining a pay structure. The process for preparing a pay structure includes job evaluation, comparison of pay to an area salary survey, and creation of pay ranges. This process provides an objective basis to define job levels. Further, the defined pay ranges help to minimize unchecked salary inflation which occurs when generous raises are passed out every year.

4. Control inflation of pay increases. Year after year, granting pay in-

creases to an employee who remains in the same job can create an unrealistically high pay level. The job has not changed; the individual's performance has probably reached a plateau, but annual pay increases are continued until the pay level far exceeds the market value of the job. There are, however, several measures which can be defined in the Pay Administration Policy to control inflationary wages.

- Conduct an annual salary trend analysis to monitor pay adjustments in the area and the industry. Consider this data along with profitability data when defining allowable pay adjustments. Communicate appropriate guidelines to supervisors each year.

- Recognize that percentage increases compound each year. As an alternative, consider a lower percent pay increase with a lump sum payment.

- Emphasize a merit or performance basis for pay adjustments. When individual performance warrants a higher pay raise, provide it. Likewise, when performance is poor, withhold, suspend, or reduce the individual's pay raise.

- Utilize bonus or incentive plans to achieve a better pay for performance relationship. See sample bonus incentive policy later in this chapter.

- Avoid reliance on cost of living increases to pay plans. Such plans, often sought by unions for their members, have a direct inflationary effect.

**Sample Policy**

**XYZ COMPANY**
**PERSONNEL POLICY & PROCEDURE**

---

SUBJECT: PAY ADMINISTRATION                    DATE: May 1, 1993

---

*Policy*: It is the policy of XYZ Company to establish employee pay rates in an equitable, objective manner which uses pay ranges and job levels based on job evaluation.

*Purpose*: To maintain pay equity within the organization, between Company locations, and in relation to area salary trends.

*Procedure*:
1. The XYZ Company pay structure has been established using a job evaluation system. The job evaluation process provides a systematic and objective method to establish a value relationship between the various jobs. The jobs are then grouped within salary grades. Job levels were established by a management consultant working closely with Corpo-

rate management and Division managers. Final responsibility for determining job levels rests with Corporate management.

2. Salary ranges are subdivided into three performance range segments:

    a) The lower third of the range is designated as the trainee range.

    b) The middle third of the range is designated as the competent range.

    c) The upper third of the range is designated as the superior range.

3. The principal objective of the pay structure is to administer the employee's salary within the established pay range in a manner which generally correlates to performance ratings. The use of a pay range assures that employees performing the same job are compensated in a comparable manner. Further, the pay range permits the supervisor to exercise some discretion to assign individual pay rates to employees reflecting performance levels, experience, job knowledge, and results achieved.

4. When a vacant position is being filled (by promotion, transfer, or selection of a job applicant), the ideal candidate should possess appropriate job qualifications and be willing to accept a pay rate which is within the pay range for the position.

5. The hiring supervisor or manager may recommend a starting pay rate for a new employee, subject to approval of the Division manager. The designated manager shall then communicate the job offer and pay rate to the new employee. Normally, the pay rate for a new employee should be set within the lower third of the pay range for the job to allow for subsequent salary growth for the employee.

6. Supervisors and managers are encouraged to confer with superiors, the Personnel Administrator, or the Vice President of Finance when formulating pay offers. Exceptions to the above guidelines may be authorized by a Vice President.

7. Salary rates for new hires and all other pay adjustments (due to promotion, transfer, demotion, pay raise, etc.) shall be recorded by the supervisor onto the Payroll Change Notice. The Payroll Change Notice shall be routed through one's superior to the Payroll Department in the Corporate office.

## Sample Employee Handbook Paragraph

*Pay and Performance*

XYZ Company endeavors to pay employees in a manner which recognizes employee job performance, as well as business conditions. To accomplish this goal, the Company undertook a study of jobs and pay practices in our region. As a result of this study, each job has a defined pay grade and salary range.

XYZ Company has established Job Descriptions for each job. The job description lists duties and responsibilities of the job. Your supervisor will provide further details.

Employee performance is evaluated on a continuous basis considering items such as ability, attendance, quantity and quality of work, timely completion of job assignments, and other performance factors. Consideration for pay changes may occur on an annual basis. However, actual pay adjustments will be made only if warranted by appropriate business conditions and satisfactory performance ratings.

As a reminder, performance evaluations may also be necessary to provide corrective job instructions or disciplinary warnings if necessary.

## Bonus Incentives

The growth of international competition in the 1980s has spurred renewed efforts in business to improve productivity and quality. Many organizations have considered bonus or incentive pay plans as a way to stimulate desired improvements.

The goal of a bonus incentive plan is to reward employees for achievement of specified performance results. The incentive plan is a form of variable compensation—that is, the compensation payout to employees varies up or down depending upon the employee's performance. When a bonus incentive plan is properly designed and administered, everyone is a winner. The employees benefit from higher compensation based upon their attainment of plan objectives. The employer benefits because increased productivity (or lower costs or reduced accidents, etc.) promotes higher profits. A good bonus incentive plan literally pays for itself.

There are a variety of plans which can be implemented under the broad term *financial incentives*. Several common examples are highlighted here.

- Premium pay is used by some firms to provide an incentive for certain kinds of work. Similar to overtime pay, premium pay is added to the employee's base pay when certain specified conditions are met. Premium pay is often used for difficult assignments, unusual hours, or hazardous working conditions. Common examples of premium pay include shift differentials for night shift work, premium pay for work on a holiday, hazardous duty pay, or pay premium for work in a high cost of living area.

- Piece rate pay is often used in a manufacturing environment where employee productivity is measured by the number of pieces produced. For best results, piece rate incentives should be developed with the aid of an industrial engineer. An industrial engineer studies the job tasks, designs efficient job procedures, and develops standards for normal performance and incentive rewards for performance that exceeds the standards.

- Many salespeople are compensated on a commission basis. The commission is a designated percent of the selling price or profits on the item sold. Some sales positions are paid solely by commission. Others may receive a base salary plus commission. Another variation is to provide a "draw" or advance in pay based on anticipated commissions. Commissions can range from 1 percent to 40 percent or more depending on the industry, product sold, commission basis, and degree of influence the salesperson has on the sale.

■ Bonus incentive plans can be designed for any type of industry or job. Bonus incentives can be keyed to individuals, work units, or the organization. Bonus plans can be an informal payout to employees after a profitable year based on management discretion. For the best incentive effect, however, a bonus plan should specify certain performance goals which are communicated to employees. Some suggestions on developing a bonus incentive are provided in the checklist which follows.

## Pitfalls to Avoid

Bonus incentives are a form of employee pay. Therefore, considerable care is needed to design a pay plan which motivates employees. A poorly designed plan or unattainable incentive goals will be demotivating. Here are some pitfalls to avoid:

1. Recognize that a bonus incentive plan can cause employees to focus activities solely toward the specified bonus incentive factor, at the expense of other job activities. For example, a performance incentive that rewards quantity of work is likely to increase output, but quality of work may be poor. To remedy this problem, the bonus incentive must be designed for high-quantity output of quality items. Poor-quality items should be deducted from output totals. The design of the bonus incentive must carefully consider the various work factors and the effect of emphasizing rewards for one factor over another.

2. Exercise considerable care in setting performance standards or goals. The standards or goals are the basis for the performance incentive. They should be attainable, but require some extra effort by the employee. If the goal is too easily attained, the employer incurs added wage costs without an increase in productivity. Conversely, if the goal is impossible to meet, the bonus becomes a disincentive. Once a goal is set and employees have increased productivity, avoid changing or raising the goal merely to push productivity higher. Frequent changes or increases in goals will cause morale problems and demotivate employees.

3. Consider implementing two bonus incentive plans. An individual incentive coupled with a group incentive helps promote teamwork throughout the organization and achieve a balance between individual and group goals. An individual incentive, by itself, can cause individuals

**CHECKLIST**
**A Bonus Incentive Policy**

- What category or classification of employees are eligible to participate in the bonus incentive?

- What eligibility criteria are defined for bonus participation, such as length of service, pay level, job class, performance rating, etc.?

- Will the bonus incentive be provided for individuals, work units, or the organization as a whole?

- What performance factor or factors will be targeted for improvement through the bonus incentive plan?

- Are current performance data or defined standards available to use as a guide for bonus achievement?

- What records will employees or supervisors maintain to track work results and compute bonus entitlement?

- What time period will be used to measure performance results and compute bonus payouts (i.e., monthly, quarterly, yearly, etc.)?

- How will the bonus incentive plan be communicated to participants?

- Will the bonus incentive formula be periodically evaluated?

to work solely toward their own incentive goals at the expense of other employees or the organization.

4. Avoid misunderstandings about the bonus or incentive plan through careful testing and communication. Evaluate the effectiveness of the incentive plan by using actual performance data to compute bonus results. Apply performance data from various employees during various times of the year to obtain a representative sampling of how the bonus will affect individual compensation. If the incentive goal appears too easy or too hard to attain, now, before implementation, is the time to make adjustments to goals or formulas. Then carefully communicate the bonus incentive plan to employees. Sample performance data applied to the incentive plan will show how the plan will affect employee earnings. Identify specific benefits—how the plan will help employees and the company.

5. Note that regular incentive pay or bonus plans are subject to overtime payment requirements for nonexempt employees. Discretionary bonuses, however, are not deemed to be regular earnings and therefore are not subject to overtime pay computations. Consider this issue when designing your bonus incentive to avoid incurring unexpected costs or liabilities.

## Sample Policy

**XYZ COMPANY
PERSONNEL POLICY & PROCEDURE**

SUBJECT: BONUS INCENTIVE                    DATE: May 1, 1993

*Policy*: It is the policy of XYZ Company to provide a bonus incentive plan to promote improved productivity and efficiency.

*Eligibility*: Full-time employees with 1500 hours of service or more in the current calendar year and a performance rating of 2.6 or more.

*Procedure*:
1. The bonus incentive is a discretionary payout based upon executive management discretion. When evaluating whether or not to issue a bonus, executive management normally considers profitability at year end, cash flow, and the overall financial condition of the company. As a discretionary plan, the bonus plan may be increased, decreased, or suspended as deemed appropriate by management.

2. To participate in the bonus, employees must meet eligibility requirements as defined above. An employee on a leave of absence who meets eligibility requirements is entitled to bonus participation. Actual time worked, company-observed holidays, paid vacation, and paid funeral absences count toward the hours-of-service requirement. A leave of absence does not count as hours of service for bonus eligibility.

3. Supervisors are responsible for preparing regular performance appraisals during the year according to the firm's performance appraisal policy. Performance appraisal ratings are one factor that is used in the bonus computation.

4. An employee's base pay is one factor for the formula. Base pay refers to the employee's regular straight time pay rate received during the current calendar year. Base pay *does not* include shift differential or overtime premiums.

5. Management customarily computes the bonus payout by mid-December. A separate bonus incentive check is issued to employees, normally timed to precede the Christmas holiday. Currently, the formula is 1 percent of base pay times the performance rating, which equals the bonus.

6. The following guidelines are provided to aid supervisors in discussing bonus incentive pay with employees:
   a) The bonus incentive plan has been a customary reward to employees following a profitable year.
   b) The bonus incentive plan is contingent upon profitability for the year (a teamwork feature that means we must all work together to achieve organizational goals).
   c) The bonus plan recognizes individual performance based upon the employee's performance rating.
   d) The bonus plan recognizes responsibility based upon a percent of base pay.

e) The bonus plan is discretionary; executive management may elect to change, suspend, or stop bonus payouts entirely.

**BONUS INCENTIVE FORMULA**
**XYZ COMPANY**

---

*Eligibility*: Full-time employees
                1500 hours of service by year end
                Performance rating of 2.6 or more

*Bonus Formula*:
1% of base pay $\times$ performance rating = bonus
Requires bonus pool of \$35,000–\$60,000

*"Average employee" computation*:
$1\% \times 20,000 \times 3.5 = \$700$

## Sample Employee Handbook Paragraph

*Bonus Compensation*

Traditionally, XYZ Company has provided a bonus compensation check for employees to aid in their enjoyment of the holiday season. The payment of a bonus at Christmas or any other time during the year is contingent upon management discretion and Company results during the year. Because of this, there may be years when the amount of the bonus may change or this practice may be suspended.

# Wage Garnishments

There are a variety of legal proceedings which can be initiated against an employee for the employee's failure to meet certain financial obligations. Among the most common proceeding that will affect many firms is a wage garnishment. Wage garnishments are a court-ordered process for an employer to withhold a portion of an employee's earnings for payment of a debt.

As a court-ordered process, the garnishment imposes a legal obligation upon the employer. An employer's failure to withhold monies as directed could create financial obligations on the company. Further, failure to properly handle deductions can create legal liabilities for the firm. For these reasons, it is important to define a policy to guide the handling of wage deduction orders.

There are a variety of wage deduction orders that a firm may receive. In addition to wage garnishments, an employer may be directed to withhold pay under the following circumstances:

- *Support order*: A support order is directed by the court for the purpose of paying support monies for an ex-spouse or dependent based upon a divorce decree.

- *Tax liabilities*: The Internal Revenue Service (IRS) has used wage deduction orders to collect back taxes owed by the employee to the government.

- *Wage assignment agreements*: Some creditors require individuals to sign a wage assignment agreement when granting credit for a large purchase. In the event the individual falls behind on payments, the creditor sends a copy of the wage assignment agreement to the employer for wage deductions and payment.

The Consumer Credit Protection Act is one law that defines employer obligations relating to wage garnishments. The Act prohibits employers from discharging an employee whose earnings have been subjected to any one indebtedness. Some interpretive court decisions on the law have held that an employee may be discharged for two or more cases of indebtedness. Further, the law limits the amount of an employee's wages that can be subject to garnishment to the lesser of 25 percent of the employee's disposable earnings or an amount equal to 30 times the federal minimum wage. Disposable earnings means that part of an employee's earnings remaining after deduction for any amount required by law to be withheld.

### Pitfalls to Avoid

Wage deduction orders present an administrative hassle for the employer. The employer must incur extra costs for a nonproductive clerical processing task. As a result, employers may be upset with the employee or the process and take inappropriate action creating legal liabilities. Here are some pitfalls to avoid.

1. Many managers erroneously believe that an employee should be fired when a wage deduction order is received. I caution employers against discharge for indebtedness, however, for several reasons as noted:

   - More restrictive state laws may apply, thus limiting or prohibiting discharge for indebtedness.

   - A discharge for indebtedness is a discharge for a non-job-related issue. Even though many states continue to assert an employment-at-will relationship, a discharge for indebtedness could be tough to defend before a jury in a wrongful discharge case.

   - Minorities and women often earn less than others and may be more likely to encounter financial difficulties, garnishments, and resulting corrective discipline or discharge by their employer. This can create a policy which has a greater adverse impact upon minorities and

**CHECKLIST**
**A Wage Garnishment Policy**

- What are the federal law requirements for handling wage deduction orders?
- What are the applicable state law requirements relating to wage deductions and voluntary wage assignments?
- Will the firm deduct a fee (as allowed by law) for the administrative costs of handling wage deductions?
- When two or more wage deduction orders are received, how and in what order will they be processed?
- Who is responsible for receiving and processing wage deduction orders?
- Who is responsible for communicating information to the employee about wage deduction orders?
- What penalties, if any, will be imposed for repeated receipt of wage deduction orders?
- What records will be maintained to process wage deductions in a timely fashion?

               females; such a practice would be in violation of Title VII of the Civil Rights Act of 1964.

2. Be alert to state as well as federal government requirements. Where a state law is more restrictive or provides greater protection for the employee, the state law will control. Check whether the law requires deduction computations based on gross earnings or disposable earnings. Also note what the deduction limits are under the applicable law. Illinois, for example, limits certain garnishments for debts other than support to 15 percent of gross income, while neighboring Kentucky specifies 25 percent of the employee's disposable income as the limit. Other deduction limits to 60 percent of the employee's disposable income may be required for court-ordered support payments.

3. Be alert for official-looking letters from collections agencies demanding wage deductions to pay off indebtedness. Generally wage deduction laws stipulate a procedure for notification to the employer. With voluntary wage assignments, the creditor provides a copy of the employee's signed authorization for a wage assignment in the event of default of payment terms specified in the credit contract.

4. Specify a priority sequence for handling multiple garnishments received on the same employee. An IRS tax garnishment takes priority over all others, then support garnishments, and then garnishments for other debts. Garnishment orders should be processed one at a time in the order received. When two or more garnishments are received,

notify the creditor that their demand notice will be satisfied upon completion of prior notices. Each demand notice is normally processed for a period of 8, 10, or 12 weeks. If the indebtedness is not satisfied in that period, the debtor must start the process over again.

## Sample Policy

**XYZ COMPANY**
**PERSONNEL POLICY & PROCEDURE**

---

SUBJECT: WAGE GARNISHMENTS                    DATE: May 1, 1993

---

*Policy*: It is the policy of XYZ Company to respond to legitimate wage garnishment orders by computing wage deductions and remitting necessary funds.

*Procedure*:

1. All wage deduction orders and wage assignment agreements received by the company shall be referred to the Human Resource Administrator. All wage garnishments and related documents shall be treated with the same confidentiality as all payroll information.

2. The Human Resource Administrator shall notify the employee upon receipt of the wage garnishment. The Human Resource Administrator shall verify with the employee that the indebtedness is accurate and explain the company policy on handling wage garnishments.

3. In the event of a question about the accuracy of the garnishment, the Human Resource Administrator may do one or more of the following:

   a) Recommend that the employee contact the creditor to correct the error.

   b) Contact the creditor directly to clarify the matter.

   c) Check to ensure that the creditor has provided proper notice and procedure for a wage garnishment.

4. The Human Resource Administrator shall route a copy of the wage garnishment to the Payroll Clerk. The Payroll Clerk shall set up a garnishment file, begin payroll deductions, and maintain a record showing pay period, employee pay, percent of deduction, and amount of deduction. Upon fulfillment of deductions for the period of the garnishment order, a check shall be authorized for payment to the creditor. A copy of the garnishment order shall be included when remitting the check.

5. In the event two or more wage garnishments are received on an employee, each garnishment shall be processed in order of receipt. The Human Resource Administrator shall contact the creditor to acknowledge receipt and notify the creditor when the next garnishment shall be processed.

6. The Payroll Clerk shall deduct any administrative fee as allowed by law. The Human Resource Administrator shall advise the Payroll Clerk about administrative fees as allowed.

7. In the event that the company repeatedly receives wage garnishments on a particular employee, the Human Resource Manager shall advise the employee about financial counseling resources available in the community.

**Sample Employee Handbook**
**Paragraph**

*Wage Garnishments*

The Company dislikes the unpleasant business of "attaching" your wages for personal debts. However, we are required to make wage deductions and assess a fee in the event garnishment notices or wage deduction orders are received. You can avoid this embarrassment by keeping your personal finances in order.

## Notes

1. *Handy Reference Guide to the Fair Labor Standards Act,* WH Publication 1282, U.S. Dept. of Labor, January, 1981, p. 7.
2. R. Green, W. Carmell, P. Gray, *1992 State by State Guide to Human Resource Law,* Panel Publishers, New York, pp. 2–17.
3. *Human Resource Policies and Practices in American Firms,* BLMR 137, U.S. Dept. of Labor, 1989, p. 56.
4. W. Hubbartt, *Performance Appraisal Manual for Managers and Supervisors,* Commerce Clearing House, Chicago, 1992, pp. 70–72. Reproduced with permission.
5. *Human Resource Policies and Practices in American Firms,* BLMR 137, U.S. Dept. of Labor, 1989, p. 57.

# 11

# Discipline, Discharges, Retirements, and Other Separations

**Read Chapter 11 for:**

Disciplinary procedures and rules

Discharge

Layoff

Resignations

Severance pay

Retirement

## Disciplinary Rules and Procedures

Regular attendance, cooperation, and timely completion of tasks are examples of acceptable on-the-job conduct. Every organization, however, must deal with occasional instances of employee misconduct. Misconduct is defined as employee behavior that is disruptive, detrimental, or destructive toward other individuals or the organization, or violates rules of the organization.

Examples of misconduct include absenteeism, tardiness, refusal to perform assigned tasks, or unauthorized use of equipment. Warnings or other disciplinary actions are customarily used to deal with misconduct.

Progressive discipline has long been recognized by human resource specialists as an effective method of controlling misconduct. With progressive discipline, the "punishment fits the crime." Minimal corrective action is taken for a minor offense. However, stronger corrective action is taken for repeated, subsequent, or serious offenses. Arbitrators, unemployment insurance hearings referees, and other third-party adjudicators have typically recognized progressive disciplinary warnings as justification for ultimate discharge of an errant employee.

Many employers have lost contested unemployment claims because of poorly defined or administered disciplinary rules and procedures. When firing an employee for misconduct, the key to beating that individual's unemployment claim is to show that

- The company had a policy or rule prohibiting the misconduct.
- The policy or rule was communicated to employees.
- The employee's actions were in clear disregard for the policy.

However, unless carefully prepared, disciplinary rules or procedures can be used against the employer. Two examples are given:

a. XYZ Company publishes its disciplinary policy, which prohibits various offenses including excessive absenteeism. As a result of a lax management attitude, the policy is not enforced. Then Tyrone, a minority employee, is fired for excessive absences. Tyrone's discrimination claim against the company is upheld because the investigation shows that other nonminorities were not disciplined for similar misconduct.

b. XYZ Company publishes its disciplinary rules and procedures in its employee handbook. The procedures clearly state, "It is our policy only to discharge an individual when there is a violation of our rules. To be fair, our rules require two prior warnings before discharge." When the Plant Manager fires an employee for insubordination, the company most likely would lose a wrongful discharge lawsuit because the immediate discharge is contrary to the pre-discharge procedure requiring two warnings.

In example a, loose or inconsistent enforcement practices which suddenly crack down on a minority employee create a likely finding of discrimination. Likewise, in example b, the company is likely to lose a wrongful discharge lawsuit because the immediate firing fails to follow the published policy requiring two prior warnings.

There are other pros and cons to defining a detailed list of disciplinary rules and procedures. To help the policy writer decide whether disciplinary rules are right for the organization, both sides of the argument are presented:

*Pro: Arguments for Disciplinary Rules and Procedures:*

Clearly defines what actions are misconduct
Communicates and helps prevent misconduct
Provides clear basis for discipline

Helps to support dismissal actions
Helps to promote uniform enforcement
Helps to prevent union organizing
Helps to beat unemployment insurance claims
Helps to control personnel costs of absenteeism, tardiness, etc.
Gives supervisor a guideline to follow

*Con: Arguments against Disciplinary Rules and Procedures:*

Listing of rules treats employees as children and not as professionals.
Many rules are for petty, unimportant issues.
Listing of disciplinary procedures limits management discretion.
Omitting an offense from the list of rules may limit management's right to deal with the issue.
Failure to follow published rules can result in discrimination or wrongful discharge claims.
Disciplinary rules may be seen as predischarge rules which limit management's prerogatives to fire at will.

When considering the pros and cons of defining disciplinary rules and procedure, it is important to consider issues such as:

*Management style*: A freewheeling, shoot-from-the-hip entrepreneurial manager would probably disregard detailed predischarge disciplinary policy; so a detailed procedure would be unadvisable.

*Organizational culture*: A large organization or governmental agency that is more procedure oriented would benefit from guidelines in the disciplinary process.

*Customary industry practice*: Unionized organizations are more likely to have detailed disciplinary procedures arising from "just cause" provisions in labor agreements.

## Pitfalls to Avoid

Disciplinary rules are an important management tool for dealing with employee misconduct. Since disciplinary actions often result in discharge—and discharges often result in litigation—disciplinary rules and procedures must be carefully defined:

1. Avoid defining a disciplinary policy which is too restrictive on management's discretion to deal with misconduct. There are several things that the policy writer can do to protect management's discretion:

    a) State that the disciplinary rules or offenses are merely examples of common forms of misconduct, that the list is not all inclusive, and that any other inappropriate or disruptive behavior or misconduct as judged by management will be grounds for corrective discipline.

    b) Describe disciplinary rules with serious and minor offenses to allow

**CHECKLIST**
**A Disciplinary Rules and Procedures Policy**

- How will disciplinary rules and procedures be communicated to employees (i.e., employee handbook, bulletin board, new employee orientation, etc.)?
- Who is responsible for communicating disciplinary rules and procedures to employees (i.e., supervisor, human resources, or other)?
- Who is responsible for enforcing disciplinary rules?
- Will disciplinary procedures be specific, correlating corrective action to offenses, or broad, allowing discretion in disciplinary matters?
- Will prior disciplinary warnings be considered when imposing corrective action? If so, for what time period?
- Will corrective discipline include any or all of the following actions: counseling, discussion, retraining, verbal warnings, written warnings, transfer, demotion, suspension, discharge?
- How will disciplinary actions be documented (i.e., warning form or letter to employer)?
- What kinds of investigation steps will be taken when imposing corrective discipline?
- What precautions or procedures will be taken in the event that discipline results in discharge?
- Will progressive disciplinary steps be taken for repeated, subsequent, or more serious offenses?
- Will the employee be permitted to appeal a disciplinary action or file a grievance?

for proper handling of the incident based upon the facts. For example, "insubordination" may be defined as a serious offense, while "failure to follow instructions" may be viewed as a less serious offense.

c) Include in the disciplinary rules one or two broadly stated offenses that can be used as a catch-all to include a broad category of misconduct. This helps to eliminate the need to define a lengthy list of rules to cover every conceivable offense. For example, "failure to follow company policies and procedures" can cover a wide range of offenses.

2. Take care to minimize a negative message when drafting a disciplinary policy. Undue emphasis of negative issues may create mistrust or contribute to an adversarial relationship between employees and management. For example, bold emphasis that all misconduct absolutely

will not be tolerated and is grounds for immediate discharge may be an unduly harsh message. Rather, a reasoned message about the importance of working together with common-sense guidelines for on-the-job conduct presents a less threatening message to employees. Such a message can include a statement that misconduct will result in corrective discipline, which may include immediate discharge. A softened statement can still alert employees that misconduct will not be allowed.

As another example, I find that many employers prefer to use the term *standards of conduct* rather than the more negative-sounding term *disciplinary rules.*

3. Make sure that your disciplinary policies do not create a binding limitation on management's right to fire at will. (See Chap. 2 for a list of states which view policy manuals as contractually binding.) Second, carefully weigh the advantages of detailed disciplinary warnings (which may limit immediate discharge at will) compared to broader guidelines (which permit greater discretion in discipline but may also result in discriminatory practices). My advice here is this: If you publish a rule, stand by it. Don't make a rule that is going to be disregarded by supervisors or managers. If supervisors, managers, or a free-wheeling entrepreneur are likely to deviate from disciplinary procedures, then I recommend use of broadly stated guidelines on misconduct and discipline.

## Sample Policy

**XYZ COMPANY**
**PERSONNEL POLICY & PROCEDURE**

---

SUBJECT: DISCIPLINARY PROCEDURES            DATE: May 1, 1993

---

*Policy*: It is the policy of XYZ Company to apply a practice of progressive discipline when needed to correct employee misconduct and improve job performance.

*Purpose*: To define common misconduct actions which may serve as a general guideline, including other similar misconduct which may be subject to disciplinary action.

*Procedure*:
1. Each Supervisor and/or Manager is responsible for communicating Company rules to subordinates and for enforcing disciplinary rules according to the guidelines of this policy.
2. Disciplinary warnings are administered on a progressive basis and may include verbal warnings, written warnings, suspension, or dismissal. Progressive disciplinary actions are cumulative; any four offenses within

one year will result in dismissal. Incidents of serious misconduct in the judgment of the Supervisor and/or Manager shall result in immediate dismissal. Refer also to Separation of Employment Policy when disciplinary action results in dismissal.

3. All disciplinary actions (including verbal warnings) are to be documented on the employee Warning Notice. The warning notice and corrective action are to be discussed with the employee, signed by the employee and the supervisor administering discipline, and then routed to the Administrative Office for inclusion in the employee's personnel file. A copy of the warning notice may be retained in the supervisor's personnel file, and the employee may receive a copy.

4. Upon learning of an employee's misconduct, the Manager or Supervisor shall consider the facts of the case and administer appropriate disciplinary action as defined below:

*Offenses Subject to Immediate Discharge*

a. Theft, unauthorized removal, or wrongful possession of Company property, merchandise, funds, or possessions of others

b. Possession or use of illegal drugs on Company time or premises

c. Unauthorized possession or use of liquor or alcoholic beverages on Company time or premises

d. Insubordination or refusal to follow work instructions

e. Flagrant disregard for safety or health endangering lives or property

f. Fighting, intimidation, or threatening fellow employees, supervisory personnel, or customers

g. Possession or use of a weapon on Company property

h. Falsification or alteration of any official Company document or form including time card, employment application, etc.

i. Unreported absence of three days or more

j. Deliberate destruction of Company property, equipment, or merchandise

k. Participation in or benefiting from unethical or illegal business practices

*Offenses Subject to Suspension without Pay or Immediate Discharge*

a. Reporting to work under the influence of drugs or alcoholic beverages or in an otherwise unfit condition to work safely

b. Reporting to work in garments which are grossly inappropriate or unsafe for performance of job responsibilities

c. Any incident involving work disruption, safety hazards, or similar conditions, pending further investigation

*Offenses Subject to Progressive Discipline as Follows*:

1st Offense—Written Warning

2nd Offense—Written Warning

3rd Offense—Written Warning and Discharge

a. Failure to follow work instructions

b. Failure to follow safety rules or safety instructions from superiors

c. Smoking in an unauthorized area

d. Failure to report reason for absence on a timely basis

e. Excessive absenteeism (two or more absences within a calendar month)

f. Excessive tardiness (two or more instances of tardiness within a calendar month)

g. Disregard for time reporting procedures

h. Abusive or negligent use of tools or equipment

i. Failure to wear clean, neat, appropriate clothing

j. Causing excessive waste or scrap

k. Unauthorized absence from work area

l. Returning late from lunch or break periods

m. Failure to wear personal protective equipment or use safety guards

## Sample List of Common Disciplinary Offenses

1. Fighting, instigating, or participating in a physical altercation on Company time or premises

2. Possession or use of a weapon on Company property

3. Possession or use of alcoholic beverages or illegal drugs on Company property, or being intoxicated by such substances while on the job

4. Possession or use of alcoholic beverages or illegal drugs on Company time or premises

5. Reporting to work under the influence of drugs or alcoholic beverages, or in an otherwise unfit condition to work safely

6. Unauthorized possession or use of alcoholic beverages on Company time or premises

7. Possession or use of illegal drugs on Company time or premises

8. Flagrant disregard for safety or health endangering lives or property

9. Failure to follow plant safety rules or safe operating procedures for your job

10. Falsification or alteration of any official Company document or form, including time card or employment application

11. Tampering with or misuse of machinery or equipment, or removing of guards

12. Destruction or defacing of Company property, equipment, or products

13. Theft or unauthorized removal of Company property, products, or possessions of others

14. Excessive absenteeism or tardiness

15. Excessive absenteeism (four or more times per month)

16. Excessive tardiness (four or more times per month)

17. Unreported absence of three days or more

18. Insubordination or refusal to follow work instructions

19. Failure to meet normal production standards or causing excessive waste or scrap

20. Gambling on Company time or premises

21. Leaving Company premises or work area during Company time without authorization

22. Causing or participating in pranks, jokes, or other similar disruptive behavior

23. Failure to report reason for absence in a timely manner

24. Loitering in other departments, loafing, or sleeping on the job

25. Failure to maintain work area in a clean and orderly manner

26. Stopping work early for breaks, lunch, or prior to the scheduled washup time at the end of the day

27. Improper use of tools or using the incorrect tool for the job

28. Intimidation, or use of threatening or abusive language toward fellow employees or supervisory personnel

29. Failure to follow work instructions

30. Failure to follow time reporting procedures

31. Failure to follow Company policies or rules

## Sample Employee Handbook Paragraph

*Standards of Conduct*

All companies must set reasonable rules in order to coordinate the many varied activities within the organization.

In recognition of this, XYZ Company has developed Standards of Conduct in order to advise employees regarding conduct which is unsuitable in a working environment. Employee misconduct which disregards the Standards of Conduct will result in corrective disciplinary action.

Violations of the Standards of Conduct accumulate within a rotating 12-month period, and any subsequent offenses progress to the next higher disciplinary action, which may include discharge. Serious misconduct or performance problems will result in immediate discharge.

Disciplinary measures are classified as shown below:

| Class | Management Action |
|-------|-------------------|
| A | Verbal Warning |
| B | Written Warning |
| C | Suspension |
| D | Discharge |

Management reserves the right to administer disciplinary rules and procedures based on its interpretation of the facts of the incident(s) and to adapt discipline procedures or use immediate discharge when such actions may be in the best interest of the Company.

**Sample Form**

### EMPLOYEE WARNING NOTICE

Name _____     Date _____

Department _____

You are hereby notified that, if you repeat the offense described below or permit the condition described to continue to be repeated, your employment relationship with this company may be terminated without further notice.

Offense: _____

_____

MANAGEMENT ACTION:     _____  Verbal Warning

                       _____  Written Warning

                       _____  Suspension (from/to)

                       _____  Termination

| _____ | _____ | _____ | _____ |
|------------------|----------|------------------|----------|
| Employee | Date | Supervisor | Date |

## Discharge

Discharge is the permanent and involuntary separation of the employment relationship. Discharge has been referred to as the capital punishment of the employment process. If all other forms of corrective action fail, discharge or involuntary separation of an employee is seen as the final alternative.

Traditionally, an employer had an unfettered right to hire and fire at will. This meant that, in the absence of an employment agreement, the employment relationship could be separated by either the employee or the employer at any time for any reason. Now, various state laws, federal laws, and court decisions have imposed limitations on discharges.

Several common examples of circumstances which should *not* be a basis for discharge are shown. Do not fire an employee for

Filing a worker's compensation claim

Filing a discrimination claim

Exercising rights under fair employment practice laws

Serving as a juror

Filing a complaint or exercising rights under the Occupational Safety and Health Act

Receiving a wage garnishment

Exercising rights protected under the National Labor Relations Act

In addition, courts in various jurisdictions have, through case decisions, outlined other limitations to the discharge process. While specific guidelines vary from state to state, here are some common circumstances under which an employee should not be fired:

For cooperating with law enforcement officials in the conduct of an investigation

For "whistle blowing" or notifying the public about a serious wrongdoing at the workplace

For refusing to participate in an illegal act

In addition, management should not fire an employee in a negligent manner which breaches a verbal promise or an implied contract (such as a predischarge procedure in an employee handbook). Further detailed discussion of wrongful discharge and employment at will is provided in Chap. 2, "The Contract Controversy."

Employers are free to discharge individuals for any other reason not specifically prohibited by law. Common reasons for discharge may include

Poor performance

Serious misconduct

Repeated instances of misconduct

Organizational change

Downsizing or job elimination

Lack of work

Because of the complexities of the employment relationship, the many laws affecting discharges, and the litigious nature of our society today, an organization needs a Discharge Policy to minimize its liability.

## Pitfalls to Avoid

Litigation relating to discharges is one of the fastest-growing areas of labor law. Wrongful discharges and discrimination claims are troublesome issues which continue to plague many firms. By avoiding several common pitfalls, however, many liabilities can be eliminated or significantly reduced.

1. Recognize that detailed predischarge procedures are likely to limit prerogatives to fire at will. When a firm defines specific procedures preceding discharge and communicates these procedures to employees in a policy manual, the courts in many states hold the employer accountable to follow the published policy.

   This creates a dilemma for the human resource specialist. Our human relations training urges guidelines for fairness, a system of prior warnings, a hearing or grievance process, and open communications of the process to employees. However, due to the trends in wrongful discharge cases, many human resource specialists now advise employers to avoid predischarge procedures and state that "the individual may be terminated at any time for any reason or no reason, with or without cause and with or without prior notice." This is a pretty heavy statement to make an employee sign after you told him or her, "welcome to the company."

   To prepare a Discharge Policy that works, consider the law in your state, management style, and organizational culture. Then write a policy that management can live with and stick to it. Second, limit definitions of pre-discharge procedures to management guidelines or supervisory instructions. Avoid listing details of discharge procedures given to employees in an employee handbook.

2. Take care to avoid deviations from published policy. Once the Discharge Policy has been defined, it is vitally important that supervisors and managers use the policy as a guide when handling discharges. One way to promote this practice is to have discharges reviewed with and approved by a second-level manager or Human Resource Specialist or both. The second look tends to be more objective and can help assure that the published policy is followed as closely as possible. Remember, when management breaks its own rule there is a greater likelihood of liability in a wrongful discharge case.

3. Be alert for unintentional discrimination. Many personnel practices are neutral on their face, but have an adverse effect on minorities, women, older workers, or other protected class individuals. In the event that

**CHECKLIST**
**A Discharge Policy**

- What circumstances are grounds for discharge?

- Who is responsible for recommending discharge (i.e., supervisor or manager)?

- Will discharges be subject to review or approval by the human resource specialist or a higher-level manager?

- Will performance appraisals, disciplinary warnings, or other forms of documentation be required to justify the discharge?

- What state or federal laws affect or limit discharges?

- Who is responsible for communicating the discharge to the employee?

- What final pay or benefits is the employee entitled to receive?

- Will there be an exit interview? if so, conducted by whom?

- Are there any contractural limitations (such as labor agreement, individual employment contract, or implied contract based on employee handbook provisions) which affect the discharge?

- When will the employee's final paycheck be provided?

- What provisions are made for return of company property prior to the individual's separation?

the investigation of a discrimination claim turns up a finding of adverse impact, the government will find that discrimination occurred. Several suggestions are offered when drafting your policy:

a) Take a careful second look at procedures to check the likelihood of unintended adverse effect. If adverse effect appears likely, adjust policy provisions to minimize this situation.

b) Periodically conduct an audit of personnel decisions to check for adverse effect. Firms that have affirmative action plans have to include mathematical comparisons of hires, separations, and other personnel actions to check for adverse affect.

4. When conducting personnel practices audits, I find that supervisors in many firms fail to adequately document performance or misconduct problems that lead up to discharge. To prevent this problem, several suggestions are offered:

a) Define adequate policy guidelines for performance appraisals and disciplinary warnings.

b) Require that appraisals and warnings be documented on an appropriate form.

c) In a management guide on discharges, include the requirement that discharges and related documentation be reviewed by a human resource specialist prior to approving discharge.

d) Include in the management guide a policy provision that urges greater use of suspension without pay or other form of documented "final warning" prior to the discharge.

5. Some states require the employer to give to separating employees a service letter detailing reasons for separation. In addition to complying with the law, a service letter helps the employer to concisely define the reason for separation. It has an added benefit of getting the employer to carefully evaluate the reason for discharge; because the reason is put in a letter to the employee.

## Sample Policy

**XYZ COMPANY**
**PERSONNEL POLICY & PROCEDURE**

SUBJECT: SEPARATION OF EMPLOYMENT          DATE: May 1, 1993

*Policy*: It is the policy of XYZ Company that the employment relationship may be terminated at any time at will by the Company or the employee.

*Purpose*: To define separation procedures and general circumstances which may result in separation of employment.

*Procedure*:
1. When an employee announces his or her intention to separate employment, it is the desire of the Company to receive two weeks' notice and for the employee to sign a resignation letter. (A copy is attached.)

2. Involuntary separation may be made at any time for any reason, normally based upon the following circumstances:

a) Layoff—Business conditions resulting in lack of work or organizational changes may result in separation by layoff. The needs of the business, and an employee's skills or abilities, are considered in determining which employees may be subject to layoff. A laid off employee is eligible for recall for three months; after that period, the layoff becomes a permanent separation.

b) Dismissal—Repeated or serious misconduct, poor performance, or any other reason deemed sufficient by management, may result in separation by dismissal.

3. When circumstances warrant, management and the employee may mutually agree on separation of employment.

4. In the event that an employee fails to perform adequately or does not respond to corrective job instructions or disciplinary measures during the orientation period or at any other time of employment with the

Company, the employee may be dismissed. Instances of serious misconduct or performance problems will result in immediate dismissal.

5. Under normal circumstances, the supervisor may recommend dismissal, with such recommendation being subject to review and approval by a second-level manager. In circumstances involving disruption to work or serious safety hazards, the supervisor has full authority to suspend an employee as defined below.

6. All involuntary separations must be made with the approval of the Company President. If immediate action must be taken, an employee may be suspended without pay for up to three days pending a final decision.

7. In the recommendation and/or approval of an involuntary separation, consideration shall be given to the facts of the case; the needs of the business; alternatives such as transfer, demotion, or suspension; and the sufficiency of any prior disciplinary warnings or corrective job instructions to assure that the separation is consistent with Company policies and relevant labor laws. The supervisor is encouraged to confer with the Personnel Manager to evaluate the adequacy of documentation to support and justify the planned separation.

8. The supervisor or manager is responsible for conducting the "final separation discussion" with the employee. The discussion should be brief, identifying the reason and effective date of the separation. A second supervisor, manager, or Personnel Manager may participate in the discussion.

9. An exit interview shall be conducted by the Personnel Manager. Separating employees shall be given an insurance continuation letter and be advised of any final compensation due and of the opportunity to continue group insurance benefits to individual coverage at the employee's cost. Final pay is to be provided on the next normal pay day following the pay period in which the separation occurs. Final pay shall include regular earnings as well as pay for any earned unused vacation as defined by Vacation Policy.

10. The supervisor and the Personnel Manager are responsible for completing an Employee Change Notice each time an employee separates employment. The Employee Change Notice is then routed to the employee's personnel file. The Employee Change Notice is intended to serve as a source of information for replying to any unemployment insurance claim.

11. All separating employees are responsible for returning any Company property, and all such matters must be settled by the time that the employee is entitled to receive the final paycheck. All records, files, designs, or computerized data generated by an employee in the course of employment are deemed to be property of the Company. Such material must be relinquished to the Company. The Company reserves the right to inspect personal property or any records which are being removed from the premises when an employee separates employment.

12. The employee's personnel file shall then be separated from the files of current employees and placed into the "separated employee file."

## Sample Employee Handbook
## Paragraph

*Separation of Employment*

We want you to understand that the employment relationship is considered to be "employment at will." This means that you may resign employment at any time, and that the Company also reserves the right to terminate the employment relationship at any time with or without notice.

In the event you find it necessary to resign or decide to retire, please notify your supervisor. Written notification is preferred, and it is customary to give at least two weeks' notice so that the Company may make arrangements for finding a replacement.

Separating associates must return any Company property, keys, credit cards, etc. The separating individual may elect to continue insurances by completing the appropriate enrollment cards and paying the designated premium costs. The final paycheck is issued on the next normal pay day following the pay period in which separation occurs.

# Layoff

A layoff is an involuntary separation of an employee due to no fault of the employee. Traditionally, layoffs affected factory employees. Employment in factory jobs rose and fell with the economic cycles and seasonal fluctuations of the employer's business. Factory workers were hired when business demands grew and laid off when there was no need for their services. For the most part, administrative support workers were not seriously affected by job loss during those cycles.

In the last 20 years, however, many charges have occurred in the working relationship. In the 1980s, there was a wave of corporate takeovers and mergers. With each new combination, excess "redundant" staff workers were released. There simply was no need for two controllers, two advertising managers, or two personnel directors. Layoffs affected administrative and management-level employees.

A recessionary economy in the early 1990s again prompted a round of layoffs. While some factory hourly jobs were affected, the white collar administrative and mid-management jobs were particularly hard hit once again. This time, the buzz words were "downsizing" and "rightsizing." The intent was to improve the corporate bottom line by eliminating excess overhead of support staff salaries added during the prosperous 1980s. To the affected employees, the bottom line was layoff—loss of one's job.

A layoff can be temporary, as in the case of a short-term separation of workers during a seasonal slowdown. These workers are typically recalled back to work when business picks up. A layoff is permanent, however, when a job is eliminated and there is no other suitable employment available for the affected employee.

Several major laws affect the terms of a layoff policy. The greatest difficulty for an employer is likely to be a violation of equal employment opportunity laws. This can occur when a layoff has a discriminatory effect on protected class individuals. If a layoff affects greater proportions of minorities or women, the employer may be faced with discrimination allegations. Likewise, if large numbers of layoff "victims" are over 40 years old, the spectre of age discrimination may be raised.

Firms with unionized employees will find that layoff procedures are a very important issue to the union. Layoff procedures are a mandatory subject for bargaining. The criteria for a layoff are usually spelled out in great detail in most labor agreements. Inappropriate use of layoff procedures to thwart union organizational activity or to reduce a union's effectiveness among current employees could result in an unfair labor practice charge.

The Worker Adjustment and Retraining Notification Act, passed in 1989, requires firms to provide advance notice of major layoffs. Referred to as the WARN Act, this law affects companies with 100 workers or more at any given site of employment. The employer is required to give 60 days' advance notice to employees or their representatives, the state dislocated worker unit providing employment and training services, and the chief elected local official. Layoff notice is required in the event of a layoff or shutdown affecting one third of the workforce or 50 or more people. A series of smaller layoffs affecting 50 or more employees within 90 days is also included.

A third issue affecting layoffs is the requirement to advise separating employees about the opportunity to continue group health insurance. This practice is required by the law and is referred to as COBRA.

When defining a layoff policy, identification of objective layoff criteria is essential. The following are several examples of layoff criteria:

- *Staffing levels*: Sales or budget levels can be quantified to specified staffing levels, providing an objective basis to determine the number of employees affected by layoff.

- *Business needs*: Sales or service requirements will dictate what business functions are needed to serve customers. Likewise, business units that are suffering from poor sales are likely targets for cutbacks, providing an objective basis to determine which departments or business segments are affected by layoff.

- *Length of service*: Length of service or seniority is a commonly used criterion at many firms. Unions in particular favor seniority as a basis for layoffs. Some large organizations define various categories of seniority including company seniority, departmental seniority, or job seniority.

- *Skill level*: Supervisors and managers are particularly concerned that after a layoff they have employees with sufficient skills to perform the work. With certain jobs to be performed, it makes little sense to lay off an individual capable of performing the work while retaining another individual with less ability but greater seniority.

■ *Performance level*: Some firms have elected to use employee performance ratings as a basis for determining which employees are affected by layoff.

## Pitfalls to Avoid

Layoffs, like discharges, are an area of significant potential liability because the employment relationship is separated. Here are some pitfalls to avoid:

1. Define your policy in a way which allows maximum flexibility to respond to business needs. Avoid getting "boxed in" by a rigid policy (or union contract) which limits seniority as the sole criterion for layoff. The layoff policy must include consideration of employee skill or performance issues to assure that the remaining employees after the layoff have adequate skills to perform available work.

2. Avoid using subjective criteria as a basis for the layoff. For example, in one company, the Chief Executive gave the directive to all department managers to reduce staff by 10 percent by eliminating marginal performers. The problem with this directive was that there was no formal performance appraisal plan in place. Each manager considered his or her own subjective assessment of subordinates in determining individuals affected by layoff. A 50-year-old black male laid off through this process filed a discrimination charge. Ultimately, a court found that a subjective performance appraisal system lacking in rating guidelines and a standardized scoring system was unfair. If performance data is going to be used as a basis for layoff, it should be from an established appraisal system or other objective quantifiable measure of job results.

3. It is one thing to identify criteria for use in planning a layoff. However, if the criteria or procedures are defined and published in an employee handbook or other form of policy communication to employees, make sure that the policy is followed to the letter when implementing the layoff. Likewise, unionized firms should follow the layoff provisions of the labor agreement. With the increasing numbers of lawsuits arising from separations, the employer who disregards his or her own policy is likely to come up on the losing side of the lawsuit.

4. Before implementing a layoff, conduct an analysis by race, sex, and age to check for adverse effect to these protected class individuals. If the data shows an adverse effect to protected class individuals, I urge consideration of two options. First, make sure that layoff criteria are based upon objective verifiable data. Second, if there is adverse effect against protected class individuals and little or no objective documentation, I recommend identifying other more objective criteria that have less adverse impact on protected class individuals.

**CHECKLIST**
**A Layoff Policy**

- What state or federal laws affect the layoff policy?

- Are there any union agreement provisions which affect the layoff policy?

- What alternative cost reduction measures can be implemented before resorting to layoff?

- What criteria will be used as a basis for determining which jobs or employees are affected by layoff?

- Who will be responsible for planning and implementing the layoff?

- Who will be responsible for communicating the layoff to affected employees? to remaining employees?

- What final pay or benefits is the employee entitled to receive?

- Will there be an exit interview? if so, conducted by whom?

- When will the employee's final paycheck be provided?

- What provisions are made for return of Company property prior to the individual's separation?

**Sample Policy**

**XYZ COMPANY**
**PERSONNEL POLICY & PROCEDURE**

SUBJECT: LAYOFF PROCEDURES                                    DATE: May 1, 1993

*Policy*: It is the policy of XYZ Company to use layoff procedures when necessary to reduce workforce levels due to economic reasons or organizational change.

*Procedure*:

1. The Company President is responsible for managing business operations and maintaining staffing levels consistent with business conditions. In the event of a need to reduce workforce levels, this layoff procedure shall serve as a guideline.

2. In the event business conditions, economics, or organizational changes prompt the need to cut costs, executive managers are directed to consider various cost cutting alternatives. Typical alternatives may include
   Curtailment/elimination of overtime
   Freeze in hiring
   Delay/freeze of pay adjustment
   Reduction of work hours
   and other operational cost cutting measures

3. When other alternatives have been considered and implemented or ruled out in the judgment of the President, then layoff procedures may be used.

4. Layoffs shall be made based on the following criteria:

   a) A reevaluation of budgets and staffing levels shall be a guide in identifying the number of positions affected by layoff.

   b) An evaluation of customer needs and department work activities shall be a guide to identify if reductions will affect certain units or cut across all Company departments.

   c) Based upon departmental evaluations and revised staffing levels, as directed by the Company President, Department Managers shall identify jobs and individuals in nonessential functions.

   d) In the event that two or more individuals are assigned to a job affected by layoff, the following criteria shall be used:

      1) Employees with the lowest overall performance rating on the most recent performance appraisal

      2) Then, if performance is equal, the employee with the least length of Company service shall be subject to layoff.

5. Prior to implementing the layoff plan, the Human Resource Administrator is responsible for verifying affected individuals who were identified correctly based upon policy. Second, the Human Resource Administrator shall check the layoff population for an adverse effect to protected class individuals. Any discrepancies shall be reported to the Company President.

6. Once the layoff is finalized, the Human Resource Administrator is responsible for preparing layoff notices, request for final pay, payroll change notice, separation checklist, and COBRA notice. These documents shall be provided to each respective Manager for use in layoff discussions.

7. Layoff discussions normally are conducted by the respective Department Manager individually with each employee. The Human Resource Administrator may participate in the discussion if deemed appropriate. The layoff discussion shall be conducted in a private office or room at a date and time as directed by the President.

8. At the layoff discussion, the Manager shall identify the reason for layoff (as directed by the Company President), explain final pay, explain benefits continuation, and provide the COBRA notice letter.

9. All separating employees are responsible for returning any Company property. If deemed appropriate, the employee shall be supervised during removal of personal property and escorted from the premises.

10. In the event of Company layoff, the employee shall be eligible for recall for a period up to three months. Thereafter, the layoff shall be considered a permanent separation.

11. The payroll change notice, COBRA notice, and separation checklist shall be referred to the Human Resource Department for inclusion in the individual's personnel file.

**Sample Employee Handbook Paragraph**

*Separation Procedures*

We realize that there are situations which may compel separation of employment; and we want you to realize that the employment relationship may be terminated at any time at will, for any reason or no reason, by yourself or the Company, typically as follows:

a) Voluntary Resignation or Retirement—Please submit a letter of resignation giving two weeks' notice.

b) Layoff—Business conditions resulting in lack of work may result in separation by layoff. An employee on layoff is eligible for recall for three months; after that period, the layoff becomes a permanent separation.

c) Dismissal—Involuntary termination may be made for any reason deemed sufficient by management such as changing business conditions requiring organizational changes, or when corrective job performance instructions or disciplinary measures have failed. Serious performance or flagrant misconduct problems may result in immediate dismissal.

All separating employees are required to return any Company property or equipment prior to receiving their final check.

**Sample Forms**

**EMPLOYEE SEPARATION—EXIT INTERVIEW CHECKLIST**

Employee _____    Date _____

Reason for Separation:

Voluntary quit _____    Layoff _____

Retirement _____    Dismissal _____

Additional comments: _____

Last day of work _____    Eligible for rehire? ____yes ____no

The following topics should be reviewed with the employee.
(Check to indicate topic discussed.)

_____ Final pay to be issued on

_____ Insurance continuation (obtain signature on COBRA insurance

form)

_____ Discuss reason for separation.

_____ Return of Company property:

_____ Pager units, car phones, etc.

*Sample Forms (Continued)*

_____ Company vehicles and vehicle keys

_____ Keys to building, files, etc.

_____ Alarm/security passes

_____ Tools or equipment

_____ Work garments

_____ Work records, documents, etc.

_____ Other:

_____ Verify address for mailing W-2 forms, etc.

Supervisor/Manager/Personnel    Employee          Date

## CONTINUATION OF INSURANCE BENEFITS

To: _____

From: _____
Insurance plan administrator

*Important*: Please respond by: _____

Employees and/or their eligible dependents are entitled by law to elect to continue group health insurance coverage if such coverage will be discontinued as a result of a qualified event as listed below:

- The employee's separation from employment
- An employee's reduction of work hours causing disqualification for health insurance
- The death of the covered employee
- The divorce or legal separation of the covered employee from his or her spouse
- The employee's becoming eligible for Medicare benefits
- A dependent child ceasing to be a dependent

Continued health insurance will provide the same level of benefits available under the group health insurance plan. The individual electing insurance coverage is responsible for paying the full insurance premium cost on a timely basis. The election to continue insurance must be made within 60 days of the event which would disqualify eligibility under the group health plan.

Sincerely,

Insurance Plan Administrator

*Sample Forms (Continued)*

Please mark below whether or not you wish to continue insurance benefits.
-----------------------------------------------------------------
Instructions: Cut on dotted line, mark your decision, and return to: XYZ COMPANY, Address, Batavia, IL 60510

\_\_\_\_\_ YES, I want to continue group health insurance at a cost of $ \_\_\_\_\_ due monthly on _____.

\_\_\_\_\_ NO, I do not wish to continue the group health insurance.

# Resignations

Employees resign from their jobs for a variety of reasons. Among common reasons for resignation are accepting other employment, seeking career advancement, a relocation to another area, or separation to care for an infant or ill family member. Employees may also quit because they dislike their supervisor or working conditions, or seek higher salary. These are factors over which the Company may exercise some control to prevent unwanted resignations or excessive turnover.

A resignation occurs when an employee voluntarily quits employment. The resignation may be with notice when the employee tells a Company representative about his or her decision. Likewise, a resignation may be put in a letter to management. Generally, it is considered customary practice for an employee to give two weeks' notice to the employer when resigning.

As employers are well aware, however, some employees quit without giving prior notice. Some merely tell their supervisor at the end of the day that they quit. Even more frustrating for employers is dealing with the employee who just walks off the job failing to give any notice at all. Many firms consider an unreported absence of three days or more as job abandonment and the employee is dropped from the payroll.

A policy on resignations helps the firm to receive timely notice of resignations in order to coordinate reassignment of tasks and find a replacement employee. Second, careful monitoring of all separations can provide an objective basis to control unwanted turnover.

A certain amount of turnover is normal and expected. Turnover provides openings in the organization, allowing for promotions, transfers, or hiring of new individuals with fresh ideas. Excessive turnover, however, is a sign of other personnel problems. Factors such as employee/supervisory relationships, working conditions, pay levels, or other similar issues may contribute to high turnover. It is important that the Human Resource Administrator track turnover and seek to identify its causes.

One of the best ways to document an employee's resignation is to get a resignation letter from the employee. Some firms have a resignation form letter and ask the employee to fill in blanks to identify date of and reason for resignation and then sign the letter. A written resignation letter has several benefits:

- It clarifies the reason for resignation.
- It serves as notice of separation so that the employer can provide timely notice of insurance continuation rights.
- It can be used to contest any subsequent unemployment insurance claim filed by the employee.

## Pitfalls to Avoid

While employee resignations may appear to be a voluntary separation beyond the control of the employer, there are several things an employer can do to minimize costs and disruption of resignations.

1. Take care to clearly document the reason for separation. There are several reasons why this is important. First, accurate information on the reason for separation provides a basis to respond to any unemployment insurance claim filed by the employee. Unemployment insurance is an employer-paid, government-administered insurance plan. The insurance provides temporary income maintenance benefits in the event of job loss at no fault of the employee. Generally, an employee who voluntarily separates employment would be ruled ineligible for unemployment benefits. Accurate documentation of separation also helps the firm to respond to any subsequent inquiries relating to the employee such as reference check information.

2. Some employees use the threat of resignation as a way to extort a raise from their employer. In my 20 plus years in human resources, I have witnessed both sides of this issue. I have seen employees tell their boss that a pay raise is necessary or they will quit. Bosses cave in to this demand with sufficient frequency that it continues to be a viable tactic for those individuals with the chutzpa to try it. Likewise, as a personnel manager I have been involved in recruiting and screening potential employees who, after accepting my job offer, returned to their former employer to negotiate a raise.

   I believe that if this type of incident occurs, it demonstrates poor compensation administration and employee relations practices. Further, if you cave in to the demands of one, this same individual or others will be back to try it again. My advice when faced with an employee who presents this ultimatum is this: "Good luck on your new job."

3. Too many resignations are an indication of other human resource problems. Don't just let turnover happen. Track it. Evaluate it. Take corrective action when necessary. Elicit reasons for resignation. Note

**CHECKLIST**
**A Resignation Policy**

- What is the desired notice period for resignations (i.e., one week, two weeks)?
- Are there any employment agreement or contract provisions which affect separation of the employment relationship?
- Are there any state or federal laws which affect resignations or separations?
- What final pay or benefits is the employee entitled to receive?
- Will a resignation letter be used to document the resignation?
- Will there be an exit interview? if so, conducted by whom?
- When will the employee's final paycheck be provided?
- What provisions are made for return of Company property prior to the individual's separation?

whether there is a pattern of resignations from a particular job, department, shift, etc.

4. Avoid creating working conditions so intolerable that the employee is forced into voluntary resignation. Such circumstances are viewed as constructive discharge. Recognize that unreasonable actions by a supervisor or manager can create a liability for the employer if the employee files a discrimination claim or a wrongful discharge lawsuit.

**Sample Policy**

**XYZ COMPANY**
**PERSONNEL POLICY & PROCEDURE**

SUBJECT: RESIGNATION                                          DATE: May 1, 1993

*Policy*: It is the policy of XYZ Company that the employment relationship may be terminated at will anytime by the employee or the Company.

*Procedure*:
1. When an employee intends to resign employment, it is the desire of the Company to receive advance notice. It is customary practice to consider two weeks' notice as reasonable advance notice.
2. When giving notice, the employee should speak with his or her Supervisor or Manager or the Human Resource Administrator.
3. Written notice is preferred. Written notice can be a letter composed by the employee or a form letter provided by the Company for the employee to complete, sign, and turn in.
4. In the event an employee is absent for three consecutive work days or

more without notice to the Company regarding reason for absence, such action shall be considered resignation by job abandonment. After the third work day, the Human Resource Administrator shall send a registered return receipt letter to the employee providing notice that absence and lack of notice is viewed as job abandonment and resignation.

5. All separating employees are responsible for returning any Company property; and all such matters must be settled before issuance of the final paycheck. The Company reserves the right to inspect an employee's tool box at time of separation.

6. The Human Resource Administrator is responsible for preparing a benefit continuation notice, for scheduling a brief meeting with the employee to discuss benefits continuation, and for obtaining the employee's enrollment or waiver of benefits. At this time, an exit interview may be conducted to identify reasons leading to separation and the employee's feelings about the Company, job, Supervisor, etc.

7. Final pay is to be provided on the next normal pay day following the pay period in which separation occurs. Final pay shall include regular earnings as well as pay for any earned unused vacation as defined by the company's Vacation Policy. Profit sharing payouts may be made in accordance with plan provisions.

8. The Human Resource Administrator is responsible for preparing a payroll change notice detailing reasons for separation. The change notice is routed to payroll for computing final pay, and a copy is retained in the individual's personnel file.

## Sample Employee Handbook Paragraph

*Resignation*

We recognize that there may be circumstances which cause an employee to resign employment. In the event you find it necessary to resign or decide to retire, please notify your supervisor. Written notification is preferred, and it is customary to give at least two weeks' notice so that the Company may make arrangements for finding a replacement.

All employees are required to return keys, uniforms, Company vehicles, supplies, or any other Company property prior to separation of employment.

## Sample Form

### SAMPLE RESIGNATION LETTER

To:  XYZ Company

From: _____     _____
            Employee name                              Date

Subject: Resignation Letter

*Sample Form (Continued)*

This is to advise you that I am resigning employment with XYZ Company

effective on _____ .
                                        (date)

Reason for resignation: _____

_____

_____

_____

_____

I understand that, if I have any questions about Company policies or benefits, I may speak to the Personnel Manager or another Company manager.

                                              _____
                                                    Signature of Employee

## Retirement

The traditional view of retirement has been that, at age 65, the elderly employee gives notice, retires to a life of leisure, and draws a pension or social security benefits. However, the days of awarding a gold watch along with a pat on the back are ending. An aging workforce is compelling management to create more productive options.

Retirement is a special form of voluntary resignation. Retirements have the added features that the employee is older (usually 55 to 70 years of age), the employee plans to draw some form of pension benefit, and he or she does not plan to pursue active full-time employment.

A firm's retirement policy should be designed to facilitate the employee's transition from employment to retirement. There are no legal requirements that an employer establish a retirement benefit or retirement program. There are, however, numerous laws and regulations relating to tax issues and benefits plans.

Age 65 is commonly thought of as a "normal" retirement age. This may be because full social security benefits are available at age 65, and many retirement plans identify age 65 as a "normal" age for retirement. However, an employee may elect to retire at an earlier age or decide to continue working up to age 70 or beyond.

The Age Discrimination in Employment Act of 1967 (ADEA) is a significant law that affects the retirement and other policies. The ADEA prohibits discrimination in employment on the basis of age. It provides protection for individuals who are age 40 or older. The law prohibits the establishment of a mandatory retirement age prior to age 70 unless there is a bona fide qualification for the requirement.

When preparing a retirement policy, I recommend that the policy be distinguished as separate from any retirement benefits. The policy should, however, guide the employer to assist the employee in the transition process from employment to retirement. Further, the policy should clarify the drawing of any applicable retirement benefits.

## Pitfalls to Avoid

The greatest stumbling blocks around the retirement issue relate to communication of benefits and the liabilities of age discrimination. Here are some pitfalls to avoid.

1. Avoid establishing a policy or practice which results in forced retirement of individuals prior to age 70. Exceptions to this requirement have been permitted where there is a bona fide occupational qualification, such as in operators of certain public transportation vehicles. However, for most firms and most jobs, a mandatory retirement plan will be in violation of ADEA.

2. Exercise care when describing the employee's entitlement to Company benefits after retirement. Take care to avoid statements which could be construed as a promise of continuation of a particular benefit for an indefinite period during retirement. Some firms, for example, have offered a Medicare supplement insurance plan for retirees. This plan, paid by the employer, is intended to supplement Medicare coverage by providing medical insurance comparable to the benefit received by employees. However, due to cost control reasons, some of these plans were cancelled by employers. Retirees who stated they were promised the benefit indefinitely filed suit, seeking reinstatement of benefits as promised. To protect against this kind of situation, such plans should include a statement that benefits may be changed or cancelled.

3. Use caution when dealing with older workers and their performance problems. Avoid making references to age or suggestions for retirement when discussing performance or recording results on a performance appraisal form. Such actions could be viewed as evidence of age discrimination in an investigation by a state or federal agency. Rather, limit the focus of job performance to work standards and performance results.

4. Actively communicate the availability of retirement plans, preretirement counseling, or other benefits to employees. Encourage interested employees to contact the designated company retirement specialist for benefits information and retirement planning advice. A lack of com-

**CHECKLIST**
**A Retirement Policy**

- What is the desired notice period for retirement (i.e., two weeks, one month, three months)?
- How much advance notice of retirement is needed to process an employee's payout request for retirement benefits?
- Are there any employment agreement or contract provisions which affect separation of the employment relationship?
- Are there any state or federal laws which affect retirement or separation?
- What final pay or benefits is the employee entitled to receive?
- Will the employee be asked to give a letter of intent to resign or make formal application for retirement benefits?
- Will preretirement planning assistance or counseling be provided?
- Will any flexible work schedule plans be permitted as part of the transition to retirement?
- When will the employee's final paycheck be provided?
- What provisions are made for return of Company property prior to the individual's separation?

munication may mean that retiring employees are not fully aware of benefits or options available to them. The result can be an individual's decision to retire without advance notice. Late notice may mean delay in processing retirement benefits, lack of coordination, promoting or hiring a replacement, and delays in transferring responsibilities to new workers.

**Sample Policy**

**XYZ COMPANY**
**PERSONNEL POLICY & PROCEDURE**

SUBJECT: RETIREMENT                                    DATE: May 1, 1993

*Policy*: It is the policy of XYZ Company to assist an employee in the transition from employment to retirement.

*Procedure*:
  1. When an employee intends to retire from employment, it is the desire of the Company to receive advance notice. It is customary practice to consider three months' notice as reasonable advance notice.

2. When giving notice, the employee should speak with his or her Supervisor or Manager or the Human Resource Administrator.

3. Written notice of retirement is required. The Company has prepared a form letter which identifies the employee, retirement data, and age at retirement. This letter shall be turned in to the Human Resource Administrator. The letter is then referred to the Retirement Plan Administrator for use in processing the retirement plan distribution.

4. Upon receipt of the notice of retirement letter, the Human Resource Administrator is responsible for meeting with the employee to provide information on retirement procedures, benefits plan continuation, and financial planning services available through a certified financial planner. Planning services are paid by the company up through retirement.

5. Upon receiving a retirement plan distribution report, the Retirement Plan Administrator shall meet with the employer, explain distribution options, and obtain employee elections for plan distribution.

6. All separating employees are responsible for returning any Company property; and all such matters must be settled before issuance of the final paycheck. The Company reserves the right to inspect an employee's tool box at time of separation.

7. Final pay is to be provided on the next normal pay day following the pay period in which separation occurs. Final pay shall include regular earnings as well as pay for any earned unused vacation as defined by the company's Vacation Policy.

8. The Human Resource Administrator is responsible for preparing a payroll change notice detailing reasons for separation. The change notice is routed to payroll for computing final pay, and a copy is retained in the individual's personnel file.

## Sample Employee Handbook Paragraph

*Retirement*

XYZ Company recognizes that the transition from employment to retirement is a major change for the employee. When you plan to retire, we encourage you to provide a minimum of three months' prior notice to the Company.

Once an employee has notified the Company about retirement, the Company's retirement planning assistance program begins. Under this plan, you and your spouse can

- learn about pension plan distribution alternatives
- learn about insurance and benefits plan continuation
- receive financial planning advice and assistance

We know that a retirement is a major life decision. Employees are encouraged to speak with their supervisor or the Human Resource Administrator for more information.

## Severance Pay

Severance pay is typically provided to a separated employee to soften the effect of job loss. Generally, severance pay is provided when job loss is initiated by the Company for reasons other than employee misconduct or poor performance.

An employer's basic legal obligation is to provide pay for time actually worked. An employer may elect to provide severance pay. Severance pay is not a requirement under federal law. Several states have defined severance pay laws.

A common misconception is that an employer must provide pay in lieu of notice. However, if an employee gives two weeks' notice of resigning, and the employer elects to separate the employee immediately, such practice is permissible unless there is an employment agreement to the contrary. Some firms, however, elect to provide up to two weeks' pay in lieu of notice and separate the employee immediately. This is done often for competitive or security reasons.

Severance pay received some notoriety in the 1980s. During a period of merger mania, executives at numerous firms negotiated severance pay agreements as a protection in the event the Board of Directors caved in to a buyout demand. These severance packages were often so lucrative that they became known as "golden parachutes."

A fairly common practice is to correlate length of Company service with the severance pay benefit. One formula that I have seen with some frequency is one week's salary for each year of service. This provides 10 weeks of severance pay for an employee with 10 years of service, 15 weeks severance for a 15-year employee, and so forth.

Severance pay plans may come under the jurisdiction of the Employee Retirement Income Security Act (ERISA) according to *Human Resource Management Personnel Practices Reporter* published by Commerce Clearing House (CCH). The report states that the ERISA definition of an employee welfare benefit plan includes "those plans which provide holiday and severance benefits." When following ERISA standards, the plan must be in writing, participants must receive a summary plan description, and employers of 100 employees or more must file a plan description and report to the government.

A second area of concern occurs when severance pay is provided with a waiver of claims against the Company. With the increasing number of wrongful discharge lawsuits being filed, growing numbers of employers are offering extra severance pay to separating employees in exchange for the employee's signature on a waiver of claims—a promise not to sue. Such waivers may come under jurisdiction of the Older Workers Benefit and Protection Act (OWBPA). This law, which is an amendment to the Age Discrimination Act, sets specific standards for ADEA releases or waivers. These requirements are

- The waiver has to be part of an agreement between the employee and the employer, and it has to be written in ordinary English.

- It must refer specifically to rights or claims arising under ADEA.

- It may not cover rights or claims that may arise after the date on which it is executed.

- It has to be exchanged for consideration, and that consideration must be in addition to anything of value to which the employee already is entitled.

## Pitfalls to Avoid

Severance plans are intended to "soften the blow" of separation by providing extra pay to the affected employee. However, because severance pay is associated with employment separation, difficulties can arise. Here are some pitfalls to avoid:

1. Take care to carefully define circumstances covered and what occurrences are exempted by the severance pay plan. Severance plans typically provide a payout to eligible employees in the event of separation through no fault of the employee. Under this definition, misconduct, poor performance, or resignation would be viewed as exempt from the policy. But what about mergers, plant closings, or shutdowns due to disaster? Such unplanned occurrences are "through no fault of the employee" but may be beyond the scope, intent, or cash flow of the firm. Also, include a statement that plan provisions are subject to continuous review, change, or discontinuance.

2. Avoid use of severance pay as a "buyout" to discourage employee claims against the Company unless the plan or agreement has been drafted or reviewed by a professional familiar with separation agreements. Such agreements must be carefully worded or they may be in violation of the law. OWBPA waiver standards must be met for any agreement with an employee over 40 years of age.

3. Prevent miscommunication of severance pay or severance benefits by centralizing responsibility for discussing these matters with separating employees. A well-intending supervisor may incorrectly explain a severance pay or benefit plan. The employee may assert in litigation that the supervisor promised greater pay or benefits than were provided.

## Sample Policy

**XYZ COMPANY**
**PERSONNEL POLICY & PROCEDURE**

SUBJECT: SEVERANCE PAY                        DATE: May 1, 1993

*Policy*: It is the policy of XYZ Company to provide severance pay for separating employees in the event of certain forms of job loss.

**CHECKLIST**
**A Severance Pay Policy**

- What categories or classes of employees are eligible to receive severance pay?
- What employment separation circumstances (i.e., layoff, merger, job elimination, reorganization, etc.) are applicable to the severance pay policy?
- Will severance pay be provided in lieu of notice if an employee is separated immediately after submitting a resignation?
- Will severance pay be a flat amount, a percent of pay, or a variable pay based on length of service?
- What formula will be used if severance pay is correlated to length of service?
- Are there any employment agreements or contract provisions which affect separation of the employment relationship?
- Will the severance pay plan be correlated to continuation of insurances or other benefits?
- Are there any state or federal laws that affect severance pay plans?
- Will severance pay be provided in one lump sum or spread out over a period of time?
- Will severance pay be provided as consideration for a specific agreement or waiver of litigation against the employer?

---

*Eligibility*: To receive severance pay, an employee must be a full-time employee.

*Procedure*:
1. Severance pay shall be paid to eligible employees in the event of a permanent separation of employment initiated by the Company and occurring through no fault of the employee. Examples of covered reasons for separation include the following:
   Job elimination
   Permanent layoff due to lack of work
   Reorganization or transfer to another location of job, department, or function
   Automation causing job loss
   Substantial change of job
   Or other similar circumstances as judged by management

2. The following are examples of job loss that *are not* covered by the severance pay plan:
   Resignation
   Involuntary separation due to poor performance
   Involuntary separation due to misconduct
   Temporary layoff subject to recall
   Leave of absence

Job elimination while on leave of absence

3. Severance pay will not be provided to any employee who is eligible for another form of compensation such as disability pay or worker's compensation pay. Receipt of unemployment insurance benefits will not be a basis to deny severance pay.

4. The severance pay benefit is computed based upon one week's pay (at 40 hours per week) for each full year of service. A year of service is the 12-month period from date of hire, including any leave of absence. A minimum severance pay benefit is two weeks. Benefits are computed in full year or full week increments only.

5. Upon learning of an individual's separation, the Human Resource Administrator shall evaluate the employee's eligibility under this policy and then compute the severance pay benefit. The benefit computation shall be reviewed and approved by a Company Officer.

6. Discussion of the severance pay benefit with the employee shall be conducted by the Department Manager together with the Human Resource Administrator.

7. Severance pay shall be provided to the employee at time of separation. At an employee's request, severance pay may be provided on a weekly basis equivalent to the employee's weekly salary at time of separation.

8. In the event of a question or complaint about severance pay benefits, the employee may request to speak with the Company President. The judgment of the Company President shall be final.

9. The amount of severance pay provided to the separating employee shall be recorded on the Employee Change Notice, which documents the employee's separation.

10. The Company reserves the right to change or withdraw the severance pay plan at any time without prior notice.

## Sample Employee Handbook Paragraph

*Severance Pay*

XYZ Company provides a severance pay plan for eligible full-time employees in the event of job loss for certain reasons. This plan is designed to provide limited income protection while the employee seeks other work. The details of this plan are defined in the Company's policy manual. The Human Resource Administrator will explain plan details to affected employees.

# 12

# Holidays, Vacations, and Other Employee Benefits

**Read Chapter 12 for:**

Holidays

Vacations

Sick pay

Educational benefits

Salary continuation

Group insurances

Retirement plans

Legislated benefits

## Holidays

In most manufacturing and administrative industries, it is customary practice to observe certain holidays by closing business operations for the day. By comparison, many retail stores are open on some holidays and may close only on a major holiday such as Christmas Day. Various service organizations are more likely to schedule holidays around the needs of their customers. Industries such as public protective services (police and fire departments), health care institutions, hospitality (hotels and restaurants), and the travel industry conduct operations 24 hours a day every day of the year.

The U.S. government and the various states designate certain dates as legal holidays. The legal holidays are designated days on which government offices are closed. Private employers are free to observe or not observe a particular day as a holiday.

The following are the basic six holidays that are observed most frequently:

| | |
|---|---|
| New Year's Day | Labor Day |
| Memorial Day | Thanksgiving Day |
| Independence Day (July 4) | Christmas Day |

In addition, the following holidays are observed by some firms:

Martin Luther King Day

Lincoln's Birthday

President's Day

Good Friday

Columbus Day

Veteran's Day

Friday following Thanksgiving

Veteran's Day

Christmas Eve Day

New Year's Eve Day

Many states have designated other dates as a local holiday. Seventeen states, for example, officially designated Sundays as a holiday under state law.

An employer is free to designate holidays for the firm. Key issues to consider are competitive practice in the area, industry practices, and the costs of time off work, lost productivity, or disruption to work and premium pay costs.

Holiday pay is another issue that needs to be determined. There are several pay options to consider:

a. *Time off without pay*: Since time off for a holiday is nonworking time, there is no obligation to pay for time not worked unless otherwise specified in an employment agreement. It is fairly common practice, for example, to provide no benefits for part-time employees. In such a case, part-time employees are given time off without pay for Company-observed holidays.

b. *Time off with pay*: An overwhelming majority of firms provide time off with pay for full-time employees on company-designated holidays. Holiday pay is normally computed based on the employee's regular straight time pay rate for a normal workday—usually eight hours. In the event that part-time employees receive holiday pay, it is customary to prorate the benefit based upon average daily pay. (A part-time employee who normally works five hours daily, or 25 hours weekly, would receive five hours of holiday pay.)

c. *Alternate day off*: Organizations that customarily work on holidays have a twofold issue to resolve. First, there is a need for adequate staffing on the holiday. Second, there is a need to provide the paid holiday time off for each employee. These organizations usually operate on a seven-day-week basis with employees on a five-day schedule, allowing two days off on designated days. When a holiday occurs, the employees work their regular schedule but receive an alternate day off with pay during the week. The alternate day off should be designated or approved by management.

d. *Premium pay for holiday work*: When an organization customarily shuts down for a holiday, there may occasionally be a need to schedule holiday work. Usually, these firms find that premium pay for work on a holiday is necessary to get employees to work. Various plans are used, such as regular pay for hours worked plus holiday pay, or time and a half (one and one-half times the employee's regular pay rate) plus holiday pay, or even double time plus holiday pay. Labor rates at these costs can add up very quickly, so carefully weigh costs of holiday work.

e. One other holiday pay issue to resolve is whether time off or paid time off for a company-observed holiday counts toward the 40-hour eligibility requirement for overtime pay for nonexempt employees. The FLSA requirement is to provide overtime pay after 40 hours actually worked; so time off for a holiday does not have to count toward overtime. As a competitive issue, however, a significant number of firms count time off on a company holiday as time worked for overtime pay eligibility.

### Competitive Practices

Table 12.1 shows competitive practices on holiday benefits.

### Pitfalls to Avoid

As noted, nearly every organization provides paid holidays for employees. Holiday policies, however, can result in some scheduling difficulties. Here are some troublespots to avoid.

1. Recognize community practices by observing holidays that are commonly observed in the locale. A publisher in a metropolitan area, for example, was reluctant to designate Martin Luther King's Birthday as a holiday. A significant portion of employees were minorities. Many

**CHECKLIST**
**A Holiday Policy**

- Are there any state or federal laws that affect the paid holiday benefit?
- What holidays will be observed?
- Will holidays be paid or unpaid?
- What will be the basis for holiday pay (eight hours pay, regular daily pay, etc.)?
- What classes or categories of employees will be eligible for holiday pay?
- Will there be a time period of eligibility (e.g., 30 days) before an employee may receive holiday pay?
- What pay will an employee receive for work on a holiday?
- Must employees work the day before and after the holiday?
- Will time off for a holiday count toward overtime pay eligibility for nonexempt employees?

employees felt that the company's refusal to recognize Dr. King's Birthday as a holiday was evidence of management's insensitivity to workers. Ultimately, company management adopted the holiday after learning that many other firms in the area observed Dr. King's Birthday as a holiday.

**Table 12.1.** Percent of Full-Time Employees Provided Paid Holidays Each Year

| Number of days | Small establishments[2] | Medium and large establishments[3] |
|---|---|---|
| Percent of Full-Time Employees Provided Paid Holidays | 84 | 97 |
| Under 5 days | 5 | 3 |
| 5 days | 5 | 2 |
| 6 days | 17 | 10 |
| 7 days | 11 | 11 |
| 8 days | 10 | 9 |
| 9 days | 8 | 8 |
| 10 days | 12 | 24 |
| 11 days | 4 | 13 |
| 12 days | 1 | 7 |
| 13 days | 1 | 5 |

2. Religious holidays can complicate the process of designating company holidays. Religious holidays such as Good Friday, Easter, Rosh Hoshana, or Yom Kippur are recognized by individuals in certain religious groups. While some employers may adopt a religious holiday to be responsive to employees or the community, it is unlikely that the firm can recognize all religious holidays as company holidays. In order to avoid discrimination on the basis of religion, the employer has a responsibility to make a reasonable accommodation for the employee's religious beliefs. The accommodation may be granting time off without pay for the religious holiday or allowing a vacation day when requested by the employee.

3. Employers complain about excessive unscheduled absences occurring around holidays. The fact is simply this: If an employee calls in sick before or after a holiday, a three-day weekend can be stretched to four days off. To counter this type of abuse, many holiday policies include a statement requiring the employee to work the regularly scheduled workday before and after the holiday in order to receive pay for the holiday. Leaving early before a holiday or arriving late after the holiday is another variation in an employee's attempt to stretch the holiday. Two alternatives have been useful in minimizing this problem. One is to require employees to work the *full* scheduled work days before and after the holiday to be eligible for holiday pay. The second alternative is to deduct from holiday pay the equivalent of time missed from work on the scheduled workdays before and after the holiday.

4. Take care when defining any premium pay received by an employee who works on a holiday. If your policy states that an employee receives "double time for holiday work," what does the policy really mean? Two interpretations are possible: (a) the employee receives two times regular pay for hours worked plus holiday pay (equivalent to three times regular pay) or (b) the employee receives regular pay for hours worked plus holiday pay. Explain this provision precisely to avoid confusion.

**Sample Policy**

**XYZ COMPANY**
**PERSONNEL POLICY & PROCEDURE**

SUBJECT: HOLIDAYS                    DATE: May 1, 1993

*Policy*: It is the policy of XYZ Company to observe designated holidays by providing time off with pay for eligible employees.

*Eligibility*: To be eligible for holiday pay, an employee must be a full-time employee, and union employees must fulfill requirements established by their respective labor agreement.

*Procedure*:

1. Paid holidays and relevant procedures for union employees are defined by their respective labor agreement. The Company observes the following holidays each year:

    New Year's Day          Thanksgiving Day
    Memorial Day            Christmas Eve Day
    Independence Day        Christmas Day
    Labor Day

2. At the beginning of each year, management announces the specific dates which will be observed as holidays. Management may elect to designate other dates as holidays from time to time. In those cases, the procedures of this policy will apply.

3. Holiday pay is computed based upon the employee's regular straight time pay rate for an eight-hour workday and pro-rated for full-time employees working less than 40 hours weekly. Time off without pay is permitted for part-time or temporary employees.

4. When an employee is scheduled to work on a holiday, the employee will receive his or her regular straight time pay rate for hours worked and the employee will be permitted an alternate day off as agreed upon between management and the employee. (The day off is paid time for full-time employees and unpaid for part-time or temporary employees.) In the event the holiday occurs on an employee's day off, the employee will receive paid time off at an agreed date. In such cases, the holiday must be used within the current pay period.

5. Time off for a holiday counts as time worked toward overtime pay for hourly paid employees.

6. When a holiday occurs during an employee's vacation, the employee may schedule an alternate day of vacation.

7. The supervisor is responsible for marking the payroll sheet to reflect paid or unpaid holidays for each employee as applicable.

## Sample Employee Handbook Paragraph

*Holidays*

XYZ Company observes the following holidays:

    New Year's Day          Thanksgiving Day
    Good Friday             Friday following Thanksgiving
    Memorial Day            Christmas Eve Day
    Independence Day        Christmas Day
    Labor Day               New Year's Eve Day

Holiday pay is based on an employee's regular pay rate per day. To be eligible for holiday pay, an employee must

a) be a full-time employee with 30 days or more of Company service

b) work the regularly scheduled workdays before and after the holiday, or be on a prior approved paid absence.

When a holiday occurs on a weekend, management will designate an alternate day to observe the holiday.

# Vacations

An annual vacation provides an important opportunity for rest and relaxation. The paid vacation benefit is a major benefit provided to employees by most firms. Vacations occur every year. Yet in my 10 years of human resource consulting and helping firms define personnel policies, I have found that a clearly defined vacation benefit seems to be a most elusive achievement at many firms. Every organization, it seems, wants to compute vacation benefits differently. Every vacation policy has some idiosyncracy which can cause confusion for employees and management alike.

The vacation policy is intended to define an annual paid absence benefit and clarify basic guidelines for scheduling employee absences. In most organizations, the amount of paid time off under the vacation benefit increases with the employee's length of service. Vacation benefits generally run from one week up to four or five weeks. Some organizations provide six or more weeks of paid vacation.

Vacation pay is computed based on the employee's regular weekly pay rate. When vacation pay is provided to employees with their normal payroll cycle, a vacation check is available to the employee upon return to work. Many firms, however, recognize that the employee needs extra funds for vacation. This can be handled by preparing a vacation pay advance and manually issuing an early paycheck on the last workday prior to the employee's vacation.

The vacation policy must direct the vacation scheduling process. Often there can be conflicts between employee vacation requests and company staffing needs. A properly written vacation policy will guide the supervisor in

- Explaining vacation benefit eligibility and entitlement
- Obtaining employee vacation requests
- Resolving conflicts on requested dates
- Defining staffing limits on number of vacations allowed in a specific period
- Establishing an approval process
- Clarifying how vacations affect overtime pay
- Determining how other absences may affect vacations

Some firms, particularly in the manufacturing sector, schedule a vacation shutdown. During a vacation shutdown, production and administrative operations are suspended and employees are released for a vacation. There are several advantages of a vacation shutdown:

- All vacations are completed at one time; there is no need to juggle work and individual vacation schedules.

- Facilities and equipment maintenance can be performed during the shutdown.

A vacation shutdown does have some disadvantages:
- New employees may be forced to take time off without pay because they have not earned enough paid vacation benefits by the shutdown period.

- The shutdown may disrupt customer requirements for products or services provided by the company.

There are no legal requirements to provide a paid vacation benefit unless negotiated in an individual employment contract or labor agreement. However, if a company does provide paid vacation, various state and federal laws may apply. State wage payment laws, for example, stipulate when wages should be paid after each pay period and at separation of employment. Various states, either by law or through court decisions interpreting the law, require that earned vacation benefits be paid pro rata through separation of employment. Check the requirements in your state when preparing a vacation policy.

State and federal equal employment opportunity laws could affect a firm's vacation policy. If a vacation policy was designed or administered in an unfair way affecting a protected class individual, a discrimination finding could result.

Another law once thought to affect vacation plans is the Employee Retirement Income Security Act (ERISA) of 1974. This law defines certain requirements for pension and other welfare plans. The law also preempts sections of state laws that regulate employee benefits. Because of this preemption, some legal authorities felt that employer wage payment and vacation plans may be subject to ERISA. In addressing this issue, the *1992 State by State Guide to Human Resource Law* reports the following: "regulations of the U.S. Department of Labor (DOL) provide that certain benefits paid out of the general assets of an employer are 'payroll practices' and do not constitute 'employee benefit plans' " (29 CFR § 2510.3-1). These payroll practices include vacation pay, holiday and overtime premiums, and sick leave pay when paid out of the employer's general assets. The U.S. Supreme Court has upheld the validity of this DOL regulation insofar as it relates to vacation benefits, in a case that specifically upheld a state statute that required employers to pay accrued vacation benefits on an employee's termination.[4]

## Competitive Practices

The charts in Fig. 12.1 show the vacation policy practices of large and small firms.

### CHECKLIST
### A Vacation Policy

- Are there any state or federal laws that affect a paid vacation benefit?

- What classes or categories of employees will be eligible for paid vacation benefits?

- What is the "Action Date" at which the employee became eligible for paid vacation benefits—i.e., employment anniversary, January 1 (calendar year), or other date, or arbitrarily defined 12-month period (vacation year)?

- How many years of service are required for one week of paid vacation? two weeks? three weeks? four weeks? etc.

- What is the basis for computing vacation pay (i.e., regular hourly or weekly pay rate)?

- Will there be a time period of eligibility (e.g., six months) before an employee may schedule paid vacation?

- When will vacation requests be solicited from employees?

- In what increments can paid vacation be scheduled (i.e., full weeks, individual days, or portions of a day)?

- Will the employee be permitted to schedule all earned vacation at one time, or will there be a limit on absences over a certain period such as two weeks?

- When will vacation pay be issued?

- Will an employee be permitted to take pay in lieu of vacation or to save unused vacation for the next year?

- If two or more employees request the same vacation dates, what will be the priority basis for granting vacations?

- Will the company schedule a vacation shutdown?

- How will unused vacation benefits be handled when an employee separates employment?

- Will paid vacation time off count toward overtime pay eligibility for nonexempt employees?

### Pitfalls to Avoid

Many firms experience difficulty in defining a clear and easy-to-administer Vacation Policy. Here are some common difficulties and suggestions for how to avoid Vacation Policy problems:

1. The most common Vacation Policy problem is failure to clearly define an action date. The action date is the date at which the employee earns and may schedule vacation benefits. The problem typically occurs like this: The employer tells the newly hired employee, "You're entitled to

| Item | All participants | Professional, technical, and related participants | Clerical and sales participants | Production and service participants |
|------|------|------|------|------|
| Paid holidays ........................................ | 9.5 | 10.6 | 9.8 | 8.7 |
| Paid vacation by length of service:[1] | | | | |
| At 1 year[1] ........................................ | 7.6 | 9.5 | 8.0 | 6.6 |
| At 3 years ........................................ | 10.0 | 11.4 | 10.2 | 9.2 |
| At 5 years ........................................ | 11.5 | 13.0 | 11.8 | 10.6 |
| At 10 years ........................................ | 13.5 | 15.2 | 13.9 | 12.5 |
| At 15 years ........................................ | 14.5 | 16.2 | 15.0 | 13.3 |
| At 20 years ........................................ | 15.0 | 16.7 | 15.6 | 13.9 |
| At 25 years ........................................ | 15.3 | 16.9 | 16.0 | 14.0 |
| At 30 years[2] ........................................ | 15.3 | 16.9 | 16.0 | 14.1 |

[1] Employees receiving vacation days, but none at 1 year of service, were included only for the service periods for which they receive vacations.

[2] The average (mean) was essentially the same for longer lengths of service.

NOTE: Computation of average included half days and excluded workers with zero holidays or vacation days and those with informal plans.

**Figure 12.1a.** Paid holidays and vacations: Average number of days for full-time participants, small establishments, 1990.[5]

| Item | All participants | Professional and administrative participants | Technical and clerical participants | Production and service participants |
|------|------|------|------|------|
| Paid holidays ........................................ | 9.2 | 9.6 | 9.2 | 8.9 |
| Paid vacation by length of service:[1] | | | | |
| At 6 months ........................................ | 6.0 | 6.6 | 6.0 | 5.3 |
| At 1 year ........................................ | 9.1 | 11.1 | 9.9 | 7.5 |
| At 3 years ........................................ | 11.0 | 12.2 | 11.2 | 10.3 |
| At 5 years ........................................ | 13.4 | 14.9 | 14.0 | 12.1 |
| At 10 years ........................................ | 16.5 | 17.8 | 16.9 | 15.6 |
| At 15 years ........................................ | 18.6 | 19.7 | 19.2 | 17.7 |
| At 20 years ........................................ | 20.4 | 21.4 | 20.6 | 19.7 |
| At 25 years ........................................ | 21.5 | 22.4 | 21.7 | 20.9 |
| At 30 years[2] ........................................ | 21.9 | 22.8 | 22.0 | 21.3 |

[1] Participants are included only for the service periods for which they receive vacations.

[2] The average (mean) was essentially the same for longer lengths of service.

NOTE: Computation of average included half days and excluded workers with zero holidays or vacation days.

**Figure 12.1b.** Paid holidays and vacations: Average number of days for full-time participants, medium and large firms, 1989.[6]

two weeks of vacation a year." (This keys vacation eligibility to the employment anniversary.) Then after a year or two, the firm customarily schedules employee vacations during each calendar year. (The action date has now shifted to a January 1 date...or has it?)

Another variation of the vacation eligibility problem is granting an employee's request for early vacation. The employee hired in the fall or at year end has not yet earned vacation by the summer vacation period. However, a good-hearted supervisor says, "Okay, you can have one week of vacation at six months." Then, after the employee's first anniversary of employment, the employee is expecting two weeks of vacation. (Remember, two weeks *after* a year!) Oops! Now the policy has been interpreted to grant three weeks of vacation in 12 months.

There are two solutions to this dilemma. Solution one is this: Define one action date and stick with it. The action date can be employment anniversary or January 1 for a calendar year vacation eligibility. In case of early vacation, compute a pro rata entitlement, allowing one-twelfth of the benefit for each month of service. Solution two is this: Compute and grant vacation on a pro rata basis during each month of employment. As the employee earns vacation each month, he or she may schedule earned vacation subject to supervisory approval. Some firms with computerized record systems use this system to record vacation earned, benefits used during the month, and the employee's current balance. Vacation benefits can be earned based on the following pro rata equivalents:

1 week of vacation  = .416 days/month
2 weeks of vacation = .833 days/month
3 weeks of vacation = 1.25 days/month
4 weeks of vacation = 1.67 days/month
5 weeks of vacation = 2.08 days/month
6 weeks of vacation = 2.50 days/month

2. Define vacation scheduling limits as needed to assure reasonable advance notice of absence, adequate staffing levels, and minimized disruption to work activities. Several examples are noted:

a. *Advance notice*: Prior notice of an employee's vacation is needed to reassign work tasks during the period of absence. Many firms like one week to 30 days of advance notice. Requiring advance notice helps prevent absentee abuses such as calling in on the day of absence to request a vacation day.

b. *One day at a time*: At one company, an employee wanted to schedule a vacation day each Friday for three-day weekends at the lakeside cabin. The employer, however, felt that day-to-day absences were disruptive and insisted that vacations be scheduled in full-week segments. At another company, management welcomed an employee's request for individual vacation days. Define your policy in a way which promotes efficiency and good employee relations.

c. *Carry forward*: Almost every organization has one employee who seems reluctant to schedule vacations. This employee wants the firm to "bank" vacations or carry the vacation forward to next year. Evaluate this issue very carefully when defining your vacation policy. Many firms have experienced difficulty with a vacation carry-forward practice, particularly if recordkeeping is poor. Disputes can arise about how much vacation the employee is owed.

The banking of vacation, however, may create an opportunity to adopt policies to meet the varying needs of employees. Vacation pay, paid or banked, is subject to IRS rules as income to the employee and an expense to the business. Extensive banking of vacation may actually create a form of deferred income with the IRS, ERISA, or other legal constraints. Get professional advice if you plan a complex policy on this issue.

d. *Use it or lose it*: Other firms have elected to define a "use it or lose it" vacation policy. With a use it or lose it policy, the employee forfeits vacation pay if the benefit is not used within a designated time period, such as by the end of the calendar year. Such a policy helps to guard against the carry forward or banking of vacation described in the preceding paragraph.

Employers must exercise caution when defining a use it or lose it vacation policy. According to the "Manager's Newsfront" column in the October, 1992 issue of *Personnel Journal*, a California Appeals court held that a use it or lose it policy violated California law prohibiting forfeiture of an employee's vested vacation time. The court however recognized a "no additional accrual" policy which limits or caps the amount of vacation an employee may earn. This very subtle difference can make the difference between a legal or an illegal policy.

e. *Vacation pay*: Your best bet is to provide vacation pay on the regular pay day following vacation, or on the last workday prior to vacation if requested by the employee. Some firms have advanced vacation pay to employees because of a personal emergency.

**Sample Policy**

**XYZ COMPANY**
**PERSONNEL POLICY & PROCEDURE**

SUBJECT: VACATION                                          DATE: May 1, 1993

*Policy*: It is the policy of XYZ Company to grant a vacation benefit based upon length of service with the Company.

*Eligibility*:

1. Employees accrue vacation during a vacation year beginning each January 1 through December 31; vacation benefits are earned on the following January 1.

2. New employees with less than one year of service accrue vacation benefits on a prorated basis for each full month of Company service. No benefits are earned during the first 60 days of service. Then, the employee earns one (1) vacation day upon completion of each full calendar month remaining in the calendar year.

3. Part-time employees are entitled to a prorated benefit based upon the number of hours normally worked compared to a 40-hour week.

4. Subsequent vacation is earned on each January 1 as shown below:

| Length of service as of January 1 | Paid vacation | Hours of vacation pay |
|---|---|---|
| Less than 1 year | See above | |
| 1 year | 1 week | 40 |
| 2 years | 2 weeks | 80 |
| 8 years | 3 weeks | 120 |
| 15 years | 4 weeks | 160 |

*Procedure*:

1. The employee must submit a vacation request at least two weeks prior to the desired time off. A vacation request form is available in the office. Request for vacation pay is submitted with the vacation request.

2. All vacation requests are subject to approval of the department supervisor after considering staffing needs and other vacation requests. As a general guide, not more than 20 percent of the department may take vacation at one time. In departments of five or fewer employees, only one individual may take vacation at one time.

3. Vacations must be used within 12 months of the date earned or be forfeited unless management has approved carryover of a vacation to the next year.

4. Vacation pay is computed based on the employee's regular straight time pay rate plus any applicable shift differential for a 40-hour work week at the time vacation is taken.

5. If a holiday occurs during the employee's vacation, the employee may receive pay for the day or schedule an alternate day of vacation, as approved by management.

6. Paid time off for vacation counts as time worked when computing overtime for hourly paid employees.

7. The supervisor is responsible for recording vacation on the employee's time and attendance records.

8. Upon separation of employment, an employee is entitled to pay for any earned unused vacation and accrued vacation prorated through the last full calendar month of service.

**Sample Employee Handbook
Paragraph**

*Vacations*

The Company believes that an annual vacation provides an important opportunity for rest and relaxation. Employees earn vacation pay on the pay period following each employment anniversary as shown below:

| Employment anniversary | Vacation pay | Vacation time off |
| --- | --- | --- |
| 1st | 40 hours | 1 week |
| 3rd | 80 hours | 2 weeks |
| 10th | 120 hours | 3 weeks |
| 20th | 160 hours | 4 weeks |

Vacation pay is based upon an employee's pay rate at the time vacation is taken multiplied by the number of hours earned.

Employees are urged to submit vacation requests early in the year. Vacation time off may be scheduled at any time during the year subject to management approval. Vacation time off must be scheduled in increments of one week or more; if less than five days vacation are scheduled in a week, the employee will forfeit the balance of the vacation days in that week. When a holiday occurs during an employee's vacation, the employee may schedule an alternate day at the beginning or end of the vacation.

# Paid Sick Leave

A sick pay benefit is designed to provide limited income protection for the employee in the event of absence due to illness. This benefit allows the employee to receive a specified amount of pay for the day when "calling in sick." It is distinguished from salary continuation or short-term disability benefits, which provide pay in the event of illness or injury lasting several weeks or months. The sick pay benefit is valued by employees.

For employers, however, the sick pay benefit is often a source of trouble. Many employees abuse sick pay benefits. A common abuse is lying about reason of absence; that is, calling in sick to take a day off work when the employee is not truly ill. Another form of sick leave abuse, according to the employer's perspective, is that many employees use all of the sick days provided under the policy. Stated one manager as he considered a new sick pay plan, "I hate to give my people five days of paid sick leave, because they will just take five days off work. It'll be like extra vacation for them."

Other employers, however, have found that a pleasant working environment with good employee relations helps to keep sick leave abuse minimal to nonexistent. One might conclude then, that abuse of paid sick leave is an indicator of more serious employee morale problems.

When defining a Sick Leave Policy, the first issue to consider is management's philosophy on providing pay to an employee who is absent due to illness. While many executives recognize paid sick leave as an important employee benefit, there are some managers who feel that an employee should not be paid for an absence.

Once the decision is made to develop a paid sick leave benefit, the next concern is to define what the benefit will be and to clarify procedures to control abuses. Among these procedures are the following:

*Call-in procedure*: The employee should call in to report absence by a specified time on the day of absence in cases of illness or other unplanned event. For absences that can be anticipated, the employee should provide advance notice.

*Number of days*: Competitive practices, costs, and attitudes of business owners will determine the number of days to be granted. Charts showing competitive practices appear later in this section.

*Pay for the absence*: While many firms provide full pay for the employee for sick days, a plan for partial pay may also be evaluated.

*Control of abuse*: Guidelines for controlling abuse and dealing with a falsified reason for absence are an important part of a sick pay policy.

Some firms have elected to define a combined paid sick/personal leave policy. This combination of benefits, they say, is done so that "the employee won't have to lie to schedule a day off." While I don't have any data on the prevalence of this practice, it does warrant consideration when dealing with sick leave and absence control issues.

Some state wage payment laws include earned unused paid sick leave benefits among the compensation that an employee should receive at separation. Be sure to check requirements in your state when defining policy guidelines. The IRS views sick pay as taxable income which is subject to employee social security and Medicare taxes.

## Competitive Practices

The charts in Fig. 12.2 show survey results on the sick pay benefit.

## Pitfalls to Avoid

The paid sick leave benefit is one benefit that is most likely to be abused by employees. Here are some pitfalls to avoid:

1. Most firms complain that there are always a few employees who are the absentee or sick leave abusers. To minimize this problem, here are some alternatives when defining the paid sick leave benefit:
   - Limit the number of days of paid sick leave. Start a new policy by

**CHECKLIST**
**A Paid Sick Leave Policy**

- Are there any state or federal laws that affect the paid sick leave benefit?

- What classes or categories of employees will be eligible for paid sick leave benefits?

- What is the action date at which time the employee becomes eligible for paid sick leave benefits (i.e., employment anniversary, January 1, or other date)?

- How many days of paid sick leave benefit are provided?

- What is the basis for computing sick leave pay (i.e., regular hourly or daily pay rate)?

- Will there be a time period of eligibility (e.g., 30 days, 6 months, etc.) before an employee may receive a paid sick day?

- In what increments can paid sick leave be used (i.e., hours, half day, full day)?

- Is sick pay for illness of the employee only or can paid sick leave be used to care for an ill child or family member?

- Can paid sick leave be scheduled in advance for medical absences which can be anticipated, such as doctor's appointments?

- By what time should the employee call in when reporting illness?

- What will be done to control abuse or falsification of reason for absence (i.e., require doctor statement or use of disciplinary action)?

- At year end, will unused days be forfeited, paid off, or banked for future use?

- At separation of employment, will unused paid sick leave benefits be forfeited or paid to employee?

- How will the paid sick leave benefit relate to family and medical leave practices?

granting only a few days, such as three or four per year. Obviously, it is easier to add to the benefit than to take days away.

- Delay the start of the benefit. Require new employees to work 60, 90, or 120 days or more before becoming eligible for sick pay benefits.

- Define sick pay as a partial pay, such as 75 percent of regular pay. This loss of pay will help minimize abuse, because it will cost the employee through lost income by calling in sick.

2. Falsification of reason for absence is probably the most common form of abuse of the paid sick leave benefit. To combat this, some firms require the employee to submit a doctor's statement as proof of being under a doctor's care. However, for a one-day absence, most employees are not likely to see a doctor. Any other verified evidence of falsification should be considered grounds for corrective discipline or discharge.

To solve sick leave abuse at one small manufacturing company, the

| Provision | All employees | Professional, technical, and related employees | Clerical and sales employees | Production and service employees |
|---|---|---|---|---|
| Total ................................. | 100 | 100 | 100 | 100 |
| Provided paid sick leave ................... | 47 | 70 | 61 | 29 |
| Sick leave provided on: | | | | |
| An annual basis only[1] ............... | 41 | 62 | 53 | 26 |
| A per disability basis only[2] ........ | 2 | 3 | 3 | 2 |
| Both an annual and per | | | | |
| disability basis ........................ | 2 | 3 | 3 | 1 |
| As needed basis[3] ....................... | 1 | 2 | 2 | 1 |
| Other basis[5] ............................ | (⁴) | (⁴) | (⁴) | (⁴) |
| Not provided paid sick leave ............. | 53 | 30 | 39 | 71 |

[1] Employees earn a specified number of sick leave days per year. This number may vary by length of service.

[2] Employees earn a specified number of sick leave days for each illness or disability. This number may vary by length of service.

[3] Plan does not specify maximum number of days.

[4] Less than 0.5 percent.

[5] Includes formal plans with provisions that change from a specified number of days per year to a specified number of days per absence after a certain service period.

NOTE: Because of rounding, sums of individual items may not equal totals. Where applicable, dash indicates no employees in this category.

**Figure 12.2a.** Paid sick leave: Percent of full-time employees by type of provision, small establishments, 1990.[8]

President started the practice of calling the employee's home to see how he or she was feeling. This immediately cut down on abuse and falsified absences.

3. Check state law on proper handling of unused sick pay benefits for separating employees. Some states require payment to the employee while others do not.

## Sample Policy

**XYZ COMPANY**
**PERSONNEL POLICY & PROCEDURE**

SUBJECT: PAID SICK LEAVE                              DATE: May 1, 1993

*Policy*: It is the policy of XYZ Company to provide a paid sick leave benefit in the event of a non-job-related illness requiring time off the job.

*Eligibility*: Full-time and part-time nonexempt employees become eligible for this benefit after three months of employment.

*Procedure*:

1. Eligible employees are permitted to schedule up to 40 hours of paid sick leave each calendar year. Benefits for part-time employees are

| Provision | All employees | Professional and administrative employees | Technical and clerical employees | Production and service employees |
|---|---|---|---|---|
| Total ............................................... | 100 | 100 | 100 | 100 |
| Provided paid sick leave .................... | 68 | 93 | 87 | 44 |
| Sick leave provided on: | | | | |
| An annual basis only[1] ............... | 51 | 62 | 64 | 37 |
| A per disability basis only[2] ........ | 9 | 16 | 10 | 5 |
| Both an annual and per | | | | |
| disability basis ......................... | 6 | 8 | 10 | 2 |
| As needed basis[3] ........................ | 3 | 7 | 2 | (⁴) |
| Other basis[5] ............................... | (⁴) | (⁴) | 1 | (⁴) |
| Not provided paid sick leave ............. | 32 | 7 | 13 | 56 |

[1] Employees earn a specified number of sick leave days per year. This number may vary by length of service.
[2] Employees earn a specified number of sick leave days for each illness or disability. This number may vary by length of service.
[3] Plan does not specify maximum number of days.
[4] Less than 0.5 percent.
[5] Includes formal plans with provisions that change from a specified number of days per year to a specified number of days per absence after a certain service period.

NOTE: Because of rounding, sums of individual items may not equal totals. Where applicable, dash indicates no employees in this category.

**Figure 12.2b.** Paid sick leave: Percent of full-time employees by type of provision, medium and large firms, 1989.[9]

prorated based upon regular weekly work schedule compared to a 40-hour work week. Benefits for newly hired employees are prorated based upon the number of full calendar months remaining in the year after the employee's eligibility period. Paid sick leave days are recorded on the employee's pay stub.

2. The paid sick leave days benefit is paid based upon the employee's regular straight time hourly pay rate.

3. The paid sick leave benefit may be used in the event of non-job-related illness for the individual, or for care of a family member. Benefits should be used in eight-hour increments. In order to receive pay for the day, an eligible employee must call in to report absence not later than one hour following the scheduled start time or request time in advance when an absence can be anticipated.

4. Time off beyond the limits of this benefit is without pay. In the event of an extended absence beyond five days, see Company Policy on Medical Leave of Absence. Repeated instances of absence beyond the limits of this policy are unexcused absences which may be subject to corrective discipline. See Company Policy on Attendance and Punctuality.

5. Unused benefits at year end are forfeited. There is no carryover to

succeeding year or pay for unused benefits. Benefits are not paid at separation of employment.

6. The Supervisor shall record the paid sick day on the employee's time card.

7. Paid time off for a sick leave day does *not* count as time worked for overtime computations for nonexempt employees.

**Sample Employee Handbook Paragraph**

*Paid Sick Leave*

XYZ Company provides a sick pay benefit for full-time and part-time employees with one year of service or more. In order to receive sick pay, an employee must call in by the normal starting time to report illness.

Eligible employees may receive up to six days of sick pay each fiscal year from February 1 through January 31. New employees meeting the one-year eligibility requirement receive a prorated benefit allowing for one-half day of sick pay for each full calendar month remaining in the fiscal year.

The sick pay benefit is paid based on the employee's regular pay rate per day. To encourage good attendance, sick pay which is unused at the end of the fiscal year will be paid to the employee. Paid or unpaid absences do not count toward hours worked for overtime computations. Unused benefits are not paid at separation of employment.

# Salary Continuation Benefit

A salary continuation benefit provides income maintenance in the event of a non-job-related illness, injury, temporary disability including pregnancy, or other absence during which the employee is placed on a medical leave of absence. The salary continuation plan is distinguished from paid sick leave. Salary continuation can continue for 8 weeks, 12 weeks, 26 weeks, or other period as specified by the employer. The paid sick leave, by contrast, often provides 5 or 10 days of benefits yearly.

Some firms define a sick pay plan which grants 5 or 10 days of paid leave benefit each year and permits unused days to be "banked" for future use. Such a plan combines the features of paid sick leave and salary continuation.

A salary continuation plan is often provided in place of an insured short-term disability plan. The employer in effect self-insures by designing a plan which is paid from general asset payroll dollars. The savings can be significant. There are no insurance premiums and, based on a Supreme Court case, the plan is not subject to ERISA standards and administration costs.[10]

Important factors to consider when defining a salary continuation plan are highlighted:

*Eligibility*: Eligibility of the employee to participate in this benefit should be defined clearly. For example, the eligibility criterion could be full-time employees with one year service or more.

*Covered illnesses*: The salary continuation plan should be limited to non-job-related illness or disability. Worker's compensation insurance will provide disability benefits for job-related medical absences. The plan can pay benefits when the employee is unable to work due to a medical condition and under the care of a physician. Be sure to require a physician's certification of the nature, extent, and anticipated duration of disability as a condition for paying benefits.

*Define benefit limits*: Identify whether the benefit will be full pay or partial pay such as 75 percent. Also, carefully spell out how long the benefits will be paid. A careful definition will help to cap the benefit and limit costs. For example:

a. Employees receive 60 percent of base pay for a period up to 12 weeks, limited to maximum salary continuation payout of 12 weeks of benefits in any calendar year.

b. Employees are credited with one (1) week of salary continuation benefits following each employment anniversary, up to a maximum of 26 weeks. An individual may use benefits up to the amount credited. Thereafter, the absence is without pay. Salary continuation benefits are based on the employee's regular salary for a 40-hour work week.

*Include administrative controls*: Since salary continuation provides a cash payout to employees, certain administrative controls are needed to prevent or control abuse of the benefit. Recommended controls include timely absence reporting, requiring a doctor's certificate of disability in order to start paying benefits and at periodic intervals, and coordination of the benefit with a medical leave policy and any other form of disability benefit.

The Pregnancy Discrimination Act of 1978 requires employers to treat pregnancy as a temporary disability and provide comparable benefits as those provided for other disabilities. This means that the same salary continuation benefits should be provided for pregnancy and other types of temporary disability. As with paid sick leave, company-funded salary continuation benefits may be affected by state wage payment laws. IRS regulations also will apply to salary continuation plans.

**Competitive Practices**

According to the U.S. Bureau of Labor Statistics, companies are providing the salary continuation benefits shown in Fig. 12.3.

**Pitfalls to Avoid**

The salary continuation benefit is not as likely to be abused as the paid sick leave benefit. However, careful definition of this benefit is necessary to prevent confusion. Here are some pitfalls to avoid:

**CHECKLIST**
**A Salary Continuation Policy**

- Are there any state or federal laws that affect the salary continuation benefit?

- What classes or categories of employees will be eligible for salary continuation benefits?

- What is the action date at which time the employee becomes eligible for salary continuation benefits (i.e., employment anniversary, January 1, or other date)?

- How many days, weeks, or months of salary continuation benefits are provided?

- Will salary continuation benefits be based on the employee's regular weekly pay, or a lesser amount such as 60 percent, 75 percent, or 80 percent of regular pay?

- Will there be a time period of eligibility (e.g., 1 month, 6 months, or 12 months) before an employee may be eligible to receive salary continuation benefits?

- Will there be an elimination period (a waiting period from onset of disability until benefits are paid)?

- In what increments will salary continuation benefits be paid (i.e., daily, weekly)?

- Will a doctor's certificate of disability be required in order to pay benefits and at subsequent periodic intervals?

- Will salary continuation be defined to coordinate with a medical leave policy, paid sick leave, long-term disability plan, or other related policy?

- What will happen to unused benefits at separation of employment?

1. The salary continuation benefit is designed to provide income continuation over a period of weeks. Benefits can be a small, one-week payout of $300 or as high as $15,000 or more for an extended medical absence. For this reason, the salary continuation benefit should be carefully defined to prevent confusion and misunderstanding. Several suggestions are offered:

   *Cap the benefit*: Define a maximum benefit payout in terms of total dollars paid, or total weeks of benefits paid during employment or during a calendar year.

   *Correlate to length of service*: The amount of salary continuation benefit can be correlated to length of service, much like vacation benefits, which increase as the employee's tenure with the firm increases.

   *Require medical certification*: Define strict policy requirements that benefits not be paid unless the firm receives a physician's statement identifying the nature and anticipated duration of absence. Also, require periodic updates from the doctor, at two-week or monthly intervals.

| Item | All participants | Professional and administrative participants | Technical and clerical participants | Production and service participants |
|---|---|---|---|---|
| **Paid annual sick leave[1] by length of service:** | | | | |
| At 6 months | 12.5 | 17.9 | 10.8 | 7.2 |
| At 1 year | 15.4 | 21.8 | 14.5 | 9.4 |
| At 3 years | 17.8 | 25.2 | 16.7 | 10.9 |
| At 5 years | 20.5 | 29.3 | 19.2 | 12.6 |
| At 10 years | 25.0 | 35.8 | 23.8 | 14.8 |
| At 15 years | 26.6 | 38.0 | 25.2 | 16.1 |
| At 20 years | 27.8 | 39.6 | 26.2 | 16.8 |
| At 25 years | 28.3 | 40.5 | 26.6 | 17.3 |
| At 30 years[2] | 28.6 | 40.8 | 26.8 | 17.4 |
| **Paid per disability sick leave[3] by length of service:** | | | | |
| At 6 months | 39.4 | 45.5 | 31.2 | 33.9 |
| At 1 year | 43.4 | 50.4 | 34.3 | 38.3 |
| At 3 years | 50.2 | 58.0 | 41.7 | 44.5 |
| At 5 years | 66.1 | 71.3 | 59.2 | 64.3 |
| At 10 years | 82.8 | 89.2 | 76.2 | 78.9 |
| At 15 years | 97.4 | 100.3 | 91.4 | 101.1 |
| At 20 years | 108.9 | 108.8 | 101.7 | 121.8 |
| At 25 years | 118.9 | 115.4 | 111.1 | 140.9 |
| At 30 years[2] | 119.3 | 115.8 | 111.4 | 141.6 |

[1] Employees earn a specified number of sick leave days per year. This number may vary by length of service.

[2] The average (mean) was virtually the same after longer years of service.

[3] Employees earn a specified number of sick leave days for each illness or disability. This number may vary by length of service.

NOTE: Computation of average excluded days paid at partial pay and workers with only partial pay days or zero days of sick leave.

**Figure 12.3.** Paid sick leave: Average number of days at full pay for full-time participants by type of plan, medium and large firms, 1989.[11]

*Define disability*: Define disability as the employee's inability to perform the substantial duties of his or her regular occupation, or other similar duties due to a non-job-related medical condition.

2. Reserve the right to get a second medical opinion if deemed necessary before approving or continuing payments of salary continuation. A like requirement should be defined in the Medical Leave of Absence Policy. A second medical opinion can serve to verify an individual's condition, or uncover possible fraud in obtaining a paid benefit. Any company-directed physical exam should be paid by the company. Carefully weigh the opinions stated in the medical reports. In the event of conflicting opinions, some organizations have opted to seek a third opinion and then base the employment decision or payment of benefits upon the predominating opinions.

3. Remember to separate the Medical Leave of Absence Policy from the Salary Continuation Policy. These two policies can and should be closely related, but eligibility for salary continuation benefits should be more specifically defined. An employee on medical leave may not be eligible for salary continuation benefits, but any employee receiving salary continuation must be on a medical leave.

4. Avoid "double dipping." Double dipping refers to the practice of collecting income from two sources at the same time. Include a provision in your policy that benefits will not be paid if the employee is receiving disability income from another source or company benefit.

## Sample Policy

**XYZ COMPANY
PERSONNEL POLICY & PROCEDURE**

**SUBJECT: SALARY CONTINUATION**          **DATE: May 1, 1993**

*Policy*: It is the policy of XYZ Company to provide a wage continuation plan which ensures a limited income maintenance for non-job-related periods of illness or disability for employees in certain job categories.

*Eligibility*: Employees become eligible to receive wage continuation on January 1 after two years of Company service. This benefit is limited to first line supervisors and management.

*Procedure*:

1. The salary continuation plan pays an employee's regular pay rate for a 40-hour work week commencing on the first day of hospitalization or the sixth workday of an illness. Wage continuation benefits are subject to normal payroll taxes. For short-term illnesses, see Sick Pay Policy.

2. The salary continuation plan accrues at a rate of one week (five workdays) of benefit for each full year of service completed as of each January 1. (Note: For new employees the first week of wage continuation benefit is earned on January 1 following two full years of service.) An additional week of salary continuation benefit is earned on each succeeding January 1, up to a maximum of six weeks.

3. During periods of disability, any earned benefits are deducted as used and the employee continues to accrue salary continuation benefits until the maximum benefit is reached.

4. The employee must submit a physician's statement documenting disability in order to receive salary continuation benefits. The physician's statement shall be updated at two-week intervals; and at the conclusion of the absence, the employee shall submit a physician's statement certifying ability to resume normal job duties.

5. During periods of disability, the absence shall be recorded on the employee's attendance record. See Medical Leave of Absence Policy.

6. The salary continuation benefit is paid solely for non-job-related illnesses or disability; and this benefit is not paid if the employee is eligible for any other disability pay plan. This benefit is not paid at separation of employment.

## Sample Employee Handbook Paragraph

*Salary Continuation*

XYZ Company provides a Company-funded salary continuation plan benefit for eligible employees in the event of extended illness or disability. To be eligible for this benefit, an employee must be a full-time or qualified part-time employee. Eligible employees accrue one week of benefit per year following each employment anniversary, up to a maximum of 26 weeks. In the event benefits are used, the employee will continue to accrue disability benefits up to the maximum allowed.

Salary continuation benefits are computed based upon the employee's regular straight time pay rate for a 40-hour work week and prorated for part-time employees. Individuals who are eligible for sick pay benefits must use their sick pay before receiving salary continuation benefits. An employee must submit a physician's statement certifying the nature and anticipated duration of disability in order to receive this benefit. Periodic updates may be required as defined in the Company's medical leave policy. This benefit is not paid on separation of employment.

# Educational Benefits

Educational benefits should not be viewed as a cost, but rather as an investment in the firm's human resources. This investment, like other investments, needs to be carefully evaluated and selected in order to achieve a maximum return. Educational benefits help employees to keep up to date with current trends and maintain skills used on the job. Properly selected educational benefits help improve employee knowledge and skill, thus increasing the employee's value to the company.

There are a wide variety of job-related educational opportunities which can benefit employee and employer alike. Common examples are highlighted:

*Seminars and workshops*: These are generally one-day or two-day concentrated programs providing specialized training related to a particular field, occupational area, or technical issue. Seminars and workshops are generally presented by consultants, universities, professional or employer associations, or other training organizations.

*Vendor schools*: Many original equipment manufacturers (OEM) offer OEM workshops or vendor schools. These programs may vary from one day to several weeks in length. Vendor schools provide participants with technical knowledge about the vendor's products, applications, equipment operations, or repair.

*Continuing education courses*: Many community colleges, trade schools, or business schools provide a variety of continuing education programs. These programs generally provide basic education or skill development related to specific occupational areas. Continuing education courses generally are not certified for college course credit.

*Apprentice training*: Apprentice training courses registered with the U.S. Department of Labor include on-the-job training coupled with classroom work over a two- or four-year period culminating in a designated job skill classification for the particular trade or craft.

*College or university education*: College or university training provides broad educational courses or professional training culminating in a college degree. Such educational programs include a variety of general courses as well as degree-specific courses.

When defining an Educational Benefit Policy, there are a variety of concerns to be addressed. One primary concern expressed by various managers is limiting education benefits to job-related topics. In most organizations, management is reluctant to authorize employee training in courses that are not reasonably related to present job responsibilities.

A second area of concern is defining eligibility requirements for the educational benefit. Generally, educational benefits are limited to full-time employees. The full-time requirement helps to assure that the employee's first priority is the job and that educational activities are secondary. Without this limitation, the employer is likely to be paying full-time college tuition for part-time employees.

The Educational Benefits Policy must also distinguish between required job training that occurs on compensable work time versus employee-elected educational programs on unpaid nonworking time.

A guideline for the handling of educational costs is another important part of this policy. Many seminars, for example, require up-front payment of fees. When authorizing continuing education or college courses, however, many firms require the employee to pay registration fees. The employee then receives reimbursement upon successful completion of the course.

Another area of concern is compliance with relevant tax laws. Improper handling of educational expenses may result in loss of their deductibility as a business expense. Further, failure to comply with IRS guidelines could cause educational benefits to be judged as taxable income to the employee. The *Tax Guide for Small Business (1991)* provides this information relating to wages paid to employees:

> If you pay the education expenses of your employees who are enrolled in courses that are not required for their present job with your company,

or are not otherwise job related, you must treat these payments as wages. The payments are includible in income and are subject to FICA, FUTA, and income tax withholding.

*Educational Assistance Programs.* The income exclusion for employer-provided educational assistance payments is extended through tax years beginning before January 1, 1992. Also, for tax years beginning after 1990, graduate-level courses can now be included as part of an educational assistance program.

Payments for educational assistance that would be includible in an employee's income solely because they are more than $5250 can be excluded if they qualify as a working condition fringe benefit, discussed in the *Tax Guide* later under "Exclusion of Fringe Benefits."[12]

Relating to business expenses, the *Tax Guide* states the following:

*Education Expenses.* You can deduct two kinds of expenses for education. One is the ordinary and necessary expenses you pay for the education and training of your employees. These expenses are discussed in Chapter 10.

The other is for amounts you spend for your own education in your trade, business, or profession, along with certain related travel, including meals (subject to the limitations discussed in Chapter 16), lodging, and transportation expenses. To qualify for deduction, you must be able to show that the education maintains or improves skills required in your trade, business, or profession, or it is required by law or regulations for keeping your pay, status, or job.

You *cannot* deduct education expenses you incur to meet the minimum requirements of your present trade, business, or profession or those that qualify you for a new trade, business, or profession, even if the education maintains or improves skills presently required in your business.[13]

## Pitfalls to Avoid

The greatest concern to the employer setting up an Educational Benefit Policy is this: "Will I get a good return on my investment?" Here are some suggestions for avoiding common problems which can occur with a poorly defined policy.

1. Define an education benefits budget to control how funds will be used. Consider whether employees will need training in new business technologies. Evaluate employee performance to identify developmental needs. And if your policy includes tuition aid, budget some funds for reimbursement of authorized educational expenses incurred by employees.

   During my 20 plus years in human resources, I have noted that employee elective participation and the associated costs of educational

**CHECKLIST**
**An Education Benefits Policy**

- What state or federal laws or regulations affect the Educational Benefit Policy?

- What class or category of employees are eligible to receive educational benefits?

- Will the policy distinguish procedures between training programs required by the company and training or educational programs requested by the employee?

- Will training or educational courses be permitted on paid time or limited to nonworking time?

- Will the policy include provision for approval of course, schools, cost, and job relatedness of subject?

- Will a special or detailed approval process be required for degree programs taking one year or more to complete?

- Will employees be required to pay tuition costs first and then receive reimbursement upon successful completion of the course?

- Will payment or reimbursement be provided for registration fees? tuition? books? lab or material fees?

- Will the employee be required to submit documented evidence of course completion such as receipts for enrollment fees, copies of grades, or completion certificates?

- Will there be a limit to number of classes, course hours, or tuition costs allowed for a specified term or year?

- Will reimbursement be provided on a 100 percent basis, or will it be on a "descending" scale related to employees' grades?

benefits often are not as high as estimated by the employer. By the end of the workday, many employees are tired and don't have the drive to pursue after-hours educational activities.

2. Retain a proper balance between employment and educational activities. During certain phases of employment, training of employees is critical. Newly hired employes and apprentices are likely to spend more time in training activities. For tuition aid educational benefits, I recommend that guidelines be defined for the number of courses or course hours taken by an employee during a particular term or other time period. This will help to keep educational activities manageable so employees can maintain adequate performance on the job and in the classroom.

3. Employee participation in degree programs requires special controls. College degree curriculums can take two to four years or more. They

represent a substantial time investment by the employee and a cost investment by the employer. For this reason, the Education Benefits Policy should define requirements for a well-thought-out request by the employee. The employee should specify the school, curriculum, cost estimate, time period to complete the program, and justification on how the educational program will benefit the company as well as the employee.

For degree programs, I recommend management approval of the whole program and approval of each course on a term-by-term basis. Approval at each term assures availability of funds and adequacy of the employee's job performance. If the employee's performance is not satisfactory, the manager may delay or deny approval until the employee's performance improves. Further, with term by term approval, the manager may reevaluate the relevance of the educational program in light of any career or job changes made by the employee.

4. To help control costs, include in the policy a requirement that the employee and supervisor identify less costly educational alternatives. The cheapest program may not always be the best, but a reasonable evaluation of the various programs and their costs will help assure that the company gets the best investment for its education dollar.

5. Some managers are reluctant to start an Educational Benefits Policy because employees quit and go to other jobs after completing their education. Here are some tips to help minimize unwanted turnover from individuals who have received educational benefits:

   a. Define career development interests. When reviewing the employee's education benefits request, explore the employee's career interests, job opportunities, and realistic career paths available in the organization. Approve only those courses that focus on a realistic assessment of business needs and opportunities in the organization.

   b. Limit educational benefit course selections to those programs which *directly relate* to skills or knowledge used on the job.

   c. Look at the big picture. If educational benefits make an employee more productive and valuable, this increased productivity may be more beneficial to the firm than an occasional separation.

**Sample Policy**

**XYZ COMPANY**
**PERSONNEL POLICY & PROCEDURE**

SUBJECT: EDUCATIONAL BENEFITS                    DATE: May 1, 1993

*Policy*: It is the policy of XYZ Company to encourage continuing education by providing reimbursement for eligible employees for certain expenses incurred in continuing job-related education.

*Eligibility*: To be eligible for educational assistance, one must be a full-time employee with one year or more of Company service.

*Procedure*:

1. All Company-sponsored or -funded training or educational programs are subject to management discretion, Company staffing needs, and the availability of budgeted funds.

2. A Supervisor may request an employee to participate in a seminar or educational program when participation in the program is essential for business operations or when it is deemed by the Supervisor that such training is essential to aid the employee in the performance of job duties. An employee participating in training required by the Company will receive regular pay for the training activity and be eligible for reimbursement of normal business travel expenses.

3. An employee may request to participate in an educational program which is related to his or her current job responsibilities or reasonable career progression within the Company. The program must be offered after normal business hours by an accredited institution of learning. It is recommended that the employee schedule only one or two courses at a given time. The employee's request must be made to the Supervisor prior to course enrollment.

4. In the event the employee requests enrollment into a program including a series of courses which may or may not lead to a degree, the educational program must be reviewed and approved by a Supervisor, Department Manager, and the Personnel Manager. Further, the employee must request and receive approval prior to enrolling in each individual course in the program.

5. An employee's participation in an evening or weekend educational program elected by the employee is not compensable time. Therefore, salary or travel expenses are not provided.

6. The Company reserves the right to suspend or withhold approval of any educational program or course. Such discretion shall be exercised by the Supervisor, Manager, or Personnel Manager after evaluating relevant factors such as business conditions, availability of funds, and the employee's performance on the job.

7. The Company will reimburse to the employee tuition fees only exclusive of expenses for books, travel, or other fees, subject to the following conditions:

    a) The course is a prior approved job-related course offered by an accredited institution as outlined by this policy.

    b) The employee provides documented evidence of costs and successful completion of the course with a grade of C or better.

    c) The employee has completed the course while remaining on the payroll as an active full-time employee.

8. In the event of an employee's economic hardship, Company management may elect to provide to the employee an advance loan for tuition fees. This loan would be cancelled upon successful completion as outlined above.

**Sample Employee Handbook
Paragraph**

*Tuition Aid*

XYZ Company recognizes the importance of changing technology and new information which can aid employees in successful performance of job duties. When appropriate, the Company may arrange for employees to participate in continuing education courses or seminars which are job related.

Also, the Company will consider employee requests for after-hours job-related educational courses. In such cases, approval is subject to budgeted funds and the employee's request must be submitted prior to course registration. Upon successful completion of the course, the employee will receive 100 percent reimbursement of tuition costs. Successful completion of the course requires a grade of C or better. Speak with your supervisor for further details.

**Sample Form**

**TUITION AID REQUEST FORM**

Employee _____       Date _____

Job _____       Dept. _____

Describe course or educational program _____

_____

Is this course part of a degree program?   YES      NO       If yes, describe

_____

School/organization _____

Location _____

Costs:

    Enrollment _____

    Tuition _____

    Lab/material fees/books _____

    Total _____

Describe how this course or program will aid your job at XYZ Company

_____

_____

_____

*Sample Forms (Continued)*

                                                  Employee

Approvals: _____
                   Supervisor

Manager                   Human Resource Manager        Date

# Group Insurances

The cost of group insurances represents approximately 7 percent of employee compensation according to the Bureau of Labor Statistics.[14] The rising cost of health care benefits is one of the major concerns of business owners and managers. Many business owners lament that insurance premiums are rising 20 percent, 40 percent, even 50 percent each year. While President Clinton has recommended health care reform, there does not appear to be any immediate relief in sight.

In keeping with the purpose of this manual, the focus of this section is to show how the policy manual can provide insurance administration instructions to supervisors and benefits information to employees.

Supervisors may become involved in group insurances during the enrollment of a new employee or when an employee has a question about an insurance claim. Unfortunately, most supervisors are as ill-informed about insurance benefit provisions as their employees. The primary goal of a personnel policy on group insurances is to instruct supervisors on insurance enrollment procedures, and to promote an awareness of benefits so supervisors can answer questions.

Information on insurance benefits can easily be combined with an Employee Orientation Policy (see Chap. 7). Important points for the supervisor to understand are what insurance benefits are offered, which employees are eligible, and when and how to complete enrollment forms. In addition, the supervisor should be provided with a current benefits booklet or plan description, and a contact either with the employer or with the insurance company in the event of questions.

## Competitive Practices

Table 12.2 shows the prevalence of various insurance plans offered by employers in the United States.

## Pitfalls to Avoid

Proper enrollment and administration of group insurances is important in maintaining good employee relations. Here are some potential problem areas to avoid:

## CHECKLIST
### A Group Insurance Policy

- What classes or categories of employees are covered by insurance benefits?
- Who is responsible for enrolling new employees into the insurance plans (Human Resource Specialist, Benefits Specialist, or supervisor)?
- By what time following the start of employment must insurance enrollment be completed?
- What enrollment form or waiver form must the employee complete and sign to enroll or decline insurance benefits?
- Who is responsible for dispensing claim forms and processing insurance claims through the insurance company?
- What provisions of the insurance plan contract will affect administration of insurances?
- Who is responsible for answering employee questions about insurance coverages or claims (supervisor, Human Resource Specialist, or Benefits Specialist)?
- Who is the designated contact person for coordinating communications with the insurance carrier?
- Is there a union agreement which affects the enrollment of employees, processing of claims, or answering of insurance questions?
- Who is responsible for notifying employees or dependents of the opportunity to continue insurances as specified by COBRA law?

1. Many families now consist of dual working spouses. When husband and wife both hold full-time jobs, both are likely to be eligible for group insurances at their respective employers. To save money, one spouse may decline insurance coverage because it is less expensive to be covered under the other's insurance plan. Many employees are unaware that insurance plans provide open enrollment for new hires, but

**Table 12.2.** Percent of Full-Time Employees Participating in Insurance Plans

| Benefit | Small establishments[15] | Medium and large establishments[16] |
|---|---|---|
| Sickness & Accident Insurance | 26 | 43 |
| Long-Term Disability Insurance | 19 | 45 |
| Medical Care Insurance | 69 | 92 |
| Dental Care Insurance | 30 | 66 |
| Life Insurance | 64 | 94 |

later enrollment is subject to evidence of insurability or a physical exam. This requirement can be an unexpected surprise to the employee. While this situation cannot be prevented, policy guidelines can instruct the supervisor or benefits specialist to advise employees of this likelihood.

2. Firms in some industries tend to experience high turnover among new hires during the first 30, 60, and 90 days of employment. Most insurance plans call for enrollment into the plan within the first 30 days of employment. A firm with high turnover, however, will be enrolling and then dropping insurance coverage for separating employees. With the COBRA insurance continuation law, all separating employees must receive notice of opportunity to continue group insurances. To minimize the disruptive effect of this practice, some employers have delayed insurance enrollment until 90 days of employment or later.

3. The COBRA insurance continuation law requires employers to notify separating employees of the opportunity to continue group insurances. When an employee leaves, most supervisors are preoccupied with reassignment of work tasks and recruiting a replacement employee. As a result, the human resource or benefits specialist may not be aware of the separation. Be sure to coordinate the Separation Policy (see Chap. 11) with insurance administration procedures so that COBRA notices are sent on time.

## Sample Policy

**XYZ COMPANY**
**PERSONNEL POLICY & PROCEDURE**

---

SUBJECT: INSURANCE ADMINISTRATION          DATE: May 1, 1993

---

*Policy*: It is the policy of XYZ Company to provide a group insurance plan for eligible employees.

*Eligibility*: To be eligible for group insurance, an employee must be a full-time employee working 30 or more hours weekly.

*Procedure*:
1. The Human Resource Administrator is responsible for conducting the benefits portion of new employee orientation. All newly hired employees meeting eligibility requirements shall be advised of group insurance plans, dependent coverage availability, and current premium costs.

2. The Human Resource Administrator shall encourage employees to enroll for group insurances within 30 days of hire. Each employee shall complete and sign an enrollment form to enroll or a waiver form if declining insurance.

3. In the event a newly hired eligible employee declines coverage, the Human Resource Administrator shall advise the employee that subse-

quent enrollment for the insurance plan will require the employee or dependents to provide evidence of insurability in the form of physical exam by a physician designated by the insurance company.

4. Each supervisor and manager is responsible for keeping a copy of the current insurance booklet handy to answer employee insurance questions. In the event the supervisor is unable to effectively answer a question, the employee shall be referred to the Human Resource Administrator.

5. The Human Resource Administrator shall maintain and dispense insurance claims forms as requested by employees.

6. Each employee is responsible for notifying his or her supervisor in the event of change of dependents, birth, marriage, divorce, or other family change affecting insurance administration. The supervisor is responsible for passing the information on to the Human Resource Administrator.

7. In the event an employee or dependent becomes ineligible for group insurances, the Human Resource Administrator shall, upon learning of the event, send notice of insurance continuation to the individual as prescribed by the COBRA insurance continuation law.

8. The Human Resource Administrator is responsible for maintaining records and files related to insurance enrollment, waivers, claims, and COBRA insurance participants.

## Sample Employee Handbook Paragraph

*Group Insurance*

XYZ Company provides a competitive array of group insurances designed to provide added financial protection for employees and eligible dependents. Insurance coverages begin after 30 days of employment. The Company pays a portion of insurance premiums to keep employee costs to a minimum. Details are explained in separate booklets. The following insurance plans are available.

*Health insurance*: Provides protection to defray the cost of hospital charges, doctor bills, and medical expenses. Additional insurance protection for your eligible dependents is available at a moderate cost.

*Life insurance*: Provides life insurance protection including provision for accidental death and dismemberment.

*Disability insurance*: Provides income maintenance protection during short-term periods of disability due to non-job-related accident or illness.

*Dental insurance*: Provides insurance protection to defray costs of dental care. Dependent coverage is available at a moderate cost.

At separation of employment, an employee may elect to continue health insurance coverages as permitted under the COBRA insurance continuation law. Also, under this law, continuation of insurance coverage is available for one's spouse or dependents in the event of marital separation, divorce, death, or other qualifying events. Speak with the Human Resource Administrator for information on costs, enrollment periods, and terms of coverage.

## Retirement Plans

A majority of organizations provide some form of retirement benefits for eligible employees. There are a wide variety of retirement plans. These plans may be classified into two broad categories: defined benefit pension plans and defined contribution plans. The defined benefit pension plans use predetermined formulas to calculate a retirement benefit and obligate the employer to provide those benefits. Benefits are computed based on salary, years of service, or both.

The defined contribution plans specify the level of employer and employee contributions to the plan, but do not specify the eventual benefits as in the defined benefit pension plan. Instead, individual accounts are set up for participants, and benefits are based upon the amounts credited to these accounts, plus investment earnings. A money purchase pension plan provides for a pension annuity or other form of retirement income that is determined by fixed contribution rules plus earnings credited to the employee's account.

There are various kinds of defined contribution plans. Cash or deferred arrangement plans, also known as 401(K) plans, allow participants to choose between receiving currently taxable income or deferring taxation by placing the money in a retirement account.

Another form of defined contribution plan is a savings and thrift plan. Under these plans, employees contribute a predetermined portion of earnings to an account, all or a part of which is matched by the employer contribution or placed into various investments such as stocks, bonds, or money market funds as directed by the employee or employer depending on plan provisions.

Profit sharing plans are another form of defined contribution plan where contributions are based on profits. Some plans provide for a cash payout to participants at year end. Others provide for deferral of benefits until retirement or other specified event. Profit sharing contributions may be made based on a formula or management discretion as specified by the plan.

Retirement plans, like the various examples described, are subject to the requirements of the Employee Retirement Income Security Act (ERISA). ERISA defines standards for plan vesting, funding, participation, and reporting both to the government and to participants. Because of these requirements, all pension plans are defined by a plan document and require that summary plan descriptions be provided to participants. The plan documents and descriptions define plan features and administrative procedures. For this reason, it is generally not necessary to define procedures in a company's personnel policy manual.

A brief summary of a pension or profit sharing plan is often highlighted in an employee handbook. The summary can identify basic plan features and eligibility requirements. Any summary in the employee handbook should refer the reader to the summary plan description or plan document for full details. Also, it is best to state that the plan document is the final authority for information on the plan.

### Competitive Practices

Table 12.3 shows employee participation in the various types of retirement plans.

### Sample Employee Handbook Paragraphs

*Profit Sharing Program*

XYZ Company provides a profit sharing plan designed to supplement an employee's social security benefits and to provide added income security upon retirement. The plan is fully Company funded, and employees become eligible to participate in the plan on January 1 following one year of Company service. Contributions to the plan may be made each year subject to the Company's profitability. Full details are described in the plan document. Speak with the Human Resource Administrator if you have additional questions.

*Pension Plan*

XYZ Company provides a pension plan for eligible employees. Employees who meet plan eligibility requirements become participants following their first anniversary of employment. At time of enrollment, pension benefits are credited back to date of hire. The plan is funded by the Company, and participants receive a periodic statement of account. Further details are defined in the plan document. Speak with the Human Resource Administrator or Controller for more information.

*401K Savings Plan*

XYZ Company has established a 401K savings plan. Employees become eligible to participate in the plan after six months of Company service and achieving 21 years of age. The employee may enter the plan on one

**Table 12.3.** Percent of Full-Time Employees Participating in Selected Retirement Plans

| Benefit | Small establishments[17] | Medium and large establishments[18] |
|---|---|---|
| All Retirement Plans | 42 | 81 |
| Defined Benefit Plans | 20 | 63 |
| Defined Contribution Plans | 31 | 18 |

of the two plan entry dates each year after meeting eligibility requirements. Participation is voluntary; the employee may elect to deduct a
portion of pay through payroll deduction.

Under current tax laws, these deductions reduce the individual's
taxable income level, and all earnings to the plan are tax deferred. This
is an excellent capital accumulation plan for added financial security
upon reaching retirement age. Speak with the Personnel Manager for
further details.

## Legislated Benefits

Various state and federal laws direct employers to contribute toward
government-required insurance plans. Since these plans are required by law,
they are referred to as legislated benefits. These benefits include unemployment insurance, worker's compensation insurance, and social security
benefits.

Unemployment insurance is intended to provide limited income maintenance protection for eligible employees in the event of job loss through no
fault of the employee. Employers pay into an unemployment insurance fund
based on employment levels and on unemployment claims filed by former
employees. The employer's contributions actually go into state and federal
funds, which are administered by state employment security agencies. These
agencies process unemployment insurance claims and refer claimants to job
openings in the community. Unemployment insurance claimants must meet
eligibility requirements defined by state law relating to covered work, tenure
of employment, and reason for separation, and be able, available, and
actively seeking work.

Worker's compensation benefits were legislated in order to assure income protection for workers or their dependents in the event of an injury,
illness, disability, or death in connection with employment. Worker's compensation insurance provides disability income and death benefit. Insurance benefits are provided by various insurance providers, subject to state
laws and regulations. Worker's compensation benefits are fully paid by the
employer.

Social security benefits were enacted into law to help assure that working
men and women received some level of income protection upon retirement.
In addition to retirement benefits, social security benefits provide disability
income in the event of permanent disability, Medicare benefits providing
hospital and medical care for retirees, and a death benefit.

The employee pays a percentage of income through payroll deduction
for social security benefits up to a specified limit. The employer pays an
equal percentage in all covered wages of employees.

The administrative details of these plans are generally handled by the
individual(s) responsible for payroll taxes and insurance/loss control func-

tions in an organization. Administrative details of these plans are normally not part of a supervisor's responsibility. For this reason, a detailed personnel policy has not been defined here. There are, however, several personnel policies which relate to the legislated benefits.

*Personnel Policies Relating to Unemployment Insurance*

a. *Layoff policies*: As a result of an involuntary separation, an employee may be eligible for unemployment insurance benefits. Include in the layoff policy procedures for referring the affected employee to the local unemployment office.

b. *Discipline and discharge policies*: As the result of an involuntary separation, an employee may file for unemployment benefits. Include in these policies provisions for assuring accurate and adequate documentation of events or circumstances which prompted discharge. Make sure that unemployment claims from discharged individuals are promptly answered.

*Personnel Policies Relating to Worker's Compensation Insurance*

a. *Safety policies and an aggressive safety program*: Promotes safety awareness, helps to prevent accidents, and reduces worker's compensation claims.

b. *Accident reporting policy*: Is an important guideline for investigating accidents. Accident investigation provides the details needed to submit a worker's compensation report to the appropriate state agency and insurance carrier. Accident reporting also helps to identify accident causes and aids in prevention of subsequent accidents.

c. *Medical leave of absence policy*: Defines policy guidelines for absence due to medical reasons. Your Medical Leave Policy can be defined to include work-related as well as non-work-related medical absences.

*Personnel Policies Relating to Social Security Insurance:*

a. *Employee orientation policy or new employee orientation checklist*: Can include a section which identifies the social security payroll deduction which will appear on the employee's payroll check.

b. *Preretirement planning and retirement policies*: Should include a reference for referring the employer to the social security office to apply for retirement and Medicare benefits.

c. *Medical leave of absence policy*: Can include guidelines for referring an employee who has a permanent total disability to the local social security office to file for disability benefits.

## Sample Employee Handbook
## Paragraph

*Government-Required Insurances*

XYZ Company makes contributions to government-required insurances, providing the following benefits for employees:

*Social security benefits*: Provides income maintenance for covered individuals in the event of permanent disability or retirement. The Company makes a contribution which matches the FICA deduction on your pay check.

*Worker's compensation insurance*: Provides insurance protection in the event of a job-related illness or injury. Coverage begins on the first day of employment for all employees.

*Unemployment insurance benefits*: Provides income maintenance for certain individuals who have lost their job through no fault of their own, such as a layoff, and meet other eligibility requirements specified by law. The Company pays the full cost of this insurance plan.

# Notes

1. *Human Resources Management, Personnel Practices/Communications Reporter*, Commerce Clearing House, Chicago, 1991, para. 4725, p. 4518.
2. *Employee Benefits in Small Private Establishments, 1990*, Bulletin 2388, U.S. Dept. of Labor, September, 1991, Table 7, p. 11.
3. *Employee Benefits in Medium and Large Firms, 1989*, Bulletin 2363, U.S. Dept. of Labor, June, 1990, Table 7, p. 12.
4. R. Green, W. Carmel, P. Gray, *1992 State by State Guide to Human Resources Law*, Panel Publishers, Inc., New York, 1992, pp. 4–77, citing Massachusetts v. Morasch, U.S. Supreme Court, No. 83-32 (April 18, 1989).
5. *Employee Benefits in Small Private Establishments, 1990*, Bulletin 2388, U.S. Dept. of Labor, September, 1991, p. 10.
6. *Employee Benefits in Medium and Large Firms, 1989*, Bulletin 2363, U.S. Dept. of Labor, June, 1990, p. 11.
7. "Manager's Newsfront Column," by Betty Southard Murphy, Wayne E. Barlow, and D. Diane Hatch, *Personnel Journal*, October, 1992, p. 24.
8. *Employee Benefits in Small Private Establishments, 1990*, Bulletin 2388, U.S. Dept. of Labor, September, 1991, p. 20.
9. *Employee Benefits in Medium and Large Firms, 1989*, Bulletin 2363, U.S. Dept. of Labor, June, 1990, p. 23.
10. *Massachusetts* v. *Morasch* (U.S. Supreme Court, No 83-32, April 18, 1989).
11. *Employee Benefits in Medium and Large Firms, 1989*, Bulletin 2363, U.S. Dept. of Labor, June, 1990, p. 26.
12. *Tax Guide for Small Businesses*, Publication 334, Dept. of Treasury, 1991, p. 30.
13. Ibid., p. 64.

14. *Employer Costs for Employee Compensation*, U.S. Dept. of Labor, Bureau of Labor Statistics, March, 1992, p. 1.

15. *Employee Benefits in Small Private Establishments, 1990*, Bulletin 2388, U.S. Dept. of Labor, September, 1991, p. 5.

16. *Employee Benefits in Medium and Large Firms, 1989*, Bulletin 2363, U.S. Dept. of Labor, June, 1990, p. 4.

17. *Employee Benefits in Small Private Establishments, 1990*, Bulletin 2388, U.S. Dept. of Labor, September, 1991, p. 5.

18. *Employee Benefits in Medium and Large Firms, 1989*, Bulletin 2363, U.S. Dept. of Labor, June, 1990, p. 4.

# 13

# Employee and Union Relations: Policies to Motivate the Workforce

**Read Chapter 13 for:**

Open door employee communications

Employee committees

Preventing and countering unions

Union agreements

Grievance and complaint policy

## Open Door Employee Communications

Motivated employees are the key to any successful enterprise. Maintaining open communications with employees is one important factor in a motivated workforce. Those organizations that earn a reputation of being a good place to work have a high level of employee communications activities.

Each of us likes to know what is going on at our firm. We have a self-interest because we want to know how events will affect our job. Too many times, employees learn significant information about their employer—information about their jobs and job security—on the six o'clock news. This form of communication fails to build employee trust.

When management communication is minimal or nonexistent, an alternative informal network of communication grows to fill the information void. That informal network is referred to as the "grapevine." The grapevine, unfortunately, often relays erroneous rumors and exaggerated misinformation.

Organizations that have conducted employee attitude surveys often find that communications issues are among the major concerns expressed by employees. These concerns often relate to the effectiveness of day-to-day communications with supervisors as well as adequacy of information from top management.

There are a wide variety of ways to actively maintain communications with employees. Various examples are highlighted here:

- *New employee orientation*: Begin the employment relationship with a proper orientation. A new employee orientation should include information on the firm, its products or services, policies, job responsibilities, benefits, and an opportunity to get acquainted with fellow workers. See policy information on new employee orientation in Chap. 7.

- *Open Door Policy*: The Open Door Policy is intended to convey a message from management to employees that says, "My door is always open. You are encouraged to come and speak with me at any time if you have a question, complaint, or problem."

- *Employee meetings*: Periodic employee meetings are an effective way to communicate information about new policies, benefits, or important news about the organization. Employee meetings give employees an opportunity to meet company managers, ask questions, or express opinions on issues of importance.

- *Employee handbook*: The employee handbook is an effective form of employee communications. It answers many employees by summarizing important employment policies and benefits information. The manager's personnel policy manual helps to clarify policy information and guide supervisors in discussing policy issues with employees.

- *Performance appraisals*: A performance appraisal system gets supervisors to talk with their subordinates about job performance issues on a periodic basis. These structured discussions can help to improve communications. See policy information on performance appraisals in Chap. 10.

- *Bulletin board*: Many organizations use a bulletin board to communicate company news, policy, and benefits information to employees. See information on Bulletin Board Policy in Chap. 15.

- *Payroll stuffers*: Employees eagerly open their pay envelope each pay day. Many firms use the pay envelope as a medium of communication to employees and their families. Payroll stuffers can be a letter explaining a new policy, brochure describing a new insurance plan, announcement about a company picnic, or other similar message of interest to employees.

- *Employee newsletter*: Many larger firms use an employee newsletter to communicate information to employees. Newsletters provide an opportunity for communicating a wide variety of information to employees. Newsletters can vary significantly, reflecting the attitudes and culture of the organization. Employee newsletters often include stories on company products or services, significant events on the job, benefits information, president's message, news about employees, and company-sponsored social activities.

- *Employee attitude surveys*: Employee attitude surveys are one way to elicit employee opinions on various job-related issues. Attitude surveys are generally administered in the form of a questionnaire filled out by each employee. To encourage frank communications, attitude surveys normally are completed anonymously. An important part of the attitude survey process is feedback of information to employees and management response to the issues raised.

A policy on employee communications needs to address several key areas. Be sure to define supervisor responsibilities for communications and, in particular, accountability to resolve employee complaints. Also, the employee communications process is an area where the Human Resource Specialist should take an active role. The Human Resource Specialist can assist in defining employee communications messages, recommend which communication medium to use, and serve as a source of information to answer employee questions. Finally, the Human Resource Specialist can serve as an independent mediator to help an employee resolve a problem with his or her supervisor.

## Competitive Practice

The chart in Fig. 13.1 shows what kinds of employee communications activities are used at various firms.

## Pitfalls to Avoid

An effective employee communications process will pay for itself in the form of lower employee costs from turnover, accidents, absenteeism, errors, or litigation. Here are some pitfalls to avoid:

1. Keep supervisors informed of important issues relating to the business, policies, benefits, or company financial condition. Your supervisors are "on the firing line" with employees. A supervisor's informed response to a question will significantly help to allay employee concerns or fears.

**CHECKLIST**
**An Employee Communications Policy**

- What responsibilities will supervisors and managers have in various employee communications activities such as new employee orientation, performance appraisal, conducting department meetings, etc.?

- What role will the Human Resource Specialist have in employee communication?

- Will there be an informal complaint resolution process or a formal grievance procedure?

- How will the complaint procedure or grievance procedure be publicized to employees?

- If an employee is not satisfied with a supervisor's response to a complaint, to whom in the organization can the employee appeal?

- If there is a union, what contract provisions relate to grievance procedures?

- Will there be any provision for independent arbitration of an issue that is not resolved to the satisfaction of the employee or the organization?

A supervisor who responds to an employee question by saying, "What do I know, they never tell me anything," contributes to lack of respect for self and management.

2. Be sure that your employee communications, open door, or grievance procedure includes a provision to appeal an employment decision to top management. While we don't want or expect every supervisor's decision to be overturned on appeal, the appeal process helps minimize liability in the event of a discrimination claim or wrongful discharge lawsuit. An appeal process can provide the following benefits:

   a. Knowing that an employment decision may be appealed to one's superior, a supervisor is more likely to exercise careful judgment in resolving a matter.

   b. An employee's use of the appeal process serves as an early warning to management of a particular concern expressed by the employee. Clearly, it is less costly and time consuming to respond to an employee's complaint than to a lawsuit.

   c. In the event of a lawsuit or discrimination claim, the firm can use the appeal process in its defense to show that the employee's complaint did receive a fair and thorough complaint resolution. One of the questions typically asked on an EEOC investigation request was whether the employee was able to appeal the supervisor's decision to a higher level of management.

| Occupational Group/Union Status | Grievance or Complaint Procedure | Employee Involvement or Participation Program | Information Sharing Program | Attitude Surveys |
|---|---|---|---|---|
| Managers | 42% (455) | 32% (418) | 59% (355) | 50% (444) |
| Nonunion Professional and Technical Employees | 45% (439) | 34% (401) | 57% (343) | 40% (426) |
| Union Professional and Technical Employees | 96% (57) | 42% (52) | 50% (44) | 51% (51) |
| Nonunion Clerical Employees | 47% (460) | 34% (420) | 53% (353) | 38% (431) |
| Union Clerical Employees | 99% (88) | 48% (82) | 64% (70) | 49% (80) |
| Nonunion Manufacturing and Production Employees | 54% (325) | 43% (296) | 57% (261) | 39% (297) |
| Union Manufacturing and Production Employees | 98% (177) | 49% (152) | 64% (137) | 44% (156) |

Sample size is in parentheses

**Figure 13.1.** Frequency of communication and involvement programs by occupation group and union status.[1]

## Sample Policy

**XYZ COMPANY**
**PERSONNEL POLICY & PROCEDURE**

SUBJECT: OPEN DOOR POLICY                     DATE: May 1, 1993

*Policy*: It is the policy of XYZ Company to encourage employee ideas or suggestions and to try to resolve any employee complaints or grievances in order to promote a harmonious working environment.

*Procedure*:
1. Each Supervisor or Manager is responsible for taking an active role in promoting good communications with employees. To achieve this goal, Supervisors are responsible for participating in new employee orientation, providing performance appraisals, and conducting departmental meetings on a monthly basis. Departmental meetings shall include discussion of one or more of the following topics: business results, departmental productivity, benefits, policies, safety, or other issues.

2. Each Supervisor or Manager is responsible for administering the Company's open door policy by being accessible and available to employees in order to answer questions, resolve work problems, and respond to complaints or grievances. Further, Supervisors or Managers should encourage employee suggestions or ideas.

3. When an employee has a question, suggestion, idea for work or product improvement, complaint, or grievance, the employee is encouraged to discuss the matter with his or her superior. The open door policy and procedure may also be used if an employee wants to make a complaint about a discriminatory employment decision, employment practice, or harassment such as sexual harassment.

4. In the event the employee is uncomfortable discussing the matter with his or her superior, the employee may speak with another Manager or representative of the Human Resource Department. In such cases, the employee should request supervisory approval to leave the work area during work time, or conduct the discussion during nonwork time.

5. The Supervisor is responsible for considering the complaint and responding to the employee. Such discussions may occur during working time, nonworking time, in work or nonwork areas as deemed appropriate by the Supervisor. In the event a discussion interferes with work activity, the Supervisor may arrange to conduct the discussion at a time or place which will not disrupt work operations.

6. The Supervisor shall make a reasonable effort to resolve the matter on a timely basis. If the matter is beyond one's scope of authority, it shall be referred to a higher-level Manager for resolution. If necessary, the matter may be brought to the attention of the General Manager. Supervisors or Managers may confer with the Human Resource Administrator for ideas or advice in resolving issues under the open door policy.

7. In those situations where a collective bargaining agreement exists, union employees may use the grievance procedure described in the agreement in order to resolve any disputes about interpretation of the agreement.

8. To aid Supervisors and Managers, a summary sheet providing Tips for Handling Complaints is included as an attachment to this policy.

### *Attachment to Open Door Policy*

### Tips for Handling Complaints

1. Listen carefully to the employee's idea or complaint. Give individual attention to the employee during the discussion.

2. Avoid criticizing the employee and his or her idea or complaint. Avoid arguments and a hasty or emotional reply.

3. Ask questions if necessary to fully understand the idea or complaint.

4. Try to address the matter on a timely basis if it can be resolved within the scope of your authority.

5. Try to be consistent when making employment decisions so that similar cases are handled in a similar manner.

6. If the matter cannot be resolved immediately, let the employee know when to expect an answer and be sure to follow up.

7. Confer with your superior and/or the Human Resource Department representative to obtain advice. Take care to protect confidential information.

## Sample Employee Handbook Paragraph

*Employee Communications*

The management of XYZ Company operates with an open management style in which each employee is encouraged to speak freely to his or her supervisor. We make a conscious effort to keep employees informed about matters affecting their jobs, and we welcome your ideas and suggestions.

If your supervisor is unable to provide assistance, you may request to speak with the Human Resource Department or the Plant Superintendent. If your complaint is unresolved at this level, it may then be referred to the Company President for a decision. We will do our best to provide a fair and timely response.

## Employee Committees

Employee involvement programs are one of the leading changes occurring in the workforce in the 1990s. Employee involvement programs reflect various management style trends, such as participative management, Japanese management styles, and quality of worklife improvement.

Under traditional management styles, managers gave the orders and employees did what they were told. The growth of international competition, the loss of manufacturing jobs, and slipping productivity prompted many firms to seek better ways to build their products.

Many of the productivity improvement efforts focused on various quality of worklife issues. There was an increasing prevalence of employee participation in various work issues. Companies that began to use mini and personal computer systems in the 1980s found employee committees to be an aid in systems implementation. Safety specialists for years have used safety committees as a way to stimulate employee participation and interest in safety. Many of the quality improvement programs implemented by firms use a committee process. The idea is to get employees together and talking about ways to improve quality, work procedures, and other efficiencies. In some organizations, management has elicited employee input for personnel policy manual preparation.

The committee process can be an effective way to elicit employee participation and ideas. Tips on working with an employee committee are covered in greater detail in Chap. 3.

While employee involvement programs are emerging as a viable management process, so too are legal constraints which affect employee committees. The topics covered by an employee committee or the manner in which committee members are selected and participate have become subject to the scrutiny of the National Labor Relations Board (NLRB). The NLRB enforces the National Labor Relations Act, which defines rules and legal guidelines for the formation of unions and employer interaction with those unions.

The NLRA defines a labor organization as "any organization of any kind, or any agency or employee representation committee or plan, in which employees participate and which exists for the specific purpose, in whole or in part, of dealing with employers concerning grievances, labor disputes, wages, rates of pay, hours of employment, or conditions of work."[2]

In another section, the Act makes it an unfair labor practice for an employer "to dominate or interfere with the formation or administration of any labor organization."[3]

Based on these two sections of the law, several questions have arisen regarding employee committees. These questions are briefly highlighted:

a. Are employee committees formed in response to an employee suggestion or complaint viewed as "concerted action" under the law? Concerted action is activities by employees acting together in concert to present a grievance or seek improvement to wages or working conditions. Concerted action is protected by the NLRA.

b. If the employee committee is viewed as a bargaining unit by the NLRB, the employer's actions directing the activities of the committee may be viewed as domination or interference with a labor organization, and an unfair labor practice.

c. If the employer has a union but fails to involve union representatives in the activities of the committee, such action may be viewed as refusal to bargain with the union, another violation of the NLRA.

To keep your employee committee free from an unfair labor practice charge, consider the following guidelines:

*Committee selection*: Elicit volunteer participation in the committee. Another approach is to select committee members by management appointment. Rotate committee participation to let others have an opportunity to be part of the committee process. One packaging firm is so actively involved in committee-based workplace improvement programs that every employee participates in at least one committee. Responsibility for committee participation is included in the individual's job description.

*Management control*: Management may issue general guidelines on topics to be discussed by the committee. Committee members may make suggestions or recommendations only, which are subject to approval or rejection by management. Within guidelines, allow the committee to set its own agenda and communications.

*Committee issues*: Focus committee activities toward a specific project and objective. Allowable topics for committee attention appear to be quality, safety, work procedures improvement, and work coordination. Do not permit the committee to deal with subjects of wages, benefits, work rules, or hours. Such topics are considered by the NLRB as mandatory subjects of bargaining—meaning that these are topics which must be bargained by a union and employer.

*Member status*: All members on an employee committee must participate as individuals speaking only for themselves. Committee members should not participate as a representative of fellow employees.

## Competitive Practices

The charts in Fig. 13.2 show the extent of employee involvement in participation initiatives and typical issues covered in employee involvement programs.

## Pitfalls to Avoid

Employee involvement programs are on the rise. Improper formation or use of an employee committee can result in violations of the National Labor Relations Act. Here are some pitfalls to avoid:

1. Avoid selection of employee committee members by any form of election process. Do not have committee members participate as representatives of a particular group of employees. Do not permit committee members to speak on behalf of others. All of these actions are characteristics of a labor union. Whether a formal union-employer relationship exists or not, if the employer deals with employees through representatives, such actions are under the jurisdiction of the NLRB and may be judged as unfair labor practice.

2. Limit the focus of employee committee activities to a specific objective related to improvement of quality or safety or work procedures. Do not permit the committee to address issues related to pay, hours, benefits, or working conditions. Such issues are proper subjects for bargaining between an employer and a union. Avoid these issues to minimize the

**CHECKLIST**
**An Employee Committee Policy**

- What work issues or subjects will be the focus of the employee committee?
- How will committee members be selected?
- How long will committee members serve (i.e., six months, one year, or other period)?
- What employees, departments, or work groups will participate in the committee process?
- What will be the effect of committee suggestions?
- When, where, and how often will the committee meet?
- Will the committee meet on company premises and time?
- Is there a union? If so, what role will the union play in the committee process?

likelihood of your committee being defined as a labor organization under NLRB criteria.

3. Do not start an employee committee in response to union organizing activity. The formation of an employee committee to counter union organizing efforts could result in an unfair labor practice charge. Rather, the start of employee involvement activities should be delayed until after the union election and contract negotiations, if the union wins the election.

4. If your firm has a union, be sure to involve the union in the employee committee process. Do not use an employee committee as a way to bypass the union or evade a duty to bargain. Further, do not involve the employee committee with wage, benefit, hours, or working condition issues that are part of the collective bargaining process.

**Sample Policy**

**XYZ COMPANY**
**PERSONNEL POLICY & PROCEDURE**

SUBJECT: EMPLOYEE COMMITTEE                          DATE: May 1, 1993

*Policy*: It is the policy of XYZ Company to encourage employee ideas or suggestions to achieve improvement in quality and productivity.

*Procedure*:
   1. Each year, Company management designates one individual to serve as the Quality and Productivity Officer (QP Officer). The term of QP

| Occupational Group | NONUNION<br>(1)<br>Average of the Percent of Employees Involved Among Firms with Initiatives | UNION<br>(2)<br>Average of the Percent of Employees Involved Among Firms |
|---|---|---|
| Managers | 48%<br>(120) | -- |
| Professional and Technical Employees | 44%<br>(120) | 23%<br>(18) |
| Clerical Employees | 40%<br>(126) | 26%<br>(29) |
| Manufacturing and Production Employees | 46%<br>(114) | 29%<br>(63) |

Sample size is in parentheses

**Figure 13.2a.** Extent of employee involvement and participation initiatives by occupation and union status.

| Issue | Managers | Professional/<br>Technical<br>Employees<br>Union | Nonunion | Clerical<br>Employees<br>Union | Nonunion | Manufacturing/<br>Production<br>Employees<br>Union | Nonunion |
|---|---|---|---|---|---|---|---|
| Product Quality | 96%<br>(140) | 96%<br>(23) | 97%<br>(133) | 95%<br>(39) | 86%<br>(139) | 95%<br>(77) | 95%<br>(128) |
| Work Unit Performance | 93%<br>(137) | 95%<br>(22) | 92%<br>(132) | 90%<br>(40) | 83%<br>(144) | 89%<br>(73) | 92%<br>(126) |
| Work and Flow Speed | 82%<br>(127) | 64%<br>(22) | 85%<br>(123) | 79%<br>(39) | 80%<br>(136) | 82%<br>(74) | 90%<br>(124) |
| Introduction of New Technology | 86%<br>(133) | 70%<br>(23) | 86%<br>(127) | 67%<br>(39) | 69%<br>(132) | 77%<br>(71) | 79%<br>(120) |
| Safety and Health | 82%<br>(133) | 68%<br>(22) | 81%<br>(127) | 71%<br>(38) | 80%<br>(136) | 88%<br>(80) | 87%<br>(125) |
| Plant Layout | 80%<br>(121) | 73%<br>(22) | 72%<br>(119) | 74%<br>(38) | 70%<br>(133) | 69%<br>(65) | 70%<br>(113) |
| Supervision | 75%<br>(125) | 45%<br>(22) | 70%<br>(120) | 44%<br>(32) | 60%<br>(129) | 52%<br>(64) | 62%<br>(113) |

Sample size is in parentheses.

**Figure 13.2b.** Issues covered by employee involvement programs.

responsibility shall run from January 1 through December 31. During this period, the QP Officer shall plan quality or productivity improvement projects, lead the employee committee, and report to employees on committee activities. The QP Officer is expected to perform regular duties during the year. However, allowance will be made to workloads to allow for 10 to 25 percent of work activities to relate to quality and productivity improvement.

2. The employee committee shall consist of one volunteer individual from each department. Employee committee members serve for a six-month period and cannot serve for two consecutive six-month periods. Committee appointments are staggered to provide some continuity of members throughout the year. Committee members from even department numbers begin in January and July. Committee members from odd department numbers begin in April and October.

3. The employee committee shall meet once a month, normally on the first Thursday of the month. Meetings are expected to run one to two hours. Regular scheduled meetings occur on Company time and premises and on paid time for all participants.

4. The employee committee shall focus its efforts toward improving quality and productivity. Committee activities may include

   a) Reviewing quality problems and discussing ways to improve quality, reduce scrap, or prevent errors.

   b) Encouraging ideas on more productive or efficient ways of performing job tasks.

   c) Encouraging ways to improve coordination and cooperation between departments and workers within departments.

   d) Recommending ideas or ways to save money or control costs of production or administration.

5. All committee members participate as individuals and not as a representative of their department or work group. In the event an employee has a question on a matter not covered by the committee, he or she is encouraged to speak with a supervisor.

6. The QP Officer shall maintain a record of discussions and submit committee recommendations to management. All committee reports and recommendations are considered purely advisory. Management may consider, accept, or reject recommendations as deemed appropriate.

**Sample Employee Handbook**
**Paragraph**

*Employee Committee*

XYZ Company believes that employees have a lot of good ideas about how to make their jobs easier and more efficient. Our company has formed an employee committee to help come up with ideas and suggestions for improvement of quality and productivity. Employees are encouraged to participate in the committee. Speak with your supervisor for more information.

## Preventing Unions and Countering Organization Attempts

During the period of the 1890s through the 1920s, the United States emerged from a rural and craft-oriented society to a manufacturing and industrial power. This period of American history is referred to as the Industrial Revolution.

It was also a period of strife and hardship for the workers, women and children included, who toiled long hours under unsafe factory conditions. These labor abuses led to the formation of labor unions. The unions sought to organize workers, seeking better working conditions, higher wages, and more worker protections. The process of organizing workers sometimes led to violence. To minimize violence and promote a more favorable labor climate, Congress passed the National Labor Relations Act in 1935.

The NLRA listed five employer activities defined as unfair labor practices:

1. Interference with employee rights protected by Section 7, namely, self-organization and bargaining collectively through freely chosen representatives

2. Domination of labor organizations or contributing financial or other support to them

3. Discrimination on account of union affiliation

4. Retaliation for filing charges or giving testimony

5. Refusal to bargain collectively[5]

Employers only were prohibited from engaging in unfair practices under the original National Labor Relations Act. It was not until the Act was amended in 1947 that unions were placed under similar restraints.

Similar to the NLRA and its amendments, the Railway Labor Act defines labor/management issues for the nation's railways and airlines. Likewise, various state laws define similar requirements for state or municipal government employers and unions seeking to represent public sector employees.

While employer or union unfair labor practices can occur at any time, unfair labor practice charges are most likely to occur during union organizing drives. To avoid unfair labor practice charges, the employer must be aware of what types of conduct violate the law.

Since supervisors are the key link in relations with employees, policy guidance can aid supervisors in avoiding actions that would be judged an unfair labor practice. Further, for those organizations that wish to remain non-union, a carefully worded policy can help promote an employee relations climate and minimize the likelihood of union organizing.

Here are some important factors to help a firm maintain its nonunion status:

- *Make a management commitment*: It takes a conscious effort to avoid a union. A statement on management's feelings about unions in an employee handbook helps to let employees know where management stands on the issue. Second, the issuance of an employee handbook is a good tool to help prevent union organizing. Third, actions speak louder than words. When you issue an employee handbook, be sure to follow its policy guidelines consistently. Disregard for your own published policies may prompt union organizing activity.

- *Coach supervisors*: The supervisor is the most visible representative of management to the employee. The supervisor's actions reflect upon management and the company. For these reasons, it is important to coach supervisors on effective employee communications and union avoidance issues. A supervisor's judgment and consistency in rules enforcement can prevent union organizing drives. One union organizer candidly admitted that his organizing efforts were focused toward firms where employees did not get along with supervision. A supervisor's policy manual can help supervisors consistently administer policies, an important preventative step in union avoidance.

- *Practice proactive employee communications*: When open and positive communications exist between employees and management, there is little likelihood that a union organizing effort will succeed. When there is poor communication between employees and management, the union is seen by employees as the force that will make sure that rules are defined and employees are treated fairly. A company's equal employment opportunity policy, grievance procedure, or open door communications policy are important tools to guide supervisors in keeping communication lines open with employees.

- *Use "due process" on discipline and discharge*: One promise made by unions is a greater guarantee of job security. The unions then negotiate for seniority and "just cause" provisions in the labor agreement to protect their members from unwarranted discipline, layoff, or discharge. Careful definition of company policies in a management policy manual can guide supervisors on proper handling of discipline, layoffs, and discharge.

- *Limit union organizers' access to employees*: An employer has a reasonable business need to direct and control employee activity on the company premises during working time. Two policy issues which the employer can (and should) control are bulletin boards and solicitations. Carefully defined policies in a management policy manual and an employee handbook can help to limit the union organizer's access to employees. See policy issues on bulletin boards and solicitations in Chap. 15.

- *Offer competitive wages and benefits*: Keeping wages and benefits competitive with other firms in the area or industry is an important element in union avoidance. A union organizer will tell employees that the union can get the employer to pay higher wages. As a preventative measure, or in response to union claims, the company should periodically compare pay and benefits to surveys. See Chap. 4, "Competitive Practices."

- *Obtain professional advice*: A union organizing drive carries significant business and legal implications for the employer. From a business perspective, the unionization of employees can change or limit the way in which an employer interacts with employees. The likelihood of a strike can severely impact business operations, profitability, and competitive position. For these reasons, an employer experiencing hand billing or other union organization tactics should not "go it alone."

The union organizer is a professional. He or she makes a living stimulating employee interest in union membership. The employer, on the other hand, may deal with a union organizing drive once or twice in a lifetime. A business owner or manager can easily get emotionally involved in a fight for employee loyalty. Such an emotional reaction can easily blind sound judgment and lead to further problems. The union organizing process is enforced by the NLRB. Many NLRB cases go to trial, and as a result there is a large body of case precedent that affects the organizing process. An unwitting employer could create an unfair labor practice finding resulting in an NLRB bargaining order. In other words, the union could win the right to represent your employees without an election.

## Pitfalls to Avoid

Union avoidance requires a proactive approach to employee relations. However, union organizing is subject to specific NLRB regulations, rulings, and court decisions. Many employer actions in response to union organizing activity may result in a costly unfair labor practice charge. Here are some pitfalls to avoid:

1. In 10 years of writing employee handbooks for firms, I have noticed two types of reaction by managers to the union avoidance issue. Managers' reactions may be summarized in this way:

   - "Out of sight, out of mind." These managers believe that any mention of the word *union* in an employee handbook will plant the idea in employees' heads. These managers insist that there be no mention of unions in their employee handbook.

**CHECKLIST**
**A Union Avoidance Policy**

- What state or federal laws affect union organizing and the collective bargaining process?

- Is company management willing to commit policy issues to writing?

- Is the company ready to define and enforce a no-solicitation rule?

- Has the company posted a no-solicitation sign on its premises?

- Is the company ready to set up and follow uniform guidelines on discipline and discharge?

- Is the company ready to set up and follow grievance or complaint procedures?

- What guidelines will be followed to prevent the likelihood of an unfair labor practice charge?

- In the event of a strike or work stoppage, does the firm have a plan for supervisors or managers to fill in to perform necessary tasks?

- In the event of an economic strike, has the Human Resource Department defined guidelines for recruiting replacements for strikers?

- Has management identified a qualified professional for advice in the event of a union organizing drive?

- "The best defense is a good offense." This philosophy states that management can best defend itself against a union organizing drive by asserting that there is no need for a union. By taking the offensive to tell employees about the company's concern for good individual communication and actively working to resolve complaints, the company also provides its best defense against a union organizing drive.

  My recommendation is this: Tell employees in a positive way that the company will actively work to resolve complaints and that there is no need for a union.

2. In the event of union organizing activity, management can and should undertake its own campaign to communicate to employees that there is no need for a union. Under the direction of an experienced labor relations professional, there are a number of things that supervisors may say and do. One source of information on countering a union organizational drive is contained in the book *Winning NLRB Elections* by the law firm of Jackson, Lewis, Schnitzler and Krupman. The authors suggest that a supervisor may:

- Tell employees that he and the company are opposed to unionization;
- Tell employees that they do not have to sign union cards and that the law says that they have an absolute right to refrain from supporting a union;
- Tell employees that they do not have to speak to union organizers or admit them into their homes if they do not desire to do so;
- Tell employees of the benefits they currently enjoy and compare these benefits with those in unionized companies;
- Tell employees that the union was not needed to get a wage increase at the time the company's usual increase was granted, and that the employer's policies with respect to wage increases will be continued;
- Tell employees that with a union they may have to take their problems to a shop steward instead of dealing directly with the supervisor;
- Tell employees of the economic disadvantages of belonging to a union, such as the payment of dues and initiation fees and the possibility of fines and assessments;
- Tell employees about the union's strikes at other companies and discuss the possibility of a strike at their company (The supervisor may not, however, state that a strike is inevitable in the event of unionization.);
- Tell employees that, if they engage in an economic strike, they may be permanently replaced and would be reinstated only when and if an opening occurs;
- Tell employees that they may be required to picket their employer, even when they are not on strike, or face union disciplinary action;
- Tell employees that a union can always out-promise an employer, but can guarantee nothing (The supervisor should nonetheless avoid characterizing the bargaining process as futile or emphasizing that employees would have nothing to gain through unionization. Rather, emphasis should be placed on the fact that negotiations are unpredictable and could leave the employees worse off.);
- Tell employees (after careful verification of the facts) about any arrest records, indictments, or convictions of union officials; and
- Urge employees to vote against the union and suggest that they encourage others to do the same.6

3. There are a number of actions which have been judged as unfair labor practices. In *Winning NLRB Elections*, the authors suggest that the supervisor should be instructed not to:

- Promise employees pay increases, promotions, improved working conditions, additional benefits, or special favors on condition that the employees refuse to join the union or vote against it;

- Threaten employees with loss of job or reduction in wages, or use threatening or intimidating language calculated to influence an employee in the exercise of his or her right to support a union;

- Tell employees they would have received a wage increase but for the start of the union campaign;

- Tell employees that there will be a strike if the union wins the election;

- Tell employees that if the union wins the company will close or move away;

- Discriminate against an employee who is taking part in union activities by separating him or her from other employees;

- Discipline an employee for soliciting another employee to sign an authorization card when both are on non-working time;

- Engage in surveillance of employees receiving union handbills or attending union meetings, or give the impression that employee union activities are being watched;

- Question employees about their union activities, internal union affairs, union meetings, or ask an employee whether he or she has signed a union card;

- Ask employees their personal opinions about the union or the feelings of other employees; or

- Visit employees at their homes on a systematic basis to urge them to vote against the union.[7]

**Sample Policy**

**XYZ COMPANY**
**PERSONNEL POLICY & PROCEDURE**

SUBJECT: UNION AVOIDANCE                              DATE: May 1, 1993

*Policy*: It is the policy of XYZ Company to recognize employee rights under law to organize and bargain collectively and to maintain a positive employee relations climate which eliminates the need for a union in the employment relationship.

*Procedure*:
1. Each Supervisor and Manager is responsible for actively maintaining open, friendly and positive communications with subordinates. Communications activities include orientation of new employees, training employees on job skills, instructing employees on work procedures, coaching for improved performance, appraising performance, and

     actively providing information about company products, policies, and benefits.

2. Each Supervisor and Manager is responsible for participating in departmental meetings, safety committees, quality circles, and other similar group process activities.

3. Each Supervisor and Manager is responsible for administering company policies and procedures in accordance with the guidelines of this policy manual. In the event of questions or unusual circumstances not covered by the policy manual, the supervisor or manager is encouraged to contact the Human Resource Administrator.

4. The Human Resource Administrator is responsible for advising management on employee relations issues, personnel policy issues, and benefits issues. The Human Resource Administrator shall assist in developing employee communications messages and disseminating information to employees. Communication methods may include memos, letters, bulletin board postings, payroll stuffers, employee meetings, and other methods deemed appropriate by management.

5. Each Supervisor and Manager shall commit a high priority to resolving employee complaints and grievances. The Human Resource Administrator shall be available to advise supervisors and assist employees to achieve a solution which is in the best interest of the employee and the company.

6. In the event that, during the normal course of daily activity, Supervisors or Managers observe evidence of union organizing activity, they should take the following actions:

   a) Avoid any form of interference, spying, interrogation, retaliation, threats, or other forms of discrimination against employees.

   b) Provide to the Human Resource Administrator any sample union notices, handbills, and authorization cards found on the premises or freely received from an employee or union representative.

   c) Continue to operate departmental activities normally, including administration of policies and enforcement of established rules.

   d) In the event of a need to discipline or discharge an employee for violation of a rule or policy, confer with the Human Resource Administrator to ensure that the corrective action is consistent with policy.

## Sample Employee Handbook Paragraph

*Our Feelings about Unions*

We believe that our union-free status is one reason why our company has continued to grow and serve our customers in a profitable and efficient manner. Union membership is not a job requirement at our company. Our company operates with an open management style where each employee has the right to deal directly with supervisors or management to discuss ideas, suggestions, or concerns.

We recognize your right to join or not to join—to belong or not to belong—to any social, political, labor, or religious organization as you see fit. We believe, however, that a union is unnecessary because no union, despite any promises, can create jobs or increase a Company's income so that higher wages may be paid.

## Union Agreements

Approximately 18 percent of employees are covered by union agreements. The union agreement is a contract negotiated between the union and the employer. The contract defines the employer/employee relationship for covered employees. Covered employees are individuals in designated job categories referred to as a bargaining unit.

Among the issues covered in a union agreement are recognition issues such as pay, benefits, hours, and other conditions of employment. The recognition issues usually include recognition of the union as the exclusive bargaining agent, definition of jobs in the bargaining unit, checkoff of union dues collected by the employer, and a union security provision.

The most common forms of union security provisions are closed shop, union shop, and agency shop. In a closed shop arrangement, all applicants to the employer must be union members. When a closed shop agreement exists, the union normally operates a hiring hall, referring its members for job openings with employers covered by the agreement. The closed shop agreement is permitted in the construction trades only.

A union shop agreement requires the employee to obtain union membership within a specified time period as a condition of continued employment. In many union contracts, the employee is required to join the union within 30 days of the start of employment.

A third form of union security agreement is called an agency shop. With an agency shop agreement, the employee is not required to join the union; however, he or she must pay the prescribed initiation fee and dues.

One section of the NLRA states that employees shall not be required to join a union as a condition of employment in any state or territory in which such a requirement is prohibited by law. This section of the law applies to so-called right-to-work laws. These are the 22 states with such laws:

| | |
|---|---|
| Alabama | Nevada |
| Arizona | New York |
| Arkansas | North Carolina |
| Florida | North Dakota |

| Georgia | South Carolina |
|---------|----------------|
| Idaho | South Dakota |
| Iowa | Tennessee |
| Kansas | Texas |
| Louisiana | Utah |
| Mississippi | Virginia |
| Nebraska | Wyoming[8] |

Pay and benefits issues are usually included in a union agreement. Contracts normally specify job titles, pay rates, and pay increases negotiated for the contract term. Some union agreements include provisions for cost of living allowances. Union-negotiated benefits often include paid holidays, paid vacation, paid funeral leave, jury service pay, pension, and health and welfare plans providing medical, life, and disability insurance protection.

In the hours and working conditions categories, unions generally negotiate overtime pay criteria, working hours or schedules, and a grievance procedure protection requiring seniority-based layoffs and just cause requirements for discharge.

In its negotiations, management seeks to retain maximum flexibility to efficiently direct work activities with a broad management rights clause. The management rights clause reserves for management discretion all issues not specifically defined or limited by the labor agreement. This can include the right to plan and organize work, determine production processes, acquire and maintain equipment and facilities, set staffing and skill requirements, and establish reasonable controls for efficient operation of the business.

Other negotiating goals for management include a no-strike clause, and minimizing wage or benefit increases to maintain a competitive and profitable financial position. Union agreements generally include a provision for any grievance or contract interpretation disputes to be submitted to binding arbitration.

The union agreement serves as a policy and benefit guide for dealing with union employees. A supervisor of union employees needs to be familiar with the contract. When questions occur on job, pay, or benefits issues, the supervisor should refer to the contract. In the event of a disagreement about contract interpretation, the Human Resource Administrator or Labor Relations Specialist who negotiated the labor agreement should be called for advice.

Another challenge to the supervisor in a union environment is working with the union steward. The steward is a company employee in the bargaining unit who is usually elected by fellow employees. The steward is the union's on-site spokesperson. He or she participates in disciplinary discussions, speaks out to ensure that the employees' contract rights are not violated, files grievances on behalf of employees, and serves as a communication link between employees, union, and company. The steward is often an outspoken advocate of unions, with leadership traits that rival those of supervisors and managers. The steward sees his or her job as making sure that management follows the labor agreement to the letter. The union steward is permitted by the contract to devote a reasonable period on company time for the performance of union duties and adjusting grievances. The steward's role is protected by the labor agreement, NLRB rules, and case decisions.

Many organizations try to resolve contract disputes through informal discussions between management and union representatives. Such informal discussions promote better labor-management cooperation and are less costly than grievance processing and arbitration.

## Pitfalls to Avoid

Improper handling of an employment issue affecting a union employee can result in time-consuming grievances, costly arbitration hearings, or devastating strikes. Here are some pitfalls to avoid:

1. Caution supervisors of union employees to be sure that their employment decisions are consistent with the union agreement. The supervisor should have handy a copy of the union agreement or reasonable access to one when dealing with issues covered in the agreement. In the event of any uncertainty on contract interpretation, encourage the supervisor to confer with the Human Resource Administrator or Labor Relations Specialist who is familiar with the labor agreement.

2. Be sure to carefully document employment decisions. Decisions that are based on misconduct or job performance issues in particular may be subject to a grievance filed by the employee. Often, the union asserts the grievance procedure to show employees that "we're fighting for you." A supervisor's effective documentation of disciplinary warnings or poor performance ratings can help justify management's action and settle the grievance. In the event that a dispute goes to arbitration, careful records by the supervisor will be a substantial aid in presenting the employer's case.

3. Avoid union disputes by keeping the union informed about policy, pay, or benefits issues that may affect the contract. Many Human Resource Administrators or Labor Relations Specialists have been effective in developing a rapport with the union business agent. Often, a potentially sensitive issue can be resolved through a phone call or two to keep the union informed of company plans. For example, an Operations Manager of a Packaging Products Company in New York notified the local

## CHECKLIST
### A Union Agreement Policy

- Are there any state or federal laws that affect the collective bargaining process?

- Does the firm have a collective bargaining agreement with one or more unions covering specified employee groups?

- Who is responsible for contract negotiations with the union (i.e., Line Manager, staff Human Resource Administrator, or a retained Labor Relations Specialist)?

- Who will receive copies of the labor agreement?

- Will bargaining unit employees be required to sign a union membership application or dues checkoff for deduction of dues payments from wages?

- Will a separate bulletin board be installed or space made available on bulletin boards for union information?

- Will supervisors receive training or instruction on labor agreement provisions and contract administration issues?

- Will supervisors be required to document disciplinary warnings or performance ratings?

- Will supervisors include the union steward in discussions with an employee when dealing with discipline, misconduct, or performance issues?

- What role will supervisors play in grievance handling?

union representative of company plans to prepare job descriptions and grant extra pay increases based on employee performance, providing an incentive for improved performance. The union's reply was "OK, as long as all employees continue to receive the base pay rates defined in the contract."

When starting any employee involvement initiatives for quality, productivity improvement, or safety, be sure to keep the union informed. Take care when establishing employee action committees to ensure that the committees are not seen as a way to exclude the union from its employee representation role.

4. When writing an employee handbook for union employees, two important points should be kept in mind: union recognition and possible contract bargaining issues. One paragraph or section of the handbook should acknowledge the union by name, recognize that the firm has a collective bargaining agreement with the union, and assert that the handbook provisions are drawn from the management rights clause and that the handbook does not alter or change the union agreement.

Second, some firms provide certain benefits for non-union employees that are not provided to union workers. (Remember, it is customary that the union negotiate for specific benefits for its members.) As an example, a firm may grant paid sick days to nonunion employees, a benefit which was not negotiated by the union for its members.

Avoid putting benefits provided exclusively to nonunion employees in the employee handbook. Such benefits could easily end up as new demands by the union at negotiating time.

**Sample Policy**

**XYZ COMPANY**
**PERSONNEL POLICY & PROCEDURE**

SUBJECT: UNION AGREEMENT                              DATE: May 1, 1993

*Policy*: It is the policy of XYZ Company to maintain a positive labor relations climate through careful administration of the union agreement.

*Procedure*:

1. The Company negotiating team consists of the Operations Vice President, Operations Manager, and Human Resource Administrator. The Chief Financial Officer is responsible for supporting union negotiations by preparing and evaluating financial data on wages and benefits. Contract provisions are subject to review and approval by the Company President.

2. Upon completion of union negotiations, the Human Resource Administrator is responsible for conducting an orientation for supervisory personnel on contract provisions and changes. At this time, supervisors shall be provided contract copies.

3. The Human Resource Administrator is responsible for explaining union membership issues, dues, and initiation fees when orientating new employees for bargaining unit jobs. At this time, the employee shall sign the union application and dues checkoff form authorizing payroll deduction. Also see Orientation Policy.

4. Each supervisor of bargaining unit employees is responsible for becoming familiar with the labor agreement. All employment decisions on matters covered by the labor agreement shall be made in accordance with the labor agreement. In the event a supervisor has a question about interpretation of a contract provision, he or she should confer with his or her superior or the Human Resource Administrator.

5. In the event that a supervisor must deal with a union employee on a disciplinary or job performance matter, such discussions shall be conducted with the union steward or other union representative present. All disciplinary warnings shall be documented on the firm's warning notice form. Also see Disciplinary Warning Policy. All performance

discussions shall be documented on the firm's performance appraisal form. Also see Performance Appraisal Policy.

6. In the event that company management is considering new issues or changes affecting pay, benefits, hours, working conditions, or other employment issues, the Operations Manager is responsible for communicating pending issues to the union representative.

## Sample Employee Handbook Paragraphs

### Union Agreements

The company has recognized a union as the collective bargaining agent for certain production and warehouse employees. A collective bargaining agreement is negotiated periodically with the union to define employment practices, wages, and benefits for union employees. Production and warehouse employees are required to join the union within 45 days of employment.

Details on Company benefits, pay practices, and certain employment procedures are described in the union agreement. When a question arises regarding issues covered in the union agreement or other union matters, you are encouraged to speak with the union steward.

This handbook is prepared pursuant to the management's rights clause of the union contract, and no information in this handbook shall be construed as altering the union agreement.

### Probationary Period

Employees hired for production or maintenance positions covered by the labor contract between the company and the union are required to join the union after 31 days of employment. Membership for this purpose means that you must pay or be willing to pay union dues and the initiation fee.

During the first 31 calendar days of employment, all employees are in a probationary period. This probationary period is intended to enable the company to carefully evaluate the employee's suitability for the job. Be sure to speak with your supervisor right away if you have any questions about job responsibilities. An employee's failure to perform adequately, failure to respond to corrective job instructions, business conditions resulting in lack of work, or any other reason deemed sufficient by management can result in discharge.

The employee is not entitled to use grievance procedures or other contract provisions until successfully completing the probationary period.

## Grievance and Complaint Policy

A Grievance and Complaint Policy is intended to provide an orderly method to address and resolve employees' grievances. A grievance is an employee's formal statement of dissatisfaction with an employment policy, practice, condition, or supervisor's decision. Unions typically negotiate a grievance procedure into the labor agreement. Many organizations, particularly large firms, say that a grievance procedure is an effective management tool.

With a grievance policy, an organization provides an outlet for employee complaints and has a systematic way to resolve the matter. By solving the matter, the Grievance Policy reduces the likelihood that an employee will seek a legal claim against the company.

A Grievance Policy can help prevent discrimination claims, formal sexual harassment charges, or even wrongful discharge lawsuits. Considering the costs of defending these kinds of charges, a grievance procedure will surely pay for itself in its first year of operation.

A grievance is generally initiated by an employee. The employee may be unhappy with an employment decision. Usually, the first step is to discuss the problem with one's supervisor. If the supervisor is unable to resolve the matter, the employee then puts the grievance in writing to the Department Manager. If the Department Manager is unable to resolve the grievance, it is then forwarded to a Human Resource Manager. Human Resources, if unable to settle the matter to the employee's satisfaction, then refers the matter to top management for a final determination.

In a grievance process, the employee is the "moving party" or individual who initiates the grievance at each step. In addition, the Grievance Policy contains time limits by which the employee must present the grievance at each step and response deadlines for management. These time deadlines assure that the grievance will be resolved on a timely basis.

In a union environment, the employee speaks to the union steward. The steward and employee then discuss the matter with the supervisor. If the grievance is not solved at the verbal level, the steward helps the employee put the grievance in writing to the Department Manager. At the next level, the grievance goes to the Human Resource Manager, but at this level, the local union business agent presents the matter on behalf of the union and the employee. If the parties aren't able to resolve the matter at the third level, it goes to top management. The local business agent or an official from the union's national office press for resolution of the issue. Depending on contract language, the next step may be arbitration or strike. The chart in Table 13.1 compares grievance procedure steps between typical union and nonunion grievance policies.

## Pitfalls to Avoid

Grievances must be processed in a fair and timely manner or the grievance process will be a cause of work disruption rather than a cure.

**CHECKLIST**
**A Grievance Policy**

- Is there a union agreement which defines grievance procedure requirements?
- How many levels of management or steps will the grievance progress through from beginning until final decision?
- Must the grievance be presented verbally or in a written format?
- Will there be a grievance form to be filled out by the employee?
- Will there be time limits for the employee to file the grievance at each level?
- Will there be any assistance (i.e., union steward or ombudsman) provided to the employee in preparing or presenting the grievance?
- Will there be provision for independent arbitration of an issue that is not resolved to the satisfaction of the employee or the organization?

1. Follow your published policy of allowing and considering grievances before making a discharge final. If an employee is entitled to file a grievance for a contested employment decision, then the employee's grievance over a discharge should receive full and careful consideration. Any policy defining a predischarge procedure such as allowing a grievance or hearing should be followed to the letter to minimize a wrongful discharge lawsuit or reinstatement order by an arbitrator.

**Table 13.1.** Comparison of Union and Nonunion Grievance Procedures

| Non-Union | Union |
| --- | --- |
| *Step 1*: Employee discusses grievance with supervisor | *Step 1*: Employee discusses grievance with steward |
| *Step 2*: Employee writes grievance and presents to Manager | *Step 2*: Steward assists in writing grievance and in presentation to Manager |
| *Step 3*: Employee presents written grievance to human resources | *Step 3*: Local Union rep presents written grievance to human resources |
| *Step 4*: Employee presents written grievance to top executive (or to a grievance hearing in the public sector) for a final decision | *Step 4*: Local or national union rep presents written grievance to top executive |
| | *Step 5*: Final alternatives may include grievance committee, arbitration, or strike |

2. Avoid a "whitewash" grievance process that upholds incorrect employment decisions. If the discussion and investigation of issues reveals that a policy or contract provision was incorrectly handled, resolve the grievance by correcting the problem. Fair and consistent administration of policies or union contract provisions will promote better supervisor-employee relations in the long run.

**Sample Policy**

**XYZ COMPANY**
**PERSONNEL POLICY & PROCEDURE**

---

SUBJECT: GRIEVANCE PROCEDURE                    DATE: May 1, 1993

*Policy*: It is the policy of XYZ Company to try to resolve employee grievances and complaints to promote a harmonious working environment.

*Procedure*:

1. Each employee is encouraged to speak to his or her supervisor whenever questions or concerns on job matters arise.

2. Each Supervisor or Manager is responsible for administering the XYZ Grievance Procedure by being accessible to employees to answer questions and resolve work problems.

3. In the event an employee has a specific complaint or grievance, the employee may file a grievance under the guidelines of this policy. An employee may file a grievance to seek redress of any job-related issue. Examples of issues which may be resolved under the grievance procedure include:
   Employment discrimination in any form
   Sexual harassment or other forms of harassment
   Disciplinary suspension
   Discharge
   Disagreement with policy interpretation
   Disagreement with an employment decision
   Or other similar issues

4. In the first step of the grievance procedure, the employee should discuss the matter with his or her immediate supervisor. The supervisor is responsible for carefully considering the employee's grievance and for responding within two workdays. The supervisor shall try to resolve the matter at the first-step level if at all possible by consistently applying relevant policy guidelines. If the matter is not resolved to the employee's satisfaction, he or she may advance the matter to the second step within five workdays.

5. In the second step of the grievance procedure, the employee shall submit a written summary of the grievance to the Department Manager. The Department Manager is responsible for carefully considering the employee's grievance and for responding within five workdays.

The Department Manager shall try to resolve the matter at the first-step level if at all possible by consistently applying relevant policy guidelines. If the matter is not resolved to the employee's satisfaction, he or she may advance the matter to the third step within five workdays.

6. In the third step of the grievance procedure, the employee shall submit a written summary of the grievance to the Human Resource Manager. The Human Resource Manager shall evaluate the employee's grievance, relevant policy guidelines, past practice, and other relevant factors. A decision shall be rendered and communicated to the employee within five working days. If the matter is not resolved to the employee's satisfaction, he or she may request that the matter be presented to the General Manager for a final decision.

7. In the fourth step, the General Manager shall evaluate the grievance, consider relevant facts, interview the employee if deemed appropriate, and then exercise discretion to resolve the matter in the best interest of the employee and the company. The General Manager's decision is final.

## Sample Employee Handbook Paragraph

*Grievance Procedure*

XYZ Company believes that it is important to resolve employee complaints and grievances to promote a harmonious working environment. Our grievance procedure is designed to resolve job problems such as discrimination, sexual harassment, or disagreement on any employment decision, disciplinary action, or discharge. Our grievance procedure works like this:

*Step 1*: Speak to your supervisor. He or she will try to resolve the matter according to company policy guidelines.

*Step 2*: Submit a written grievance to the Department Manager. He or she will try to resolve the matter according to company policy guidelines.

*Step 3*: Submit a written grievance to the Human Resource Administrator. He or she will try to resolve the matter according to company policy guidelines.

*Step 4*: If the grievance hasn't been resolved to the employee's satisfaction, the matter will be considered by the General Manager. The General Manager's decision shall be final.

## Sample Form

### EMPLOYEE GRIEVANCE

Employee _____ Dept _____ Date ____

Date of incident giving rise to grievance _____

*Sample Form (Continued)*

Describe issue or event giving rise to grievance _____

_____

_____

Describe action sought _____

_____

_____

_____

Management Action:

Approved

*Step 1*: Date of verbal discussion _____ Declined

Approved

*Step 2*: Date grievance received _____ Declined

Comment _____ Mgr Initial _____

Approved

*Step 3*: Date grievance received _____ Declined

Comment _____ Mgr Initial _____

Approved

*Step 4*: Date grievance received _____ Declined

Comment _____ Mgr Initial _____

## Notes

1. *Human Resource Policies and Practices in American Firms*, BLMR 137, U.S. Dept. of Labor, 1989, p. 59.
2. National Labor Relations Act. 49 Stat. 450, 29 U.S. Code 152 (5).
3. National Labor Relations Act. 49 Stat. 452, 29 U.S. Code 158 (2).
4. *Human Resource Policies and Practices in American Firms*, BLMR 137, U.S. Dept. of Labor, 1989, p. 61.

5. National Labor Relations Act. 49 Stat. 452, 29 U.S. Code 158 (1), (2), (3), (4), (5).
6. Jackson, Lewis, Schnitzler & Krupman, *Winning NLRB Elections: Management's Strategy and Preventative Programs*, 3rd ed., Executive Enterprises Publication Co., Inc., New York, N.Y., 1991, pp. 60–61.
7. Ibid., pp. 67, 68.

# 14

# Controlling Use of Telephones, Protecting Confidentiality, Setting Dress Codes, and Handling Related Administrative Issues

**Read Chapter 14 for:**

Telephone use
Dress codes
Confidentiality
Relocation
Secondary employment
Use of vehicles
Ethical business practices

## Telephone Use

The telephone plays a major role in business communications. It is used for communication between employees and the organization. The telephone is also a vital tool for contact with customers, vendors, suppliers, job seekers, and others outside the organization.

For many employees, much of their workday is spent talking on the telephone. In some businesses, disruption of telephone service results in a complete cessation of business activities. A 1989 fire in a telephone switching station, for example, disrupted telephone service in Chicago's western suburbs, causing millions of dollars of business losses.

There are three common policy concerns about employee telephone use: pleasant telephone manners, use of proper telephone procedures, and controlling abuse of telephones.

*Pleasant telephone manners*: Every telephone contact with a customer, vendor, supplier, job applicant, or the general public conveys an image of the organization. Employees trained in effective telephone techniques present a positive company image to the caller. Prompt answering of telephones, a pleasant voice, together with identification of employee, Company, and department are important elements of pleasant telephone manners. Lack of professionalism on the telephone and discourteous treatment of callers will harm the Company image and turn customers away.

*Proper telephone procedures*: Among the most frustrating experiences for a caller is to have his or her phone call transferred, misdirected, or "cut off." These telephone problems are often the result of an employee's lack of knowledge about proper telephone procedures. One reason for improper telephone procedures is that today's telephone systems are more complex, with many service features. Another reason is poor orientation and training of new employees.

*Telephone abuse*: One of the biggest complaints that managers have is, "How can I control excessive personal telephone calls by my employees?" Another form of employee telephone abuse is unauthorized use of Company telephones for long-distance personal calls. While many firms try to take a flexible approach to employees' personal use of telephones, managers find that occasional abuses occur, prompting the need for policy guidelines.

A three-phase approach is recommended to improve telephone professionalism and control common abuses. First, take care to include telephone training in new employee orientation. Periodic retraining also is recommended for employees who frequently use the telephone on the job. Telephone training should cover telephone system features and use. Be sure that employees are familiar with proper telephone techniques to transfer, hold, forward, and conference telephone calls, along other similar procedures. Also, orientation should cover telephone etiquette and instructions on the proper salutation when answering the phone.

The second recommended approach for effective telephone use is to periodically evaluate the telephone system. Determine whether equipment and service options meet your needs. Consider adding control features as needed to deal with telephone abuses. For example, call accounting features can track phone usage. Certain phones can be programmed for local calls only to minimize unauthorized long-distance calls. In addition, pay telephones can be installed on the premises for use by employees for personal calls.

Finally, employers need to define reasonable guidelines on telephone use. Unless told otherwise, employees will assume that personal calls are permissible. If personal calls are permissible, what limits are reasonable for timing or frequency of calls? These and similar issues are identified in the Telephone Use policy checklist that follows.

**Pitfalls to Avoid**

A policy on telephone use needs to promote professionalism on the telephone and to control abuses without seeming petty. Here are some pitfalls to avoid.

1. Avoid pettiness by finding the proper "rule of reason" for telephone use in your organization. Most managers recognize that an occasional personal call is reasonable. Unfortunately, some individuals seem to spend more time on the phone than others. Is one call home per day allowable? Are two calls daily allowable or excessive? Most organizations are reluctant to quantify this issue. Several telephone use guidelines are offered:

   a. Limit outgoing personal calls to nonworking time such as lunch and breaks.

   b. Limit incoming personal calls to employees, particularly those in public contact jobs.

   c. Route incoming personal calls to voice mail, message center, or supervisor.

   d. Do not allow employees in production, service, or public contact jobs to be interrupted from work tasks by personal phone calls.

   e. Limit outgoing calls to a pay telephone in the plant or work area.

2. Focus on job performance issues when dealing with telephone abuse. Avoid getting caught up in an individual's personal family difficulties. Instead, policy guidelines should instruct the supervisor to address the employee's job performance through performance ratings or warnings. If personal problems persist, refer the employee for help through an employee assistance program or other similar services.

**CHECKLIST**
**A Telephone Use Policy**

- Which jobs will require use of a telephone on the job? Which jobs will not?
- Which supervisor, manager, or staff specialist is responsible for phone system administration and training?
- How will new employees be instructed on telephone system features and desired salutation when answering the telephones?
- Will there be any guidelines or control procedures on long-distance telephone calls?
- Will there be any instructions or limits on personal telephone calls?
- Will a pay telephone be provided in those areas where employees do not have regular access to a telephone on the job?
- What measures will be taken to screen or control excessive incoming personal telephone calls?
- Will telephone use and etiquette be included in new employee orientation?
- Will there be specified time periods for personal telephone calls, such as lunch breaks or other nonworking times?
- Will employees be instructed to advise family or friends not to call unless there is an emergency?
- Will there be a procedure to take messages, which are routed to employees who cannot be disturbed during meetings or while operating certain equipment?

**Sample Policy**

**XYZ COMPANY**
**PERSONNEL POLICY & PROCEDURE**

SUBJECT: TELEPHONE USE                                    DATE: May 1, 1993

*Policy*: It is the policy of XYZ Company to train employees in proper telephone procedures.

*Procedure*:
  1. The Administrative Manager is responsible for telephone system management. Responsibilities include
     a) ordering and coordinating telephone installation
     b) coordinating system repair
     c) supervising training of employees
     d) maintaining current telephone directory to be updated at the start of each year

2. The Administrative Manager and Department Manager jointly determine when and where telephones are installed. The following general guide is provided for telephone assignment:

   a) Supervisor, management, professional staff, and secretary receive full-service telephones with voice mail features.

   b) Clerical and service personnel receive local service telephones.

   c) Warehouse and other employees without customer contact responsibilities do not receive telephones.

3. The Administrative Manager shall train new supervisors and managers on telephone system features, telephone procedures, and telephone etiquette.

4. Each supervisor and manager is responsible for training newly hired employees on telephone system features, telephone procedures, telephone etiquette, and the guidelines defined in this policy.

5. The following telephone use guidelines are provided:

   a) Individuals with telephone voice mail are responsible for checking their messages at least twice daily.

   b) Employees are expected to answer the telephone by the second ring.

   c) The proper telephone salutation is "(department name) (your name) speaking, may I help you?"

   d) Avoid repeated transfers of the caller, and refer to the telephone directory when making a transfer. Stay on the line with the caller until you are sure that the caller is speaking with the proper XYZ employee to provide assistance.

   e) Notify a fellow employee or your supervisor when leaving the work area so that your calls will be properly handled.

6. The supervisor or manager is responsible for notifying switchboard personnel of absences, vacations, promotions, or other job changes which affect the routing of telephone calls.

7. Personal telephone calls must be kept to a minimum. The following guidelines are provided:

   a) Outgoing personal calls must be made during nonworking time periods.

   b) Incoming personal calls are routed to employees with phones and to the supervisor of an employee without a telephone. It is our practice not to interrupt an employee's job activity with personal calls except in an extreme emergency. The supervisor shall take a message and give it to the employee.

   c) Personal long-distance telephone calls are not permitted unless approved by the Department Manager.

   d) In the event the supervisor observes that an employee is receiving or making an excessive number or long personal phone calls, the supervisor shall remind the employee to handle personal matters on nonworking time.

   e) Abuse of telephone privileges shall be reflected in disciplinary warnings and performance ratings.

**Sample Employee Handbook
Paragraph**

*Telephone Use*

A large portion of our business is conducted through telephone contacts with our customers and suppliers. Pleasant telephone manners are important because with each telephone call placed or received, we project an image of our company to customers and the public. Always answer the telephone promptly and pleasantly.

In order to keep Company telephone lines open for business calls, personal calls are to be kept to a minimum and limited to nonworking periods. The use of Company phones for long-distance personal calls is not permitted unless you have management approval. Additional telephone instructions will be provided by your supervisor.

# Dress Codes

Dress codes are a matter of concern in many organizations. Company management usually defines a dress code to present a particular image to customers and the public. Some organizations provide or require employees to procure certain work garments or uniforms. Dress codes or specified work garments help to achieve several objectives:

- *Identification of individuals as employees of the firm*: Common examples include airline workers, police officers, parcel delivery personnel, pest control technicians, and fast food counter workers.

- *Identification of department or work function*: Common examples might include distinctive garments for doctors, nurses, technicians, and orderlies. Another example could be color coded shirts or hard hats to distinguish supervisors, quality inspectors, and workers in production or construction industries.

- *Safety and accident prevention*: Certain work environments necessitate the wearing of appropriate work apparel to help prevent injury. Employers often require production employees to wear long-sleeved shirts for arm protection. Lab workers often wear a three-quarter-length lab coat for protection against splashes or spills. Further details on safety issues are covered in Chap. 15.

- *Public image*: For many organizations with employees who have public contact, public image is a significant concern. Banks, retail stores, law firms, accounting firms, and other professional service organizations want their employees to convey a clean, neat professional appearance. Management's feeling is that a professional image of employees builds customer confidence and is good for business.

- *Prevention of distractions*: Individuals have a wide variety of preferences in the selection of clothing. In some organizations, dress codes have been defined as a result of outlandish garments worn by some which caused distraction to others. For this reason, dress codes sometimes include prohibitions against the wearing of casual garments such as short-shorts, halter tops, tank tops, imprinted T shirts, fishnet T shirts, jeans, etc.

Fair employment practice laws generally apply to all terms and conditions of employment. Because of this, the policy writer must exercise care when defining a dress code policy. Dress code policies have come under fire through employment discrimination charges. A common challenge to a dress code can arise when a policy applies different dress standards for men and women, resulting in a sex discrimination charge. Likewise, if a dress code policy prohibits garments that are unique to a particular race, ethnic group, or religion, the policy would be grounds for a discrimination finding.

A Dress Code Policy should recognize the employer's obligations to make a reasonable accommodation in the event of an individual's religious beliefs or physical or mental disability. However, the employer may refuse to accommodate the dress or grooming requirements of an employee based on the individual's religion only when justified by undue hardship or business necessity such as safety hazards to the employee or others.

## Pitfalls to Avoid

Dress code policies can create a clash between individual preferences and corporate cultures. Here are some pitfalls to avoid:

1. Carefully evaluate and reread your dress code policy to guard against the likelihood of a discrimination charge. Check to eliminate guidelines that apply different standards to men and women, adversely affect minorities, or fail to allow for accommodation of religious beliefs.

2. Avoid misunderstandings by using precise terminology to define dress or grooming guidelines. A policy statement stating that employees must wear "conservative business attire" in the office is a very broad statement subject to many interpretations. A listing of examples of allowable garments and styles can help supervisors to understand and enforce the policy.

   Another alternative with a dress code is to list styles or garments that are prohibited. In many offices, prohibited wear includes athletic garments, jeans, shorts, or T shirts. The list of "don'ts" tends to grow as employees experiment with different styles.

   One garment category, jeans, probably has been the topic of countless hours of management discussion on dress codes. The traditional view of many managers is that jeans are not proper office attire. But jeans, a denim pant, come in many colors and styles. Does your policy against jeans also prohibit white or beige denim garments? Does it prohibit dresses, vests, or men's or women's sport coats tailored from

**CHECKLIST**
**A Dress Code Policy**

- Is there a state or federal law which affects the dress code policy?

- Will there be a requirement to make a reasonable accommodation for an employee because of religious beliefs or physical or mental disability?

- Will the firm require use of specified work garments or uniforms?

- What class or category of employees are covered by the Dress Code Policy?

- Will dress code guidelines be included in new employee orientation materials?

- Will the cost of uniforms (and laundry service) be paid by the company, the employee, or both?

- Will there be defined time periods when work garments or uniforms must be worn or when they may not be worn?

- Will there be a definition or guideline describing which kinds of garments should be worn?

- Will there be a definition or guideline describing which kinds of garments may not be worn?

- Who is responsible for enforcing the dress code?

- What actions will be taken to enforce the policy?

- What provisions will be made for the return of work garments or uniforms at separation of employment?

---

denim material? Try to anticipate these issues and achieve a consensus or interpretive guideline for your policy.

3. Grooming standards also represent a potential troublesome area for employers. As with dress codes, grooming guidelines should not have an adverse impact on a particular protected class group. A prohibition against "Afro" hair styles, for example, would be deemed discriminatory because it affects only blacks. Rather, grooming guidelines should focus on the importance of a clean, neat appearance.

**Sample Policy**

**XYZ COMPANY**
**PERSONNEL POLICY & PROCEDURE**

---

SUBJECT: DRESS CODE                          DATE: May 1, 1993

---

*Policy*: It is the policy of XYZ Company to define a basic dress code to convey a positive and professional image to our customers and the public.

*Procedure*:

1. Each supervisor and manager is responsible for interpreting and enforcing the dress code in his or her area of responsibility. This includes explaining the dress code to new employees, counseling employees who are inappropriately dressed, and setting a good example with proper dress for the job. In the event of questions about suitability of a particular garment, the Human Resource Administrator may be consulted.

2. Each employee is responsible for reporting to work in a clean, neat manner dressed for work as defined in these guidelines.

3. XYZ Company tries to maintain a relaxed yet professional working atmosphere that promotes a positive Company image. The following guidelines are provided:

    a) Appropriate attire for men in the office: Business suit or sport coat, dress shirt, slacks, tie, dark socks, and leather dress shoes. Sweaters are permissible.

    b) Appropriate attire for women in the office: Business suit or dress, or blouse with dress slacks or skirt, stockings, and dress shoes or heels. Jewelry is permissible so long as it is not distracting.

    c) Appropriate attire for service employees: Company-issued work garments bearing employee name and company logo, including shirt or blouse and slacks. Dark leather or flat shoes are recommended. Company uniforms must be worn while on the job. Work garments shall not be worn before or after work when engaging in personal activities.

4. Employees are not permitted to wear garments to work that may be distracting, unusually revealing of the body, or unsafe. Examples of inappropriate garments include the following:

    a) Alteration or destruction of uniform or logo or only wearing half of uniform

    b) Athletic-style clothes such as jogging suits or sweat suits

    c) Revealing or distractive clothes such as lycra tights, short-shorts, tank tops, halter tops, beachwear, or other similar garments

5. If an employee wears an inappropriate garment, he or she shall be advised that the item is contrary to the policy and should not be worn again. If an employee's garments are unsafe or distracting, he or she may be sent home (without pay) to change clothes.

6. The supervisor or manager shall make a reasonable accommodation in the event an employee wears or seeks to wear garments related to a religious belief. In the event an employee has a question or complaint about this policy, he or she may seek redress through the Company's Open Door Policy.

7. In the event of an employee's repeated or deliberate disregard of dress code guidelines, the supervisor shall take appropriate corrective action. Corrective action may include performance appraisal, disciplinary warnings, or other procedures defined in the Disciplinary Policy.

**Sample Employee Handbook**
**Paragraph**

*Personal Appearance*

Valued customers and prominent suppliers visit our office frequently. In order to present a professional Company image and working atmosphere, employees are expected to dress in a clean and neat businesslike fashion appropriate for their job responsibilities. Dress attire such as slacks, suit, and tie for men, or dresses, suits, skirts, or slacks for women are deemed appropriate. Casual garments such as denims, halters, sweatshirts, thongs, or sandals are not permitted. Your supervisor will provide further details on our dress policy.

# Confidentiality

Employees in every organization deal with confidential information. Private sector enterprises have various operational data which, if it fell into the hands of competitors, could be very detrimental to the business. Examples include customer lists, formulas, recipes, or blueprints. Such information in the possession of a competitor could result in its use to counter or improve upon products or services. Employees have a responsibility to protect the confidentiality of their employer's records.

An even higher level of confidentiality protection is needed for firms performing sensitive defense contract work. On some projects, the employer and individual employees are subject to the scrutiny of government background checks that go with top-secret clearances.

Many service organizations, in the course of providing their services, routinely collect and use business information relating to their clients or customers. Banks have financial records and account levels on their customers. Insurance companies have health, personal, or financial records on insureds. Medical care facilities have personal medical files on patients. Even employees of service organizations such as equipment repair technicians, janitorial services, pest control technicians, and property management firms all have access to work areas and records of their customers. These employees have a responsibility to protect the confidentiality of customer or client records.

Even in public sector organizations, where government records are supposed to be open to the public, certain information must be properly handled to protect confidentiality. Certain personal, health, or financial records are handled with confidentiality.

In some firms, a trade secret agreement is used to help prevent unauthorized release of confidential matters. The trade secret agreement defines specific requirements for the employee to protect confidentiality of business information. In consideration of employment, the employee signs an agreement limiting unauthorized release of company information and records.

The purpose of a policy on confidentiality is to identify confidential information and to alert employees about the importance of protecting confidentiality of records. The policy may also specify corrective action in the event of unauthorized release of confidential information.

Business records that are commonly defined as confidential information are as follows:

Business plans

Marketing strategies

Payroll data

Personnel records

Employee or patient medical records

Client records held by employer

Customer or client lists

Research and development tests or data

Blueprints

Production processes

Recipes

Product formulas

Other similar information

## Pitfalls to Avoid

A primary concern with a confidentiality policy is to get employees to realize the importance of protecting confidentiality of company records. Here are some pitfalls to avoid:

1. Avoid the tendency to take confidentiality issues for granted. An employee sometimes can forget about the importance of protecting the confidentiality of job information which he or she works with daily. The employee has ready access to the information in normal day-to-day job tasks. The information is casually passed along to others as job duties are performed. As a result, the employee may get careless in handling confidential information. Common examples of carelessness include openly discussing confidential matters, careless handling of confidential records which allows others to view information, failure to follow proper security procedures which limit access to offices or records, or failure to properly dispose of information. To emphasize the importance of confidentiality, several important points must be included in your confidentiality policy.

**CHECKLIST**
**A Confidentiality Policy**

- Is there any state or federal law that relates to records confidentiality?
- What business records are deemed confidential?
- Will there be different levels of records confidentiality?
- Will access to records be limited?
- Will records sign-out procedures be initiated?
- Will employees be required to sign a confidentiality or trade secret agreement?
- What instructions will be given to employees regarding locking of files, discussion of confidential matters, and disposal of records?
- Will responsibility for protecting confidentiality be included in the employee's job description?
- Will the employee receive instructions during orientation on protecting records confidentiality?
- Will there be any special precautions or procedures for protecting confidentiality of computer records?

 

- Define confidentiality of records and information in the employee's job description.
- Be sure to emphasize the importance of protecting confidentiality during orientation and training of new employees.
- Include confidentiality issues in desk or work procedures.

2. Require separating employees to return company property, records, files, policy manuals, etc. One of the best ways to insure that items are returned is through control procedures for issuing material at the start of work and securing its return at separation of employment. Such control procedures are recommended for issuance and return of keys, computer access codes, policy manuals, and sensitive files or records in the possession of the employee.

**Sample Policy**

**XYZ COMPANY**
**PERSONNEL POLICY & PROCEDURE**

SUBJECT: CONFIDENTIALITY                    DATE: May 1, 1993

*Policy*: It is the policy of XYZ Company to develop necessary guidelines and controls to protect confidential Company information.

*Procedure*:

1. All employees work with information, processes, or data that must be kept confidential in order to protect the interests of the Company. Employees are reminded that information such as product specifications, production procedures, financial data, customer lists, personnel or payroll data, and other similar records are confidential details which must not be disclosed to others.

2. Certain jobs by their nature involve frequent use and possession of confidential data. To protect confidentiality, employees are reminded to

   a) Store confidential information in appropriate locked files when not in use.

   b) Avoid displaying confidential data where it can be easily observed.

   c) Avoid discussing confidential information except when required to perform the job.

   d) Immediately inform the Supervisor of any loss of confidential information.

3. Each Department Manager is responsible for identifying confidential information used in the department, and for assuring proper handling of confidential records.

4. Each Supervisor is responsible for specifying in an employee's job description when job responsibilities include handling of confidential records. The supervisor is responsible for instructing employees on proper handling of confidential records.

5. All confidential records must be disposed of through shredding. To protect against accidental shredding of currently needed information, authorization of the Supervisor and Department Manager is needed.

6. Each Supervisor or Manager is responsible for administering this policy within his or her respective area of authority and for reporting any misconduct to superiors.

## Sample Employee Handbook Paragraph

*Confidential Information*

All employees are reminded that Company records such as customer lists, pricing, blueprints, or production processes are confidential business information. Please exercise proper care of this information and avoid discussing confidential business matters with persons not employed by XYZ Company.

# Relocation

Relocation of employees and their families is a matter of concern to large and small firms alike. Many large, multi-location organizations transfer employees from one location to another to meet staffing needs. Smaller firms also may become involved in relocation issues when hiring an employee from another area.

Relocation of an employee, his or her family, and personal belongings can be a costly proposition. According to *Personnel Practices Communications Reporter*, published by Commerce Clearing House, the average cost to transfer a home-owning employee and family in 1990 was $45,620.[1]

However, relocation of the right employee for the job can pay tremendous dividends when the desired performance results are achieved. In spite of relocation costs, there are a number of important benefits to relocating an employee:

- A relocation policy opens applicant recruiting to a wider geographical area beyond the immediate community. The consideration of candidates from a wider area helps assure that the firm is getting the best individual for the job.

- Relocation of an individual from one Company location to another provides a trained employee who knows the organization and can be immediately productive. Hiring of new employees, even if experienced, still means learning job issues unique to the organization. Hiring and training costs can be greater than relocation costs.

- Many organizations want to fill top-level job openings with individuals who have specific industry experience. Other firms in the industry may be located in different geographical areas. As a result, relocation is necessary to hire an individual with industry-specific skills or experience.

- Career development for staff or management personnel can be achieved by rotation through various job assignments. In a large, multilocation organization, the practice may require some relocations. The long-term benefit to the organization is the "grooming" of staff personnel or managers who have had diversified experience.

The primary objectives of a Relocation Policy are to define how relocations are arranged and clarify what moving costs are covered by the employer. These issues must be clarified for three important reasons. First, the employee is unlikely to accept a job requiring relocation without some financial support from the employer covering the costs of the move. Second, the employee who accepts a job requiring relocation is unlikely to be fully effective on the job until the relocation is complete and family members are settled in the new community. Third, the employer needs some basis to plan and control the costs associated with the relocation.

Major issues covered in a Relocation Policy include defining which relocations are covered by the policy, specifying what moving costs are covered, and listing related expenses such as sale of home, legal fees, real estate fees, mortgage costs, and home hunting costs. Examples of expenses covered by the Relocation Policy include

Packing, moving, and unpacking of household goods

Insurance on household goods during move

Transportation or mileage for personal auto(s)

Travel, meals, and lodging during move

Travel, meals, and lodging while looking for new residence

Temporary rental or living expenses pending completion of move to new area

Real estate broker's fee

Legal or professional service fees related to sale or purchase of residence

Advertising and selling expenses

Temporary storage of personal or household goods

In addition to defining covered expenses, a Relocation Policy can help to control relocation expenses in several ways. Actual dollar limits can be defined for each expense category. In addition, costs for professional services for real estate sales, appraisals, legal services, moving, home buying services, etc. can be controlled by negotiating companywide agreements at "group rates" and specifying use of the designated vendors.

## Pitfalls to Avoid

Employee relocation is a complicated process involving a new job, movement to a new residence, getting family assimilated into a new community, and reimbursement of related expenses. Here are some pitfalls to avoid:

1. One of the biggest challenges facing employers involved with relocations is accommodating the working spouse. A generation ago, fewer than 20 percent of married women with children were in the labor force. Most relocations involved a job change for the husband and a residence change for housewife and family. Now, according to government data, in more than 55 percent of all marriages, wives work outside the home.

   Clearly, dual income families add a new variable to an employee's consideration of a job change involving relocation. The pay increase or promotion of the relocation is now weighed against the spouse's likelihood of reemployment in the new area. Often, this new relocation equation means that the employee declines the transfer and relocation opportunity.

   To address this issue, the firm needs to include a provision in its relocation policy for assisting spouses in reemployment in the new area. Job search assistance and referral for job placement are two common kinds of assistance provided. Some firms even hire the spouse if a suitable job opening is available.

**CHECKLIST**
**A Relocation Policy**

- Is there any state or federal law or administrative regulation that affects relocations?

- What class or category of employees are covered by the Relocation Policy?

- What relocations are covered by the Relocation Policy?

- Will there be specified dollar limits for expense amounts?

- Will there be specified vendors or professional service providers which the employee should use?

- Will the company provide or make arrangements for any form of cash advance or short-term loan to help the employee pay immediate out-of-pocket expenses?

- What expense documentation will be needed?

- Will the company provide any job finding or employment referral assistance for the employee's spouse?

- What relocation expenses are covered by the policy?

- What expenses related to relocations are not covered by the policy?

2. Relocation expenses, like other business expenses, are subject to Internal Revenue Service regulations. The employer needs to exercise care in properly handling relocations, expense reporting, and payment to the employee to avoid creating unintended taxable income. The *Tax Guide for Small Business* provides the following explanation:

> Payments to employees as an allowance or reimbursement for the cost of moving to a new job site must be included in the employee's income, but are not considered wages for purpose of income tax withholding, FICA, and FUTA if it is reasonable to believe at the time payments are made that the employee will be allowed a deduction for moving expenses in computing income tax.
>
> However, payments to an employee for non-deductible moving expenses are wages for purposes of income tax withholding, FICA, and FUTA. For example, if you reimburse your employee for a loss on the sale of a residence, the amount is considered wages and is subject to income tax withholding, FICA, and FUTA.
>
> You must give your employees a statement describing any amounts paid to or on behalf of them for moving expenses. The statement must contain sufficient information to allow your employees to properly figure their allowable moving expense deduction. You may use Form 4782. You must give this information to your employees by January 31 of the year after the year in which you make the payments.

Any reimbursement for moving expenses must be shown on the employee's Form W-2.[2]

Additional information on moving is covered in IRS Publication 521, Moving Expenses.

**Sample Policy**

**XYZ COMPANY**
**PERSONNEL POLICY & PROCEDURE**

SUBJECT: EMPLOYEE RELOCATION          DATE: May 1, 1993

*Policy*: It is the policy of XYZ Company to reimburse employees for reasonable expenses incurred in connection with a Company-initiated relocation.

*Procedure*:
1. The employee relocation reimbursement benefit applies to full-time employees in jobs paying $20,000 annually or more who accept a Company-initiated transfer or promotion resulting in a relocation.

2. An employee relocation must be approved by a Company officer prior to any reimbursement made or money paid under this policy. At the discretion of a Company officer, the relocation policy may be used as a general guide for negotiating with new hires incurring relocation expenses.

3. At the time that an employment decision causing a relocation is being considered, the hiring supervisor or manager is responsible for preparing and submitting a relocation estimate to the respective Company officer. (A Relocation Expense Estimate Form is attached.) Upon receiving approval, the hiring manager may communicate the job offer/employment decision to the employee and explain relocation benefits defined by this policy.

4. Reasonable relocation expenses, as judged by Company management, are covered under the guidelines of this policy. Examples of covered expenses include the following:
   a) Transportation of household goods; including packing, shipping, unpacking, and insuring normal household belongings of employee. Insurance limit is $50,000.
   b) Travel, meals, and lodging expenses incurred in moving from a former to a new residence.
   c) Premove travel, meals, and lodging expenses incurred while searching for a new residence.
   d) Temporary living expenses in new location or area.
   e) Qualified expenses attributable to sale, purchase, or lease of a residence (see paragraph #10).
   f) Relocation allowance (see paragraph #10).
   g) In-transit storage for up to 30 days.

5. Current business travel expense reimbursement practices shall serve as a guideline for suggested limits on expense reimbursements. The employee is responsible for maintaining receipts of all moving expenses.

6. Relocation expenses must be listed on the Employee Relocation Expense form with receipts or copies attached. The employee is responsible for submitting the Employee Relocation Expense Form with receipts to the Corporate Accounting Department in order for the employee to receive reimbursement.

7. If necessary, an employee may receive a cash advance of up to $1000 to cover premove travel, lodging, or other moving expenses associated with the relocation. A cash advance may be authorized by the hiring supervisor or manager.

8. An equity advance may be made to the relocating employee in the event the employee needs to make a down payment before the sale of the former residence is complete. The equity advance is an interest-free swing loan made by the Company to the employee, and it must be paid back upon the sale of the former residence. An equity advance must be authorized by the Chief Financial Officer. It is limited to the lesser of the required down payment or 80 percent of the equity value of the former residence, based on the appraisal of the home buying service.

9. The Company engages the service of a home buying service which will conduct its own appraisals and offer to purchase the residence. This purchase offer is valid for 60 days. During this time, the relocating employee may elect to sell his or her former residence by owner or through a local realtor selected by the employee. Thereafter, the employee must accept the home buying service offer.

10. The relocating employee is eligible to receive the following payments:

    a) A relocation allowance is provided for miscellaneous expenses which are incurred as a result of relocation. The relocation allowance is computed based on one month's salary for a homeowner and one-half of one month's salary for renters.

    b) A purchase allowance of up to 3 percent of the purchase price is provided for the various expenses incurred through the purchase transaction of the new residence. Typical expenses may include
        Legal fees
        Appraisal fees
        Mortgage application fees
        Mortgage or transfer taxes
        Title insurances
        Escrow fees
        Mortgage costs or "points"
        Other usual and customary fees associated with a home purchase transaction
        All purchase allowance expenses must be itemized on the Employee Relocation Expense Form with receipts or copies attached.

11. All relocation expense reimbursements and allowances are subject to applicable income tax regulations. Relocating employees are referred

to their personal tax advisor or the attached IRS Publication 523, *Tax Information on Selling Your Home*, for information about tax requirements.

12. The administration of this benefit is subject to the interpretation and discretion of Company management. This policy is designed to serve as a general guide to aid in the equitable handling of relocations in order to minimize economic risk and uncertainty associated with a relocation. The Company reserves the right to adapt the policy in response to unique situations.

## Sample Employee Handbook Paragraph

*Employee Relocation*

XYZ Company is a growing firm with various locations around the country. As professional and managerial job opportunities occur at the various locations, it has been our practice to consider current employees for transfer or promotion. When a Company-initiated transfer or promotion results in relocation to a new geographical area, XYZ Company will provide relocation assistance to the employee.

Our relocation policy provides reimbursement for certain specified moving expenses such as costs of finding a new residence, sales of residence, moving, and other authorized costs. In the event you are offered a job change and relocation under this policy, the Human Resource Administrator will explain our relocation policy and procedures.

## Sample Relocation Expense Estimate Form

Employee _____ Job _____

Moving from _____ to _____

Estimate prepared by _____

Instructions: The hiring supervisor or manager is responsible for preparing an estimate of the cost of relocating the employee to the new job and area by supplying the information requested below.

| *Eligibility* | YES | NO |
|---|---|---|
| 1. Is the employee in a full-time job paying $20,000 or more? | ___ | ___ |
| 2. Is this relocation due to a Company-initiated promotion or transfer? | ___ | ___ |
| 3. Have other local candidates been screened and ruled out for this job? | ___ | ___ |

*Sample Form (Continued)*

COMMENTS: (Explain any NO response here)

_____

_____

| *Expense* | *Estimate* |
|---|---|
| 1. One house hunting trip | _____ |
| 2. Sale of former residence | _____ |
| 3. Purchase of new residence (allowance to 3% of purchase price) | _____ |
| 4. Packing, moving, transportation of household goods | _____ |
| 5. Storage of household goods | _____ |
| 6. Travel, meals, lodging in moving from old to new residence | _____ |
| 7. Temporary living for employee, family | _____ |
| 8. Relocation allowance (1 month's pay for homeowner) (1/2 month's for renter) | _____ |
| TOTAL ESTIMATE | _____ |

*Approvals*

Hiring supervisor/manager _____ date _____

Location manager _____ date _____

Company officer/treasurer _____ date _____

**Sample Relocation Expense Form**

Employee _____ Job _____

Moving from _____ to _____

_____

Instructions: The employee is responsible for maintaining a detailed record of costs incurred due to relocation on this expense form, showing an itemized list of expenses with receipts attached in order to receive reimbursement.

_____

*Sample Form (Continued)*

*Summary of Expenses*

1. Travel:

Date                    Purpose                    $ Total

_____

_____

                                        Total Travel        $_____

2. Sale of former residence                                _____

3. Purchase of new residence                               _____

4. Transportation of household goods                       _____

5. Storage of household goods—from _____ to _____        _____

6. Temporary living expenses—from _____ to _____         _____

    Total Expenses                                     _____

    Less Advance Received                              _____

    Net Reimbursement to Employee                      _____

I certify that the above listed expenses are a true, accurate record of actual expenses incurred due to relocation.

_____        _____

Employee signature                           Date

*Side Two—Itemized Detail of Relocation Expenses*

1. Travel

Date       Purpose                    Meals    Lodging    Travel    Total

_____

_____

_____

Record total on line 1 of reverse side.        Total _____

2. Sale of former residence

    Title fees _____    Other (itemize)

    Survey fees _____     _____        _____

    Legal fees _____    _____        _____

    Real Est Com ____      _____        _____

Record total on line 2 of reverse side.        Total _____

*Sample Form (Continued)*

3. Purchase of new residence

Title fees _____       Other (itemize)

Apprasl fees _____          _____       _____

Loan applic _____           _____       _____

Loan cost(pts) ____           _____       _____

Taxes _____            _____       _____

Record total on line 3 of reverse side.            Total _____

4. Transportation of household goods

Packing, moving, transportation _____       Other _____ _____

Record total on line 4 of reverse side.            Total _____

5. Storage of household goods from _____ to _____

Record total on line 5 of reverse side.            Total _____

6. Temporary living expenses from _____ to _____

Daily rental rate _____ ×(days) _____ = _____

Record total on line 6 of reverse side.            Total _____

Attach copies of receipts for all expenses reported.


## Secondary Employment

Employees at many organizations hold second jobs. These second jobs are often part-time employment, work performed after hours, or weekend jobs. Sometimes the secondary job is in a similar field as the primary job, and sometimes it is in a totally different occupational area.

An individual may seek secondary work for a variety of reasons. Common reasons for secondary or part-time work include need for more money, interest in learning a new field or occupation, or using special skills or talents to produce supplemental income.

For the employer, however, secondary employment by employees can create some problems. In one manufacturing company, for example, the shipping clerk was working a night job as a limousine driver. The combined work schedules of both jobs meant that the employee was working 16 to 20 hours daily. After about two weeks on this grueling schedule, the employee's performance deteriorated and he began falling asleep on the daytime shipping job. Corrective action was needed.

Secondary employment created different problems for a retail building center and lumber yard. Many of the center's counter sales personnel were handy with tools and enjoyed working on home improvement projects. Some of these individuals developed their home repair hobby into weekend projects for hire. Ultimately, problems arose when building center customers complained that they were being solicited for home repair jobs when buying merchandise. Once again, secondary employment began to interfere with the primary job.

The opportunities for some form of conflict between the first job and secondary employment are many. Often, the secondary job starts as a harmless part-time activity to make a few extra dollars. Time or work demands in the second job can easily grow and overlap into the primary job.

Employers complain that employees who work a second job are often unavailable to work overtime on short notice. Another problem is that the employee may become tired, careless, or even injured as a result of secondary employment. In some instances, the secondary work may cause a conflict of interest, such as the sales personnel at the building center. If secondary work is performed for a competitor, security and confidentiality concerns become significant.

Another common problem occurs when an employee begins to perform tasks of the secondary job while working on the primary job. Use of telephone, copier, computer, or other equipment is also common when an employee performs other work on company time. Occasionally, an employee's secondary job may reflect poorly on the primary employer. One such example was a bank secretary who was fired when management learned that she was moonlighting as a stripper at a local nightclub. Unless there is a specific law, labor agreement, or employment contract covering the secondary employment issue, an employer is free to define a policy regarding secondary employment. Likewise, an employee is free to seek secondary employment during off-duty hours, unless otherwise limited by labor agreement, employment contract, or employer policy.

A labor agreement, for example, may require the employer to hire only craft union workers. The labor agreement or union membership rules may require members to perform only union work as referred through the union hall.

Specific employment agreements can also limit secondary employment. Some employment agreements, such as noncompete or trade secret agreements, define specific limitations upon employees who are a party to the agreement.

There is one other issue that may limit employer controls on secondary employment. State privacy laws are being enacted by more and more states. Several states have passed laws limiting termination of employees for lawful off-duty conduct.

For example, the state of New York recently passed a law prohibiting discrimination against employees for legal off-work activities. The law, however, does not afford protection to activities that create a material conflict of interest related to the employer's business, trade secrets, or proprietary information.[3]

Key elements of a policy on secondary employment should include a business reason for the limits, the need for employees to be able and available for all work as scheduled, and provisions for corrective action if the employee encounters performance problems. In addition, a policy on secondary employment may cross reference other policies related to conflict of interest, noncompete limitations, or use of company property.

## Pitfalls to Avoid

A policy on secondary employment creates a potential conflict between organizational goals and an employee's individual needs. Here are some pitfalls to avoid:

1. Carefully consider organizational goals and corporate culture when defining a policy on secondary employment. If company policies lean toward the "family friendly" side, then limits on secondary employment are less likely. However, if the job duties or corporate culture require employees to subordinate personal interests to company needs, then a more restrictive policy is called for.

2. Consider whether other policy topics can effectively address the secondary employment issue. If management's main concern is to prevent a conflict of interest or prohibit an employee from working for a competitor, then prohibitions against these actions may be sufficient. This will avoid an unnecessary limitation which prohibits employees from taking a second job.

3. Avoid unnecessary prying into employees' off-duty lives. Rather, coach supervisors to monitor employee performance. If outside interests or secondary employment begin to affect the employee's job performance, then there is a basis for action through performance appraisal procedures.

## Sample Policy

**XYZ COMPANY**
**PERSONNEL POLICY & PROCEDURE**

---

SUBJECT: SECONDARY EMPLOYMENT                    DATE: May 1, 1993

---

*Policy*: It is the policy of XYZ Company that secondary employment will not be permitted if it affects the employee's performance or results in a conflict of interest, or results in competition.

## CHECKLIST
### A Secondary Employment Policy

- Are there any state or federal laws relating to secondary employment?

- Are there any labor agreement or employment contract provisions which apply to secondary employment?

- What business necessity reasons can be identified as a basis for limiting secondary employment?

- Will your policy require employees merely to report secondary employment, or specify limits or complete prohibition of secondary employment?

- Does the company want to encourage outside interests and activities to broaden employee perspectives, or does the company want individuals dedicating job requirements over personal interests?

- Will the policy limit or prohibit secondary employment due to job performance issues, availability issues, conflicts of interest, competitive issues, or unauthorized use of company equipment or supplies?

- Will employees be advised of secondary employment limits at time of hire?

- Will employees be required to sign an agreement or letter of understanding about secondary employment?

- What corrective action will be taken when secondary employment affects an individual's performance or the employment relationship?

*Procedure*:

1. At time of new hire orientation, new employees shall be advised by the Human Resource Administrator of the Company policy regarding secondary employment. Employees shall be advised that

   a) The Company recognizes that an employee may accept secondary employment or participate in other activities or organizations.

   b) Employees are expected to be available for all scheduled work, including overtime work, as needed.

   c) Any outside interests or employment which affect job performance or result in conflict of interest or competition will not be permitted.

2. In the event that an employee becomes or may become involved in an incident or activity which results in a conflict of interest or competition with the Company, the employee is responsible for reporting the situation to his or her supervisor. In such cases, the supervisor shall confer with the Department Manager, Human Resource Administrator, and, if necessary, legal counsel to determine appropriate resolution to the situation.

3. The supervisor is responsible for continually monitoring employee performance. In the event an employee encounters job performance problems (whether related to secondary employment or other factors),

the supervisor shall provide constructive performance instructions. (See Performance Appraisal Policy for further details.)

**Sample Employee Handbook Paragraph**

*Secondary Employment*

The Company recognizes that an employee may accept secondary employment or participate in other activities or organizations. Employees are expected to be available for all scheduled work, including overtime work, as needed. Any outside interests or employment which affect job performance or result in conflict of interest or competition will not be permitted. Speak to your supervisor if you encounter a situation which appears to be in violation of this policy.

## Use of Vehicles

Employees in a large number of organizations are involved in business travel and operation of a vehicle on the job. The employee may operate his or her own personal vehicle or a company vehicle. Vehicles used on the job may range from autos, light delivery trucks, to large trucks or construction equipment.

The operation of a vehicle on the job raises many concerns for the employer. Chief among those concerns are safety, complying with the law, and controlling insurance costs. Fleet operators are also concerned with vehicle maintenance. Firms which operate trucks over a specified weight in interstate commerce are subject to Department of Transportation (DOT) regulations relating to licenses, physical exams, and drug tests. Many states have imposed similar requirements on organizations which operate trucks within the state.

Employees who operate personal vehicles on the job are concerned about receiving reimbursement for out-of-pocket expenses.

An organization's policy on vehicles must clarify each of these issues as listed here:

*Licensing requirements*: The employer should require that the employee operating a vehicle on the job have a valid driver's license with a classification appropriate for the vehicle operated. This requirement should be a condition of employment for jobs requiring operation of a vehicle. Likewise, suspension or revocation of licenses by the state is grounds to suspend or transfer the employee to a non-driving position.

*Insurance requirements*: Employees operating their own vehicle should be required to provide to the employer a current certificate of insurance with specified and reasonable liability insurance provisions. Employees operating company vehicles must possess an insurable driving record. These requirements can be a condition of employment.

*Safety responsibility*: Employee safety responsibility must be clearly defined and communicated through the policy information given to individuals who operate vehicles on the job. Safety responsibility can include a listing of vehicle safety rules, reminder to observe traffic laws, and accident reporting instructions. In addition, the vehicle operator must be held personally accountable for traffic safety and parking citations.

*Operator maintenance*: Employees operating company vehicles must be assigned specified vehicle maintenance safety checks to be completed at the start of the day. The maintenance safety check will help insure that the vehicle is properly maintained for safe operations.

*Expense reimbursement*: Whether operating a personal or company vehicle, policy guidelines are needed to address the handling of fueling, maintenance, and reimbursement of these costs. The Internal Revenue Service defines mileage reimbursement expense limits for companies and individuals.

*Compliance with DOT requirements*: Operators of large vehicles weighing 10,000 pounds or more which transport property or passengers in interstate commerce are subject to federal motor carrier safety regulations. These regulations are defined in Title 49 of the Code of Federal Regulations (CFR) in parts 390 and 391. These regulations define certain standards related to driver licensing, driver physical exams and drug tests, driver hours, and safety.

## Pitfalls to Avoid

The safe operation of a vehicle on the road imposes certain responsibilities upon the driver and significant potential liabilities upon the employer. Here are some pitfalls to avoid:

1. Take care to thoroughly screen job candidates who will be operating a vehicle on the job. Don't just assume that anyone can drive. Verify the driver's references. Make a copy of the driver's license and insurance certificate. Some firms even contact the state driver's licensing agency for a copy of the applicant's driving record. Because of the potential for serious accident, an employer who fails to screen a driver with a record of accidents or DUI convictions could be on the losing end of a negligent hiring lawsuit.

2. Be sure to comply with all relevant Department of Transportation (DOT) and federal motor carrier safety regulations. Failure to make a

**CHECKLIST**
**A Vehicle Use Policy**

- What are the requirements of state or federal laws that relate to operation of vehicles on the job?
- What jobs require operation of a vehicle while working?
- Will the employee be required to provide evidence of (or ability to obtain) a current driver's license appropriate for the vehicle to be operated?
- Will the employee be required to provide proof of adequate insurance coverage?
- Will designated drivers be assigned to operate company vehicles?
- What responsibilities will drivers be given for vehicle maintenance and cleaning?
- What arrangements will be made for purchase of fuels, use of charge cards, or reimbursement of vehicle operational expenses?
- What expense records must the vehicle operator maintain and submit to receive reimbursement for travel expenses?
- What instructions or procedures should be followed in case of accident?
- Will the vehicle operator be accountable for traffic or parking citations?
- Will the vehicle operator be equipped to keep vehicle maintenance records?
- What safety rules or guidelines must be followed while operating the vehicle?
- What corrective action will be taken in the event of an avoidable accident, traffic citation, or conviction for driving under the influence (DUI) of alcohol or drugs?

good-faith effort to show compliance with DOT regulations can result in citations, delivery or travel delays, and potential suspension of delivery operations.

3. Avoid the tendency to arbitrarily reject job candidates with a disability. The Americans with Disabilities Act (ADA) prohibits employers from discriminating against qualified disabled workers. Thoroughly evaluate candidates based on their ability to perform essential job requirements. If an individual with a disability applies for work as a driver, examine what reasonable accommodations may be made for the individual. Several examples are provided:

   a. Individuals who have successfully completed a drug or alcohol treatment program are afforded protection under ADA. On the other hand, a current drug user who tests positive on a drug screen can be legitimately rejected from employment.

   b. Avoid defining selection standards that exclude an entire class of individuals with a disability. An example would be "no person who has epilepsy, diabetes, or a heart or back condition is eligible for a job." Such a blanket exclusion would violate ADA. Rather, define specific skills and abilities needed on the job, include these criteria in a written job description, and assess the individual's current ability to perform on the job safely and effectively.

c.  An employer may require as a qualification standard that an individual not pose a "direct threat" to the health or safety of the individual or others, if this standard is applied to all applicants for a particular job. However, an employer must meet very specific and stringent requirements under the ADA to establish that such a direct threat exists. The employer must be prepared to show the following:

- There is a *significant* risk of substantial harm.

- The *specific* risk must be identified.

- It must be a *current* risk, not one that is speculative or remote.

- The assessment of risk must be based on objective medical or other factual evidence regarding a particular individual.

- Even if a genuine significant risk of substantial harm exists, the employer must consider whether the risk can be eliminated or reduced below the level of a direct threat by *reasonable accommodation*.[4]

**Sample Policy**

**XYZ COMPANY**
**PERSONNEL POLICY & PROCEDURE**

SUBJECT: USE OF VEHICLES                    DATE: May 1, 1993

*Policy*: It is the policy of XYZ Company to define guidelines regarding use of vehicles on the job to assure compliance with applicable laws and promote safety of employees and the public.

*Procedure*:
1.  Employees hired for jobs involving operation of a delivery vehicle or significant auto/truck travel are required to demonstrate safe driving skills and meet applicable legal requirements to operate a vehicle on public roads. To achieve these requirements, employees hired for delivery, field service, and sales jobs must meet the following conditions of employment:

   a)  They must possess (or obtain by start of employment) a current valid driver's license appropriate for the vehicle to be operated on the job. A chauffeur's license is needed for delivery truck drivers.

   b)  Employees operating their own vehicle on the job must provide evidence of liability insurance meeting current liability standards set by state law.

   c)  Individuals hired for delivery drivers must meet all DOT health and safety standards including successful completion of physical exam and drug test.

2. An individual's failure to comply with the above requirements is sufficient grounds to deny or withdraw an offer of employment.

3. The Department Manager is responsible for designating qualified drivers for Company vehicles. Only qualified and designated drivers may operate a Company vehicle. Company vehicles must be used solely for business purposes.

4. All drivers are responsible for the safe operation of their vehicle in compliance with applicable traffic laws. Drivers shall

    a) Observe traffic laws.

    b) Follow safe operating procedures.

    c) Perform operator maintenance, including checking and replenishing fluid levels and testing vehicle operation before operation on public roads.

    d) Make sure that Company-owned vehicles are equipped with first aid kit, fire extinguisher, emergency light, and accident report kit.

5. Drivers of Company vehicles are issued a credit card for charging fuel and routine maintenance expenses. The credit card must be turned in to the Department Manager at separation of employment.

6. Employees operating personal vehicles on the job are required to maintain an expense report detailing travel, location, and business purpose. The expense report must be turned in to the supervisor for approval and then routed to Accounting for expense reimbursement.

7. All drivers are responsible for paying any traffic or parking citations incurred while on the job.

8. In the event of an accident, the driver is responsible for completing an accident report form and submitting it to his or her supervisor. The supervisor shall investigate the accident and provide information as needed for police department accident report, insurance claim, or worker's compensation claim.

9. In the event of an avoidable accident, traffic citation, or other incident involving improper use of a vehicle, the supervisor shall take corrective action designed to prevent recurrence of the incident. Corrective action may include any of the following: training, retraining, performance appraisal, disciplinary warning, suspension, or other corrective actions up to and including dismissal.

10. Operation of a vehicle on the job with a suspended or revoked driver's license, or a conviction for driving under the influence of alcohol or drugs, is sufficient grounds for dismissal.

## Sample Employee Handbook Paragraph

### Vehicle Use

All Company vehicles bear the Company name and paint scheme. As you operate your vehicle on job sites and public roads, you are—in effect—a traveling billboard providing continuous advertising for the Company. This means that your courteous behavior and careful driving help to build customer and public relations. Good customer relations help to provide more job opportunities and work.

Each individual operating a Company vehicle is responsible for operating the vehicle in a safe manner, observing all traffic laws and relevant regulations. In the event of any incident or driver neglect resulting in a traffic citation, the driver is responsible for paying the traffic fine. Repeated citations will result in corrective disciplinary action.

All traffic accidents and citations will be thoroughly investigated by the Company. Management reserves the right to evaluate all circumstances and any mitigating evidence in determining corrective action which may include dismissal. In the event your driver's license is suspended or revoked, you are responsible for notifying the Company. Any individual found to be operating a Company vehicle with a suspended or revoked license is subject to disciplinary action, which can include dismissal.

## Ethical Business Practices

Ethical business practices are good business practices. Many business enterprises have built their reputation on values such as integrity and honest dealings with customers. Unfortunately, some overzealous individuals give in to greed and get involved in unethical business schemes.

One example of the effect of unethical business dealings was the insider trading scandals of the late 1980s. Contrary to government securities regulations, securities dealers and stock brokers learned of pending mergers prior to public announcement and used this "inside information" to buy stock, amassing huge personal fortunes. Once these stories broke, criminal prosecutions resulted. The reputations of several major Wall Street securities firms were seriously tarnished by these unethical business practices.

In another example, a government defense contractor learned that a purchasing employee was negotiating special deals with several suppliers and receiving illegal gifts or "kickbacks" in return. These arrangements turned up in a Defense Department audit. Upon learning of the special deals, the contractor dismissed the employee and found a new supplier. The contractor's prompt corrective action prevented the loss of a major contract and possible debarment from future contracts.

Clearly, based on these examples, it makes good business sense to commit to using ethical business practices. Unfortunately, an employee's understanding of what actions may be ethical or unethical, legal or illegal, may not be clear. Without some guidance, the employee may not recognize that a particular business transaction is illegal or unethical. For these reasons, a policy which defines unethical practices and instructs employees on how to deal with them is important.

Any employee who makes business decisions in the course of performing job duties could become involved in unethical transactions. It is easy to see how sales representatives or purchasing personnel could get involved in unethical practices; their job consists of continuously negotiating deals. Many other employees also make commitments on behalf of their employer. Common examples include

- A supervisor or manager who hires a job applicant referred by an employment agency
- A maintenance worker who authorizes purchase of parts, supplies, or machines
- An engineer who "specs" a design to use certain material or products
- An accountant who transfers funds between banks or accounts
- A bookkeeper who schedules payment of invoices or handles collections
- A service technician who specifies repair services
- A retail sales worker who recommends products for purchase by the customer

In each of these examples, an employee could be faced with a situation which may be unethical.

Many firms have a practice of providing a "token of appreciation for your business." In each of the preceding examples, the vendor may provide a gift item as a way of saying thank you. The problem occurs when gifts become frequent or are of significant value.

Also, the promise of rewards or presentation of gifts or compensation to sway the outcome of a decision are examples of inappropriate conduct.

An Ethical Business Practice Policy will help employees to understand and avoid unethical situations.

## Pitfalls to Avoid

A firm's failure to prevent or stop unethical business practices can result in serious economic and legal difficulties. Here are some pitfalls to avoid:

1. The biggest mistake that an organization can make is failure to recognize the significance of an Ethics Policy. When management takes ethical issues for granted by failing to publish a policy, employees are guided solely by their own judgment of what is right or wrong. With clearly communicated management concern for profitable financial results, employees can be swayed toward business decisions which emphasize personal financial rewards. These actions can lead to unethical or illegal business practices.

   Sooner or later, ethics violations are noticed, resulting in serious liabilities for the firm. Among the losses incurred are loss of goodwill

**CHECKLIST**
**An Ethical Business Practices Policy**

- What laws or regulations affect ethical business practices?

- What classes or categories of employees are covered by the Ethics Policy?

- Will the policy prohibit or define limits on receipt of gifts?

- Will the policy prohibit receipt of compensation beyond monies paid by the employer?

- Will the policy require the employee to identify any actual or potential conflict of interest in which the employee or family member stands to receive nonsalary financial gain as a result of a business decision?

- Will the policy define as unethical receipt of gift items, or other forms of indirect compensation such as paid vacation, business transactions favoring family members, payment of debts, or other transaction resulting in significant value received?

- Will the employee be required to sign a statement of understanding about conflicts of interest or ethical business practices?

- What corrective action will be taken if an employee knowingly violates the Ethics Policy?

in the business community, loss of customers who refuse to deal with an unethical firm, loss of valued employees who do not want to be associated with an unethical employer, or criminal prosecutions of offending individuals.

The solution is to recognize the importance of the ethics issue, define policy guidelines, and communicate the policy to employees.

2. Avoid the tendency to "look the other way" or cover up unethical behavior. Be sure that your Ethics Policy or other employment policies include procedures for policy violation. Failure of management to stop unethical or illegal behavior is just as bad as actually participating in the conduct. However, if the firm's policy is used to take appropriate corrective action, the firm can lessen liabilities while showing employees the importance of following ethical practices.

**Sample Policy**

**XYZ COMPANY**
**PERSONNEL POLICY & PROCEDURE**

SUBJECT: ETHICAL BUSINESS PRACTICE          DATE: May 1, 1993

*Policy*: It is the policy of XYZ Company to conduct all business transactions in an ethical manner without conflict of interest or unjust personal gain.

*Procedure*:

1. Employees responsible for making commitments on behalf of the Company (i.e., buying, selling, or recommending such decisions) are reminded that all business transactions should be conducted in an ethical manner. To remain free of a conflict of interest, employees should not use their position for personal gain beyond regular compensation.

2. Examples of unethical conduct are listed below to guide employees on proper business conduct:

   a) Receipt by employee or family member of gifts of significant value—deemed to be $25 or more

   b) Offer or receipt by employee or family member of compensation or other items of significant value in order to influence a pending business decision

   c) Participation in a business decision in which the employee or a family member may receive financial gain or reward (beyond normal compensation paid by the Company)

   d) Offering or giving to others any gift, compensation, or item of value in order to influence or show appreciation for a business decision

3. In the event an employee or family member is offered or receives any form of value as defined by this policy, he or she must report the situation to the Department Manager and turn the gift over to the Company.

4. In the event an employee has an outside interest or employment which affects job performance, results in a conflict of interest, or results in competition with the Company, such activity must not be permitted.

5. Each Supervisor or Manager is responsible for administering this policy within their respective area of authority and for reporting any misconduct to superiors. Disregard for this policy is sufficient grounds for discharge.

## Sample Employee Handbook Paragraph

*Ethical and Legal Business Practices*

XYZ Company and each employee have a responsibility for maintaining a high standard of ethical and legal conduct in all business transactions or activities. Ethical business conduct includes any business decision relating to clients, client personnel, competitors, government agencies, etc. Employees are reminded that it is unethical and illegal conduct to solicit, offer, or accept, directly or indirectly, any gift, favor, loan, or other item of significant monetary value in order to influence a business decision or receive any financial enrichment beyond normal compensation provided by XYZ Company. In the event you are faced with circumstances which may appear to conflict with this policy, you are encouraged to speak with your supervisor. Disregard for this policy is sufficient grounds for discharge.

# Notes

1. *Personnel Practices Communications, Human Resource Management Reporter*, Commerce Clearing House, Chicago, 1991, p. 4283.
2. *Tax Guide for Small Business*, Dept. of the Treasury, Publication 334, Rev. November, 91, p. 31.
3. *Personnel Practices Communications, Human Resource Management Report Number 129*, Commerce Clearing House, Chicago, September 25, 1992, p. 9.
4. *Americans with Disabilities Act of 1990, EEOC Technical Assistance Manual*, Commerce Clearing House, Chicago, February 14, 1992, p. IV–9.

# 15

# Miscellaneous Policy Issues: Safety, Hazard Communication, Security, Sanitation, and Others

**Read Chapter 15 for:**

Safety responsibility

Accident investigation

Hazard communication

Security

Sanitation

Highlights on 15 other policy topics

## Safety Responsibility

Firms that have successful safety programs typically share three common characteristics: a management commitment to safety, active employee participation in safety activities, and thorough investigation of accidents.

Successful safety programs reduce accidents. Fewer accidents means less work interruptions, fewer worker's compensation claims, and lower insurance costs.

An active safety program helps the organization to comply with government safety laws. The U.S. Occupational Safety and Health Administration (OSHA) is the federal government agency responsible for defining and enforcing job safety standards. Also, a number of states have agreements with OSHA, permitting a state safety agency to enforce state laws. Currently, the states with their own safety plans are

| | |
|---|---|
| Alaska | New Mexico |
| Arizona | North Carolina |
| California | Oregon |
| Hawaii | South Carolina |
| Indiana | Tennessee |
| Iowa | Utah |
| Kentucky | Vermont |
| Maryland | Virginia |
| Michigan | Washington |
| Minnesota | Wyoming[1] |
| Nevada | |

Employers with facilities in these states should review state safety requirements when preparing safety policies. Organizations operating in the remaining 29 states are subject to the Occupational Safety and Health Act and the regulations issued by OSHA.

The OSHA law covers all employers engaged in a business affecting commerce, but excludes self-employed individuals, family firms, and workplaces covered by other federal safety laws. Employers covered by OSHA have a general duty to maintain a safe and healthful workplace. The general duty requirement means that the employer must become familiar with safety standards that affect the workplace, educate employees on safety, and promote safe practices in the daily operation of the business. There are numerous safety regulations defining standards on a wide range of industrial practices. Safety standards specify requirements for the following activities:

| | |
|---|---|
| Construction and shipbuilding | Materials handling and storage |
| Medical records access | Machinery and machine guarding |
| Walking and working surfaces | Hand and power tools |
| Means of egress | Welding operations |
| Powered platforms | Special industries |
| Workplace environment | Electrical systems |
| Hazardous materials | Commercial diving operations |
| Personal protective equipment | Hazard communication |
| General environmental controls | Toxic and hazardous substances |
| First aid | Fire protection[2] |
| Compressed gas and air equipment | |

When writing safety policies, consider these safety success characteristics: management commitment, employee participation, and accident investigation.

Focus first on identifying responsibility for workplace safety. I recommend several key points: Identify the chief executive as having ultimate responsibility for directing workplace safety. Designate a safety manager to coordinate day-to-day safety activities. The safety manager may be a full-time job (or even a department) in a large organization. In a smaller firm, the safety manager role is one responsibility assigned to a supervisor, manager, or other staff specialist such as the Human Resource Administrator. Also, be sure to define specific safety responsibilities for supervisors.

A safety responsibility policy serves as the framework for additional policy guidelines which direct safety activities. Typical safety activities include safety orientation, safety training, safety committee, workplace inspections, and accident investigation. Also effective in promoting safe work practices are safe operating procedures, job safety analysis, and publishing of safety rules.

Safety policy guidelines provide a basis to promote employee participation in safety activities. Active participation in safety is one important way to keep safety in everyone's mind. A safety mindset helps to prevent accidents.

## Pitfalls to Avoid

An effective safety and loss control program doesn't just happen. It requires active involvement of employees and management alike. Here are some pitfalls to avoid:

1. Don't wait for the OSHA inspector to appear at the door in regard to a workplace injury or death before taking safety seriously. Unfortunately, too many firms do just that. Recently, I assisted an electronics manufacturing firm in the preparation of a written Hazard Communication Program. The company was developing its safety policies after an employee complaint, OSHA inspection, and a $1000 citation for failure to comply with the Hazard Communication Standard issued in 1985. As another example, a firm involved with environmental issues was sending its consultants and technicians out to various job sites without adequate safety training. Only after a workplace death did the employer begin to define safety guidelines and train employees on safety precautions.

   In both of these cases, costly and unfortunate situations could have been avoided if management had taken the initiative to define safety guidelines.

2. An effective safety program is more than a few slogans and posters. When defining your safety policy, identify specific activities and assign specific responsibilities. Hold supervisors and managers accountable for safety in their respective areas. Include safety results on a supervisor's performance evaluation. Expect supervisors to set a good

**CHECKLIST**
**A Safety Responsibility Policy**

- Overall responsibility for workplace safety will be assigned to which management official?

- What state or federal laws or regulations relate to workplace safety?

- Will a safety coordinator be assigned to monitor and direct day-to-day safety activities?

- Will the safety coordinator be a full-time function, or will safety coordination responsibilities be assigned to a supervisor, manager, or other staff specialist?

- What safety activities will be started to promote safe practices at the firm?

- Will a safety committee be formed, and if so, who will participate?

- Will supervisors be given specific responsibilities in safety orientation, training, inspections, or accident investigations?

- Who will be responsible for maintaining accident records and the OSHA log?

- Will disciplinary procedures be defined and used if necessary to enforce employee compliance with safety rules and practices?

- Will jobs be analyzed to identify personal protective equipment requirements?

- Will periodic workplace inspections be conducted to identify and eliminate hazardous conditions?

- Who will be responsible for monitoring safety regulations and recommending or implementing compliance programs?

example on safety for their employees. Safety is an important area where "actions will speak louder than words."

3. Avoid the tendency to publish a few safety rules and then let things slide. Under the law, an employer will be held liable for failing to enforce safety rules. If a company publishes a safety rule, but neglects to require employees to comply with the rule, the firm may be subject to a citation.

**Sample Policy**

**XYZ COMPANY**
**PERSONNEL POLICY & PROCEDURE**

SUBJECT: SAFETY RESPONSIBILITIES                    DATE: May 1, 1993

*Policy*: It is the policy of XYZ Company to define safety responsibilities in order to provide a safe and healthful working environment and to comply with relevant government regulations.

*Procedure*:

1. Top management is responsible for planning, directing, and conducting Company operations in a manner which provides a safe and healthful working environment. This responsibility includes keeping informed of current safety regulations and issues, specifying and procuring appropriate personal protective equipment, maintaining appropriate management controls, and directing safety-related activities.

2. Each employee is responsible for performing job duties in a safe manner, following safe operating procedures, and wearing personal protective equipment as specified. In the event of an accident, illness, or injury on the job, the employee must report the incident immediately to his or her supervisor.

3. Pursuant to any incident involving injury, illness, or property damage, the supervisor is responsible for

   a) arranging for any necessary medical care or first aid

   b) directing clean-up or other similar activities to return to normal production

   c) conducting an accident investigation and providing an accident report to the Plant Manager within 24 hours

4. The supervisor is responsible for proper orientation and training of employees on safe work practices, and operation of any equipment or machines. Only trained and authorized employees are permitted to operate equipment or machines.

5. The supervisor is responsible for communicating and enforcing safety rules, including the use of progressive discipline when appropriate.

6. The supervisor is responsible for conducting a periodic inspection of the work area, to ensure proper housekeeping, equipment maintenance, and prevention or elimination of hazardous conditions.

7. The Office Administrator is responsible for maintaining records and files needed for compliance with OSHA, worker's compensation, or related information useful for management control of safety activities. Records shall include

   a) Company investigation reports

   b) Worker's compensation first report of injury

   c) OSHA log

   d) Training or orientation files

   e) Safety committee reports

   f) Other related files and records

## Sample Employee Handbook Paragraph

*Safety First*

At XYZ Company, we are committed to providing a safe and healthful working environment for employees. Our commitment includes providing proper tools and machines, purchasing necessary safety equipment, affording insurance coverages, and defining important safety rules.

However, safety on the job requires active participation by employees as well as management. You can help assure your own safety by performing job duties in a safe manner, wearing personal protective equipment when exposed to hazards, and using common sense to protect yourself and fellow employees from injury.

Accident prevention is our goal, so please maintain your work area in a clean and orderly manner, and report any hazardous conditions to your supervisor.

## Accident Investigation

One of the keys for accident prevention is thorough accident investigation. The purpose of accident investigation is to identify the accident's cause so that future accidents can be avoided. In addition to prevention of accidents, accident investigation serves several other important functions:

- *Eliminate unsafe conditions*: When an accident investigation identifies an unsafe condition, management should take action to correct the condition.

- *Identify training needs*: An individual's unsafe act causing an accident indicates the need for training or retraining in proper and safe job procedures.

- *Job redesign*: Accident investigation can reveal that job procedures or equipment used are unsafe. To correct this problem, it may be necessary to redesign job procedures or change equipment used on the job.

- *Prevent/combat fraud*: Prompt accident investigation is the best way to combat fraudulent worker's compensation claims. A thorough investigation can identify inconsistencies of fraudulent claims and discourage unethical attempts to "beat the system."

- *Analyze accident data*: Accident investigations provide a source of data on accident trends. Where data shows that certain kinds of accidents are recurring, management needs to take appropriate corrective action to prevent or eliminate these causes of accidents.

- *Government reporting*: Accidents resulting in medical treatment or care must be reported to the respective state worker's compensation agency. In addition, the employer is responsible for maintaining the OSHA form 200 log of illnesses and injuries. OSHA does not require the employer to submit specific accident data or reports. Rather, OSHA requires the employer to post the prior year's accident log in the workplace during each February. In addition, the log must be made available to OSHA inspectors upon request. A sample OSHA form 200 is reproduced on pages 438–439.

An accident investigation policy should guide the supervisor in conducting a prompt and thorough investigation. The policy needs to identify who is responsible for conducting the investigation, provide deadlines to assure timely reporting, include instructions on accident investigation techniques, and clarify reporting government requirements.

Accident investigation should begin immediately following the accident after the injured have received appropriate first aid or medical care. An accident investigation form can guide the supervisor or investigator in eliciting information about events that led up to the accident. The investigation should include

- A statement from the employee explaining how the accident occurred

- Statements of any witnesses explaining their view of the accident

- An examination of the accident site to evaluate workplace conditions and verify facts given by the employer

- A review of specific work procedures being used by the employee when the accident occurred

In the mid-1980s, a midwestern meat packing company received hefty fines from OSHA for underreporting accidents in the workplace. Part of the company's defense was that many accidents were minor and did not qualify as OSHA reportable accidents.

In another similar case, a northeastern paper company agreed to pay a negotiated settlement of $475,000 in OSHA penalties as a result of underreporting illnesses and injuries occurring in the workplace.

OSHA has issued instructions and various publications providing guidelines on what accidents are "recordable." A flow chart showing recordability of accidents appears in Fig. 15.1. A sample of the OSHA log appears in Fig. 15.2. The following publications are available from the regional OSHA offices:

*Recordkeeping Requirements under the Occupational Safety and Health Act of 1970*

*What Every Employer Needs to Know about OSHA Recordkeeping*

*A Brief Guide to Recordkeeping Requirements for Occupational Injuries and Illnesses*

*Recordkeeping Guidelines for Occupational Injuries and Illnesses*

## Pitfalls to Avoid

Conducting an accident investigation and taking corrective action are important cost control techniques. Here are some pitfalls to avoid:

1. Avoid using accident investigation as a fault finding process. Remember that the purpose is not to fix blame, but to identify the cause and eliminate recurrence of the accident. Except in cases of deliberate and

## CHECKLIST
### An Accident Investigation Policy

- What state or federal laws or regulations deal with accident investigation?
- Who will be responsible for conducting an accident investigation?
- When should the accident investigation be conducted?
- When and to whom should the accident investigation report be submitted?
- What investigation procedures will be required, such as employee statement, witness statements, tour of accident site, or examination of equipment?
- What kinds of accidents are recordable, and what accidents are not?
- Will instructions be provided for processing worker's compensation claims through the insurance company or state worker's compensation agency?
- Will policy guidelines be provided to clarify proper OSHA recording?
- What action will be taken as a result of accident report information?

gross disregard for safety guidelines, the outcome of accident reporting should be training, retraining, or action to correction unsafe conditions. Only in cases clearly demonstrating employee negligence would disciplinary actions or dismissal be appropriate.

2. Prevent fraudulent worker's compensation claims by thorough accident investigation and contesting unwarranted cases based upon the evidence. Managers at a medium-sized metal fabricating company were distressed about a rush of back injuries and worker's compensation claims. An analysis of their safety practices revealed a cursory accident investigation by supervisors in order to process worker's compensation claims filed by employees. Further investigation revealed that a former employee had filed a claim alleging a back injury. The insurance company negotiated a sizable settlement. The former employee had come back to visit fellow workers driving a new car and bragging about his cash windfall.

The solution to fraud prevention begins with accident investigation. Also, work closely with your insurance carrier to contest questionable claims.

**Sample Policy**

**XYZ COMPANY**
**PERSONNEL POLICY & PROCEDURE**

SUBJECT: ACCIDENT INVESTIGATION                    DATE: May 1, 1993

*Policy*: It is the policy of XYZ Company to investigate all accidents in order to determine accident cause and take appropriate steps to prevent recurrence.

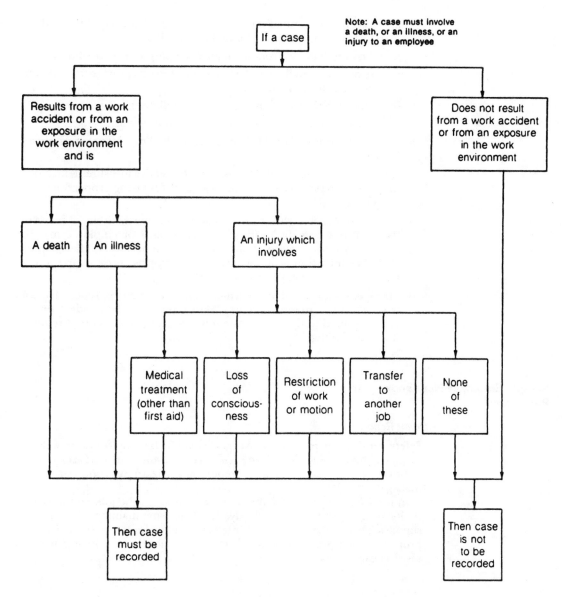

**Figure 15.1.** Guide to recordability of cases under the Occupational Safety & Health Act.[3]

*Procedure*:

    1. The supervisor is responsible for conducting an accident investigation following any job-related illness, injury, or accident.

    2. The accident report shall be prepared on the "Supervisor's Accident Investigation Report" form (sample attached). In preparing the accident report, the supervisor should

      a. Observe the scene of the accident to identify any conditions which may have contributed or caused the accident.

      b. Obtain statements from the injured employee and/or witness.

      c. Ask questions to determine sequence of events prior to, during, and following the accident.

      d. Determine if correct procedures were followed.

      e. Answer all questions on the accident report form.

3. The accident report shall be submitted to the Plant Manager within 24 hours.

4. A chart of common accident causes and corrective measures is included as an aid to the supervisor and management for taking proper follow-up action.

5. The Plant Manager shall review all accident reports within 72 hours of the occurrence of the incident. The supervisor or employee may be called in for clarification of information when necessary. Management shall then initiate appropriate corrective action as necessary to prevent a recurrence of a similar accident.

6. Management shall then determine if the accident is reportable for worker's compensation and/or OSHA reporting. The accident report is then routed to the Office Administrator for preparation of reports, if any, and filing.

**Sample Employee Handbook Paragraph**

*Accident Reporting*

Safety on the job requires active participation by employees as well as management. Each employee has a responsibility to perform job duties in a safe manner and to report any hazardous condition to management.

In the event of any accident, injury, or illness on the job, you must notify your supervisor immediately. The Company maintains first aid supplies on the premises, and designated individuals are trained in proper first aid procedures. In the event of serious injury, emergency medical care is nearby.

**Sample Form**

**SUPERVISOR'S ACCIDENT INVESTIGATION REPORT**

Date _____     Time _____

Employee involved _____

Position _____     Date employed _____

Supervisor _____     Department _____

*Sample Form* (cont'd)

How long was employee performing this operation _____

Was the employee instructed _____

Did the accident result in an injury _____

Nature and extent of injury _____

Date injury reported _____  Was first aid given _____

If so, when and by whom _____

How did accident occur _____

_____

_____

Cause of accident _____

_____

_____

Recommendations to prevent recurrence _____

_____

_____

What action has been taken _____

_____

_____

Signed _____  Dept _____  Date _____

Safety committee comments and recommendations: _____

_____

_____

Signed _____  Date _____

Executive special orders: _____

_____

Signed _____  Date _____

# Hazard Communication

There are an estimated 575,000 existing chemical products used in the workplace. As a result, approximately 32 million workers are exposed to one or

Bureau of Labor Statistics
Log and Summary of Occupational
Injuries and Illnesses

| NOTE: | This form is required by Public Law 91-596 and must be kept in the establishment for 5 years. Failure to maintain and post can result in the issuance of citations and assessment of penalties. (See posting requirements on the other side of form.) | **RECORDABLE CASES:** You are required to record information about every occupational **death**; every nonfatal occupational **illness**; and those nonfatal occupational injuries which involve one or more of the following: loss of consciousness, restriction of work or motion, transfer to another job, or medical treatment (other than first aid). (See definitions on the other side of form.) | Company Name |
| | | | Establishment Name |
| | | | Establishment Address |

| Case or File Number | Date of Injury or Onset of Illness | Employee's Name | Occupation | Department | Description of Injury or Illness | Extent of and Outcome of INJURY | | | |
| | | | | | | Fatalities | Nonfatal Injuries | | |
| | | | | | | Injury Related | Injuries With Lost Workdays | | |
| Enter a nonduplicating number which will facilitate comparisons with supplementary records. | Enter Mo./day. | Enter first name or initial, middle initial, last name. | Enter regular job title, not activity employee was performing when injured or at onset of illness. In the absence of a formal title, enter a brief description of the employee's duties. | Enter department in which the employee is regularly employed or a description of normal workplace to which employee is assigned, even though temporarily working in another department at the time of injury or illness. | Enter a brief description of the injury or illness and indicate the part or parts of body affected.<br><br>Typical entries for this column might be: Amputation of 1st joint right forefinger; Strain of lower back; Contact dermatitis on both hands; Electrocution—body. | Enter DATE of death.<br><br>Mo./day/yr. | Enter a CHECK if injury involves days away from work, or days of restricted work activity, or both. | Enter a CHECK if injury involves days away from work. | Enter number of DAYS away from work. |
| (A) | (B) | (C) | (D) | (E) | (F) | (1) | (2) | (3) | (4) |
| | | | | | PREVIOUS PAGE TOTALS ➝ | | | | |
| | | | | | | | | | |
| | | | | | | | | | |
| | | | | | | | | | |
| | | | | | | | | | |
| | | | | | | | | | |
| | | | | | | | | | |
| | | | | | | | | | |
| | | | | | | | | | |
| | | | | | | | | | |
| | | | | | | | | | |
| | | | | | | | | | |
| | | | | | | | | | |
| | | | | | | | | | |
| | | | | | | | | | |
| | | | | | TOTALS (Instructions on other side of form.) ➝ | | | | |

OSHA No. 200

FOLD

Certification of Annual Summary Totals By _____

OSHA No. 200

**Figure 15.2.** Sample of OSHA log.

For Calendar Year 19 _____          Page ____ of ____

Form Approved
O.M.B. No. 1220-0029

Type, Extent of, and Outcome of ILLNESS

| | Injuries Without Lost Workdays | Type of Illness | | | | | | | Fatalities | Nonfatal Illnesses | | | | |
|---|---|---|---|---|---|---|---|---|---|---|---|---|---|---|
| | | CHECK Only One Column for Each Illness (See other side of form for terminations or permanent transfers.) | | | | | | | Illness Related | Illnesses With Lost Workdays | | | | Illnesses Without Lost Workdays |
| Enter number of DAYS of restricted work activity. | Enter a CHECK if no entry was made in columns 1 or 2 but the injury is recordable as defined above. | Occupational skin diseases or disorders | Dust diseases of the lungs | Respiratory conditions due to toxic agents | Poisoning (systemic effects of toxic materials) | Disorders due to physical agents | Disorders associated with repeated trauma | All other occupational illnesses | Enter DATE of death. Mo./day/yr. | Enter a CHECK if illness involves days away from work, or days of restricted work activity, or both. | Enter a CHECK if illness involves days away from work. | Enter number of DAYS away from work. | Enter number of DAYS of restricted work activity. | Enter a CHECK if no entry was made in columns 8 or 9. |
| (5) | (6) | (a) | (b) | (c) | (d) | (e) | (f) | (g) | (8) | (9) | (10) | (11) | (12) | (13) |
| | | | | | (7) | | | | | | | | | |
| | | | | | | | | | | | | | | |
| | | | | | | | | | | | | | | |
| | | | | | | | | | | | | | | |
| | | | | | | | | | | | | | | |
| | | | | | | | | | | | | | | |
| | | | | | | | | | | | | | | |
| | | | | | | | | | | | | | | |
| | | | | | | | | | | | | | | |
| | | | | | | | | | | | | | | |
| | | | | | | | | | | | | | | |
| | | | | | | | | | | | | | | |
| | | | | | | | | | | | | | | |
| | | | | | | | | | | | | | | |
| | | | | | | | | | | | | | | |
| | | | | | | | | | | | | | | |
| | | | | | | | | | | | | | | |
| | | | | | | | | | | | | | | |
| | | | | | | | | | | | | | | |
| | | | | | | | | | | | | | | |

_____ Title _____          _____ Date _____

**POST ONLY THIS PORTION OF THE LAST PAGE NO LATER THAN FEBRUARY 1.**

more chemical hazards on the job. Improper use of chemicals on the job can cause fire, explosion, contamination of water or sewer systems, and other serious accidents. Further, employees who fail to follow proper chemical handling procedures may be subject to serious health elements such as heart conditions, kidney and lung damage, sterility, cancer, burns, and rashes.[4]

All of these factors are reasons why the Occupational Safety and Health Administration (OSHA) issued the Hazard Communication Standard. The Hazard Communication Standard is intended to help prevent employee illness or injury from chemical products. The standard requires chemical manufacturers and distributors to identify chemical hazards and communicate this information to employers using the products. Employers, in turn, are responsible for educating employees about workplace hazards.

The Hazard Communication Standard has six main requirements:

- Determine what chemical hazards are in the workplace.
- Establish a written Hazard Communication Program.
- Develop and/or use warning labels on containers of hazardous chemicals.
- Maintain a file of Material Safety Data Sheets which describe properties and precautions of each chemical used in the workplace.
- Train employees to recognize chemical hazards and follow safety precautions.
- Provide disclosure of limited trade secret information when requested by health care professionals dealing with employee chemical exposures.[5]

A major portion of the Hazard Communication Standard appears at 29CFR 1910.1200. The standard deals with hazardous substances listed in 29CFR 1910 Subpart Z, Toxic and Hazardous Substances. Reprints of these regulations are available from OSHA offices, federal government bookstores, and numerous other commercial publishers.

When the Hazard Communication Standard took effect in 1986, it applied to chemical manufacturers, importers, and manufacturing industries. In 1987, OSHA issued its final standard, expanding coverage to include nonmanufacturing firms subject to OSHA jurisdiction.

Many states also passed similar laws. Often referred to as "right to know" laws, the state laws generally contained similar provisions. An employer with facilities in a state which has a state hazard communication law may be subject to requirements of both laws, except in states with OSHA-approved state job safety and health laws. In those areas, the state plan that provides equal or greater protection for the employee will control.

The following states have enacted a state hazard communication law:

| | |
|---|---|
| Alabama | New Hampshire |
| Alaska | New Jersey |
| Arizona | New Mexico |

| | |
|---|---|
| California | New York |
| Connecticut* | North Carolina |
| Delaware | North Dakota |
| Florida | Oklahoma |
| Hawaii | Oregon |
| Illinois | Pennsylvania |
| Indiana | Rhode Island |
| Iowa | South Carolina |
| Kentucky | Tennessee |
| Louisiana | Texas |
| Maine | Utah |
| Maryland | Vermont |
| Massachusetts | Virginia |
| Michigan | Washington |
| Minnesota | West Virginia |
| Missouri | Wisconsin |
| Montana | Wyoming[6] |

*Applies to state and local government employees only.

Highlights of the OSHA Hazard Communication Standard are summarized:

1. *Hazard determination*: The requirement for hazard determination primarily affects the chemical manufacturers and importers. These organizations are required to review available scientific evidence concerning the hazards of chemicals manufactured or imported. This information must be summarized and distributed to organizations which use the substance. The hazard determination information is summarized into Material Safety Data Sheets. Manufacturing and nonmanufacturing firms which use chemical substances in the workplace may rely on the hazard determination conducted by the chemical manufacturer or importer. The employer must, however, develop a thorough listing of all substances used in the workplace. An OSHA inspector will want to see this list, compare it to substances observed in the workplace, and check the list against Material Safety Data Sheets on file.

2. *Written hazard communication plan*: All covered employers must develop a written hazard communication plan. The plan must include instructions on container labeling, filing and availability of Material Safety Data sheets, instructions on employee training, and definition of responsibilities for carrying out the plan. The written program must be made available to employees, their representatives, or OSHA personnel on request.

3. *Labels and other forms of warning*: The regulations require chemical manufacturers and importers to affix to hazardous substances an appropri-

ate label. The label must indicate the material identity, an appropriate hazard warning, and the name and address of the manufacturer or distributor.

In the workplace, the employer is responsible for ensuring that chemical containers have a proper label, tag, or other form of warning. Labels must be legible, in English, and prominently displayed. Signs or placards may be used at stationary containers. Batch tickets, production orders, or other similar operating procedures may be used to communicate warning label information.

4. *Material safety data sheets*: The employer is responsible for procuring Material Safety Data Sheets (MSDS) for each substance used in the workplace. The MSDS forms, normally prepared by the chemical manufacturer or importer, contain information such as

Chemical identity
Physical and chemical characteristics
Known health effects
Exposure limits
Precautionary handling measures
Recommended personal protective equipment
Emergency and first aid procedures
Identification of manufacturer, importer, or distributor

The employer is responsible for maintaining a file of MSDS forms in an area that is readily accessible to employees during each workshift. Many organizations keep MSDS forms in a three-ring looseleaf binder. The MSDS forms should be readily available in case of questions about chemical handling procedures, protective equipment, spill control, or first aid.

5. *Employee training*: The hazard communication must include training materials or information for use in educating employees about workplace hazards. The training should include the following:

Information about the Hazard Communication Standard
Information about the employer's Hazard Communication Plan
Identification of where hazardous substances are used in the workplace
Information about reading and understanding labels
Information about reading and understanding MSDS forms
Identification of chemicals in the work area
Discussion of precautions and proper protective equipment
Information about recognizing chemical exposures

The employer should conduct training for all individuals routinely exposed to chemical hazards on the job. Training should be conducted at program implementation, when hiring new workers, when transferring an employee to a new job, and whenever a new hazard is introduced into the workplace.

6. *Trade secrets*: The Trade Secrets Section stipulates that the employer provide information on chemical identity when requested by a health care professional involved in the treatment of an employee exposed to hazardous chemicals.

## Pitfalls to Avoid

A firm's Hazard Communication Program does not have to be lengthy or complicated. OSHA regulations define guidelines permitting employers to develop programs which reflect their unique needs. Here are some pitfalls to avoid:

1. Distributors of chemicals and other raw materials used in industry generally provide MSDS forms with the first purchase of a product. As a result, most manufacturing employers receive numerous MSDS forms in the mail from suppliers. It is important to take the time to review the MSDS forms and to keep the MSDS file up to date. Too many firms fail to handle MSDS forms properly, resulting in lost forms, incomplete files, and inadequate information for responding to an emergency.

2. Various business publishers have marketed commercially prepared generic Hazard Communication Programs. These programs often consist of "fill in the blank" policy statements and a training outline. Such a plan by itself, however, may not be adequate to comply with the regulations. Your Hazard Communication Plan must be sufficiently individualized to detail actual chemical hazards at the workplace. Several examples of specific information unique to a particular company include the list of chemicals used on site, identification of nonroutine tasks, special production operations, or employment of service technicians who visit customer job sites. Failure to develop a Hazard Communication Plan which deals with the workplace hazards of your firm could result in OSHA citations.

3. Some managers confide that they are reluctant to discuss chemical hazard issues with employees for fear of generating employee concerns about job safety. During my 20 years in human resources and safety issues, I have found that employees are pleased to see that management is willing to deal with job safety issues. Following hazard communication training, employees tend to be cautious and more likely to use personal protective equipment. An employer's failure to address chemical safety issues on the job, however, is more likely to prompt employee concerns and fears.

## Sample Policy

**XYZ COMPANY**
**PERSONNEL POLICY & PROCEDURE**

SUBJECT: HAZARD COMMUNICATION                     DATE: May 1, 1993

*Policy*: It is the policy of the Company to exercise reasonable and proper controls in the handling of chemical and toxic substances, and to comply

**CHECKLIST**
**A Hazard Communication Policy**

- What state or federal laws or regulations apply?
- What workplace processes and procedures will be affected by the Hazard Communication requirements?
- Who will have overall responsibility to write and implement the Hazard Communication Plan?
- Who will be responsible for ensuring that containers bear proper labels?
- Who will be responsible for requesting and maintaining the MSDS file?
- Who will be responsible for conducting employee training?
- Who will be responsible for evaluating workplace procedures to define safety precautions and specify personal protective equipment?
- Will training be documented with an employee sign-off sheet?
- Where will Material Safety Data Sheets be stored?
- Will Hazard Communication issues be discussed with new employees at time of orientation?

with relevant government regulations related to communication of workplace chemical hazards to employees.

*Purpose*: To define management and supervisor responsibilities for developing and implementing programs for toxic hazard identification and communication.

*Procedure*:

1. The Vice President of Operations has ultimate responsibility for assuring compliance with government safety regulations. This responsibility shall include the planning and development of Company policies related to hazard communication. Responsibility for coordinating certain day-to-day activities is delegated to other personnel as defined in this policy.

2. The Personnel Manager is responsible for implementing a hazard communication program which includes elements related to hazard determination, communication of information to employees and service contractors, use of proper labeling and warnings, maintaining Material Safety Data Sheets (MSDS), and training employees regarding workplace chemical hazards and appropriate protective measures.

3. The Personnel Manager is responsible for scheduling and conducting training for employees who are routinely exposed to hazardous substances. Training shall be conducted at the implementation of this

policy, annually thereafter, when a new employee is hired, and whenever a new hazard is introduced to the workplace or an employee is reassigned to work with routine exposure to new hazardous substances. Employee training shall include

a) Information about state and federal laws/regulations related to hazard communication and toxic substance disclosure

b) Identification of toxic substances in the work area

c) Instruction on reading and understanding labels and Material Safety Data Sheets

d) Protective measures which should be taken to prevent illness or injury

4. The Personnel Manager is responsible for conducting a hazard communication orientation for newly hired employees assigned to jobs in which there is a routine exposure to hazardous substances.

5. Each supervisor is responsible for orientating new employees to job responsibilities, explaining safe operating procedures for equipment, alerting employees to hazardous or toxic substances in the workplace, directing employees to maintain clean work areas, and correcting or reporting hazardous conditions to superiors.

6. The Purchasing Manager is responsible for procuring Material Safety Data Sheets (MSDS) for all toxic or hazardous substances used in Company operations.

7. An MSDS file showing characteristics of substances shall be maintained by the Personnel Manager for ready access by employees during work time. MSDS forms shall be maintained on file for 10 years. A duplicate file of MSDS forms shall be maintained in a file on the shop floor by the Production Superintendent.

8. Incoming inspection personnel are responsible for checking incoming materials to ensure proper labeling.

9. The Personnel Manager is responsible for maintaining records and files related to employee exposures to toxic substances, accident investigations or reports, and worker's compensation reporting. Records related to any employee exposure must be maintained for 30 years.

10. Each field service representative performing work at a customer work site is responsible for notifying the customer about hazards brought to the premises by XYZ personnel. Such notification shall include precautions to other workers, explanation of availability of MSDS forms, and request of hazard information necessary for protection of XYZ Company employees.

11. Company management may reassign responsibilities for safety or hazard communication if deemed necessary in response to business conditions, staffing changes, organizational changes, etc.

NOTE: The foregoing policy defines responsibility for administration of a Hazard Communication Program. This policy by itself, however, does not contain sufficient detail to serve as a firm's written Hazard Communication Plan.

## Sample Employee Handbook Paragraph

*Hazard Communication*

The nature of our business involves the use of or storage of small quantities of various chemical substances, oils, and cleaning solvents. The Company maintains a file of Material Safety Data Sheets in the office. These sheets provide information on safety precaution, spill control, and protective equipment. You may ask to see the Safety Data Sheets any time you have a question about a chemical substance. Your supervisor and the Plant Safety Manager will provide additional guidelines on chemical safety.

## Sample Form

**Hazard Communication Training Certification**

This certifies that I have participated in the Company's Hazard Communication Training Program which included information on the following topics:

- Highlights of the OSHA Hazard Communication Standard and the Illinois Toxic Substances Disclosure Act
- Information about the Company's Hazard Communication Program
- Information about reading and understanding the Material Safety Data Sheets
- Information about chemical substances used on the job and proper safety precautions

"I understand that I may speak with the Personnel Manager and/or review Material Safety Data Sheets if I have any further questions about chemical substances used on the job."

_____     _____
Date                          Employee Signature

# Security

Management in every organization is concerned about protecting company assets from loss and protecting employees from harm. Security issues can range from protecting the premises from unauthorized entry, guarding against unauthorized release of business records, protecting the safety of employees or customers, and preventing theft.

A security policy assigns responsibilities and defines plans to help the firm prevent and control losses. Firms that fail to define certain security guidelines generally incur greater losses than organizations with comprehensive security practices.

Security issues are a matter of great concern in certain industries. Banks define stringent procedures for handling and storage of cash. Health care facilities and drug stores follow rigid procedures in the handling of drugs. Certain government defense contractors are required to establish sophisticated systems and controls to protect confidentiality of classified defense projects.

For a majority of firms, routine security matters focus on the following issues:

*Security services*: A variety of security services are available, ranging from guard services, installation of alarms and video monitoring systems, to off-site monitoring of alarm and video systems.

*Locks and key control*: Good old-fashioned locks and careful control of keys remains one of the best security systems. Locked doors prevent access, which prevents opportunity for theft.

*Locked files and administrative controls*: Records are vulnerable to theft or unauthorized access. A system of locking files, controlling keys, and limiting access helps protect against unauthorized disclosure of confidential information.

*Documented asset and inventory control*: Organizations which tag assets and record inventory transactions have a much better chance for preventing theft and controlling inventory shrinkage.

*Visitor control*: Many retail and service organizations routinely have customers or the general public on their premises. Also, offices in large office buildings have added security concerns in controlling access by nonemployees.

*Computer security*: New computer technologies have placed a terminal on every desk with real-time access to computer files and storage memories. Certain computer records are confidential, requiring codes to access the data.

*Personal safety*: Employers in certain areas need to provide security measures to protect the safety of employees entering or leaving the premises or parking areas. Employee identification systems may be part of this process.

*Employee selection*: Firms in security-conscious industries must also include security check issues in their employee selection process. Background checks, reference checks, and surity bonds may be part of this process.

Employers are no longer permitted to use polygraph or "lie detector machines" in the employee selection process. The Employee Polygraph Protection Act of 1988 prohibits the use of lie detectors to test an employee or prospective employee. The law also prohibits discipline, discharge, or other discrimination against an employee based on polygraph tests or refusal to take a test. Private security firms, drug companies, and government units are exempted from the law.[7]

The law does permit an employer to test current employees if suspected of workplace theft or other incident causing economic loss. In order to refer an employee for a polygraph test, the employee must have had access to the property under investigation, and the employer must have a reasonable suspicion that the employee was involved. Also, the employer must provide the employee a written statement giving reasons for testing.

Various state worker privacy laws have provisions against polygraph testing. State laws which are more restrictive providing greater protection for the employee are not preempted by the federal law.

## Pitfalls to Avoid

The increases in theft and property crimes have lead to use of greater security measures by many organizations. Workplace security measures have the potential for conflict with individual privacy concerns. Here are some pitfalls to avoid:

1. In a working environment, it is easy to become lax about security issues. Employees can become relaxed when performing routine tasks, and troublesome security procedures are overlooked. Unfortunately, laxity allows security breaches and theft to occur. The best way to prevent theft, according to security specialists, is to eliminate the opportunity. There are a number of things that can be done to prevent opportunity for theft. Maintain doors and gates for proper operation. Lock secure areas. Limit access to those with legitimate business purpose. Implement documented inventory controls. Be sure to follow the control procedures that have been established.

2. Minimize employee privacy concerns by communicating the importance and purpose of security precautions. No one likes an invasion of privacy. For example, we accept the security and parcel inspection procedures at airports because we recognize their effectiveness in preventing airplane hijackings. When security problems arise, communicate an appropriate message to the workforce. Also, employees performing their routine jobs can be the "eyes and ears" to report suspicious activity to management.

3. Limit or control visitor access to facilities. Unescorted visitors on the premises pose potential safety problems as well as security concerns. Visitors should enter through a designated entrance, be authorized by management, and be escorted by an employee while on the premises. Several common problems and solutions are summarized:

   *Former employees*: Former employees often feel that they have free access to work areas like they did as employees. However, their return to the workplace will distract workers. Treat former employees just like other visitors.

   *Family members*: On occasion, an individual's spouse, children, or

## CHECKLIST
### A Security Policy

- What state or federal laws or regulations relate to company security practices?
- Who is responsible for planning and directing security procedures?
- What security systems, procedures, or services will be used?
- Will certain work areas be designated restricted access?
- Will employees be required to wear identification cards or badges?
- What procedures will be defined to regulate access of visitors?
- Will signout procedures be used for issuance and return of company property, keys, etc.?
- Will company management reserve the right to inspect lockers, parcels, or packages leaving the premises?
- Will camera, electronic, or other systems be used to monitor employees in the workplace?
- Will polygraph testing be used in the investigation of theft or other economic loss?
- Will security or reference checks be conducted prior to hire of new employees?

other family members will visit the employee at work. I recommend that these visits be kept to a minimum and limited to nonworking times and nonworking areas.

*Service technicians*: Service technicians have been called to the premises to perform a specific service such as machine repair, installation, delivery, etc. The manager or individual responsible for the service activity being performed should supervise the service technician. This can include authorizing entrance to the facility, escorting the technician into and out of the building, and actual supervision of work performed.

*Customers*: In a retail setting, the customer has free access to the sales floor area. However, in office manufacturing and service environments, the customer should be escorted by an employee while on the premises. The escort can explain work activities and avoid exposure of confidential information.

*Sales representatives*: Sales personnel should be interviewed in a private office, conference room, lobby, or vestibule. If the sales presentation requires access to a part of the facility, the manager or individual responsible for the purchase should escort the sales representative while on the premises.

*Solicitors/street vendors*: I recommend that nonemployee solicitors or street vendors be prohibited from access to the premises or employees.

Sometimes, street vendors will enter a back door and begin peddling their wares to employees on the job. These vendors should be escorted from the premises immediately. Likewise, a strictly enforced policy against nonemployee solicitors can be used to bar union organizers from the premises without creating an unfair labor practice.

*Delivery drivers*: Many plants, warehouses, and large office buildings have receiving docks. Truck drivers generally do not personally load or unload their trucks. Some may wander around while their trucks are being loaded or unloaded. As with other visitors, the drivers' access to the premises should be limited to the area(s) related to the delivery. Generally, it is best to limit driver access to the following areas: shipping office, dock, and restroom. Also, a shipping department employee should monitor the truck loading and verify all items listed on the trucker's bill of lading.

*Employee safety*: In recent years, there have been increasing incidents of workplace violence involving weapons. Some of these incidents, unfortunately, caused deaths of employees on the job. Regrettably, the development of a security policy should also consider emergency response to an individual with a weapon in the workplace. Consider issues such as locking doors, emergency notifications, posted escape routes (these should be displayed for emergency fire escape procedures), and security guard service. Consult with your local police department for advice on weapons issues.

**Sample Policy**

**XYZ COMPANY**
**PERSONNEL POLICY & PROCEDURE**

---

SUBJECT: SECURITY                                        DATE: May 1, 1993

---

*Policy*: It is the policy of XYZ Company to protect the security of Company property and records through the establishment of necessary controls and procedures.

*Procedure*:
1. A designated Vice President has overall authority for security of Company property and records. For making management decisions affecting the security of Company assets, the following positions are on 24-hour call:
   President
   Vice President
   Facilities Manager
   Maintenance Supervisor
2. The Company may install alarm or surveillance equipment as needed. Designated individuals will be trained to activate and deactivate such systems. Employees who are issued keys to buildings, vehicles, files, etc. are responsible for proper care of keys.

3. All visitors to the premises must enter through the reception area, sign the guest register, be approved by a Supervisor or Manager, and be escorted by an employee while on the premises. This guideline applies to vendors, service technicians, former employees, family members, and other visitors. Delivery drivers may enter shipping/receiving doors but must remain in the dock area.

4. In the event of theft, suspicious activity, or dangerous incident, an employee should report the situation to the Department Manager. The Department Manager shall assess the situation and, if appropriate, contact local police.

5. The Company reserves the right to inspect bags, parcels, or containers being removed from the premises. Further, in the interest of health and safety, the Company reserves the right to inspect the workplace, including lockers, desks, files, etc.

6. Employees are expected to use designated entrances and exits. In addition, the attached security guidelines are provided for employees.

7. All keys, access codes, Company records, documents, and other property must be turned in at separation of employment.

## SECURITY GUIDELINES FOR EMPLOYEES

Employees should observe the following security measures:

1. Observe all regulations regarding closing or locking of doors or safekeeping enclosures.

2. Do not enter restricted areas without permission from your Supervisor.

3. Company property or confidential information in the possession of an employee should be carefully safeguarded.

4. An employee should immediately report to his or her Supervisor any security irregularities such as acts of theft, sabotage, vandalism, or damage to Company property.

5. The presence of any unauthorized persons should be reported immediately to your Supervisor.

6. Employees will be responsible for properly safeguarding their own personal property.

7. The Company shall have the right to inspect nonauthorized packages within the plant.

8. Report any lost or found building keys to your Supervisor.

## Sample Employee Handbook Paragraph

*Security*

Company facilities are protected by an alarm system which is activated after business hours. Our fire alarm systems are wired directly to the Fire Department to ensure fast response time.

Employees are issued an identification card (ID) at time of hire. Please remember to keep the card with you while on Company premises. A replacement cost may be charged if the ID is lost. Your ID card must be turned in on separation of employment.

Certain employees receive a Company key because job duties occasionally may include weekend or evening work. If you are issued a Company key, please remember that along with your possession of the key there is a responsibility for protecting the security of Company facilities, equipment, and records. The Company key must be returned on separation of employment.

# Sanitation

A Sanitation Policy is important to food manufacturing firms, food processors, restaurants, and firms involved in food services. Also, firms which manufacture packaging for food products need to be concerned with sanitation policies.

Sanitation policies are commonly referred to as Good Manufacturing Practices (GMP) in the food production industry. Generally, GMP rules are defined as part of the Quality Control Policy guidelines. Since supervisors in food-related industries need to know sanitation policies, and since employees must follow GMP rules, sanitation issues are an appropriate topic for a personnel policy manual or employee handbook.

The purpose of a Sanitation Policy is to define guidelines for preventing contamination of food products. A Sanitation Policy can also help a firm to comply with regulations of the Food and Drug Administration.

A Sanitation Policy should define management responsibilities for setting and enforcing GMP rules. In addition, a Sanitation Policy typically specifies product handling procedures, personal hygiene requirements, protective garments needed, and guidelines for work area clean-up.

In a food handling work environment, it is important that employees learn sanitation policies and procedures. The new employee orientation can include discussion of sanitation rules, issuance of protective work garments, and explanation of clean-up procedures.

Because of the importance of sanitation procedures, the policy should include provisions for stopping production until sanitation guidelines are followed. Further, the policy should give supervisors authority to discipline an employee for disregard of sanitation policies.

## Pitfalls to Avoid

An effective Sanitation Policy is closely coordinated with policies relating to safety and housekeeping. Here are some pitfalls to avoid:

1. Employees in a food handling position need to clean work areas daily or even more frequently. One food processing firm, for example,

## CHECKLIST
## A Sanitation Policy

- Are there any state or federal laws which regulate food handling procedures?

- Who is responsible for defining sanitation procedures or good manufacturing practices?

- Who is responsible for enforcing sanitation procedures (i.e., quality inspectors, supervisors)?

- What protective garments must be worn?

- What personal hygiene and washup procedures must employees follow?

- What procedural issues will be defined in the Sanitation Policy (i.e., product handling procedures, hygiene requirements, protective garments, etc.)?

- What clean-up or other housekeeping responsibilities will employees have?

- What guidelines will be provided on use of hand or power tools?

- What provisions will be made for dealing with employees who have infectious or communicable disease?

- When and how will new employees receive instructions on sanitation procedures or GMP rules?

- Will sanitation procedures or GMP Rules be defined in an employee manual or handbook?

---

requires its employees to wash down work tables any time that a new food product is being handled. Without cleaning between the handling of different food items, residue from one food material would contaminate the next item handled. Also, thorough clean-up at the end of the workday, is critical in assuring the cleanliness of facilities the next day.

2. Extra care is needed in food handling environments to prevent accidents. Slipping and falling accidents are likely because of the frequent use of water to clean work areas. Standing water must be brushed into drains. Employees need to wear sturdy footwear with antislip soles.

3. Food handling employers need to pay attention to employee health matters. Employee health can affect product quality. Employees must report to work in a fit condition to work. Personnel policies defining sick leave, medical leave, and physical exam screening are essential.

4. Recognize your responsibilities for limiting the spread of infectious and communicable diseases in food handling jobs. Pursuant to the passage of ADA, the Secretary of Health and Human Services is responsible for preparing a list of diseases which can be transmitted through the handling of food. If an individual is disabled by one of the infectious

or communicable diseases included on this list, and if the risk of transmitting the disease associated with the handling of food cannot be eliminated by reasonable accommodation, an employer may refuse to hire an applicant or may remove an employee from the food handling position.

**Sample Policy**

**XYZ COMPANY**
**PERSONNEL POLICY & PROCEDURE**

---

SUBJECT: SANITATION AND QUALITY                    DATE: May 1, 1993
              CONTROL RESPONSIBILITIES
APPLIES TO: All Plant and QC Employees

---

*Policy*: It is the policy of the Company to maintain high quality standards through a priority attention to quality control and adherence to Good Manufacturing Practices (GMP).

*Procedure*:

1. The Quality Assurance Manager is responsible for establishing and administering a quality control program including supervision of quality and lab personnel, recommending quality policies, developing quality/testing procedures, creating Good Manufacturing Practices, enforcing quality policies and rules, conducting product inspections, and other tasks related to an effective quality assurance program.

2. All plant employees shall receive and sign receipt for GMP rules at the start of employment. Plant personnel are responsible for observing standard operating procedures for equipment operations, handling of food material and product, and packing product in order to assure quality control.

3. All plant personnel are responsible for complying with GMP rules and other instructions from Supervisors or the Quality Assurance Manager. Plant personnel must wear hair covering, frock, beard cover if necessary, and sturdy shoes with nonslip soles.

4. Work areas must be washed down at the start of the workday, whenever a new food product is being handled, and at the end of the workday.

5. In the event of any accident or incident causing food material or product to become contaminated or tainted, the employee is responsible for notifying superiors and/or quality control personnel. Any negligent handling of food material or product, causing of intentional damage or contamination, or willful concealment of damage or contamination is grounds for immediate discharge.

6. All material and product is subject to inspection and testing by quality control personnel. Inspection and testing will occur on incoming material, or in-process material, and on finished product, according to procedures prescribed by the Quality Assurance Manager.

7. Lab technicians are responsible for performing designated visual checks

and lab tests to check product quality. In the event that product does not meet customary or specified standards, the lab technician shall notify the Quality Assurance Manager. The Quality Assurance Manager shall exercise authority to pass or reject the product and to suspend production on a machine or work area in the event of quality problems.

8. Employees are responsible for reporting to work in a fit condition to work and for observing proper health/hygiene habits. In the event of illness, the employee shall report the condition to his or her supervisor. In situations involving infectious or communicable disease, the supervisor shall confer with the Human Resource Administrator to identify a reasonable accommodation for the condition. If an accommodation is not possible, the employee may be temporarily reassigned, placed on sick leave, referred for a medical exam, or placed on a medical leave as appropriate. The Human Resource Administrator is responsible for maintaining a reference of information for guidance in implementing this policy.

9. Plant employees, lab technicians, and the Quality Assurance Manager shall maintain records and files for quality control as needed.

## Sample Employee Handbook Paragraph

*Sanitation Practices*

As a manufacturer and packager of food products, XYZ Company is subject to stringent government regulations regarding cleanliness of facilities and equipment, employee hygiene practices, and job safety. The Company Sanitation Supervisor has full authority over all matters related to sanitation, and his or her instructions must be obeyed.

Sanitation and clean-up procedures are posted in work areas where food products are measured, mixed, or packaged. Adherence to these procedures will be strictly enforced. Hair nets or hats are provided, and their use is mandatory. Employees with beards must wear protective beard covers. Eating and smoking are permitted only in specified areas of the plant.

## Sample Good Manufacturing Practices (GMP) Rules

Good manufacturing practices are work procedures which protect the product from becoming soiled or contaminated. Since most of our products are used as packaging for the food industry, we must provide quality products which will not cause contamination to food products. Each employee is responsible for using good manufacturing practices and for complying with the instructions from supervisors, lab technicians, or the Quality Assurance Manager.

*Clothing and Protective Equipment*

All persons entering the production area must wear sanitation hat or hair net and beard guard as appropriate. The requirement applies to employees, visitors, and any other person entering the production area. Company management will specify hair length which requires use of hair net. All employees assigned to work in the production area must wear safety shoes.

All employees assigned to work in the production area must wear personal protective equipment (such as safety glasses, goggles, hearing protection, etc.) as specified for protection from job hazards.

All employees should dress in a clean and neat fashion appropriate for job responsibilities. Work garments should be laundered as necessary to avoid product contamination from contact with soiled garments.

### Personal Hygiene

Rashes, sores, infections, colds, or other contagious medical conditions that may contaminate the product must be reported to your supervisor before production begins. Company management will determine whether the conditions will affect product quality. An employee may be referred for a medical evaluation if deemed appropriate by management. Regular bathing and hair washing is an important personal hygiene practice.

Employees must wash hands prior to the start of work, when returning from lunch or breaks, after using the restroom, or following any other activity which may cause contamination when handling product.

Avoid situations which may cause perspiration to contact and contaminate product.

Avoid coughing, spitting, sneezing, etc. in a way which would contaminate product or material.

### Tools and Equipment

A utility knife must be used when cutting product. Hand-held or uncovered razor blades must not be used to cut product.

Use bacteriacide spray on slitter blades, cores, and rollers at the start of each job and whenever a new product material is mounted for slitting.

Periodically clean or wipe down tools and equipment to avoid accumulation of inks, solvents, oils, or other material which may contaminate product.

Stay alert and continually observe production or machine operation to prevent or correct problems which may affect product quality and sanitation.

### Material Handling

Make sure that raw material is placed and stored properly on pallets, avoiding contact with the floor.

Make sure that work in process and finished product is properly stored on pallets to prevent direct contact with the floor.

Clean gloves may be worn when handling material or product. Gloves should not be worn when working with turning or spinning equipment or rolls of material.

Use material handling equipment when necessary to effectively handle heavy rolls of product or material. Handle material or product carefully to prevent it from being soiled.

*Housekeeping*

Smoking is not permitted in the plant area.

Storage, preparation, or consumption of food is not permitted in the plant area. Food must be stored, prepared, and consumed in the lunchroom or other designated areas.

Keep your work area clean and free of trash or waste material. Dispose of trash and report housekeeping problems or spills to the Maintenance Department for clean-up.

*Quality Problems*

Report any quality problems or contamination of product to your supervisor. Do not overlook or conceal problems relating to product contamination.

# Fifteen Additional Policy Topics

In this section, 15 additional policy topics are highlighted. To guide the policy writer, key policy points are identified to help the organization formulate a policy. A sample employee handbook paragraph is also provided.

The following topics are covered here:

| | |
|---|---|
| Benefits continuation | First aid |
| Bulletin boards | I-9 employment eligibility |
| Call-in pay | Office parties |
| Customer relations | Parking |
| Employee activities | Report-in pay |
| Exit interview | Seniority |
| Fetal protection | Solicitations |
| Fire drills | |

## Benefits Continuation

Employers with 20 or more employees are subject to the Consolidated Omnibus Budget Reconciliation Act of 1986 (COBRA). COBRA defines requirements for employers to offer continued health insurance coverage for employees or covered dependents who become ineligible for benefits. Likewise, 40 states have similar laws requiring insurance continuation under certain conditions. States which do not have insurance continuation laws are Alabama, Alaska, Delaware, District of Columbia (DC), Idaho, Indiana, Michigan, Mississippi, Pennsylvania, and Wyoming.[8]

When certain qualifying events occur under COBRA, the individual must be offered the opportunity to continue group health insurance. Qualifying events include termination of employment, reduction of hours, layoff, divorce, death, or losing dependent status due to age. The law specifies time limits for period of continued coverage. Also, there are notification responsibilities and limits. Employee notification to the Plan Administrator of divorce, separation, retirement, or aged out dependent must occur within 60 days. Employer notification to the Plan Administrator of employee death, termination, or reduction of hours must occur within 30 days. The Plan Administrator has 14 days to advise employees of continuation rights. The employee then has 60 days to decide to elect coverage and pay the full premium cost on a timely basis. Upon expiration of the benefit continuation period, the employee may exercise conversion rights. This means that the employee's coverage is converted to an individual policy with a higher premium rate.

A sample employee handbook paragraph follows:

> At separation of employment, an employee may elect to continue health insurance coverages as permitted under the COBRA insurance continuation law. Also, under this law, continuation of insurance coverage is available for one's spouse or dependents in the event of marital separation, divorce, death, or other qualifying events. Speak with the Human Resource Administrator for information on costs, enrollment periods, and terms of coverage.

## Bulletin Boards

Many organizations have a bulletin board to communicate information to employees. In addition, various state and federal labor laws require employers to post notices about certain employee rights under the law. A bulletin board is company property, so the employer has full authority to regulate what items are posted. Bulletin boards may be used to post information on holidays, benefits, company policies, advancement opportunities, company rules, or other Company news. The following are federal labor law posters which must be displayed in the workplace.

1. *Equal employment*: The poster "Equal Employment is the Law" must be displayed by all employers of 15 or more employees. Be sure that your poster reflects the new ADA law.

2. *Minimum wage, overtime, child labor*: A poster entitled "Your Rights Under the Fair Labor Standards Act" (WH 1088) is required of all employers covered under the Fair Labor Standards Act. There is a special version for state and local government employers (WH 1385).

3. *Federally financed construction*: The poster "Notice to Employees Working on Federal or Federally Financed Construction Projects" (WH 1321) must be posted at the job site if the company is engaged in federal or federally assisted construction.

4. *Federal government contracts*: The poster "Notice to Employees Working on Government Contracts" (WH 1313) must be posted by contrac-

tors and subcontractors with contracts which exceed $10,000 under Walsh-Healy Public Contract Act or contracts in excess of $2500 under the Service Contract Act.

5. *Occupational Safety and Health Act*: The OSHA poster "Job Safety and Health Protection" (OSHA 2203) is required of all employers covered by the federal OSHA law.

6. *Polygraph*: "Notice—Employee Polygraph Protection Act" (WH 1462) must be posted by private employers where employees and applicants can see it to advise them of the general prohibition against the use of lie detectors in employment.

7. *Family and medical leave*: The new family and medical leave law requires employers to post a notice summarizing the law's provisions.

   *Note*: Publications and posters issued by the Wage-Hour Division are denoted by "WH" and an identifying number. Publications and posters issued by the Occupational Safety and Health Administration are denoted by "OSHA" and an identifying number.

Employee postings may be prohibited so long as the practice is uniformly administered for all employees. Some organizations permit employee postings subject to requirements that postings must be approved by management. If employees are permitted to post items for sale, it may be wise for the employer to post a disclaimer that the company is not responsible for accuracy of the notice. Items should be dated and removed after a specified period of time. Avoid postings on non-work-related activities of organizations. Uniform application of this rule allows removal or refusal to post union organizing literature in the event of a union drive. Unionized firms typically provide a union bulletin board for posting of union information.

A sample employee handbook paragraph follows:

> The Company maintains a bulletin board to communicate information to employees. You are encouraged to check the bulletin board periodically to keep informed of Company announcements and information. The Company has customarily allowed employees to post items for sale or other similar notices which are in good taste; however, please check with your supervisor before posting anything on the bulletin board.

## Call-in Pay

A Call-in Pay Policy defines compensation guidelines for employees who are called in to work after having completed their regular work shift or on a day when the employee was not scheduled to work. Call-in work sometimes takes only 15 minutes or a half-hour. However, such minimal pay is hardly worth it to the employee, particularly if travel time to the job is a half-hour or more. The intent of call-in pay is to provide some extra pay to the employee to compensate for the disruption to personal activities. Call-in pay practices are generally defined for hourly paid non-exempt workers usually performing emergency work. Service, repair, maintenance, or computer systems personnel are most likely to be affected by a call-in pay policy.

Call-in pay is generally a minimum of two hours' work or pay. Some firms provide up to three or four hours' minimum work or pay. Thereafter, the employee receives regular pay for hours actually worked.

A sample employee handbook paragraph follows:

> There are occasions when it is necessary to call employees in to work after a normal workday. We recognize that this practice can be disruptive to an individual's personal activities.
>
> In the event an hourly paid employee is called in to work on a scheduled day off or after having worked his or her regular shift, the employee shall receive a minimum of two hours' pay at the regular hourly pay rate. Overtime pay may be provided based on the Company's overtime pay policy.

## Customer Relations

Employees in retail and service organizations deal directly with their customers every day. For these organizations, employee professionalism and good customer service are essential ingredients of the job. Every contact with the public or customer presents an opportunity for the employer to build better customer relations. Well-regarded retail and service firms devote a significant amount of time to training employees on customer relations issues. Policy issues can relate to importance of customer relations, greeting the customer, handling "tough" customers, and/or responding to customer complaints.

A sample employee handbook paragraph follows:

> The customer is the most important person in our organization. He or she deserves the most courteous and attentive treatment we can give. Remember that the customer is not an interruption to our work; rather, he or she is the purpose of our work. The customer does us a favor by patronizing our store. The customer is not dependent on us...it is our livelihood that is dependent on the customer.
>
> In the event of a customer accident on our premises, please observe the following guidelines:
> - Offer assistance and comfort to the individual. If necessary, make arrangements for first aid or emergency assistance.
> - Notify your department manager.
> - Obtain the individual's name, address, telephone number, and any relevant information about the cause of the accident. Prepare a detailed accident report for management as soon as possible following the incident.

## Employee Activities

Social or recreational activities contribute to good employee relations in an organization. Social and recreational activities promote employee interaction in a relaxed environment. Employee activities can include bowling leagues, golf leagues, softball or basketball teams, company picnics, or other similar events.

Company policy on employee activities should focus on several key issues. Participation should be voluntary; encourage employee participation but don't make attendance mandatory. Plan some events for family members. Employee activities are subject to equal employment opportunity laws, so do not restrict activities to a certain class, race, sex, or other category of employees. Also, recognize that sexual harassment prohibitions apply after hours as well as on the job.

A sample employee handbook paragraph follows:

> XYZ Company encourages employee participation in various employee activities which occur after work hours. Many XYZ employees enjoy participating in our golf league, bowling league, and softball teams. Company-sponsored recreational activities are "coed," and all are encouraged to participate. In addition, the Company has an annual summer picnic and a Christmas party for employees, families, and guests. Information on these activities is posted on the bulletin board.

## Exit Interview

An exit interview is an important human resource tool for controlling unwanted turnover. An exit interview also promotes compliance with COBRA insurance continuation requirements. In an exit interview, the human resource specialist interviews a separating employee to discuss reasons for separation, explain benefits entitlements, and secure return of company property. When there appears to be an unusually large number of employee quits, the exit interview can help identify causes such as poor supervisory relations, poor employee selection decisions, pay concerns, working conditions, or other problems. The first policy concern is to assign responsibility for exit interviews, preferably to an independent third party such as a human resource specialist. The second policy concern is to act on the information received.

A sample employee handbook paragraph follows:

> It is the practice of the Company to conduct an exit interview with the separating employee and to provide an opportunity to convert group insurances to individual coverages. The separating employee is entitled to receive salary earned up to the date of separation and pay for earned, unused vacation.
>
> All employees are required to return keys, uniforms, Company vehicles, supplies, or any other Company property prior to separation of employment.

## Fire Safety

Every organization needs to recognize the potential hazard of fire. Certainly, manufacturing and construction industries which work with flammable materials have a greater concern for fire safety than office environments. But even office workers need to know basic fire safety procedures. Several years ago, an advertising agency employee working late in her high rise office building became trapped by fire and died because she was unable to escape.

Fire safety policies generally contain instructions on proper handling/storage of flammables, fire reporting, fire drills, maintenance and availability of fire extinguishers, smoking prohibitions when working with flammables, and marking of exits.

Much of the guidelines for fire safety practices can be found in OSHA regulations. In addition to fire protection standards, OSHA regulations also require employers of 10 or more employees to define written emergency action plans and fire prevention plans. Guidelines for these plans are found in the OSHA regulations at Section 1910.38.

A sample employee handbook paragraph follows:

> Due to the nature of our business and products, every employee must recognize the potential danger of fire and take an active role in fire prevention. Flammable liquids and oily rags must be properly stored in covered metal containers. Please comply with the requirement for no smoking in the plant area and take note of fire extinguisher locations and emergency exits. Do not block fire doors, exits, or fire extinguishers.
>
> An evacuation plan is posted in the locked bulletin board. In the event of an emergency, an evacuation order will be announced over the plant intercom. Smoking is strictly prohibited at the machines and throughout the plant area. Smoking is permitted in the lunchroom, washroom, and locker areas only. Disregard for fire safety is grounds for dismissal.

## First Aid

First aid requirements are another policy issue that is covered by OSHA regulations. At Section 1910.151, the regulations state that "the employer shall ensure the ready availability of medical personnel for advice and consultation on matters of plant health. In the absence of an infirmary, clinic, or hospital in near proximity to the workplace which is used for the treatment of all injured employees, a person or persons shall be adequately trained to render first aid... ."[9]

This section of the regulations also requires the employer to provide eye wash stations in work areas where employees are exposed to injurious or corrosive materials.

The recommended policy is to have first aid supplies available in an accessible area with designated individuals trained in providing first aid. Dispensing of aspirin or other over-the-counter pain remedies by the company is not recommended. Some medicines have side effects; antihistamines can cause drowsiness on the job; and employees may take more than recommended dosages. Because of the potential liabilities of these actions, it is better to refer an ill employee to his or her physician for treatment.

A sample employee handbook paragraph follows:

> Safety on the job requires active participation by employees as well as management. Each employee has a responsibility to perform job duties in a safe manner.
>
> Accident prevention is our goal, so please maintain your work area in a clean and orderly manner. In the event of an accident or injury, *no matter how slight,* report to your supervisor. He or she will immediately notify designated employees who are trained in first aid procedures. Emergency medical care is available if needed at a nearby clinic.

## I-9 Employment Eligibility

The I-9 Employment Eligibility Verification Form must be completed by all employees hired after November 6, 1986. The completion of this form is a requirement of the Immigration Reform and Control Act of 1986. The purpose of the law is to eliminate employment opportunities that attract illegal aliens to the United States. The law makes it the employer's responsibility to verify that the employee is a U.S. citizen or an alien authorized to work in the United States.[10]

An employer's policy should guide personnel responsible for hiring on complying with the law. The basic requirements are these:

1. The new employee must complete the I-9 form, or a translator may assist the employee.

2. The employee must present two original forms of identification showing employment eligibility and identity. Acceptable documents are listed on the I-9 form.

3. The employer must check the documents and complete the employer portion of the I-9 form within three days of hiring the employee. Photocopies of the documents may be retained.

4. Employers must retain the forms for three years and present the forms for inspection if requested by officials of the Department of Labor or the Immigration and Naturalization Service.[11]

An employer may refuse to hire an individual who fails to provide appropriate documents. However, it is illegal to discriminate against an individual because of national origin or citizenship status. Additional information is available in *Handbook for Employers–Instructions for Completing Form I-9* (Publication M-274, U.S. Department of Justice, Immigration and Naturalization Service, Rev. 11/21/91).

A sample employee handbook paragraph follows:

> The Company has established the following conditions of employment to promote a safe working environment and comply with government regulations:
>
> You must be legally qualified for employment in the United States by showing evidence of citizenship or work authorization and personal identification.
>
> All newly hired employees must present two original forms of identification and complete the I-9 Employment Eligibility Verification Form.

## Independent Contractors

Independent contractors are self-employed individuals who contract with firms to provide a particular service. Some employers treat certain employees as independent contractors. Whether an individual is an employee or an independent contractor depends on a number of factors defined either in common law or under various statutes.

A number of state and federal laws define and regulate the employment relationship. The Internal Revenue Service defines employee status and requires income tax withholding from employees. State and federal unemployment insurance laws require employer contributions for employees. Worker's compensation laws require insurance coverages for employees. Wage hour laws stipulate minimum wage and overtime pay requirements for covered employees. Clearly, the determination of whether an individual is an employee or independent contractor has a significant effect on business costs and legal liability.

Unfortunately, there is no single definition for independent contractor. Each government agency that enforces laws relating to the employer-employee relationship has its own definitions and tests to determine whether a covered employment relationship exists. There are some common trends to aid in defining employment relationships.

The following factors are typical of independent contractor status:

- Individual operates a separate business on a profit and loss basis.
- Individual performs services for other businesses.
- Individual exercises initiative and judgment in how work is performed.
- Individual maintains own tools, equipment, and separate office or facility.
- Individual is paid on a per-job basis.

The following factors are typical of an employer-employee relationship:

- Employer exercises direction and control over employee, work methods, and hours of work.
- Employee generally performs tasks at employer's facility.

- Employee works only for employer.
- Employee is compensated on an hourly or weekly salary basis.

Note: The preceding examples are provided as a general guide only. The IRS uses a 20-point checklist to evaluate the employment relationship. Obtain professional assistance if unsure of all criteria for evaluating independent contractor status.

A sample employee handbook paragraph follows:

> XYZ Company occasionally retains the services of independent contractors for special projects. Independent contractors are not actually our employees. They are, instead, self-employed individuals who work on contract. Independent contractors have been used for computer programming, design engineering, interior decoration, and other related professional services.
>
> Please give these individuals your fullest cooperation.

## Office Parties

Office parties can be an excellent social activity providing a lot of fun for employees. Office parties also can be disruptive to work activities and create potential liabilities when alcoholic beverages are involved.

Employee marriages, birthdays, employment separation, and retirement are common reasons for employee parties on company premises. Management may overlook an occasional party, but if parties become frequent, it becomes difficult to control. Party planning, organizing, and collecting funds to cover costs are activities that interfere with regular work activities. A recommended policy on parties should limit frequency (i.e., not more than one per month; combine celebrations if two or more events occur in a month), prohibit party planning on work time, and designate a time and space for parties which minimizes work disruption.

Parties on or off premises which include the serving of alcoholic beverages create special concerns and liabilities. An employer serving alcoholic beverages should avoid serving minors and limit drinks or provide designated drivers to prevent intoxicated employees from driving home after the party. If alcoholic beverages are used frequently at business, sales, or social functions, the employer ought to obtain special liability coverage for this kind of event.

A sample employee handbook paragraph follows:

> XYZ Company recognizes that employee parties are an opportunity for celebrating weddings, retirements, or other events. In order to allow employee parties which do not disrupt our daily work activities, several guidelines have been defined.
>
> The individual planning a party must notify the Human Resource Administrator at least one week in advance. Parties are permitted on the first Friday of the month in the employee lunchroom, beginning after

4:00 p.m. Party preparations must be conducted during nonworking time (breaks or lunch period). Up to $25 may be spent from the employee activities fund for a party.

## Report-in Pay

Report-in pay is compensation provided when employees report to work for their regular work shift and there is no available work. Report-in pay is used in cases of facilities emergency or power outage. Report-in pay provides compensation to hourly paid employees for a minimum period. There is no legal requirement to provide report-in pay, although the practice is commonly negotiated by unions into labor agreements.

A Report-in Pay Policy should identify circumstances under which report-in pay will be provided, specify the number of hours of pay (two to four hours is common), and define advance notification procedures by the company which would void eligibility for report-in pay. If the company can provide advance notice to employees through telephone calls or radio announcements, then no report-in pay is provided.

A sample employee handbook paragraph follows:

> When an employee reports to work on his/her regularly scheduled shift without being properly notified that there will be no work, he or she will receive a minimum of four (4) hours work, or four (4) hours pay at his or her regular straight-time hourly rate. The hours paid, but not worked, shall accumulate toward a 40-hour week for overtime pay eligibility.
>
> This policy will not apply if inability to supply work is due to causes beyond the Company's control such as power failure, fire, flood, civil disturbance, other "acts of God"; or if proper notice cannot be given due to an employee's absence from home or failure to provide current address/telephone, thus preventing timely notification by the Company.

## Solicitations

Solicitations or distributions of literature in the workplace can be disruptive and interfere with work. For this reason, many firms define a solicitation policy prohibiting such activity. Solicitations can range from sale of cookies or food products for fundraising, seeking contributions for employee parties, or distribution of literature about clubs or activities in the community.

Solicitations also can be an integral part of a union organizing drive. Union organizers may seek to distribute literature to employees in the workplace, or enlist the aid of sympathetic employees to distribute literature to others on the job. An employer most likely will stop a union solicitor or employee from distributing literature on company premises.

Union organizing activities such as solicitations or handbilling are protected under the National Labor Relations Act. This means that the employer who permitted candy sales but stopped union solicitations may be charged with an unfair labor practice.

A Solicitation Policy needs to be carefully defined to prevent workplace disruption but allow employee freedom of speech rights guaranteed by federal labor laws. A Solicitation Policy can include these key points:

- Nonemployee solicitors generally can be prohibited from the premises.
- Employee solicitations must be limited to nonworking times and nonworking areas.

A sample employee handbook paragraph follows:

> In order to avoid disruption to Company operations, XYZ Company has established the following rules related to solicitations and distribution of literature on Company property.
> a) Nonemployees may not solicit or distribute literature on Company property at any time for any purpose.
> b) Employees may not solicit or distribute literature during working time for any purpose.
> c) Employees may not distribute literature at any time in public areas or in working areas.

Working time includes the working time of both the employee doing the soliciting and distributing and the employee to whom the soliciting or distributing is being directed. Working time does not include break periods, meal periods, or any other specified periods during the workday when employees are properly not engaged in performing their work tasks.

## Seniority

Seniority is a term which defines length of service with an organization. The measure of seniority typically begins at the start of employment. Seniority is an artificial concept created by unions to accord greater status or benefits to individuals with greater service. Seniority can be used as a basis to grant preference in vacation schedules, layoff, transfer, promotion, assignment of overtime, or other similar employment conditions. Seniority does define a uniform basis for employment decisions.

However, nonunion employers complain that seniority can severely limit management discretion to make employment decisions in the best interest of the organization. Often, the best qualified individual for a particular job assignment is not the most senior worker. Managers of nonunion facilities prefer to avoid seniority policies. If a Seniority Policy is defined based on past practice or through collective bargaining, try to define seniority as a deciding factor after skills, abilities, and job performance have been considered.

A sample employee handbook paragraph follows:

> Each employee begins accruing seniority after successfully completing the 90-day orientation period. Seniority is a measure of length of Company service based upon date of hire, and it is one factor which is considered in certain employment decisions such as promotions, vacation scheduling, layoff, or recall. An employee loses seniority upon permanent separation of employment.

## Company Information

An employee handbook is an excellent medium for providing company information to employees. Company information can include highlights of company history, details on company products and services, and explanation of company goals or philosophy. Learning information about the company helps employees to feel a better sense of belonging to the organization.

Company information presents a positive and less harsh message, helping to reduce the "rule book" effect of some employee handbooks. One sales-oriented company was concerned that employees be really responsive to the customer. To address this concern, various segments of the handbook explained company goals for friendly service and fast response to customer requests.

In another company, quality control was stressed as a high priority. This organization included in its employee handbook various statements about the employee's role in achieving quality.

Several sample paragraphs are shown:

*Working Together*

> The success of our organization depends upon each individual effectively handling daily job tasks and performing his or her fair share of the group effort. Your cooperation with fellow employees and dedication by performing job duties to the best of your ability will receive appropriate recognition by Company management. Our salary and benefits programs are designed to provide compensation and rewards which are competitive with other firms in the area.
>
> We hope that you will share our commitment to quality and dedication to efficiently serve the customer's needs. Anything less than your best effort fails to meet our standard of a day's work for a day's pay.

*History and Growth*

> XYZ Company was founded in 1946 by J. Jones. The new company began operations in Chicago, Illinois as a mold making shop.
>
> In 1950, the Company acquired additional equipment and began its plastic molding operations. This strategic business decision placed XYZ into the newly emerging plastics industry and contributed significantly toward the Company's continued growth. By 1970, the Company pur-

chased and built its present modern facility, providing an efficient and attractive working environment.

XYZ builds molds and performs injection molding assembly of a variety of plastic parts and components. Our products are used in pharmaceutical, automotive, housewares, electronics, telecommunications, and other industries throughout North America. The Company has established its reputation as a leading plastic molder because of our commitment to quality and on-time delivery. We optimistically predict continued growth in the years ahead.

*Quality Comes First*

At XYZ, we strive to constantly produce quality printing. Each employee plays an important role in meeting this objective by taking pride in his or her work, performing each task with care, and paying careful attention to each customer order to eliminate errors or reruns.

# Notes

1. R. Green, W. Carmell, P. Gray, *1992 State by State Guide to Human Resource Law*, Panel Publishers, New York, 1992, pp. 8–3.
2. *OSHA Safety and Health Standards* (29CFR 1910), U.S. Dept. of Labor, OSHA 2206, June, 1981, pp. i–vi.
3. *A Brief Guide to Recordkeeping Requirements for Occupational Injuries and Illnesses*, U.S. Dept. of Labor, June, 1986, p. 7.
4. *Chemical Hazard Communication*, U.S. Dept. of Labor, OSHA 3084, 1987, p. 1.
5. 29 CFR 1910.1200, *Hazard Communication*, November 2, 1983.
6. *Occupational Safety and Health Hazard Communication Federal/State Right to Know Laws*, Commerce Clearing House, Chicago, 1985, pp. 7–8.
7. Title 29 U.S.C.A., Chapter 22, Employee Polygraph Protection.
8. R. Green, W. Carmell, P. Gray, *1992 State by State Guide to Human Resource Law*, Panel Publishers, New York, 1992, pp. 4–51.
9. OSHA Safety and Health Standards, Subpart K, Medical & First Aid, 29 CFR 1910.151, OSHA publication 2206, June 1981, p. 304.
10. *Handbook for Employers, Instructions for Completing Form I-9*, U.S. Dept. of Justice, M 274 (Rev. 11-21-91), p. 1.
11. Ibid., pp. 3–5.

# 16

# Current Issues: Addressing Workplace Drug Abuse, Smoking, Disability Accommodation, Etc.

**Read Chapter 16 for:**

Smoking

Drug testing

Drug-free workplace

Disability accommodation

Workplace AIDS policy

## Smoke-free Workplace

Employee attitudes about smoking have changed significantly over the past 20 years. Smoking was a widely accepted practice in the 1940s and 1950s. According to the American Cancer Society, per capita cigarette consumption reached its peak in 1963. Then, the U.S. Surgeon General's office released the first of a series of statements that smoking is a health hazard. Since that time, the Surgeon General's warning statements have grown increasingly critical of smoking, advertising limits have been imposed, and the prevalence of smoking has declined.

According to Cancer Society data, 37 percent of the U.S. adult population were smokers in 1976. A decade later, the proportion of smokers had decreased to 30 percent. Public opinion surveys conducted by the Society in the early 1980s revealed that 79 percent of all Americans, including 76 percent of smokers, thought that workplace smoking should be restricted to designated areas.[1]

Along with the changes of public attitudes about smoking, growing numbers of governmental units have defined laws or regulations restricting smoking. A number of these actions are highlighted:

- OSHA regulations prohibit use of smoking materials when working near flammable substances.

- The federal government and the military adopted policies limiting use of smoking materials in governmental buildings.

- The Federal Aeronautics Administration now prohibits use of smoking materials on all domestic commercial airplane flights.

- Minnesota's Clean Indoor Air Act, which went into effect in 1975, was the first state law to prohibit use of smoking materials in public places except in designated areas. Since that time, over 30 states have passed similar laws. (See Chap. 5.)

- Over 400 cities have passed ordinances restricting smoking in public areas.

According to the U.S. Department of Health and Human Services, smokers create added costs to business—costs which cut into profits. An HHS publication cites these costs:

- Absenteeism rates for smokers are approximately 50 percent higher than for nonsmokers.

- The smoking ritual takes up about 6 percent of the workday.

- Smokers have twice as many job-related accidents as nonsmokers.

- Average annual health insurance claims for smokers are $300 higher than for nonsmokers.

- Smokers are 50 percent more likely to be hospitalized than those who do not smoke.[2]

In light of the social, legal, and economic reasons cited, growing numbers of employers are developing policies which restrict workplace smoking. One important element in the success of a smoking policy is willing commitment by top managers. Managers who smoke must set a good example by observing smoking prohibitions or actively participating in stop-smoking clinics.

Employee involvement in developing a new Smoking Policy is recommended. Employee involvement can range from completion of a survey questionnaire on smoking issues to actual participation in defining policy elements.

Advance notice to employees about the new Smoking Policy is essential. Since quitting smoking is a major lifestyle change, advance notice of the policy change allows time for employees as well as the company to prepare for the adjustment. Three months, six months, or more time is not unreasonable. The process of involving employees in policy planning helps to provide advance notice and general employee support for the new policy.

The scope of the Smoking Policy is a major issue to consider. The policy can range from a total ban on smoking in the workplace to limited restrictions such as OSHA's prohibition against smoking when working with flammable substances. Any state or local smoking ordinances should be evaluated for effect on the policy. A common practice is to designate certain areas as nonsmoking and other areas where smoking is permitted. When possible, many firms permit employees to designate their office or immediate work area as a smoke-free area. Whenever possible, it is best to try to separate smokers and nonsmokers into different areas or rooms. In the event that separation is not feasible, the recommended solution is to designate shared work spaces as nonsmoking.

Communication of the Smoking Policy is needed to resolve the many questions that may occur. Try to anticipate questions and define appropriate answers based on the policy. Communicate the policy through employee meetings, memos, payroll stuffers, bulletin board announcements, and other similar methods.

A positive approach which reconciles individual differences within the policy guidelines is a recommended enforcement approach. Disciplinary measures may be used as a last resort or whenever smoking practices show disregard for sanitation or safety requirements.

Consider incentives to promote employee interest in stopping smoking. Offering stop-smoking clinics on site or off site helps provide support and direction to employees who are trying to stop smoking. The costs of such programs can be borne by employee participants, but company funding can provide an incentive for broader participation. Bonuses or financial rewards have also been offered to motivate employee efforts to kick the smoking habit.

## Pitfalls to Avoid

When employees are quibbling about smokers' rights versus nonsmokers' rights, work tasks are not getting done. Here are some pitfalls to avoid when defining a smoking policy.

1. Lack of planning will create many questions later. Smoking is one of those issues which creates strong feelings and emotions. Smokers' and nonsmokers' battle lines can easily be created by secondhand smoke wafting through a shared work area. One important planning key is to elicit employee opinions on the desired extent of the Smoking Policy.

## CHECKLIST
## A Smoking Policy

- What federal, state and local laws apply to workplace smoking issues?

- What safety or fire safety regulations apply to workplace smoking issues at your firm?

- Is management committed to developing a policy that limits or prevents smoking in the workplace?

- What kinds of smoking materials will be controlled by the smoking policy?

- Are there any union agreement or insurance plan requirements that will affect a smoking policy?

- Will your smoking policy totally ban smoking on the job or limit smoking to designated areas or times of day?

- Will your smoking policy extend beyond working time to prohibit off-workers use of smoking materials, or are such prohibitions limited by law in your state?

- Will employees be permitted to designate their own work area as smoke-free?

- What sort of conflict resolution or enforcement steps will be taken to assume that the policy is followed?

- Will the preferences of the smoker or the nonsmoker prevail in the event of a conflict?

- Will the smoking policy apply to employees, management, visitors, customers, or general public?

- Will the policy be announced in advance, such as 6 months or one year?

- Will the firm encourage and pay for participation in stop smoking clinics, health screening programs, or the use of stop smoking devices available on the market?

- How will the policy be publicized and introduced to employees?[3]

Then work through the "what ifs" to identify possible questions and answers under the Smoking Policy.

2. Once a Smoking Policy is in place, several likely side effects will occur. Some common difficulties and suggested solutions are offered:

   *The smoking room*: Many firms limit smoking to designated areas such as lunchroom or washrooms. These designated areas become smoky rooms because the concentration of smoke cannot be dissipated. Limiting smoking to larger rooms, or rooms with enhanced ventilation may be needed.

   *Smoking on the front steps*: When driving through many office or industrial parks, it is easy to spot those firms with Smoking Policies. These are the firms where employees are seen smoking on the front steps (rain or shine, hot or cold). This practice certainly creates a poor image of the company. If management elects to designate "outside the building" as the designated smoking area, I recommend that a back door or other area be designated to prevent smokers gathering on the front steps.

*Smoke breaks*: Smoking is a habit-forming activity as well as an addiction. The smoking act becomes correlated to various work activities. When a smoking ban is instituted, smokers will "feel the urge" based on work habits or routines and will take a smoke break. A smoke break means stopping work and going to the designated area for a smoke. This individual will probably also expect to take the full limits of regular break periods and lunch. Smoke breaks should not be allowed. If a smoking ban in the workplace is instituted, smokers should be limited to smoking only during nonworking times such as lunch, break periods, before work, or after work.

3. Be alert to the effect of new privacy laws being passed in various states. These laws make it illegal for an employer to discipline or otherwise discriminate against an employee for legal off-duty activities. The intent of these laws is to prevent an employer from taking action against an employee for smoking off the job and may serve to bar broad policy criteria such as hiring only non-smokers or banning employees from smoking on or off the job.

**Sample Policy**

**XYZ COMPANY**
**PERSONNEL POLICY & PROCEDURE**

---

SUBJECT: SMOKING                                    DATE: May 1, 1993
APPLIES TO: All Employees

---

*Policy*: It is the policy of the Company to define restrictions on workplace smoking in order to promote employee safety and health.

*Procedure*:
1. The XYZ Smoking Policy applies to all Company facilities, all employees, as well as customers and vendors visiting our facilities. Our policy becomes effective January 1, 1994.

2. In the interest of promoting employee health and safety, use of smoking materials is prohibited on Company time and premises, except in designated smoking areas. Use of smoking materials refers to the lighting and smoking of cigarettes, cigars, pipes, or other similar items.

3. Smoking is permitted during nonworking time periods in designated smoking areas. Designated smoking areas include the smoking section of the lunchroom, break area in the warehouse, and the picnic area by the employee entrance. Smoking materials must be properly disposed

       of in ashtrays provided, and exhaust ventilation fans must be turned on. Nonworking time periods include lunch, breaks, or before or after work. Special "smoke breaks" are not permitted.

4. The XYZ Smoking Policy applies to customers, vendors, and visitors to our facility. The individual hosting the visitor is responsible for advising the visitor of XYZ Smoking Policy. A sign describing our Smoking Policy shall be displayed in our lobby.

5. Each supervisor is responsible for enforcing the Smoking Policy in his or her respective area. Disregard for smoking guidelines should be handled by discussions or warnings as defined in our Disciplinary Policy.

6. XYZ Company encourages employees to use the policy as an opportunity to stop smoking. The Company will, as this policy is implemented, pay the full cost of employee participation in a designated stop-smoking clinic. The Human Resource Administrator is responsible for coordinating program enrollments.

7. Any questions or disputes arising under this policy shall be referred to the Human Resource Administrator. Final authority in policy interpretation rests with the General Manager.

**Sample Employee Handbook Paragraph**

*Smoking Policy*

XYZ Company has a sincere interest in the health of employees and in maintaining pleasant working conditions. For this reason, it is Company policy to prohibit the use of smoking materials in
a) open office areas
b) lunchroom
c) conference room
d) shared offices if shared with a nonsmoker who objects to smoking
Please cooperate with these limits. In the event of conflicts, management shall resolve the matter in the best interests of employees, the Company, and workplace efficiency.

# Drug Testing

The prevalence of drug abuse in our society today is underscored by frequent reports of drug-related stories in our daily newspapers and evening television news. The drug abuse problem has reached crisis proportions in various inner city neighborhoods. Suburban and rural areas are not immune to the social and workplace problems caused by drugs. An estimated 10 percent to 25 percent of the population is affected directly or indirectly by alcohol or drug abuse. The substance abuser may be your employee,

employee's spouse, family member, or close friend. With this many individuals being affected by substance abuse, these problems are certain to enter and affect the workplace.

Indeed, substance abuse costs American business $40 billion a year in lost productivity according to the National Council on Alcoholism. In a 1986 survey of human resource directors conducted by the American Management Association, an overwhelming 93.5 percent of firms surveyed reported dealing with employee drug abuse problems.[4]

Data from the U.S. Department of Health and Human Services reveals the following characteristics of a typical drug-abusing worker:

- Late three times more often than other nonabusing employees
- Requested early dismissal or time off during work 2.2 times more often than nonabusing coworkers
- Had 2.5 times as many absences of eight days or more
- Used three times the normal level of sick benefits
- Was five times more likely to file a worker's compensation claim
- Was involved in accidents 3.6 times more often than other employees[5]

For employers, drug abuse by employees causes greater absences, lower productivity, quality problems, higher insurance costs, increased worker's compensation claims, and lower profits.

During the last decade, drug testing has grown as a means to combat drug abuse on the job. There are a variety of ways in which firms have used drug testing. These are highlighted:

*New hire testing*: The testing of job applicants for drugs is intended to identify drug abusers before hire and to screen them out. Firms that use preemployment drug testing make successful completion of the drug test a condition of employment. A positive test result showing presence of drugs in the body is considered grounds to deny or withdraw a job offer. Preemployment drug testing is not limited by the Americans with Disabilities Act.

*Transportation and public safety testing*: Government regulations dealing with certain public safety jobs require drug testing of workers. Jobs such as nuclear plant workers, truck drivers, and railway engineers are subject to drug testing requirements.

*Reasonable cause testing*: Reasonable cause testing is used to test current employees of an organization. With reasonable cause testing, there must be some incident, accident, or other unusual event which creates adequate justification (reasonable cause) for a drug test.

*Random testing*: Random testing is the unscheduled or surprise testing of an employee or group of employees for presence of drugs. The random and surprise approach is intended to catch drug-using individuals who may be able to remain drug-free in anticipation of a scheduled drug test in order to pass the test.

*Universal testing*: Universal testing involves the scheduled or unscheduled drug testing of all employees. An example of universal testing would be the requirement that all Olympic athletes undergo drug tests following competition.

There are a number of legal issues to consider when implementing a drug testing program. Constitutional issues, federal laws, state laws, and various regulations must be considered when defining drug testing programs. The U.S. Constitution restricts governmental interference with individual rights. This means that public sector employees have been accorded privacy rights from unreasonable search and seizures of drug tests. Private sector employees, on the other hand, have not been accorded the same protection from their employers. Some state constitutions, however, contain privacy protections applicable to both private and public sector conduct.

Handicap discrimination issues can impact on drug or alcohol policy issues. The Rehabilitation Act of 1973 and the Americans with Disabilities Act prohibit employment discrimination on the basis of handicap. Under both laws, individuals who have successfully completed drug or alcohol treatment programs are considered handicapped and protected from discrimination. Likewise, any use of drug testing in a manner which discriminates against individuals on the basis of age, sex, race, religion, national origin, or color would violate equal employment opportunity laws.

Fifteen states have laws dealing with drug test issues. Drug test restrictions are defined by the following states:

| | |
|---|---|
| Connecticut | Minnesota |
| Florida | Mississippi |
| Hawaii | Montana |
| Iowa | Nebraska |
| Louisiana | Nevada |
| Maine | Rhode Island |
| Maryland | Utah |
| | Vermont[6] |

Federal government regulations on drug testing for motor carriers appear at Title 49 Code of Federal Regulations, Parts 391 and 394. In addition, the U.S. Department of Health and Human Services published mandatory guidelines for federal workplace drug testing programs in the *Federal Register* at volume 53, number 69, on April 14, 1988. These guidelines provide technical safeguards useful for any employer establishing a drug testing program.

The National Labor Relations Board has ruled that drug testing is a mandatory subject for bargaining.[7] This means that firms with a union must bargain with the union before implementing drug testing policies or procedures which affect bargaining unit employees. Preemployment drug testing or alcohol testing of job applicants, however, is permissible. Job applicants are not employees within the meaning of the National Labor Relations Act.

Currently, the most common method of drug testing is by urinalysis. The procedure, referred to as immunoassay, involves lab testing of a urine sample given by the employee or applicant. The National Institute on Drug Abuse (NIDA) recommends a second confirmation test if the urinalysis is positive. In a NIDA publication entitled *Employee Drug Screening,* the NIDA suggests

> If an initial screening assay shows a sample as being positive, a second assay should be employed to confirm the initial result. Two different assays operating on different chemical principles having both given a positive result greatly decreases the possibility that a methodological problem or a "cross reacting" substance could have created the positive. A confirmation assay usually should be carried out by a method which is of comparable sensitivity and which is more specific (or selective) than a screening assay. Examples of confirmation methods currently in use include gas chromatography (GC), gas chromatography/mass spectrometry (GC/MS), and high performance liquid chromatography (HPLC). These are sophisticated instrumental methods requiring highly trained technicians to operate them. Properly run, they are capable of providing highly selective assays for a variety of drugs.
>
> Gas chromatography coupled with mass spectrometry (GC/MS) has evolved as the preferred method for confirmation of a positive urine screening test, primarily because it provides the greatest level of specificity and therefore the greatest margin of certainty and legal defensibility. Additionally, it is the only method which provides a documented data record suitable for review and interpretation by an outside expert. This method of confirmation is required of laboratories which are certified for urine drug testing for Federal employee programs.[8]

There are some limitations to drug testing. Drug tests merely detect the presence of certain chemicals in the body. Drug tests cannot identify degree of intoxication or performance impairment resulting from drug use. Drug tests do not prove that drugs were used on the job. Further, drug tests can produce "false positives." A false positive is a test result reporting the presence of a tested chemical when the employee in fact did not use drugs. A false positive can be due to a lab error, or it can be due to the employee consumption of certain legal substances. One example was the use of over-the-counter pain killers containing Ibuprofen. Test procedures have been adjusted to prevent these false positives.

Another similar problem can occur when employees consume over-the-counter substances such as diet pills, cold remedies, and even bakery goods containing poppy seeds. These items have been found to produce a positive result on the urinalysis test. The confirmation tests, however, can more specifically identify whether a substance is an illegal drug.

Another recommended procedure is the use of a specially trained doctor referred to as a medical review officer. According to the *Employee Drug Screening* publication,

> One essential part of any drug-testing program is the medical review of laboratory results. A positive drug test result does not automatically identify an employee/applicant as a user of illegal drugs. Confirmed positive test results for amphetamines, barbiturates, opiates, and even cocaine can result from legitimate medical treatment.
>
> The DHHS Guidelines for drug testing by Federal agencies require that a licensed physician, with knowledge of substance-abuse disorders, be contracted to review and interpret any positive test results. The Guidelines specify:
>
>> In carrying out this responsibility, the Medical Review Officer shall examine alternate medical explanations for any positive test result. This action could include conducting a medical interview with the individual, review of the individual's medical history, or review of any other relevant biomedical factors. The Medical Review Officer shall review all medical records made available by the tested individual when a confirmed positive test could have resulted from legally prescribed medication.
>
> If procedures such as those prescribed for the Federal drug testing program are followed, the chances of an individual being wrongfully accused of using illicit substances will be virtually eliminated.[9]

Some individuals view drug testing as an intrusive invasion of privacy. Others view testing as a necessary weapon in the war on drugs. Since these emotional attitudes can influence individual careers and organization livelihoods, a decision to begin drug testing must be carefully weighed.

For those organizations subject to drug testing regulations, compliance with government rules can be the foundation of the policy. For other organizations, an assessment of the scope of the problem is recommended.

A Labor Department publication offers these suggestions:

> To try to determine whether an organization has a substance abuse problem or the potential for developing a problem, the following steps can be taken.
> - Identify organizational indicators of substandard performance such as increases in accidents, theft and property losses, security breaches, benefits utilization, absenteeism, training costs, and worker compensation claims.
> - Call together representatives of key units within the organization such as occupational safety and health, security, employee benefits, personnel, and the EAP to get a company-wide sense of the problem. Employee representatives should be a part of the process.
> - Obtain national, State or local statistics gathered by substance abuse agencies (health or law enforcement), medical or health societies,

hospitals or treatment facilities, chapters of the National Council on Alcoholism, business and industry or trade organizations.

- Gather workers' views, formally or informally, as to whether drug use is present and whether it is undermining health, safety, security, or other aspects of work activity.

- Compare hard data with subjective views to get some idea of the productivity toll exacted by drugs.[10]

## Competitive Practices

The number of companies doing drug testing continues to increase. According to the NIDA, various surveys conducted during 1986 and 1987 found that 20 to 33 percent of firms have drug testing programs in place. NIDA reports that

> In general, the larger the company, the more likely it is to have a drug testing program. One survey by the American Management Association found that 15% of companies doing under $15 million do testing, while 36% of companies doing over $1 billion do some testing. Other surveys have also documented this relationship. In a College Placement Council survey, while overall 28% of companies did testing, 58% of those over 5,000 employees have testing programs. Larger companies are leading in the adoption of drug testing programs.
>
> There are also significant differences by industry. Federally regulated industries are more likely to test—utilities (91%) and transportation (81%); followed by manufacturing (44.8%), communications (34.5%), mining/construction (15.3%), and with the lowest rates in retail (13.0%), services (12.6%) and finance and insurance (8.7%) industries.[12]

## Pitfalls to Avoid

The sensitivity of an individual's right to privacy is a major employee concern. An employer's insensitivity to employee privacy concerns or failure to adequately implement a testing program can cause serious morale problems and costly litigation. Here are some pitfalls to avoid:

1. Do not start drug testing without careful research and planning. A written policy is essential (and even required under various state laws). Often, drug tests influence decisions to hire or to fire an employee. Policy guidelines will help management to recognize when testing is needed and how to deal with the situation in an appropriate manner.

2. As a general guide, I recommend that firms avoid use of random or universal drug testing. These two approaches to drug testing present the greatest privacy threat to employees without apparent justification. Exceptions to this recommendation are when government require-

## CHECKLIST
## A Drug Testing Policy

- Is management committed to addressing substance abuse?

- Can an effective policy be developed internally or will outside assistance be required?

- What substances will be included under the policy (illegal drugs, marijuana, alcohol, prescription drugs)?

- What federal, state, and local laws might apply to the proposal?

- Will the policy be limited to referral procedures for testing or encompass a range of employee-relations issues?

- Will the tests be used for new applicants, certain positions, employee evaluation following an accident or misconduct, or across-the-board searches for drug abuse?

- Will a second confirmation test be used in the event of a positive test report?

- Will the employee or applicant be advised of test results, referred for counseling or treatment in the event of a positive finding, or permitted to file a grievance or complaint or obtain an independent test?

- Will an employee be disciplined for refusing to submit to a drug test?

- Will drug tests or related records remain confidential?

- Will an employee be permitted a medical leave to enter in-patient treatment for substance abuse?

- Does health insurance cover substance-abuse treatment or will it be modified to provide such coverage?

- Will an employee-assistance plan be implemented as part of the policy?

- What actions will be taken to communicate policies to employees and to train supervisors?[11]

ments specify such testing or if a drug problem is found to be so pervasive that extreme measures are needed.

As a general guide for most firms, I recommend that preemployment drug testing be the first priority. Safety concerns of hiring only individuals without evidence of drug use can be easily justified. Applicants can be given prior notice that passing the drug test is a condition of employment. Discrimination against current drug users is permissible. For these reasons, a preemployment drug screen is the least likely to cause legal liabilities.

The second best area for drug testing is probable cause or incident-based testing. This means that testing is done when some action or inaction by the employee creates an incident providing reasonable justification for management to refer the employee for a drug test. Courts and arbitrators generally have held that an individual's privacy claims are secondary to the organizations need to maintain a safe and healthful workplace.

3. When drug testing is used, avoid relying exclusively on the test results as the sole basis for a hiring or firing decision. Secondary or confirmation drug tests are recommended. Also, consider the drug test results as one of the various factors which influence the employment decision. Where there is a pattern of information pointing to a conclusion, a better employment decision will result.

**Sample Policy**

**XYZ COMPANY**
**PERSONNEL POLICY & PROCEDURE**

SUBJECT: INCUMBENT EMPLOYEE        DATE: May 1, 1993
             DRUG/ALCOHOL SCREENING
APPLIES TO: All Employees

*Policy*: It is the policy of the Company to use a health evaluation when investigating suspected drug or alcohol abuse.

*Purpose*: To assure a safe and healthful working environment by alerting management to employee problems caused by drug or alcohol abuse.

*Procedure*:
1. The General Manager or the Plant Superintendent is responsible for orientating new employees under his or her direction to the Company's comprehensive drug/alcohol program. The orientation shall include a discussion of Company policies and philosophy and obtaining the employee's signed certification about the program.

2. Each employee is responsible for reporting to work in a fit condition for duty. Reporting to work under the influence of alcohol or drugs (including prescription or "over-the-counter" drugs which impair judgment or coordination) is deemed to be unfit for duty.

3. The employee is responsible for advising superiors when he or she is ill or unable to work, or under a physician's care and taking prescription or over-the-counter drugs which may impair job performance. In such cases, management reserves the right to temporarily transfer an employee, to send the employee home for a sick day, or to place an employee on medical leave of absence until such time as the employee is able to resume normal job duties.

4. In the event an employee voluntarily advises a manager or supervisor regarding a chemical dependency problem such as drug abuse or

alcoholism, the employee shall be referred to the General Manager or Plant Superintendent for assistance. In such cases, it is recommended that the employee be immediately referred to a qualified chemical dependency counselor or treatment center for evaluation and assistance. If in-patient treatment for chemical dependency is warranted, the employee shall be placed on a medical leave of absence. The employee shall be assured of full confidentiality and there shall be no disciplinary penalties imposed upon an employee solely because he or she voluntarily sought medical assistance.

5. The supervisor is responsible for being continually alert to employee behavior, giving careful attention to unusual behavior, significant behavior or mood changes, performance problems, accidents, or misconduct. In the event of an unusual or adverse incident, the following procedures shall apply:

   a) The supervisor shall discuss the incident with the General Manager or Plant Superintendent as appropriate.

   b) The employee shall be called in to a private office for a confidential discussion/investigation of the incident. (A union steward shall be included if the employee is a member of the bargaining unit.)

   c) Statement of witnesses or any other evidence to corroborate the incident shall be considered; and the employee shall be given reasonable opportunity to explain or provide mitigating evidence.

   d) If the supervisor has reasonable cause to suspect that the use of drugs or alcohol is a contributing factor to the adverse incident, management may elect to refer the employee to a Company-designated medical facility for a health evaluation.

   e) In the event that the General Manager or Plant Superintendent are not available for discussion at the time of the incident (i.e., during night shift) the supervisor may exercise discretion to refer the employee for a health evaluation. In such cases, the supervisor shall provide full details of the incident to management as soon as possible on the next workday.

6. When management elects to refer an employee for a health evaluation, the following procedures shall apply:

   a) The supervisor shall prepare a written statement and duplicate copy describing the incident and the employee's behavior; one copy shall be retained in Company personnel files and the second copy shall be carried to the medical facility.

   b) The employee shall be driven to the medical facility by a Company supervisor or manager. The supervisor or manager shall remain at the medical facility or coordinate return transportation arrangements for the employee.

   c) The employee is expected to sign a consent form for the health evaluation.

   d) In the event any test shows a positive result indicating presence of drugs or alcohol, a second confirmation test shall be conducted.

   e) The employee shall receive regular pay for time lost from work, up to eight hours for the day.

7. When a drug/alcohol test shows a confirmed positive finding, the employee shall be referred to a drug/alcohol treatment center for a chemical dependency evaluation. An employee's agreement to participate in a health evaluation exam and treatment, if warranted, shall result in no disciplinary penalty for the first adverse incident. The employee will receive regular pay for time lost from work, up to eight hours for the day, for a chemical dependency evaluation. If the chemical dependency evaluation results in in-patient treatment, the employee will be placed on a medical leave of absence.

8. In the event an employee refuses to submit to a health evaluation exam, or denies existence of a chemical dependency problem (when there is reasonable evidence to indicate chemical dependency), the employee shall be subject to normal disciplinary measures up to and including dismissal as a result of the adverse incident prompting investigation regardless of whether the incident was drug or alcohol related. In addition, the supervisor may elect to impose discipline for insubordination resulting from the employee's refusal to submit to a drug/alcohol exam.

9. In the administration of this policy, the Company reserves the right to schedule an employee for a complete physical exam or any other lab tests deemed appropriate by management or the Company-designated physician or other health care professional.

10. Under this policy, an employee may elect to exercise the following rights:

    a) Union employees may file a grievance in the manner prescribed by their union contract if there is a contract issue at dispute.

    b) Nonunion employees may present any complaint to management in the manner described by the Company's open door policy.

    c) An employee whose health evaluation shows a confirmed positive test result may request a second confirmation test at his or her own expense. Specimens must be taken at the same time, and testing must be performed by an approved lab facility. Such test results will receive appropriate consideration by management.

## Sample Employee Memorandum

To: All XYZ Employees

From: General

Subject: Comprehensive Drug/Alcohol Program

Abuse of chemical substances such as alcohol and drugs is a serious problem in our society today, causing personal grief for many workers and their families and creating significant costs to business and industry. According to some estimates, one person in 10 experiences difficulty at work or at home due to excessive use of alcohol or drugs.

The management of XYZ Company recognizes that chemical dependence may be a disease. With proper medical care and treatment, chemical dependency can be controlled so that the troubled individual can resume productive employment and normal relationships with friends or family members. With this objective in mind, the Company has initiated a Comprehensive Drug/Alcohol Program.

One part of our program is designed to screen out those job applicants who show a confirmed presence of drugs or alcohol in their body when applying for work. We believe that employment of these individuals would present a safety hazard to fellow workers and could seriously jeopardize efficient business operations.

More importantly, we are committed to providing confidential assistance, without penalty, to any XYZ employee who voluntarily seeks medical help to deal with a drug or alcohol dependency problem. An employee who seeks help under this program will be referred to a qualified chemical dependency counselor or treatment center for evaluation and assistance. If in-patient care is warranted, the employee will be placed on a medical leave of absence during the period of treatment. During treatment, eligible employees may receive disability income and/or medical care insurance coverages, subject to the limitations and terms of Company insurance plans.

In addition to the disciplinary rules outlined in the Company Employee Handbook, our Comprehensive Drug/Alcohol Program also provides procedures for dealing with an employee reporting or attempting to work while under the influence of a chemical substance. If any such instances occur and management believes that there is a reasonable cause to suspect that drugs or alcohol are a contributing factor, the employee may be referred to a medical facility for a drug or alcohol screening test. If the test shows confirmed presence of drugs or alcohol in the body, the employee will be referred for a medical evaluation by a qualified chemical dependency counselor.

We believe that this policy provides a fair balance between an individual's concern for personal privacy and the Company's obligation to provide a safe working environment for employees while efficiently providing products and services to meet the needs of our customers. This policy in no way attempts to regulate one's personal lifestyle, but it does call for firm action when personal matters affect job performance.

For all XYZ employees, efficient job performance remains the key ingredient to a successful employment relationship. You may speak with your supervisor if you have any questions.

## Substance Abuse Policy

Substance abuse can be defined as inappropriate or excessive use of alcoholic beverages, over-the-counter drugs, prescription drugs, or any use of illegal drugs. Substance abuse by employees is a contributing factor to workplace accidents, poor productivity, increased errors, and absenteeism.

Often, the substance abusing employee seems perfectly normal. He or she shows up to work on time and gets work assignments done on time. However, the substance abuse has one unique characteristic: It is a big secret. The substance abuser works very hard at masking his or her craving. The work environment is often the last place in which the substance abuser's problem becomes evident.

The substance abuser does not fit our perception of an alcoholic wino or a crazed druggie. Instead, the substance abuser often fits a more normal pattern, such as

A sales manager with a reputation that he's the "life of the party" and can hold his liquor

A single parent in a customer service job using over-the-counter medicines to get "up" for the high-stress workday and taking sleeping pills to relax at night

A service technician who is always on the road but was recently questioned by authorities investigating a theft ring and cocaine dealings

An accounting supervisor with a ruddy face and a liking for breath mints

Each of the foregoing examples represents a valued experienced employee with a potential or real substance abuse problem. An organization with a substance abuse policy has guidelines for dealing with these individuals. A substance abuse policy lets employees know how the company will deal with substance abuse problems. It provides guidance and instructions for supervisors to focus on job performance issues and referral for assistance. A substance abuse policy identifies specific action steps that a supervisor can take rather than covering for the employee and enabling the substance abuser to continue.

A substance abuse policy typically defines specific prohibitions against possession or use of drugs or alcoholic beverages on company time or premises. The policy may also extend to abuse of legal drugs available by prescription or over the counter. In the event an employee recognizes his or her substance abuse problem, the policy needs to guide management in referring the employee for assistance. Confidentiality must be assured. Supervisors must enforce normal work standards and take appropriate disciplinary action if warranted to enforce the policy. If drug testing will be used, these issues must be clarified as well.

When preparing a substance abuse policy, several state and federal labor laws may impact on the policy. Government contractors are subject to the Drug-free Workplace Act of 1988. This law requires employers receiving a government contract of $25,000 or more to certify that they maintain a drug-free workplace with a written plan to comply with the law. The employer's drug-free workplace program should include the following elements:

- A written policy distributed to employees regarding illegal drugs

- A drug awareness program that includes information about hazards of drug use on the job, penalties for violating the policy, and education about available counseling or rehabilitation programs

- Employee compliance with the policy including the reporting of an employee conviction of a drug offense in the workplace

- Corrective action that the employer will take against an employee for policy violation or drug conviction
- The employer's good-faith effort to comply with the law[13]

The Drug-free Workplace Act does not require drug testing. Also, the law does not require sanctions for job use or possession of alcoholic beverages. Both of these issues, however, may be included in a substance abuse policy if elected by the employer.

State laws limiting drug testing may apply to a firm's substance abuse policy if the policy includes drug testing requirements.

The Americans with Disabilities Act specifically defines recovered alcoholics and recovered former drug users as individuals with a disability subject to the law's protection.

Other potential liabilities could result from a substance abuse policy if the employer discharged an employee in a manner contrary to procedures published in a policy manual or employee handbook. Also, careless release of confidential facts or release of false information about an employee in the course of employment or reference check could result in litigation.

## Pitfalls to Avoid

A Substance Abuse Policy needs to achieve a balance between two key issues: referral for assistance and corrective action policy violations. Here are some pitfalls to avoid.

1. Define your Substance Abuse Policy in a way to encourage employees to seek voluntary treatment for substance abuse. Under this approach, the priority is helping to salvage a valuable employee rather than focusing on discharge of the individual. A Substance Abuse Policy can include several features to encourage employees to seek help. First, publicize the goal of the policy to help employees. Second, encourage confidential referral to help without any disciplinary penalty if an employee voluntarily seeks help. Third, offer referral for treatment without disciplinary penalty as an alternative to discipline for the *first* violation of the policy. Fourth, provide health and leave of absence benefits which will aid the employee to accept in-patient care in a substance abuse treatment center when warranted. Fifth, communicate effectively with spouse or dependents so that family members have an adequate understanding of company benefits.

2. Define policy guidelines and train supervisors to focus on performance issues when dealing with employee substance abuse issues. The supervisor should not attempt to diagnose an employee's substance abuse problem. Nor should the supervisor lecture or debate substance abuse

## CHECKLIST
### A Substance Abuse Policy

- What state or federal law or regulations affect a substance abuse policy?

- Will the substance abuse policy relate to illegal drugs? alcoholic beverages? prescription drugs? over-the-counter drugs?

- Will the policy relate to possession, use, selling, or working under the influence of drugs or alcoholic beverages?

- Will there be different corrective action taken for possession or use of substances on company time or premises compared to reporting under the influence?

- Will employees be encouraged to seek treatment or assistance for substance abuse problems?

- Will an employee assistance plan or other referral services be provided?

- Will substance abusers be held to normal performance standards?

- What actions will be taken to protect confidentiality of substance abuse issues?

- Will drug testing be part of the substance abuse policy?

- Will supervisors receive information or training to recognize and deal with substance abuse issues?

- Will transportation home be arranged for an individual who is found "under the influence" on the job?

issues with an employee. The supervisor's job should relate to defining work requirements, setting performance goals or standards, and coaching employees for improved performance. When substance abuse issues interfere with work, the supervisor's responsibility should focus on referring the employee to human resources, or an employee assistance plan, or to another trained specialist.

3. Recognize privacy concerns when dealing with substance abuse issues. Several examples are noted. Protect the confidentiality of an employee's request for assistance and referral for assessment or treatment in a substance abuse center. Maintain records of medical treatment or health insurance claims in separate files. In the event that substance abuse was a factor in discharge, limit release of substance abuse information in reference checks.

4. Do not permit an intoxicated employee to drive home after he or she has been suspended for working while intoxicated. Various court decisions have found employers liable for death or injuries caused by an intoxicated employee who was found unfit for work but then permitted to drive home.

**Sample Policy**

**XYZ COMPANY**
**PERSONNEL POLICY & PROCEDURE**

SUBJECT: SUBSTANCE ABUSE                          DATE: May 1, 1993
APPLIES TO: All Employees

*Policy*: It is the policy of the Company to maintain a drug-free workplace to comply with the Drug-free Workplace Act of 1988.

*Procedure*:

1. The Company President is responsible for supervising development and implementation of workplace practices and controls as summarized by this policy to comply with the law. Day-to-day coordination of Drug-free Workplace Policy issues shall be handled by the Personnel Administrator.

2. Each employee is responsible for complying with the Company policy as a condition of employment and for acknowledging receipt of the Company policy.

3. The Personnel Administrator is responsible for orientating his or her respective employees about the Company's Drug-free Workplace Policy and providing drug awareness information. Also, the Personnel Administrator shall periodically provide drug-free workplace employee awareness messages such as bulletin board postings, payroll stuffers, etc.

4. In the event of an altercation, accident, near-miss accident, or other incident, the Personnel Administrator or a department manager may direct an employee to a designated medical facility for a chemical dependency evaluation as part of the investigation of the incident. The following guidelines are provided:

   a) A supervisor shall drive the employee to the facility and coordinate any return transportation.

   b) The employee shall sign a consent form and receive regular pay for time lost from work, up to eight hours for the day.

   c) In the event the chemical dependency evaluation recommends in-patient or out-patient treatment, the employee is encouraged to participate in the recommended treatment program. If the employee refuses to cooperate in referral or recommended treatment, or in cases of subsequent incidents, the employee shall be subject to corrective discipline, which may include discharge.

5. Any illegal manufacture, distribution, dispensing, possession, or use of illegal drugs; or unauthorized possession or use of alcoholic beverages on Company time or premises is grounds for discharge.

6. Alcoholic beverages may be served at Company business or social functions as authorized by a Company officer. In such instances, employees should use common sense and demonstrate moderation.

7. Any employee reporting to work under the influence of drugs, alcohol, or in an otherwise unfit condition to work may be subject to suspension

without pay, or referral for testing, or discharge, or other action as deemed appropriate by management.

8. Each supervisor or manager is responsible for enforcing Company rules on policies through use of corrective discipline up to and including discharge if necessary. Supervisors and managers are encouraged to confer with the Personnel Administrator when dealing with discipline/discharge issues.

9. In the event management becomes aware of an employee's drug-related criminal conviction occurring in the workplace, the Personnel Administrator is responsible for taking the following actions:

   a) Notify the contracting agency of the drug conviction within 10 days.

   b) Within 30 days, refer the employee for chemical dependency treatment if a first offense/incident, or take appropriate disciplinary action up to discharge if there are prior drug/alcohol-related incidents occurring on the job by the employee.

10. If an employee voluntarily seeks help regarding a drug or alcohol problem, he or she shall be referred to the Personnel Administrator on a confidential basis. The Personnel Administrator shall then refer the employee to an appropriate counseling or medical facility for assistance. In such cases, the employee may be placed on a medical leave of absence. Any medical costs arising from treatment may be filed under the group insurance plan as applicable.

11. In the event of a question or complaint arising under this policy, the employee should speak first to his or her supervisor. If the matter cannot be resolved by the supervisor, it may be referred to the Personnel Administrator and then the Company President for a final determination. All matters under this policy shall be treated as confidential.

12. This policy, management actions, and records shall be checked annually by the Personnel Administrator to ensure a good-faith effort to be in compliance.

**Sample Employee Handbook Paragraph**

*Drug-free Workplace*

Abuse of chemical substances such as alcohol and drugs is a serious problem in our society, causing personal grief for afflicted individuals and significant costs to business. The Company does not want to become involved in an individual's personal lifestyle, but when abuse of chemical substances affects job performance, the Company is also affected. Our goal is to maintain a drug-free workplace in order to prevent errors, injuries, and other problems stemming from abuse of chemical substances.

In the event an employee encounters personal or job problems resulting from excessive use of alcohol or drugs, the employee is encouraged to seek counseling and treatment through an appropriate medical facility. If an individual refuses to accept assistance and is unable to maintain satisfactory performance, the employee will be subject to disciplinary action, which may include dismissal.

Unauthorized possession or use of alcoholic beverages is not permitted on Company time or premises. Any unlawful manufacture, distribution, dispensing, possession, or use of illegal drugs or other controlled substances is strictly prohibited on Company time, premises, or at any Company business or social function. In the event an employee is convicted for a drug-related offense occurring at the workplace, the employee is responsible for reporting the conviction to the Company. Disregard for these policies may result in dismissal.

The Company reserves the right to use drug or alcoholic screening tests during employment if deemed necessary.

## Accommodating Disabilities

The Americans with Disabilities Act (ADA) of 1990 prohibits discrimination against individuals with disabilities. This far-reaching law deals with discrimination issues in employment, public services, public transportation, accessibility or public accommodations, and telecommunications. This section is limited to addressing employment-related issues. The employment sections of ADA become effective on July 26, 1992 for firms of 25 or more employees. Firms with 15 or more employees become subject to the law on July 26, 1994.[14]

Prohibitions against handicap discrimination are not new, however. Firms doing business with the federal government have been subject to the Rehabilitation Act of 1973. This law requires federal government contractors to avoid discriminatory practices and take affirmative action to promote employment opportunities of handicapped individuals. Also, nearly every state has a Fair Employment Practice statute which includes handicap discrimination as a prohibited employment practice.

A policy providing guidance to supervisors on accommodating disabilities will help an organization to comply with the law. The policy can focus on those employment practices which involve supervisor decisions affecting disabled persons. The most likely areas for supervisor guidance are hiring processes, reemployment following medical leave or job accident, and other job changes such as promotions or transfers. Important policy points are noted:

- The firm's employment application should be revised to eliminate inquiries about prior illnesses, physical limitations, or prior worker's compensation claims. These kinds of preemployment inquiries, common in most application forms published prior to 1992, are now improper inquiries under ADA.

- The ADA specifically recognizes job descriptions prepared before advertising and interviewing candidates as evidence of essential job functions. Old job descriptions need updating to reflect actual job tasks performed on the job. New job descriptions should be prepared where no descriptions currently exist. Responsibility for job description preparation can rest with supervisors.

- All interview questions, hiring criteria, exams, or tests must be based on job-related standards consistent with business necessity in order to comply with ADA. Such qualification standards should not have the effect of discriminating against disabled individuals unless the standards are consistent with business necessity. However, a job qualification standard may require that the individual be able to perform essential job functions without posing a direct threat to the health or safety of the individual or others.

- Preemployment medical exams to determine the nature or severity of a disability are prohibited by ADA. A medical examination evaluating the individual's ability to perform job-related functions may be conducted after making an offer of employment but before the applicant begins performing job duties. Any medical exam should be administered to all entering employees in the same job category. An individual's employment may be conditioned on the results of the examination.

- Separate medical records from regular personnel files protect confidentiality of medical records and limit release of medical information to supervisors who need to know work restrictions or accommodations, to first aid personnel providing emergency treatment, or to government officials investigating ADA compliance.

- Develop and use a worksheet to evaluate reasonable accommodations that may be made when considering an employment decision affecting a disabled worker. Consider as reasonable accommodations one or more of the following actions:

  a. Modification or adjustment of the job application process

  b. Modification or adjustment to the work environment

  c. Modification or adjustment of policies, procedures, or benefits

  d. Making facilities accessible to disabled persons

  e. Restructuring job duties, assignments, or schedules

  f. Acquisition of equipment or devices to aid the disabled worker in performing job tasks

  g. Any other work-related modification which enables a qualified individual with a disability to perform essential job functions without imposing excessive cost or undue hardship on the operation

## Pitfalls to Avoid

Enforcement of the employment sections of the ADA rests with the Equal Employment Opportunity Commission (EEOC). Many employers are familiar with the EEOC enforcement process. Enforcement can include an informal investigation questionnaire, fact finding conference, conciliation, settlement, dismissal, or federal court enforcement action. Remedies can include reinstatement, back pay, or other actions available under Title VII of the Civil Rights Act. In addition, complainants will be eligible for jury trials and compensatory damages under the Civil Rights Act of 1991. Also, ADA allows the court to grant reasonable attorneys' fees for counsel of the prevailing party. To minimize claims and avoid discrimination findings, here are some pitfalls to avoid:

1. Carefully consider the definitions of a disability. ADA defines a disability as

   a. A physical or mental impairment that substantially limits one or more of the major life activities of such individual

   b. Having a record of such an impairment

   c. Being regarded as having such impairment

   Further guidelines are defined in *A Technical Assistance Manual on the Employment Provisions (Title I) of the Americans with Disabilities Act*, U.S. Equal Employment Opportunity Commision, January, 1992.

2. Make sure that job descriptions are accurate and current. The job description can provide an objective summary of job tasks and responsibilities for comparing applicant skills or abilities. An inaccurate, vague, or generic job description will be useless for comparison and can contribute toward a finding of apparent discrimination.

3. Document reasonable accommodation efforts on a worksheet. When a qualified individual with a disability has requested a reasonable accommodation to assist in the performance of a job, the employer, using a problem-solving approach, should

   a. Analyze the particular job involved and determine its purpose and essential functions.

   b. Consult with the individual with a disability to ascertain the precise job-related limitations imposed by the individual's disability and how those limitations could be overcome with a reasonable accommodation.

   c. In consultation with the individual to be accommodated, identify potential accommodations and assess the effectiveness each would have in enabling the individual to perform the essential functions of the position.

   d. Consider the preference of the individual to be accommodated and

**CHECKLIST**
**An Accommodating Disabilities Policy**

- What state or federal law or regulations affect a substance abuse policy?

- Will job descriptions be developed to define job duties, hiring criteria, working environment, and other essential job functions?

- Who will be responsible for setting job standards and hiring criteria?

- What checks or audits will be performed to ensure that job standards do not tend to discriminate against disabled workers unless there is a business necessity or no direct threat to the individual or others?

- What steps will be taken to prevent use of preemployment medical inquiries?

- If medical exams are used, what steps will be taken to ensure that the exam is job related, scheduled post offer, and required of all candidates of the designated job category? What steps will be taken to insure that tests or exams are job related, valid, and adjusted if needed to fairly measure skills of a disabled individual?

- What analysis or evaluation will be made to identify reasonable accommodations of qualified disabled individuals?

- What personnel practice issues will be covered by the Accommodating Disabilities Policy such as recruiting, hiring, pay, benefits, or other employment terms and conditions?

- Will current disabled employees be invited to identify themselves in order to receive accommodations offered by the firm?

- Will a complaint procedure be adopted to consider employee complaints under this policy?

select and implement the accommodation that is most appropriate for both the employee and the employer.

In the event an appropriate accommodation cannot be identified, or if the accommodation creates an undue hardship on the business, another applicant may be selected. In the event of any subsequent discrimination complaint, the reasonable accommodation worksheet will show a good-faith effort to comply with the law and justify the decision not to select the disabled individual. See reasonable accommodation decision flow chart in Fig. 16.1.

4. Build a file of resource information. Refer to the resource file when evaluating disabilities. The resource file should include organizations like the Job Accommodation Network where trained specialists can assist in identifying effective accommodations for disabled individuals.

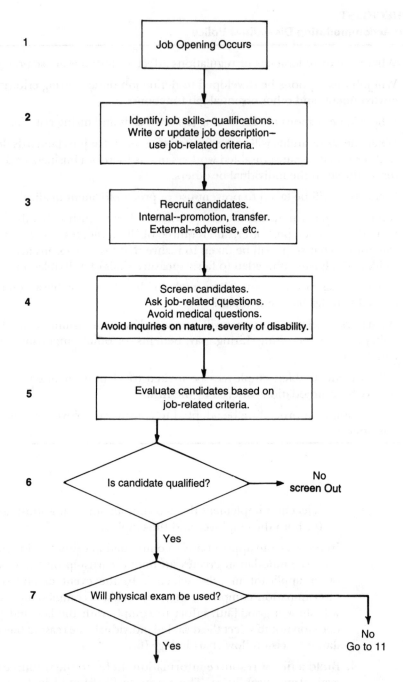

**Figure 16.1.** Reasonable accommodation decision flowchart.

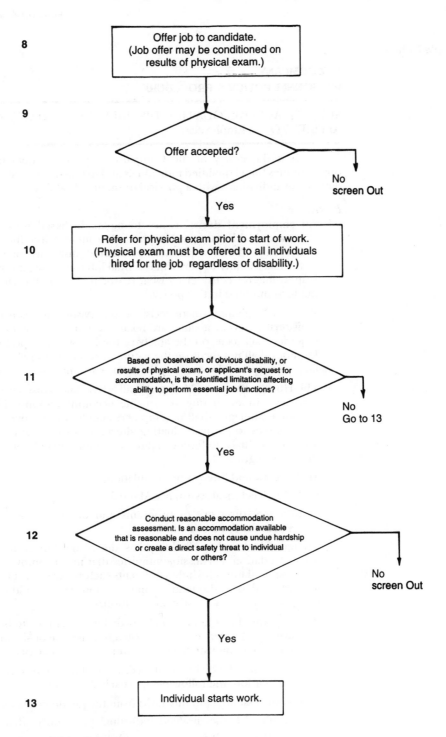

**Figure 16.1.** *(Continued)*

**Sample Policy**

**XYZ COMPANY**
**PERSONNEL POLICY & PROCEDURE**

---

SUBJECT: ACCOMMODATING DISABILITIES          DATE: May 1, 1993
APPLIES TO: All Employees

---

*Policy*: It is the policy of the Company to provide equal employment opportunities for all qualified individuals and to make reasonable accommodations for individuals with a physical or mental disability.

*Procedure*:

1. All employment decisions are to be made based upon job-related criteria and without regard to physical or mental disability of qualified individuals. When a physical or mental disability may affect the individual's ability to perform essential job functions, the supervisor is responsible for considering what reasonable accommodations may be made as outlined in this policy.

2. When making employment decisions, supervisors must consider how the individual's skills or abilities are related to job requirements. Evaluation inquiries shall focus on the ability of the individual to perform the job. Inquiries shall not focus on the nature or severity of disabilities, physical limitations, prior illnesses, or prior worker's compensation claims.

3. The Human Resource Manager shall advise and assist supervisors and managers in evaluating reasonable accommodations. The Human Resource Manager shall develop and maintain reference information or resources to aid in evaluating alternatives for accommodating disabled individuals. Reference materials should include one or more of the following:

   a) ADA law and interpretive regulations

   b) EEOC Technical Assistance Manual

   c) Resource directory of programs and organizations that provide services for the disabled

4. An individual with a disability has the responsibility to request an accommodation. Permissible inquiries that may prompt identification of accommodations include statements such as: Are you able to perform job tasks with or without an accommodation? How would you perform the tasks and with what accommodation?

5. If an applicant has a known disability that would appear to interfere with or prevent performance of a job-related function, he or she may be asked to describe or demonstrate how this function would be performed.

6. When a qualified individual with a disability has requested a reasonable accommodation, the following approach should be used:

   a) Identify essential job functions from the job description.

   b) Consult with the disabled individual to identify what limitations affect performance of which job duties.

   c) Elicit suggestions from the disabled individual about possible accommodations.

d) If necessary, confer with the Human Resource Manager to identify accommodations or other resources to aid in identifying accommodations.

e) Consider the preferences of the disabled individual and implement the accommodation(s) that are in the best interest of the individual and the company.

7. All accommodations shall be made on the Reasonable Accommodation Worksheet which is attached to this policy.

8. As a general guide, accommodations may be approved based on the following authorizations:

a) Accommodations costing $100 or less may be authorized by the supervisor.

b) Accommodations costing $500 or less may be authorized by the controller.

c) Accommodations costing over $500 must be authorized by the General Manager.

**Sample Form**

### REASONABLE ACCOMMODATION ASSESSMENT

*Instructions*: Use this assessment worksheet when considering accommodations for an individual's religious practices, disability, or physical or mental condition.

1. Is the individual qualified to perform the essential functions of the job?
Yes _____   No _____
(If no, an accommodation assessment is not needed.)

2. What specific job task/requirement may need accommodation?

_____

_____

3. What limitation has been identified by the individual which affects the performance of job duties?

_____

_____

4. List possible accommodations, cost, and degree of reasonableness. Elicit and consider any accommodations suggested by the individual.

| Accommodation | Estimated cost | Reasonable? |
|---|---|---|
| a) _____ | | |
| _____ | | |
| _____ | _____ | Yes      No |

*Sample Form* (cont'd)

b) _____

_____

_____            _____        Yes        No

c) _____

_____

_____            _____        Yes        No

| Supervisor | Manager | Date |
| --- | --- | --- |

## Sample Employee Handbook Paragraph

*Accommodating Disabled Workers*

Employment opportunities at XYZ Company are based on ability to do the job. We recognize our moral and legal obligation to employ qualified disabled individuals. It is our goal to make reasonable accommodations when necessary to aid the employment of disabled workers who are qualified to perform essential job functions.

Current employees with a disability are encouraged to request an accommodation if needed to perform your job tasks more effectively. Speak with your supervisor or the Human Resource Administrator.

## Workplace AIDS Policy

AIDS was first recognized in the United States in 1981. AIDS is an acronym for the disease Acquired Immune Deficiency Syndrome. It is a bloodborne and sexually transmitted virus which invades the body, damages the immune system, and allows other infectious agents to invade the body and cause disease. ARC, or AIDS Related Complex, refers to a variety of conditions caused by infection with the AIDS virus. Currently, there is no known cure for AIDS. Various treatments can help prolong life; but eventually the AIDS victim dies from an infection that has invaded the body.

According to *Worker Exposure to AIDS and Hepatitis B*, a publication of the U.S. Department of Labor, the AIDS virus is spread through body fluids, primarily blood and semen. The disease is transmitted by sexual contact, by needle sharing, and through contaminated blood products. The AIDS virus is not transmitted by casual contact, touching or shaking hands, eating food prepared by an infected person, or from drinking fountains, telephones, toilets, or other surfaces.

Workers at risk of blood, body fluid, or needle stick exposures are at the highest risk of infection. They include, but are not limited to, nurses, physicians, dentists, and other dental workers, podiatrists, laboratory and blood bank technologists and technicians, phlebotomists, dialysis personnel, medical technicians, medical examiners, morticians, housekeepers, laundry workers, and others whose work involves contact with blood or other body fluids, or with corpses. Other personnel such as paramedics, emergency medical technicians, law enforcement personnel, firefighters, lifeguards, and others whose jobs might require first-response medical care and potential contact with blood or body fluids are also at risk.[15]

In most manufacturing service, distribution, or administrative working environments, the likelihood of contracting AIDS is considerably less than in the foregoing high-risk occupations. However, once an individual acknowledges that he or she has the disease, fellow employees often react with emotion and fear. In fact, fear of AIDS can cause greater disruption to the business than the disease itself. Further, AIDS is now a condition protected by ADA and other fair employment practice laws. For these reasons, an employer should define policy guidelines for dealing with AIDS cases.

Various state and federal labor laws and regulations now deal with the AIDS issue. In the early 1980s when the disease was first discovered, however, labor laws did not specifically identify AIDS victims as a protected class. A court decision on a related issue, dismissal of an employee with a contagious disease, began a new policy direction for AIDS. A teacher, Gene Arline, had been dismissed by the Nassau County School Board because of a relapse caused by tuberculosis. In a lawsuit brought under Section 504 of the Rehabilitation Act of 1973, the U.S. Supreme Court in 1988 ruled that tuberculosis is a contagious condition protected by the Act. That same year, the U.S. Department of Justice issued an opinion which said persons with AIDS or HIV are considered individuals with handicaps covered by Section 504. Section 504 deals with federal government contractors and contracts of $25 or more.[16]

AIDS is among the conditions specifically identified as covered by the Americans with Disabilities Act (ADA). ADA prohibits discrimination because of AIDS or other physical or mental disabilities. Further, the employer is required to make a reasonable accommodation for individuals with HIV or AIDS.

AIDS is also subject to a variety of state laws. According to the *1992 State by State Guide to Human Resources Law*, 32 states have passed a law or defined regulations relating to AIDS:

| | |
|---|---|
| Arizona | Nebraska |
| California | New Jersey |
| Colorado | New Mexico |
| Delaware | New York |
| District of Columbia | North Carolina |

| | |
|---|---|
| Florida | North Dakota |
| Georgia | Ohio |
| Hawaii | Oregon |
| Iowa | Pennsylvania |
| Kansas | Rhode Island |
| Kentucky | South Carolina |
| Maine | Texas |
| Massachusetts | Vermont |
| Michigan | West Virginia |
| Minnesota | Washington |
| Missouri | Wisconsin[17] |

Provisions of the laws vary from state to state. Some states classify AIDS as a handicap, others do not. Some states prohibit mandatory employment testing for AIDS while other states are silent on this issue. A number of states prohibit any use of a positive AIDS test to discriminate in employment decisions.

Requirements to protect the confidentiality of AIDS test results are specified by some of the states in the preceding list. In addition, the following states have enacted statutes to protect the confidentiality of HIV test results: Connecticut, Illinois, Indiana, Montana, Nevada, New Hampshire, North Dakota, Oklahoma, Virginia, and Wyoming.[18]

Recently, the Occupational Safety and Health Administration issued a regulatory standard on bloodborne pathogens. The standard defines specific requirements designed to protect an estimated 5.3 million workers against AIDS, Hepatitis B, viruses, and other bloodborne pathogens.

The standard requires covered employers, typically health care or related organizations, to evaluate worker exposures, develop a written infection control plan, provide protective clothing and equipment, assure sanitary housekeeping conditions, and observe universal precautions for handling infectious material.

Many individuals with HIV and early stages of AIDS want to continue to work. This means that as the AIDS virus continues to spread, more and more firms will face the AIDS issue. Because of employee fears, the employer may encounter conflicts between the AIDS victim, fellow employees, and even customers. An AIDS policy can help to put these issues in proper perspective. Here are some key points to consider.

- Protect confidentiality of the individual's health condition. As with any other medical or personnel data, an employee's personnel file or medical information should be kept confidential. Release of confidential information to others should be only with the consent of the individual, unless there is a specific business necessity.

- Avoid HIV or AIDS testing as part of preemployment screening or general workplace physical exams, unless specifically required or author-

**CHECKLIST**
**An AIDS Policy**

- What state or federal law requirements affect the AIDS policy?

- What steps will be taken to protect confidentiality of an individual's health status and health records?

- What kinds of employee benefits are available for individuals with AIDs or other medical conditions?

- Will the AIDS policy require that accommodations be made for leaves or absences associated with the medical condition?

- Will the AIDS policy specify that reasonable accommodations should be made to facilitate the employment of an employee with AIDS?

- Will the policy prohibit discrimination or discharge of the employee with AIDS?

- Will medical exams or tests be used if there is a business necessity to evaluate an individual's fitness to perform job duties?

- Will the policy be broadly defined to serve as a guideline for other contagious diseases?

- Will employees be required to observe reasonable precautions and seek appropriate medical care to protect the health and safety of themselves, fellow workers, customers, the public, or products handled on the job?

- Will HIV/AIDS-infected employees be referred for counseling or other services available through an Employee Assistance Plan?

- Will employees and supervisors be educated about AIDS issues?

- Will the HIV/AIDS-infected employee be consulted when defining reasonable accommodations?

- Will a grievance procedure be available to resolve employee complaints relating to the AIDS policy?

ized in a health care or related environment. ADA requires medical or other tests to be job related. Based on this requirement, AIDS testing in most occupational areas would be a violation of the law.

- Provide reasonable accommodation for an employee who has HIV or AIDS. In the early stages of HIV, little or no accommodation may be needed. In later or advanced stages of AIDS, accommodation may include one or more of the following:
  Flexible work hours
  Part-time work schedules
  Liberal use of sick leave
  Approval of leave of absence for medical or personal reasons
  Light-duty assignments

Arrangement for work at home
Modifications to equipment or facilities
Job restructuring
Voluntary transfer, reassignment, or demotion

- Educate employees about AIDS. Firms that have provided educational programs find that employees have a better understanding of the disease and greater compassion for the AIDS victim. Hospitals and other health care institutions, for example, deal with AIDS-infected individuals on a daily basis without significant employee relations problems.

- Continue insurance and other benefits without regard for the AIDS condition. Failure to enroll an HIV or AIDS-infected individual into benefit plans, or refusal to pay benefits when others are accorded such benefits, would be a discriminatory practice.

- Provide counseling or assistance for the AIDS-infected employee. Referral to an Employee Assistance Plan or other counseling service can provide vitally needed psychological support. The AIDS victim will need support to deal with personal fears and uncertainties that lie ahead.

### Pitfalls to Avoid

The AIDS issue creates a dual concern for employers. The federal law now protects the HIV/AIDS-infected employee from discrimination. Coworkers' concerns, however, can cause significant disruption to the workplace. Here are some pitfalls to avoid when reconciling these conflicting issues:

1. Responding to coworker's concerns is likely to be more frustrating to the employer than dealing with an AIDS-infected employee. The Ryan White story is an example of how fear of AIDS can affect a community or a workplace. Ryan White was a grade school youth who had contracted AIDS from tainted blood received during an operation. The small Indiana community in which he lived created such a furor over his disease that the board of education banned him from attending school.

   Likewise, in a working environment, coworkers have expressed concerns about working alongside AIDS-infected employees. One right that coworkers may assert is the employer's "general duty obligation to provide a safe and healthful workplace." Using this argument, the employee may file an OSHA complaint. The employee's complaint may be valid in a high-risk environment with exposure to contaminated blood, such as health care, particularly if the employer failed to comply with the OSHA bloodborne pathogen standard. In most other working environments involving casual contact with an AIDS-infected employee, it is unlikely that OSHA would consider the condition likely to cause death or serious harm.

A provision of OSHA permits employees to refuse to work by not performing an assigned task if they will be subject to serious injury or death. Such action has been upheld by the U.S. Supreme Court. Employees also have protections under the National Labor Relations Act.

Commerce Clearing House, a publisher of topical law reports, explains employee rights in this fashion:

Employees are also protected from hazards in the workplace under the National Labor Relations Act. Section 7 of the NLRA provides that employees may engage in "protected, concerted activity" to protest issues affecting their wages, hours, and working conditions. This means that two or more employees are protected if they walk off the job because their working conditions are unsafe. Further, Section 502 of the Labor Management Relations Act protects employees' right to stop working because of "abnormally dangerous" working conditions.

In addressing the issue of whether employees protesting what they regard as an "abnormally dangerous condition" would be protected, the U.S. Supreme Court rules that it is not sufficient that an employee merely believes that he faces such a condition. Rather, the employee must establish by "ascertainable objective evidence" that the "abnormally dangerous condition" exists. Because medical evidence does not support the contention that the workplace is "abnormally dangerous" from casual contact with an AIDS-infected employee, it is unlikely that employees who refuse to work with an AIDS-infected employee could successfully argue that they were legitimate in protesting an "abnormally dangerous condition."[19]

A personnel policy which focuses on reasonable accommodations for the AIDS victim and education of co-workers will be the best response to employee concerns.

2. Avoid rumors and confidentiality leaks. AIDS policy guidelines need to stress the importance of protecting confidentiality of medical information. The ADA law, for example, requires that medical records be separated from other personnel records. Supervisors directing the activities of an HIV/AIDS-infected employee may be informed of an individual's disability and reasonable accommodations made to facilitate employment.

Prevention and control of rumors should be an important priority when dealing with employee concerns about AIDS in the workplace. The informal network of employee communication, referred to as the "grapevine," may buzz with rumors about an employee with AIDS. Supervisors should not condone or participate in rumor discussions. Instead, the supervisor should act to prevent rumors. One publication that provides useful ideas is *Managers' Guidelines for Dealing with Individual Cases of AIDS,* published by the U.S. General Accounting Office, available from the Superintendent of Documents.

3. Make sure that a grievance procedure is available as a part of the AIDS policy or as a separate policy. The grievance procedure can serve as an outlet for employee concerns or complaints. When an employee files a grievance, the company has an opportunity to resolve the complaint internally. Solving the problem within the company is obviously less costly than litigation.

**Sample Policy**

**XYZ COMPANY**
**PERSONNEL POLICY & PROCEDURE**

SUBJECT: AIDS AND CONTAGIOUS DISEASES          DATE: May 1, 1993
APPLIES TO: All Employees

*Policy*: It is the policy of the Company to ensure a safe and healthful workplace for all employees and to prohibit arbitrary discrimination in the event an employee becomes afflicted with HIV/AIDS or other contagious medical condition.

*Procedure*:
1. HIV/AIDS and other chronic contagious diseases are considered a disability under XYZ Company policies. Company procedures summarized under this policy are based upon the Company's understanding of current knowledge about AIDS and other contagious diseases. This policy shall be subject to periodic review and revision as necessary to reflect good safety and health practices.

2. Supervisors and managers are responsible for making all employment decisions relating to individuals with HIV/AIDS or other chronic contagious diseases in a non-discriminatory manner. This includes hiring, promotion, pay benefits, training, discipline, discharge, or other terms or conditions of employment.

3. Each employee is responsible for reporting to work in a fit condition to work. In the event of illness, employees are encouraged to use company benefits such as sick pay, medical leave, health insurance, etc. in order to receive proper medical care.

4. In the event that an employee incurs a medical condition or contagious disease which may affect health or safety of the individual, coworkers, customers, the general public, or the sanitation of company products, the employee has a responsibility to seek appropriate medical care. Further, the employee is expected to exercise reasonable precautions to prevent the spread of disease to others.

5. At the time that a supervisor, manager, or other company representative becomes aware of an employee's medical condition or contagious disease, he or she shall confer with the employee to identify appropriate action, such as

   a) Continuation of normal work if allowed by employee's physician

   b) Consideration of reasonable accommodations that may be necessary (See Accommodating Disabilities Policy.)

c) Referral for a job-related physical exam paid by the company to evaluate fitness to work

d) Placement on a medical leave of absence if deemed appropriate

e) Referral of the employee to the Employee Assistance Program for support and advice

6. The supervisor and department manager shall evaluate each situation based on the facts of the individual case. The Human Resource Manager may be consulted for advice. Final authority on policy matters rests with the General Manager.

7. All medical information, medical records, health insurance claims, or other related information is deemed to be confidential. Confidential records or information on an individual must not be disclosed to other employees. A supervisor may be told of an individual's medical condition and reasonable accommodation in order to effectively direct an individual's work activities. An employee with AIDS or other contagious disease or medical condition, subject to normal eligibility requirements, is entitled to participate in regular benefits plans, insurances, sick leave, medical leave, and other Company policies.

8. Each supervisor and manager is responsible for maintaining open communications with employees, responding to employee concerns, and taking appropriate action to minimize co-worker or customer anxieties relating to AIDS or other contagious disease. Supervisors are encouraged to contact the Human Resource Administrator or employee Assistance Program for advice. Coworkers shall be told that based on guidelines from the U.S. government, AIDS is not transmitted by casual contact that occurs on the job.

9. In the event an employee has a question or complaint about this policy or employment decisions based on this policy, he or she may register a complaint under the Company's Grievance Procedure.

## Sample Employee Handbook Paragraph

### AIDS and Contagious Diseases

XYZ Company recognizes its responsibility to provide a safe and healthful work environment for all employees. Further, we recognize our moral and legal obligations to provide a workplace in which each individual is treated with dignity and without any form of discrimination.

In response to inquiries raised by various employees, XYZ Company has defined guidelines concerning AIDS or other contagious diseases. This policy has been developed following extensive research on health, safety, medical care, and relevant labor law matters.

We believe that each employee is responsible for reporting to work in a fit condition to work. If you become ill or require medical care, we urge you to see your doctor. In the event that an employee incurs a medical condition or contagious disease which may affect health or safety of the individual, coworkers, customers, the general public, or the sanitation of company products, the employee has a responsibility to seek appropriate medical care.

At the time that the Company becomes aware of an employee's medical condition, we will take appropriate action based upon the doctor's recommendations about your ability to work. Employees with AIDS or other medical conditions are subject to normal benefits eligibility requirements. Eligible employees are entitled to participate in regular benefits plans, insurances, sick leave, medical leave, and other practices defined by Company policies.

In the event of any questions about this policy, you are encouraged to speak with your supervisor or the Human Resource Manager.

## Notes

1. *Facts and Figures on Smoking*, American Cancer Society, Chicago, 1986, pp. 2–3.

2. *A Decision Maker's Guide To Reducing Smoking at the Worksite*, U.S. Dept. of Health and Human Services, 1985, p. 5.

3. W. Hubbartt, "Smoking at Work—An Emerging Office Issue," *Administrative Management*, February, 1986, p. 23.

4. D. Masi, "Company Responses to Drug Abuse from AMA's Nationwide Survey," *Personnel*, March, 1987, p. 41.

5. T. Backer, Ph.D., *Strategic Planning for Workplace Drug Abuse Programs*, U.S. Dept. of Health and Human Services, DHHS Publication No. (ADM), 87-1538, 1987, p. 4.

6. State Drug Testing Laws, *Personnel Practices/Communications Section, Human Resource Management Reporter*, Commerce Clearing House, Chicago, 1992, Para. 2484.

7. *Johnson Bateman Co.*, 295 NLRB, No. 26, 1989.

8. J. M. Walsh, Ph.D., R. L. Hawks, Ph.D., *Employee Drug Screening–Detection of Drug Use by Urinalysis*, U.S. Dept. of Health and Human Services, DHHS Publication No. (ADM) 88-1442, Rev. 1988, pp. 7–8.

9. Ibid., p. 12.

10. *What Works: Workplaces Without Drugs*, U.S. Dept. of Labor (undated), p. 5.

11. W. Hubbartt, "Are You Ready to Test Employees for Drugs?," *Office Systems '87*, January, 1987, p. 26.

12. J. M. Walsh, Ph.D., R. L. Hawks, Ph.D., *Employee Drug Screening–Detection of Drug Use by Urinalysis*, U.S. Dept. of Health and Human Services, DHHS Publication No. (ADM) 88-1442, Rev. 1988, pp. 2–3.

13. *Federal Register*, Vol. 54, No. 19, January 31, 1989, p. 4946.

14. Public Law 101-336, American's with Disabilities Act of 1990, July 26, 1990.

15. *Worker Exposure to Aids and Hepatitis B*, U.S. Dept. of Labor, OSHA 3102, 1987.

16. School Board of Nassau County, *Florida* v. *Arline* (U.S., 1987) 42 EPD, pp. 36, 791.

17. R. Green, W. Carmell, P. Gray, *1992 State by State Guide to Human Resources Law*, Panel Publishers, New York, 1992, Table 7.2-3, pp. 7-19 through 7-22.

18. Ibid.

19. *Human Resource Management–Personnel Practices/Communications Reporter*, Commerce Clearing House, Chicago, pp. 4163, 4164.

# PART 3

# Auditing Your Policy Manual

# 17

# Personnel Policy Audit: A Comprehensive 50-Item Checklist

**Read Chapter 17 for:**

An audit of any current policy manual to identify areas in need of improvement

A final check on your newly prepared or revised policy manual

The Personnel Policy Audit was defined to meet two goals. For firms with an existing Personnel Policy Manual, the audit provides a way to identify areas where improvement is needed. Second, the audit serves as a final check of the newly prepared or revised Personnel Policy Manual.

Review the audit questions listed in this chapter. This audit checklist has been designed so that a "yes" is the desired response to indicate a satisfactory written personnel policy. When a "no" response is checked, additional writing or editing is recommended. Check each policy with the audit checklist. If your manual has a shortcoming in a particular area, read the designated chapter for information on improving the policy.

For each "no" response, read relevant portions of this book to identify recommended ways to improve your policy manual.

To audit specific issues on the various policies, see the checklists of issues to consider for each policy topic in Part II of this book.

| **Audit Questionnaire** | **Action Required** | |
|---|---|---|
| 1. Does your Policy and Procedure Guide include a prominently displayed employment-at-will disclaimer? (See Chap. 2) | Yes | No |
| 2. Does the disclaimer assert that the Policy Manual is not a contract and that employment may be terminated at any time for any reason? (See Chap. 2.) | Yes | No |
| 3. Does the disclaimer reserve the right to add, change, or withdraw policies or benefits at any time? (See Chap. 2.) | Yes | No |
| 4. Is the Policy and Procedure Guide written as an instructional guideline for management rather than an information summary for employees? (See Chap. 6.) | Yes | No |
| 5. Does the Policy and Procedure Guide avoid stating a just cause requirement for dismissals? (See Chaps. 2 and 11.) | Yes | No |
| 6. Are predischarge procedures defined as guidelines appearing in a management Policy and Procedure Guide only? (See Chaps. 2 and 11.) | Yes | No |
| 7. Does the Policy Manual recognize the union if there is a collective bargaining agreement at the organization? (See Chaps. 5 and 13.) | Yes | No |
| 8. Does the Policy Manual assert that policies and procedures are defined pursuant to the management rights clause of the contract? (See Chaps. 5 and 13.) | Yes | No |
| 9. Is the union informed when contract provisions or mandatory bargaining subjects are defined as policies or procedures? (See Chaps. 5 and 13.) | Yes | No |
| 10. If a union contract exists, are contract-related policies defined in a manner consistent with the contract? (See Chaps. 5 and 13.) | Yes | No |
| 11. Has each policy been checked for compliance with relevant federal labor laws? (See Chap. 5 and Part II.) | Yes | No |
| 12. Has each policy been checked for compliance with relevant federal laws and regulations? (See Chap. 5 and Part II.) | Yes | No |
| 13. Has each policy been checked for compliance with relevant state laws or regulations? (See Chap. 5 and Part II.) | Yes | No |
| 14. Has each policy been checked for compliance with relevant local ordinances or regulations? (See Chap. 5 and Part II.) | Yes | No |
| 15. Have policies been reviewed for consistency with relevant court decisions? (See Chaps. 3, 5, and Part II.) | Yes | No |
| 16. Are written policies defined where required by law or regulations? (See Chap. 5 and Part II.) | Yes | No |

17. Do policies and procedures define requirements for documenting personnel decisions? (See Part II.)     Yes     No

18. Are sample forms included in the Policy Manual? (See Part II.)     Yes     No

19. Do policies and procedures provide adequate instructions for completing and filing personnel forms? (See Chap. 6 and Part II.)     Yes     No

20. Does each policy specify who is accountable for recommending actions and approving employment decisions? (See Chap. 6 and Part II.)     Yes     No

21. Are responsibilities defined by job title? (See Chap. 6 and Part II.)     Yes     No

22. Are gender neutral terms or titles used throughout the Policy Manual? (See Chap. 6.)     Yes     No

23. Has each policy or benefit been compared to a local or industry survey to evaluate competitiveness? (See Chap. 4 and Part II.)     Yes     No

24. Does the number of policies defined correlate to organization size or critical issues of concern, such as the following guidelines:

| Number of employees | Number of policies and procedures |
|:---:|:---:|
| 1– 14 | 0–15 |
| 15– 49 | 10–25 |
| 50–199 | 15–30 |
| 200–499 | 15–50 |
| 500 | 20–75 |

    (See Chap. 3)     Yes     No

25. Is each policy and procedure written concisely with three to four pages or less? (See Chap. 6.)     Yes     No

26. Is the Policy and Procedure Guide written in an impersonal, semiformal, or instructional writing style? (See Chap. 6.)     Yes     No

27. Is the Policy and Procedure Guide written in the third-person voice? (See Chap. 6.)     Yes     No

28. Are there sufficient details and procedural instructions for supervisors to consistently administer each policy? (See Chap. 6.)     Yes     No

29. Is the Policy and Procedure Guide organized into sections, with each section covering similar topics? (See Chap. 6.)     Yes     No

| | | |
|---|---|---|
| 30. Are policy and procedure statements written in short sentences that average between 10 and 20 words per sentence? (See Chap. 6.) | Yes | No |
| 31. Do all sentences observe basic grammar guidelines with a subject and predicate? (See Chap. 6.) | Yes | No |
| 32. Are sentences written in a simple, straightforward style limited to one or two main thoughts? (See Chap. 6.) | Yes | No |
| 33. Do policy statements use common terms used in daily communications? (See Chap. 6.) | Yes | No |
| 34. Are policy statements written at a level appropriate for the reading audience, using one-, two-, or three-syllable words? (See Chap. 6.) | Yes | No |
| 35. Are terms in the Policy and Procedure Guide used consistently throughout the Guide? (See Chap. 6.) | Yes | No |
| 36. Are time intervals and cumulative time periods carefully defined to avoid confusion? (See Chap. 6.) | Yes | No |
| 37. Are eligibility criteria cut-offs clearly explained to avoid misinterpretation? (See Chap. 6.) | Yes | No |
| 38. Is the term *may* used when the policy describes an event that is a possibility or a decision in which management retains flexibility or discretion? (See Chap. 6.) | Yes | No |
| 39. Is the term *shall* used when the policy describes an imperative event or a command that is followed without discretion? (See Chap. 6.) | Yes | No |
| 40. Are proper distinctions made between the terms *day, workday, week, calendar week*, etc.? (See Chap. 6.) | Yes | No |
| 41. Are lists, such as a list of disciplinary rules, defined as not all inclusive, but instead as representative of other similar terms? (See Chap. 6.) | Yes | No |
| 42. Does your Policy and Procedure Guide have a contents page? (See Chap. 6.) | Yes | No |
| 43. Does your Policy and Procedure Guide contain an alphabetical index? (See Chap. 6.) | Yes | No |
| 44. Does your Policy and Procedure Guide contain a revision list? (See Chap. 6.) | Yes | No |
| 45. Does your Policy and Procedure Guide follow a consistent format? (See Chap. 6.) | Yes | No |
| 46. Does each policy specify what class or category of employees are covered by the policy? (See Chap. 7.) | Yes | No |
| 47. Does the Policy and Procedure Guide avoid defining employees in a "permanent" status? (See Chap. 7.) | Yes | No |

48. Do procedural steps start at the beginning of the decision-making process and continue step by step through the conclusion? (See Chap. 6.)    Yes    No

49. Does each policy and procedure identify effective date, revision date, and policy revised? (See Chap. 6.)    Yes    No

50. Is (or will) the Policy and Procedure Guide be consistently administered by supervisors and managers? (See Chaps. 1, 2, and 20.)    Yes    No

# 18

# Employee Handbook Audit: A Comprehensive 50-Item Checklist

**Read Chapter 18 for:**

An audit of any current employee handbook to identify areas in need of improvement

A final check on your newly prepared or revised employee handbook

The Employee Handbook Audit was defined to meet two goals. For firms with an existing Employee Handbook, the audit provides a way to identify areas where improvement is needed. Second, the audit serves as a final check of the newly prepared or revised Employee Handbook.

Review the audit questions listed in this chapter. This audit checklist has been designed so that a "yes" response is the desired response to indicate a satisfactory written Employee Handbook. When a "no" response is checked, additional writing or editing is recommended. If your handbook has a short-coming in a particular area, read the designated chapter for information on improving the policy.

For each "no" response, read relevant portions of this book to identify recommended ways to improve your Employee Handbook.

To audit specific issues on the various policies, see the checklists of issues to consider for each policy topic in Part II of this book.

| **Audit Questionnaire** | **Action Required** | |
| --- | :---: | :---: |
| 1. Does your Employee Handbook include a prominently displayed employment-at-will disclaimer? (See Chap. 2.) | Yes | No |
| 2. Does the disclaimer assert that the Employee Handbook is not a contract and that employment may be terminated at any time for any reason? (See Chap. 2.) | Yes | No |
| 3. Does the disclaimer reserve the right to add, change, or withdraw policies or benefits at any time? (See Chap. 2.) | Yes | No |
| 4. Is the Employee Handbook written as an information summary for employees, in a friendly, personalized, or informal style? (See Chap. 6.) | Yes | No |
| 5. Does the Employee Handbook avoid stating a just cause requirement for dismissals? (See Chaps. 2 and 11.) | Yes | No |
| 6. Are predischarge procedures avoided in the Employee Handbook and appearing as guidelines in a management Policy and Procedure Guide only? (See Chaps. 2 and 11.) | Yes | No |
| 7. Does the Employee Handbook avoid defining a "probationary period" to evaluate new employees? (See Chaps. 2 and 7.) | Yes | No |
| 8. Do statements of corporate philosophy avoid an implied promise of lifetime employment, career tenure, guaranteed or steady work? (See Chap. 2.) | Yes | No |
| 9. Does the Employee Handbook recognize the union if there is a collective bargaining agreement at the organization? (See Chaps. 5 and 13.) | Yes | No |
| 10. Does the Employee Handbook assert that company policies are defined pursuant to the management rights clause of the contract? (See Chaps. 5 and 13.) | Yes | No |
| 11. Is the union informed when contract provisions or mandatory bargaining subjects are defined as policies or procedures?(See Chaps. 5 and 13.) | Yes | No |
| 12. If a union contract exists, are contract-related policies defined in a manner consistent with the contract? (See Chaps. 5 and 13.) | Yes | No |
| 13. Has each policy or benefit summary been checked for compliance with relevant federal labor laws? (See Chap. 5 and Part II.) | Yes | No |
| 14. Has each policy or benefit summary been checked for compliance with relevant federal regulations? (See Chap. 5 and Part II.) | Yes | No |
| 15. Has each policy or benefit summary been checked for com- | Yes | No |

pliance with relevant state laws or regulations? (See Chap. 5 and Part II.)

16. Has each policy or benefit summary been checked for compliance with relevant local ordinances or regulations? (See Chap. 5 and Part II.)            Yes        No

17. Have policies or benefit summaries been reviewed for consistency with relevant court decisions? (See Chaps. 3, 5, and Part II.)            Yes        No

18. Are written policies defined where required by law or regulations? (See Chap. 5 and Part II.)            Yes        No

19. Does the Employee Handbook identify a contact person for additional information? (See Part II.)            Yes        No

20. Does the Employee Handbook avoid defining detailed management procedures which belong in a Personnel Policy and Guide for Supervisors? (See Chap. 6.)            Yes        No

21. Are responsibilities defined by job title? (See Chap. 6 and Part II.)            Yes        No

22. Are gender neutral terms or titles used throughout the Employee Handbook? (See Chap. 6.)            Yes        No

23. Has each policy or benefit been compared to a local or industry survey to evaluate competitiveness? (See Chap. 4 and Part II.)            Yes        No

24. Does the size of the Employee Handbook correlate to organization size or critical issues shown by the following guidelines:

| Number of Employees | Number of employee handbook topics |
|:---:|:---:|
| 1– 14 | 5– 20 |
| 15– 49 | 10– 30 |
| 50–199 | 20– 40 |
| 200–499 | 30– 50 |
| 500+ | 30–100 |

(See Chap. 3.)            Yes        No

25. Is each Employee Handbook topic written in one to three paragraphs or a quarter to half page per topic? (See Chap. 6.)            Yes        No

26. Is the Employee Handbook written in a friendly, personalized, or informal style? (See Chap. 6.)            Yes        No

27. Are procedural details in the handbook broadly written or avoided when necessary to preserve management flexibility or discretion? (See Chap. 2.)                Yes        No

28. Does the Employee Handbook include a receipt for the employee to sign indicating receipt and understanding of company policies? (See Chaps. 2 and 20.)                Yes        No

29. Is the Employee Handbook organized into sections with each section covering similar topics? (See Chap. 6.)                Yes        No

30. Are Employee Handbook topics written in short sentences that average between 10 and 20 words per sentence? (See Chap. 6.)                Yes        No

31. Do all sentences observe basic grammar guidelines with a subject and predicate? (See Chap. 6.)                Yes        No

32. Are sentences written in a simple, straightforward style limited to one or two main thoughts? (See Chap. 6.)                Yes        No

33. Do employee handbook topics use common terms used in daily communications? (See Chap. 6.)                Yes        No

34. Is the Employee Handbook written at a level appropriate for the reading audience, using one-, two-, or three-syllable words? (See Chap. 6.)                Yes        No

35. Are terms in the Employee Handbook used consistently throughout the Handbook? (See Chap. 6.)                Yes        No

36. Are time intervals and cumulative time periods carefully defined to avoid confusion? (See Chap. 6.)                Yes        No

37. Are eligibility criteria cut-offs clearly explained to avoid misinterpretation? (See Chap. 6.)                Yes        No

38. Is the term *may* used when the policy describes an event that is a possibility or a decision in which management retains flexibility or discretion? (See Chap. 6.)                Yes        No

39. Is the term *shall* used when the policy describes an imperative event or a command that is followed without discretion? (See Chap. 6.)                Yes        No

40. Are proper distinctions made between the terms *day, workday, week, calendar week*, etc.? (See Chap. 6.)                Yes        No

41. Are lists, such as a list of disciplinary rules, defined as not all inclusive, but instead as representative of other similar terms? (See Chap. 6.)                Yes        No

42. Does your Employee Handbook have a contents page? (See Chap. 6.)                Yes        No

43. Does your Employee Handbook contain an alphabetical index? (See Chap. 6.)                Yes        No

44. Does your Employee Handbook indicate that it supersedes prior editions? (See Chap. 6.)　　Yes　　No

45. Does your Employee Handbook follow a consistent format? (See Chap. 6.)　　Yes　　No

46. Does each policy specify what class or category of employees are covered by the policy? (See Chap. 7.)　　Yes　　No

47. Does the Employee Handbook avoid defining details of insurance plans already defined in other insurance booklets? (See Chaps. 6 and 12.)　　Yes　　No

48. Does the Employee Handbook avoid defining details of pension or profit sharing plans already defined in other summary plan descriptions? (See Chaps. 6 and 12.)　　Yes　　No

49. Does the Employee Handbook contain information about an employee complaint or grievance procedure? (See Chap. 13.)　　Yes　　No

50. Is (or will) the Employee Handbook be consistently administered by supervisors and managers? (See Chaps. 1, 2, and 20.)　　Yes　　No

# PART 4

# Implementing Your Policy Manual

# 19
# Publishing Ideas and Suggestions

**Read Chapter 19 for:**

Tips on publishing alternatives

Analyzing image, audience and cost concerns

Evaluating bound or looseleaf formats

Understanding printing terms

## Publishing: The Next Phase

After the research, writing, and editing of your Personnel Policy Manual, the next phase is publishing. The writing process produces a manuscript which must be put into a final form for distribution to employees or supervisors.

A wide variety of publishing alternatives are available. In some companies, the policy manual is turned over to the Company Art Department or advertising agency. The result may be a slick and colorful publication similar to a glossy annual report of a *Fortune* 500 corporation. At the other extreme, numerous smaller firms have a few typed pages of policy information which is reproduced on the office copier.

Publishing your policy manual is—in a very real sense—the packaging of policy information. Packaging can influence how your policy manual is perceived and used by the reader. A policy manual that is easy to read will be used. On the other hand, a poorly organized, unattractive collection of typed sheets can convey a negative image about the organization.

## Publishing Considerations

There are four main publishing issues to consider: readability, cost, image, and maintenance.

**Readability.**   Any policy manual must be readable or it will be useless. Readability begins with clear, concise writing. An easy-to-read written message should be the top priority. Readability is enhanced by logical organization of policy information. Finally, readability is aided by careful placement of information on the page.

The *Federal Register*, for example, looks like it would be hard to read. The print is small. There is little space between lines. Sentences are often long and legalistic. The full page is jam packed with words. Because of these characteristics, the *Federal Register* may seem intimidating and difficult to read.

When preparing a Personnel Policy Manual, consider readability issues as you organize information on the page. Design the page to provide information in a way that is easy to read.

**Cost.**   The cost of publishing a policy manual is always a concern. Management expects the cost to be somewhat reasonable. Clearly, the organization that orders looseleaf binders, textured paper stock, and multicolor printing will spend more than the firm that produces copies from a word processor or speedi-printer. There are, however, a variety of ways to control costs while producing an attractive readable policy manual.

**Image.**   Image is an intangible impression that is created by the design and format of the policy manual. A large consumer products company is more likely to convey its corporate image through all publications, including its Personnel Policy Manual. Another organization that hires predominantly unskilled laborers is less likely to be concerned about the image of its Personnel Policy Manual. The image of the organization can be enhanced by the policy manual. The design, style, and costs of the policy manual or other employee communication pieces will reflect corporate philosophies and cultures. The importance of image will also affect cost.

**Maintenance.**   Many human resource specialists are concerned about the maintenance of their Personnel Policy Manual. Once the manual is published, it will need to be updated from time to time. Managers in many firms prefer a looseleaf form of binding so that revised pages can be inserted when policies are revised or new policies are added. The looseleaf format appears more prone for inserting revisions than a bound booklet. Other alternatives, however, may be more cost effective for some firms.

## Publishing Alternatives

Personnel policy information can be published in a variety of formats. Commonly used formats are summarized here. A chart for evaluating publishing alternatives appears in Table 19.1.

**Typed Manuscript.**   For many smaller organizations, a typed manuscript remains the most economical way to produce the policy manual. The typed manuscript can be reproduced in the office copier or sent to a speedi-printer. A good typist can produce a manuscript that organizes information into sections for ease in reading.

**Word Processing Manuscript.**   A great majority of organizations today use dedicated word processors or computers with word processing software. The word processing programs provide a number of advantages over conventional typing. The computerized systems contain features which aid in editing, changing, deleting, inserting, or moving copy without retyping. Most word processing programs also contain a spell check feature to aid in preventing spelling errors. The word processing manuscript is then printed out by the computer's printer unit.

As with typing, a good word processor can organize the manuscript for ease in reading. Policy manual copies can be printed out from the computer as needed. Also, the computer-generated manuscript can be photocopied on the office copier or turned over to a speedi-printer for printed reproduction.

**Desktop Publishing.**   Desktop publishing systems are computerized software programs which interface with word processing software to add special design features. With a desktop publishing system, the user can create a manuscript, select desired type styles and sizes, design a page layout, and produce a manuscript with headlines and illustrations. Depending upon the type of computer printer used, the desktop publishing system can produce "camera ready" material for printing.

A carefully designed policy manual from desktop publishing can be reproduced on the office copier, by a speedi-printer, or by a commercial printer.

**Typesetting.**   The typesetting process is a commercial or "heavy duty" version of desktop publishing. Typesetting services are available through printers, small newspapers, and typesetting firms. Typesetting, like desktop publishing, is a computerized system in which the operator can select type styles, type sizes, line spacing, and other design features. Commercial artists generally perform layout and pasteup of the typeset copy and headlines. Typesetting produces crisp, sharp images in a wide variety of type styles or fonts. Generally, all work done by commercial printers is from typeset copy.

**On-Line Computer Data.**   In this era of office automation with a computer

**Table 19.1.** Evaluating Publishing Alternatives

| Publishing Alternatives | Publishing considerations | | | |
| --- | --- | --- | --- | --- |
| | Readability | Cost | Image | Maintenance |
| Typed manuscript | 0/− | + | 0/− | + |
| Word Processing | 0/− | + | 0 | + |
| Desktop publishing | + | + | + | + |
| Typesetting | + | 0/− | + | 0/− |
| Online computer display | 0/− | 0/− | 0 | + |

Key: + = favorable, 0 = neutral, − = unfavorable.

terminal on nearly every desk, some organizations have elected to put their policy manual on the computer. The on-line display of the policy manual makes policy or benefits information readily available to employees. Separate displays are recommended for a Supervisor's Policy Guide and for an Employee Handbook. Special access passwords can be used to limit policy guide access to supervisors. And, of course, any computerized display of policy information should be programmed for display only. Access codes to enter the policy manual program to change policy information should be limited to Human Resource personnel.

## Should Your Policy Manual Be Bound or Looseleaf?

Several factors influence whether your policy manual should be bound or looseleaf. These factors are quantity, cost, image, and maintenance. Some practical suggestions are offered. Policy manual binding alternatives appear in Table 19.2.

The quantity of policy manuals to be produced affects unit cost. Printing and binder fabrication are manufacturing processes. Therefore, large quantities are needed to bring unit costs down. Looseleaf binding formats are economical for less than 100 manual copies. Smaller firms can purchase looseleaf report covers (similar to those used by students for term papers) or dual pocket portfolios.

However, when producing quantities of 100 to 500 policy manuals, I recommend "saddlestitch" binding. Saddlestitch binding is typically used for softbound booklets. With saddlestitch binding, the information is printed and folded to form a booklet with a heavy paper stock cover stapled on the spine.

In the 100 to 500 quantity range, custom imprint of looseleaf binders can

**Table 19.2.** Policy Manual Binding Alternatives

| Quantity | Binding Alternatives | | |
| | Saddlestitch Binding | Looseleaf report cover | Looseleaf 3-ring binder |
|---|---|---|---|
| 1– 99 | – | + | – |
| 100–500 | + | – | 0/– |
| 500+ | + | – | + |

Key: + = favorable—economic approach, 0 = neutral—not as cost effective, – = unfavorable or costly approach.

be quite costly. A small firm can print one booklet and two or three revisions before reaching a break-even cost with the purchase of customized three-ring binders. When producing quantities of 500, 1000, or more, however, bound or looseleaf formats may be suitable.

Customarily, personnel policy guides for supervisors are done in the looseleaf fashion. These facilitate easy insertion of new policies or policy revisions.

Employee handbooks, on the other hand, are seen in a wider variety of formats. Many human resource specialists in mid-sized firms prefer the looseleaf format until they see how costly it can be. As a general guide, larger firms tend to use looseleaf or softbound employee handbook booklets.

Mid-sized firms tend to use the softbound booklets. Saddlestitch binding of booklets in the 100 to 500 quantity range will generally be more economical than other reproduction formats.

## Selecting Manual Size

The selecting of manual page size is largely a matter of preference and cost. The use of standard sheet sizes will be a significant factor in controlling printing costs. When you select a standard sheet size of $8\frac{1}{2} \times 11$, your printer can use paper that is already in stock without making special cuts. Odd sizes or unusual booklet shapes will add to the cost. When you request an odd-sized page dimension, your printer will need to order larger sheets and cut them to size. These added production steps add to your printing cost. Common booklet sizes are shown:

$17 \times 11$ inch—folded to $8\frac{1}{2}'' \times 11''$

$8\frac{1}{2} \times 11$ inch—used as is

$8\frac{1}{2} \times 11$ inch—folded to $5\frac{1}{2}'' \times 8\frac{1}{2}''$

$11 \times 8\frac{1}{2}$ inch—folded to $8\frac{1}{2}'' \times 5\frac{1}{2}''$

## Selecting Type Styles

Type styles are referred to as fonts. The selection of an appropriate font is important for readability. With the new type setting and desktop publishing systems, there are literally hundreds of type styles available. However, it is best to avoid unused, scripted, artistic, or italic typefaces. Bold type styles may be used for headlines or topic headings.

The recommended typefaces are Helios or English Times. Samples appear in Fig. 19.1.

## Selecting Type Sizes

The size of type is measured in "points," a printer's term. A point is a unit of measurement to designate the height of typeset characters or the space between lines. There are 72 points to the inch. A commonly used type size is 10-point type on 11-point spacing between lines, referred to as leading.

Other alternatives on the type size are shown:

Body of copy (policy)—10 pt, 9 pt, 8 pt

Subheads—12 pt or 10 pt in bold

Headlines—14 pt, 18 pt, or 24 pt in standard or bold characters

A sample of type sizes is shown in Fig. 19.2.

## Eight Ideas on Ordering Printing

1. Give the printer exact specifications. Printing specifications can include quantity, date required, paper color, texture and weight of paper, ink color, bindery or finishing tasks, and other special instructions. Ask to see samples of inks and papers if you are unsure. Show the printer samples if you have a particular design in mind.

2. Recognize that standard practice in the printing industry is to consider plus or minus 10 percent of the ordered quantity as an acceptable delivery. If you absolutely must have 1000 copies, clearly state *1000 minimum* on your order.

3. Check your page counts when preparing booklets that will be saddlestitch bound. The page count should come in a multiple of four. If your manuscript comes to 33 pages, order a 36-page booklet.

4. Specify your page count in two ways to make sure that you are not paying extra. If your policy manual will be on $8\frac{1}{2} \times 11$ sheets printed on front and back, specify "25 double-sided sheets providing 50 pages." Likewise, when ordering a saddlestitch bound booklet, specify "9 double-sided sheets providing 36 pages." (I caught one printer trying

## HELIOS II

WHEN SOMEONE CAN REDUCE THE COST OF DOING business in these days of increasing prices, that is real news! Booklet Publishing Company has devised a revolutionary new way to offer you low-cost, fast-delivery quality printing for all of your needs. We have eliminated unnecessary frills and standardized our operations, thereby eliminating special press and bindery operations. Of course, we can customize your booklets for you at a slight additional cost, if your requirements so dictate.

ABCDEFGHIJKLMNOPQRSTUVWXYZ
abcdefghiklmnopqrstuvwxyz          1234567890 ½ ¼ ¾ ²/₃ ⅓
*¢$1234567890[]&?()!-;:'' ★ ✓ –® ● □ %¢——1234567890

## HELIOS BOLD II

**WHEN SOMEONE CAN REDUCE THE COST OF DOING business in these days of increasing prices, that is real news! Booklet Publishing Company has devised a revolutionary new way to offer you low-cost, fast-delivery quality printing for all of your needs. We have eliminated unnecessary frills and standardized our operations, thereby eliminating special press and bindery operations. Of course, we can customize your booklets for you at a slight additional cost, if your requirements so dictate.**

**ABCDEFGHIJKLMNOPQRSTUVWXYZ
abcdefghiklmnopqrstuvwxyz          1234567890 ½ ¼ ¾ ²/₃ ⅓
*¢$1234567890[]&?()!-;:'' ★ ✓ –® ● □ %¢——1234567890**

**Figure 19.1a.** Sample type styles. *(Courtesy of Booklet Publishing Company, Elk Grove Village, Ill.)*

## ENGLISH TIMES

WHEN SOMEONE CAN REDUCE THE COST OF DOING business in these days of increasing prices, that is real news! Booklet Publishing Company has devised a revolutionary new way to offer you low-cost, fast-delivery quality printing for all of your needs. We have eliminated unnecessary frills and standardized our operations, thereby eliminating special press and bindery operations. Of course, we can customize your booklets for you at a slight additional cost, if your requirements so dictate.

ABCDEFGHIJKLMNOPQRSTUVWXYZ
abcdefghiklmnopqrstuvwxyz                              1234567890½¼¾⅔⅓
*¢$1234567890[]&?()!-;:'" ★ ✔–®  ●□%℀__1234567890

## ENGLISH TIMES BOLD

**WHEN SOMEONE CAN REDUCE THE COST OF DOING business in these days of increasing prices, that is real news! Booklet Publishing Company has devised a revolutionary new way to offer you low-cost, fast-delivery quality printing for all of your needs. We have eliminated unnecessary frills and standardized our operations, thereby eliminating special press and bindery operations. Of course, we can customize your booklets for you at a slight additional cost, if your requirements so dictate.**

**ABCDEFGHIJKLMNOPQRSTUVWXYZ**
**abcdefghiklmnopqrstuvwxyz**                              **1234567890½¼¾⅔⅓**
**\*¢$1234567890[]&?()!-;:'" ★ ✔–®  ●□%℀__1234567890**

**Figure 19.1b.**  Sample type styles.

| | |
|---|---|
| 6 pt | ABCDEFGHIJKLMNOPQRSTUVWXYZ 1234567890 |
| 7 pt | ABCDEFGHIJKLMNOPQRSTUVWXYZ 1234567890 |
| 8 pt | ABCDEFGHIJKLMNOPQRSTUVWXYZ 1234567890 |
| 9 pt | ABCDEFGHIJKLMNOPQRSTUVWXYZ 1234567890 |
| 10 pt | ABCDEFGHIJKLMNOPQRSTUVWXYZ 123456789 |
| 11 pt | ABCDEFGHIJKLMNOPQRSTUVWXYZ 12345 |
| 12 pt | ABCDEFGHIJKLMNOPQRSTUVWXYZ 1: |
| 14 pt | ABCDEFGHIJKLMNOPQRSTUVWX\ |
| 18 pt | ABCDEFGHIJKLMNOPQRS |
| 24 pt | ABCDEFGHIJKLMN( |
| 30 pt | ABCDEFGHIJKL |
| 36 pt | ABCDEFGHIJ |

**Figure 19.2.** Sample type sizes.

to charge me the full page price, in effect quadrupling the cost of the job.)

5. Exercise care with photos to prevent damage. Photos mounted on a card backing with a tissue cover are recommended. Do not write on the photos.

6. Colors add class...and cost. If your budget is tight, consider using a colored paper stock with black ink. Or, use a color other than black, such as blue, throughout the printed reproduction. Use of two colors means two passes through the press. Also, your artwork submitted to the printer must show the color separations.

7. Use camera-ready art for best results. Camera-ready art includes typeset headlines, copy, illustrations, or pictures exactly as they will appear on the printed page. Remember: The better the original, the better your printed copy will appear.

8. Check any typesetting carefully for errors. Ask for a proof of the job if you are having the printer or a commercial artist do layout and design. Careful checking is the policy writer's responsibility to prevent errors.

## Summary

There are a variety of ways to publish your policy manual. Issues such as cost, quantity, and image must be considered. An effectively designed policy manual conveys the firm's philosophy and image as well as written policy information. Now that your policy manual is produced, Chap. 20 gives instructions on implementing and maintaining the manual.

# 20

# Distributing and Updating Your Policy Manual

**Read Chapter 20 for:**

Instructions on distributing your personnel policy manual

Tips on orientating supervisors to proper use of personnel policy information

Ideas for announcing new policies to employees

Sample employee letters

Keeping your manual up to date

## Distributing Your Personnel Policy Manual

The weeks or months of research, writing, editing, checking, and rewriting are over. Your Personnel Policy Manual has been prepared and published. It is now time to distribute the policy manual.

If you prepared a Personnel Policy and Procedure Guide with management instruction, its distribution will be limited to supervisors and managers. If you prepared an Employee Handbook, plan on distributing the handbook to supervisors and employees alike.

Distribution is an important phase of the policy manual project. Distribution of the manual provides an important opportunity for positive communication with employees. Some managers fear that employees will view a policy manual as a restrictive rule book. However, an effective policy manual helps to clarify many policy and benefit questions. Employees want to know "the rules of the game" and be assured that management will follow its own rules. From this perspective, a policy manual is welcomed by employees and supervisors.

Distributing the policy manual also provides an opportunity for management to "sell" the benefits of employment with the organization. In addition to informing employees about the manual, communications can include highlights of current benefits, overview of policy or benefits changes, and information on new benefits or policies.

## Allow Supervisor Preview of Employee Handbooks

Supervisors and managers are on the firing line for answering benefits questions and interpreting policy issues. For this reason, it is important to give supervisors an opportunity to preview a new employee handbook before its official release to employees. Once the handbook is released to employees, there is likely to be a flurry of questions. A preview period together with training or explanation of new policy issues helps supervisors to better understand company policies and benefits.

When distributing a Personnel Policy Manual to supervisors, here are some key points to emphasize.

1. Explain reasons or events that led to the development of the policy manual. A proactive positive reason for preparing the policy manual is best. ("We wanted to announce the new family leave benefit and improve communications with employees," or "The recent attitude survey pointed to the need to update our Employee Handbook.")

2. Review key points of policies and benefits. Focus comments to ensure supervisors clearly understand policy issues which occur on a frequent basis. Common recurring issues may include vacation scheduling, sick leave abuse, absence or tardiness control, or disciplinary procedures. Recap policy provisions which clarify these common problems.

3. Describe how past practice has affected current policies defined in the manual. Does the manual merely document past practice as the policy? Or does the newly defined policy solve problems or clarify issues which were misunderstood in the past?

4. Identify new or revised policies or benefits. Explain what factors prompted the change. Define in detail what is new or different about the new policies or benefits.

5. Provide instructions on policy interpretations or sources for clarification of policy questions. Should unresolved issues be clarified through one's superior or the human resource specialist?

6. Anticipate employee questions or concerns. Identify policy provisions or suggested responses to questions which are likely to be raised by employees.

7. Supervisors are employees too. So encourage supervisor questions. Supervisors may identify important concerns that need to be clarified before release of the policy manual to the employee population at large.

## Sample Memo to Supervisors

### POLICY MANUAL REVISION TRANSMITTAL MEMO

To:       Division Managers, Facility Managers, Department Supervisors
From:    Company President
Subject: Revisions to Personnel Policy and Procedure Guide and to Employee Handbook

In 1986, the Company issued its Personnel Policy and Procedure Guide and an Employee Handbook. Over the past few years, there have been changes in Company policy and in various labor laws which affect employment policies. Attached are revisions to certain personnel policies in response to these changes:

| *New/Revised Policy* | *Old Policy* |
|---|---|
| 1. Introduction | Replaces old introduction. |
| 2. Page 1 of each policy has been updated to reflect the new Company name. | Replaces Page 1 of old policies. |
| 3. Policy No. 401 Hiring Procedures Page 1, Page 2. Revision adds a procedure for the I-9 Immigration forms, and a 30-day evaluation procedure. | Replaces old Policy 401. |
| 4. Policy No. 402 Equal Employment Opportunity, Page 1. Revision adds other protected class categories | Replaces Page 1 of Policy 402. |
| 5. Policy No. 408 Drugs & Alcohol. | New policy. |
| 6. Policy No. 411 Eligibility for Benefits Page 1, Page 2. Revision adds pro rata vacation benefit for part-time employees. | Replaces Page 2 of Policy 411. |
| 7. Policy No. 413 Vacation Page 1, Page 2. Revision clarifies that benefits are earned "at the rate" of 1/12th of the annualized benefit following each full calendar month. | Replaces Policy 413. |

## Announcing Policy Information to Employees

There are a variety of ways to announce policy information to employees. These are highlighted here. (Also see Chap. 13.)

- Bulletin board postings can be used to announce policy or benefits information.

- An employee memo or letter distributed to all employees at work is a common practice for policy or benefits information at many firms.

- A letter to employees and family at home is recommended to announce policy or benefits issues which have a significant impact on family members.

- Payroll stuffers are another way to communicate policy or benefits information to employees.

- Articles in an employee newsletter can help to announce or explain policy or benefits information.

- Departmental meetings by supervisors or managers are a useful communications method. Meetings also provide an opportunity for questions and answers.

- Group or company-wide meetings by top management or human resource personnel convey the importance of an issue. Also, these meetings provide an opportunity for questions and answers.

- Employee handbooks and other benefits booklets provide an excellent medium for communicating policy or benefits information to employees.

I recommend that several of these communication methods be used simultaneously.

## Distributing Employee Handbooks

Employee handbooks can be distributed to employees individually or in group meetings. If the organization is issuing a revised Employee Handbook with minimal revisions, a letter to employees highlighting the changes is recommended.

However, if there are major revisions to a handbook or a handbook is released for the first time, more involved communications are recommended. In these cases, I recommend an employee letter with departmental or group presentation on policy or benefits issues.

During employee meetings, explain policies or benefits, identify changes or revisions, and specify where the employee can go for more information.

Recognize that there will be employee questions about policy or benefits issues described in the employee handbook. Questions will be particularly critical when changes have the effect of reducing benefit levels or making policies (such as attendance) more restrictive. Try to anticipate these questions and be prepared with appropriate answers.

When a restrictive policy or reduced benefit is being introduced, consider these strategies:

- Identify alternative policies or benefits that can be used as a "trade off." The trade-off approach allows management to eliminate a troublesome policy or benefit by substituting it with a less troublesome alternative. A small midwestern metalworking company, for example, eliminated an abuse-prone sick pay benefit and replaced it with a salary continuation plan which paid benefits after five days of illness.

- Explain problems and their effect on business operations which caused the need for the policy or benefit change.

- Identify costs or other quantifiable data which support the need for the change in policy or benefits. Explain how these costs affect the company, employees, products, quality, service, etc.

One important aspect of employee handbook distribution is getting the employee's signature on a handbook receipt. The signature verifies that the employee received the handbook. In a legal proceeding such as unemployment claim or employee lawsuit, the employee's signature on an employee handbook receipt means that the employee can be held accountable for complying with the company policy.

### Sample Employee Handbook Receipt

"I have received an employee handbook and understand that I am responsible for becoming familiar with its contents.

I further understand that this information is not a contract.

I further acknowledge that this handbook does not guarantee my continued employment at XYZ Company, and that I or the Company may terminate employment at any time for any reason, with or without cause."

| | |
|---|---|
| Employee | Date |
| Supervisor | Date |
| Personnel Manager | Date |

### Tips on Effective Use of the Employee Handbook

For years, an Employee Handbook has been a trusted tool for good employee relations. Even now, a carefully prepared Employee Handbook will withstand legal challenges and continue to serve a positive role in employee communications. Here are some tips for getting the most out of your Employee Handbook.

1. Provide Employee Handbooks to new employees as part of the new employee orientation process. Obtain a signed receipt for the handbook. Assign responsibility to supervisors and human resource specialists to explain designated policy or benefits sections to the employee.

2. Make sure that all employees receive Employee Handbooks when first issued and when revised handbooks are released. Obtain signed receipt on each revision.

3. Encourage employees to refer to the handbook for answers to questions about personnel policies or benefits.

4. Refer to the handbook as necessary when addressing performance or discipline problems. Encourage supervisors to record any disciplinary action for the employee's file.

5. Avoid the tendency to deviate from the policies defined in your handbook. If you find it necessary to change a policy or create a new policy, make sure that the policy is communicated to supervisors and employees. Then make employment decisions based on the revised policy. Note: This is important to minimize liability.

6. Always refer to the Employee Handbook when handling a discharge situation. Review handbook provisions that deal with the situation and with the discharge process. Take care to handle the situation in a manner which is consistent with the handbook. An employer's failure to follow policies published in an Employee Handbook is a leading cause of wrongful discharge lawsuits.

## Keeping Your Policy Manual Current

Some human resource administrators lament, "My policy manual was out of date the day after I published it!" At the other extreme, some of my clients with a policy manual that I prepared five years earlier have told me, "The manual you prepared is fine, answers our questions, and we have no need for updating." The frequency of policy manual revisions at your company will depend upon the number of policy or benefit changes.

A Personnel Policy Manual in a looseleaf format can be updated at any time. For a bound manual or handbook, I recommend periodic revisions at two- to three-year intervals. Personnel Policy Manuals require revision for several reasons:

- New policies are defined.
- New benefits are added.
- Policies or benefits are changed or eliminated.
- Policies need to be clarified for better interpretation.

- New laws require a new or changed policy.
- Government regulations require a new or changed policy.
- A landmark court decision changes the interpretation of a law or regulation.

There are a number of things that a human resource administrator can do to keep the firm's Personnel Policy Manual current.

1. Maintain a central file of policy and benefits information. Establish a Personnel Policy Manual Revision file to collect policy or benefits changes which will be included in the next edition of the handbook or policy guide.

2. As policy or benefit changes occur, issue a notice of changes in a memo or letter format to employees. Save these memos for future revision of your policy manual. If you have a looseleaf binding format, you can issue policy revisions for insertion directly into the policy manual.

3. Keep a record of recurring policy interpretation questions or problems. Make sure that these issues are resolved when updating the policy manual.

4. Keep an inventory of Employee Handbooks. As the inventory level declines when handbooks are given to new employees, identify a reorder point. When the level of handbooks reaches the reorder point, survey managers on policy issues which should be changed in the handbook. Then begin revisions and reorder so that the new handbooks arrive about the same time that the supply of old books is depleted.

5. Keep abreast of labor law changes by reading newspapers, trade magazines, newsletters, topical reporter subscriptions, or similar news sources. When necessary, contact the appropriate government agency for copies of laws or regulations. Review your policy manual to note where revisions are needed. Request professional advice if uncertain how to define policy issues to comply with labor laws.

6. Draw information from the aforementioned sources to update and revise your policy manual. As policies are revised, keep a historical file of old policies or policy manuals for five years. After that period, old materials may be destroyed.

## Manual Maintenance

When a revised Employee Handbook or policy booklet is issued, it replaces the prior edition. Instruct employees to turn in old manuals for destruction when issuing the revised edition. A signed receipt documents who received the manuals.

However, when working with a looseleaf manual format, there is always a concern that revisions may not be inserted into the manual. There are several ways to control proper insertion of policy revisions.

- Specify on the revised policy which policy or page it replaces. For example, "Policy 1.05 Personal and Family Leave replaces Policy 1.05 Personal Leave of Absence."

- Provide revision instructions to supervisors or employees on a cover sheet or transmittal letter when issuing policy revisions. For example, "Remove Policy 1.05 Personal Leave of Absence. Insert Policy 1.05 Personal and Family Leave."

- Maintain a Revision Index which lists all current policies and replacement policies.

***Sample Memo to Employees*—Announcing new Employee Handbook**

To: XYZ Company Employees
From: Vice President, Finance & Administration
Subject: Employee Handbook

Attached is the new XYZ Company Employee Handbook. This handbook is being distributed to all current employees, and all future employees will receive a handbook at the start of employment.

In preparing this Employee Handbook, we have summarized many of the informal personnel practices and benefits which have been administered over the years. Company management has elected to provide this information in order to enhance positive and open communications with employees.

Please take a few minutes to read through your new handbook, and keep it as a handy reference when questions arise. In the event you would like additional information on a particular subject, feel free to speak with your supervisor.

After you have had an opportunity to review your new handbook, please sign and return the "new employee orientation" and the "chemical hazard orientation" forms at the back of the handbook.

**Sample Revision Control Sheet**

**RECORD OF POLICY ADDITIONS/REVISIONS**

| Policy | Title | Effective Date | Revision Date |
|--------|-------|----------------|---------------|
| 1.01 | Employment Classifications | 1-1-93 | |
| 1.02 | Staffing Procedures | 1-1-93 | |

| Policy | Title | Effective Date | Revision Date |
|--------|-------|----------------|---------------|
| 1.03 | Orientation of New Employees | 1-1-93 | |
| 1.04 | Open Door Policy | 1-1-93 | |
| 1.05 | Equal Employment Opportunity | 1-1-93 | |
| 1.06 | Sexual Harassment | 1-1-93 | |
| 1.07 | Personnel Records | 1-1-93 | 7-1-93 |
| 1.08 | Promotions and Transfers | 1-1-93 | |
| 1.09 | Substance Abuse | 1-1-93 | |
| 1.10 | Disciplinary Procedures | 1-1-93 | |
| 1.11 | Separation of Employment | 1-1-93 | |
| 2.01 | Working Hours | 1-1-93 | |
| 2.02 | Attendance and Punctuality | 1-1-93 | 7-1-93 |
| 2.03 | Voting Time Off | 1-1-93 | |
| 2.04 | Jury Service | 1-1-93 | |
| 2.05 | Funeral Leave | 1-1-93 | |
| 2.06 | Military Leave | 1-1-93 | |
| 2.07 | Medical Leave | 1-1-93 | |
| 2.08 | Personal Leave | 1-1-93 | |
| 3.01 | Benefits Enrollment | 1-1-93 | |
| 3.02 | Holidays | 1-1-93 | |
| 3.03 | Vacations | 1-1-93 | 7-1-93 |
| 3.04 | Paid Personal Days | 1-1-93 | |
| 3.05 | Short-Term Disability | 1-1-93 | |
| 3.06 | Educational Assistance | 1-1-93 | |
| 4.01 | Performance Reviews | 1-1-93 | |
| 4.02 | Pay Reviews (nonunion) | 1-1-93 | |
| 5.01 | Confidentiality and Conflict of Interest | 1-1-93 | |
| 5.02 | Security | 1-1-93 | |
| 5.03 | Business Travel | 1-1-93 | |
| 5.04 | Interruption of Operations | 1-1-93 | |
| 6.01 | Safety | 1-1-93 | |
| 6.02 | Hazard Communication | 1-1-93 | |

## Summary

*Personnel Policy Handbook: How to Develop a Manual That Works* has provided a step-by-step look at the policy manual preparation process. The process begins with planning, and then moves to developing policy, auditing your efforts, and finally implementing your completed policy manual. When the ideas and suggestions of this book are implemented, your investment will be amply repaid.

# APPENDIXES

Appendix **A**

# Sample Employee Handbook

**XYZ COMPANY**
1234 ANY STREET
ANY TOWN, USA
PHONE NUMBER

## THE PRESIDENT'S MESSAGE

I want to take this opportunity to welcome each new employee.

In accepting employment at XYZ Company, you have joined a dynamic team of employees working together to uphold traditions begun by the XYZ Company years ago.

For more than 80 years, our organization has been supplying production equipment to manufacturers throughout the United States, Canada, Central and South America, and overseas. We are proud of our reputation for providing quality products through ethical business practices. We believe that our dedication to quality and service has been an important factor in our success.

We have prepared this Employee Handbook to help acquaint you with our company's principles, employment policies, and highlights of certain benefits. Since we cannot be all inclusive here, feel free to speak with your supervisor if there are any questions about our employment practices.

I sincerely hope that your employment with XYZ Company will be challenging and rewarding.

Chairperson & President

January, 19XX

## YOUR EMPLOYEE HANDBOOK

This Employee Handbook has been prepared to provide information about current Company personnel policies and benefits for XYZ Company employees. An employee handbook, by its very nature, is brief and not all inclusive. Employees are referred to their supervisor or Personnel Manager when further information is desired.

XYZ Company is a dynamic organization operating in a competitive and changing business environment. Because of this, our personnel policies and benefits are under constant review and may be changed at any time with or without notice based on the needs of the business or the interests of employees. Final authority for information summarized in this handbook rests with management discretion, management interpretation of policies, or insurance or benefit plan contracts as applicable. In the event policies or benefits are changed, we will do our best to keep you informed.

This handbook does not constitute a contract, and it does not guarantee employment security or specific benefits. Any individual may voluntarily leave employment upon proper notice, and employment may be terminated by the Company at any time for any reason. Any oral or written statements or promises to the contrary are hereby expressly disavowed and should not be relied upon by any prospective or existing employee.

The policies and benefits defined in this handbook are intended to be in conformance with applicable state and federal laws related to employment. XYZ Company employees are located in many areas of the country. In the event a particular state law or local ordinance conflicts with a policy stated herein, management reserves the right to modify or adapt the policy to conform with state or local practice.

## CONTENTS

## GETTING ACQUAINTED

### A Brief History

In 1922, the XYZ brothers formed a merchandising company in Chicago.
This Company began selling tools, wheels, gears, and other equipment

used by manufacturers. The XYZ brothers saw tremendous opportunities in supplying the needs of the many new manufacturing firms that were formed during the industrial growth period. From the beginning, the XYZ organization has been dedicated to a philosophy of providing quality merchandise at a fair price. Innovations in marketing also helped the Company to succeed. The XYZ Company offered consumers a free trial with a money back guarantee, a practice which was considered unusual in those days.

Now, Company operations are located in modern facilities at Milwaukee, Wisconsin; Rockford, Illinois; Denver, Colorado; as well as the headquarters and distribution center in Chicago, Illinois. Our products are sold through a network of independent dealers.

XYZ Company maintains its leadership position in the industry by developing new products, services, and technology for the manufacturer. New electronic controls and computer information systems developed by XYZ aid progressive manufacturers to efficiently compete in the international market. Dealers and employees receive comprehensive training from the XYZ Company Training Center.

### Our Mission Statement

The purpose of a mission statement is to define the overall objective of an organization. We believe that each employee will better understand his or her responsibilities by being familiar with our mission statement, as reproduced below:

> XYZ Company is in the business of providing a quality line of production equipment, supplies, and services which integrate into systems that satisfy the requirements of our customers on a global basis. The key to our long-term success is to provide customers with new, innovative products and services providing superior value. We are committed to leadership in the industry, yet we seek new growth opportunities which capitalize on our strengths.

### Our Objectives

The manner in which we operate our business and relate to our employees is defined in the following objectives. It is the objective of XYZ Company management to

- Treat each employee as an individual
- Be fair, ethical, and honest in all business transactions
- Provide a safe and healthful working environment
- Provide open and positive communication of Company policies, guidelines, benefits, and employment practices
- Maintain the high standards of quality and service upon which our company was founded
- Make XYZ Company a good place in which to work

### Quality

The XYZ Company recognized very early that poor-quality work injures the Company's reputation and hampers prospects for the financial security which is important to all of us. Because of this, quality products and service have always been a top priority at XYZ Company.

In order to emphasize our commitment to quality, the Company has adopted a quality policy. Please realize that quality is everyone's responsibility—your attention to detail contributes to quality and the success of the Company.

The XYZ Company Quality Policy reads as follows:

- We will perform defect-free work for our customers and associates by doing things right the first time.
- We will seek out and fully understand the requirements of our jobs, the systems that support us and our customers.
- We will conform to those requirements at all times or have them officially changed to better meet the needs of our customers and associates.

### Quality Improvement Teams

In the past year, XYZ Company created Quality Improvement Teams at each company location. These teams are an important part of the Company's efforts to achieve zero defects and maintain the high standards of quality attained by XYZ Company over the years. Designated employees and managers participate in various activities of the teams in order to educate employees, define and establish quality standards, take corrective action, and promote a greater awareness of each individual's role in achieving quality products and service. The Company began publishing a newsletter to promote and communicate quality program activities among the various locations. We want each employee to assume an active role in maintaining high-quality standards on the job.

### Equal Employment Opportunity

It is the policy of XYZ Company to afford equal opportunity for employment. All employment decisions are made without regard to race, color, age, sex, religion/creed, national origin, ancestry, marital status, physical or mental disability which can be reasonably accommodated, arrest/conviction record, pregnancy, sexual orientation, or unfavorable discharge from military service.

### Sexual Harassment

XYZ Company has a strict policy against sexual harassment of any kind. Sexual harassment may include unwanted sexual advances, requests for sexual favors, or any other sexually oriented conduct that may be intimidating or unwelcomed by the recipient. This Company will not tolerate any form of harassment or discrimination, and any complaint relating to such matters may be brought directly to the attention of top management.

## Open Door Policy

Good "two way" communications are necessary in order for each employee and the Company to be successful. We want to keep employees informed about matters which affect their job, and likewise please speak up when you have questions or concerns about job responsibilities or work assignments.

XYZ Company maintains an Open Door Policy and encourages employees to speak openly with supervisory or management personnel. Your ideas or suggestions on improved work methods and procedures are welcomed. Feel free to discuss work matters or issues of concern with your supervisor. If your supervisor is unable to provide assistance, you may request to speak with a higher-level manager. We will do our best to provide a fair and timely response.

## Our Feeling about Unions

At XYZ Company, we believe that our union-free status is one reason why our company has continued to grow and serve our customers in a profitable and efficient manner. Union membership is not a job requirement at our company. Our company operates with an open management style where each employee has the right to deal directly with supervisors or management to discuss ideas, suggestions, or concerns.

We recognize your right to join or not to join—to belong or not to belong—to any social, political, labor, or religious organization as you see fit. We believe, however, that a union is unnecessary because no union, despite any promises, can create jobs or increase a Company's income so that higher wages may be paid.

## EMPLOYEE BENEFITS

XYZ Company provides a competitive array of employee benefits designed to make your job more rewarding and to provide added protection for eligible employees and their dependents. XYZ Company benefits include paid holidays and vacations, group insurances, retirement benefits, income maintenance plans, as well as government-required insurances.

Brief highlights of current Company benefits are summarized here. Certain benefits or insurance plans are defined in detail by their respective plan document or contract. Such documents (and not this handbook) represent the final authority for plan eligibility, coverages, etc. Feel free to speak with your supervisor when questions arise.

## Eligibility for Benefits

At time of hire, each new employee is placed into an employment category based upon work schedule. The employment category determines one's eligibility for benefits as defined below:

a) *Full-Time Employee*—One who is hired to work for an indefinite period with a work schedule averaging 40 hours per week. Full-time employees meeting appropriate length-of-service requirements are eligible to participate in all Company benefits programs. These benefits include paid holidays, paid vacations, health insurance, life insurance, dental insurance, long-term disability insurance, sick pay, wage continuation, pension plan, 401K savings investment plan, paid time off in the event of funeral, military reserve training, jury service, and a Section 125 Cafeteria Plan.

b) *Reduced Hours Full-Time Employee*—One who is hired to work for an indefinite period for a work schedule which normally averages 30 or more hours but less than 40 hours weekly. Reduced hours full-time employees meeting appropriate length-of-service requirements are eligible to participate in all Company benefits programs, except that benefits providing pay for time off are prorated based on the number of weekly hours normally worked compared to 40 hours. Paid time off benefits include vacation, holiday, sick pay, wage continuation, military leave pay, jury service pay, and funeral leave pay.

c) *Part-Time or Temporary Employee*—One who is hired to work less than 25 hours per week or is hired for short-term periods such as summer employment. Part-time and temporary employees meeting eligibility requirements are entitled to receive holiday pay. Part-time and temporary employees are not eligible for other Company benefits except for government-required benefits defined later in this booklet.

Temporary changes in the number of hours do not affect your status, and the preceding definitions are not to be construed as a guarantee of work hours.

### Holidays

XYZ Company observes 10 holidays during the year. Management identifies the specific dates which are observed as holidays and announces the holiday schedule each year. A nonexempt employee must have 30 days employment or more to receive holiday pay. Full-time and reduced hours full-time employees are entitled to holiday pay computed based on the employee's regular straight time pay rate for an eight-hour workday and prorated for the reduced hours employees.

In the event a nonexempt employee works on a holiday, the employee is entitled to holiday pay plus one-half times of the employee's regular pay rate for all hours actually worked. Nonexempt part-time and temporary employees who work on a holiday are entitled to receive their regular straight time pay rate for hours worked, plus any overtime pay if applicable.

### Vacations

Full-time and reduced hours full-time employees become eligible for paid vacation benefits based upon length of service as of December 31 of each year, as follows:

| Length of service as of December 31 of the year the vacation is taken if hired prior to July 1 | Paid vacation benefit |
|---|---|
| 6 months but less than 1 year | 1 week |
| 1 year but less than 8 years | 2 weeks |
| 8 years but less than 15 years | 3 weeks |
| 15 years but less than 25 years | 4 weeks |
| 25 years or more | 5 weeks |

A full-time or reduced hours full-time employee who was hired prior to July 1 is entitled to take one (1) week of vacation after four months service, to be scheduled in the second half of the year between July and December. During the following calendar year, the employee is entitled to two (2) weeks vacation after completing one (1) year employment.

When the employee advances from two to three weeks vacation, or three to four weeks, etc., the employee is eligible for the extra week of vacation as follows: If the employee is hired prior to July 1, the additional week vacation may not be taken until after the qualifying anniversary date. If hired on or after July 1, the individual will not be entitled to an additional week vacation until the following calendar year.

Vacation pay is computed based upon the employee's regular straight time pay rate for a 40-hour work week and prorated for reduced hours full-time employees. Employees who do not meet eligibility requirements may receive time off without pay.

Employees are encouraged to submit vacation requests early in the year so that vacation schedules can be established in each department or work group. All vacation requests are subject to management approval. Please recognize that there may be occasions when an individual's vacation request may be denied or delayed because absence would adversely affect departmental staffing. Normally, vacation requests above two consecutive weeks will not be approved. In the event two or more employees request conflicting vacation dates, our practice is to give preference based on the earliest request received or length of service depending upon local practice, except where seniority is a factor.

All vacations must be used within the calendar year immediately following the January 1 eligibility date. There is no carryover to future years except as defined herein, and unused vacation benefits are not paid at year end. At separation of employment, an employee is entitled to receive pay for any earned unused vacation.

### Insurance Plans

Full-time and reduced hours full-time employees are eligible for group insurances beginning on the first day of the month following one full calendar month of employment and timely completion of the insurance enrollment forms. XYZ Company pays a significant portion of the insurance premium cost for individual and family coverage.

Employees and eligible dependents must enroll within 30 days of hire; if an employee or dependents fail to enroll within this enrollment period, any subsequent enrollment will be subject to providing evidence of insurability (a physical exam at the employee's expense) in order to be accepted into the insurance plan. Further details on group insurances are defined in a separate booklet. The following insurance plans are available:

*Health Insurance*—Provides protection to defray the cost of hospital charges, doctor bills, and medical expenses. Additional insurance protection for your eligible dependents is available.

*Life Insurance*—Provides life insurance protection including provision for accidental death and dismemberment.

*Dental Insurance*—Provides insurance protection to defray costs of dental care. Dependent coverage is available.

*Long-Term Disability Insurance*—Provides income maintenance protection during an employee's extended disability.

*HMO*—The HMO or Health Maintenance Organization is provided at certain locations as an alternative to the health insurance plan. HMO benefits include coverage of hospital charges, medical expenses, as well as periodic physical exams and preventative health care for service performed by an HMO participating physician.

*PPO*—The PPO or Preferred Provider Organization is provided at certain locations as another health insurance alternative. PPO benefits include reimbursement for specified health care services provided by participating doctors and organizations.

### Section 125 Benefit Plan

XYZ Company provides a Section 125 Benefit Plan for eligible employees. Also referred to as a Cafeteria Plan, this benefit allows eligible employees to designate funds through payroll deduction to be applied to the cost of certain benefits. This plan helps to reduce an individual's income tax liability by directing pretax income to pay certain benefit costs.

### Pension Plan

XYZ Company provides a Pension Plan which is designed to provide added financial security for eligible employees upon retirement. Further details are defined in a separate booklet. If you have specific questions about retirement benefits, speak to your supervisor, who will refer you to the appropriate person for answers.

### 401K Plan

XYZ Company provides a 401K Savings Investment Plan for eligible employees. Under this plan, participants may elect to contribute a portion of earnings into the plan; these funds are then invested by plan administrators and held until the employee's retirement. Current tax laws allow for favorable tax treatment to both the contributions and earnings from this plan. Full details are defined in a plan description. Speak with your supervisor for more information.

## Wage Continuation

XYZ Company provides a Wage Continuation benefit for full-time and reduced hours full-time employees. Eligibility for this benefit is defined by length-of-service criteria established by management. This benefit provides limited income maintenance protection in the event of a non-job-related illness, injury, or disability. Benefits may be paid upon receipt of a physician's statement certifying the nature of disability and completion of a 14-day waiting period. Speak with your supervisor for more information.

## Service Awards

XYZ Company has established a service award program to recognize long-term service to the Company. Employees receive a service award following their fifth employment anniversary and each succeeding five-year anniversary.

## Government-Required Insurances

XYZ Company contributes toward the costs of the following government-required insurances, which are designed to provide income maintenance protection for employees:

*Worker's Compensation Insurance*—Provides insurance protection in the event of a job-related illness or injury. Coverage begins on the first day of employment for all employees.

*Social Security Insurance*—Provides retirement and disability income protection for covered workers. The Company matches the contribution deducted from your paycheck each pay period.

*Unemployment Insurance*—Provides limited income protection for eligible employees in the event of job loss through no fault of the employee.

## EMPLOYMENT POLICIES

---

## Continuous Service

An employee's length of service is a factor which influences certain Company benefits. Your continuous service date is the date on which you began active employment at XYZ. This date serves as a basis to measure continuous service with the Company. Continuous service may be interrupted by a medical leave, personal leave, or other absence causing a break in service as defined by the pension, 401K, or other similar benefit plans. In the event of any leave of absence, you are urged to speak with your supervisor to clarify the effect of absence upon benefits plans.

In the event of separation of employment due to voluntary resignation, dismissal, layoff exceeding one year, or other similar separation, the employee loses all continuous service credits. Any reemployment of an individual following separation would establish a new continuous service date. (Under law, former employees returning to work after military service are entitled to retain their latest continuous service date preceding military duty.)

### Pay Day

Employee paychecks normally are distributed according to the following schedule:

| Pay Period | Pay Day |
| --- | --- |
| Weekly | Friday following the end of the pay period |
| Biweekly | Tuesday following the end of the pay period |
| Semimonthly | 15th and the last workday of the month |
| Monthly | 15th of the following month |

In the event the designated pay day occurs on a holiday or a weekend, management will designate another date as a pay day. If there is a question regarding your paycheck, speak with your supervisor.

### Personnel Records

In order to keep Company personnel records current, please notify your supervisor if there is a change of address, telephone number, name, tax exemption, insurance beneficiary, marital status, or number of dependents. Please cooperate with this request in order to keep payroll and benefits information up to date.

### Advancement Opportunities

As the Company continues to grow and expand, there will be new job opportunities for employees. We believe in the idea of promotion from within, and when possible qualified employees are promoted as suitable vacancies occur. Please realize, however, that XYZ Company cannot guarantee promotions; there will be occasions when it is necessary to hire job candidates from outside the Company.

### Outside Employment

Employees may, at their option, seek outside employment during hours other than their normally scheduled working hours. However, no employee may work in any capacity for any competitor. Violation of this rule will result in immediate discharge. To remove any doubts as to whether an outside employer is a competitor, we request that you inform your supervisor of your plans before you accept outside employment.

Employees should avoid any outside activities which interfere with their work performance. If this occurs, the employee will be asked to make a decision about priority of employment or other activities.

### Temporary Transfer

XYZ Company is a growing company where all employees must work together to make our operation a success. There are occasions when it is necessary to transfer employees from one job to another on a temporary basis in order to meet the needs of our customers. Please cooperate when your supervisor asks you to handle a special assignment.

### Smoking Policy

XYZ Company advocates no smoking in order to promote a smoke-free environment. General office, warehouse, and other areas are designated no-smoking areas. Certain areas are specified as allowable for smoking based on local practice. For example, the Chicago office lunchroom is an allowable smoking area except from 11:00 a.m. to 1:30 p.m. when smoking is not allowed.

### Separation of Employment

We realize that there are situations which may compel separation of employment; and we want you to realize that the employment relationship may be terminated at any time at will, for any reason or no reason, by yourself or the Company. In the event of voluntary resignation or retirement, please submit a letter of resignation giving two weeks notice.

All separating employees are required to return any Company property, equipment, keys, manuals, etc. prior to receiving their final check.

## ATTENDANCE POLICIES

### Working Hours

Full-time employees normally work a 40-hour work week Monday through Friday. Your specific work hours and starting times will be set by facility management based upon department needs and workloads. Employee work schedules or starting times may be changed or adjusted in response to business needs.

Employees working a full-time work schedule are entitled to a lunch period at a time designated by their supervisor. The scheduling and length of lunch periods are established by each facility manager based upon business needs. In some areas, lunches may be scheduled in a way which permits uninterrupted telephone coverage or continuous business operations throughout the workday.

### Overtime

Due to the nature of our business, there may be peak periods when extra work hours are scheduled. Employees are expected to work hours as scheduled, and the Company reserves the right to schedule and require overtime work if necessitated by business needs. All overtime work must be approved by your supervisor.

Nonexempt employees are entitled to receive overtime pay computed at one and one-half times their regular straight time pay rate for all time worked over 40 hours per week.

Time not worked due to Company-observed holidays and prior approved paid vacations counts as time worked for overtime eligibility.

### Time Records

Certain employees are required to maintain a record of hours worked. Your supervisor will provide time recording instructions to you as applicable. Be sure that your time records are accurate, because these records affect computation of pay and certain benefits.

### Attendance and Punctuality

Each employee performs an important job at XYZ Company. Employees are expected to report to work regularly, to be at their work station ready to work at start time, and to work the full scheduled workday. When you are absent or late for work, fellow employees must fill in and assume extra responsibilities to meet production needs.

In the event you will be absent or late for work, you are expected to call in to your supervisor or other designated individual, within one hour of your scheduled start time, to report your absence and anticipated date or time of return to work. In the event of a medical-related absence of three days or more, the employee must submit a doctor's statement. (Also, see the Company policy on medical leave of absence.)

An unreported absence of three days or more will be viewed as a voluntary quit. Please be conscientious about attendance habits, because excessive absenteeism or tardiness is subject to disciplinary action, which may include dismissal.

### Jury Service

The Company recognizes an employee's civic responsibility for serving as a juror. Full-time and reduced hours full-time employees who are summoned to and participate in jury service will receive pay for the difference between their regular straight time daily pay rate (prorated for reduced hours employees) and the daily jury pay for a period up to three weeks.

Please notify your supervisor by providing a copy of the juror summons immediately upon receipt. Also, upon return to work remember to bring in to work a copy of the juror pay warrant. Part-time and temporary employees will receive time off without pay for jury service.

### Military Leave

Full-time and reduced full-time employees who participate in military reserve training or emergency national guard duty will receive pay for the difference between their regular straight time daily pay rate (prorated for reduced hours employees) and the daily military service pay for a period up to 30 days for each instance of active service.

Please notify your supervisor by providing a copy of military orders immediately upon receipt. Also, upon return to work remember to bring in to work a copy of the military pay warrant. Part-time and temporary employees will receive time off without pay for military obligations.

Employees may be released, without pay, for extended military obligations. Reemployment from such absence is consistent with federal laws on veterans' reemployment.

### Funeral Leave

In the event of a death in the family, an employee may be permitted time off work as authorized by management to attend to funeral matters. Full-time and reduced hours full-time employees may receive up to three days of funeral leave pay for time off from regularly scheduled workdays for bereavement and attending to funeral matters for members of one's immediate family. Time off without pay may be allowed for part-time or temporary employees.

Funeral leave pay is computed based on the employee's regular straight time pay rate for eight hours and prorated for reduced hours full-time employees. You must be on active payroll at the time of payment; funeral leave pay will not be paid during a leave of absence, vacation, or holiday.

Immediate family is defined as husband, wife, mother, father, sister, brother, daughter, son, father-in-law, or mother-in-law. Remember to keep your supervisor advised regarding your absence.

### Medical Leave

An employee who becomes seriously ill or disabled for three days or more may be placed on medical leave. Medical leaves are normally approved for periods up to 30 days and may be extended at 30-day intervals at management discretion. A medical statement is required to place the employee on leave, when requesting extensions, and upon return to work. Absence for maternity is treated in a manner similar to sustained illness or disability.

In the event of a question regarding a medical leave or an employee's ability to perform available work, the Company may elect to obtain a second medical opinion prior to considering or extending a medical leave of absence.

The employee's regular pay is suspended during leave. The employee may be entitled to income maintenance protection under the Company's wage continuation benefit, long-term disability insurance, or worker's compensation insurance as applicable.

In the event an employee incurs a medical condition which may affect the employee's ability to work safely or which may adversely affect other employees, the employee has a responsibility to report the condition to management and to seek appropriate medical care. In such cases, the Company may elect to schedule the individual for medical exams, tests, make reasonable accommodation for the condition, or arrange a medical leave of absence as appropriate.

### Personal and Family Leave

In the event urgent personal or family matters require time off work, an employee may request an unpaid personal leave of absence. Approval of any personal leave of absence is at management discretion after considering the circumstances of the case and staffing needs of the business. A personal leave is limited to employees with one year or more of continuous service.

### Conditions of Leave

All requests for leave of absence are subject to management approval after considering the Company needs and the nature of the employee's request. A leave of absence is approved with the understanding that the employee intends to return to work at the conclusion of the leave. Every effort is made to place the returning employee into the same or similar position if possible. During any period of leave, the Company reserves the right to fill, alter, or eliminate a vacant position if required by business needs.

During a leave, the employee is responsible for paying the normal contributory portion of insurance premiums. The Company-paid portion of insurance premiums continues through the end of the next full calendar month following the month in which the leave began. Thereafter, the employee must pay the full premium cost of insurances if uninterrupted coverage is desired. Accrual of vacation benefits is prorated for any leave of 30 days or more. The employee's continuous service accumulation is suspended during any period of medical leave or personal leave. Extended absences may affect eligibility for pension, 401K, or similar benefits. Speak with your supervisor for further details.

### ADMINISTRATIVE POLICIES

### Confidential Information

All employees are reminded that Company records such as customer lists, pricing, blueprints, or production processes are confidential business information. Please exercise proper care of this information and avoid discussing confidential business matters with persons not employed by XYZ Company.

## Security

Every employee shares a responsibility to exercise reasonable precautions to protect the security of Company property and equipment. Our facilities are protected by locks and alarm systems which are activated after business hours. In the event you are scheduled to work outside of normal business hours, you will be advised regarding any special entrance, exit, or security procedure.

## Visitors

For safety and security reasons, all visitors to the Company must enter through the office reception area, be approved by management, and escorted by an employee while on the premises. This requirement applies to all outside visitors including former employees. As a reminder, employees are not permitted to loiter about the premises after your work shift has ended.

## Solicitations

In order to avoid disruption to Company operations, XYZ Company has established the following rules related to solicitations and distribution of literature on Company property.

a) Nonemployees may not solicit or distribute literature on Company property at any time for any purpose.

b) Employees may not solicit or distribute literature during working time for any purpose.

c) Employees may not distribute literature at any time in working areas.

Working time includes the working time of both the employee doing the soliciting and distributing and the employee to whom the soliciting or distributing is being directed. Working time does not include break periods, meal periods, or any other specified periods during the workday when employees are properly not engaged in performing their work tasks.

## Telephones

In order that Company telephone lines remain clear for business use, employees are reminded that personal calls from family or friends should be kept to a minimum. As a general rule, employees will not be called off their job to accept a phone call unless there is a true emergency. Outgoing personal calls may be made from designated telephones on your own time. Additional telephone instructions will be provided by your supervisor.

## Dress and Appearance

Please remember that the reputation of the Company, as well as your own reputation, is judged partly by your personal conduct and appearance.

Employees are expected to dress in a clean and neat manner, appropriate for their respective job responsibilities and a business environment. Dress guidelines for each facility may be established by the respective facility manager or other designated manager.

Please cooperate with dress guidelines established by management.

### Travel Expenses

Employees incurring authorized business or travel expenses associated with the performance of job duties will receive reimbursement.

The employee is responsible for preparing a detailed expense voucher with attached receipts for approval by management. Speak with your supervisor for further details.

### Bulletin Boards

The Company maintains bulletin boards to communicate information to employees. You are encouraged to check the bulletin board in your area periodically to keep informed of Company announcements and information. Any employee postings must be approved by management.

### Lockers

Lockers are provided in certain areas for storage of personal belongings and any work garments. Remember to lock your locker; the Company is not responsible for loss or damage to one's personal possessions.

In the interest of maintaining safety and health, the Company reserves the right to inspect lockers if deemed necessary by management.

### Lunchroom

Lunchrooms are provided at most facilities for the convenience of employees. Please cooperate in cleaning any spills and properly disposing of trash.

### SAFETY

### Safety First

At XYZ Company, we are committed to providing a safe and healthful working environment for employees. Our commitment includes providing proper tools and machines, purchasing necessary safety equipment, affording insurance coverages, and defining important safety rules. However, safety on the job requires active participation by employees as well as management.

You can help assure your own safety by performing job duties in a safe manner, wearing personal protective equipment when exposed to hazards, and using common sense to protect yourself and fellow employees from injury.

### Accident Reporting

Please report any injury or illness on the job to your supervisor as soon as possible so that proper medical treatment may be provided. In the event of a serious accident, emergency medical care is nearby.

### Housekeeping

XYZ Company provides a modern attractive working environment for employees. Each employee is responsible for keeping his or her work area clean and neat throughout the day. Dispose of trash properly and do your part to keep the lunch-room, washrooms, locker area, and parking lot clean. Good housekeeping is an important part of accident prevention.

### Dress for Safety

Employees are reminded that wearing of appropriate work garments and personal protective equipment is an important way to prevent painful injuries. For example, sturdy work-type or safety shoes must be worn when working in the plant area. Employees are required to wear personal protective equipment such as safety glasses, or goggles, which may be specified when performing job duties exposed to potential hazards. Your supervisor will provide further details and Company safety rules for your work area.

### Chemical Safety

The nature of our business involves the use of or storage of small quantities of various chemical substances, oils, and cleaning solvents.

The Company maintains a file of Material Safety Data Sheets in the office. These sheets provide information on safety precaution, spill control, and protective equipment. You may ask to see the Material Safety Data Sheets any time you have a question about a chemical substance. Your supervisor will provide additional guidelines.

### Accident Prevention

Take care to follow safe operating procedures for your job. When operating motor vehicles, always wear safety belts, observe traffic laws, and adjust speed for weather and road conditions. Motorcyclists should always wear helmets when operating their vehicles.

### Safety Rules

- Report all injuries or illnesses immediately following their occurrence.
- Safety guards or devices are not to be altered in any way.
- Employees are required to wear personal protective equipment, such as safety glasses or goggles, which may be specified when performing job duties exposed to potential hazards.
- Loose clothing, loose sleeves, ties, or jewelry should not be worn when operating machinery.
- Defective tools or equipment must not be used and should be turned in to your supervisor.
- Lift objects properly by bending knees and keeping back straight to avoid strains. Ask for assistance on heavy loads.
- Keep your work area clean and free of dangerous hazards.
- Long hair must be restrained and beards trimmed to avoid exposure to machinery.
- Open-toed, casual, or sport-type shoes may not be worn when working in the plant. Sturdy work-type or safety shoes are recommended.
- Store flammable liquids or oily rags in fire-resistant containers and observe posted no-smoking signs.
- Only trained and authorized employees are permitted to operate machines, equipment, or lift trucks.
- Never hitch a ride or permit riders on material handling equipment.
- Do not touch or surprise someone who is working on a machine. Participation in jokes or pranks is prohibited.
- Only trained and authorized employees are permitted to make machine adjustments or repairs. Respect safety locks.
- Observe all safe operating procedures and instructions from your supervisor.

## STANDARDS OF CONDUCT

All companies must set reasonable rules in order to coordinate the many varied activities within the organization. In recognition of this, XYZ Company has developed Standards of Conduct in order to advise employees regarding conduct which is unsuitable in a working environment.

Employee misconduct which disregards the Standards of Conduct will result in corrective disciplinary action.

Disciplinary actions may include verbal warnings, written warnings, suspension without pay, or discharge. The severity of the corrective action reflects the nature of the offense, and increasingly severe measures will be taken for more serious or repeated offenses. Serious offenses will result in immediate discharge.

The following is not designed to be a complete list of prohibited behaviors, but is intended to serve as a general guideline. Other similar behaviors may be subject to disciplinary action.

1) Fighting or participating in a physical altercation on Company time or premises

2) Unauthorized possession or use of a weapon on Company property

3) Unauthorized possession or use of liquor on Company time or premises

4) Possession or use of illegal drugs on Company time or premises

5) Flagrant disregard for safety or health endangering lives or property

6) Falsification of alteration of any official Company document or form, including time card or employment application

7) Destruction or defacing of Company property, equipment, or products

8) Theft or unauthorized removal of Company property, products, or possessions of others

9) Insubordination or refusal to follow work instructions, or walking off the job to avoid assigned work

10) Gross incompetence, repeated failure to perform job duties, or inability to meet expected norms of work performance

11) Sleeping on the job

12) Immoral or indecent actions on Company time or premises or other similar behavior at any time which reflects poorly upon the Company

13) Intimidation, or use of threatening or abusive language toward fellow employees or supervisory personnel

14) Reporting to work under the influence of drugs or liquor or in an otherwise unfit condition to work safely

15) Failure to follow plant safety rules or safe operating procedures for your job

16) Tampering with or misuse of machinery or equipment, or removing of guards

17) Excessive absenteeism or tardiness

18) Failure to meet normal production standards or causing excessive waste or scrap

19) Failure to report reason for absence in a timely manner

20) Loitering in other departments, or loafing

21) Failure to maintain work area in a clean and orderly manner

22) Stopping work early for breaks, lunch, or prior to the end of the day

23) Unauthorized absence from work area or premises

24) Operating a motor vehicle in an unsafe manner on Company time or premises, or disregard for parking procedures

25) Use of profane or obscene language on Company property, or acting in an offensive or insulting manner toward a fellow employee, supervisor, guest, or customer

26) Unauthorized posting, removing, or altering of notices or signs on Company property

## NEW EMPLOYEE ORIENTATION

This checklist is designed to assist the supervisor in orienting new employees to personnel practices and their new job at XYZ Company (Remove from handbook, complete, and return to employee's personnel file.)

_____ Orientation to Company, department, and work area

_____ Review of job responsibilities

_____ Review of attendance policy and call-in procedures

_____ Review of relevant personnel policies, disciplinary rules, safety rules

_____ Review of benefits and eligibility requirements

_____        _____
Supervisor                                                       Date

"I have received an XYZ Company employee handbook and understand that I am responsible for becoming familiar with its contents. I understand that this information is provided on an advisory basis and that policies or benefits may change from time to time. I further understand that employment is at will for an indefinite period unless terminated at any time by myself or the Company."

_____        _____
Employee                                                        Date

# Topic List for Personnel Policy Manual

Absence Reporting
Absenteeism Control
Accidents
Administrative Exemption
Affirmative Action
Age Discrimination
Alcohol and Drugs
Aliens
Appearance and Dress
Apprenticeship Training
Arrests and Convictions
Attendance Bonus
Bonus Payments
Breaks
Bulletin Boards
Callback Pay/Report-in
  Pay
Carpooling
Childcare/Daycare
Child Labor
Confidential Information
Conflict of Interest
Counseling Services
Court Appearance
Credit Union

Death of Employee
Death in Family
Deductions from Pay
Disability Insurance
Discipline
Discharge
Discounts
Disease
Dress Codes
Drug Testing
Election Day
Emergencies
Employee Associations
Employee Definitions
Employee Handbooks
Employment Agencies
Employment Contracts
Employment at Will
Equal Employment Opportunity
Executive Exemption
Exempt Personnel
Exit Interviews
Fingerprinting
Fire Drills
First Aid

# Index